Seventh Edition

COUNSELING

A COMPREHENSIVE PROFESSION

Samuel T. Gladding
Wake Forest University

Boston Columbus Indianapolis New York San Francisco Upper Saddle River
Amsterdam Cape Town Dubai London Madrid Milan Munich Paris Montréal Toronto
Delhi Mexico City São Paulo Sydney Hong Kong Seoul Singapore Taipei Tokyo

To Dr. Thomas M. Elmore of Wake Forest University who first taught me the art and science of being a counselor and who encouraged me to dream beyond the possible.

Vice President and Editorial Director: Jeffrey W. Johnston
Acquisitions Editor: Meredith D. Fossel
Associate Editor: Anne Whittaker
Editorial Assistant: Andrea Hall
Vice President, Director of Marketing: Margaret Waples
Senior Marketing Manager: Chris Barry
Senior Managing Editor: Pamela D. Bennet
Senior Project Manager: Mary M. Irvin
Senior Operations Supervisor: Matt Ottenweller

Senior Art Director: Diane Lorenzo
Cover Designer: Ali Mohrman
Art: SuperStock
Cover Image: Don Paulson Photography/Purestock/SuperStock
Project Coordination and Composition: S4Carlisle Publishing Services
Printer/Binder: Courier
Cover Printer: Courier
Text Font: Times LT Std

Photo Credits: Rhoda Sidney/PH College, p. 2; John Deeks/Photo Researchers, Inc., p. 29; © Paul Vasarhelyi/iStockphoto.com, p. 53; Ron Chapple/Getty Images, Inc. – Taxi, p. 77; VCL/Getty Images, Inc. – Taxi, p. 99; Lane V. Erickson/Shutterstock, p. 120; Jim Varney/Photo Researchers, Inc., p. 142; Stephen Coburn/Shutterstock, p. 163; © Andrew Moss/Alamy, p. 178; Anthony Magnacca/Merrill, p. 203; © Senthil Photography/Alamy, p. 234; © Amy Etra/PhotoEdit, p. 253; Monkey Business Images/Shutterstock, p. 269; Tek Image/Photo Researchers, Inc., p. 288; Scott Cunningham/Merrill, pp. 312, 355; Getty Images – Stockbyte, p. 337; Getty Images, Inc. – Photodisc/Royalty Free, p. 383; © UpperCut Images/Alamy, p. 402; © Mark McEvoy/Alamy, p. 425.

Every effort has been made to provide accurate and current Internet information in this book. However, the Internet and information posted on it are constantly changing, so it is inevitable that some of the Internet addresses listed in this textbook will change.

Library of Congress Cataloging-in-Publication Data

Gladding, Samuel T.
  Counseling : a comprehensive profession / Samuel T. Gladding. — 7th ed.
    p. cm.
  Includes bibliographical references and index.
  ISBN-13: 978-0-13-265797-6
  ISBN-10: 0-13-265797-X
1. Counseling. I. Title.
  BF637.C6G53 2013
  158.3—dc23   2011038696

10 9 8 7 6 5 4 3 2 1

ISBN 10:   0-13-265797-X
ISBN 13: 978-0-13-265797-6

PREFACE

Counseling is a dynamic, ever-evolving, and exciting profession that deals with human tragedy and possibility in an intensive, personal, and caring way. It is a profession dedicated to prevention, development, exploration, empowerment, change, wellness, and remediation in an increasingly complex and chaotic world. In the past, counseling emphasized guidance by helping people make wise choices. Now guidance is but one part of this multidimensional profession.

This text presents counseling in a broad manner covering its history, theories, activities, specialties, and trends. In addition, this book concentrates on the importance of the personhood of counselors and of the multicultural, ethical, and legal environments in which counselors operate. By focusing on the context and process of counseling, this book provides you with a better idea of what counselors do and how they do it.

Materials in *Counseling: A Comprehensive Profession,* Seventh Edition, have been divided into four main sections. Part I, Historical and Professional Foundations of Counseling, contains chapters dealing with an overview of the development of counseling and important competencies of contemporary counselors. Specific chapters that will orient you to the counseling profession as it was and is are:

Chapter 1: History of and Trends in Counseling
Chapter 2: Personal and Professional Aspects of Counseling
Chapter 3: Ethical and Legal Aspects of Counseling
Chapter 4: Counseling in a Multicultural Society
Chapter 5: Counseling with Diverse Populations

Part II, Counseling Processes and Theories, highlights the main processes, stages, and theories of the counseling profession. This section addresses the universal aspects of popular counseling approaches and zeros in on specific theories and ways of dealing with client concerns. The five chapters are:

Chapter 6: Building Counseling Relationships
Chapter 7: Working in a Counseling Relationship
Chapter 8: Closing Counseling Relationships
Chapter 9: Psychoanalytic, Adlerian, and Humanistic Theories of Counseling
Chapter 10: Behavioral, Cognitive, Systemic, Brief, and Crisis Theories of Counseling

Part III, Core Counseling Activities in Various Settings, emphasizes universal skills required in almost all counseling environments. Counselors use group counseling, consultation, research, and assessment skills in various areas. The chapters in this section include:

Chapter 11: Groups in Counseling
Chapter 12: Consultation
Chapter 13: Evaluation and Research
Chapter 14: Testing, Assessment, and Diagnosis in Counseling

Finally, Part IV, Counseling Specialties, contains six chapters that focus on specific populations with whom counselors work or professional practices in which they are engaged that are unique. The chapters are titled:

Chapter 15: Career Counseling over the Life Span
Chapter 16: Marriage, Couple, and Family Counseling
Chapter 17: Professional School Counseling

A common theme woven throughout this book is that counseling is both a generic and specialized part of the helping field. Although it is a profession that has come of age, it is still growing. It is best represented in professional organizations such as the American Counseling Association (ACA) and its divisions. There are also numerous other professional groups—social workers, psychologists, psychiatric nurses, psychiatrists, marriage and family therapists, and pastoral counselors—that use and practice counseling procedures and theories on a daily basis. In essence, no one profession owns the helping process. However, being a counselor is distinct.

This text is the result of a lifetime of effort on my part to understand the counseling profession as it was, as it is, and as it will be. My journey has included a wide variety of experiences—working with clients in all ages and stages of life in clinical settings and with students who are interested in learning more about the essence of how counseling works. Research, observation, dialogue, assimilation, and study have contributed to the growth of the content contained in these pages.

NEW TO THIS EDITION

Counseling is changing so rapidly that it is difficult to keep up. Four years makes a world of difference in the profession. So, updating and expanding a comprehensive text like this is a challenge. What is new? Plenty!

- This edition of *Counseling: A Comprehensive Profession* has over 275 new citations within its pages, and dozens of older references that are not as relevant anymore have been deleted. Most of the new additions are from the flagship journal of the profession: *Journal of Counseling & Development.* However, a number of other articles drawn from ACA divisional journals and related periodicals are included.
- This edition is much more multicultural than ever before. Counseling is becoming more diverse in regard to the people who are seen. This text reflects the change in demographics that are a part of the United States. Infused within almost every chapter is material on working in a diverse and multicultural climate.
- To help readers pick up concepts and information more quickly, essential ideas have now not only been italicized but boldfaced as well. Thus, when going through a chapter, the reader should be able to highlight crucial facts without having to use a marker. This feature of the book makes it much more helpful for students of counseling as they seek to learn the essentials in single chapters and in the book as a whole.
- New graphs and tables have been inserted into the text. Many times those who study need visual cues as to what is being described. The new visuals will meet this need while not affecting the narrative surrounding them.
- At the beginning of each chapter is a brief, focused section on learning objectives. This feature is followed by some suggestions readers should consider regarding these objectives. This new feature will help those who study this text reflect in a more focused way and learn chapter material more easily.
- New sections or expanded sections on history, wellness, trauma, social justice, multiculturalism, rehabilitation, motivational interviewing, bullying, microaggression, international counseling, process addiction, abuse, and ethical and legal issues in counseling have been added. I honestly do not think any major topic dealing with the world of counseling has been left out.

- Finally, this edition of *Counseling*, while having a similar chapter layout to the sixth edition, contains an even stronger emphasis on counseling as a profession and counseling as an identity. With the passage of counselor licensure in all 50 states, a new definition of counseling endorsed by 29 professional counseling associations, the generation of significant counseling research, and a stronger American Counseling Association, the profession of counseling is no longer beholden to other disciplines. Thus, the distinctiveness of counseling in general and in particular areas is highlighted within these pages.

MyCounselingLab

Help your students bridge the gap between theory and practice with **MyCounselingLab**. **MyCounselingLab** connects your course content to video- and case-based real world scenarios, and provides:

- *Assignments & Activities* assess students' understanding of key concepts and skill development. Hints and feedback provide scaffolding and reinforce key concepts.
- *Building Counseling Skills* exercises offer opportunities for students to develop and practice skills critical to their success as professional helpers. Suggested responses are available to instructors, making grading easy.
- *Multiple-Choice Quizzes* help students gauge their understanding of important topics and prepare for success on licensure examinations.

Access to **MyCounselingLab** can be packaged with this textbook or purchased standalone. To find out how to package student access to this website and gain access as an Instructor, go to www.mycounselinglab.com, email us at counseling@pearson.com, contact your Pearson sales representative.

ACKNOWLEDGMENTS

I am particularly indebted to input from my original mentors, Thomas M. Elmore and Wesley D. Hood, Wake Forest University, and W. Larry Osborne, University of North Carolina, Greensboro. Other significant colleagues who have contributed to my outlook and perception of counseling include C. W. Yonce, Peg Carroll, Allen Wilcoxon, Jim Cotton, Robin McInturff, Miriam Cosper, Charles Alexander, Chuck Kormanski, Rosie Morganett, Jane Myers, Diana Hulse, Ted Remley, Jerry Donigian, Donna Henderson, Debbie Newsome, Art Lerner, and Thomas Sweeney. Then, of course, there have been graduate students who have contributed significantly to this endeavor, especially Shirley Ratliff, Marianne Dreyspring, Hank Paine, Don Norman, Tom McClure, Paul Myers, Virginia Perry, Pamela Karr, Jim Weiss, and Tim Rambo. I am especially indebted to my graduate assistants, Sheryl Harper, Brandi Flannery, Elizabeth Cox, and Joe Wilkerson for their hard work and contributions in helping me put together the last four editions of this text.

I am also grateful to the current reviewers for their comments and suggestions for improvement: Jesse A. Brinson, University of Nevada, Las Vegas; Sharon Jones, University of Georgia; Kristin A. Smiley, Oakland University; and Brian L. Turner, University of West Florida.

Also appreciated is the valuable input of reviewers of the previous editions: Lisa Costas, University of South Florida; Stuart Itzkowitz, Wayne State University; John Krumboltz, Stanford University; Sally Murphy, George Mason University; Julie Yang, Governors State

University; Irene M. Ametrano, Eastern Michigan University; Jamie Carney, Auburn University; James S. DeLo, West Virginia University; Thomas DeStefano, Northern Arizona University; Michael Duffy, Texas A&M University; Thomas M. Elmore, Wake Forest University; Stephen Feit, Idaho State University; David L. Fenell, University of Colorado–Colorado Springs; Joshua M. Gold, University of South Carolina; Janice Holden, University of North Texas; Roger L. Hutchinson, Ball State University; Robert Levison, California Polytechnic State University–San Luis Obispo; Michael Forrest Maher, Sam Houston University; A. Scott McGowan, Long Island University; Karen N. Ripley, Georgia State University; Simeon Schlossberg, Western Maryland College; Holly A. Stadler, University of Missouri–Kansas City; Arthur Thomas, University of Kansas; JoAnna White, Georgia State University; Mark E. Young, University of Central Florida; and Scott Young, Mississippi State University. Their feedback and excellent ideas on how to improve this book were invaluable. I also owe a debt of gratitude to my past editors at Merrill, including Vicki Knight, Linda Sullivan, and Kevin Davis, and to my present associate editor Anne Whittaker and my editor Meredith Fossel. They have been extremely helpful and a real joy to work with.

Finally, I am grateful to my parents, Russell and Gertrude Gladding, who gave me the opportunities and support to obtain a good education and who called my attention to the importance of serving people. Their influence continues to be a part of my life. Likewise, I am thankful to Claire, my wife, who has given me support over the years in writing and refining this text. She has been patient, understanding, encouraging, and humorous about this book, even in the midst of three pregnancies, three moves, and the launching or almost launching of three children who are now young adults. She exemplifies what an ally in marriage should be. Her presence has brightened my days and made all the hard work a joy.

Samuel T. Gladding

ABOUT THE AUTHOR

 **Samuel T. Gladding** is a professor of counseling and chair of the Department of Counseling at Wake Forest University in Winston-Salem, North Carolina. He has been a practicing counselor in public as well as private agencies since 1971. His leadership in the field of counseling includes service as president of the following groups: the American Counseling Association (ACA), the American Association of State Counseling Boards (AASCB), the Association for Counselor Education and Supervision (ACES), the Association for Specialists in Group Work (ASGW), and Chi Sigma Iota (counseling academic and professional honor society international).

Gladding is the former editor of the *Journal for Specialists in Group Work* and the author of seven dozen or so professional publications. In 1999, he was cited as being in the top 1% of contributors to the *Journal of Counseling & Development* for the 15-year period 1978–1993. Some of Gladding's other recent books are *Clinical Mental Health Counseling in Community and Agency Settings* (with Debbie Newsome) (3rd ed., 2009); *Group Work: A Counseling Specialty* (6th ed., 2012); *Family Therapy: History, Theory, and Practice* (5th ed., 2011); *Becoming a Counselor: The Light, The Bright, and the Serious* (2nd ed., 2009); *The Counseling Dictionary* (3rd ed., 2011); and *The Creative Arts in Counseling* (4th ed., 2011).

Gladding's previous academic appointments have been at the University of Alabama at Birmingham and Fairfield University (Connecticut). He received his degrees from Wake Forest, Yale, and the University of North Carolina—Greensboro. He is a National Certified Counselor (NCC), a Certified Clinical Mental Health Counselor (CCMHC), and a practicing Licensed Professional Counselor (North Carolina). Gladding is a Fellow in the American Counseling Association and a recipient of the Gilbert and Kathleen Wrenn Award for a Humanitarian and Caring Person, the Arthur A. Hitchcock Distinguished Professional Service Award, and the David K. Brooks Distinguished Mentor Award.

Dr. Gladding is married to Claire Tillson Gladding and is the father of three young adult men—Ben, Nate, and Tim. Outside of counseling, he enjoys tennis, swimming, and humor.

CONTENTS

Prologue

Counseling is a distinct profession that has developed in a variety of ways since the early years of the 20th century. The personalities of previous counselors, government actions to promote counseling, advocacy on the part of counselors, change within the American Counseling Association, and a bit of serendipity as well as thoughtful planning have made counseling what it is today. It is exciting to explore counseling's many dimensions, and I hope you will enjoy reading and reflecting on what has preceded you and what possibilities lay ahead. This is a great time to be in the profession, and I trust you will realize in reading this text that there is much to learn as well as much to look forward to as you develop your skills and abilities as a counselor.

I have outlined what is in the text in the preface of this book, so I will not repeat that material here. I will simply tell you I have been a professional counselor for over 40 years and I can honestly say I have loved almost every moment of it (there are always a few rough times). I have never thought of doing anything else. Why? The number one reason is that I think counseling allows you to make a profound difference in the lives of people regardless of their background. It is rare in life that you get to be in touch with people from various levels of society. Most of us live within the artificial boundaries of groups with whom we are comfortable. It is even rarer that you are privileged to work with these individuals in a humanitarian, caring, and productive way that can change their lives for the better. I am moved and humbled almost every day in my work as a counselor. I cannot think of a better way to spend a life. As a counselor you matter and make meaning in multiple ways.

As you read, try to personally put yourself in the context of each chapter's material. In that way you will get a feel for what is being conveyed and not just a cognitive understanding of what counselors do and where they do it. As you will see, the chapters are organized in such a way that you will be able to tell where to concentrate your time. **Important points** are highlighted in **bold type** and **definitions** of important concepts **both highlighted in bold type and *italicized***.

Hopefully within these pages you will get a feel for the topics that are a part of the counseling profession. Hopefully you will have a positive learning experience as well, and you may even find yourself enjoying the book! Regardless, as one of my mentors used to say: "Studying counseling will never hurt you"—and you just might find it changes your life!

PART I

Historical and Professional Foundations of Counseling

1   History of and Trends in Counseling

Chapter Overview

From reading this chapter you will learn about

- The consensus definition of counseling adopted by 29 diverse counseling associations
- The history of counseling and important events and people that have shaped the profession during different decades
- Current trends in counseling and where the profession of counseling is headed

As you read consider

- What you believe most people think counseling is and how that differs from what it is
- How world events, governments, and strong personalities shape a profession such as counseling
- What trends you see on the horizon that you think may influence the future of counseling including developing needs in humanity

There is a quietness that comes
    in the awareness of presenting names
        and recalling places
            in the history of persons
                who come seeking help.
Confusion and direction are a part of the process
    where in trying to sort out tracks
        that parallel into life
            a person's past is traveled.
Counseling is a complex riddle
    where the mind's lines are joined
        with scrambling and precision
            to make sense out of nonsense,
a tedious process
    like piecing fragments of a puzzle together
        until a picture is formed.

Reprinted from "In the Midst of the Puzzles and Counseling Journey," by S. T. Gladding, 1978, *Personnel and Guidance Journal, 57*, p. 148. © S. T. Gladding.

MyCounselingLab™

Visit the MyCounselingLab™ site (www.MyCounselingLab.com) for *Counseling: A Comprehensive Profession,* Seventh Edition to enhance your understanding of chapter concepts. You'll have the opportunity to practice your skills through video- and case-based Assignments and Activities as well as Building Counseling Skills units and to prepare for your certification exam with Practice for Certification quizzes.

A *profession* is distinguished by having

- **a specific body of knowledge,**
- **accredited training programs,**
- **a professional organization of peers,**
- **credentialing of practitioners such as licensure,**
- **a code of ethics,**
- **legal recognition,** and
- **other standards of excellence** (Myers & Sweeney, 2001).

Counseling meets all the standards for a profession and has done so for a significant period of time. It is unique from, as well as connected with, other mental health disciplines by both its emphases and at times its history. Counseling emphasizes growth as well as remediation over the course of a life span in various areas of life: childhood, adolescence, adulthood, and older adulthood. Counselors within the counseling profession specialize in helping individuals, couples, groups, families, and social systems that are experiencing situational, developmental, and long- or short-term problems. Counseling's focus on development, prevention, wellness, and treatment makes it attractive to those seeking healthy life-stage transitions and productive lives.

Counseling has not always been an encompassing and comprehensive profession. It has evolved over the years from diverse disciplines "including but not limited to anthropology, education, ethics, history, law, medical sciences, philosophy, psychology, and sociology" (Smith, 2001, p. 570). Some people associate counseling with educational institutions or equate the word "guidance" with counseling because they are unaware of counseling's evolution. As a consequence, outdated ideas linger in their minds in contrast to reality. They misunderstand the essence of the profession and those who work in it. Even among counselors themselves, those who fail to keep up in their professional development may become confused as to exactly what counseling is, where it has been, and how it is moving forward. As C. H. Patterson, a pioneer in counseling, once observed, some writers in counseling journals seem "ignorant of the history of the counseling profession . . . [and thus] go over the same ground covered in publications of the 1950s and 1960s" (Goodyear & Watkins, 1983, p. 594).

Therefore, it is important to examine the history of counseling because a counselor who is informed about the development and transformation of the profession is likely to have a strong professional identity and subsequently make significant contributions to the field. By understanding counseling's past, you may better appreciate present and future trends of the profession.

PERSONAL REFLECTION

What do you know about your family and personal history that has helped you in your life? Why do you find this type of information valuable? What parallels do you see between knowing your family history and the history of counseling?

DEFINITION OF COUNSELING

There have always been "counselors"—people who listen to others and help them resolve difficulties—but the word "counselor" has been misused over the years by connecting it with descriptive adjectives to promote products. Thus, one hears of carpet counselors, color coordination counselors, pest control counselors, financial counselors, camp counselors, and so on. These counselors are mostly glorified salespersons, advice givers, and supervisors of children or services. They are to professional counseling what furniture doctors are to medicine.

Counseling as a profession grew out of the **progressive guidance movement** of the early 1900s. Its **emphasis** was on **prevention** and **purposefulness**—on helping individuals of all ages and stages avoid making bad choices in life while finding meaning, direction, and fulfillment in what they did. Today professional counseling encompasses within its practice clinicians who still focus on the avoidance of problems and the promotion of growth, but the profession is much more than that. The focus on wellness, development, mindfulness, meaningfulness, and remediation of mental disorders is the hallmark of counseling for individuals, groups, couples, and families across the life span. To understand what counseling is now, it is important first to understand the history of the profession and how counseling is similar to and different from concepts such as guidance and psychotherapy.

Guidance

Guidance focuses on helping people make important choices that affect their lives, such as choosing a preferred lifestyle. Although the decision-making aspect of guidance has long played an important role in the counseling process, the concept itself, as a word in counseling, "has gone the way of 'consumption' in medicine" (Tyler, 1986, p. 153). It has more historical significance than present-day usage. Nevertheless, it sometimes distinguishes a way of helping that differs from the more encompassing word "counseling."

One distinction between guidance and counseling is that guidance centers on helping individuals choose what they value most, whereas counseling helps them make changes. Much of the early work in guidance occurred in schools and career centers where an adult would help a student make decisions, such as deciding on a course of study or a vocation. That relationship was between unequals and was beneficial in helping the less experienced person find direction in life. Similarly, children have long received "guidance" from parents, religious leaders, and coaches. In the process they have gained an understanding of themselves and their world. This type of guidance will never become passé. No matter what the age or stage of life, a person often needs help in making choices. But guidance is only one part of the overall services provided by professional counseling.

Psychotherapy

Traditionally, *psychotherapy* (or *therapy*) has focused on serious problems associated with intrapsychic, internal, and personal issues and conflicts. It has dealt with the "recovery of adequacy" (Casey, 1996, p. 175). As such, psychotherapy, especially analytically based therapy, has emphasized (a) the past more than the present, (b) insight more than change, (c) the detachment of the therapist, and (d) the therapist's role as an expert. In addition, psychotherapy has historically involved a *long-term relationship* (20 to 40 sessions over a period of 6 months to 2 years) that concentrated on reconstructive change as opposed to a more *short-term relationship* (8 to 12 sessions spread over a period of less than 6 months). Psychotherapy has also been more of a process associated with *inpatient settings*—some of which are residential, such as mental hospitals—as opposed to *outpatient settings*—some of which are nonresidential, such as community agencies.

However, in more modern times, the distinction between psychotherapy and counseling has blurred, and professionals who provide clinical services often determine whether clients receive counseling or psychotherapy. Some counseling theories are commonly referred to as therapies as well and can be used in multiple settings. Therefore, the similarities in the counseling and psychotherapy processes often overlap.

Counseling

The term *counseling* has eluded definition for years. However, in 2010, 29 counseling associations including the American Counseling Association (ACA) and all but two of its 19 divisions, along with the American Association of State Counseling Boards (AASCB), the Council for the Accreditation of Counseling and Related Educational Programs (CACREP), the National Board for Certified Counselors (NBCC), the Council of Rehabilitation Education (CORE), the Commission of Rehabilitation Counselor Certification (CRCC), and the Chi Sigma Iota (counseling honor society international) accepted a consensus definition of counseling. According to the **20/20: A Vision for the Future of Counseling** group, *counseling* is defined as follows:

"Counseling is a professional relationship that empowers diverse individuals, families, and groups to accomplish mental health, wellness, education, and career goals" (www .counseling.org/20-20/index.aspx).

This definition contains a number of implicit and explicit points that are important for counselors as well as consumers to realize.

- *Counseling deals with wellness, personal growth, career, education, and empowerment concerns.*   In other words, counselors work in areas that involve a plethora of issues including those that are personal and those that are interpersonal. These areas include concerns related to finding meaning, adjustment, and fulfillment in mental and physical health, and the achievement of goals in such settings as work and school. Counselors are concerned with social justice and advocate for the oppressed and powerless as a part of the process.
- *Counseling is conducted with persons individually, in groups, and in families.*   Clients seen by counselors live and work in a wide variety of settings. Their problems may require short-term or long-term interventions that focus on just one person or with multiple individuals who are related or not related to each other.
- *Counseling is diverse and multicultural.*   Counselors see clients with varied cultural backgrounds. Those from minority and majority cultures are helped in a variety of ways depending on their needs, which may include addressing larger societal issues, such as discrimination or prejudice.
- *Counseling is a dynamic process.*   Counselors not only focus on their clients' goals, they help clients accomplish them. This dynamic process comes through using a variety of theories and methods. Thus, counseling involves making choices as well as changes. Counseling

is lively and engaging. In most cases, "counseling is a rehearsal for action" (Casey, 1996, p. 176) either internally with thoughts and feelings or externally with behavior.

In addition to defining counseling in general, the ACA has defined a professional ***counseling specialty***, which is an area (within counseling) that is "narrowly focused, requiring advanced knowledge in the field" of counseling (www.counseling.org). Among the specialties within counseling are those dealing with educational settings such as schools or colleges and those pertaining to situations in life such as marriage, mental health, rehabilitation, aging, addiction, and careers. According to the ACA, becoming a specialist is founded on the premise that "all professional counselors must first meet the requirements for the general practice of professional counseling" (www.counseling.org).

PERSONAL REFLECTION

What special talents do you have? How did they develop from your overall definition of yourself as a person? How do you see your personal circumstances paralleling the general definition of counseling and counseling specialties?

HISTORY OF COUNSELING

Before 1900

Counseling is a relatively new profession (Aubrey, 1977, 1982). It developed in the late 1890s and early 1900s, and was interdisciplinary from its inception. "Some of the functions of counselors were and are shared by persons in other professions" (Herr & Fabian, 1993, p. 3). Before the 1900s, most counseling was in the form of advice or information. In the United States, counseling developed out of a humanitarian concern to improve the lives of those adversely affected by the Industrial Revolution of the mid- to late 1800s (Aubrey, 1983). The **social welfare reform movement** (now known as **social justice**), the spread of public education, and various changes in population makeup (e.g., the enormous influx of immigrants) also influenced the growth of the fledgling profession (Aubrey, 1977; Goodyear, 1984). Overall, "counseling emerged during a socially turbulent period that straddled the ending of one century and the beginning of another, a period marked by great change that caused a major shift in the way individuals viewed themselves and others" (Ginter, 2002, p. 220).

Most of the pioneers in counseling identified themselves as teachers and social reformers/advocates. They focused on teaching children and young adults about themselves, others, and the world of work. Initially, these helpers were involved primarily in child welfare, educational/vocational guidance, and legal reform. Their work was built on specific information and lessons, such as moral instruction on being good and doing right, as well as a concentrated effort to deal with intra- and interpersonal relations (Nugent & Jones, 2009). They saw needs in American society and took steps to fulfill them. Nevertheless, "no mention of counseling was made in the professional literature until 1931" (Aubrey, 1983, p. 78). Classroom teachers and administrators were the main practitioners.

One way to chart the evolution of counseling is to trace important events and personal influences through the 20th century. Keep in mind that the development of professional counseling, like the activity itself, was and is a process. Therefore, some names and events do not fit neatly into a rigid chronology. They overlap.

1900–1909

Counseling was an infant profession in the early 1900s. During this decade, however, three persons emerged as leaders in counseling's development: Frank Parsons, Jesse B. Davis, and Clifford Beers.

Frank Parsons, often called the **founder of guidance**, focused his work on growth and prevention. His influence was great in his time and it is "Parson's body of work and his efforts to help others [that] lie at the center of the wheel that represents present day counseling" (Ginter, 2002, p. 221). Parsons had a colorful life career in multiple disciplines, being a lawyer, an engineer, a college teacher, and a social worker before ultimately becoming a social reformer and working with youth (Hartung & Blustein, 2002; Pope & Sweinsdottir, 2005; Sweeney, 2001). He has been characterized as a broad scholar, a persuasive writer, a tireless activist, and a great intellect (Davis, 1988; Zytowski, 1985). However, he is best known for founding **Boston's Vocational Bureau** in 1908, a major step in the institutionalization of vocational guidance.

At the Bureau, Parsons worked with young people who were in the process of making career decisions. He "envisioned a practice of vocational guidance based on rationality and reason with service, concern for others, cooperation, and social justice among its core values" (Hartung & Blustein, 2002, p. 41). He theorized that **choosing a vocation** was a matter of relating **three factors: a knowledge of work, a knowledge of self, and a matching of the two through "true reasoning."** Thus, Parsons devised a number of procedures to help his clients learn more about themselves and the world of work. One of his devices was an extensive questionnaire that asked about

> experiences ("How did you spend each evening last week?"), preferences ("At a World's Fair, what would you want to see first? second? third?"), and morals ("When have you sacrificed advantage for the right?") (Gummere, 1988, p. 404).

Parsons's book *Choosing a Vocation* (1909), published one year after his death, was quite influential, especially in Boston. For example, the superintendent of Boston schools, Stratton Brooks, designated 117 elementary and secondary teachers as vocational counselors. The "Boston example" soon spread to other major cities as school personnel recognized the need for vocational planning. By 1910, 35 cities were emulating Boston (Lee, 1966).

Jesse B. Davis was the first person to set up a systematized guidance program in the public schools (Aubrey, 1977; Brewer, 1942). As superintendent of the Grand Rapids, Michigan, school system, he suggested in 1907 that classroom teachers of English composition teach their students a lesson in guidance once a week, to accomplish the goal of building character and preventing problems. Influenced by progressive American educators such as Horace Mann and John Dewey, Davis believed that proper guidance would help cure the ills of American society (Davis, 1914). What he and other progressive educators advocated was not counseling in the modern sense but a forerunner of counseling: *school guidance* (a preventive educational means of teaching students how to deal effectively with life events).

Clifford Beers, a former Yale student, was hospitalized for depression several times during his life (Kiselica & Robinson, 2001). He found conditions in mental institutions deplorable and exposed them in his book, *A Mind That Found Itself* (1908), which became a popular best seller. Beers used the book as a platform to advocate for better mental health facilities and reform in the treatment of people with mental illness by making friends with and soliciting funds from influential people of his day, such as the Fords and Rockefellers. His work had an especially powerful influence on the fields of psychiatry and psychology. "Many people in these fields referred to what they were doing as counseling," which was seen "as a means of helping people adjust to themselves and society" (Hansen, Rossberg, & Cramer, 1994, p. 5). Beers's work was the impetus for the mental health movement in the United States, as well as advocacy groups that exist today including the National Mental Health Association and the National Alliance for the Mentally Ill. His work was also a **forerunner of mental health counseling**.

CASE EXAMPLE

Doug Deliberates

After reading about the three major pioneers in the profession of counseling, Doug deliberated about who among them was most important. At first he was sure it must be Frank Parsons because Parsons seemed the most scientific and influential of the group. Yet as he thought, he was not sure. Where would counseling be without Clifford Beers's influence on mental health and Jesse Davis's work in the school?

   Who do you think was the most important of these three? Why?

1910s

Three events had a profound impact on the development of counseling during the 1910s. The first was the 1913 founding of the *National Vocational Guidance Association (NVGA)*, which was the forerunner of the American Counseling Association. It began publishing a bulletin in 1915 (Goodyear, 1984). In 1921, the *National Vocational Guidance Bulletin* started regular publication. It evolved in later years to become the *National Vocational Guidance Magazine* (1924–1933), *Occupations: The Vocational Guidance Magazine* (1933–1944), *Occupations: The Vocational Guidance Journal* (1944–1952), *Personnel and Guidance Journal* (1952–1984), and, finally, the *Journal of Counseling and Development* (1984 to the present). NVGA was important because it established an association offering guidance literature and united those with an interest in vocational counseling for the first time.

   Complementing the founding of NVGA was congressional passage of the *Smith-Hughes Act* of 1917. This legislation provided funding for public schools to support vocational education.

   World War I was the third important event of the decade. During the war "counseling became more widely recognized as the military began to employ testing and placement practices for great numbers of military personnel" (Hollis, 2000, p. 45). In this process, the Army commissioned the development of numerous psychological instruments, among them the **Army Alpha and Army Beta intelligence tests**. Several of the Army's screening devices were employed in civilian populations after the war, and *psychometrics* (psychological testing) became a popular movement and an early foundation on which counseling was based.

   Aubrey (1977) observes that, because the vocational guidance movement developed without an explicit philosophy, it quickly embraced psychometrics to gain a legitimate foundation in psychology. Reliance on psychometrics had both positive and negative effects. On the positive side, it gave vocational guidance specialists a stronger and more "scientific" identity. On the negative side, it distracted many specialists from examining developments in other behavioral sciences, such as sociology, biology, and anthropology.

1920s

The 1920s were relatively quiet for the developing counseling profession. This was a period of consolidation. **Education courses for counselors**, which had begun at Harvard University in 1911, almost exclusively emphasized vocational guidance during the 1920s. The dominant influences on the emerging profession were the progressive theories of education and the federal government's use of guidance services with war veterans.

A notable event was the **certification of counselors** in Boston and New York in the mid-1920s. Another turning point was the development of the first standards for the preparation and evaluation of occupational materials (Lee, 1966). Along with these standards came the publication of **new psychological instruments** such as Edward Strong's *Strong Vocational Interest Inventory (SVII)* in 1927. The publication of this instrument set the stage for future directions for assessment in counseling (Strong, 1943).

A final noteworthy event was Abraham and Hannah Stone's 1929 establishment of the **first marriage and family counseling center** in New York City. This center was followed by others across the nation, marking the beginning of the specialty of marriage and family counseling.

Throughout the decade, the guidance movement gained acceptance within American society. At the same time, the movement's narrow emphasis on vocational interests began to be challenged. Counselors were broadening their focus to include issues of personality and development, such as those that concerned the family.

1930s

The 1930s were not as quiet as the 1920s, in part because the **Great Depression influenced researchers and practitioners**, especially in university and vocational settings, to emphasize helping strategies and counseling methods that related to **employment**. A highlight of the decade was the development of the **first theory of counseling**, which was formulated by **E. G. Williamson** and his colleagues (including John Darley and Donald Paterson) at the University of Minnesota. Williamson modified Parsons's theory and used it to work with students and the unemployed. His emphasis on a **direct, counselor-centered approach** came to be known by several names—for example, as the *Minnesota point of view* and *trait-factor counseling*. His pragmatic approach emphasized the counselor's teaching, mentoring, and influencing skills (Williamson, 1939).

One premise of Williamson's theory was that persons had *traits* (e.g., aptitudes, interests, personalities, achievements) that could be integrated in a variety of ways to form *factors* (constellations of individual characteristics). Counseling was based on a scientific, problem-solving, empirical method that was individually tailored to each client to help him or her stop nonproductive thinking/behavior and become an effective decision maker (Lynch & Maki, 1981). Williamson thought the task of the counselor was to ascertain a deficiency in the client, such as a lack of knowledge or a skill, and then to prescribe a procedure to rectify the problem. Williamson's influence dominated counseling for the next two decades, and he continued to write about his theory into the 1970s (Williamson & Biggs, 1979).

Another major occurrence was the **broadening of counseling beyond occupational concerns**. The seeds of this development were sown in the 1920s, when Edward Thorndike began to challenge the vocational orientation of the guidance movement (Lee, 1966). The work of **John Brewer** completed this change in emphasis. Brewer published a book titled *Education as Guidance* in 1932. He proposed that every teacher be a counselor and that guidance be incorporated into the school curriculum as a subject. Brewer believed that all education should focus on preparing students to live outside the school environment. His emphasis made counselors see vocational decisions as just one part of their responsibilities.

During the 1930s the U.S. government became more involved in guidance and counseling. For example, in 1938 Congress passed the **George-Dean Act** that created the **Vocational Education Division** of the U.S. Office of Education and an **Occupational Information and Guidance Service** (Sweeney, 2001). Evolving from this measure was the creation of state supervisors of guidance positions in state departments of education throughout the nation. Thus, school counseling, still known as guidance in the 1930s, became more of a national phenomenon. Furthermore, the government established the **U.S. Employment Service** in the 1930s. This agency published the first edition of the *Dictionary of Occupational Titles (DOT)* in 1939. The *DOT*, which became a major source of career information for guidance specialists working with students and the unemployed, described known occupations in the United States and coded them according to job titles.

1940s

Three major events in the 1940s radically shaped the practice of counseling: the theory of Carl Rogers, World War II, and government's involvement in counseling after the war.

Carl Rogers rose to prominence in 1942 with the publication of his book *Counseling and Psychotherapy*, which challenged the counselor-centered approach of Williamson as well as major tenets of Freudian psychoanalysis. Rogers emphasized the importance of the client, espousing a **nondirective approach to counseling**. His ideas were both widely accepted and harshly criticized. Rogers advocated giving clients responsibility for their own growth. He thought that if clients had an opportunity to be accepted and listened to, then they would begin to know themselves better and become more congruent (genuine). He described the role of the professional helper as being nonjudgmental and accepting. Thus, the helper served as a mirror, reflecting the verbal and emotional manifestations of the client.

Aubrey (1977, p. 292) has noted that, before Rogers, the literature in guidance and counseling was quite practical, dealing with testing, cumulative records, orientation procedures, vocations, and placement functions. In addition, this early literature dealt extensively with the goals and purpose of guidance. With Rogers, there was a new emphasis on the importance of the relationship in counseling, research, refinement of counseling technique, selection and training of future counselors, and the goals and objectives of counseling. Guidance, for all intents and purposes, suddenly disappeared as a major consideration in the bulk of the literature and was replaced by a decade or more of concentration on counseling. The Rogers revolution had a major impact on both counseling and psychology. Not only did Rogers's ideas come to the forefront, but a considerable number of alternative systems of psychotherapy emerged as well (Corsini, 2008).

With the advent of **World War II**, the U.S. government needed counselors and psychologists to help select and train specialists for the military and industry. The war also brought about a **new way of looking at vocations for men and women**. Many women worked outside the home during the war, exemplified by such personalities as Rosie the Riveter. Women's contributions to work and the well-being of the United States during the crisis of war made a lasting impact. Traditional occupational sex roles began to be questioned, and greater emphasis was placed on personal freedom.

After the war, the U.S. government further promoted counseling through the **George-Barden Act** of 1946, which provided vocational education funds through the U.S. Office of Education for **counselor training institutes** (Sweeney, 2001). In addition, the **Veterans**

Administration (VA) funded the training of counselors and psychologists by granting stipends and paid internships for students engaged in graduate study. The VA also "rewrote specifications for vocational counselors and coined the term **'counseling psychologist'**" (Nugent, 1981, p. 25). Money made available through the VA and the GI bill (benefits for veterans) influenced teaching professionals in graduate education to define their curriculum offerings more precisely. Counseling psychology, as a profession, began to move further away from its historical alliance with vocational guidance.

1950s

"If one decade in history had to be singled out for the most profound impact on counselors, it would be the 1950s" (Aubrey, 1977, p. 292). Indeed, the decade produced at least **five major events** that dramatically changed the history of counseling:

1. The establishment of the **American Personnel and Guidance Association (APGA)**;
2. The charting of the **American School Counselor Association (ASCA)**;
3. The establishment of **Division 17** (Society of Counseling Psychology) within the American Psychological Association (APA);
4. The passage of the **National Defense Education Act (NDEA)**; and
5. The introduction of **new guidance and counseling theories**.

AMERICAN PERSONNEL AND GUIDANCE ASSOCIATION.   APGA grew out of the **Council of Guidance and Personnel Associations (CGPA)**, a loose confederation of organizations "concerned with educational and vocational guidance and other personnel activities" (Harold, 1985, p. 4). CGPA operated from 1934 to 1951, but its major drawback was a lack of power to commit its members to any course of action (Sheeley & Stickle, 2008). APGA was formed in 1952 with the purpose of formally organizing groups interested in guidance, counseling, and personnel matters. Its original four divisions were the American College Personnel Association (Division 1), the National Association of Guidance Supervisors and Counselor Trainers (Division 2), the NVGA (Division 3), and the Student Personnel Association for Teacher Education (Division 4) (Sheeley, 2002). During its early history, APGA was an interest group rather than a professional organization because it did not originate or enforce standards for membership (Super, 1955).

THE CHARTERING OF THE AMERICAN SCHOOL COUNSELOR ASSOCIATION (ASCA).   In 1953, the American School Counselor Association was chartered. It joined APGA as its fifth member shortly thereafter. By joining APGA, ASCA strengthened the association numerically, pragmatically, and philosophically.

DIVISION 17.   In 1952, the Society of Counseling Psychology (Division 17) of APA was formally established. It was initially known as the **Division of Counseling Psychology**. Its formation required dropping the term "guidance" from what had formerly been the association's Counseling and Guidance Division. Part of the impetus for the division's creation came from the VA, but the main impetus came from APA members interested in **working with a more "normal" population** than the one seen by clinical psychologists (Whiteley, 1984).

Once created, Division 17 became more fully defined. Super (1955), for instance, distinguished between counseling psychology and clinical psychology, holding that counseling psychology was more concerned with normal human growth and development and was influenced in its approach by both vocational counseling and humanistic psychotherapy. Despite Super's work, counseling psychology had a difficult time establishing a clear identity within the APA (Whiteley, 1984). Yet the division's existence has had a major impact on the growth and development of counseling as a profession. In fact, luminaries in the counseling profession such as Gilbert Wrenn and Donald Super held offices in both Division 17 and in APGA divisions for years and published in the periodicals of both.

NATIONAL DEFENSE EDUCATION ACT.   A fourth major event was the passage in 1958 of the National Defense Education Act (NDEA), which was enacted following the Soviet Union's launching of its first space satellite, *Sputnik I.* The act's primary purpose was to identify scientifically and academically talented students and promote their development. It provided funds through **Title V-A for upgrading school counseling programs**, established counseling and guidance institutes, and offered funds and stipends through **Title V-B** to train counselors. In 1964, the NDEA was extended to include elementary counseling. The results were impressive. From 1908 to 1958, the number of school counselors grew to 12,000. "In less than a decade, the number of school counselors quadrupled and counselor to student ratio decreased from 1 to 960 in 1958 to 1 to 450 by 1966–1967" (Bradley & Cox, 2001, p. 34). Indeed, the end of the 1950s began a boom in school counseling that lasted through the 1960s thanks to the cold war and the coming of school age of the baby boom generation (Baker, 1996).

PERSONAL REFLECTION

Much of the growth of counseling in the 1950s came as a reaction to external events or pressures. What other positive outcomes have you seen emerge from crises, such as natural or person-initiated disasters? For example, the state of New York passed legislation licensing counselors as mental health professionals after September 11, 2001.

NEW THEORIES.   The last major event during this decade was the emergence of new guidance and counseling theories. Before **1950, four main theories** influenced the work of counselors: (a) psychoanalysis and insight theory (e.g., Sigmund Freud); (b) trait-factor or directive theories (e.g., E. G. Williamson); (c) humanistic and client-centered theories (e.g., Carl Rogers); and, to a lesser extent, (d) behavioral theories (e.g., B. F. Skinner). Debates among counselors usually centered on whether directive or nondirective counseling was most effective, and almost all counselors assumed that certain tenets of psychoanalysis (e.g., defense mechanisms) were true.

During the 1950s, debate gradually shifted away from this focus as new theories of helping began to emerge. Applied behavioral theories, such as Joseph Wolpe's systematic desensitization, began to gain influence. Cognitive theories also made an appearance, as witnessed by the growth of Albert Ellis's rational-emotive therapy, Eric Berne's transactional analysis, and Aaron Beck's cognitive therapy. Learning theory, self-concept theory, Donald Super's work in career development, and advances in developmental psychology made an impact as well (Aubrey, 1977). By the end of the decade, the number and complexity of theories associated with counseling had grown considerably.

1960s

The initial focus of the 1960s was on **counseling as a developmental profession. Gilbert Wrenn** set the tone for the decade in his widely influential book, *The Counselor in a Changing World* (1962a). His emphasis, reinforced by other prominent professionals such as Leona Tyler and Donald Blocher, was on working with others to resolve developmental needs. Wrenn's book had influence throughout the 1960s, and he, along with Tyler, became one of the strongest counseling advocates in the United States.

The impact of the developmental model lessened, however, as the decade continued, primarily because of **three events: the Vietnam War, the civil rights movement, and the women's movement**. Each event stirred up passions and pointed out needs within society. Many counselors attempted to address these issues by concentrating their attention on special needs created by the events.

Other powerful influences that emerged during the decade were the **humanistic counseling theories** of Dugald Arbuckle, Abraham Maslow, and Sidney Jourard. Also important was the phenomenal growth of the **group movement** (Gladding, 2012). The emphasis of counseling shifted from a one-on-one encounter to small-group interaction. **Behavioral counseling** grew in importance with the appearance of **John Krumboltz's** *Revolution in Counseling* (1966), in which learning (beyond insight) was promoted as the root of change. Thus, the decade's initial focus on development became sidetracked. As Aubrey notes, "the cornucopia of competing counseling methodologies presented to counselors reached an all-time high in the late 1960s" (1977, p. 293).

Another noteworthy occurrence was the passage of the 1963 **Community Mental Health Centers Act**, which authorized the establishment of community mental health centers. These centers opened up opportunities for counselor employment outside educational settings. For instance, alcohol abuse counseling and addiction counseling, initially called **drug abuse counseling**, began in the 1960s and were offered in mental health centers among other places. Marriage and family counseling also emerged in such centers during this time because of the increase in the divorce rate (Hollis, 2000).

Professionalism within the APGA and the continued professional movement within Division 17 of the APA also increased during the 1960s. In 1961, APGA published a "sound code of ethics for counselors" (Nugent, 1981, p. 28). Also during the 1960s, Loughary, Stripling, and Fitzgerald (1965) edited an APGA report that summarized role definitions and **training standards** for school counselors. Division 17, which had further clarified the definition of a counseling psychologist at the 1964 Greyston Conference, began in 1969 to publish a professional journal, *The Counseling Psychologist*, with **Gilbert Wrenn** as its **first editor**.

A final noteworthy milestone was the establishment of the **ERIC Clearinghouse on Counseling and Personnel Services (CAPS)** at the University of Michigan. Founded in 1966 by Garry Walz and funded by the Office of Educational Research and Improvement at the U.S. Department of Education, ERIC/CAPS was another example of the impact of government on the development of counseling. Through the years ERIC/CAPS would become one of the largest and most used resources on counseling activities and trends in the United States and throughout the world. It also sponsored conferences on leading topics in counseling that brought national leaders together.

1970s

The 1970s saw the emergence of several trends that were influenced by actions apart from and within counseling circles. New initiatives related to diversity such as working with women, minorities, and people with disabilities were initiated. They were partly the result of the passage of Title IX, affirmative action, and legislation for disabled persons. Within counseling, occurrences that propelled the profession forward were the formation of **helping skills programs**, the beginning of **licensure**, and the further development of the APGA.

DIVERSIFICATION IN COUNSELING SETTINGS.   The rapid growth of counseling outside educational institutions began in the 1970s when mental health centers and community agencies began to employ counselors. This hiring occurred for several reasons including the passage of new federal legislation, which opened up human services activities more to girls and women, minorities, and persons with disabilities. Specifically, **Title IX** of the Education Amendments came online, along with **affirmative action** laws, and **antidiscrimination legislation** against people with disabilities.

The diversification of counseling meant that specialized training began to be offered in counselor education programs. It also meant the development of new concepts of counseling. For example, Lewis and Lewis (1977) coined the term *community counselor* for a new type of counselor who could function in multidimensional roles regardless of employment setting. Many community counseling programs were established, and counselors became more common in agencies such as mental health clinics, hospices, employee assistance programs, psychiatric hospitals, rehabilitation centers, and substance abuse centers. Equally as striking, and as dramatic in growth, was the formation of the **American Mental Health Counseling Association (AMHCA)** within APGA. Founded in 1976, AMHCA quickly became one of the largest divisions within APGA and united mental health counselors into a professional organization where they defined their roles and goals.

HELPING SKILLS PROGRAMS.   The 1970s saw the development of *helping skills programs* that concentrated on relationship and communication skills. Begun by Truax and Carkhuff (1967) and Ivey (1971), these programs taught basic counseling skills to professionals and nonprofessionals alike. The emphasis was humanistic and eclectic. It was assumed that certain fundamental skills should be mastered to establish satisfactory personal interaction. A bonus for counselors who received this type of training was that they could teach it to others rather easily. Counselors could now consult by teaching some of their skills to those with whom they worked, mainly teachers and paraprofessionals. In many ways, this trend was a new version of Brewer's concept of education as guidance.

STATE LICENSURE.   By the mid-1970s, state boards of examiners for psychologists had become restrictive. Some of their restrictions, such as barring graduates of education department counseling programs from taking the psychology licensure exam, caused considerable tension, not only between APA and APGA but also within the APA membership itself. The result was APGA's move toward state and national licensure for counselors. Thomas J. Sweeney (1991) chaired the first APGA Licensure Committee and he and his successors did so with much success. **Virginia was the first state to adopt a professional counselor licensure law**, doing so in 1976. It was followed quickly by Arkansas and Alabama before the decade ended (Figure 1.1). In regard to licensure, it should be noted that California passed a marriage, family, and child counselor law in 1962. The problem with the California law was it defined the term "counselor" broadly and later replaced the term with the word "therapist," which was strictly defined, and which ultimately disenfranchised counselors. It was not until 2010 that the California legislature passed a professional counselor licensure law.

A STRONG APGA.   During the 1970s, APGA emerged as an even stronger professional organization. Several changes altered its image and function, one of which was the building of its own headquarters in Alexandria, Virginia. APGA also began to question its professional

FIGURE 1.1 All states legally regulate counselors

identification because guidance and personnel seemed to be outmoded ways of defining the organization's emphases.

In 1973, the **Association of Counselor Educators and Supervisors (ACES)**, a division of APGA, **outlined the standards for a master's degree in counseling**. Robert Stripling of the University of Florida spearheaded that effort. In 1977, ACES approved guidelines for doctoral preparation in counseling (Stripling, 1978). During the decade, APGA membership increased to almost 40,000. Four new divisions (in addition to AMHCA) were chartered: the Association for Religious and Value Issues in Counseling, the Association for Specialists in Group Work, the Association for Non-White Concerns in Personnel and Guidance, and the Public Offender Counselor Association.

CASE EXAMPLE

Justin Feels Justified

Justin received his counseling degree in the mid-1970s. Although counseling was not as developed as it is now, Justin feels considerable pride in how the profession grew during "his decade." He feels justified telling others that the 1970s was the best decade for becoming a counselor. How is his claim supported? What might he be overlooking?

1980s

The 1980s saw the continued growth of counseling as a profession, exemplified by proactive initiatives from counselors associated with APGA and Division 17. Among the most noteworthy events of the decade were those that standardized the training and certification of counselors, recognized counseling as a distinct profession, increased the diversification of counselor specialties, and emphasized human growth and development.

STANDARDIZATION OF TRAINING AND CERTIFICATION.   The move toward standardized training and certification was one that began early in the decade and grew stronger yearly. In **1981**, the **Council for Accreditation of Counseling and Related Educational Programs (CACREP)** was formed as an affiliate organization of APGA. It refined the standards first proposed by ACES in the late 1970s and initially accredited four programs and recognized others that had been accredited by the California state counselor association and ACES (Steinhauser & Bradley, 1983). In 1987, **CACREP achieved membership in the Council on Postsecondary Accreditation** (COPA), bringing it "into a position of accreditation power parallel to" such specialty accreditation bodies as the APA (Herr, 1985, p. 399). CACREP standardized counselor education programs for master's and doctoral programs in the areas of school, community, mental health, and marriage and family counseling, as well as for personnel services for college students.

Complementary to the work of CACREP, the **National Board for Certified Counselors (NBCC)**, which was formed in **1982**, began to certify counselors on a national level. It developed a standardized test and defined eight major subject areas in which counselors should be knowledgeable: (a) human growth and development, (b) social and cultural foundations, (c) helping relationships, (d) groups, (e) lifestyle and career development, (f) appraisal, (g) research and evaluation, and (h) professional orientation. To become a National Certified Counselor (NCC), examinees have to pass a standardized test and meet experiential and character reference qualifications. By the end of the decade, there were approximately 17,000 NCC professionals.

Finally, in collaboration with CACREP, the **National Academy of Certified Clinical Mental Health Counselors** (NACCMHC), an affiliate of the AMHCA, continued to define training standards and certify counselors in mental health counseling, a process it had begun in the late 1970s (Seiler, Brooks, & Beck, 1987; Wilmarth, 1985). It also began training supervisors of mental health counselors in 1988. Both programs attracted thousands of new professionals into counseling and upgraded the credentials of those already in the field.

COUNSELING AS A DISTINCT PROFESSION.   The **evolution of counseling in the 1980s as a distinct helping profession** came as a result of events, issues, and forces, both inside and outside APGA (Heppner, 1990b). Inside APGA was a growing awareness among its leaders that the words "personnel" and "guidance" no longer described the work of its members (Sheeley, 2002). In **1984**, after considerable debate, the **APGA changed its name to the American Association for Counseling and Development (AACD)** to "reflect the changing demographics of its membership and the settings in which they worked" (Herr, 1985, p. 395). The name change was symbolic of the rapid transformation in identity that APGA members had been experiencing through the implementation of policies regarding training, certification, and standards. External events that influenced APGA to change its name and ultimately its focus included legislation, especially on the federal level, that recognized mental health providers and actions by other mental health services associations.

Moreover, there was a newness in professional commitment among AACD members. **Chi Sigma Iota, an international academic and professional honor society**, was formed in **1985** by Thomas J. Sweeney to promote excellence in the counseling profession. It grew to more than 100 chapters and 5,000 members by the end of the decade (Sweeney, 1989). Furthermore, liability insurance policies, new counseling specialty publications, legal defense funds, legislative initiatives, and a variety of other membership services were made available to AACD members by its national headquarters (Myers, 1990). By 1989, over 58,000 individuals had become members of AACD, an increase of more than 18,000 members in 10 years.

The founding of CSI was followed the next year, **1986**, by the establishment of the **American Association of State Counseling Boards (AASCB)** by Ted Remley. AASCB from the beginning was an association of bodies that were legally responsible for the registration, certification, or licensing of counselors within their jurisdictions in the United States. The first meeting of the group was in Charleston, South Carolina.

Division 17 also continued to grow at a steady rate (Woody, Hansen, & Rossberg, 1989). In 1987, a professional standards conference was assembled by its president, George Gazda, to define further the uniqueness of counseling psychology and counseling in general.

PERSONAL REFLECTION

What's in a name? Think of your own name and how it has influenced your relationships. If you have changed your name, write down some of the impacts of that change. What might be some of the ramifications of a counseling organization changing its name?

MORE DIVERSIFICATION OF COUNSELING.   During the 1980s, counselors became more diversified. Large numbers of counselors continued to be employed in primary and secondary schools and in higher education in a variety of student personnel services. Mental health counselors and community/agency counselors were the two largest blocks of professionals outside formal educational environments. In addition, the number of counselors swelled in mental health settings for business employees, the aging, and married persons and families. Symbolic of that growth, the Association for Adult Development and Aging (AADA) and the International Association for Marriage and Family Counselors (IAMFC) were organized and chartered as divisions of AACD in 1987 and 1990, respectively.

Strong membership in AACD divisions dedicated to group work, counselor education, humanistic education, measurement and development, religious and value issues, employment and career development, rehabilitation, multicultural concerns, addiction and offender work, and military personnel further exemplified the diversity of counseling during the 1980s. Special issues of AACD journals focused on topics such as violence (*Journal of Counseling and Development*, March 1987), the gifted and talented (*Journal of Counseling and Development*, May 1986), the arts (*Journal of Mental Health Counseling*, January 1985), and prevention (*Elementary School Guidance and Counseling*, October 1989). These publications helped broaden the scope of counseling services and counselor awareness.

INCREASED EMPHASIS ON HUMAN GROWTH AND DEVELOPMENT.   Counseling's emphasis on human growth and development during the 1980s took several forms. For example, a new spotlight was placed on developmental counseling across the **life span** (Gladstein & Apfel, 1987). New behavioral expressions associated with Erik Erikson's first five stages of life development were formulated as well (Hamachek, 1988), and an increased emphasis on the development of adults and the elderly resulted in the formation of the Association for Adult Aging and Development (AAAD).

A second way that human growth and development was stressed was through increased attention to **gender issues** and **sexual preferences** (O'Neil & Carroll, 1988; Pearson, 1988; Weinrach, 1987). Carol Gilligan's (1982) landmark study on the development of moral values in females, which helped introduce **feminist theory** into the counseling arena, forced human growth specialists to examine the differences between genders.

An emphasis on **moral development** was the third way in which human growth issues were highlighted (Colangelo, 1985; Lapsley & Quintana, 1985). There was a renewed emphasis on models of moral development, such as Lawrence Kohlberg's theory (1969), and increased research in the area of enhancing moral development. In counselor education, it was found that moral development was closely related to both cognitive ability and empathy (Bowman & Reeves, 1987).

Finally, the challenges of working with different ethnic and **cultural groups** received more discussion (Ponterotto & Casas, 1987). In focusing on multicultural issues, the Association for Multicultural Counseling and Development (AMCD) took the lead, but multicultural themes, such as the importance of diversity, became a central issue among all groups, especially in light of the renewed racism that developed in the 1980s (Carter, 1990).

1990s

The 1990s continued to see changes in the evolution of the counseling profession, some of them symbolic and others structural. One change that was significant was the **1992** decision by the AACD to modify its name and become the **American Counseling Association (ACA)**. The new name better reflected the membership and mission of the organization.

A second noteworthy event in the 1990s also occurred in 1992, when **counseling**, as a **primary mental health profession**, was included for the **first time** in the health care human resource statistics compiled by the Center for Mental Health Services and the National Institute of Mental Health (Manderscheid & Sonnenschein, 1992). This type of recognition put counseling on par with other mental health specialties such as psychology, social work, and psychiatry. By the beginning of the 21st century, it was estimated that there were approximately 100,000 counselors in the United States (Wedding, 2008).

A third event in counseling that also originated in 1992 was the writing of the **multicultural counseling competencies and standards** by Sue, Arredondo, and McDavis (1992). Although these competencies mainly applied to counseling with people of color, they set the stage for a larger debate about the nature of multicultural counseling—for instance, the inclusion within the definition of other groups, such as people with disabilities. Thus, a lively discussion occurred during the decade about what diversity and counseling within a pluralistic society entailed (Weinrach & Thomas, 1998).

A fourth issue in the 1990s was a focus on health care and an **increase in managed health care organizations**. Conglomerates emerged, and many counselors became providers under these new organized ways of providing services. As a result, the number of independent counselor practitioners decreased as did the number of sessions a counselor could offer under managed health care plans. A new emphasis on legislation connected with these organizations forced counselors to become increasingly informed and active as legislative proponents (Barstow, 1998).

In addition, there was a renewed focus within the decade on counseling issues related to the whole person. Counselors became more aware of social factors important to the development and maintenance of mental disorders and health including the importance of organism-context interaction (i.e., ***contextualism***) (Thomas, 1996). These factors include spirituality, family environment, socioeconomic considerations, the impact of groups and group work, and prevention (Bemak, 1998).

Other developments in the 1990s included the following:

- The merger of the National Academy of Clinical Mental Health Counselors with NBCC to credential counselors.
- The growth of CACREP-accredited programs in counselor education on both the doctoral and master's levels.
- An increase in the number of publications on counseling by ACA, commercial publishers, and ERIC/CASS (Counseling and Student Services Clearinghouse).
- The growth of Chi Sigma Iota to over 200 chapters and 20,000 members.
- Growth of state counselor licensure laws.

CURRENT TRENDS IN THE TWENTY-FIRST CENTURY

In **2002, counseling** formally **celebrated its 50th anniversary** as a profession under the umbrella of the ACA. However, within the celebration was a realization that counseling is ever changing and that emphases of certain topics, issues, and concerns at the beginning of the 21st century would most likely change with the needs of clients and society. The changing roles of men and women, innovations in media and technology, poverty, homelessness, trauma, loneliness, and aging, among other topics, captured counseling's attention as the new century began (Lee & Walz, 1998; Webber & Mascari, 2010). Among the most pressing topics were dealing with violence, trauma, and crises; managed care; wellness; social justice; technology; leadership; and identity.

Dealing with Violence, Trauma, and Crises

Conflict is a part of most societies, even those that are predominantly peaceful. It occurs "when a person perceives another to be interfering or obstructing progress toward meeting important needs" (Corcoran & Mallinckrodt, 2000, p. 474). ***Violence*** results when one or more parties address conflict in terms of win–lose tactics. In the United States concerns about conflict and safety from both a prevention and treatment standpoint have emerged in the past couple of decades from a rash of school shootings, such as **Columbine**, and the **Oklahoma City** bombing where in each a number of innocent people were killed (Daniels, 2002). A defining moment in conflict and violence occurred on **9/11/2001** when terrorists crashed commercial airliners into the World Trade Center towers in New York City and the Pentagon in Washington, DC. These acts signaled the beginning of an active and new emphasis in counseling on preparing and responding to **trauma and tragedies** such as those associated with **Hurricane Katrina, the Iraq and Afghanistan Wars**, and the **Virginia Tech shootings** (Walz & Kirkman, 2002; Webber & Mascari, 2010). Within this new emphasis is a practical focus, such as developing crisis plans and strategies for working with different age groups from young children to the elderly in order to provide psychological first aid and facilitate the grieving and healing process.

Trauma is a normal response to a very abnormal situation. "Natural disasters, ongoing wars, terrorist attacks, plane crashes, school violence and abuse are among the most widely recognized causes of trauma . . . trauma can also stem from events that don't necessarily make the national news" (Shallcross, 2010, p. 26). Indeed, there are the tragedies of daily life—auto accidents, or the sudden loss of family members, friends, classmates, or coworkers that have a traumatic effect on individuals as profound as any major occurrence in the world. These events and the people who experience them are those with whom counselors interact with most. Some of the signs and symptoms associated with **trauma-induced stress** include sleep disturbance, emotional instability, impaired concentration, and an inability to perform routine and regular daily tasks. However, not all signs of trauma are visible. Nevertheless, early intervention for trauma survivors should emphasize helping them to connect with natural social support systems and resources that are available to them in their communities.

In the area of dealing with trauma, a renewed emphasis has been focused in recent years on the treatment of stress and both *acute stress disorder (ASD)* and *post-traumatic stress disorder (PTSD)* (Jordan, 2002; Marotta, 2000; Taylor & Baker, 2007). Both ASD and PTSD develop as a result of being exposed to a traumatic event involving actual or threatened injury (American Psychiatric Association, 1994). Threats are associated with intense fear, helplessness, or horror. ASD is more transient; people develop symptoms within about 4 weeks of a situation and resolve them within about another 4 weeks (Jordan, 2002). However, PTSD differs in that, whereas, except in cases of delayed onset, symptoms occur within about a month of an incident, they may last for months or years if not treated. People who develop PTSD may display a number of symptoms including reexperiencing the traumatic event again through flashbacks, avoidance of trauma-related activities, and emotional numbing plus other disorders such as substance abuse, obsessive-compulsive disorders, and panic disorders (Jones, Young, & Leppma, 2010).

Many survivors of the 9/11 World Trade attacks suffered from PTSD years later. A survey of over 3,200 evacuees of the Twin Towers found that nearly all suffered at least one PTSD symptom and 15% had PTSD 2 or 3 years after the attacks. The likelihood of PTSD was greater for those who evacuated later, were on a high floor, or worked for a company that lost employees in the disaster (Columbia University's Mailman School of Public Health, 2011s).

Counselors who are employed in the area of working with ASD or PTSD clients need specialized training to help these individuals. Crises often last in people's minds long after the events that produced them. **Crisis counseling** as well as long-term counseling services are often needed, especially with individuals who have PTSD. For example, psychosocial and moral development may be arrested in PTSD war veterans making it more difficult for them to have successful relationships and to cope by themselves "with the trauma, confusion, emotion, brutality, and fear associated with combat" (Taylor & Baker, 2007, p. 368). "It is only by recognizing and treatment of PTSD that trauma victims can hope to move past the impact of trauma and lead healthy lives" (Grosse, 2002, p. 25).

The Challenge of Managed Care

"*Managed care* involves a contractual arrangement between a mental health professional and a third party, the managed care company, regarding the care and treatment of the first party, the client" (Murphy, 1998, p. 3). Managed care is and will be a major concern to counselors during the 21st century and indeed has already become the new gatekeeper for mental health practice

(Lawless, Ginter, & Kelly, 1999). There are only a few dominant companies in the managed care business, but their influence is tremendous. They determine how health care providers, including counselors, deliver services and what rights and recourses consumers have.

"Although managed care models have promoted accountability in treatment through an emphasis on quality over quantity of services, such models often fail to acknowledge critical differences in treatment needs related to specific issues or specific populations" (Calley, 2007, p. 132). Managed care arrangements often require clients first to see a gatekeeper physician before they can be referred to a specialist such as a counselor. This restriction, along with limited financial reimbursement, and limitations on sessions allowed under managed care has had mixed results.

Managed care has advanced the counseling profession by including counselors on both managed care boards and as providers of services (Goetz, 1998). However, managed care has also had a negative impact on the profession (Daniels, 2001). As a group, counselors have not been well compensated under most managed care arrangements. Client consumers have often been limited in getting the services they need. Likewise, counselors have been frustrated in being able to offer adequate treatment or be seated on managed care boards. In addition, managed care companies have shifted the focus of treatment from treatment that was relationship based, such as counseling, to treatment that is more medication only based even though the research does not support such an emphasis (Nordal, 2010). Finally, there are ethical concerns in managed care services offered by counselors to clients. These concerns are around issues like informed consent, confidentiality, maintaining records, competence, integrity, human welfare, conflict of interest, and conditions of employment (Daniels, 2001).

The challenge for counselors in the future is to find ways to either work more effectively with managed care companies or work outside such companies and still be major players in the mental health arena. If counselors stay with managed care services, it will become increasingly important for them to be on managed care provider boards, for it is these boards that will ultimately determine who is credentialed and for what with managed care organizations. Regardless, it will be essential for counselors to attain a national provider number if they are to maintain flexibility in the services they provide.

CASE EXAMPLE

The Limitations on Lauren

Lauren was well established as a counselor. She was known for her effectiveness. She was into long-term counseling relationships, though, and thought that anything less than a 3-month commitment to the counseling process was a waste for both the client and the counselor.

Lauren's philosophy and her commitment to the process of counseling bothered her when a new client, Lucy, who appeared quite depressed showed up in her office with a managed care contract that allowed for only six sessions. Lauren knew she could not help Lucy very effectively in six sessions. Yet, she knew that to turn her away might make her more disturbed.

What would you do if you were in Lauren's shoes?

Promoting Wellness

In recent years, the idea of promoting wellness within the counseling profession has grown (Lawson, Venart, Hazler, & Kottler, 2007; Myers & Sweeney, 2005, 2008). Wellness involves many aspects of life including the physical, intellectual, social, psychological, emotional, and environmental. Myers, Sweeney, and Witmer (2000) define *wellness* as a way of life oriented toward optimal health and well-being in which body, mind, and spirit are integrated by the individual to live life more fully within the human and natural community. "Ideally, it is the optimum state of health and well-being that each individual is capable of achieving" (p. 252).

A model for promoting wellness has been developed by Myers et al. (2000). It revolves around **five life tasks: spirituality, self-direction, work and leisure, friendship,** and **love**. Some of these tasks, such as self-direction, are further subdivided into a number of subtasks, such as sense of worth, sense of control, problem solving and creativity, sense of humor, and self-care. The premise of this model is that healthy functioning occurs on a developmental continuum that is interactive, and healthy behaviors at one point in life affect subsequent development and functioning as well.

More and more, "professional counselors seek to encourage wellness, a positive state of well-being, through developmental, preventive, and wellness-enhancing interventions" (Myers & Sweeney, 2008, p. 482). There is still debate over the exact definition of wellness and how it is measured (Roscoe, 2009). However, it appears that wellness will be one of the major emphases within counseling in the 21st century because of the counseling profession's focus on health and well-being as a developmental aspect of life.

Concern for Social Justice and Advocacy

Early pioneers in what evolved to be counseling were interested in the welfare of people in society. Therefore, it is not surprising that counselors of today are drawn to social justice causes and to advocacy. *Social justice* "reflects a fundamental valuing of fairness and equity in resources, rights, and treatment for marginalized individuals and groups of people who do not share the power in society because of their immigration, racial, ethic, age, socioeconomic, religious heritage, physical abilities, or sexual orientation status groups" (Constantine, Hage, Kindaichi, & Bryant, 2007, p. 24). Major elements of a social justice approach include "helping clients identify and challenge environmental limits to their success," "challenging systematic forms of oppression through counselor social action," and "liberating clients from oppressive social practices" (Astramovich & Harris, 2007, p. 271). Social justice also helps counselors become more attuned to social injustices and thereby work with clients in a more sensitive and just manner (Hays, Prosek, & McLeod, 2010).

Among the active involvement counselors are taking in social justice causes now are advocacy, along with community outreach, and public policy making (Constantine et al., 2007). **Advocacy** involves "helping clients challenge institutional and social barriers that impede academic, career, or personal-social development" (Lee, 1998, pp. 8–9). The purpose is to "increase a client's sense of personal power and to foster sociopolitical changes that reflect greater responsiveness to the client's personal needs" (Kiselica & Robinson, 2001, p. 387).

In order to be effective as an advocate, counselors need to have "the capacity for commitment and an appreciation of human suffering; nonverbal and verbal communications skills; the

CASE EXAMPLE

The Tragic Death of Deamonte – A True Story

Lee and Rodgers (2009) tell the story of the death of a 12-year old boy in the metropolitan DC area whose name was Deamonte. His mother was a wage-reliant worker with no health insurance and whose family Medicaid coverage had temporarily lapsed. When Deamonte got a toothache, his mother could not afford the $80 dental bill so he initially went untreated. By the time he was seen the bacteria from the abscess in his rotting tooth had spread to his brain. "After two operations and 6 weeks of hospital care, Deamonte ultimately died. It was later revealed that Deamonte and his younger brother, DaShawn, never received dental attention at any time during their young lives" (p. 284).

How does this story personalize the need for social justice and advocacy? What do you think counselors can or should do when they encounter situations where a tragedy of this magnitude may happen?

ability to maintain a multisystems perspective"; individual, group, and organizational intervention skills; "knowledge and use of the media, technology, and the Internet; and assessment and research skills" (Kiselica & Robinson, 2001, p. 391). Advocates must also be socially smart, knowing themselves, others, and the systems around them. Likewise, they must know when to be diplomatic as well as confrontational. In addition, they must have a knowledge and passion for the cause or causes they advocate for and be willing to be flexible and compromise to obtain realistic goals.

In the American Counseling Association, Counselors for Social Justice (CSJ) and ACES are the leading groups for advocacy and social justice. Chi Sigma Iota (Counseling Academic and Professional Honor Society International) and NBCC are the leading advocacy groups outside the ACA for these causes. "Counselors have an ethical and moral mandate to work toward social justice" (Bryan, 2009, p. 510).

Greater Emphasis on Technology

Technology use has grown rapidly in counseling (Kennedy, 2008b; Shaw & Shaw, 2006). What once was considered promising has now become reality, and technology "is having a profound impact on almost every aspect of life including education, business, science, religion, government, medicine, and agriculture" (Hohenshil, 2000, p. 365). For example, technology, particularly the Internet, is now a major tool for career planning (Harris-Bowlsbey, Dikel, & Sampson, 2002).

Initially, technology was used in counseling to facilitate record keeping, manipulate data, and do word processing. More attention is now being placed on factors affecting technology and client interaction, especially on the Internet and on telephones (Reese, Conoley, & Brossart, 2006). "The number of network-based computer applications in counseling has been increasing rapidly" (Sampson, Kolodinsky, & Greeno, 1997, p. 203). Listservs and bulletin board systems (BBSs) have become especially popular for posting messages and encouraging dialogue between counselors. One of the most popular listservs in counseling, at least among counselor educators, is CESNet. E-mail is also used in counselor-to-counselor interactions as well as counselor-to-client conversations. Websites are maintained by counseling organizations, counselor education programs, and individual counselors (Pachis, Rettman, & Gotthoffer, 2001). For instance the American Counseling Association's website is www.counseling.org. There are even **"online" professional counseling journals**, the first being the *Journal of Technology in Counseling* (Layne & Hohenshil, 2005; (www.jtc.colstate.edu/) and the most recent being *The Professional Counselor: Research and Practice* (www.tpcjournal.nbcc.org/).

The similarities between working with certain aspects of technology (e.g., computers or telephones) and working with clients are notable (e.g., establishing a relationship, learning a client's language, learning a client's thought process, setting goals, and taking steps to achieve them). However, the practice is fraught with ethical and legal risks, such as (a) the issue of confidentiality, (b) how to handle emergency situations, (c) the lack of nonverbal information, (d) the danger of offering online services over state judicial lines, (e) the lack of outcome research on the effectiveness of online counseling services, (f) technology failures, and (g) the difficulties of establishing rapport with a client who is not visually seen (Pollock, 2006; Shaw & Shaw, 2006).

Despite drawbacks, a number of counselors and counseling-related organizations offer services across the Internet (e.g., suicide prevention; Befrienders International, 2007) and through the telephone (adolescent smokers cessation help; Tedeschi, Zhu, Anderson, Cummins, & Ribner, 2005). This trend is understandable given the fact that people are pressed for time, phone services are readily available, and Internet use is ubiquitous.

Telephone counselors can use web technology to enhance the services they offer if they follow guidelines adopted by the NBCC on Internet counseling (www.nbcc.org/ServiceCenter/Ethics). Clients who may be especially well served through the use of **online counseling** are those who (a) are geographically isolated, (b) are physically disabled, (c) would ordinarily not seek counseling, and (d) are more prone to writing than speaking (Shaw & Shaw, 2006).

Competencies for counselors continue to be developed in regard to the use of technology in therapy. These competencies include skills they should master such as being able to use word processing programs, audiovisual equipment, e-mail, the Internet, Listservs, and CD-ROM databases. Although the Internet, the telephone, and other technologies will never fully replace face-to-face counseling, clearly they are here to stay. They offer a unique experience with both benefits and limitations (Haberstroh, Duffey, Evans, Gee, & Trepal, 2007). They require a unique set of skills as well as personality traits, such as patience and persistence (Haberstroh, Parr, Bradley, Morgan-Fleming, & Gee, 2008).

Cybercounseling, the practice of professional counseling and information delivery through electronic means, usually the Internet, when clients and counselors are in separate or remote locations, is growing as a modality by which counseling services are delivered. It is a phenomenon occurring worldwide, for example, in South Korea as well as the United States (Maples & Han, 2008). The Center for Credentialing and Education, an affiliate of NBCC, now even offers a **Distance Certified Counselor credential**, providing national visibility and certification for counselors delivering online services (Center for Credentialing and Education, 2011).

Streaming video and wireless connectivity are two of the more cutting-edge technologies that will affect how counselors function in the future (Layne & Hohenshil, 2005). Counselors "would be wise to educate themselves on the ethical and technical issues emerging in this new arena" (Pollock, 2006, p. 69).

Leadership

With the rapid changes in society and counseling, there is an increased need for counselors to develop their leadership and planning skills. By so doing, they become a more positive and potent force in society. Although many counseling skills can be readily applied to effective leadership such as empathy, group processing, and goal setting, other "specific leadership practices, such as completing performance reviews, communicating compensation philosophies and practices, addressing colleagues' performance problems, and being accountable for team camaraderie and productivity, are not taught in traditional counseling programs" (Curtis & Sherlock, 2006, p. 121). Therefore, counselors are particularly challenged in agencies and schools to move beyond clinical supervision and into *managerial leadership* roles. In such roles they influence "a group of individuals to achieve a goal" (p. 120). Managerial leadership is an important topic in counseling because there is considerable evidence that "it makes a difference in an organization's performance" (p. 121).

The ACA is engaged in leadership activities through working nationally and regionally to provide training for new leaders and legislative training for counselors. Divisions within the ACA also focus on leadership development and legislative training. Chi Sigma Iota (Counseling Academic and Professional Honor Society International) is especially strong in providing leadership training and services to counselors through workshops and seminars.

One area of leadership, *strategic planning*, involves envisioning the future and making preparations to meet anticipated needs. Similar to the counseling skill of leading, it is usually accomplished in a group and involves hard data as well as anticipations and expectations (C. Kormanski, personal interview, June 20, 1994). In 2005 the ACA and 30 other counseling groups initiated the *20/20 Future of Counseling* initiative in order to map out the future of the profession for the year 2020. By the fall of 2007, the group had agreed on seven principles that unite the counseling profession (Kaplan & Gladding, 2011). By 2010 it has come to a consensus definition of counseling.

Identity

Since 1952 most counselors in the United States and a number in other countries have held membership in ACA. The composition of ACA has been mixed, "like a ball of multicolored yarn," and sometimes within ACA there has been an emphasis within the specialties of counseling as opposed to the overall profession (Bradley & Cox, 2001, p. 39). Other professions, such as medicine, have overcome the divisiveness that comes within a profession where there is more than one professional track that practitioners can follow. ACA has not been as fortunate. Part of the reason is that counseling has not adapted as much of a postmodern stance regarding its identity as some other professions such as medicine (Hansen, 2010).

However, as counseling has grown stronger as a profession with more counselor education programs that promote identity, with a stronger national professional association (ACA), with more research literature being generated, and with more professionals who see themselves as counselors first and foremost, its identity has become more widely accepted by the public. Thus, the emphasis on modifying adjectives to the noun "counselor" has begun to diminish in many cases (Myers & Sweeney, 2001). Clearly, as ACA and related organizations, such as CACREP, NBCC, and AASCB become stronger, all counselors stand to benefit as does the public.

The following divisions and affiliates now operate under ACA's structure:

1. *National Career Development Association (NCDA)*—founded in 1913; formerly the National Vocational Guidance Association
2. *Association for Humanistic Counseling (AHC)*—founded in 1931; formerly the *Student Personnel Association for Teacher Education* (SPATE), *Association for Humanistic Education and Development*, and *Counseling Association for Humanistic Education and Development (CAHEAD)*
3. *Association for Counselor Education and Supervision (ACES)*—founded in 1938; formerly the National Association of Guidance Supervisors and Counselor Trainers
4. *American School Counselor Association (ASCA)*—founded in 1953
5. *American Rehabilitation Counseling Association (ARCA)*—founded in 1958; formerly the Division of Rehabilitation Counseling
6. *Association for Assessment in Counseling and Education (AACE)*—founded in 1965; formerly the Association for Measurement and Evaluation in Guidance
7. *National Employment Counselors Association (NECA)*—founded in 1966
8. *Association for Multicultural Counseling and Development (AMCD)*—founded in 1972; formerly the Association for Non-white Concerns in Personnel and Guidance
9. *International Association of Addictions and Offender Counselors (IAAOC)*—founded in 1972; formerly the Public Offender Counselor Association
10. *Association for Specialists in Group Work (ASGW)*—founded in 1973
11. *Association for Spiritual, Ethical, and Religious Values in Counseling (ASERVIC)*—founded in 1974; formerly the National Catholic Guidance Conference
12. *American Mental Health Counselors Association (AMHCA)*—founded in 1976
13. *Association for Counselors and Educators in Government (ACEG)*—founded in 1984
14. *Association for Adult Development and Aging (AADA)*—founded in 1986
15. *International Association of Marriage and Family Counselors (IAMFC)*—founded in 1989
16. *American College Counseling Association (ACCA)*—founded in 1991
17. *Association for Lesbian, Gay, Bisexual, and Transgender Issues in Counseling (ALGBTIC)*—founded in 1996
18. *Counselors for Social Justice*—founded in 1999
19. *Association for Creativity in Counseling*—founded in 2004

MyCounselingLab™

Go to Topic 10: *History of Counseling*, in the MyCounselingLab™ site (www .MyCounselingLab.com) for *Counseling: A Comprehensive Profession*, Seventh Edition, where you can:

- Find learning outcomes for *History of Counseling* along with the national standards that connect to these outcomes.
- Complete Assignments and Activities that can help you more deeply understand the chapter content.
- Apply and practice your understanding of the core skills identified in the chapter with the Building Counseling Skills unit.
- Prepare yourself for professional certification with a Practice for Certification quiz.
- Connect to videos through the Video and Resource Library.

Summary and Conclusion

Counseling is a distinct profession. It is concerned with wellness, prevention, development, and situational difficulties as well as with helping persons with particular psychological disorders. It is based on principles and a definition that has evolved over the years. It contains within it a number of specialties.

An examination of the history of counseling shows that the profession has an interdisciplinary base. It began with the almost simultaneous concerns and activities of Frank Parsons, Jesse B. Davis, and Clifford Beers to provide, reform, and improve services in vocational guidance, character development of school children, and mental health treatment. Counseling became interlinked early in its history with psychometrics, psychology, anthropology,

ethics, law, philosophy, and sociology. In addition to the development of theory and the generation of practical ways of working with people, important events in the development of counseling include the involvement of the government in counseling during and after World War I, the Great Depression, World War II, and the launching of *Sputnik*.

Ideas from innovators such as E. G. Williamson, Carl Rogers, Gilbert Wrenn, Donald Super, Leona Tyler, and Thomas J. Sweeney have shaped the development of the profession and broadened its horizon. The emergence and growth of the American Counseling Association (rooted in the establishment of the National Vocational Guidance Association in 1913) has been a major factor in the growth of the counseling profession.

Challenges for the profession in the 21st century include dealing with violence, trauma, and crises; interacting positively with managed care organizations; promoting wellness; using technology wisely and effectively; promoting social justice and advocating for client needs; providing leadership; and working on establishing a stronger identity for the profession. The timeline that follows (Figure 1.2) provides highlights in the history of counseling and spotlights current and future issues.

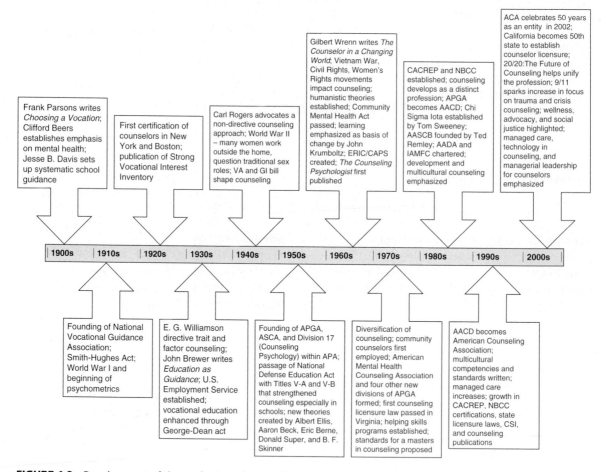

FIGURE 1.2   Development of the profession of counseling from 1900 to 2012

Personal and Professional Aspects of Counseling

Chapter Overview

From reading this chapter you will learn about

- The important personality factors and background qualities of counselors
- Professional aspects of being a counselor
- Credentialing of counselors
- Attribution and systematic framework of counseling
- Engaging in professional counselor-related activities

As you read consider

- What has motivated you to enter the profession of counseling
- What qualities you need to cultivate more of in order to be successful as a counselor
- The many facets in credentialing and the differences in the types of credentials available

In the midst of a day
    that has brought only gray skies, hard rain,
        and two cups of lukewarm coffee,
You come to me with Disney World wishes
    waiting for me to change into:
        a Houdini figure with Daniel Boone's style
Prince Charming's grace and Abe Lincoln's wisdom
Who with magic words, a wand,
    frontier spirit, and perhaps a smile
        can cure all troubles in a flash.
But reality sits in a green-cushioned chair,
    lightning has struck a nearby tree,
        yesterday ended another month,
I'm uncomfortable sometimes in silence,
And unlike fantasy figures
I can't always be
    what you see in your mind.

Reprinted from "Reality Sits in a Green-Cushioned Chair," by S. T. Gladding, 1973, *Personnel and Guidance Journal, 54*, p. 222. © S. T. Gladding.

MyCounselingLab™

Visit the MyCounselingLab™ site (www.MyCounselingLab.com) for *Counseling: A Comprehensive Profession,* Seventh Edition to enhance your understanding of chapter concepts. You'll have the opportunity to practice your skills through video- and case-based Assignments and Activities as well as Building Counseling Skills units and to prepare for your certification exam with Practice for Certification quizzes.

Counseling is "an altruistic and noble profession." For the most part, "it attracts caring, warm, friendly and sensitive people" (Myrick, 1997, p. 4). According to the Bureau of Labor Statistics, counselors held about 665,000 jobs in 2008, and the profession is projected to increase 18% in employment between 2008 and 2018.

However, individuals aspire to become counselors for many reasons. Some motivators, like the people involved, are healthier than others, just as some counselor education programs, theories, and systems of counseling are stronger than others. It is important that persons who wish to be counselors examine themselves before committing their lives to the profession. Whether they choose counseling as a career or not, people can be helped by studying counseling and their own lives in relationship to the field. By doing so they may gain insight into their thoughts, feelings, and actions, learn how to relate better to others, and understand how the counseling process works. They may also further develop their moral reasoning and empathetic abilities.

The **effectiveness of a counselor** and of counseling depends on numerous variables, including

- the **personality and background of the counselor**;
- the **formal education of the counselor**; and
- the **ability of the counselor to engage in professional counseling-related activities**, such as continuing education, supervision, advocacy, and the building of a portfolio.

Counselors and the counseling process have a dynamic effect on others. If counseling is not beneficial, it is most likely harmful (Carkhuff, 1969; Ellis, 1984; Mays & Franks, 1980). In this chapter, personal and professional factors that influence the counseling profession are examined.

THE PERSONALITY AND BACKGROUND OF THE COUNSELOR

A counselor's personality is at times a crucial ingredient in counseling. Counselors should possess personal qualities of maturity, empathy, and warmth. They should be altruistic in spirit and not easily upset or frustrated. Unfortunately, such is not always the case, and some people aspire to be in the profession of counseling for the wrong reasons.

Negative Motivators for Becoming a Counselor

Not everyone who wants to be a counselor or applies to a counselor education program should enter the field. The reason has to do with the motivation behind the pursuit of the profession and the incongruent personality match between the would-be-counselor and the demands of counseling.

A number of students "attracted to professional counseling . . . appear to have serious personality and adjustment problems" (Witmer & Young, 1996, p. 142). Most are screened out or decide to pursue other careers before they finish a counselor preparation program. However, before matriculating into graduate counseling programs, candidates should explore their reasons for doing so. According to Guy (1987), **dysfunctional motivators for becoming a counselor** include the following:

- *Emotional distress*—individuals who have unresolved personal traumas
- *Vicarious coping*—persons who live their lives through others rather than have meaningful lives of their own
- *Loneliness and isolation*—individuals who do not have friends and seek them through counseling experiences
- *A desire for power*—people who feel frightened and impotent in their lives and seek to control others
- *A need for love*—individuals who are narcissistic and grandiose and believe that all problems are resolved through the expression of love and tenderness
- *Vicarious rebellion*—persons who have unresolved anger and act out their thoughts and feelings through their clients' defiant behaviors

Fortunately, most people who eventually become counselors and remain in the profession have healthy reasons for pursuing the profession, and a number even consider it to be a "calling" (Foster, 1996). Counselors and counselors-in-training should always assess themselves in regard to who they are and what they are doing. Such questions may include those that examine their development histories, their best and worst qualities, and personal/professional goals and objectives (Faiver, Eisengart, & Colonna, 2004).

CASE EXAMPLE

Roberta's Rotation

Roberta had been a business student pursuing an MBA. However, she found dealing with facts and figures boring. So she quit. "What now?" she wondered. After a few months of floundering, she went to see a career specialist. In examining her interests, she found she liked working with people. "That's it!" she said excitedly. "I'll become a counselor! That way I can 'assist' all those overwrought and overeducated business types who are bored to death with their jobs. And all I'll have to do is listen and, of course, give them advice. Sweet!"

Would you want Roberta in your counseling program? Why? What else do you think she should consider?

Personal Qualities of an Effective Counselor

Among the functional and **positive factors that motivate individuals to pursue careers in counseling** and make them well suited for the profession are the following qualities as delineated by Foster (1996) and Guy (1987). Although this list is not exhaustive, it highlights aspects of one's personal life that make a person best suited to function as a counselor.

- *Curiosity and inquisitiveness*—a natural interest in people
- *Ability to listen*—the ability to find listening stimulating

- *Comfort with conversation*—enjoyment of verbal exchanges
- *Empathy and understanding*—the ability to put oneself in another's place, even if that person is totally different from you
- *Emotional insightfulness*—comfort dealing with a wide range of feelings, from anger to joy
- *Introspection*—the ability to see or feel from within
- *Capacity for self-denial*—the ability to set aside personal needs to listen and take care of others' needs first
- *Tolerance of intimacy*—the ability to sustain emotional closeness
- *Comfort with power*—the acceptance of power with a certain degree of detachment
- *Ability to laugh*—the capability of seeing the bittersweet quality of life events and the humor in them

In addition to personal qualities associated with entering the counseling profession, a number of personal characteristics are associated with being an effective counselor over time

---

Effective Counselor Self Examination

Answer the following questions as you see yourself in regard to the peer group with whom you most identify. What do the results tell you about yourself?

	not like me 1	somewhat like me 2	like me 3	a quality I aspire to 4
Intellectually Curious				
Energetic				
Flexible				
Self-Aware				
Sense of Humor				
Able to Listen				
Empathic				
Emotionally Insightful				
Introspective				
Comfortable with Conversation				
Comfortable with Power				
Tolerant of Intimacy				

(Patterson & Welfel, 2005). They include stability, harmony, constancy, and purposefulness. Overall, the potency of counseling is related to counselors' personal togetherness (Carkhuff & Berenson, 1967; Gladding, 2009; Kottler, 2010). The personhood or personality of counselors is as important, if not more crucial in bringing about client change, than their mastery of knowledge, skills, or techniques (McAuliffe & Lovell, 2006; Rogers, 1961). Education cannot change a person's basic characteristics. Effective counselors are growing as persons and are helping others do the same both personally and globally. In other words, effective counselors are sensitive to themselves and others. They monitor their own biases, listen, ask for clarification, and explore racial and cultural differences in an open and positive way (Ford, Harris, & Schuerger, 1993).

Related to this sensitive and growth-enhancing quality of effective counselors is their appropriate use of themselves as instruments in the counseling process (Brammer & MacDonald, 2003; Combs, 1982). Effective counselors are able to be spontaneous, creative, and empathetic. "There is a certain art to the choice and timing of counseling interventions" (Wilcox-Matthew, Ottens, & Minor, 1997, p. 288). Effective counselors choose and time their moves intuitively and according to what research has verified works best. It is helpful if counselors' lives have been tempered by multiple life experiences that have enabled them to realize some of what their clients are going through and to therefore be both aware and appropriate.

The ability to work from a perspective of resolved emotional experience that has sensitized a person to self and others in a helpful way is what Rollo May characterizes as being a ***wounded healer*** (May, Remen, Young, & Berland, 1985). It is a paradoxical phenomenon. Individuals who have been hurt and have been able to transcend their pain and gain insight into themselves and the world can be helpful to others who struggle to overcome emotional problems (Miller, Wagner, Britton, & Gridley, 1998). They have been where their clients are now. Thus, "counselors who have experienced painful life events and have adjusted positively can usually connect and be authentic with clients in distress" (Foster, 1996, p. 21).

Effective counselors are also people who have successfully integrated scientific knowledge and skills into their lives. They have achieved a balance of interpersonal and technical competence (Cormier, Nurius, & Osborn, 2009). **Qualities of effective counselors over time** other than those already mentioned include the following:

- ***Intellectual competence***—the desire and ability to learn as well as think fast and creatively
- ***Energy***—the ability to be active in sessions and sustain that activity even when one sees a number of clients in a row
- ***Flexibility***—the ability to adapt what one does to meet clients' needs
- ***Support***—the capacity to encourage clients in making their own decisions while helping engender hope
- ***Goodwill***—the desire to work on behalf of clients in a constructive way that ethically promotes independence
- ***Self-awareness***—a knowledge of self, including attitudes, values, and feelings and the ability to recognize how and what factors affect oneself (Hansen, 2009).

According to Holland (1997), specific personality types are attracted to and work best in certain vocational environments. The environment in which counselors work well is primarily social and problem oriented. It calls for skill in interpersonal relationships and creativity. The act of creativity requires courage (Cohen, 2000; May, 1975) and involves a selling of new ideas and ways of working that promote intrapersonal as well as interpersonal relations (Gladding, 2011). The more aligned counselors' personalities are to their environments, the more effective and satisfied they will be.

In an enlightening study, Wiggins and Weslander (1979) found empirical support for Holland's hypothesis. They studied the personality traits and rated the job performance of 320 counselors in four states. In general, those counselors who were rated "highly effective" scored highest on the social (social, service oriented) and artistic (creative, imaginative) scales of John Holland's *Vocational Preference Inventory*. Counselors who were rated "ineffective" generally scored highest on the realistic (concrete, technical) and conventional (organized, practical) scales. Other factors, such as gender, age, and level of education, were not found to be statistically significant in predicting effectiveness. The result of this research and other studies like it affirms that the personality of counselors is related to their effectiveness in the profession. Nevertheless, the relationship of persons and environments is complex: Individuals with many different personality types manage to find places within the broad field of counseling and make significant contributions to the profession.

CASE EXAMPLE

Pass the Pain Please

Patricia grew up in a comfortable environment. She went to private schools, was extensively tutored, toasted by her parents' associates, and was on the path to succeeding her father as CEO of a large corporation when she realized she wanted to work with people in a therapeutic way. She applied to a number of counseling programs and was accepted. However, she decided that before she entered a program she would take a year to work with poor people in a third-world country so she could "suffer" some and become more empathic.

What do you think of her idea? Do you think her plan would help her?

Maintaining Effectiveness as a Counselor

Persons who become counselors experience the same difficulties as everyone else. They must deal with aging, illness, death, marriage, parenting, job changes, divorce, loneliness, success, and a host of other common problems and occurrences that fill the lives of ordinary people. Some of these life events, such as marrying for the first time late in life or experiencing the death of a child, are considered developmentally "off time," or out of sequence and even tragic (Skovholt & McCarthy, 1988). Other events consist of unintended but fortuitous chance encounters, such as meeting a person with whom one develops a lifelong friendship (Bandura, 1982; Krumboltz & Levin, 2004).

Both traumatic and fortunate experiences are problematic because of the stress they naturally create. A critical issue is how counselors handle these life events. As Roehlke (1988) points out, Carl Jung's idea of *synchronicity,* "which he [Jung] defined as two simultaneous events that occur coincidentally [and that] result in a meaningful connection," is perhaps the most productive way for counselors to perceive and deal with unexpected life experiences (p. 133).

Besides finding meaning in potentially problematic areas, other strategies counselors use for coping with crisis situations include remaining objective, accepting and confronting situations, asserting their own wishes, participating in a wellness lifestyle, and grieving (Shallcross, 2011b; Witmer & Young, 1996). Counselors who have healthy personal lives and learn from both their mistakes and their successes are more likely than others to grow personally and therapeutically and be able to concentrate fully and sensitively on clients' problems. Therefore, counselors, and those who wish to enter the profession, need to adapt to losses as well as gains in life and remain relatively free from destructive triangling patterns with persons, especially parents, in their families of origin (McGoldrick, Gerson, & Petry, 2008). Such a stance enables them to foster and maintain intimate yet autonomous relationships in the present as desired (Gaushell & Lawson, 1994).

Other ways effective counselors maintain their health and well-being include taking preventive measures to avoid problematic behaviors, such as burnout (Grosch & Olsen, 1994; Morkides, 2009). *Burnout* is the state of becoming emotionally or physically drained to the point that one cannot perform functions meaningfully. There are a number of reasons why professional counselors become burned out (Sang Min, Seong Ho, Kissinger, & Ogle, 2010). However, in a burnout state, counselors develop a negative self-concept, a negative job attitude, and even loss of concern, compassion, and feeling for others (Lambie, 2007). They often feel physically exhausted and emotionally spent. Burnout is the single most common personal consequence of working as a counselor. It is estimated that approximately 39% of school and community/agency counselors experience a high to moderate amount of burnout during their careers (Emerson & Markos, 1996; Lambie, 2007).

To avoid burnout, counselors need to modify environmental as well as individual and interpersonal factors associated with it (Wilkerson & Bellini, 2006). For example, counselors need to step out of their professional roles and develop interests outside counseling. They must avoid taking their work home, either mentally or physically. They also must take responsibility for rejuvenating themselves through such small but significant steps as refurbishing their offices every few years; purging, condensing, and creating new files; evaluating new materials; and contributing to the counseling profession through writing or presenting material on which they are comfortable (McCormick, 1998). Other **ways in which counselors can avoid or treat burnout** include the following:

- Associate with healthy individuals
- Work with committed colleagues and organizations that have a sense of mission
- Be reasonably committed to a theory of counseling
- Use stress-reduction exercises
- Modify environmental stressors
- Engage in self-assessment (i.e., identify stressors and relaxers)
- Periodically examine and clarify counseling roles, expectations, and beliefs (i.e., work smarter, not necessarily longer)
- Obtain personal therapy
- Set aside free and private time (i.e., balance one's lifestyle)
- Maintain an attitude of detached concern when working with clients
- Retain an attitude of hope

In summing up previous research about the personalities, qualities, and interests of counselors, Auvenshine and Noffsinger (1984) concluded, "Effective counselors must be emotionally mature, stable, and objective. They must have self-awareness and be secure in that awareness, incorporating their own strengths and weaknesses realistically" (p. 151).

PERSONAL REFLECTION

What do you do that invigorates you or that you enjoy? What other activities or hobbies would you like to include in your life? What keeps you from doing so? How might you get around any real or potential barriers?

PROFESSIONAL ASPECTS OF COUNSELING

Levels of Helping

There are **three levels of helping relationships**: nonprofessional, paraprofessional, and professional. To practice at a certain level requires that helpers acquire the skills necessary for the task (Figure 2.1).

The first level of helping involves ***nonprofessional helpers***. These helpers may be friends, colleagues, untrained volunteers, or supervisors who try to assist those in need in whatever ways they can. Nonprofessional helpers possess varying degrees of wisdom and skill. No specific educational requirements are involved, and the level of helping varies greatly among people in this group.

A second and higher level of helping encompasses what is known as ***generalist human services workers***. These individuals are usually human services workers who have received some formal training in human relations skills but work as part of a team rather than as individuals. People on this level often work as mental health technicians, child care workers, probation personnel, and youth counselors. When properly trained and supervised, generalist human services workers such as residence hall assistants can have a major impact on facilitating positive relationships that promote mental health throughout a social environment (Waldo, 1989).

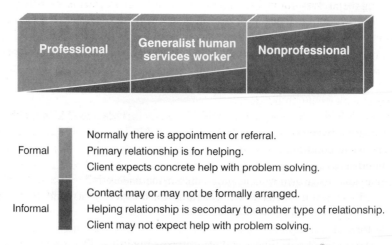

FIGURE 2.1   Kinds of helping relationships   *Source:* From *Effective Helping: Interviewing and Counseling Techniques,* 5th edition by Barbara R. Okun. © 1997. Reprinted with permission of Wadsworth, a division of Thomson Learning: www.thomsonrights.com. Fax 800-730-2215

Finally, there are ***professional helpers***. These persons are educated to provide assistance on both a preventive and a remedial level. People in this group include counselors, psychologists, psychiatrists, social workers, psychiatric nurses, and marriage and family therapists. Workers on this level have a specialized advanced degree and have had supervised internships to help them prepare to deal with a plethora of situations.

In regard to the education of helpers on the last two levels, Robinson and Kinnier (1988) found that self-instructional and traditional classroom training were equally effective at teaching skills.

Professional Helping Specialties

Each helping profession has its own educational and practice requirements. Counselors need to know the educational backgrounds of other professions in order to use their services, communicate with them in an informed manner, and collaborate with them on matters of mutual concern. **Three helping professions with which counselors frequently interact** are psychiatrists, psychologists, and social workers.

Psychiatrists earn a medical degree (MD) and complete a residency in psychiatry. They are specialists in working with people who have major psychological disorders. They are schooled in the ***biomedical model***, "which focuses on the physical processes thought to underlay mental and emotional disorders" (MacCluskie & Ingersoll, 2001, p. 8). Frequently, they prescribe medications and then evaluate the results, especially in agencies such as mental health clinics. Generally, psychiatrists take almost an exclusive biopsychological approach in treatment, and as a group they are not heavily engaged in counseling activities. They must pass both national and state examinations to practice. Their clients are called ***patients.***

Psychologists earn one of the following advanced degrees in psychology: a doctor of philosophy (PhD), a doctor of education (EdD), or a doctor of psychology (PsyD). Their coursework and internships may be concentrated in clinical, counseling, or school-related areas. All states license psychologists, but the requirements for licensure differ from state to state. Most clinically oriented psychologists are listed in the ***National Register of Health Service Providers***, which has uniform standards for inclusion. Graduates of counseling psychology programs follow a curriculum that includes courses in scientific and professional ethics and standards, research design and methodology, statistics and psychological measurement, biological bases of behavior, cognitive–affective bases of behavior, social bases of behavior, individual behavior, and courses in specialty areas. Counseling psychology and counselor education share many common roots, concerns, and significant persons in their histories but they differ too (Elmore, 1984; Gladding & Evans, 2010).

Social workers usually earn a master's of social work degree (MSW), although some universities award a bachelor's degree in social work. There is also advanced training at the doctoral level. Regardless of their educational background, social workers on all levels have completed internships in social agency settings. Social workers vary in regard to how they function. Some administer government programs for the underprivileged and disenfranchised. Others engage in counseling activities. "Social work differentiates itself from counseling, psychology, and psychiatry in that its mission includes mandates to negotiate social systems and advocate for change, to understand clients' ***habitats*** (physical and social settings within cultural contexts) and ***niches*** (statuses and roles in community) and to provide social services" (MacCluskie & Ingersoll, 2001, p. 13). The National Association of Social Workers (NASW) offers credentials for members who demonstrate advanced clinical and educational competencies.

The Education of Professional Counselors

Few, if any, people have the ability to work effectively as counselors without formal education in human development and counseling (Kurpius, 1986b). The level of education needed is directly related to the intensity, expertise, and emphasis of work in which one engages. Professional *counselors* obtain either a master's or a doctorate in counseling from a counselor education or closely related program and complete internships in specialty areas such as school counseling; rehabilitation counseling; mental health counseling; career counseling; gerontological counseling; addiction counseling; or marriage, couple, and family counseling. They are usually certified by the **National Board of Certified Counselors (NBCC)** (the primary national agency that certifies counselors) as a **National Certified Counselor (NCC)** (the entry level of national credentialing). Often they are credentialed on a specialist level, such as school, mental health, or addiction. In addition, they are licensed to practice by individual states.

An *accredited counselor education program* is one recognized at either the master's or doctoral level. The accrediting body for counselor education programs is the **Council for Accreditation of Counseling and Related Educational Programs (CACREP)**. This independent body evolved from the efforts of the Association for Counselor Education and Supervision (ACES) and the American Counseling Association (ACA) to establish standards and guidelines for counseling independent of the **National Council for Accreditation of Teacher Education (NCATE)**, which is the primary accreditation agency for teacher education programs.

On the master's level, CACREP accredits programs in career counseling; mental health counseling; school counseling; marital, couple, and family counseling/therapy; student affairs; and college counseling. Graduates from accredited master's programs have an advantage over graduates from nonaccredited programs in (a) obtaining admittance to accredited counselor education doctoral programs, (b) meeting the educational requirements for counselor licensure and certification, and (c) obtaining employment as a counselor.

Although accreditation standards are periodically changing, the following broad standards must be met in an accredited counselor education master's degree program (CACREP, 2009):

- The entry-level program must be a minimum of 2 full academic years in length, with a minimum of 48 semester hours required of all students. The entry-level program in mental health counseling must be 60 semester hours long, and the entry-level program in marriage, couple and family counseling must also be 60 semester hours.
- Curricular experiences and demonstrated knowledge and skill competence is required of all students in each of **eight common core areas of counseling: (a) human growth and development, (b) social and cultural foundations, (c) helping relationships, (d) groups, (e) lifestyles and career development, (f) appraisal, (g) research and evaluation, and (h) professional orientation.**
- Clinical experiences are required under the direction of supervisors with specific qualifications. The student must complete 100 clock hours of a supervised practicum with 1 hour per week of individual supervision and 1.5 hours per week of group supervision with other students in similar practice.
- The program must require that each student complete 600 clock hours of a supervised internship, which is to begin only after successful completion of the student's practicum.
- Three full-time faculty members must be assigned to the academic unit in counselor education.

CACREP accredits programs on the doctoral level too in counselor education and supervision (EdD and PhD). In 2011 there were 60 doctoral programs in counselor education accredited by CACREP. Standards at this level assume that an individual has completed an entry-level master's degree in counseling. Doctoral-level programs require more in-depth research, supervised field experiences, and specialization. A growing number of graduate schools are applying for CACREP accreditation because of the benefits and recognition such accreditation brings to themselves and to their students. Overall, counselor education programs have become deeper in course offerings and broader developmentally as a result of accreditation standards and procedures.

CREDENTIALING OF COUNSELORS

With the recognition of counseling as a separate professional entity, professional issues have arisen that must be addressed in a positive way. One of the most important of these is credentialing. Obtaining proper credentials to practice as a counselor is important to individual counselors and to the counseling profession as a whole. "Credentialed counselors possess enhanced visibility and credibility" (Clawson & Wildermuth, 1992, p. 1).

There are basically **four types of professional credentials**, two of which, certification and licensure, have considerable prestige. In the past, most credentials were awarded by states, but now certification is also the function of a professional organization, the National Board for Certified Counselors (NBCC). Before deciding on what credentials to pursue, counselors need to know which are legally required for their practice and will enhance their credibility and development.

Credentialing procedures have four levels: inspection, registration, certification, and licensure.

Inspection

In the *inspection* process "a state agency periodically examines the activities of a profession's practitioners to ascertain whether they are practicing the profession in a fashion consistent with the public safety, health, and welfare" (Swanson, 1983b, p. 28). Many state agencies that employ counselors, such as mental health centers, are subject to having their personnel and programs regularly inspected. Such an inspection may include a review of case notes on treatment during a specific period, a review of agency procedures, and personal interviews.

Registration

Registration requires practitioners to submit information to the state concerning the nature of their practice. Usually a professional organization, such as a state division of the ACA, assumes the responsibility for setting standards necessary to qualify as a registrant and maintains a list of names of those who voluntarily meet those standards. This method is employed as a way to gain legal recognition for counselors who used the title "registered professional counselor."

Certification

Certification is a professional, statutory, or nonstatutory process "by which an agency or association grants recognition to an individual for having met certain predetermined professional qualifications. Stated succinctly, certification . . . is a 'limited license,' that is, the protection of title only" (Fretz & Mills, 1980, p. 7). In this case, a state or national board or department issues a certificate to an individual in a specialty. Certification basically implies that the person meets the minimum skills necessary to engage in that profession and has no known character defects that would interfere with such a practice. Often states require candidates for certification to pass a competency test and submit letters of reference before a certificate is issued. School counselors were among the first counselors to be certified.

NBCC is the main national organization that certifies counselors. Certification specialties are available from NBCC in school counseling, mental health counseling, addiction counseling, and supervision (Figure 2.2).

Counselors who wish to become a **National Certified Counselor (NCC)** must have a minimum of 48 semester or 72 quarter hours of graduate study in counseling or a related field, including a master's degree in counseling from a regionally accredited institution of higher education. They must include courses in their program of study that cover the eight core areas of counseling: human growth and development, group work, research and program evaluation, counseling theories/helping relationships, professional orientation, career and lifestyle development, ethics, social/cultural foundations, and appraisal. They must also have a minimum of two academic terms of supervised field experience in a counseling setting. In addition, they must pass the **National Counselor Examination (NCE)**. In the case of individuals graduating from a non-CACREP program, 2 years of postmaster's field experience with 3,000 client contact hours and 100 hours of weekly face-to-face supervision with an NCC or equivalent is also required.

Counselors should obtain both NBCC certification and state licensure for four reasons (Clawson & Wildermuth, 1992). First, national certification is broader than state licensure and based on a larger population. Second, licensure is more susceptible than national certification to state politics. Third, national certification more readily provides referral sources and networking across state lines. Finally, most state counseling licenses do not recognize specialty areas, whereas national certification does.

Licensure

Fretz and Mills (1980) define *licensure* as "the statutory process by which an agency of government, usually a state, grants permission to a person meeting predetermined qualifications to engage in a given occupation and/or use a particular title and to perform specified functions" (p. 7). Licensure differs in purpose from certification but requires similar procedures in terms of education and testing for competence. Once licensure requirements are established, individuals cannot practice a profession legally without obtaining a license (Anderson & Swanson, 1994; Wheeler & Bertram, 2008). Licensure is almost exclusively a state-governed process, and those states that have licensure have established boards to oversee the issuing of licenses. "A licensee who commits an offense that violates the legal or ethical codes adopted by the board to regulate practice is subject to the board's disciplinary authority. Disciplined providers of mental health services who do not face revocation or suspension of a license are generally permitted to continue to practice with one or more of the following requirements:

- participating in corrective education,
- obtaining therapy,
- agreeing to be monitored,
- limiting the scope of their practice, and/or
- having their practice supervised by specified colleagues (Cobia & Pipes, 2002, p. 140).

In general, the licensing of professional helpers is always under scrutiny from the public, other professions, and state legislatures. The licensing of counselors gained momentum in the 1970s and 1980s, just as the licensing of psychologists did in the 1960s and 1970s. By 2010, all 50 states, plus Puerto Rico and the District of Columbia legally regulated the practice of counseling.

NATIONAL BOARD FOR
CERTIFIED COUNSELORS

Understanding NBCC's National Certifications

The National Certified Counselor (NCC)

The NCC certification was launched by NBCC in 1982 as a result of the efforts of members of the American Counseling Association (ACA). Since that time, NBCC has become an independent entity and more than 80,000 counselors have become NCCs. The NCC is one of two NBCC certifications that are accredited by the National Commission for Certifying Agencies (NCCA). The NCC is the prerequisite for all specialty certifications (below) with NBCC.

The **National Counselor Examination for Licensure and Certification (NCE)** is required for this certification.

Specialty Certifications

NBCC also offers three specialty certifications. All three require the National Certified Counselor certification as a prerequisite or corequisite.

The Certified Clinical Mental Health Counselor (CCMHC)

The CCMHC was launched originally in 1979 by the National Academy for Certified Clinical Mental Health Counselors. In 1993, the Academy and NBCC reached an agreement for NBCC to take over administration and testing for the CCMHC certification. Nearly 1,000 NCCs currently hold the CCMHC certification.

The **National Clinical Mental Health Counselor Examination (NCMHCE)** is required for this certification.

The National Certified School Counselor (NCSC)

The NCSC certification was launched in 1991 in cooperation with the American School Counselor Association (ASCA). There are more than 2,500 NCCs who also hold the NCSC certification.

The **National Certified School Counselor Examination (NCSCE)** is required for this certification.

The Master Addictions Counselor (MAC)

The MAC certification was first offered in 1995 and testing with the EMAC began in 1996. The MAC is one of two NBCC certifications that is accredited by the National Commission for Certifying Agencies (NCCA). The MAC is also recognized and accepted by the U.S. Department of Transportation (DOT) as qualifying for the Substance Abuse Professional (SAP) training and credential. More than 600 NCCs currently hold the MAC.

The **Examination for Master Addictions Counselors (EMAC)** is required for this certification.

FIGURE 2.2 About NBCC *Source:* About NBCC and Ethics NBCC: The Practice of Internet Counseling from www.nbcc.org. Reprinted with permission of the National Board for Certified Counselors®, Inc. and Affiliates; 3 Terrace Way, Greensboro, NC 27403-3660.

To coordinate efforts at uniformity and growth in counselor licensure, the **American Association of State Counseling Boards (AASCB)** was formed in 1986 (Dingman, 1990). It holds annual conferences where counselor licensure board members meet to discuss and resolve mutual problems and concerns.

CASE EXAMPLE

Alice and the Alphabet

When she moved to a new state, Alice set about making sure she was licensed. She worked hard, and in time the state licensure board granted her a license. Alice was thrilled but when she showed her new business cards to her friend, Luke, his response was: "Why do you want to put the alphabet after your name?" Who cares about letters like "LPC"?

Alice was taken back initially but then she thought: "I want to do it because it indicates my professional status. I have earned it and the credential is important not only to me but to my clients."

What do you think of Luke's reaction? How about Alice's answer?

ATTRIBUTION AND SYSTEMATIC FRAMEWORK OF COUNSELING

Attribution and the systematic framework of counselors makes a difference in what counselors do and how effectively they do it. *Attribution* is what the counselor attributes the cause of a client's problem to (e.g., an external circumstance or an internal personality flaw). A *system* is a unified and organized set of ideas, principles, and behaviors. Systems associated with counseling are concerned with how the counselor approaches clients and are interrelated to attributes and theories. Two systems, one based on developmental issues and one based on the diagnosis of disorders, will be examined here because it is from these two perspectives (and the places in between) that counselors work.

Attributes

Both counselors and clients enter a relationship with some assumptions about what may have caused a problem. Often these personal perceptions are far apart. However, "diagnostic decisions, symptom recognition, and predictions concerning treatment response and outcome can be [and often are] influenced by counselors' explanations for the cause [or causes] of clients' presenting problems" (Kernes & McWhirter, 2001, p. 304). For example, if clients are seen as being responsible for their problems, such as bad decision making, they may be blamed, whereas if the cause of a problem is viewed as beyond their control, such as the trauma of an unexpected death, they may be treated sympathetically.

There are **four main attribution models that counselors use** on either a conscious or unconscious basis (Kernes & McWhirter, 2001). They are as follows:

Medical Model—"In this model, clients are not held responsible for either the cause of their problem or its solution" (p. 305). Counselors who adopt this model act basically as experts and provide the necessary services for change. Although clients are not blamed, they may become dependent.

Moral Model—This model is best typified by the self-help movement and is basically the opposite of the medical model. "Clients are seen as responsible for both causing and solving their problems" (p. 305). Counselors are viewed primarily as coaches or motivators. The drawback to this model is that those who may be victims of circumstances may be held responsible for their own victimization.

Compensatory Model—In the compensatory model, clients are held "responsible only for solving their problems but not for causing them" (p. 304). Essentially, clients are viewed as "suffering from the failure of their social environments to meet their needs" (p. 304). Therefore, counselors and clients form a partnership to overcome problems with the counselor taking a subordinate role and acting as a teacher who provides education, skills, and opportunities for clients. The drawback to this model is that clients may "feel undue pressure at having to continually solve problems they did not create."

Enlightenment Model—This model holds "clients responsible for causing their problems but not for solving them" (p. 304). Clients are seen as "guilty individuals whose lives are out of control" (p. 304). They need enlightenment into the nature of their problems and ways of resolving these problems that the counselor can provide. Whereas clients may feel relief in such an approach, the disadvantage in this model is that they may become dependent on the counselor who acts in the role of an authority figure, or they may structure their lives around external sources of authority after they have completed counseling.

PERSONAL REFLECTION

Think of difficulties you have had in your life. Which of the attribution models just discussed do you think you would feel most comfortable with had you gone to a counselor for help with most of these problems?

Systems of Counseling

Effective counselors adhere to certain systems of counseling as well as theories of counseling. Indeed, the strength of counseling ultimately depends on a continuation of that process.

That counseling is not governed by one dominant system approach is hardly surprising considering its historical development. Counseling started like a person who mounted a horse and rode off in all directions; that is, the person had no focus or planned direction (Ungersma, 1961).

As far back as the late 1940s, professionals noticed the lack of a system for counseling. Robert Mathewson (1949) observed that counseling was in "a search for a system . . . to win free from inadequate frames borrowed from traditional philosophy and education, from psychology, from political formulations underlying democratic government, from the concepts of physical science, etc." (p. 73).

Until the late 1940s, counseling used a variety of systems. Because the profession was without an organizational base, different factions defined what they did according to the system that suited them best. Competition among points of view, especially those connected with theories, was often spirited. For example, E. G. Williamson and Carl Rogers debated the merits of their approaches with passion. Some counselors recognized the need for a unifying systematic approach to their discipline, but the unplanned growth of the profession proved an obstacle. However, by the 1990s several systems of counseling had emerged, the two most dominant being the developmental/wellness approach and the medical/pathological approach.

THE DEVELOPMENTAL/WELLNESS APPROACH.   The *developmental/wellness perspective* to counseling is based on stages various personality theorists have outlined that people go through as a normal part of human growth. Counseling from this perspective is premised on whether a problem a client is having is part of a developmental task of life or not. For example, establishing an identity is a developmental task in life that individuals in early adulthood may struggle with. However, it is not a task that those in their 70s would. Thus, behaviors that are appropriate at one stage of life are not as healthy at another stage of life, although, if unresolved they may well be present.

Allen Ivey (1990) was not the first to suggest that counseling systems be based on a developmental perspective, but his integration of developmental growth with counseling strategies stands out as one of the most unique expressions of this approach. Basically, Ivey suggests applying *Piagetian concepts of cognitive levels* (i.e., sensorimotor, concrete, formal, and postformal) to clinical interviews with adults and children. Therefore, if clients do not initially recognize their feelings, counselors will work from a sensorimotor level to bring out emotions. In a similar way, clients who are interested in planning strategies for change will be helped using a formal pattern of thought. *Developmental counseling and therapy (DCT)* "specifically addresses the sequence and process of development as it occurs in the natural language of the interview" (Ivey & Ivey, 1990, p. 299).

Wellness goes even further than development in emphasizing the positive nature and health of human beings (Myers & Sweeney, 2005). "Counselors have historically been in the business of helping their clients identify their strengths and build on their strengths" (Rak & Patterson, 1996, p. 368). In this perspective, individuals are seen as having the resources to solve their own problems in a practical, immediate way. "Problems are not evidence of an underlying pathology" (Mostert, Johnson, & Mostert, 1997, p. 21). Indeed, as Rak and Patterson (1996) point out, even most at-risk children show *resilience* (the ability to recover relatively quickly from setbacks and trauma) and become coping adults. Indeed, as Zautra, Hall, and Murray (2010) argue, resilience is an integrative construct that provides an approach to understanding how people and their communities achieve and sustain health and well-being in the face of adversity.

An example of a counseling approach based on the wellness model is *solution-focused theory*. In this approach, the emphasis is on health and strength and to help clients tap into their inner resources and find solutions to situations that already exist in their lives, some of which are universal in nature. *Stress inoculation training (SIT)* (Meichenbaum, 1993), a proactive, psychoeducational intervention that can be used in schools and with adults, is another example of a present and future wellness emphasis approach (Israelashvili, 1998). In this model, individuals are helped to understand their problematic situations, acquire skills for coping with them, and apply this knowledge to present and even future events through the use of imagery or simulated rehearsal.

A cornerstone of the developmental/wellness approach is its stress on prevention and education (Kleist & White, 1997). Counselors and clients function best when they are informed about the mental, physical, and social spheres of human life as represented in the wellness wheel developed by Myers and Sweeney (2005). Through gaining knowledge of the multiple nature of wellness, counselors and clients recognize how they can focus on avoiding or minimizing disruptive forces that are either internal or external in nature.

THE MEDICAL/PATHOLOGICAL MODEL. In contrast to the developmental/wellness view of counseling is the *medical/pathological model* of human nature represented by those who base treatment plans in accordance with the *Diagnostic and Statistical Manual of Mental Disorders (DSM)* (American Psychiatric Association, 2013). The DSM is compatible with the *International Classification of Diseases* manual (ICD), published by the World Health Organization, in codifying psychiatric disorders. The fifth edition of the DSM contains different clinical diagnoses with much more information about each than the 106 diagnoses in the initial edition of this manual published in 1952.

The chapters in the fifth edition of the DSM are organized in a developmental life span fashion. Neurodevelopmental Disorders, which often are diagnosed in infancy and early childhood, are explained first. Then, in a progressive fashion, diagnostic areas more commonly having an onset in adulthood, such as Sleep-Wake Disorders, are focused on. Within each diagnostic category, individual disorders are similarly arranged. This chapter ordering makes an attempt to closely situate diagnostic areas that seem to be related to one another, "such as creating a specific category for Bipolar and Related Disorders and placing it immediately after Schizophrenia Spectrum and Other Psychotic Disorders" (Proposed DSM-5 Organizational Structure and Disorder Names, www.dsm5.org/proposedrevision/Pages/proposed-dsm5-organizational-structure-and-disorder-names.aspx).

DSM-5 Organizational Structure of the DSM V

Neurodevelopmental Disorders
Schizophrenia Spectrum and Other Psychotic Disorders
Bipolar and Related Disorders
Depressive Disorders
Anxiety Disorders
Obsessive-Compulsive and Related Disorders
Trauma- and Stressor-Related Disorders
Dissociative Disorders
Somatic Symptom Disorders
Feeding and Eating Disorders
Elimination Disorders
Sleep-Wake Disorders
Sexual Dysfunctions
Gender Dysphoria
Disruptive, Impulse Control, and Conduct Disorders
Substance Use and Addictive Disorders
Neurocognitive Disorders
Personality Disorders
Paraphilias
Other Disorders

Overall, the DSM is an extremely interesting but controversial medical/pathology model. It is atheoretical and frames mental disorders as dispositional, that is something that is within the individual and part of his or her psychological makeup. Social problems such as racism, discrimination, patriarchy, homophobia, and poverty may "become lost in the DSM's focus on disorders being rooted in the individual" (Kress, Eriksen, Rayle, & Ford, 2005, p. 98). Furthermore, the DSM does not substantially deal with anything but individual diagnoses, many of which are severe. Therefore, this classification system is of limited value to group workers, marriage and family counselors, and counseling professionals who are not working with highly disturbed populations or who work from a humanistic orientation. However, the DSM-5 is logically and developmentally organized and is sophisticated in its use of neurobiological research.

Counselors should not be naive to the limitations of the DSM or alternatives. However, they should master DSM terminology regardless of their setting, specialty, or even agreement with the classification system for the following reasons (Geroski, Rodgers, & Breen, 1997; Kress et al., 2005; Seligman, 2004, 1999):

1. The DSM system is universally used in other helping professions and forms the basis for a common dialogue between counselors and other mental health specialists.
2. The DSM system helps counselors recognize patterns of mental distress in clients who need to be referred to other mental health professionals or treated in a certain way.
3. By learning the DSM system, counselors establish accountability, credibility, uniform record keeping, informed treatment plans, research, and quality assurance.

PERSONAL REFLECTION

How exciting is diagnosing clients through the DSM to you? Did you expect that you would have to diagnose when you decided to become a counselor? What appeals to you most in regard to the two models just presented (medical vs. wellness)? More specifically, which do you like best and why?

ENGAGING IN PROFESSIONAL COUNSELING-RELATED ACTIVITIES

Becoming a counselor is a lifelong process (Gladding, 2009). It continues well past the formal education of obtaining a master's or doctoral degree and includes participation in professional counseling-related activities. Granello (2010a) found that counselors with more years in the counseling profession had higher levels of *cognitive complexity* (the ability to absorb, integrate, and make use of multiple perspectives). Earning highest degrees in the counseling profession also contributed to the prediction equation. However, becoming more cognitively complex with all the benefits it brings, such as the ability to tolerate ambiguity, listen carefully, suspend judgments, look for evidence, and adjust opinions when new information becomes available, is not automatic. Counselors must work at it! One way they help themselves in this journey is by obtaining **continuing education units (CEUs)** to stay up-to-date on theories and practice, getting needed supervision to ensure excellence in treatment, and advocating for both their clients and the profession of counseling. In addition, they must learn and stay up-to-date on government regulations, especially the Health Insurance Portability and Accountability Act (HIPAA).

Continuing Education

There is a need for continuing education for all counselors, especially after graduation from a counseling program. The reason is that new ideas in the treatment and practice of clients are always evolving and must be evaluated, incorporated, and, if necessary, mastered. Counselors who stop reading professional publications or stop attending in-service workshops and conventions quickly become dated in the delivery of skills. Therefore, counselors must obtain a certain number of CEUs annually to stay abreast of the latest and best methods of working.

CEUs are offered by approved professional counseling organizations on the local, state, regional, and national levels. It is possible to earn CEUs through correspondence courses as well as attending workshops. CEUs are even offered free for reading some ACA counseling journals and ACA's monthly magazine, *Counseling Today*. Counselors who are licensed or certified have to earn a certain number of CEUs to retain their credentials. Engaging in such continuous efforts is sometimes expensive in terms of time and money, but the cost of not keeping up professionally (i.e., becoming incompetent or outdated) is much higher.

Supervision

Supervision is another way of improving professional counseling skills. In fact, "the supervision process, particularly in counselor training programs, is central to counselors' development" (Lawson, Hein, & Stuart, 2009, p. 449). *Supervision* is an interactive and evaluative process in which someone with more proficiency oversees the work of someone with less knowledge and skill to enhance the professional functioning of the junior member (Bernard & Goodyear, 2009). At its best, supervision is a facilitative experience that combines didactic and experiential learning in the context of a developmental relationship. It allows the acquiring of expertise in theory and practice that is not possible to gain in any other way (Borders & Leddick, 1988).

Supervision is a required area of instruction in all CACREP-accredited programs. In addition, counselors may undergo supervision from members of the profession who have received advanced training and in the process obtain approved supervisor status. Standards for counseling supervisors have been developed for counselors, and the NBCC now offers a specialty credential in supervision. Often, those already licensed as counselors can count supervised experiences toward CEUs.

To be effective, supervision must be given on a counselor's developmental level and help the novice counselor conceptualize better what counseling is like. Often beginning graduate students have a high level of anxiety and are a bit fearful when they start supervision. In some respects they are at a self-centered stage where they are focused on their general skills performance and dependent on their supervisor (Ward, 2010). Thus, supervisors are most potent if they assume a highly structured teaching role (Ronnestad & Skovholt, 1993). For example, supervisors may be more authoritarian, didactic, and supportive in their interactions with beginning counselors in this stage of supervision. Therefore, a supervisor might help counselor trainees increase their case note conceptual skills by using Prieto and Scheel's (2002) **format for organizing and structuring thinking about a case** using the acronym **STIPS**, in which the letters stand for the following:

S = signs and symptoms

T = topics discussed in counseling

I = counseling interventions used

P = clients' progress and counselors' continuing plan for treatment

S = any special issues of importance regarding clients (e.g., suicidality) (p. 11)

By using this acronym, counselor trainees enhance their "ability to acquire relevant facts about clients, better understand clients' presenting problems, better monitor counseling processes, and better evaluate and adjust treatment interventions" (p. 11). They also may gain enhanced skills in becoming more methodical in monitoring relevant elements of the counseling process, such as diagnosis and treatment planning. These skills can help them become more verbally interactive and astute in their interactions with supervisors.

With advanced graduate students or experienced counselors, such a teaching modality is usually not appropriate. Instead, supervisors help supervisees work through what is known as the ***client centered stage***—where those being supervised fluctuate between being dependent and autonomous—and then on to a ***process centered stage***—where supervisees exhibit increased professional self-confidence, with increased insight beyond specific skills (Ward, 2010). If all goes well, supervisees enter a ***context centered stage***, where they become more integrated in regard to personal autonomy, insightful awareness, and stable motivation. In essence, supervision, like counseling, may increase one's self-awareness and skills. This process is focused on professional as well as personal growth (Ronnestad & Skovholt, 1993).

In setting up supervisory situations, one must address several myths and many realities. Myths are made up of extreme views—for example, "one supervisor can perform all supervisory roles," "individual supervision is best," or "individuals do not need training to supervise" (McCarthy, DeBell, Kanuha, & McLeod, 1988). Realities include the following facts:

- There is not just one theoretical model of supervision but several (e.g., behavioral, facilitative, dynamic, systemic) (Landis & Young, 1994).
- Before a productive supervisory relationship can be established, the developmental level of the supervisee must be verified and a written plan of realistic goals must be completed (Borders & Brown, 2005).
- There is a significant relationship between a supervisor's credibility, such as trustworthiness, and a supervisee's performance (Carey, Williams, & Wells, 1988).
- Supervision relationships may last for years, and there are potential challenges including transference, countertransference, anxiety, and resistance that must be addressed when this happens (Pearson, 2000).

Overall, the literature and the sophistication of supervisory techniques in counseling are growing (Borders & Brown, 2005; Ladany & Bradley, 2010). For example, the ***reflective team model*** is an innovative way of providing group supervision, especially in working with couples and families (Landis & Young, 1994). In this model, graduate students are asked to collaborate, brainstorm, and take their clients' perspectives as they advance hypotheses about client behaviors, view situations from the clients' framework, and work cooperatively. ***Triadic supervision***, described by CACREP as two supervisees working with one supervisor, in a process that involves all three members simultaneously, is also a promising method of supervision in which fledgling counselors can gain insight from both their supervisor and a peer (Lawson, Hein, & Stuart, 2009).

Counselors who take advantage of supervisory opportunities after they are in practice, especially opportunities for ***peer supervision*** (supervision among equals), can both gain and give information about themselves and their clinical abilities. This increased awareness is the bedrock on which other positive professional experiences can be built.

Advocacy and Social Justice

In addition to other characteristics and qualities connected with themselves and the counseling process, effective counselors engage in advocacy and social justice work. "***Advocacy*** can be defined simply as promoting an idea or a cause through public relations. It involves networking and education" (Tysl, 1997, p. 16). **Social justice** refers to the idea of creating a society or institution that is based on the principles of equality, that values human rights, and that recognizes the dignity of every human being.

Counselors need to support and actively espouse client concerns and the profession of counseling on multiple levels. By doing so, they correct injustices and improve conditions for individuals, groups, and society (Goodman, 2009; Osborne et al., 1998). This process can be achieved in a number of ways, such as making presentations to clubs and civic groups, writing articles for newspapers, contacting legislators, and focusing on community issues through giving one's time and effort as a leader or a proponent. It is especially important to make others aware of social concerns of needy populations, since such groups do not have a voice or recognition.

At times, advocacy involves speaking on the behalf of disadvantaged people and promoting ways of ensuring that their rights are respected and that their needs are taken care of through social action (McClure & Russo, 1996). Professionals who subscribe exclusively to what Bemak and Chung (2008) describe as the "***nice counselor syndrome***" do not exercise their needed roles as multicultural/social justice leaders, advocates, and change agents. The reason is that they are too focused on promoting harmony to move beyond the status quo. Such a stance reinforces inequities. Thus, part of being an advocate is for counselors to overcome fears of being rejected and personal discomforts.

Besides speaking to individuals and groups, another form of advocacy is for counselors to work through the political process. By doing so they are acting in the tradition of Mahatma Gandhi, Nelson Mandela, and Martin Luther King, Jr. in standing up for social justice (Roysicar, 2009). Thus, not only must counselors be knowledgeable about social matters, but they must also influence the passage of laws when conditions adversely affect either their clients or the profession of counseling. Counselors can make a difference by writing letters or visiting with legislators. However, the more personal contact they have with those who make laws, the more likely they are to be influential. According to Lee and Rogers (2009), the **process of creating change** entails "establishing a sense of social/political urgency regarding an issue, organizing and educating a group of people to initiate social/political change, developing a vision and strategy for such change, communicating the vision for that change, empowering broad-based action, and generating actual change" (p. 284). That is the way passage of socially enhancing bills (such as the Elementary and Secondary School Counseling Program) or the reauthorization of initiatives (such as the Rehabilitation Act) have come to fruition.

Advocacy occurs at multiple levels, such as the county, state, or federal (Goetz, 1998). Counselors can work to positively impact the passage of laws in a number of ways. The first is to stay informed and know what bills are being considered. The ACA Office of Public Policy and Information is an excellent resource for federal legislative initiatives and can be accessed through the ACA website (www.counseling.org).

A second way to advocate is to know the rules for effective communication with legislators. The use of jargon, exaggeration, or rambling hurts a counselor's presentation. Therefore, it is important to be organized, concise, and concrete in advocating for certain actions. Flexibility and anticipation of opposite points of view are crucial to being successful.

Finally, be persistent. As in counseling, follow-up is essential in dealing with legislative situations. Initiatives may require years of lobbying before they are enacted. For instance, counselor licensure was passed in Maryland in 1998, but only after a 20-year effort! Counselors can expand their role in advocacy by using the American Counseling Association Advocacy Competencies (Ratts, Toporek, & Lewis, 2010).

Portfolios

A *portfolio* is a form of communication that documents "an individual's training, work, and pertinent life experiences" (James & Greenwalt, 2001, p. 161). Counselors need to keep portfolios to be proactive in regard to documentation they may need to quickly retrieve for licensure, managed care organizations, employer evaluations, and even new jobs.

Counselor portfolios may be either working portfolios or presentation portfolios. A *working portfolio* is a continuous collection of unabridged artifacts counselors can use as evidence of professional competence. These portfolios typically contain the following kinds of information: vita/resume, documentation on counseling courses as well as practicum and internships taken for a degree, postdegree supervision, work experience, professional credentials, continuing education, presentations, publications, and professional service. A *presentation portfolio* is more limited in nature and usually consists of materials needed for a particular project, such as becoming an expert witness in a court of law.

Regardless of which type of portfolio a counselor works on, it is important to keep the portfolio up-to-date. Such a process should be done regularly, such as once a month or once a quarter.

Health Insurance Portability and Accountability Act (HIPAA)

HIPAA is an acronym that refers to federal legislation passed in 1996. The act was intended to:

- Improve "efficiency in healthcare delivery by standardizing electronic data interchange," and
- Protect "confidentiality and security of health data through setting and enforcing standards" (www.hhs.gov/ocr/hipaa/).

More specifically, HIPAA works with the Department of Health and Human Services (HHS) to publish new rules that ensure the following:

- Standardization of electronic patient health, administrative, and financial data
- Unique health identifiers for individuals, employers, health plans, and healthcare providers
- Security standards protecting the confidentiality and integrity of "individually identifiable health information," past, present or future. (HIPAAdvisory — www.csun.edu/~lisagor/.../494BEE%20What's%20HIPAA_.pdf)

Under HIPAA, providers of health services, including counselors, must comply with requirements and regulations laid out in the act in transmitting any healthcare information in an electronic form. Therefore, it is crucial that counselors not only know about HIPAA, but that they also keep up-to-date on the law. The consequences for noncompliance include fines and imprisonment.

Compliance requirements vary from setting to setting, but for large organizations they include the following:

- Building initial organizational awareness of HIPAA
- Comprehensive assessment of the organization's privacy practices, information security systems and procedures, and use of electronic transactions

- Developing an action plan for compliance with each rule
- Developing a technical and management infrastructure to implement the plans
- Implementing a comprehensive implementation action plan, including
  - Developing new policies, processes, and procedures to ensure privacy, security, and patients' rights
  - Building business associate agreements with business partners to support HIPAA objectives
  - Developing a secure technical and physical information infrastructure
  - Updating information systems to safeguard protected health information (PHI) and enable use of standard claims and related transactions
  - Training of all workforce members
  - Developing and maintaining an internal privacy and security management and enforcement infrastructure, including providing a Privacy Officer and a Security Officer. (HIPAAdvisory; www.csun.edu/~lisagor/.../494BEE%20What's%20HIPAA_.pdf)

MyCounselingLab™

Go to Topic 3: *Characteristics of the Effective Counselor,* in the MyCounselingLab™ site (www.MyCounselingLab.com) for *Counseling: A Comprehensive Profession,* Seventh Edition, where you can:

- Find learning outcomes for *Characteristics of the Effective Counselor* along with the national standards that connect to these outcomes.
- Complete Assignments and Activities that can help you more deeply understand the chapter content.
- Apply and practice your understanding of the core skills identified in the chapter with the Building Counseling Skills unit.
- Prepare yourself for professional certification with a Practice for Certification quiz.
- Connect to videos through the Video and Resource Library.

Summary and Conclusion

The qualities and behaviors necessary to become an effective counselor will probably increase as counseling evolves as a profession. Yet there will always be some basic qualities and abilities that all counselors must embody to become effective.

One such quality is the core personality of counselors. Persons feel comfortable working in counseling environments because of their interests, backgrounds, and abilities. The majority of effective counselors have social and artistic interests and enjoy working with people in a variety of problem-solving and developmental ways. Effective counselors are generally characterized as warm, friendly, open, sensitive, patient, and creative. They are consistently working on their own mental health and strive to avoid becoming burned out and ineffective.

Education is a second quality related to the effectiveness of counselors. Effective counselors have gone through an accredited counseling program or its equivalent on either a doctoral or master's level.

Many have also achieved the skills and experience necessary to work in counseling specialty areas.

A third area related to effectiveness in counseling is theory and systems. Effective counselors know that theory is the *why* behind the *how* of technique and practice and that nothing is more practical than mastering major theoretical approaches to counseling. These counselors are not unsystematic and capricious in using theories and methods in their practice. Many use a healthy type of eclecticism in their work. They operate systematically from a developmental/wellness approach, a medical/pathological model, or someplace in between. Regardless, effective counselors know how individuals develop over the life span and also know the terminology and uses of the latest edition of the *Diagnostic and Statistical Manual (DSM)*.

Finally, effective counselors are active in counseling-related activities. They realize the importance of keeping their knowledge up-to-date by participating in continuing education programs and supervisory activities. Furthermore, they advocate for both the needs of their clients and the profession of counseling from a social justice perspective. In addition, they keep their credentials current and available through the use of a portfolio or some other organized way of maintaining important documents and credentials. Finally, effective counselors learn and keep up-to-date on federal legislation that impacts counseling such as HIPAA regulations.

Ethical and Legal Aspects of Counseling 3

Chapter Overview

From reading this chapter you will learn about

- How ethics, morality, and the law are defined and how counseling incorporates ethics
- How ethical decisions are made and how counselors can learn ethical decision making
- The role of ethics in specific counseling situations
- The relationship between the law and counseling
- Liability, legal issues involving minors, client rights, records, and the counselor in court

As you read consider

- The multiple steps in making an ethical decision
- The many domains where ethical decision making is called for
- How you might work with another professional who has acted unethically
- How you feel about the law and legal matters
- Your thoughts about record keeping
- How you would feel about going to court in various capacities

In the cool grey dawn of early September,
I place the final suitcase into my Mustang
and silently say "good-bye"
to the quiet beauty of North Carolina.
Hesitantly, I head
for the blue ocean-lined coast of Connecticut
bound for a new position and the unknown.
Traveling with me are a sheltie named "Eli"
and the still fresh memories of our last counseling session.
You, who wrestled so long with fears
that I kiddingly started calling you "Jacob,"
are as much a part of me as my luggage.
Moving in life is bittersweet
like giving up friends and fears.
The taste is like smooth, orange, fall persimmons,
deceptively delicious but tart.

Reprinted from "Bittersweet," by S. T. Gladding, 1984, *Counseling and Values, 28,*
p. 146. © S. T. Gladding.

MyCounselingLab™

Visit the **MyCounselingLab**™ site (www.MyCounselingLab.com) for *Counseling: A Comprehensive Profession,* Seventh Edition to enhance your understanding of chapter concepts. You'll have the opportunity to practice your skills through video- and case-based Assignments and Activities as well as Building Counseling Skills units and to prepare for your certification exam with Practice for Certification quizzes.

Counseling is not a value-free or neutral activity (Cottone & Tarvydas, 2007; Welfel, 2010). Rather, it is an active profession based on values, which are "orienting beliefs about what is good . . . and how that good should be achieved" (Bergin, 1985, p. 99). Values are at the core of counseling relationships. All goals in counseling, "whether they are goals for symptom relief or goals to modify a lifestyle, are subtended by value systems" (Bergin, 1992, p. 9). In addition, because counseling is such a complex and multifaceted profession, counselors, by necessity, must be dependent on codes of ethics as well as external codes of law (Remley & Herlihy, 2010).

Counselors who are not clear about their values, ethics, and legal responsibilities, as well as those of their clients, can cause harm despite their best intentions (Remley, 1991; Wilcoxon, Remley, & Gladding, 2012). Therefore, it is vital for counselors to be knowledgeable about themselves in addition to the ethics of and laws pertaining to the profession of counseling.

In this chapter, ethical standards and legal constraints under which counselors operate are explored. Both ethics and the law are crucial in the work and well-being of counselors and the counseling process. They promote the professionalism of counseling both directly and indirectly. In some cases, ethical and legal considerations overlap. However, counseling and the law may be quite different and operate according to different premises (Hermann, 2011a; Rowley & MacDonald, 2001).

DEFINITIONS: ETHICS, MORALITY, AND LAW

Ethics involves "making decisions of a moral nature about people and their interaction in society" (Kitchener, 1986, p. 306). The term is often used synonymously with morality, and in some cases, the two terms overlap. Both deal with "what is good and bad or the study of human conduct and values" (Van Hoose & Kottler, 1985, p. 2). Yet each has a different meaning.

"*Ethics* is generally defined as a philosophical discipline that is concerned with human conduct and moral decision making" (Van Hoose & Kottler, 1985, p. 3). Ethics are normative in nature and focus on principles and standards that govern relationships between individuals. "*Professional ethics* are beliefs about behavior and conduct that guide professional practices," such as those between counselors and clients (Calley, 2009, p. 477). *Morality*, however, involves judgment or evaluation of action. It is associated with such words as *good, bad, right, wrong, ought,* and *should* (Brandt, 1959; Grant, 1992). Counselors have morals, and the theories counselors employ have embedded within them moral presuppositions about human nature that explicitly and implicitly question first "what is a person and second, what should a person be or become?" (Christopher, 1996, p. 18).

Law is the precise codification of governing standards that are established to ensure legal and moral justice (Hummell, Talbutt, & Alexander, 1985; Remley & Herlihy, 2010). Law is created by legislation, court decision, and tradition, as in English common law (Wheeler & Bertram, 2012). The law does not dictate what is ethical in a given situation but what is legal. Sometimes what is legal at a given time (e.g., matters pertaining to race, age, or sex) is considered unethical or immoral by some significant segments of society. An example is the controversy between law and ethics in the 1994 Helms-Smith Amendment to the *Elementary and Secondary Education Act* (ESEA), an attempt to cut off funds to schools that provide counseling for gay and lesbian students.

ETHICS AND COUNSELING

As a group, professional counselors are concerned with ethics and values. Indeed, many counselors treat ethical complaints with the same seriousness that they treat lawsuits (Chauvin & Remley, 1996). However, some counselors are better informed or more attuned to these issues. Patterson (1971) has observed that counselors' professional identity is related to their knowledge and practice of ethics. Welfel (2010) has added that the effectiveness of counselors is connected to their ethical knowledge and behavior as well.

Unethical behavior in counseling can take many forms. The temptations common to people everywhere exist for counselors. They include "physical intimacy, the titillation of gossip, or the opportunity (if the gamble pays off) to advance one's career" (Welfel & Lipsitz, 1983b, p. 328). Some forms of unethical behavior are obvious and willful, whereas others are more subtle and unintentional. Regardless, the harmful outcome is the same. The following are some of the most prevalent forms of unethical behaviors in counseling (American Counseling Association (ACA), 2005; Herlihy & Corey, 2006):

- Violation of confidentiality
- Exceeding one's level of professional competence
- Negligent practice
- Claiming expertise one does not possess
- Imposing one's values on a client
- Creating dependency in a client
- Sexual activity with a client
- Certain conflicts of interest, such as ***dual or multiple relationships***—in which the role of the counselor is combined with another relationship (either personal or professional) and not monitored for appropriateness of boundaries (Hermann, 2011a; Moleski & Kiselica, 2005)
- Questionable financial arrangements, such as charging excessive fees
- Improper advertising
- Plagiarism

CASE EXAMPLE

Carl Considers What to Do with a Client

After working for a mental health agency, Carl decided to go into private practice. His first few months were quite slow. In fact, he wondered if he would have to quit and go to work for an agency again. One day, however, he received two referrals for anger management.

Carl was mild-mannered and had not dealt with anger management cases before. Nevertheless, considering his financial situation, he accepted both and made appointments for the next day. That night he read everything he could on anger management. Yet as the time drew near for the appointments, he felt uneasy.

If you were Carl, what might you consider besides the stability of your private practice? What ethical principles might Carl violate if he actually sees clients with anger problems?

A division within the American Counseling Association (ACA)—the **Association for Spiritual, Ethical, and Religious Values in Counseling (ASERVIC;** www.aservic.org/)— is especially concerned with the values and ethics of counseling professionals. This division, which regularly deals with ethical concerns, addressed issues such as counseling the aged, values education, and feminism long before they were concerns of counselors in general. ASERVIC has even published ethical guidelines for leaders in professional counseling organizations. In addition to the vanguard work on ethics and values that ASERVIC has done, it also publishes a journal, *Counseling and Values*, which contains articles on ethical situations.

PROFESSIONAL CODES OF ETHICS AND STANDARDS

To address ethical situations, counselors have developed professional codes of ethics and standards of conduct based on an agreed-on set of values. Professionals in counseling voluntarily abide by such codes for many reasons. "Among its many purposes, a code of ethical conduct is designed to offer formal statements for ensuring protection of clients' rights while identifying expectations of practitioners" (Wilcoxon, 1987, p. 510). Another reason for ethical codes is that "without a code of established ethics, a group of people with similar interests cannot be considered a professional organization" (Allen, 1986, p. 293). Ethics not only help professionalize an association on a general level but "are designed to provide some guidelines for the professional behavior of members on a personal level" (Swanson, 1983a, p. 53). Three other reasons for the existence of ethical codes according to Van Hoose and Kottler (1985) are as follows:

1. Ethical codes protect the profession from government. They allow the profession to regulate itself and function autonomously instead of being controlled by legislation.
2. Ethical codes help control internal disagreements and bickering, thus promoting stability within the profession.
3. Ethical codes protect practitioners from the public, especially in regard to malpractice suits. If counseling professionals behave according to ethical guidelines, the behavior is judged to be in compliance with accepted standards.

In addition, ethical codes help increase public trust in the integrity of a profession and provide clients with some protection from charlatans and incompetent counselors (Vacc, Juhnke, & Nilsen, 2001). Like counselors, clients can use codes of ethics and standards as a guide in evaluating questionable treatment.

The Development of Codes of Ethics for Counselors

The first counseling code of ethics was developed by the American Counseling Association (ACA) (then the American Personnel and Guidance Association, or APGA) based on the original American Psychological Association code of ethics (Allen, 1986). The initial ACA code was initiated by Donald Super and approved in 1961. It has been revised periodically since that time (in 1974, 1981, 1988, 1995, and 2005). The ACA also produces an *Ethical Standards Casebook* (Herlihy & Corey, 2006).

The ACA's latest *Code of Ethics* is comprehensive in nature and a major sign that counseling has developed into a mature discipline. ACA (2005) proposed five main purposes for its code of ethics: (a) to clarify the nature of ethical responsibilities, (b) to support the mission of the organization, (c) to establish principles that inform best practice, (d) to assist members in constructing a course of action, and (e) to serve as the basis for processing ethical complaints and inquiries (Ponton & Duba, 2009, p. 119). The **ACA** *Code of Ethics* (www.counseling.org/Resources/CodeOfEthics/TP/Home/CT2.aspx) contains **eight topical sectional headings**. They include material similar to that found in many other ethical codes (Merrill Education, 2007), yet they are unique to the profession of counseling.

Section 1 deals with the **counseling relationship**, including counselors' professional responsibilities to clients and their welfare (e.g., roles and relationships with clients and use of technology in counseling). The section also discusses ways to handle troublesome subjects such as fees, bartering, referrals, and termination. For example, in this section the ACA clearly states that sexual or romantic intimacies between counselors and former clients must be examined carefully before commencing and are prohibited for a period of 5 years following the last professional contact.

Section 2 covers **confidentiality, privileged communication, and privacy in counseling**, including exceptions to the right to privacy, records, minor or incompetent clients, consultation, and research and training. **Section 3** focuses on issues related to **professional responsibility**, such as professional competence, advertising and solicitation, credentials, and public responsibility. **Section 4** covers **relationships with other professionals**, including colleagues, employers, and employees.

Section 5 deals with **evaluation, assessment, and interpretation**. In addition to general information, it includes material on competence to use and interpret tests, informed consent, release of information to competent professionals, proper diagnosis of mental disorders, conditions of assessment administration, multicultural issues in assessment, forensic evaluation, and test scoring and interpretation. **Section 6** focuses on issues related to **teaching, training, and supervision**, including expectations and responsibilities of counselor educators and students and counselor education programs. **Section 7** deals with **research and publications** and delineates research responsibilities, rights of research participants, and reporting of research results (including publications). Finally, **Section 8** addresses **ways to resolve ethical issues**, including how to handle conflicts between ethics and the law, suspected violations, and cooperation with ethics committees.

A. The Counseling Relationship
B. Confidentiality, Privileged Communication, and Privacy
C. Professional Responsibility
D. Relationships with Other Professionals
E. Evaluation, Assessment, and Interpretation
F. Supervision, Training, and Teaching
G. Research and Publication
H. Resolving Ethical Issues

Eight Main Sections of the ACA *Code of Ethics*

PERSONAL REFLECTION

Although the 2005 ACA *Code of Ethics* covers multiple topics, it does not cover all counseling situations. What other topics can you think of that are related to counseling but not mentioned in the eight sections of the Code?

Limitations of Ethical Codes

Remley (1985) and Kocet (2006) note that ethical codes are general and idealistic; they seldom answer specific questions. Furthermore, they point out that such documents do not address foreseeable professional dilemmas. Rather, they provide guidelines, based on experiences and values, of how counselors should behave. In many ways, ethical standards represent the collected wisdom of a profession at a particular time.

A number of specific limitations exist in any code of ethics. Here are some of the limitations most frequently mentioned (Beymer, 1971; Corey, Corey, & Callanan, 2011; Talbutt, 1981):

- Some issues cannot be resolved by a code of ethics.
- Enforcing ethical codes is difficult.
- There may be conflicts within the standards delineated by the code.
- Some legal and ethical issues are not covered in codes.
- Ethical codes are historical documents. Thus, what may be acceptable practice at one time may be considered unethical later.
- Sometimes conflicts arise between ethical and legal codes.
- Ethical codes do not address cross-cultural issues.
- Ethical codes do not address every possible situation.
- There is often difficulty in bringing the interest of all parties involved in an ethical dispute together systematically.
- Ethical codes are not proactive documents for helping counselors decide what to do in new situations.

Thus, ethical codes are useful in many ways, but they do have their limitations. Counselors need to be aware that they will not always find all the guidance they want when consulting these documents. Nevertheless, whenever an ethical issue arises in counseling, the counselor should first consult ethical codes to see whether the situation is addressed.

Conflicts Within and Among Ethical Codes

The adoption of ethical codes and the emphasis placed on them has paralleled the increased professionalism of counseling (Remley & Herlihy, 2010). However, the presence of such standards poses a potential dilemma for many counselors, for three reasons. First, as Stadler (1986) points out, to act ethically counselors must be aware of ethical codes and be able to differentiate an ethical dilemma from other types of dilemmas—a differentiation that is not always easy. For example, a person may take a stand on a controversial issue, such as gay rights, that he or she seemingly supports with ethical principles but in reality supports only with personal beliefs or biases.

Second, sometimes different ethical principles in a code offer conflicting guidelines about what to do in a given situation. An example is the potential conflict over confidentiality and acting in the client's best interest when a client reveals that he or she is going to attempt to harass someone or harm himself or herself. In such a situation, the counselor who keeps this information confidential may actually act against the best interests of the client and the community in which the client resides.

Third, conflicts may occur when counselors belong to two or more professional organizations whose codes of ethics differ, such as the codes of the APA and the ACA. Such counselors may become involved in situations in which ethical action is unclear. For instance, the APA code of conduct states that psychologists do not engage in sexually intimate relationships with former clients for at least 2 years after cessation or termination of treatment, whereas the ACA *Code of Ethics* requires at least 5 years. If a professional belongs to both organizations and is dealing with this dilemma, which code should he or she follow?

MAKING ETHICAL DECISIONS

Ethical decision making is not always easy, yet it is a part of being a counselor. It requires virtues such as character, integrity, and moral courage as well as knowledge (Hermann, 2011b; Welfel, 2010). Some counselors operate from personal ethical standards without regard to the ethical guidelines developed by professional counseling associations. They usually function well until faced with a dilemma "for which there is no apparent good or best solution" (Swanson, 1983a, p. 57). At such times, ethical issues arise and these counselors experience anxiety, doubt, hesitation, and confusion in determining their conduct. Unfortunately, when they act, their behavior may turn out to be unethical either because it is not grounded in an ethical code or it is grounded in only part of a code that they have extracted to justify their behavior.

In a study conducted in New York (Hayman & Covert, 1986), researchers found five types of ethical dilemmas most prevalent among the university counselors they surveyed there: (a) confidentiality, (b) role conflict, (c) counselor competence, (d) conflicts with employer or institution, and (e) degree of dangerousness. The situational dilemmas that involved danger were the least difficult to resolve, and those that dealt with counselor competence and confidentiality were the most difficult. The surprising finding of this study, however, was that less than one third of the respondents indicated that they relied on published professional codes of ethics in resolving dilemmas. Instead, most used "common sense," a strategy that at times may be professionally unethical and at best unwise.

It is in difficult, murky, and personally troubling situations that counselors need to be aware of resources for ethical decision making such as books and articles on ethics and more experienced colleagues (Welfel, 2010). Such resources are especially important when questions arise over potentially controversial behaviors such as setting or collecting fees, conducting multiple relationships, or working with individuals whose beliefs and styles counselors do not agree with. **Ethical reasoning**, "the process of determining which ethical principles are involved and then prioritizing them based on the professional requirements and beliefs," is crucial (Lanning, 1992, p. 21).

In making ethical decisions, counselors should take actions "based on careful, reflective thought" about responses they think are professionally right in particular situations (Tennyson & Strom, 1986, p. 298). Six ethical principles relate to the activities and ethical choices of counselors:

- *beneficence* (doing good and preventing harm),
- *nonmaleficence* (not inflicting harm),
- *autonomy* (respecting freedom of choice and self-determination),

- *justice* (fairness),
- *fidelity* (faithfulness or honoring commitments and promises), and
- *veracity* (truthfulness) (Hermann, 2011b; Remley & Herlihy, 2010).

All these principles involve conscious decision making by counselors throughout the counseling process. Of these principles, some experts identify nonmaleficence as the primary ethical responsibility in the field of counseling. Nonmaleficence not only involves the "removal of present harm" but the "prevention of future harm, and passive avoidance of harm" (Thompson, 1990, p. 105). It is the basis on which counselors respond to clients who may endanger themselves or others and why they respond to colleagues' unethical behavior (Daniluk & Haverkamp, 1993).

PERSONAL REFLECTION

When have you acted in a way to avoid harm (nonmaleficence)? When have you acted in a way that promoted good (beneficence)?

Other Guidelines for Acting Ethically

Swanson (1983a) lists **guidelines for assessing whether counselors act in ethically responsible ways**. The first is *personal and professional honesty*. Counselors need to operate openly with themselves and those with whom they work. Hidden agendas or unacknowledged feelings hinder relationships and place counselors on shaky ethical ground. One way to overcome personal or professional honesty problems that may get in the way of acting ethically is to receive supervision (Kitchener, 1994).

A second guideline is *acting in the best interest of clients*. This ideal is easier to discuss than achieve. At times, a counselor may impose personal values on clients and ignore what they really want (Gladding & Hood, 1974). At other times, a counselor may fail to recognize an emergency and too readily accept the idea that the client's best interest is served by doing nothing.

A third guideline is that counselors *act without malice or personal gain*. Some clients are difficult to like or deal with, and it is with these individuals that counselors must be especially careful. However, counselors must be careful to avoid relationships with likable clients either on a personal or professional basis. Errors in judgment are most likely to occur when the counselor's self-interest becomes a part of the relationship with a client (St. Germaine, 1993).

A final guideline is whether counselors can *justify an action* "as the best judgment of what should be done based upon the current state of the profession" (Swanson, 1983a, p. 59). To make such a decision, counselors must keep up with current trends by reading the professional literature; attending in-service workshops and conventions; and becoming actively involved in local, state, and national counseling activities.

The *ACA Ethical Standards Casebook* (Herlihy & Corey, 2006) contains examples in which counselors are presented with issues and case studies of questionable ethical situations and given both guidelines and questions to reflect on in deciding what an ethical response would be. Each situation involves a standard of the ethical code.

As helpful as the casebook may be, the proper behavior is not obvious in many counseling situations (Wilcoxon et al., 2012). For example, the question of confidentiality in balancing the individual rights of a person with AIDS and society's right to be protected from the spread of the disease is one with which some counselors struggle (Harding, Gray, & Neal, 1993). Likewise, there are multiple ethical dilemmas in counseling adult survivors of incest, including those of confidentiality and the consequences of making decisions about reporting abuse (Daniluk & Haverkamp, 1993). Therefore, when they are in doubt about what to do in a given situation, it is crucial for counselors to consult and talk over situations with colleagues, in addition to using principles, guidelines, casebooks, and professional codes of ethics (Hermann, 2011b).

EDUCATING COUNSELORS IN ETHICAL DECISION MAKING

Ethical decision making in counseling can be promoted in many ways, but one of the best is through taking courses and continuing education credits that are now required in most graduate counseling programs and for the renewal of professional counselor licenses. Such classes can bring about significant attitudinal changes in students and practicing professionals, including increased knowledge about the ethical areas of self-awareness, dual and multiple relationships, impairment, and multiculturalism (Coll, 1993). Because ethical attitudinal changes are related to ethical behavioral changes, courses in ethics on any level are extremely valuable.

Van Hoose and Paradise (1979) conceptualize the **ethical behavior of counselors** in terms of a **five-stage developmental continuum of reasoning**:

1. *Punishment orientation.*   At this stage the counselor believes external social standards are the basis for judging behavior. If clients or counselors violate a societal rule, they should be punished.
2. *Institutional orientation.*   Counselors who operate at this stage believe in and abide by the rules of the institutions for which they work. They do not question the rules and base their decisions on them.
3. *Societal orientation.*   Counselors at this stage base decisions on societal standards. If a question arises about whether the needs of society or an individual should come first, the needs of society are always given priority.
4. *Individual orientation.*   The individual's needs receive top priority at this stage. Counselors are aware of societal needs and are concerned about the law, but they focus on what is best for the individual.
5. *Principle (conscience) orientation.*   In this stage, concern for the individual is primary. Ethical decisions are based on internalized ethical standards, not external considerations.

As Welfel and Lipsitz (1983a) point out, the work of Van Hoose and Paradise is especially important because it "is the first conceptual model in the literature that attempts to explain how counselors reason about ethical issues" (p. 36). It is *heuristic* (i.e., researchable or open to research) and can form the basis for empirical studies of the promotion of ethical behavior.

Several other models have been proposed for educating counselors in ethical decision making. Gumaer and Scott (1985), for instance, offer a method for training group workers using case vignettes and Carkhuff's three-goal model of helping: self-exploration, self-understanding, and action. Kitchener (1986) proposes an integrated model of goals and components for an ethics education curriculum based on research on the psychological processes underlying moral behavior and current thinking in applied ethics. Her curriculum includes "sensitizing . . . counselors to ethical issues, improving their abilities to make ethical judgments, encouraging responsible ethical actions, and tolerating the ambiguity of ethical decision making" (p. 306). Her model and one proposed by Pelsma and Borgers (1986) are process oriented and assume that counselors do not learn to make ethical decisions on their own. Pelsma and Borgers particularly emphasize the *how* **as opposed to the** *what* **of ethics**—that is, how to reason ethically in a constantly changing field.

Other practitioner guides for making ethical decisions are a seven-step decision-making model based on a synthesis of the professional literature (Forester-Miller & Davis, 1996), a nine-step ethical decision-making model based on critical-evaluative judgments (Welfel, 2010), and seven other models created between 1984 and 1998 (Cottone & Claus, 2000). These ethical decision-making models follow explicit steps or stages and are often used for specific areas of counseling practice. "As to whether one model is better than another is yet to be determined" (p. 281). However, through empirical comparisons and continued dialogue, the effectiveness of the models may be validated.

In addition to the models already mentioned, the ACA Ethics Committee offers a variety of educational experiences. For example, members of the committee offer learning institutes at ACA conferences. In addition, they publish articles in the ACA newsletter, *Counseling Today* and the *Journal of Counseling and Development*.

ETHICS IN SPECIFIC COUNSELING SITUATIONS

Ethical behavior is greatly influenced by the prevalent attitudes in the setting in which one works, by one's colleagues, and by the task the counselor is performing (e.g., assessing, diagnosing). Therefore, implementing ethical decisions and actions in counseling sometimes involves substantial personal and professional risk or discomfort (Faiver, Eisengart, & Colonna, 2004). The reasons are multiple, but as Ladd (1971) observes, the difficulty in making ethical decisions can sometimes be attributed to the environments in which counselors work. "Most organizations that employ counselors are organized not collegially or professionally, as is in part the case with universities and hospitals, but hierarchically. In a hierarchical organization, the administrator or executive decides which prerogatives are administrative and which are professional" (p. 262).

Counselors should check thoroughly the general policies and principles of an institution before accepting employment because employment in a specific setting implies that the counselor agrees with its policies, principles, and ethics. When counselors find themselves in institutions that misuse their services and do not act in the best interests of their clients, they must act either to change the institution through educational or persuasive means or find other employment.

CASE EXAMPLE

Fred's First Job

Fred was excited about his first job as a counselor in an outpatient mental health facility. He was skilled and competent. Therefore, he found it troubling when his supervisor requested that he "hedge a bit" about the number of clients he was seeing each month. The supervisor said that because of the impact of what he was doing, he should record that he was treating about 10% more clients than he actually was. Fred stated he did not think that kind of practice was ethical. His supervisor then told him to "forget ethics" and think about his paycheck. Fred really needed the job in order to help his elderly parents and, because he was working in a rural area, he knew he would not find another job like this one.

What would you advise Fred to do and why? Is his case clear-cut?

School Counseling and Ethics

The potential for major ethical crises between a counselor and his or her employer exists in many school settings (Davis & Ritchie, 1993; Stone, 2010). School counselors are often used as tools by school administrators (Boy & Pine, 1968; Hermann, 2011a). When the possibility of conflict exists between a counselor's loyalty to the employer and the client, "the counselor should always attempt to find a resolution that protects the rights of the client; the ethical responsibility is to the client first and the school [or other setting] second" (Huey, 1986, p. 321). One way school counselors can assure themselves of an ethically sound program is to realize that they may encounter multiple dilemmas in providing services to students, parents, and teachers. Therefore, before interacting with these different groups, school counselors should become familiar with the ethical standards of the American School Counseling Association (www.schoolcounselor .org/content.asp?contentid=136), which outlines counselors' responsibilities to the groups with whom they work (Remley, Hermann, & Huey, 2011).

Computers, Counseling, and Ethics

The use of computers and technology in counseling is another area of potential ethical difficulty. With hundreds of websites now being run by individual counselors, the possibility exists for a breach of client information when computers are used to transmit information among professional counselors.

Other ethically sensitive areas include client or counselor misuse and even the validity of data offered over computer links (Sampson, Kolodinsky, & Greeno, 1997). In addition, the problem of ***cyber counseling or webcounseling***—that is, counseling over the Internet in which the counselor may be hundreds of miles away—is fraught with ethical dilemmas. Thus, the National Board of Certified Counselors has issued ethical guidelines regarding such conduct.

Marriage, Couple, and Family Counseling and Ethics

Another counseling situation in which ethical crises are common is marriage, couple, and family counseling (Corey et al., 2011; Margolin, 1982; Wilcoxon et al., 2012). The reason is that counselors are treating a number of individuals together as a system, and it is unlikely that all members of the system have the same goals (Wilcoxon, 1986). To overcome potential problems, Thomas (1994) has developed a dynamic, process-oriented framework for counselors to use when working with families. This model discusses six values that affect counselors, clients, and the counseling process: (a) responsibility, (b) integrity, (c) commitment, (d) freedom of choice, (e) empowerment, and (f) right to grieve.

Other Counseling Settings and Ethics

Other counseling settings or situations with significant potential for ethical dilemmas (and often legal consequences) include counseling older adults (Myers, 1998), multicultural counseling (Baruth & Manning, 2012), working in managed care (Murphy, 1998), diagnosis of clients (Braun & Cox, 2005; Rueth, Demmitt, & Burger, 1998), and counseling research (Jencius & Rotter, 1998). In all these areas, counselors face new situations, some of which are not addressed by the ethical standards of ACA. For instance, counselors are challenged by ethical and legal dilemmas when using diagnostic codes in managed health care (Braun & Cox, 2005). The reason is that some DSM codes are not reimbursed by managed care companies. However, intentional misdiagnosis is a breach of the American Counseling Association *Code of Ethics* as well as fraud. Such action has legal consequences.

In working with older adults, counselors must also make ethical decisions. They must assess the unique needs of the aging who have cognitive impairments, a terminal illness, or who have been victims of abuse (Schwiebert, Myers, & Dice, 2000). In order to do so, counselors may apply ***principle ethics*** to these situations that are based on a set of obligations that focus on finding socially and historically appropriate answers to the question: "What shall I do?" (Corey et al., 2011). In other words, "Is this action ethical?" They may employ ***virtue ethics*** as well, which focus on the "character traits of the counselor and nonobligatory ideals to which professionals aspire" (p. 13). Rather than solving a specific ethical question, virtue ethics are focused on the question: "Am I doing what is best for my client?" Counselors are wise to integrate both forms of ethical reasoning into their deliberations if they wish to make the best decisions possible.

In making ethical decisions where there are no guidelines, it is critical for counselors to stay abreast of current issues, trends, and even legislation related to the situation they face. In the process, counselors must take care not to stereotype or otherwise be insensitive to clients with whom they are working. For instance, "a primary emphasis of **research ethics** is, appropriately, on the protection of human subjects [people] in research" (Parker & Szymanski, 1996, p. 182). In the **area of research** in particular, there are **four main ethical issues** that must be resolved:

- **informed consent**,
- **coercion and deception**,
- **confidentiality and privacy**, and
- **reporting the results**. (Robinson & Gross, 1986, p. 331)

All these areas involve people whose lives are in the care of the researcher. Anticipation of problems and implementation of policies that produce humane and fair results are essential.

PERSONAL REFLECTION

Ethical issues in research grew out of experiments where people were deceived into believing they were actually torturing others or acting in ways that they later regretted and were upset about. If someone signs up to do research with you and then changes his or her mind, what do you think you should do? Would it make a difference if you needed only one more person to complete your research, no one else had signed up, and you had only 2 days left to collect your data or you would fail the research course?

MULTIPLE RELATIONSHIPS

The matter of multiple relationships as an ethical consideration is relatively new, emerging from debates in the 1970s on the ethical nature of counselor–client sexual relations. When professional groups concluded that sexual relationships between counselors and clients were unethical, questions were raised about the formation of other types of relationships between counselors and clients, such as business deals or friendship. Such relationships are not built on mutuality because of the past therapeutic nature of the people involved. In other words, one (the client) was more vulnerable than another (the counselor).

Discussions among professional groups have concluded that nonsexual multiple relationships should be avoided whenever possible, and when not possible, appropriate boundaries should be constructed and adhered to (e.g., in rural areas where nonsexual multiple relationships may be unavoidable). The reason for these guidelines is that no matter how harmless such relationships seem, "a conflict of interest almost always exists, and any professional counselor's judgment is likely to be affected" (St. Germaine, 1993, p. 27). What follows may be harmful because counselors lose their objectivity and clients may be placed in a situation in which they cannot be assertive and take care of themselves. For example, if a business transaction takes place between a counselor and a client at the same time that counseling is occurring, either party may be negatively affected if the product involved does not work well or work as well as expected. The thought and emotion that take place as a result will most likely have an impact on the therapeutic relationship. Therefore, as a matter of ethics, counselors should remove themselves from socializing or doing business with present or former clients, or accepting gifts from them. Entering into a counseling relationship with a close friend, family member, student, lover, or employee is to be avoided.

Although the principles underlying the ethics of multiple relationships seem clear, implementing them is sometimes difficult and in some situations even unavoidable (Corey, 2009). For instance, as mentioned before, in rural areas counselors may not be able to avoid doing business with someone who is also a client. Likewise, many substance abuse counselors are in recovery. "For these individuals, existing ethical codes do not specifically or adequately address the unique circumstances in which they periodically find themselves" (Doyle, 1997, p. 428). Therefore, multiple relationships may be inescapable at times. Among the issues that are problematic and require thoughtful consideration in these cases are those involving confidentiality and anonymity, such as attending self-help groups with clients, social relationships among self-help group members, employment, and sponsorship in self-help programs.

Given these potential problems, counselors should approach multiple relationships with caution. However, since they sometimes cannot be avoided in certain circumstances, a focus of benefits, consequences, and boundaries may become uppermost in dealing with them. Assessing benefits and consequences of multiple relationships on a case-by-case basis is prudent. Setting healthy boundaries at the beginning of such relationships is essential. Counselors should be clear with clients concerning the complexity of multiple relationships and what boundaries need to be established. They should be willing to talk with clients about any unforeseen problems and conflicts that may arise. They should also seek supervision and/or consultation if they find themselves in situations in which they are uncomfortable or think that the relationship is not working beneficially.

WORKING WITH COUNSELORS WHO MAY ACT UNETHICALLY

Violating codes of ethics is serious. It can result in the suspension or revocation of a counseling license, the termination of a counselor from a professional organization, or even legal consequences (Hermann, 2011a). Although most counselors act ethically, occasional situations arise in which such is not the case. In these circumstances, counselors must take some action. Otherwise, by condoning or ignoring a situation they risk eroding their own sense of moral selfhood and find it easier to condone future ethical breaches, a phenomenon known as the "***slippery slope effect.***"

Herlihy (1996) suggests several steps to take in working through potential ethical dilemmas, especially with impaired professionals. The first is to identify the problem as objectively as possible and the counselor's relationship to it. Such a process is best done on paper to clarify thinking.

The second step in the process is for a counselor to apply the current ACA *Code of Ethics* to the matter. In such cases, clear guidance as to a course of action may emerge. Next, a counselor should consider moral principles of the helping profession discussed earlier in this chapter, such as beneficence, justice, and autonomy. Consultation with a colleague is also an option.

If action is warranted, the colleague in question should first be approached informally. This approach involves confrontation in a caring context, which hopefully will lead to the counselor in question seeking help. If it does not, the confronting counselor should consider the potential consequences of all other options and then define a course of action. Such a course might include filing an ethical complaint with the ACA and/or a state licensure or national certification board. A complaint may be filed by either the professional, who has queried his or her colleague, or by a client who believes he or she has been treated unethically.

In examining courses of action, a counselor must evaluate where each potential action might lead. Criteria for judgment include one's comfort surrounding (a) "**publicity**" (i.e., if the actions of the confronting counselor were reported in the press), (b) "**justice**" (i.e., fairness), (c) "**moral traces**" (i.e., lingering feelings of doubt), and (d) "**universality**" (i.e., is this a course I would recommend others take in this situation?).

Finally, a course of action is chosen and implemented. In such a case, the counselor must realize that not everyone will agree. Therefore, he or she must be prepared to take criticism as well as credit for what has been done.

THE LAW AND COUNSELING

The profession of counseling is also governed by legal standards. *Legal* refers to "law or the state of being lawful," and *law* refers to "a body of rules recognized by a state or community as binding on its members" (Shertzer & Stone, 1980, p. 386). Contrary to popular opinion, "law is not cut and dried, definite and certain, or clear and precise" (Van Hoose & Kottler, 1985, p. 44). Rather, it always seeks compromise between individuals and parties. It offers few definite answers, and there are always notable exceptions to any legal precedent.

There is "no general body of law covering the helping professions" (Van Hoose & Kottler, 1985, p. 45). However, there are a number of court decisions and statutes that influence legal opinions on counseling, and counselors need to keep updated. The 1993 Napa County, California, case involving Gary Ramona is one such legal decision. In this widely publicized trial, Ramona sued his daughter's therapists, "charging that by implanting false memories of sexual abuse in her mind they had destroyed his life" (Butler, 1994, p. 10). Ramona was awarded $475,000 after the jury "found the therapists had negligently reinforced false memories" (p. 11). The legal opinion on which the case was decided was *duty to care*—health providers' legal obligation not to act negligently.

Another important legal case in recent years was the 1996 U.S. Supreme Court decision in *Jaffee* v. *Redmond* that held that communications between licensed psychotherapists and their patients are privileged and do not have to be disclosed in cases held in federal court (Remley, Herlihy, & Herlihy, 1997). The importance of the case for counseling is that a legal precedent was set regarding confidentiality between a master's-level clinician (in this case a social worker) and her client. The case also brought positive attention to mental health services, including counseling.

Yet a third legal case that has affected counselors is the Amicus Curiae brief argued before the United States Supreme Court in 1997. This brief dealt with mental health issues associated with "physician-assisted suicide" (Werth & Gordon, 2002). In this court action, the ACA joined with several other mental health groups to protect the rights of counselors and other helping specialties to play a part in hastened death, in particular by protecting the suffering person, the person's significant others, and society as a whole from the potential problems associated with aid-in-dying.

In most cases, the law is "generally supportive or neutral" toward professional codes of ethics and counseling in general (Stude & McKelvey, 1979, p. 454). It supports licensure or certification of counselors as a means of ensuring that those who enter the profession attain at least minimal standards. It also supports the general "confidentiality of statements and records provided by clients during therapy" (p. 454). In addition, the law is neutral "in that it allows the profession to police itself and govern counselors' relations with their clients and fellow counselors" (p. 454). The only time the law overrides a professional code of ethics is when it is necessary "to protect the public health, safety, and welfare" (p. 454). This necessity is most likely in situations concerning confidentiality, when disclosure of information is necessary to prevent serious and foreseeable harm (Hermann, 2011a). In such cases, counselors have a duty to warn potential victims about the possibility of a client's violent behavior (Costa & Altekruse, 1994).

LEGAL RECOGNITION OF COUNSELING

Swanson (1983b) points out that, in part, counseling gained professional recognition and acceptance through the legal system. As recently as 1960, counseling did not have a strong enough identity as a profession to be recognized legally. In that year, a judge ruled in the case of *Bogust* v. *Iverson* that a counselor with a doctoral degree could not be held liable for the suicide of one of his clients because counselors were "mere teachers" who received training in a department of education.

It was not until 1971, in an *Iowa Law Review Note*, that counselors were legally recognized as professionals who provided personal as well as vocational and educational counseling. The profession was even more clearly defined in 1974 in *Weldon* v. *Virginia State Board of Psychologists Examiners*. The judgment rendered in this case stated that counseling was a profession distinct from psychology. The U.S. House of Representatives further refined the definition of counseling and recognized the profession in H.R. 3270 (94th Congress, 1976), stating that counseling is "the process through which a trained counselor assists an individual or group to make satisfactory and responsible decisions concerning personal, educational and career development."

Swanson (1983b) notes that state laws regulating counseling, such as the first one passed in Virginia in 1976 exclusively recognizing counseling as a profession, saw counseling as a "generic profession" with specialties such as career counseling (p. 29). Further impetus for defining counseling as a profession came with the adoption and implementation of minimum preparation standards, such as those adopted by CACREP in the late 1970s.

LEGAL ASPECTS OF THE COUNSELING RELATIONSHIP

Counselors must follow specific legal guidelines in working with certain populations. For example, **PL 94–142** (the Education of All Handicapped Children Act of 1975) provides that schools must make provisions for the free, appropriate public education of all children in the least restrictive environment possible. Part of this process is the development of an ***individualized education plan (IEP)*** for each child as well as the provision for due-process procedures and identifying and keeping records on every child with a disability (Cobia & Henderson, 2007;

Humes, 1978). School counselors who work with children with disabilities have specific tasks to complete under the terms of this act.

Similarly, counselors have a legal obligation under all child abuse laws to report suspected cases of abuse to proper authorities, usually specific personnel in a state social welfare office (Henderson, 2007). Such situations may be especially difficult when counselors are working directly with families in which the abuse is suspected (Stevens-Smith & Hughes, 1993). Furthermore, the legal obligations of counselors are well defined under the **Family Educational Rights and Privacy Act (FERPA)** of 1974, known as the **Buckley Amendment**. This statute gives students access to certain records that educational institutions have kept on them.

Counselors have considerable trouble in situations in which the law is not clear or a conflict exists between the law and professional counseling ethics. Nevertheless, it is important that providers of mental health services be fully informed about what they can or cannot do legally. Such situations often involve the sharing of information among clients, counselors, and the court system.

Sharing may be broken down into confidentiality, privacy, and privileged communication. **Confidentiality** is "the ethical duty to fulfill a contract or promise to clients that the information revealed during therapy will be protected from unauthorized disclosure" (Arthur & Swanson, 1993, p. 7). Confidentiality becomes a legal as well as an ethical concern if it is broken, whether intentionally or not. It is annually one of the most inquired about ethical and legal concerns received by the ACA Ethics Committee including "dilemmas/questions regarding right to privacy, clients' right to privacy, and counselors avoiding illegal and unwarranted disclosures of confidential information (exceptions, court ordered disclosure and records)" (Williams & Freeman, 2002, pp. 253–254).

"**Privacy** is an evolving legal concept that recognizes individuals' rights to choose the time, circumstances, and extent to which they wish to share or withhold personal information" (Herlihy & Sheeley, 1987, p. 479). Clients who think they have been coerced into revealing information they would not normally disclose may seek legal recourse against a counselor.

Privileged communication, a narrower concept, regulates privacy protection and confidentiality by protecting clients from having their confidential communications disclosed in court without their permission. It is defined as "a client's legal right, guaranteed by statute, that confidences originating in a therapeutic relationship will be safeguarded" (Arthur & Swanson, 1993, p. 7). Most states recognize and protect privileged communication in counselor–client relationships (Glosoff, Herlihy, & Spence, 2000). However, there are nine categories of exceptions:

(a) in cases of a dispute between counselor and client;
(b) when a client raises the issue of mental condition in legal proceedings;
(c) when a client's condition poses a danger to self or others;
(d) in cases of child abuse or neglect (in addition to mandated reporting laws);
(e) when the counselor has knowledge that the client is contemplating commission of a crime;
(f) during court ordered psychological evaluations;
(g) for purposes of involuntary hospitalization;
(h) when the counselor has knowledge that a client has been a victim of a crime; and
(i) in cases of harm to vulnerable adults. (p. 455)

As opposed to individuals, the legal concept of privileged communication generally does not apply in group and family counseling (Wheeler & Bertram, 2012). However, counselors should consider certain ethical concerns in protecting the confidentiality of group and family members.

One major difficulty with any law governing client and counselor communication is that laws vary from state to state. It is essential that counselors know and communicate to their clients potential situations in which confidentiality may be broken (Glosoff et al., 2000; Woody, 1988).

A landmark court case that reflects the importance of limiting confidentiality is ***Tarasoff* v. *Board of Regents of the University of California*** (1976). In this case, Prosenjit Poddar, a student who was a voluntary outpatient at the student health services on the Berkeley campus of the University of California, informed the psychologist who was counseling him that he intended to kill his former girlfriend, Tatiana Tarasoff, when she arrived back on campus. The psychologist notified the campus police, who detained and questioned the student about his proposed activities. The student denied any intention of killing Tarasoff, acted rationally, and was released. Poddar refused further treatment from the psychologist, and no additional steps were taken to deter him from his intended action. Two months later, he killed Tarasoff. Her parents sued the Regents of the University of California for failing to notify the intended victim of a threat against her. The California Supreme Court ruled in their favor, holding, in effect, that a therapist has a ***duty to protect*** the public that overrides any obligation to maintain client confidentiality (Haggard-Grann, 2007).

Thus, there is a limit to how much confidentiality a counselor can or should maintain. When it appears that a client is dangerous to himself or herself or to others, state laws specify that this information must be reported to the proper authorities. For example, when a child is at risk of being suicidal, the courts hold that school personnel, including counselors, are in a position to make a referral and "have a duty to secure assistance from others" (Maples et al., 2005, p. 401).

Knapp and Vandecreek (1982) note that state laws vary in regard to confidentiality, and reporting information about potentially dangerous situations is often difficult. In addressing this area, they suggest that when client violence seems to be at risk, a counselor should try both to defuse the danger while also satisfying any legal duty. They recommend consulting with professional colleagues who have expertise in working with violent individuals and documenting the steps taken. In addition, Haggard-Grann (2007) advocates using risk-assessment tools whenever possible and appropriate. She also recommends in **risk assessment** that a number of variables be included such as situational aspects, including life situation (e.g., living conditions), behavioral patterns (e.g., substance abuse, medication), and foreseeable events or stressors (e.g., child custody, dilemmas, separation/divorce).

CIVIL AND CRIMINAL LIABILITY

The *Tarasoff* case raises the problem of counselor liability and malpractice. Basically, ***liability*** in counseling involves issues concerned with whether counselors have caused harm to clients (Wilcoxon et al., 2012). The concept of liability is directly connected with malpractice. ***Malpractice*** in counseling is defined "as harm to a client resulting from professional negligence, with ***negligence*** defined as the departure from acceptable professional standards" (Hummell et al., 1985, p. 70). Until recently, there were relatively few counselor malpractice lawsuits. But with the increased number of licensed, certified, and practicing counselors, malpractice suits have become more common. Therefore, professional counselors need to make sure they protect themselves from such possibilities.

Three ways to protect oneself from malpractice are (a) to **follow professional codes of ethics**, (b) to **follow normal practice standards**, and (c) to **act in a professional, attentive, and courteous manner at the beginning of a counseling relationship so communication is enhanced and clients perceive that the counselor really cares about them** (Crawford, 1994; Saxton, 2008; Wheeler & Bertram, 2012). Regardless of how careful counselors are, however, malpractice lawsuits can still occur. Therefore, carrying liability insurance is a must (Bullis, 1993).

Liability (legal responsibility for something) can be classified under three main headings: civil, criminal, and administrative (Leslie, 2004). Liability can also involve a combination of these three. *Civil liability* means that one can be sued for acting wrongly toward another or for failing to act when there is a recognized duty to do so (Wheeler & Bertram, 2012). Usually, civil liability results in a lawsuit from a client against the counselor for professional malpractice (i.e., negligence) or gross negligence. *Criminal liability* involves a counselor working with a client in a way the law does not allow. Examples of criminal liability are the commitment of a crime by a counselor (such as failing to report child abuse), engaging in sexual relations with a client, or insurance fraud. *Administrative liability* "means that the therapist's license to practice is threatened by an investigation from the licensing board, which has the power to revoke or suspend a license" (Leslie, 2004, p. 46). Additionally, a client can file a complaint with the ethics committee of a professional association to which the counselor belongs. The association has the power, among other options, to terminate the counselor's membership.

The concept of civil liability rests on the concept of *tort*, a wrong that legal action is designed to set right (Wheeler & Bertram, 2012). The legal wrong can be against a person, property, or even someone's reputation and may be unintentional or direct. **Counselors are most likely to face civil liability suits for malpractice** in the following situations: (a) **malpractice in particular situations** (birth control, abortion, prescribing and administering drugs, treatment), (b) **illegal search**, (c) **defamation**, (d) **invasion of privacy**, and (e) **breach of contract** (Wheeler & Bertram, 2012). Three **situations in which counselors risk criminal liability** are (a) **accessory to a crime**, (b) **civil disobedience**, and (c) **contribution to the delinquency of a minor** (Wheeler & Bertram, 2012).

LEGAL ISSUES INVOLVED WHEN COUNSELING MINORS

Minors are children under the age of 18. Many school counselors work with children in this age group. Other counselors interact with children in this age range in community agencies. Working with minors in nonschool settings involves legal (and ethical) issues different from those in an educational environment (Lawrence & Kurpius, 2000). For example, since the "client-counselor relationship is fiduciary it falls under the legal jurisdiction of contract law. Typically, a minor can enter into a contract for treatment in one of three ways: (a) with parental consent, (b) involuntarily at a parent's insistence, or (c) by order of the juvenile court" (p. 133). Whereas court-ordered treatment of a child does not require parental consent, the other two conditions do and, even with court-ordered treatment, parents or guardians should be informed. "If informed parental consent is not obtained, counselors risk the possibility of being sued for battery, failure to gain consent, and child enticement" (p. 133). It is important in obtaining consent both in school and agency settings that the custodial parent's permission be obtained if a child's parents are divorced. Furthermore, it is prudent and necessary to find out what information, if any, noncustodial parents are entitled to.

In working with minors and their families, Lawrence and Kurpius (2000, p. 135) give a number of suggestions including the following:

- "Be thoroughly familiar with state statutes" especially regarding privileged communication.
- "Clarify your policies concerning confidentiality with both the child and parents at the initiation of the therapeutic relationship and ask for their cooperation. Provide a written statement of these policies that everyone signs."
- "Keep accurate and objective records of all interactions and counseling sessions."
- "Maintain adequate professional liability coverage." Such coverage should be above the minimum.
- If you need help, "confer with colleagues and have professional legal help available."

CLIENT RIGHTS AND RECORDS

There are **two main types of client rights**: implied and explicit (Hansen, Rossberg, & Cramer, 1994). Both relate to due process. *Implied rights* are linked to substantive due process. When a rule is made that arbitrarily limits an individual (i.e., deprives the person of his or her constitutional rights), he or she has been denied substantive due process. *Explicit rights* focus on procedural due process (the steps necessary to initiate or complete an action when an explicit rule is broken). An individual's procedural due process is violated when an explicit rule is broken and the person is not informed about how to remedy the matter. A client has a right to know what recourse he or she has when either of these two types of rights is violated.

The records of all clients are legally protected except under special circumstances. For example, in some instances, such as those provided by the Buckley Amendment, an individual has the right legally to inspect his or her record. There are also some cases in which third parties have access to student information without the consent of the student or parent. In the vast majority of cases, counselors are legally required to protect clients of all ages by keeping records under lock and key, separate from any required business records, and not disclosing any information about a client without that person's written permission (Mitchell, 2007). The best method to use in meeting a request for disclosing information is a **release-of-information form**, which can be drawn up by an attorney (Rosenthal, 2005). Counselors should not release client information they have not obtained firsthand.

Because record keeping is one of the top five areas pertaining to legal liability of counselors (Snider, 1987), the question often arises about what should go into records. Basically, records should contain "all information about the client necessary for his or her treatment" (Piazza & Baruth, 1990, p. 313). The number and types of forms in a **client record** vary with the agency and practitioner, but **six categories of documents** are usually included:

1. *Identifying or intake information:* name, address, telephone number(s), date of birth, sex, occupation, and so on
2. *Assessment information:* psychological evaluation(s), social/family history, health history, and so on
3. *Treatment plan:* presenting problem, plan of action, steps to be taken to reach targeted behavior, and so on (i.e., clearly define the purpose of counseling)
4. *Case notes:* for example, documentation of progress in each session toward the stated goal; if documentation is not provided it is almost impossible to verify something happened

5. *Termination summary:*   outcome of treatment, final diagnosis (if any), after-care plan, and so on
6. *Other data:*   client's signed consent for treatment, copies of correspondence, notations about rationale for any unusual client interventions, administrative problems, and so on

It is vital for counselors to check their state legal codes for exact guidelines about record keeping. After doing so, counselors should establish a timeline for purging sole-possession records or case notes applying careful discretion and deliberation before shredding information related to child abuse, suicide, sexual harassment, or violence (Hermann, 2011a).

It is critical for counselors who receive third-party reimbursement to make sure that their client records refer to progress in terms of a treatment plan and a diagnosis (if required) (Hinkle, 1994b; HPSO, February 24, 2011). In no case, however, should confidential information about a client be given over the telephone. Counselors are also ethically and legally bound to ensure that a client's rights are protected by not discussing counseling cases in public. Never alter a client's records. Altering records is a criminal act. However, records can and should be updated when clients are seen or there is a significant change in the client's circumstances. At such times, the updated record should be signed and dated. Overall, good record keeping is good for both the client and the counselor (Barnett & Johnson, 2010).

CASE EXAMPLE

Diane Deletes

Diane kept her records on her computer. It was easier for her to keep up-to-date and she figured she could always make changes or edits without anyone knowing. However, when Diane received a court order regarding one of her clients, she not only had to appear but so did her computer. One of the questions asked was: "Have you made any modifications of this client's record?"

Diane wanted to answer "no" but she knew that was not true. She was constantly making corrections or inserting new impressions in her notes.

If you were Diane, what would you say and how? Do you think that modifying client records on a computer is unethical? Why or why not?

MINIMIZING LEGAL LIABILITY

Besides keeping excellent records, adhering to ethical codes, being aware of clients' rights, and knowing professional counselor responsibilities, there is at least one other step counselors can take to minimize their legal liability. That step is to use a model to determine their legal responsibilities. Hermann (2011c), who is both a counselor and an attorney, has devised such a model. While it is designed primarily for school counselors, the eight steps in it, all formulated in a question format, are applicable for counselors in other specialty areas too. They are as follows:

1. Is there a state statute or federal law related to the dilemma? If there is specific information on the situation a counselor is considering, such as child abuse, the statute will provide it.
2. What is the spirit of the law? In other words, why was the law written? In the case of child abuse laws, these statutes were written to protect children and keep them out of danger.

3. Is there a ***binding case law***? A binding case is one that emulates state court decisions. The important point here is that the case must come from the state or the federal appeals courts within the jurisdiction in which the counselor resides or from the U.S. Supreme Court.

4. Is there ***persuasive case law***? "Persuasive case law is law from a case in another jurisdiction. For example, Eisel v. Board of Education held that school counselors have a duty to use reasonable means to attempt to prevent student suicide and this duty includes contacting parents" (pp. 9–10). While this case law is binding in Maryland, it is persuasive case law in other states.

5. Is there a workplace policy? "Workplace policies are extremely important" (p. 10). If an agency or educational institution does not follow its own policies, it is more likely to increase its liability.

6. What would a reasonable person do? The standard here is that if most counselors would do what the counselor who is being questioned would do, than the liability risk is lowered.

7. What would a colleague who has similar education and experience do? Determine this by consulting with colleagues who have comparable education and experience. In such circumstances, it is "important to keep records of this consultation" (p. 10).

8. Act reasonably based on the information elicited from the questions in the model and act in the best interest of the client. Basically, this last point is mostly a summary and a reminder that there are many aspects to protecting yourself and others from liability. These include making sure you have done everything you can before you receive a "request" to appear in court.

THE COUNSELOR IN COURT

The court system in the United States is divided into federal and state courts. Each is similarly patterned with trial courts, a middle-level appellate court, and a supreme court (Wheeler & Bertram, 2012). Most counselors who appear in court do so on the state level because the federal courts deal with cases arising primarily under the laws of the United States or those involving citizens of different states where the amount of controversy exceeds $50,000.

Most counselors wind up in court in two main ways. One is voluntary and professional: when the counselor serves as an ***expert witness*** (Murphy, 2011). "An expert witness is an objective and unbiased person with specialized knowledge, skills, or information, who can assist a judge or jury in reaching an appropriate legal decision" (Remley, 1992, p. 33). The expert witness's job is almost like a teacher in court—to inform the court, to help the court resolve some kind of issue (Wheeler & Bertram, 2012). A counselor who serves as an expert witness is compensated financially for his or her time.

The other way in which a counselor may appear in court is through a ***court order*** (a subpoena to appear in court at a certain time in regard to a specific case). Such a summons is issued with the intent of having the counselor testify on behalf of or against a present or former client. Because the legal system is adversarial, counselors are wise to seek the advice of attorneys before responding to court orders (Remley, 1991; Remley & Herlihy, 2010). By so doing, counselors may come to understand law, court proceedings, and options they have in response to legal requests. For example, once a subpoena is issued, counselors do not have to produce their records or give testimony until the client–counselor privilege has been waived or the court orders the counselor "to turn over the records or to testify" (Leslie, 2004, p. 46). Role-playing possible situations before appearing in court may also help counselors function better in such situations.

Overall, in preparing for legal encounters, counselors may find it helpful to read some or all of the 12 volumes in the ACA Legal Series. These volumes, edited by Theodore P. Remley, Jr., are written by experts in the field of counseling who have either legal degrees or expert knowledge on important legal issues such as preparing for court appearances, documenting counseling records, counseling minors, understanding confidentiality and privileged communication, receiving third-party payments, and managing a counseling agency.

ETHICS AND THE LAW: TWO WAYS OF THINKING

In ending this chapter, it should be apparent that attorneys and counselors tend to think in different ways. The professionals in these specialties live for the most part in two different cultures and base their practices on unique worldviews. For this reason, there is a "strong rationale for considering counseling and the legal system from a cross-cultural perspective" (Rowley & MacDonald, 2001, p. 423).

To become successful in a litigious society, counselors, who are part of a minority culture, must become acculturated into the majority culture, the law. There are several ways they can accomplish this goal, including:

- becoming "knowledgeable with those elements that are common to both mental health and the law";
- understanding and being prepared to "work with those elements of the law that differ from the culture of mental health" such as seeking information from a counselor without an appropriate release;
- reviewing the ACA *Code of Ethics* and other relevant ethical codes annually;
- participating in continuing education programs that review laws pertinent to one's counseling specialty;
- learning more about the legal system through "organizations and publications that interface the mental health and legal system" (e.g., *American Psychology-Law Society News* or *The Forensic Examiner*);
- creating a collaborative relationship with a lawyer, a judge, or other legal practitioner;
- developing a relationship with a counselor who is knowledgeable about the world of law; and
- consulting and receiving feedback on possible decisions when there is an ethical–legal dilemma (Rowley & MacDonald, 2001, pp. 427–428).

Even though thinking styles may differ, there are times when legal and ethical outlooks reach similar conclusions even for different reasons. Such has occurred for instance in *Bruff* v. *North Mississippi Health Services, Inc.*, 2001 (Hermann & Herlihy, 2006). In this situation, a therapist refused on religious grounds to treat an openly lesbian woman who requested assistance in having better sexual relations with her partner. The counselor assumed that she would have to perform only those duties she found acceptable and, in addition, cited sections A.11.b and C.2.a (which deal with competence and boundary issues) of the 2005 ACA *Code of Ethics* to support her referral of the client to another counselor. The court found that "providing counseling only on issues that do not conflict with a counselor's religious beliefs is an inflexible position not protected by the law" (p. 416). The court cited legal precedents in *Romer* v. *Evans*, 1996, and *Lawrence* v. *Texas*, 2003, upholding the Equal Protection Clause of the Fourteenth Amendment to the U.S. Constitution and the unconstitutionality of state sodomy laws. Ethically, the "moral principles of justice (fairness), beneficience (doing good), nonmaleficence (doing no harm), and respect for autonomy" (p. 417) all applied to this case.

In somewhat related 2010 cases, the state courts in Georgia and Michigan respectively found in *Keeton* v. *Anderson-Wiley* and *Julea Ward* v. *Roy Wilbanks et al.* that graduate counseling students cannot refuse to counsel same sex couples based on their religious beliefs. Counseling programs are responsible for upholding the ethics standards of the profession as expressed through the ACA *Code of Ethics.* A refusal to counsel a client on the basis of his or her sexual orientation is a clear violation of the nondiscrimination section within the ACA ethics code according to the two opinions rendered by these courts.

MyCounselingLab™

Go to Topic 7: *Ethical and Legal Considerations,* in the MyCounselingLab™ site (www .MyCounselingLab.com) for *Counseling: A Comprehensive Profession,* Seventh Edition, where you can:

- Find learning outcomes for *Ethical and Legal Considerations* along with the national standards that connect to these outcomes.
- Complete Assignments and Activities that can help you more deeply understand the chapter content.
- Apply and practice your understanding of the core skills identified in the chapter with the Building Counseling Skills unit.
- Prepare yourself for professional certification with a Practice for Certification quiz.
- Connect to videos through the Video and Resource Library.

Summary and Conclusion

Counselors are like other professionals in having established codes of ethics to guide them in the practice of helping others. The ACA *Code of Ethics* is one of the main documents counselors consult when they face ethical dilemmas. Acting ethically is not always easy, comfortable, or clear (Barnett & Johnson, 2010).

In making an ethical decision, counselors may rely on personal values as well as ethical standards and legal precedents. They can also consult with professional colleagues, casebooks, and principles. It is imperative that counselors become well informed in the area of ethics for the sake of their own well-being and that of their clients. It is not enough that counselors have an academic knowledge of ethics; they must have a working knowledge and be able to assess at what developmental level they and their colleagues are operating.

In addition, counselors must be informed about state and national legislation and legal decisions. These will affect the ways in which they work. Counselors are liable for civil and criminal malpractice suits if they violate client rights or societal rules. One way for counselors to protect themselves legally is to follow the ethical standards of the professional organizations with which they are affiliated and operate according to recognized normal practices. There are models for making both ethical and legal decisions that can be helpful to counselors. It is imperative that counselors be able to justify what they do. Counselors should also carry malpractice insurance.

Ethical standards and legal codes reflect current conditions and are ever-evolving documents. Revisions of ethical standards and court opinions are primary ways that these two entities change. Present standards and codes do not cover all situations, but they do offer help beyond that contained in counselors' personal beliefs and values. As counseling continues to develop as a profession, its ethical and legal aspects will probably become more complicated, and enforcement procedures will become stricter.

Ignorance of ethics and the law is no excuse for any practicing counselor. It is important that counselors realize that, with notable exceptions, they think differently from attorneys. Therefore, as the minority culture, they need to take the initiative in learning how to deal with legal matters and lawyers.

Counseling in a Multicultural Society 4

In the dark, through a steady rain,
*　　we pass through the ancient hills of Pennsylvania,*
Chatting as if we were old friends
*　　when the fact is*
*　　　　we have known each other for minutes.*
He, a native born Arab,
I, a southern born American,
*　　together, in a yellow taxi.*
We mix and mingle words and accents
*　　as if they were the greens in a salad*
*　　　　while cars on the interstate pass us by*
*　　　　　　unaware of what is transpiring.*
In only moments we will separate
I going south to Charlotte on a plane
*　　while he heads back to Pittsburgh for another fare*
But for now we are one
*　　Muslim and WASP united*
pouring out our opinions with passion
*　　about George Bush and Osama Bin Laden*
*　　　　through the commerce of the morning.*

Reprinted from "In the Commerce of the Morning," by S. T. Gladding, © 2007
S. T. Gladding.

MyCounselingLab™

Visit the MyCounselingLab™ site (www.MyCounselingLab.com) for *Counseling: A Comprehensive Profession*, Seventh Edition to enhance your understanding of chapter concepts. You'll have the opportunity to practice your skills through video- and case-based Assignments and Activities as well as Building Counseling Skills units and to prepare for your certification exam with Practice for Certification quizzes.

The effectiveness of counseling depends on many factors, but among the most important is for the counselor and client to be able to understand and relate to each other. Such a relationship is usually easier to achieve if the client and counselor are from the same culture or similar to each other in beliefs. For instance, data from 61 Asian American clients at a university counseling center showed that both a strong match on belief about problem etiology and a high client expectation for counseling success were associated with strong client-counselor working alliance (Kim, Ng, & Ahn, 2009).

Regardless of whether a natural match between counselors and clients occurs, it is imperative that counselors be acutely sensitive to their clients' backgrounds and special needs and equally attuned to their own values, biases, and abilities (Atkinson, 2004; Brinson, 1996; Holiday, Leach, & Davidson, 1994). Otherwise, counselors may misunderstand and frustrate clients or even harm them by making bad decisions regarding their treatment (Hays, Prosek, & McLeod, 2010). Understanding and dealing positively with differences in cultures is a matter of **developing self-awareness** (from the inside out) as well as **developing an awareness of others** (from the outside in) (Okun, Fried, & Okun, 1999). Differences between counselors and clients should never be allowed to influence the counseling process negatively.

This chapter considers distinct populations and issues that impact counseling in a culturally diverse world, especially North America. "As the racial and ethnic diversity of the United States [and Canada] continues to increase, the need for mental health professionals to tailor their mental health services to the needs of various cultural populations has become more germane" (Constantine, Hage, Kindaichi, & Bryant, 2007, p. 24). Culturally neutral counseling does not exist.

Topics covered here focus on working with clients who are culturally and ethnically distinct from their counselors. Methods that work best with one population may be irrelevant or even inappropriate for others. Indeed, "a particular characteristic may be valued and desirable in certain cultures and denigrated and seen as a weakness in others" (Harris, Thoresen, & Lopez, 2007, p. 5). Therefore, counselors must be constant lifelong learners and implementers of new and effective methods of working with those in cultures distinct from their own.

COUNSELING ACROSS CULTURE AND ETHNICITY

Many cultural and ethnic groups live in the United States and Canada. In the 2010 Census, European Americans make up the largest group (64%), with four other distinct groups— African Americans (13%), Native American Indians (1.0%), Asian Americans (5%), and

Hispanics/Latinos (16%)—composing the majority of the rest of the population that report being of just one backgroup (i.e., not of two or more races or a different race from these five). In addition, Arab Americans, a small but significant group, are important to understand because of the ties between the North American and Arab worlds.

The minority cultural and ethnic groups just mentioned, along with numerous other distinct populations, are growing rapidly in number and as a percentage within the United States and Canada. Non-Whites make up a majority of the inhabitants in nearly 1 in 10 counties in the United States and are a majority in almost one third of the most populous counties in the country. For example, Chicago now has more Asians than Honolulu, Washington has more Hispanic residents than El Paso, and Houston has overtaken Los Angeles in regard to the Black population (Roberts, 2007).

Several factors influence the counseling of cultural and ethnic groups, but the harsh reality is that over 50% of minority-culture clients who begin counseling terminate after one session, as compared with about 30% of majority-culture clients (Sue & Sue, 2008). This statistic suggests that, as a rule, minority-culture clients have negative experiences in counseling. As a group, ethnic minorities underutilize counseling services because of the treatment they receive or fail to have provided. The results work against these clients, their families, and society in general.

PERSONAL REFLECTION

Think of when you have been misunderstood by someone else. What did it feel like? What did it make you want to do or not want to do in regard to the situation? Then think about what you would feel like if misunderstood by a counselor—a professional who is supposed to be sensitive and attuned to others!

DEFINING CULTURE AND MULTICULTURAL COUNSELING

Culture may be defined in several ways. Definitions include "*ethnographic variables* such as ethnicity, nationality, religion, and language, as well as *demographic variables* of age, gender, place of residence, etc., *status variables* such as social, economic, and educational background and a wide range of formal or informal memberships and affiliations" (Pedersen, 1990, p. 550). A culture "structures our behavior, thoughts, perceptions, values, goals, morals, and cognitive processes" (Cohen, 1998, p. B4). It may do so on an unconscious or a conscious level.

A broad definition of *culture* that is inclusive as well as accurate is "any group of people who identify or associate with one another on the basis of some common purpose, need, or similarity of background" (Axelson, 1999, p. 2). Shared elements of a culture include learned experiences, beliefs, and values. These aspects of a culture are "webs of significance" that give coherence and meaning to life (Geertz, 1973). Whereas some cultures may define themselves partially in regard to similar physical features, others do so more in terms of a common history and philosophy, and still others combine the two. What people claim as a part of their culture and heritage is not always apparent at first sight. However, culture is important in counseling for numerous reasons including the fact that "a client's cultural identity, cultural match between a client and counselor, and cultural bias—affects the clinical decision making process" (Hays, Prosek, & McLeod, 2010).

Just as the word "culture" is multidimensional, the term ***multicultural*** has been conceptualized in a number of different ways. There is no universal agreement as to what it includes, although accrediting bodies, such as CACREP, have defined the term broadly. "The lack of a concrete definition for multiculturalism has been a continuing problem" (Middleton, Flowers, & Zawaiza, 1996, p. 19). The most prominent foci of multiculturalism are distinct group uniquenesses and concepts that facilitate attention to individual differences (Locke, 1998).

Therefore, ***multicultural counseling*** may be viewed generally as counseling "in which the counselor and client differ" (Locke, 1990, p. 18). The differences may be the result of socialization in a unique cultural way, developmental or traumatic life events, or the product of being raised in a particular ethnic environment. The debate in the multicultural counseling field is how broad differences should be defined. On one hand, some proponents advocate what is known as an ***etic perspective,*** stating universal qualities exist in counseling that are culturally generalizable. On the other hand, the ***emic perspective*** assumes counseling approaches must be designed to be culturally specific.

"The etic approach can be criticized for not taking important cultural differences into account. The emic approach can be criticized for placing too much emphasis on specific techniques as the vehicle for client change" (Fischer, Jome, & Atkinson, 1998, p. 578). Some professionals have tried to find common elements shared by these two approaches. For example, Fischer et al. (1998) have proposed four conditions common to any type of counseling treatment:

- the therapeutic relationship,
- a shared worldview between client and counselor,
- client expectations for positive change, and
- interventions believed by both client and counselor to be a means of healing (p. 531).

However, this proposal has received only limited support. Thus, in the 21st century, the definition of multicultural counseling continues to be argued. There are those who are more inclusive and more exclusive of others. In this chapter, multiculturalism will be dealt with using an emic approach that should be combined with diversity factors (which are covered in the next chapter). In order to really understand clients, counselors must realize the persons sitting before them are complex and multifaceted. Therefore, combining cultural and diversity factors as a part of understanding is essential.

HISTORY OF MULTICULTURAL COUNSELING

Although a number of scholars had previously pointed out the cultural limits of counseling, Gilbert Wrenn (1962b) was the first prominent professional to call attention to the unique aspects of counseling people from different cultures. In a landmark work, he described the ***culturally encapsulated counselor*** as one who disregards cultural differences and works under the mistaken assumption that theories and techniques are equally applicable to all people. Such a counselor is insensitive to the actual experiences of clients from different cultural, racial, and ethnic backgrounds and therefore may discriminate against some persons by treating everyone the same. Clemmont Vontress (1966, 1967, 1996) was also an early active pioneer in defining culture and showing how it influences counseling relationships. In 1973, Paul Pedersen chaired a panel on multicultural counseling at the APA's annual convention and, with his colleagues in 1976, later published the first book specifically on the subject, *Counseling Across Cultures*. The book is now in its 6th edition (Pedersen, Lonner, Draguns, & Trimble, 2007)! Since that time, numerous other publications and workshops have highlighted different aspects of multicultural counseling.

The history of offering counseling services for culturally distinct populations in the United States is rather brief and uneven (Arredondo, 1998). For example, in a survey of experts in the field, Ponterotto and Sabnani (1989) found "only 8.5% of the most frequently cited books in the field [were published] before 1970" (p. 35). Indeed, the focus of multicultural counseling has shifted in its relatively short history from an emphasis on the client (1950s), to the counselor (1960s), to the total counseling process itself (1970s to the present). In the late 1980s, multicultural counseling was described as "the hottest topic in the profession" (Lee, 1989, p. 165). Throughout the 1990s and into the 21st century, it has remained so with a significant increase in counseling journals that focus on multicultural issues from an exploratory and developmental, rather than a pathology-oriented, view (Arredondo, Rosen, Rice, Perez, & Tovar-Gamero, 2005). Indeed, multicultural issues in counseling now account for 12% of the quantitative articles published in the flagship journal of the American Counseling Association, the *Journal of Counseling and Development*, which is only slightly less than the leading subject published in the journal, career/academic issues with 14% (Nisson, Love, Taylor, & Slusher, 2007). That is why multicultural counseling is often called "*the fourth force*"—following psychoanalysis, behaviorism, and humanistic concepts of counseling.

As a major force in counseling, multicultural counseling has changed the profession in a number of ways (D'Andrea & Heckman, 2008). Four are particularly pertinent. The first is by "describing the between-groups differences that are commonly manifested among persons in diverse racial/ethnic/cultural groups." The second is by illuminating "the within-group psychological differences that are routinely manifested among persons in the same racial/cultural groups." A third change has been "the introduction of additional theoretical models that highlight the multidimensionality of human development" (p. 356) Among these has been an acronym model for assessing cultural components of a client: **RESPECTFUL** counseling framework (**R = religious/spiritual issues, E = economic class issues, S = sexual identity issues, P = psychological developmental issues, E = ethnic/racial identity issues, C = chronological issues, T = trauma and threats to well-being, F = family issues, U = unique physical issues, L = language and location of residence issues**) (D'Andrea & Daniels, 2001). Finally, "new professional competencies counselors need to acquire to work effectively and ethically in a culturally diverse society have been generated" (D'Andrea & Heckman, 2008, p. 356) as a result of the multicultural counseling movement. The most prominent of these is the *Multicultural Counseling Competencies* (Sue, Arredondo, & McDavis, 1992).

The **Association for Multicultural Counseling and Development (AMCD;** www .amcdaca.org/amcd/default.cfm), a division within the ACA, is dedicated primarily to defining and dealing with issues and concerns related to counseling across cultures within the United States. Originally known as the Association for Non-White Concerns in Personnel and Guidance (ANWC), the division became part of the ACA in 1972 (McFadden & Lipscomb, 1985). It publishes a quarterly periodical, the *Journal of Multicultural Counseling and Development*, which addresses issues related to counseling in a culturally pluralistic society. The AMCD has also sponsored training to help counselors understand competencies needed in working with clients from non-European backgrounds and to promote the *Multicultural Counseling Competencies Standards* (Sue, Arredondo, & McDavis, 1992). "*Multicultural competence* generally is defined as the extent to which counselors possess appropriate levels of self-awareness, knowledge, and skills in working with individuals from diverse cultural backgrounds" (Constantine et al., 2007, p. 24).

The AMCD, in cooperation with the ACA, regularly holds conferences and meetings to address real or perceived problems related to counseling relationships involving clients and counselors from different cultural groups. The focus of such training is to help counselors obtain **cultural expertise** (effectiveness in more than one culture) and **cultural intentionality** (awareness of individual differences within each culture). The need for such educational efforts continues to be great because of the changing demographics within North America and the world and because of the limited and general training in multicultural counseling that many counselors have received.

DIFFICULTIES IN MULTICULTURAL COUNSELING

While multicultural counseling is a noble and necessary part of counseling, one of the difficulties of this process is measurement. For example, Hays (2008) has reviewed the instruments used to measure the multicultural counseling competencies as first set forth by Sue et al. (1992). Her research considered individual and program evaluation instruments. In general, current assessments appear to have little statistical support, might be measuring different constructs even though they are using similar labels, and may be evaluating multicultural counseling self-efficacy more than anything else. Thus, more sophistication in measuring multicultural counseling competencies is needed.

Smith and Vasquez (1985) caution that it is important to distinguish differences that arise from cultural backgrounds from those that are the result of poverty or deprived status. A failure to make this distinction can lead to **overculturalizing**: "mistaking people's reactions to poverty and discrimination for their cultural pattern" (p. 533). In the United States, "people of color are overrepresented among Americans living in poverty relative to their proportions in the general population" (Smith, Foley, & Chaney, 2008, p. 304).

The problem of overculturalizing is compounded by a persistent third difficulty: **language** patterns. If the primary language of the client is not English, both verbal utterances and non-verbal behaviors may be misunderstood by counselors outside the client's own culture. Such a situation may well arise when counselors steeped in a country's or region's traditions try to work with individuals from immigrant populations.

Racism is a fourth problematic area in working across cultures (Utsey, Ponterotto, & Porter, 2008). **Racism** is prejudice displayed in blatant or subtle ways due to recognized or perceived differences in the physical and psychological backgrounds of people. It demeans all who participate in it. Essentially, racism is a form of projection usually displayed out of fear or ignorance.

A final difficulty in multicultural counseling involves **acculturation,** "the process by which a group of people give up old ways and adopt new ones" (Romero, Silva, & Romero, 1989, p. 499). In the acculturation process, individuals are simultaneously being influenced by elements of two distinct cultures to some extent. The process is not easy, and research indicates difficulties in trying to balance contrasting values of two different cultures include "psychological stress, guilt, apathy, depression, delinquency, resentment, disorientation, and poor self-esteem" (Yeh & Hwang, 2000, p. 425). Therefore, it is crucial to know where clients are located on a continuum of acculturation in order to provide them with appropriate services (Weinrach & Thomas, 1998).

Each of these difficulties in multicultural counseling must be recognized, understood, and empathetically resolved if counselors are to be effective with clients who are different from them (Ridley, 2005).

CASE EXAMPLE

Mary and the *Mayflower*

Mary was proud of her strong New England heritage and rightfully so. Her family had originally come over on the *Mayflower*, and her ancestors had made noteworthy contributions to society. However, Mary had a problem. She was so enthralled with her family's past that she failed to respond to present reality. That became apparent when Mary saw her first Hispanic client, Maria, in her private practice office just outside Boston.

Mary was annoyed initially with Maria's accent but she became even more upset when she found her client took pride in her "foreign culture." Soon Mary found herself in a psychological battle with Maria on whose culture was "better." Counseling took a backseat to conflict.

What do you think Mary should have done in this situation besides the path she chose to pursue? What is wrong with engaging in cultural competition?

ISSUES IN MULTICULTURAL COUNSELING

A primary issue of concern for some multicultural counselors in the United States, especially those with an emic perspective, is the dominance of theories based on European/North American cultural values. Some of the **predominant beliefs of European/North Americans** are the value of individuals, an action-oriented approach to problem solving, the work ethic, the scientific method, and an emphasis on rigid time schedules (Axelson, 1999). A liability of these values in counseling is that theories built around them may not always be applicable to clients from other cultural traditions (Lee, 2006b; Nwachuku & Ivey, 1991; Sue, 1992). If this fact is not recognized and dealt with, bias and a breakdown in counselor–client relationships may occur (Pedersen, 1987).

A second issue in multicultural counseling is **sensitivity to cultures** in general and in particular. Pedersen (1982) believes that it is essential for counselors to be sensitive to cultures in three areas:

1. **knowledge** of the worldviews of culturally different clients,
2. **awareness** of one's own personal worldview and how one is a product of cultural conditioning, and
3. **skills** necessary for work with culturally different clients.

These three areas have been used by the AMCD as a basis for developing the Multicultural Counseling Competencies in 1992 and for operationalizing them (Arredondo et al., 1996). Prior to this development, Pedersen (1977, 1978) developed a **triad model for helping counselors achieve a deeper understanding of cultures** in general. The four areas in the model are "articulating the problem from the client's cultural perspective; anticipating resistance from a culturally different client; diminishing defensiveness by studying the trainee's own defensive responses; and learning recovery skills for getting out of trouble when counseling the culturally different" (1978, p. 481). In this model, an ***anticounselor***, who functions like an alter ego and deliberately tries to be subversive, works with a counselor and a client in a videotaped session. The interaction and feedback generated through this process help break down barriers and foster greater understanding and sensitivity in counselors (Parker, Archer, & Scott, 1992).

Another model for understanding specific cultures has been devised by Nwachuku and Ivey (1991). They propose that counselors first study a culture and its values before trying to adapt a theory to fit a particular client. A starting point in achieving this goal is to view popular diversity-focused films about specific cultures. Pinterits and Atkinson (1998) list some films that can help counselors understand different cultures and experience the issues within these cultures vicariously.

A third issue in multicultural counseling involves understanding how cultural systems operate and influence behaviors. Counselors who have gained knowledge and awareness from within the cultural system are more likely to be skilled in helping members from a specific cultural group. These counselors are able to share a particular worldview with clients, make skillful and appropriate interventions, and yet maintain a sense of personal integrity. This type of cultural sensitivity requires "active participation on the part of the practitioner" including self-awareness (Brinson, 1996, p. 201).

A fourth issue in multicultural counseling is providing effective counseling services across cultures. Sue (1978a) established **five guidelines for effectively counseling across cultures** that are still applicable:

1. Counselors recognize the values and beliefs they hold in regard to acceptable and desirable human behavior. They are then able to integrate this understanding into appropriate feelings and behaviors.
2. Counselors are aware of the cultural and generic qualities of counseling theories and traditions. No method of counseling is completely culture-free.
3. Counselors understand the sociopolitical environment that has influenced the lives of members of minority groups. Persons are products of the milieus in which they live.
4. Counselors are able to share the worldview of clients and do not question its legitimacy.
5. Counselors are truly eclectic in counseling practice. They are able to use a wide variety of counseling skills and apply particular counseling techniques to specific lifestyles and experiences.

A final issue in multicultural counseling is the development and employment of counseling theories. *Cultural bias* (the tendency to think one's own culture is superior to others) is present in majority and minority counselors (Wendel, 1997) and in the past has spilled over into counseling theories and practices. To deal with culturally limited counseling theories and bias, and to help transcend cultural limitations, McFadden (1999) and a number of leading counselor educators have devised ways to overcome ideas and methods developed before there was any awareness of the need for multicultural counseling. McFadden's model is a **transcultural perspective** that focuses on three primary dimensions counselors must master. They are:

• the **cultural–historical**, where counselors must possess knowledge of a client's culture;
• the **psychosocial**, where counselors must come to understand the client's ethnic, racial, and social group's performance, speeches, and behaviors in order to communicate meaningfully; and
• the **scientific–ideological**, where counselors must use appropriate counseling approaches to deal with problems related to regional, national, and international environments.

Explanations of existing theories and their applicability to certain populations and problems have also become popular (e.g., Corsini & Wedding, 2010; Sue, Ivey, & Pedersen, 2009;

Vontress, 1996). Existential counseling is one such approach that, like McFadden's transcultural perspective, is holistic and applicable across "all cultures and socioeconomic groups" (Epp, 1998, p. 7). As a theoretical approach, it deals with meaning and human relationships and with the ultimate issues of life and death.

Another exciting development in multicultural counseling is the renewed emphasis on theories specifically designed for different cultures (Lee, 2006b). For example, traditional Asian psychotherapies, which have existed for more than 3,000 years, have recently become more popular in the West (Walsh, 2000). Many of these traditions stress existential and transpersonal health and development over pathology, employing such techniques as meditation and yoga. They have a beneficial effect on wellness and psychological growth whether used alone or in concert with other approaches.

CASE EXAMPLE

Katie's Knowledge

Katie was a quick study. Her mind was like a machine in being able to size up and solve a task. Therefore, she thought her high intellectual skills would translate well into helping her clients when she became a counselor. With her first few clients, that's exactly what happened. However, her next client was culturally different from Katie in a number of ways. To her credit, Katie listened well and seemed to grasp the client's worldview. However, after that she felt stuck, and the session seemed to go nowhere.

What does Katie's situation tell you about the power of knowledge and intellectual understanding? What would you suggest Katie do to become more culturally competent?

COUNSELING CONSIDERATIONS
WITH SPECIFIC CULTURAL GROUPS

In addition to general guidelines for working with culturally different clients, counselors should keep in mind some general considerations when working with specific cultural groups. In reviewing these considerations, it is crucial that counselors remind themselves that *each individual, like each counseling session, is unique.* There are *more within-group differences than between-group differences in counseling people from specific cultural traditions* (Atkinson, 2004; Swartz-Kulstad & Martin, 1999). Therefore, knowing a cultural tradition is only a part of the information counselors need in order to be effective. They must work to know their clients, problems, and themselves equally well.

In examining themselves, counselors who are from minority cultures need to be aware that they may harbor "**historical hostility**" at either a conscious or unconscious level toward members of majority cultures (Wendel, 1997). They also need to be aware that, because of their minority status within a society, they have developed a within-group racial identity as well as a personal identity that is known as **minority racial identity development (MRID)**. MRID is impacted by the historic and contemporary sociopolitical environments in which minority culture groups live (Warner, 2009). Its development is most productive when it progresses from an identity with and conformity to the majority culture to recognizing the uniqueness of one's own cultural heritage. In such a movement, deeper understanding of the implication of race for all people develops with a commitment to improving the lives of everyone.

On the opposite side, counselors from majority cultures may carry attitudes of superiority and privilege. In American society, such privilege is based on skin color and is commonly referred to as **White privilege**. It is a reward that is not based on merit and is often ignored by those who have it, which can cause them to neglect or be prejudiced to those who are not the same as them. Connected with this privilege in the United States, but the opposite from it, is **White racial identity development**. This model purposes a development movement of those with White skin through a stage process to a nonracist White identity (Modak & Sheperis, 2009). All the models of identity mentioned here are still undergoing research and refinement, but their points are well made and should be kept in mind as we examine different ethnic groups: European Americans, African Americans, Hispanics/Latinos/as, Asian Americans, Native American Indians, and Arab Americans.

European Americans

BACKGROUND OF EUROPEAN AMERICANS. As a group, European Americans are a diverse population. Within the United States alone "there are 53 categories of European Americans" (Baruth & Manning, 2012, p. 198). Although Europe is their common ancestral homeland, there are large differences between the cultural heritages of people from Sweden, Italy, France, England, Poland, Germany, Russia, Sweden, and Austria. (In addition, many people from Spain or from Spanish ancestry consider their heritage distinct from other Europeans in general.) Europeans who have recently arrived in the United States differ widely from those whose families settled in North America generations ago, many of whom now identify themselves as simply "American," forsaking their European ancestries (El Nasser & Overberg, 2002). Overall, there is no typical European American.

However, European Americans have a long and dominant history in the United States that has some common threads. As a group, European Americans have blended together more than most other cultural groups. Reasons include a history of intergroup marriages and relationships that have simultaneously influenced the group as a whole and made it more homogeneous. European Americans are more likely than not to espouse a worldview that "values linear, analytical, empirical, and task solutions" and stresses that "rugged individualism should be valued, and that autonomy of the parts and independence of action are more significant than group conformance" (Sue, 1992, p. 8).

In addition, most European Americans are White with the term **White ethnic** referring "to all non-Hispanic White families of European American heritage" (Baruth & Manning, 2012, p. 198). Whiteness and majority status within the United States for generations has led to what is known as **White privilege**, by which White people have achieved "societal rewards on the basis of skin color and other socially determined indicators of race as compared with merit" (Utsey, Ponterotto, & Porter, 2008, p. 341). While this privilege is an advantage to Whites, it is a detriment to other cultural groups unless, as mentioned at the beginning of this section, Europeans develop an identity that is nonracist.

APPROACHES THAT WORK WITH EUROPEANS AND EUROPEAN AMERICANS. Some professionals argue that the vast majority of counseling theories in Europe and the United States are applicable for either Europeans or European Americans. The reason is that members from this group generated the majority of the most popular theories used in Western society. Their point has considerable merit. Most counseling theories employed with these populations are more in tune with the lifestyle and values of these groups than not. However, not all theories work well for all European Americans. Those theories that do work well emphasize many of the shared values of European Americans. For example, many European Americans gravitate toward rational or logical methods in understanding themselves and others. Therefore, cognitive and cognitive-behavioral approaches may work well with this group as a whole. However, existential, psychoanalytic, Adlerian, person-centered, and other affective counseling theories may be appropriate for some within this population. Just as there is no typical European American, there is no one counseling theory or approach that will work with all members of this group.

PERSONAL REFLECTION

What has been your experience in dealing with European Americans? If you are a European American, how do you see yourself the same as and different from other European Americans? If you are not European American, ask yourself the question: "How are European Americans the same as and different from one another?"

African Americans

BACKGROUND OF AFRICAN AMERICANS.   When counseling African Americans, counselors must understand African American history, cultural values, conflicts, and coping mechanisms and be aware of their own attitudes and prejudices about this group (Atkinson, 2004; Garretson, 1993; Vontress & Epp, 1997). It is possible for counselors from different cultural backgrounds to work effectively with African American clients if they understand the nature of racism and the fact that individual, institutional, and cultural racism are "major quality of life issues for African Americans living in contemporary society" (Utsey, Ponterotto, Reynolds, & Cancelli, 2000, p. 72) and that racial discrimination and self-esteem are inversely related. They must further be aware that although blatant racist behaviors, or racial assaults, are seldom acted out in American society, **racial microaggressions** (actions that "communicate hostile, derogatory, or negative racial slights and insults to the target person or group") are (Sue et al., 2008, p. 330). "The power that these microaggressions have to hurt and oppress people of color is due to their invisible nature" (p. 331). They take three forms:

microassaults, which are similar to old-fashioned racism and are deliberate, conscious, and overt, such as refusing to serve someone because of the color of the person's skin;

microinsults, which verbally, nonverbally, or environmentally demean a person's racial identity of heritage, such as "You are a credit to your race"; and

microinvalidations, which are actions that "exclude, negate, or nullify psychological thoughts, feelings, or experiences" (p. 331) of a person, such as being ignored or served last.

African Americans are a diverse group and display a broad range of feelings, thoughts, and behaviors (Baruth & Manning, 2012; Harper, 1994; Smith, 1977). Therefore, no one single counseling or helping approach works best for everyone. Often "counseling is frequently perceived by African Americans as a process that requires the client to relinquish his or her independence by first having to 'tell your business to a stranger' and then having to 'heed the unsolicited advice of that stranger'" (Priest, 1991, p. 215). Therefore, many African Americans are unwilling to voluntarily commit themselves to a counseling relationship.

Another factor that influences African American participation in counseling is the perception that the relationship takes place among unequals. Given the history of slavery in America and the common misdiagnosis of African Americans in mental health centers, members of this group who enter into an unequal relationship do so with great reluctance (Garretson, 1993; Schwartz & Feisthamel, 2009).

A third factor that affects African Americans in counseling is the emphasis on the collective in most of their community tradition. "In historical times the collective was the clan or tribe" (Priest, 1991, p. 213). Today, it is the family and those who live, work, or worship nearby. This emphasis on the collective and the therapeutic power of the group (i.e., the village concept) is the antithesis of individual responsibility for resolving difficulties (McRae, Thompson, & Cooper, 1999).

Spirituality and the role of the minister and the church in African American culture are factors influencing members of this group as well (Baruth & Manning, 2012). Rather than a counselor, a minister is usually sought out as a "source of mental and emotional sustenance" (Priest, 1991, p. 214).

APPROACHES THAT WORK WITH AFRICAN AMERICANS. One place to begin in counseling African Americans is to carefully identify their expectations. Because there are a number of within-group differences among African Americans, as with any group, clients come to counseling for different reasons and with different variations of a worldview. Therefore, it is important to determine what has brought clients to seek counseling services now and what, as well as how, they hope to be different as a result of the experience (Parham, 2002; Sue & Sue, 2008). If the client and counselor are from different cultural and ethnic backgrounds, that factor should be examined (Brammer, 2012; Sue & Sue, 2008). Likewise, the impact of discrimination and racism on African American clients should not be ignored. Racial identity is a further factor to hone in on.

In practical terms, an egalitarian relationship should be established between African American clients and their counselors (Sue & Sue, 2008). Beyond the relationship, there should be an emphasis on pragmatics. "For many African Americans, the purpose for coming to therapy is to receive some practical steps to ease the pain. This may take the form of education and job training, drug treatment, or parenting skills. Therapeutic interventions will work best when connected with related services" (Brammer, 2012). Overemphasizing their feelings does not work with African Americans.

In addition to being practical, counselors should focus on African Americans' strengths and address individuals within the context of their families, neighborhoods, and cities (Brammer, 2012). Family members or neighbors can often be brought in to help. Likewise, spiritual resources within the client's community should be tapped whenever possible because the church and spirituality are an integral part of African American life (Ahia, 2006).

Hispanics/Latinos/as

BACKGROUND OF HISPANICS/LATINOS/AS. Both "Hispanic" and "Latino/a" are terms used to describe a heterogeneous people whose ancestors came from the Spanish-speaking countries of the Americas. The common denominator for **Hispanics** is the Spanish language, but Hispanics are a very diverse group. The word ***Latino/a*** describes "people of Spanish and Indian descent whose ancestors lived in areas of the Southwest United States that were once a part of Mexico" and in countries in Central and South America where the predominant language, usually Spanish, has Latin roots (Fontes, 2002, p. 31). Regardless of their background, most Hispanics and Latinos/as in the United States are bicultural. However, they vary in their degree of acculturation (Baruth & Manning, 2012). Overall, their ethnic histories and cultures play a major part in influencing their worldviews, family dynamics, and health (Miranda, Bilot, Peluso, Berman, & Van Meek, 2006). Many within-group differences exist among Hispanics and Latinos/as (Atkinson, 2004; Romero et al., 1989).

APPROACHES THAT WORK WITH HISPANICS/LATINOS/AS.   As a group, Hispanics and Latinos/as are reluctant to use counseling services. Part of this hesitancy is cultural tradition (e.g., pride), and part is cultural heritage (e.g., reliance on extended family ties). Cultural reasons revolve around the fact that Hispanic and Latino/a individuals and families as a group are poorer than most other cultural groups and have historically been the victims of discrimination and racism (Sue & Sue, 2008). More practical reasons are the distance to service agencies (especially in the Southwest), inadequate transportation, a lack of health insurance, and the absence of counseling professionals fluent in Spanish and familiar with Hispanic and Latino/a cultures (Gonzalez, 1997; Sue & Sue, 2008).

While Hispanic and Latino/a individuals, couples, and families have unique and personal problems, many Hispanics and Latinos/as perceive psychological problems as similar to physical problems (Lopez-Baez, 2006; Ruiz & Padilla, 1977). Therefore, they expect the counselor to be active, concrete, and goal directed. This perception is especially true for clients who are "very" Hispanic (Ruiz, 1981).

Overall, counselors of Hispanics and Latinos/as must address numerous topics and work within cultural concepts and beliefs. This usually means involving families because family loyalty is very important in Latin culture. An evidence-based therapeutic approach that primarily focuses on the family is filial therapy. In **filial therapy**, "positive behavioral or symptomatic changes result from a changed parent-child relationship rather than specific problem-focused strategies. Filial therapy is both a therapeutic intervention and a preventive approach" (Garza & Watts, 2010, p. 108). It involves parents being taught to work with their children on an emotional level in child-centered play therapy with special kits of toys. "Four Hispanic values that, when interfaced with filial therapy, help facilitate effective culturally responsive treatment: (a) the importance of *familismo* (family), (b) *respeto* (respect), (c) *personalismo* (personal relationships), and (d) *confianza* (trust)" (p. 110).

In working therapeutically with a Hispanic and Latino/a person, it is helpful to do so in harmony with the client's spiritual or religious tradition. Since the majority of Hispanics and Latinos/as are Catholic (Baruth & Manning, 2012), knowing the practices of this faith can be beneficial. In addition, it is often helpful if the counselor is bilingual because many Hispanic and Latino/a individuals prefer Spanish to English, especially when expressing their emotions. In addition, bilingual European American counselors are seen as culturally competent by Mexican Americans (Ramos-Sánchez, 2009). Bilingual classes, especially in schools, can help promote cultural identity, acculturation, self-esteem, and learning among students (Cavazos-Rehg, & DeLucia-Waack, 2009) who can in turn serve as translators, if needed, in a counseling session.

CASE EXAMPLE

Collin Considers the Collective

Collin was a counselor of few words. As a former athlete, he believed in showing rather than telling individuals how to stay mentally healthy. Therefore, when he first came across a client, Margareta, who referred to her family as a crucial part of her life, he was baffled. None of his individualistic techniques worked. Therefore, he asked a colleague for help. "Ah," said the colleague who was about at Collin's same age and level of maturity, "You are doing just the right thing. The client will eventually see that."

What do you think of Collin's colleague's remark? What more should Collin do in regard to preparing himself to work with clients who stress the importance of family and their collective identity? What should he do in regard to Margareta now?

Asian Americans

BACKGROUND OF ASIAN AMERICANS.   Asian Americans include those whose original heritage is Chinese, Japanese, Filipino, Indochinese, Indian, and Korean, among others. They vary widely in cultural background (Atkinson, 2004; Morrissey, 1997). The demographic profile of Asian Americans includes an array of more than 40 disparate cultural groups" (Sandhu, 1997). Historically, they have faced strong discrimination in the United States and have been the subject of many myths (Sue & Sue, 1972, 2008). A combination of factors has promoted stereotypes of Asian Americans.

Because of bias and misunderstandings, Asian Americans have "been denied the rights of citizenship, forbidden to own land, locked in concentration camps, maligned, mistreated, and massacred" (Sue & Sue, 1973, p. 387). Ironically, a combination of factors has also promoted a positive image of them. They are collectively described as hardworking and successful and not prone to mental or emotional disturbances. Sometimes they are referred to as the "*model minority*" (Bell, 1985). Like all stereotypes, there are kernels of truth in this last descriptor, but it is still not realistic or accurate. The model minority myth glosses over the real social, economic, and psychological problems experienced by Asian Americans. More important, it diverts attention away from the racism and discrimination that affect their lives.

In many quarters, Asian Americans are resented and envied on the dimension of competent while also being perceived as unsociable (Kohatsu, Victoria, Lau, Flores, & Salazar, 2011). The model minority myth is perpetuated as a **color-blind racial ideology**. Inherent in color blindness is the idea that race and racism do not matter and do not play important roles in the current social and economic climate. Thus, color-blind racial attitudes often justify **blaming the victim** and rationalize beliefs that racial minority groups who cannot succeed in this society are "culturally" inferior. Research has shown that counselors "subscribing to a color-blind perspective are less skilled at communicating empathy, less sensitive to issues pertaining to cultural diversity, and more likely to attribute responsibility for the resolution of a therapy issue to a client of color than to a European American client. Therefore, it is crucial that therapists who work with clients of color develop an awareness of their color-blind racial attitudes" (p. 64).

APPROACHES THAT WORK WITH ASIAN AMERICANS.   As a group "Asian Americans use mental health services two thirds less frequently than do Whites" (Gloria, Castellanos, Park, & Kim, 2008, p. 419). Part of the reason is due to indigenous beliefs among some Asian cultures about the nature of mental health and mental disorders and the need to seek counseling services (Yamawaki, 2010). Therefore, counselors must see and appreciate Asian Americans in the context of their cultural heritage, or they will be unable to offer them help in mentally healthy ways (Henkin, 1985).

There are many subtleties in Asian American cultures, and often communication is more indirect and discrete. One cultural factor in some Asian Americans' worldviews is that psychological distress and disorders are explained within a religious framework. If persons are troubled, they may be possessed by a bad spirit, or they may be suffering because they have violated some religious or moral principle. Thus, religious tradition plays a strong role in some of their views about the origins of mental health and mental illness. Similarly, they may see healing take the form of "invoking the help of some supernatural power or restoring the sufferer to a state of well being through prescribing right conduct and belief" (Das, 1987, p. 25).

Another important subtlety, which may have an impact in career counseling, is that many Asian Americans typically eschew occupations that call for forceful self-expression (Watanabe, 1973). Genteel ways of communicating stem from cultural traditions and must be dealt with positively if a strong counseling relationship is to be established.

It is critical that counselors appreciate the history and unique characteristics of select Asian American groups in the United States, such as the Chinese, Japanese, and Vietnamese (Atkinson, 2004; Axelson, 1999; Sandhu, 1997). This sensitivity often enables counselors to facilitate the counseling process in ways not otherwise possible (Lum, 2007). For example, counselors may promote self-disclosure with Chinese Americans through educational or career counseling rather than direct, confrontational psychotherapeutic approaches.

Native American Indians

BACKGROUND OF NATIVE AMERICAN INDIANS.   Native Americans, mistakenly called Indians by the first European settlers in America, are the indigenous peoples of the Western Hemisphere who were the first inhabitants of the American continents (Garrett & Pichette, 2000). Today, they are made up of 517 tribes recognized by the U.S. Bureau of Indian Affairs. Tremendous diversity prevails among Native Americans, including close to 300 languages with "a plethora of unique cultures, histories, and traditions" (Hinson, 2010, p. 22). However, they also have a common identity that stresses values such as harmony with nature, cooperation, holism, a concern with the present, and a reliance on one's extended family (Heinrich, Corbin, & Thomas, 1990). In general, Native Americans have strong feelings about the loss of ancestral lands, a desire for self-determination, conflicts with the values of mainstream American culture, and a confused self-image resulting from past stereotyping (Atkinson, 2004). Anger from or about past transgressions of people from other cultures is a theme that must be handled appropriately (Hammerschlag, 1988). Native American Indians, as a group, have high suicide, unemployment, and alcoholism rates and a low life expectancy (Garrett & Pichette, 2000). "American Indians continue to have the highest dropout rate of any ethnic group at the high school level, regardless of region or tribal affiliation" (Sanders, 1987, p. 81). In short, as a group "Native Americans face enormous problems" (Heinrich et al., 1990, p. 128).

APPROACHES THAT WORK WITH NATIVE AMERICAN INDIANS.   A number of counseling approaches, from existentialism to directed counseling, have been tried with Native Americans. Effective counseling, however, depends in part on whether they live on a reservation; whether other Native Americans help facilitate the counseling process; and whether their acculturation is traditional, bicultural, or assimilated (Avasthi, 1990; Garrett, 2006; Valle, 1986). Regardless, it is crucial that counselors understand Native American cultures and avoid imposing culturally inappropriate theories on them (Herring, 1996, 1997; Ivey, 1990).

In the case of Native Americans who are still attached to traditions and ancestral ways of living, healing practices revolve around a circular and holistic model for understanding human issues. "The model of organization is the medicine wheel, from which counselors and others can examine diverse dimensions of the human condition" (Rybak, Eastin, & Robbins, 2004, p. 25).

One way to assess the degree of cultural values held by Native American clients is by using the Native American Acculturation Scale (Garrett & Pichette, 2000). This scale measures individuals' levels of acculturation along a continuum ranging from traditional Native American to assimilated mainstream American.

According to Richardson (1981), four ideas to be considered when counseling Native Americans are silence, acceptance, restatement, and general lead. Richardson has used vignettes to model ways of using these techniques. The use of the *vision quest,* a rite of passage and religious renewal for adult men, is recommended in some cases (Heinrich et al., 1990). The use of the **creative arts** (music, drama, visual art, literature/writing, dance/movement) is also an approach that has considerable merit because emotional, religious, and artistic expression is "an inalienable aspect of Native culture" (Herring, 1997, p. 105). The creative arts do not require verbal disclosure. In addition, they may focus on rituals and wellness in Native American culture. Using multiple counseling approaches in a synergetic way, such as network therapy, home-based therapy, indigenous-structural therapy, and traditional native activities such as "the talking circle," "the talking stick," and storytelling, are also recommended (Garrett, 2006; Herring, 1996).

More important than specific ways of working is the crucial nature of a sense of "realness" when in a counseling relationship with a Native American. Being willing to be a learner and to admit one's mistakes can help a counselor and a Native American bond.

Arab Americans

BACKGROUND OF ARAB AMERICANS.   Arab Americans are a fast-growing and mosaic group in the United States, coming from 22 countries as diverse as Egypt, Lebanon, Morocco, Yemen, Tunisia, and Palestine. There are over 3.5 million Arab Americans, most of whom are Christian with a sizable portion being Muslim (www.aaiusa.org/arab-americans/22/demographics, retrieved August 29, 2007; Negy, 2008). However, "Arabic and Muslim cultures often overlap. Thus, although the majority of Arab Americans are Christian, Muslim traditions and values are often upheld by Muslim and Christian Arab Americans alike" (Nassar-McMillan & Hakim-Larson, 2003).

Arab Americans vary among themselves. Potential differences include social class, level of education, language (Arabic has distinct dialects), relative conservatism of the country of origin, time of immigration, and level of acculturation (Abudabbeh & Aseel, 1999). "Age, gender, income, and education, variables such as age at migration, length of time in the United States, religion, and discrimination experiences are significant predictors of mental health problems for

Arab Americans" (Aprahamian, Kaplan, Windham, Sutter, & Visser, 2011, p. 88). Despite such cultural variations, sufficient commonalities exist that special attention from service providers is warranted.

Arab cultures tend to be of a high context rather than of a low context such as in North American society. Therefore, Arab Americans as a group usually differ significantly from traditional Americans in that they emphasize social stability and the collective over the individual.

The family is the most significant element in most Arab American subcultures with the individual's life dominated by family and family relations. Men are the patriarchs in family life and women are expected to uphold the honor of the family. Education is valued in Arab American households with approximately 4 in 10 Americans of Arab descent having earned a bachelor's degree or higher (www.aaiusa.org/arab-americans/22/demographics, retrieved August 29, 2007).

APPROACHES THAT WORK WITH ARAB AMERICANS.   When working with Arab Americans, especially immigrants, it is crucial for counselors to remember that there is a sharp delineation of gender roles in such families. Furthermore, patriarchal patterns of authority, conservative sexual standards, and the importance of self-sacrifice prevail. There is also an emphasis on the importance of honor and shame because people in Arab cultures seek outside help from helpers, such as counselors, only as a last resort (Abudabbeth & Aseel, 1999). Complicating matters even more is the fallout, tension, and distrust from 9/11 (Beitin & Allen, 2005).

Therefore, clinical recommendations for working with members of this population include

- being aware of their cultural context,
- being mindful of the issue of leadership and the importance that authority figures play in their lives,
- being attentive to the part that the extended family plays in decision making,
- being sensitive to the large part culture plays as an active and tangible co-participant in treatment,
- being conscious of the fact that a strength-based approach to treatment is both desirable and works better, and
- being active as a counselor and balancing the role so as not to be seen as a rescuer or a threat.

Counselors can also assist Arab Americans by helping them access groups where they can find support and become members of a larger community that is dealing with issues as they are. Working in and with groups presents "some potentially problematic issues for particular clients. This is especially true for the war refugees from Iraq, due to the paranoid symptoms that often accompany the diagnosis of PTSD in clients who have experienced wartime trauma. On the other hand, parenting groups and 12-step programs seem to be effective with some nonrefugee Arab immigrant groups, perhaps due to the collectivist nature of the Arab culture in the countries of origin" (Nasser-McMillan & Hakim-Larson, 2003).

Overall in helping Arab Americans, counselors need to go beyond individual or limited group work with clients and do what they can to reduce prejudice and discrimination in the majority culture of the United States. This is a social justice focus and, if carried out by counselors, can help Arab Americans improve their mental health and overall functioning in multiple ways (Aprahamian et al., 2011).

International Counselling/Counseling

Counseling is a worldwide phenomenon frequently spelled in the English language with double *ll*s (i.e., **counselling**). The cultural perspective of the United States regarding counseling is just one among many in the world. Indeed, some continents have their own counseling associations (specifically, Africa—African Counselling Association—and Europe—European Association for Counselling and European Branch of the American Counseling Association). A number of other countries (over 40) have counseling associations as well (see chart below).

Countries with Counselling/Counseling Associations	
Argentina	Kyrgyzstan
Australia	Lebanon
Botswana	Malawi
Brazil	Malaysia
Canada	Mexico
China	New Zealand
Czech Republic	Nigeria
Denmark	Philippines
Equador	Romania
France	Russia
Germany	Singapore
Great Britain	South Africa
Greece	South Korea
Guatemala	Switzerland
Haiti	Taiwan
Honduras	Thailand
India	Turkey
Ireland	Uganda
Israel	United States
Japan	Venezuela
Kenya	Zimbabwe

In addition, the practice of counseling is evolving in a number of regions, particularly Singapore (Rivera, Nash, Chun, & Ibrahim, 2008) and Hong Kong, where counseling associations are blossoming. Furthermore, there are worldwide associations of therapists who ascribe to particular theories, such as Adlerian, transactional analysis (TA), and reality therapy. In some countries without formal counseling associations, such as Italy, literally dozens of training institutes for theories exist (Gemignani & Giliberto, 2005). Finally, there is the **International Association for Counseling** (IAC; www.iac-irtac.org), which holds annual meetings in countries around the world and publishes the *International Journal for the Advancement of Counseling*.

Super (1983) questioned more than 20 years ago whether counseling, as practiced in North America, is adaptable to other countries. His analysis of culture and counseling concluded that prosperous and secure countries view counseling as a way of promoting individual interests and abilities. Economically less fortunate countries and those under threat of foreign domination view counseling services as a way of channeling individuals into areas necessary for cultural survival (Super, 1954b). Knowledge about such cultural differences must be considered in international counseling, especially as it relates to counseling specialties (Watkins, 2001).

Such knowledge is crucial in counseling internationally. For instance, in Poland career counseling is more highly prized than other forms of counseling because of the developing nature of the country (Richard Lamb, personal communication, June 7, 1997). In other countries, such as Japan, counseling is both therapeutic and psychosocial—for example, working with Japanese men on fathering (Seto, Becker, & Akutsu, 2006). However, Japan still lacks a unified licensure standard, and occupational security is an issue (Iwasaki, 2005). On the other hand, in Malaysia, counselling is modeled after counseling in the United States and England, except the initial degree that is granted is the bachelor's (the same as in Japan). Furthermore, almost all graduates are assigned to school settings where they are qualified to teach one subject as well as counsel.

Regardless of their knowledge of counseling, international students who attend colleges and universities in the United States may be reluctant to receive counseling services (Mori, 2000). This reluctance is in spite of the fact that many international students experience a host of stressors beyond those that are mainly developmental in nature. These stressors include "difficulties with linguistics, academic, interpersonal, financial, and intrapersonal problems" (p. 137). The networks of family and friends these students have relied on are absent, and the fear of being seen as a failure and sent home adds to their daily stress (Boyer & Sedlacek, 1989). There is empirical evidence that international students experience greater stress than their American counterparts, which often reaches a crisis level in the first 6 months of study (Schneller & Chalungsooth, 2002).

In order to **help international students who use counseling services**, Mori (2000) suggests the following areas of focus:

- developing stress management techniques,
- learning assertive communication skills,
- becoming fully aware of the American educational system, and
- developing career- and life-planning skills.

Henkin (1985) proposes a number of practical guidelines for counselors interacting on an international level as well. Besides establishing a clear-cut structure for the counseling process and explaining the process to the client, Henkin recommends that counselors educate themselves about the culture of their clients, including the importance of family and community life. Indeed, "a direct application of Western approaches to persons of Eastern descent may have negative consequences" (Raney & Cinarbas, 2005, p. 157). What is needed instead is "an integration of Western and indigenous counseling approaches" that may include family and friends in counseling sessions along with supporting a client's religious practices (p. 158).

PERSONAL REFLECTION

Reflect on the sources of encouragement and support you had while growing up (e.g., an adult leader of a group you were in, siblings, friends, parents, etc.). Were these individuals able to support you and/or help you with your problems satisfactorily? Imagine what it would be like to use such people in a therapeutic way if you were working with someone in or from another country. What do you think?

MyCounselingLab™

Go to Topic 12: *Multicultural Considerations,* in the MyCounselingLab™ site (www
.MyCounselingLab.com) for *Counseling: A Comprehensive Profession*, Seventh Edition,
where you can:

- Find learning outcomes for *Multicultural Considerations* along with the national
  standards that connect to these outcomes.
- Complete Assignments and Activities that can help you more deeply understand the
  chapter content.
- Apply and practice your understanding of the core skills identified in the chapter with the
  Building Counseling Skills unit.
- Prepare yourself for professional certification with a Practice for Certification quiz.
  Connect to videos through the Video and Resource Library.

Summary and Conclusion

In this chapter we have examined counseling issues
related to culture and internationalism. There is a
wealth of material in the professional literature on
the general concerns of each group discussed here
and on the counseling theories and techniques
most appropriate for working with these populations (i.e., European American, African American,
Hispanic/Latino/a, Asian American, Native American Indian, and Arab American). Indeed, specialty
courses and counseling approaches that focus on
one or more of these groups are offered in most
graduate counselor education programs.

Although information on special cultural
aspects of a population may appear unrelated to other
factors in counseling, they are not. A common theme
is that counselors who work with a variety of culturally different clients must be knowledgeable about
them collectively, in subgroups, and individually.
They must be able to deal effectively with concerns
that transcend stereotypes and prescribed roles. Cultural limitations restrict not only the growth of the
people involved in them but the larger society as
well. Overcoming traditions, prejudices, fears, and
anxieties and learning new skills based on accurate
information and sensitivity are major parts of counseling in a multicultural society.

International counseling is growing. As such,
it is adding to cultural understanding of how people
are helped both within and outside a particular context. Countries and continental groups of counselors
are forming their own associations, which numbered
over 40 in 2012. Thus, counseling is a worldwide
phenomenon with integrated and interrelated theories and methods being developed and exchanged.
In the United States, it is important that counselors
pay attention to the needs of international students as
well as keep up with counseling on the international
level.

Counseling with Diverse Populations 5

Chapter Overview

From this chapter you will learn about

- The challenges and rewards of counseling older adults
- Concerns, issues, and theories of counseling women
- Concerns, issues, and theories of counseling men
- Counseling with persons of different sexual orientations
- Counseling and spirituality

As you read consider

- Your biases and beliefs about older adults
- Your thoughts and feelings about counseling with women and men
- Your views about people who differ from you in their sexual orientation
- The part spirituality plays in the lives of most people and where it belongs in counseling

When you wake up one morning
  and feel you've grown old
Take this poem down from your shelf
  and slowly read its well-wrought lines
    which fade like memories of our youth.
Those were the days on the knolls of Reynolda
  when times were measured in looks not words,
Those were the moments we wrote in our memories
  and now, like fine parchment, though faded, they remain
    clear impressions in the calmness of age,
bringing warmth and smiles to the chill of the season:
  brightness in a world full of grey.

"A poem in parting," by S. T. Gladding, © 1968/1989 S. T. Gladding.

MyCounselingLab™

Visit the MyCounselingLab™ site (www.MyCounselingLab.com) for *Counseling: A Comprehensive Profession,* Seventh Edition to enhance your understanding of chapter concepts. You'll have the opportunity to practice your skills through video- and case-based Assignments and Activities as well as Building Counseling Skills units and to prepare for your certification exam with Practice for Certification quizzes.

Diversity is a major aspect of human life. People differ in multiple ways. This chapter deals with diversity in counseling. Specifically, it focuses on counseling different populations based on age, gender, sexual orientation, and spirituality. Each of the populations addressed has distinct, unique needs and concerns as well as issues that are universal in nature. All these groups are at times stereotyped and may become marginalized, discounted, oppressed, or abused. Therefore, persons who are members of one or more of these subgroups of humanity are sometimes not recognized for their talents and possibilities.

Honoring diversity in all of its many forms is fundamental to counseling. Without such a stance, the welfare of clients is endangered, and the respect and dignity that should be accorded every person is ignored. Indeed, negative attitudes toward clients because of their age, sex, sexual orientation, ethnicity, or spirituality "have been found to influence counseling processes" for the worse (Miller, Miller, & Stull, 2007, p. 325).

In examining the populations covered here, as well as the ones discussed in the previous chapter, ask yourself what opinions you hold of each. How have those thoughts and feelings influenced your interactions? How are you like and unlike each of the groups explored? How can the research help modify your beliefs and actions?

Fixed opinions are almost always deleterious in counseling those who differ from us. When trying to work with diversity, it is crucial not to reduce individuals to caricatures who are less than human or to pathologize them.

COUNSELING AGED POPULATIONS

Development is traditionally defined as any kind of systematic change that is lifelong and cumulative. Throughout their lives, individuals develop on a number of levels: cognitively, emotionally, physically, spiritually, and otherwise. When development occurs within an expected time dimension, such as physical growth during childhood, individuals generally have only minor transitional or adjustment problems, if they have any difficulties at all. However, if life events are accelerated or delayed or fail to materialize, the well-being of persons and their associates is negatively affected (Goodman, Schlossberg, & Anderson, 2006).

The **Association for Adult Development and Aging (AADA)** is the division within the ACA that particularly focuses on chronological life-span growth after adolescence, but it is concerned ultimately with the entire life span. It focuses on theorists such as Jean Piaget, Lawrence Kohlberg, Erik Erikson, Carol Gilligan, and Nancy Schlossberg who have addressed issues associated with developmental stages from infancy to old age. Erikson's stages and their challenges are probably the most well known and are outlined here. Although the aged (**late adulthood**) are dealt with in this section of this chapter, the stages before late adulthood have a deep impact on

Stage/Age	Challenge	Strength
1. Infant (birth to 18 months)	Basic trust vs. basic distrust	drive, hope
2. Toddler (18 months to 3 years)	Autonomy vs. shame/doubt	self-control/courage
3. Preschooler/Play Age (3 to 5 years)	Initiative vs. guilt	purpose
4. School Age (6 to 12 years)	Industry vs. inferiority	method/competence
5. Adolescence (12 to 18 years)	Identity vs. role confusion	devotion/fidelity
6. Young Adulthood (18 to 35 years)	Intimacy vs. isolation	devotion/love
7. Middle Adulthood (35 to 55/65 years)	Generativity vs. stagnation	production/care
8. Late Adulthood (55/65 to death)	Ego integrity vs. despair	wisdom

Erikson's Stages of Human Development

how this time of life is handled. Gender, ability, ethnicity, health, physiology, environment, and drive all affect this stage of life and the ones that come before it and will be highlighted throughout this book.

The aged are defined here as persons over age 65. Since 1935 and the passage of the Social Security Act, age 65 has been seen as the beginning of old age or late adulthood. Even with people living longer than before, most "senior" rates and discounts begin around that time and some actually start around age 55. When the United States was founded, only 2% of its population was 65 years or older; by 1900 it was 4%; by 2010 it was almost 13%; and by 2030 it will be approximately 20% or 71.5 million (Erber, 2010; Piercy, 2010; U.S. Census Bureau, 2010; Zalaquett & Stens, 2006).

Today, the average **life expectancy** of a baby born in the United States is 78.2 years, with women's life expectancy at 80.2 years and men's at 75.6 years (National Center for Health Statistics of the Centers for Disease Control and Prevention, 2011; www.cdc.gov/nchs/). Whites have a higher life expectancy than other groups, but overall the life expectancy for all segments of the U.S. population is increasing. Reasons for the remarkable growth in the older U.S. population include high birthrate during the 20th century, immigration policies that favored the admittance of persons who are now growing older, improved health care, better nutrition, and the reduction of infectious diseases (Lefrancois, 1999; National Center for Health Statistics of the Centers for Disease Control and Prevention, 2011). Therefore, counselor attention needs to focus on this group, especially with the baby boomer generation beginning to fill up this age range (Maples & Abney, 2006).

There are a number of myths and misconceptions about aging, many of which are negative. Most center around loss and dysfunctionality. However, the vast majority of individuals who reach older adulthood are active and well functioning. For instance, Sophocles was still productive past age 100. Indeed, Cohen (2000) has found that some of the most significant and creative works of individuals have come after age 65. For instance, in the field of counseling Carl Rogers published more books after age 65 than he did before then.

Historically, counseling older adults has been a neglected area of the profession. For instance, as a group, members of this population receive only 6% of all mental health services (less than half of what might be expected because approximately 15% of the older adult population in the United States manifest at least moderate emotional problems) (Hashimi, 1991). In part, this situation stems from the group's unique developmental concerns, especially those involving financial, social, and physical losses.

In the mid-1970s, Blake (1975) and Salisbury (1975) raised counselor awareness about counseling older adults by respectively noting a lack of articles on this population in the counseling literature and a dearth of counselor education programs offering an elective course on the aged and their special needs. By the mid-1980s, the situation had changed. Based on a national survey, Myers (1983) reported that 36% of all counseling programs offered one or more courses on working with older people. That percentage has continued to increase along with new studies on the aged (Hollis, 1997; Myers, Poidevant, & Dean, 1991). Now there are standards for working with geriatric populations (Myers, 1995), and counseling with this age group has increased. Case studies have also increased awareness of the common issues faced by older adults today so that they do not appear to be extraordinary to counselors who work with members of this population group (Golden, 2009).

Old Age

Several prominent theories of aging, many of them multidimensional, have been proposed. For instance, Schaie and Willis (2011) view aging from a biological, psychological, and social perspective, recognizing that the multidimensional process may be uneven. Aging is a natural part of development (DeLaszlo, 1994; Erikson, 1963; Friedan, 1994). People have specific tasks to accomplish as they grow older. For example, Erikson views middle and late adulthood as a time when the individual must develop a sense of generativity and ego integrity or become stagnant and despairing. Jung believes spirituality is a domain that only those over age 40 are uniquely qualified to explore.

Neugarten (1978), stressing development, sees three major periods of older adulthood. The **young-old** are those between ages 65 and 75. They are still active physically, mentally, and socially, whether they are retired or not. The **old** are individuals beyond age 75 whose physical activity is far more limited. Finally, there are those classified as the **old-old**, 85 years and older who are in decline. The effects of deterioration are usually more apparent in the old-old population, although patterns of aging are clearly unique. For instance, the comedian George Burns was still physically active and mentally sharp until shortly before his death at age 100. Altogether, these three age groups of older adulthood are "collapsed into one group called the ***third phase of life***" (Richmond & Guindon, 2010, p. 281).

Despite an increased understanding of aging and an ever-growing number of older adults, those in this category of life have to deal with age-based expectations and prejudices; for instance, "older people often are tagged with uncomplimentary labels such as senile, absent-minded, and helpless" (McCracken, Hayes, & Dell, 1997, p. 385). These negative attitudes and stereotypes, which are known as ***ageism***, prevent intimate encounters with people in different age groups and sometimes lead to outright discrimination (Angus & Reeve, 2006; Butler, 2001). Unfortunately, individuals who are growing older frequently deny and dread the process, a phenomenon that Friedan (1994) calls "***the age mystique***." Even counselors are not immune to ageist attitudes (Blake, 1982; Maples & Abney, 2006).

Needs of the Aged

Older adults in the United States must deal with a wide variety of complex issues in their transition from midlife to "senior citizen" status, including changes in physical abilities, social roles, relationships, and even residential relocation (Cox, 2009; Kampfe, 2002).

Many of these changes have the potential to spark an identity crisis within the person. The developmental demands of older adults are probably second only to those of young children. According to Havighurst (1959), older adults must learn to cope successfully with (a) the death of friends and spouses, (b) reduced physical vigor, (c) retirement and the reduction of income, (d) more leisure time and the process of making new friends, (e) the development of new social roles, (f) dealing with grown children, and (g) changing living arrangements or making satisfactory ones.

Some of the required changes associated with aging are gradual, such as the loss of physical strength. Others are abrupt, such as death. Overall, aging is a time of both "positive and negative transitions and transformations" (Myers, 1990a, p. 249). Positive transitions for older adults involve a gain for the individual, such as becoming a grandparent or receiving a discount on purchases and for cultural events such as musical performances or movies. Transitions that involve a high level of stress are those connected with major loss, such as the death of a spouse, the loss of a job, or the contraction of a major illness. In these situations, many older adults struggle because they lack a peer support group through which to voice their grief and work through emotions (Morgan, 1994).

Major problems of the aged include loneliness, physical illness, retirement, idleness, bereavement, and abuse (Morrissey, 1998; Williams, Ballard, & Alessi, 2005). In addition, members of this group suffer more depression, anxiety, and psychosis as they grow older, with approximately 30% of the beds in mental hospitals being occupied by older adults. About 25% of all reported suicides are committed by persons over age 60, with White males being especially susceptible. *Domestic elder abuse*—"any form of maltreatment by someone who has a special relationship with the elderly," including neglect—is problematic as well (Morrissey, 1998, p. 14). Among the most common forms of maltreatment for older adults, with nearly 600,000 cases a year, are physical abuse, psychological abuse, financial exploitation, and violation of rights, including personal liberty, free speech, and privacy (Welfel, Danzinger, & Santoro, 2000). In addition, alcohol abuse is a prevalent but often undiagnosed disorder in older adults, ranging from 6% to 16% of the population (Williams et al., 2005).

CASE EXAMPLE

Gene and His Low Self-Esteem

Gene grew up in a household of 12 brothers and sisters. His parents worked hard, but the little money they made was stretched thin. Thus, Gene wore clothes that were either hand-me-downs or that were bought at secondhand stores. His parents could not afford to pay dues for clubs or sports teams, so Gene did not have an opportunity to mix much with his peers. To make matters even worse, Gene had to work part-time jobs as soon as he was old enough to help out the family. Most of the jobs involved manual labor, and often Gene was dirty and unkempt. He never married and now, at age 65, he still carries around a low self-concept. He has come to counseling to "get better" and to "get over" his history so he can live more productively.

Do you think counseling can do him any good considering his past? If so, how do you suppose it might help? What other activities do you think would be good for Gene?

Counseling the Aged

Most counselors interested in working with the aged need additional professional training in this specialty (Blando, 2011; Schlossberg, 1990). Many simply do not understand older adults and therefore do not work with them. Such may be especially true in regard to new phenomena regarding older adults needing help in taking on new and unexpected roles in life, such as grandparents raising grandchildren (Leder, Grinstead, & Torres, 2007; Pinson-Milburn, Fabian, Schlossberg, & Pyle, 1996). In such situations, counseling-related services may need to be offered on multiple levels, such as direct outreach interventions that teach new coping strategies and skill training. In addition, indirect or supportive interventions may be needed, such as grandparent support groups, family support groups, and the sponsoring of events such as "Grandparents Day" at school.

Another reason that older people do not receive more attention from mental health specialists is the *investment syndrome* described by Colangelo and Pulvino (1980). According to these authors, some counselors feel their time and energy are better spent working with younger people "who may eventually contribute to society" (p. 69). Professionals who display this attitude are banking on future payoffs from the young and may well be misinformed about the possibilities for change in older adults.

A third reason that older adults may not receive attention from counselors and mental health specialists is the irrational fear of aging and the psychological distancing from older persons that this fear generates (Neugarten, 1971). This phenomenon may be best explained in the proverbial saying: "Out of sight, out of mind."

The final reason older adults do not receive more or better treatment by counselors in regard to their needs is that their problems may be mistaken for conditions related to aging (Williams et al., 2005). For example, many older adults have a number of ailments, such as depression, which may be attributed to old age but which has always been a part of their lives.

One broad and important approach to working successfully with the aged is to treat them as adults (Cox & Waller, 1991). Late adulthood is a unique life stage and involves continuous growth. When counselors display basic counseling skills such as reflecting feelings, paraphrasing content, identifying patterns, asking open-ended questions, validating feelings and thoughts, and gently confronting inconsistencies, older adults feel free to explore difficulties or adjustment issues and are likely to respond appropriately (Blando, 2011; Kampfe, 2002).

Xu (2010) advocates for incorporating logotherapy principles into working with older adults. Present models of successful aging, and the interventions they encourage, tend to focus on maintaining physical and cognitive functioning and continuing engagement in active living. Xu notes, however, that such models neglect what Frankl (1962) identified as the "*noetic*," *or spiritual*, *dimension of human existence*. A more holistic model of aging, the author concludes, attends to the spiritual tasks and the Will to Meaning of older individuals. It assists them in integrating and transcending their lived experience and making meaning in late life.

Another strategy for promoting change in the aged is to modify the attitudes of people within the systems in which they live (Colangelo & Pulvino, 1980; Sinick, 1980). Many societal attitudes negatively influence older people's attitudes about themselves. Often, older adults act old because their environments encourage and support such behavior. American society "equates age with obsolescence and orders its priorities accordingly" (Hansen & Prather, 1980, p. 74). Therefore, counselors must become educators and advocates for change in societal attitudes if destructive age restrictions and stereotypes are to be overcome. "We need to develop a society that encourages people to stop acting their age and start being themselves" (Ponzo, 1978, pp. 143–144).

In addition to treating the aged with respect and working for changes in systems, counselors can help older adults deal with specific and immediate problems. Tomine (1986) asserts that counseling services for older adults are most helpful if they are portable and practical, such as being educational and focused on problem solving. For example, Hitchcock (1984) reviewed successful programs that help older adults obtain employment. A particularly successful program was a job club for older job seekers, where participants at regular meetings shared information on obtaining employment.

For older adults with Alzheimer's disease, counseling based on Rogers's theories and Carkhuff's practical application is beneficial in the early stages of the disease. Group counseling, based on Yalom's existential writings, may be productive in helping family members cope as the disease progresses (LaBarge, 1981).

A structured life-review process has also proven beneficial in working with older adults (Beaver, 1991; Bohlmeijer, Smit, & Cuijpers, 2003). This approach helps them integrate the past and prepare themselves for the future.

Short-term cognitive-behavior therapy has been used successfully with some older adults in increasing rational thinking and decreasing depression (James, 2008). Likewise, 12-step programs and bibliotherapy have proven successful in helping older adults who abuse alcohol.

The following **groups** are among the **most popular for adults age 65 and older** (Gladding, 2012):

- *Reality-oriented groups,* which help orient confused group members to their surroundings
- *Remotivation therapy groups,* which are aimed at helping older clients become more invested in the present and the future
- *Reminiscing groups,* which conduct life reviews focused on resolving past issues in order to help members become more personally integrated and find meaning in the present (Zalaquett & Stens, 2006)
- *Psychotherapy groups,* which are geared toward specific problems of the aging, such as loss
- *Topic-specific groups*, which center on relevant areas of interest to the aging, such as health or the arts
- *Member-specific groups,* which focus on particular transition concerns of individual members, such as hospitalization or dealing with in-laws

In working with the aged, counselors often become students of life, and older persons become their teachers (Kemp, 1984). When this type of open attitude is achieved, clients are more likely to deal with the most important events in their lives, and counselors are more prone to learn about a different dimension of life and be helpful in the process.

PERSONAL REFLECTION

Aging is a state of mind as well as a physical reality. Think of people you know age 65 or above. Which ones do you consider to be adjusting well to their age? What factors do you think make that so?

GENDER-BASED COUNSELING

The second population considered in this chapter focuses on counseling based on *gender* (i.e., the sex of a person). Clients have distinct needs and concerns that are determined in part by the cultural climates and social groups in which they live and develop (Cook, 1993; Hoffman, 2006; Sue & Sue, 2008). Women and men are "basically cultural-social beings" (McFadden, 1999,

p. 234), or put another way, they are ***biopsychosocial*** (i.e., influenced by their biology, psychology, and society). Counselors who are not fully aware of the influence of societal discrimination, stereotypes, and role expectations based on gender are not likely to succeed in helping their clients in counseling. Effective counseling requires special knowledge and insight that focuses on particular and common aspects of sexuality and sexual orientation of people. "This attention to unique and shared experiences of women and men is the paradoxical challenge of counseling" (Lee & Robbins, 2000, p. 488).

There is no longer any debate over the question of whether counselors need to possess specialized knowledge and skill in counseling women and men as separate groups as well as genders that have much in common. However, because women and men "experience different developmental challenges," they may need different styles of interaction from professionals (Nelson, 1996, p. 343). Furthermore, counselors who work more with one gender than another may need in-depth training and experience in particular counseling areas. For example, women in the United States suffer from more mood, anxiety, and eating disorders than men (Eriksen & Kress, 2008). Part of the reason may be that women are socialized to suppress anger because it is seen as incompatible with the feminine gender role, whereas "anger has been hypothesized to be one of the few emotions that are compatible with the traditional masculine role" (Newman, Fugua, Gray, & Simpson, 2006, p. 157). In addition, compared to employed men, employed women continue to bear greater responsibility for household tasks and caregiving responsibilities (Pearson, 2008). Thus, working with women in mental health and career domains may well differ from working with men in these same two areas.

Counseling Women

Women are the primary consumers of counseling services (Wastell, 1996). They have special needs related to biological differences and socialization patterns that make many of their counseling concerns different from men's (Cook, 1993; Hoffman, 2006; Huffman & Myers, 1999). Women still lack the degree of freedom, status, access, and acceptance that men possess, although their social roles and career opportunities have expanded considerably since the 1960s when the women's movement influenced substantial changes (Kees, 2005).

As a group, women have quite different concerns than men in many areas. For instance, they differ in their interest and involvement in such fundamental issues as intimacy, career options, and life development (Kopla & Keitel, 2003). That is why the American Counseling Association and other professional helping associations have devoted special issues of their publications to the subject of women and counseling (see, for instance, the Summer 2005 issue of the *Journal of Counseling and Development*). "Women grow and/or develop in, through, and toward relationship" (Jordan, 1995, p. 52). When they feel connected with others, women have an increased sense of energy and a more accurate view of themselves and others. Furthermore, they feel empowered to act outside their relationships because they are active within them. They also feel a greater sense of worth and desire more connection (Miller & Stiver, 1997). Among the group's major concerns are development and growth, depression, eating disorders, sexual victimization, widowhood, and multiple roles.

Counseling women "is not a simple matter of picking a counseling theory or approach and commencing treatment" (Hanna, Hanna, Giordano, & Tollerud, 1998, p. 181). Rather, counselors' attitudes, values, and knowledge may either facilitate or impede the potential development of women clients, especially at an international level (Chung, 2005). Women are basically relational beings, and counselors' approaches should be geared toward that fact (Davenport &

Yurich, 1991; Nelson, 1996). An examination of the literature indicates that professionals who counsel women should be "highly empathic, warm, understanding, and sufficiently well developed as a person to appreciate the predicament in which women find themselves" (Hanna et al., 1998, p. 167).

Unfortunately, evidence indicates that some counselors and health professionals still hold sex-role stereotypes of women (Mollen, 2006; Simon, Gaul, Friedlander, & Heatherington, 1992), and some counselors are simply uninformed about particular difficulties that women face in general or at different stages of their lives. On a developmental level, there is "a noticeable gap in the literature with respect to studies on women in midlife who are childless, single, disabled, lesbian, ethnic minorities, or members of extended family networks" (Lippert, 1997, p. 17). For example, in working with voluntarily childfree women, Mollen (2006) stresses the importance of acceptance and empowerment of these women as well as helping them manage the stigma they may face in society because of their choices or lifestyles.

False assumptions, inaccurate beliefs, and a lack of counselor understanding may all contribute to the problems of women clients (e.g., those who have primary or secondary infertility) (Gibson & Myers, 2000). It is important that counselors consider sociopolitical as well as other factors when counseling members of this population for "regardless of the presenting problem, women often blame themselves for inadequacies that were [are] actually the products of unrecognized forced enculturation" (Petersen, 2000, p. 70).

Committees and task forces within professional counseling organizations have been formed to address issues related to counseling women. For instance, there is a national Commission on Women within ACA. Furthermore, ACA has published a special issue on women and counseling in its flagship periodical, the *Journal of Counseling and Development* (Volume 83, Summer 2005).

CONCERNS IN COUNSELING WOMEN. One of the major concerns in counseling women revolves around the issue of adequate information about their lives. Many early theories of the nature and development of women, especially those based on psychoanalytic principles, tended to characterize women as innately "passive, dependent, and morally inferior to men" (Hare-Mustin, 1983, p. 594). Those theories promoted the status quo in regard to women and limited their available options (Lewis, Hayes, & Bradley, 1992). The general standard of healthy adult behavior came to be identified with men, and a double standard of mental health evolved with regard to adult females (Lawler, 1990; Nicholas, Gobble, Crose, & Frank, 1992). This double standard basically depicted adult female behavior as less socially desirable and healthy, a perception that lowered expectations for women's behavior and set up barriers against their advancement in nontraditional roles (Broverman, Broverman, Clarkson, Rosenkrantz, & Vogel, 1970)—a view that unfortunately continues in many places (Eriksen & Kress, 2008).

However, the literature in the field of women's studies and female psychology has grown from only three textbooks in the early 1970s to a plethora of texts and articles today. Many of these publications have been written by women, for women, often from a feminist and feminist therapy perspective to correct some older theoretical views generated by men without first-hand knowledge of women's issues (Enns, 1993; Evans, Kincaide, Marbley, & Seem, 2005). For example, some theorists have proposed that women's development is in marked contrast to Erikson's psychosocial stages of development. These theorists stress the uniqueness of women and connectedness rather than separation. Furthermore, they outline female identity development from several points of view and compare and contrast it to ethnic identity models (Hoffman, 2006).

A second major concern in counseling women involves sexism, which Goldman (1972a) describes as "more deep rooted than racism" (p. 84). *Sexism* is the belief (and the behavior resulting from that belief) that females should be treated on the basis of their sex without regard to other criteria, such as interests and abilities. Such treatment is arbitrary, illogical, counterproductive, and self-serving. In the past, sexism has been blatant, such as limiting women's access to certain professions and encouraging them to pursue so-called **pink-collar jobs** that primarily employ women (e.g., nurse, receptionist). Today, sexism is much more subtle, involving acts more of "omission rather than commission" (Leonard & Collins, 1979, p. 6). Many acts of omission result from a lack of information or a failure to change beliefs in light of new facts. In either case, sexism hurts not only women but society in general.

ISSUES AND THEORIES OF COUNSELING WOMEN. One of the main issues in counseling women involves the counselor's research knowledge about them and proven ways of responding to them as individuals and in groups (Leech & Kees, 2005). Women are diverse, and it is important for counselors to react to women in regard to their uniqueness as well as their similarity (Cook, 1993; Kopla & Keitel, 2003; Worrell & Goodheart, 2006). Counselors should recognize that specialized knowledge is required for counseling women at various stages of life, such as childhood and adolescence, midlife, and late adulthood. Counselors must also understand the dynamics of working with females under various conditions, such as eating disorders (Marino, 1994), sexual abuse and rape (Enns, 1996), suicide (Range, 2006), and career development (Cook, Heppner, & O'Brien, 2002).

Johnson and Scarato (1979) have presented a model that outlines major areas of knowledge about the psychology of women. It proposes seven areas in which counselors should increase their knowledge of women and thereby decrease prejudice: (a) history and sociology of sex-role stereotyping, (b) psychophysiology of women and men, (c) theories of personality and sex-role development, (d) life-span development, (e) special populations, (f) career development, and (g) counseling/psychotherapy. In the last area, the authors focus on alternatives to traditional counseling approaches as well as specific problems of women.

Thames and Hill (1979) assert that, beyond the issue of basic knowledge, effective counselors of women need to be skilled in four areas of counseling: verbal, nonverbal, process, and techniques. They must also be able to apply appropriate intervention skills for special populations of women. Finally, counselors must be aware of personal difficulties they may have in dealing with female clients.

A major approach to working with women (and even some men) in counseling is **feminist theory** (Brown, 2010; Mejia, 2005). Feminist views of counseling sprang from the eruption of the women's movement in the 1960s. Initially, this movement was a challenge to patriarchal power, but as it grew, its focus centered on the development of females as persons with common and unique qualities (Okun, 1990). Beginning with the publication of Carol Gilligan's *In a Different Voice* (1982), there has been an increased integration of feminist theory into counseling. This approach encourages individuals to become more aware of socialization patterns and personal options in altering traditional gender roles as they make changes, and encourages clients to become involved in social change activities that stress equality as a way of bringing about change (Enns & Hackett, 1993). Thus, the theory and the therapeutic expressions of it recognize the role of the larger community in creating problems, especially for women, and "encourages intervention in the larger community" (Eriksen & Kress, 2008, p. 159).

In many respects, feminist theory is more an approach to counseling rather than a well-formulated set of constructs. It is assertive in challenging and questioning attitudes of traditional counseling theories because these models often advocate the maintenance of the status quo of a male-dominated, hierarchical society. **Two main emphases in the feminist position** distinguish it from other forms of helping:

- Its emphasis on **equality in the helping relationship**, which stems from a belief that women's problems are inseparable from society's oppression of women (Okun, 1997)
- Its emphasis on **valuing social, political, and economic action as a major part of the process of treatment**

Androgyny, the importance of relationships, the acceptance of one's body "as is," and nonsexist career development are also stressed in feminist thought. Overall, "feminist theory starts with the experience of women and uses women's values and beliefs as the assumptive framework" (Nwachuku & Ivey, 1991, p. 106).

CASE EXAMPLE

Paula Assumes People Are People

Paula was not the hardest working counseling student ever, but she managed to get by. However, when she was about to see her first client in her practicum, a childless woman of 36, Paula's lack of rigor caused her on-site supervisor some concern. When discussing how she would handle the intake interview, Paula simply said, "People are people. I don't care what their background or station in life is."

How would you respond to Paula having just read the section on counseling women? Is there any truth in what Paula is saying? What would be a better response on her part?

Counseling Men

An outgrowth of the focus on counseling women and eliminating sexism is new attention to the unique concerns and needs of men. In the early 1980s, Collison (1981) pointed out that "there seem to be fewer counseling procedures tailored to men than to women" (p. 220). Since that time, there has been an increase in conducting research on "men, masculinity, and the male experience" (Wade, 1998, p. 349) with "the burgeoning interest in men's psychology" leading "to a greater demand for clinical services tailored explicitly for men" (Johnson & Hayes, 1997, p. 302). Yet, most counselors lack formal education on men's issues (Gold & Pitariu, 2004).

CONCERNS IN COUNSELING MEN. Concerns related to counseling men often stem from their socialization. Part of men's general social behavior can be explained by the fact that men's traditional sex roles are more narrowly defined than women's, and beginning in childhood, there are stricter sanctions against boys adopting feminine behaviors than exist among girls adopting those deemed as masculine (Robinson-Wood, 2009). In addition, during childhood, girls are rewarded for being emotionally or behaviorally expressive; boys are reinforced primarily for nonemotional physical actions. Thus, many men internalize their emotional reactions and seek to be autonomous, aggressive, and competitive (Scher & Stevens, 1987). They are oriented to display fighter rather than nurturing behavior, and they often "perceive themselves as losing power and status by changing in the direction of androgyny," especially in young adulthood (Brown, 1990, p. 11). Specific diagnoses for men, as compared to women, center around substance abuse, sexually related disorders, and antisocial behavior (Eriksen & Kress, 2008), which may explain why more men end up in prison and more women end up in therapy. Often, well-socialized men, especially White men, "run the risk of being under-diagnosed for mental disorders with the possible implication that they do not receive the services that they may need to address these disorders" (p. 154).

When not focused on behavior, as a group, men operate primarily from a cognitive perspective (Pollack & Levant, 1998; Scher, 1979). Affective expression is usually eschewed because of a lack of experience in dealing with it and the anxiety it creates.

In such constrictive roles, insensitivity to the needs of others and self often develops, and a denial of mental and physical problems becomes lethal in the form of shorter life spans (Jourard, 1971). In addition, "men find psychological safety in independence and fear closeness" (Davenport & Yurich, 1991, p. 65). Therefore, counselors who work with men need to be aware that many of them will be loners and reticent to talk. Because of this isolation, they may well minimize their behaviors and others' actions. Most times, they are not being obstinate but simply displaying behaviors for which they have been reinforced. In childhood, many men incorporate social taboos about self-disclosure, especially before other men, for it is not seen as "masculine" (Mejia, 2005).

Scher (1981) provides guidelines to assist counselors in understanding the realities of men's situations, including (a) an emphasis on the difficulty of change for most men, (b) the constraints imposed by sex-role stereotypes, (c) the importance of asking for assistance and dealing with affective issues, and (d) the need to distinguish between differences of roles and rules in one's personal and work life.

As a group, men are more reluctant than women to seek counseling (Gertner, 1994; Worth, 1983). Most men enter counseling only in crisis situations, such as in trauma, because they are generally expected to be self-sufficient, deny needs, and take care of others (Mejia, 2005; Moore & Leafgren, 1990). Different age and stage levels of men may be especially relevant as to whether they consider counseling or not. Race may cause minority men to be particularly vulnerable, especially to gender role identity (Wester, Vogel, Wei, & McLain, 2006). Thus, when working with men, it is important to consult developmental models and culturally related research that underscore developmental and culture-specific themes.

ISSUES AND THEORIES IN COUNSELING MEN. Many myths as well as realities exist about counseling men (Kelly & Hall, 1994; Wexler, 2009). When males are able to break through traditional restrictions, they usually work hard in counseling and see it as if it were another competition. They have high expectations of the process and want productive sessions. Thus, as a group, they are likely to be clear and sincere in the process and express themselves directly and honestly.

The dominance of cognitive functioning in men creates special challenges for counselors. Marino (1979) advises counselors to stay away from the cognitive domain in working with men and explore with them the feeling tones of their voices, the inconsistencies of their behaviors and feelings, and their ambivalence about control and nurturance. Scher (1979) also advises moving the client from the cognitive to the affective realm and recommends that the process be started by explaining to male clients the importance of owning feelings in overcoming personal difficulties and then working patiently with men to uncover hidden affect.

In contrast to eschewing the cognitive domain, Burch and Skovholt (1982) suggest that Holland's (1997) model of person–environment interaction may serve as the framework for understanding and counseling men. In this model, men are most likely to operate in the realistic dimension of functioning. Such individuals usually lack social skills but possess mechanical–technical skills; therefore, the authors recommend that counselors adopt a cognitive–behavioral approach to establish rapport and facilitate counseling. Giles (1983) disagrees with this idea, pointing out that no conclusive research supports it. He believes that counselors are not necessarily effective when they alter the counseling approach to fit the personal typology of clients.

Cultural, as well as cognitive, factors must be taken in when working with men as well. For instance, minority men, particularly African Americans, are often caught in a conundrum. If they attempt to meet one set of gender roles, such as those of the dominant European American culture, "they likely frustrate the other set of gender roles (African American) while societal racism often does not allow them to fully meet either set" (Wester et al., 2006, p. 420). In such cases, counselors must work with the intersection of identities and male gender-role conflict (i.e., traditional versus nontraditional behaviors) such as that between work and interpersonal relationships.

Given the emphasis on interpersonal learning in groups, working with men in this way may be an effective intervention strategy (Andronico, 1996; Corey, 2012; Jolliff, 1994). The goals of men's groups are to increase personal awareness of sex-role conditioning, practice new desired behaviors, and promote a lifestyle based on the individual's needs. Three types of men—male sex offenders, gay men, and homeless men—may especially benefit from group work (DeAngelis, 1992). Men who do not do well in groups are those who are manic, very depressed, in severe crisis, addicted, inebriated, or paranoid (Horne & Mason, 1991).

Group work for men in general can be powerful in cutting through defenses, such as denial, and building a sense of community. To be effective, the counselor must publicize the availability of such a group, screen potential candidates carefully, identify specific behaviors on which to focus, institute opening and closing rituals, and develop intervention strategies aimed at resolving deep psychological issues such as conflict management (Corey, 2012; Hetzel, Barton, & Davenport, 1994; Horne & Mason, 1991).

In working with men in groups, Moore and Haverkamp (1989) found, in a well-controlled study, that "men age 30 to 50 are able to increase their level of affective expression, as measured by both self-report and behavioral tests" (p. 513). During this developmental stage of life, many men are seeking to become more intimate, deepen their relationships, and deal directly with their emotions. Thus, a group for men at this level of maturity can be very effective in producing change, especially, as the authors state, when it follows a social-learning paradigm in which other men serve as models and reinforcers for new behaviors. The impact of Robert Bly and the mythopoetic movement (the use of myths and poetry with men in groups) is one example of the power of such a paradigm for change (Erkel, 1990).

While promoting change and an exploration of affective issues, it is crucial that counselors be aware that rules within most men's world of work differ from those within the personal domain. Counselors must caution men not to naively and automatically introduce newly discovered behaviors that work in their personal lives into what may be a hostile environment—that is, the world of work.

Counseling with men, as with all groups, is a complex phenomenon, but the potential benefits are enormous. They include helping men develop productive strategies for dealing with expectations and changing roles (Gladding, 2012; Moore & Leafgren, 1990). Through counseling, men may also develop new skills applicable to "marital communication, stress-related health problems, career and life decision making, and family interaction" (Moore & Haverkamp, 1989, p. 516). A particularly powerful procedure that may be employed with select men involves having them interview their fathers. Using a series of structured, open-ended questions about family traditions, these men make discoveries about themselves by understanding their fathers more clearly. This new understanding can serve as a catalyst for implementing different behaviors within their own families.

PERSONAL REFLECTION

A number of distinctions exist between counseling women as opposed to counseling men. What factors do you think you need to be most aware of? What overlap is there in counseling members of both sexes?

COUNSELING AND SEXUAL ORIENTATION

Whether one approves or not, individuals have different lifestyles and distinct social and sexual orientations. Approximately 1.4% of the population in the United States (approximately 5 to 6 million people) is primarily gay or lesbian, although there are a number of individuals who do not divulge their sexual orientation (National Center for Health Statistics and Centers for Disease Control and Prevention, 2011). As a group, individuals who self-report as lesbian or gay exist in all age categories and approximate racial mixes as the population as a whole (Degges-White & Shoffner, 2002). Demographics on the percentage of bisexual and transgender people are not as clear.

Regardless, individuals with minority sexual orientations are often stereotyped, stigmatized, and discriminated against (Savage, Harley, & Nowak, 2005). Stereotypes include statements that members of sexual minority populations are child molesters, and that same-sex relationships never last (Chen-Hayes, 1997). Sexual stigmatizing and discrimination devalues sexual minorities and "may lead to hostility (from either the dominant or marginalized group), restricted identity, exclusion . . . and less access to power and resources" (Dermer, Smith, & Barto, 2010, p. 328). Within the ACA, the **Association for Lesbian, Gay, Bisexual and Transgender Issues in Counseling (ALGBTIC;** algbtic.org/) deals with concerns specifically related to these populations and, like other responsible organizations, dispels myths with factual information.

Difficulties usually begin for LGBT early in life. Children who are oriented toward any of these lifestyles frequently have trouble growing up in regard to their identity. They often have feelings of isolation and stigmatization, and trouble with peer relationships, as well as family disruptions (Marinoble, 1998). Many are frequently harassed. Even some counselors are less accepting of members of these populations than one might expect (Matthews, 2005). Some of this discomfort may be a holdover from previous times because the *Diagnostic and Statistical Manual* of the American Psychiatric Association considered homosexuality a disorder until the mid-1970s. As Rudolph (1989) states, "ministering to the psychotherapy needs of homosexuals [and bisexuals] has historically been an exercise in dissatisfaction and discomfort for many clients and counselors" (p. 96).

The majority culture, which professional helpers represent, has a predominantly negative view of persons who do not have a heterosexual orientation. When these views are voiced in strong, dogmatic ways, they can have a detrimental impact on the mental health and well-being of GLBTs and may severely disrupt their total development. For example, in career decision making, gays and lesbians often lack role models and are often directed into socially stereotyped occupations with little consideration for their total relationship (Hetherington, Hillerbrand, & Etringer, 1989; O'Ryan & MacFarland, 2010). In any minority culture that is treated with prejudice, people suffer and the overall culture is negatively affected.

Counseling with Gays, Lesbians, Bisexuals, and Transgenders

GLBTs are diverse in their lifestyles and in the problems they bring to counseling. Therefore, individuals who embrace these lifestyles do not come to counseling with a few typical concerns. In fact, members of these groups may have many of the same types of problems as those who are heterosexuals. For instance, in a 2-year analysis of the Lesbian Connection's discussion forum, Erwin (2006) found the top five themes important to lesbians were "(a) isolation, safety, and aging; (b) children; (c) lesbian relationships and sexuality; (d) physical and mental health; and (e) political issues" (p. 99). If "lesbian relationships" are simply interpreted to be "interpersonal relationships," this list is very similar to lists of people from various backgrounds. Therefore, it is important not to make any assumptions before hearing what clients have to say.

However, there are some fairly frequent issues faced by GLBTs that may surface in a counseling relationship. These difficulties include "coming out," forming community organizations, following religious practices, and coping with AIDS and relationships (House & Miller, 1997). *Coming out*—letting others know that one is gay, lesbian, bisexual, or transgender—is a developmental process (Barret & Logan, 2007; Bieschke, Perez, & DeBord, 2007). First, it involves recognizing one's own sexual identity and working toward self-acceptance. Part of that process is realizing that **sexuality is on a continuum**, and everyone is not at the same place on the continuum. Reflecting as to where one is can help in resolving this conflict. Once the decision is made, there are a number of positive outcomes such as increased self-esteem, greater honesty in one's life, and a sense of greater personal integrity. There is also often a sense of relief, a reduction of internal tension, and a greater freedom of self-expression and honesty with others.

However, the process is not easy and not the same for everyone. Reading about how others have dealt with coming out can be helpful. Coming out may raise strong feelings, such as anger, in a person's family and friends and rupture relationships. The same may be true for members of these populations trying to form community organizations or follow religious practices. Therefore, rehearsing how to act and what to say prior to such an event can be helpful. Cognitive approaches, in regard to modifying the self-talk a person generates, likewise may be therapeutic (Martell, Safren, & Prince, 2004).

Gay men may need special help in dealing with the stigma that is attached to them. "Society's reactions can lead to internalized homophobia, resulting in guilt, fear, or self-hatred that can affect many other, seemingly unrelated areas of their lives" (Granello, 2004, p. 59). One area where some gay men may have difficulty, outside of external factors, is in the loss of friends and significant others to the AIDS epidemic (Moursund & Kenny, 2002; Springer & Lease, 2000). Bereavement counseling may be needed to avoid developing major depressive episodes or posttraumatic stress disorder (PTSD).

Savage et al. (2005) advocate that a **social empowerment model (SEM)** be used with lesbians and gay men, rather than counseling, because it increases this group's collective and personal self-advocacy. In such a model, clients come to know that the origins of sexual orientation "are not clearly understood or completely known" (p. 135). Likewise, they learn that lesbians and gay men have a variety of lifestyles and "lead fulfilling and satisfying lives" (p. 135). Furthermore, they come to recognize that being lesbian or gay is not a pathological condition and that counseling is about dealing with concerns rather than focusing on attempts to persuade clients to change their sexual orientation.

To work effectively with transgender adults, counselors need to familiarize themselves with the social, medical, career, and family challenges that these clients face (Moundas et al., 2009). Such a task is a huge undertaking and needs to be personalized to the clients counselors encounter. In working with transgenders, a **gender role conflict** (GRC) model is recommended (Wester, McDonough, White, Vogel, & Taylor, 2010).

> "GRC occurs when an individual experiences negative consequences resulting from the competition between rigid, sexist, or overly restrictive gender roles and incompatible situational demands. In applying GRC theory in counseling, the focus is on the situational constraints placed on people by their socialized gender role while allowing for an understanding of the experience of distress without blaming individuals for their situation. . . . Thus, counseling based on GRC theory addresses the gender role messages learned from society, how these messages can be used to understand the client's experiences, and how the client can move beyond that societal teaching to live life on his or her own terms." (p. 214)

Singh, Hays, & Watson (2011) have found that despite often living in a hostile environment, transgenders have resiliency. "The authors identified 5 common resiliency themes (evolving a self-generated definition of self, embracing self-worth, awareness of oppression, connection with a supportive community, and cultivating hope for the future) and 2 variant themes (social activism and being a positive role model for others)" (p. 20). Thus despite hardships, transgenders have found ways to help themselves outside counseling. These strategies hold promise for other cultural minority groups as well.

Working with gays, lesbians, bisexuals, and transgenders is bound to be an unpopular activity in some locales but one that can do much good if conducted properly. It involves not only working with clients who are in the minority regarding their sexual orientations, but also focusing on transforming the cultural contexts in which these clients live and promoting understanding in the process (Carroll, Gilroy, & Ryan, 2002). One way to do that, other than advocacy, is to attend workshops that focus on learning how to help affirm the lifestyles of gay men and lesbians and other sexually oriented minorities (Granello, 2004). After such workshops, counselors who wish may sponsor community symposiums dealing with sexually oriented minority groups.

PERSONAL REFLECTION

Sexuality is a controversial subject that stimulates strong views from many sides. What views do you currently hold? Have your views changed or remained the same? Explain.

COUNSELING AND SPIRITUALITY

Spirituality is not a new concept in counseling (Cashwell & Young, 2011; van Asselt & Senstock, 2009). However, it has been highlighted more in recent decades. "Spirituality is increasingly recognized as an important cultural and coping factor that may affect counseling relationships, processes, or outcomes" (Harris et al., 2007, p. 4). Luminaries such as Carl Jung, Victor Frankl, Abraham Maslow, and Rollo May have emphasized the importance of spirituality in counseling. It is a complex, multidimensional construct. "At present, there is no generally agreed on definition of spirituality" (Ganje-Fling & McCarthy, 1996, p. 253), but those immersed in the study of this phenomenon concur that "spirituality includes concepts such as transcendence, self-actualization, purpose and meaning, wholeness, balance, sacredness, altruism, and a sense of a Higher Power" (Stanard, Sandhu, & Painter, 2000, p. 209). Thus, as an entity, spirituality usually refers to a unique, personally meaningful experience of a transcendent dimension that is associated with wholeness and wellness (Hinterkopf, 1998; Miller, 2003; Westgate, 1996).

Within counseling, there is an increased emphasis on the importance of spirituality in the well-being of those seeking help, those wishing to maintain their own health, and those who are aging in a healthy manner (Burke & Miranti, 1995; Hudson, 1998; Snyder, 2005). For many average people who seek out counselors, spirituality and religion "are significant aspects of their life" (Burke et al., 1999, p. 251). Two thirds of Gallup poll respondents indicated they would prefer to see a counselor who held spiritual values and beliefs similar to theirs (Young, Wiggins-Frame, & Cashwell, 2007, p. 47), and, in a national survey of ACA counselors, these same researchers found that 82% agreed or strongly agreed when responding to the statement "I consider myself to be a spiritual person."

In recent years "a burgeoning literature has emerged concerning religion and spirituality in psychotherapy" as well as in life (Ottens & Klein, 2005, p. 32). Religious faith can work to the benefit or detriment of individuals, groups, couples, and families. On the positive side, it can boast "psychological well-being, including career satisfaction, the ability to cope, a sense of meaning and purpose in life and overall levels of happiness" (Rollins, 2009a,b, p. 34). On the negative side, it can narrow people's worldview, promote fear and hatred, and even lead to the death of believers as happened in the Jim Jones People's Temple mass suicide of 900 followers in 1978.

Ingersoll (1994) was an early pioneer in developing a comprehensive overview of spirituality, religion, and counseling. Specifically, he pointed out the importance of defining spirituality, in contrast to religion, and listed dimensions that describe it. The following characteristics were included in Ingersoll's definition of spirituality:

- A concept of the divine or a force greater than oneself
- A sense of meaning
- A relationship with the divine
- Openness to mystery
- A sense of playfulness
- Engagement in spiritually enhancing activities
- Systematic use of spiritual forces as an integrator of life

The positive place spirituality plays in a person's life stands out in this definition. Indeed, spirituality seems to be an important dimension in most people's lives.

For most people, a spiritual journey is developmental in nature. It involves an active search toward overcoming one's current centricity to becoming more connected with the meaning of life, including a oneness of ultimate being (Chandler, Holden, & Kolander, 1992; Kelly, 1995). Indeed, Gill, Barrio Minton, & Myers (2010) found spirituality and religiosity accounted for a large percentage of the variables for wellness among low-income, rural women and provided them with a coping strategy as well as with meaning. Related to age, Snyder (2005) relates how personal storytelling is one way aging populations can create community and achieve spirituality simultaneously. She recommends an exercise in which aging adults divide their lives into sections of 5 years each and mark how decisions they made altered their fate and helped them reclaim a well-lived life with meaning.

Three events have profoundly affected the attitude about spirituality in America at large and indirectly in counseling. One has been the "informal spirituality promulgated by Alcoholics Anonymous, Adult Children of Alcoholics, and other 12-step programs" (Butler, 1990, p. 30). Another has been the writings of Scott Peck, whose books, especially *The Road Less Traveled*

(1978), bridge the gap between traditional psychotherapy and religion. The final event has been the film series featuring Joseph Campbell, as interviewed by Bill Moyers, in which Campbell gives "respectability to the spiritual-psychological quest itself, even in modern-times" (Butler, 1990, p. 30).

The **Association for Spiritual, Ethical, and Religious Values in Counseling (ASERVIC)**, a division within ACA, is devoted to exploring the place of spirituality in counseling. In 1995, ASERVIC held a "Summit on Spirituality" and generated nine counselor competencies on spiritual and religious issues in counseling that still influence the counseling profession (Young et al., 2007). These competencies were revised in 2009 at a second ASERVIC summit (Cashwell & Watts, 2010).

Prior to the ASERVIC competencies, Ingersoll (1994) states that counselors interested in working well with clients committed to a particular spiritual view can best do so by affirming the importance of spirituality in the client's life and engaging in treatment that is congruent with the client's worldview. Consulting with other "healers" in the client's life such as ministers, priests, or rabbis is also recommended. As Briggs and Rayle (2005) emphasize, it is not whether to include spirituality in counseling when appropriate, but how to do it. The process calls for cultural sensitivity as well as ethical practices of the highest standard. One specific way to help clients in their spiritual quest is to assess at what level they are on developmentally. Parker (2011) recommends the use of James Fowler's (1995) **seven stages of faith** through which humans may pass as one way of determining how to help them on their journey to growth and development as a more complete and fully functioning person. The focus of this approach is on universal structures that belong to "all faiths that allow the counselor to diagnose and assess the nature and role of a person's faith apart from its specific beliefs" (Parker, 2011, p. 118). Thus, this stage emphasis offers a growth-oriented model of spiritual and religious development.

Asking about a client's spirituality or spiritual resources has become more of a fundamental intake question in many counseling practices, as counselors address the total person of the client. Sometimes, spirituality is manifested in a particular philosophy or religious belief, such as Taoism or Christianity. At other times, it is more nebulous. When spirituality is in the form of religious beliefs, counselors need to be respectful and work with clients to maximize the positive nature of their beliefs and values in connection with the difficulties they are experiencing. Counselors who work best with **religious issues** in counseling are either **pluralistic** (i.e., "recognizing the existence of a religious or spiritual absolute reality" but allowing for multiple interpretations and paths toward it) or **constructivist** (i.e., recognizing a client worldview that includes God or spiritual realities) (Zinnbauer & Pargament, 2000, p. 167).

Regardless of the form spirituality takes, spiritual aspects of clients' lives can be enhanced through creating rituals or other ways for clients to focus on their lives that help them appreciate life rather than depreciate themselves (Cashwell & Young, 2011; Miller, 2003). For example, one ritual distraught clients might be invited to engage in is writing down five things for which they are grateful (Hudson, 1998). Such an assignment can help them move away from bitterness and transcend the adversity of the moment. In addition to helping clients, forms of spirituality, such as meditation and prayer, may be important aspects of counselors' lives as well.

Kelly (1995) found in a nationally representative sample of ACA-affiliated counselors that the majority of respondents valued spirituality in their lives (even more than institutionalized religion). In many cases, a "counselor's personal spirituality/religiousness may prove a value base for being attuned to clients' spiritual and religious issues" (p. 43). Likewise, van Asselt and Senstock (2009) found when a counselor is more spiritually aware, his or her ability to recognize a client's spiritual concerns is also greater. Personal spirituality and spirituality training do make a difference when working with clients presenting spiritual concerns. Therefore, counselors should assess their own spirituality as well as that of their clients.

CASE EXAMPLE

Agnostic Agony

Juan is an agnostic and has been a counselor for approximately 5 years. His private practice has thrived, and he loves working by himself. He has had to be eclectic and a generalist to earn a living. Recently, his client load has fallen off sharply. His newest client, Mag, with whom he seems to have established a good rapport, tells Juan that she would like to start exploring the spiritual side of her life because she is turning 50 next month and has neglected that aspect of herself since she was a teenager. Juan is uncertain what to do. What would you advise him to do and why?

MyCounselingLab™

Go to Topic 2: *Career/Individual/Development Counseling* in the MyCounselingLab™ site (www.MyCounselingLab.com) for *Counseling: A Comprehensive Profession,* Seventh Edition, where you can:

- Find learning outcomes for *Career/Individual/Development Counseling* along with the national standards that connect to these outcomes.
- Complete Assignments and Activities that can help you more deeply understand the chapter content.
- Apply and practice your understanding of the core skills identified in the chapter with the Building Counseling Skills unit.
- Prepare yourself for professional certification with a Practice for Certification quiz.
- Connect to videos through the Video and Resource Library.

Summary and Conclusion

This chapter has focused on counseling four different populations based on age, gender, sexual orientation, and spirituality. Each of the areas highlighted impacts clients and counselors for better or worse. When those involved are open to exploring age, gender, sexual orientation, and spirituality factors, productive insights and new behaviors may be generated. When there is fear or avoidance of examining

these aspects of life, people may regress or become stressed. They may even develop disorders.

In counseling the aged, it is important to help them realize that growing older is a natural part of life. It can be exciting and fulfilling as well as difficult at times. Likewise, gender—being male or female—has advantages and disadvantages. Concentrating on unique as well as universals related to gender in either a group or individual setting can help to resolve hurt or misfortune that have occurred because of one's biology, socialization, and environment.

Sexual orientation, like the two preceding subject areas, is still relatively new as a focus for counselors. Yet gays, lesbians, transgenders, and bisexuals face an array of common concerns, as well as unique circumstances for which counseling can be helpful. Prejudice and discrimination occur in regard to members of this population, just as they do with other groups, but probably more frequently and blatantly.

Spirituality differs, at least on the surface, from the other three topics explored in this chapter. In most cases, those who want to work on spiritual matters are not distinguishable from others. Yet, individuals who have spiritual concerns need to resolve past conflicts and focus on the present so they can live life to the fullest.

In working with any of the populations covered in this chapter, counselors must constantly ask themselves how clients in these domains are similar to and different from others with whom they work. What are within- and between-group universals and uniquenesses? Such awareness will help counselors be more effective and will help clients as well. Overall, in working with diverse, multicultural, and other populations, a constructive acronym for counselors to keep in mind is **ADRESSING** (Hayes, 1996). Letters of this model stand for "**Age and generational influences, Disability, Religion, Ethnicity (which may include race and culture), Social status, Sexual orientation, Indigenous heritage, National origin, and Gender**" (p. 332). In ADDRESSING clients, it is most likely their needs will be met.

Counseling Processes and Theories

Building Counseling Relationships

8

Chapter Overview

From this chapter you will learn about

- Factors that influence the counseling process such as seriousness of a problem
- The importance of initiative and structure in counseling
- How the physical setting of an office and client qualities can influence a counseling sesssion
- Types of counseling interviews
- Helpful and nonhelpful ways of responding to clients
- The importance of goals in directing counseling

As you read consider

- What you would put in a professional disclosure statement
- How you would like to decorate a counseling office
- Your tendencies now in responding to others
- What goals you might feel most comfortable in helping a client achieve

Your words splash heavily upon my mind
  like early cold October rain
    falling on my roof at dusk.
The patterns change like an autumn storm
  from violently rumbling thundering sounds
    to clear, soft steady streams of expression.
Through it all I look at you
  soaked in past fears and turmoil;
Then patiently I watch with you in the darkness
  for the breaking of black clouds
    that linger in your turbulent mind
And the dawning of your smile
  that comes in the light of new beginnings.

Reprinted from "Autumn Storm," by S. T. Gladding, 1975, *Personnel and Guidance Journal, 54,* p. 149. © Samuel T. Gladding.

MyCounselingLab™

Visit the MyCounselingLab™ site (www.MyCounselingLab.com) for *Counseling: A Comprehensive Profession,* Seventh Edition to enhance your understanding of chapter concepts. You'll have the opportunity to practice your skills through video- and case-based Assignments and Activities as well as Building Counseling Skills units and to prepare for your certification exam with Practice for Certification quizzes.

The process of counseling develops in definable stages with recognizable transitions. The first stage involves building a relationship and focuses on engaging clients to explore issues that directly affect them. Two struggles take place at this time (Napier & Whitaker, 1978). One is the ***battle for structure***, which involves issues of administrative control (e.g., scheduling, fees, participation in sessions). The other is the ***battle for initiative***, which concerns the motivation for change and client responsibility. It is essential that counselors win the first battle and clients win the second. If there are failures at these points, the counseling effort will be prematurely terminated, and the counselor and client may feel worse for the experience.

Other factors that influence the progress and direction of counseling are the physical setting, the client's background, the counselor's skill, and the quality of the relationship established. They will be examined here as well as the nature of the first interview and the exploration stage of counseling. Carkhuff (1969, 2000) and Daniel and Ivey (2007) have demonstrated that some counseling responses cut across theoretical and cultural lines in helping build a counselor–client relationship. These responses are sometimes known as **microskills** and include atheoretical and social-learning behaviors such as attending, encouraging, reflecting, and listening. When mastered, these abilities allow counselors to be with their clients more fully, "act in a culturally appropriate manner, and find positives in life experience" (Weinrach, 1987, p. 533). Thus, part of this chapter will focus on microskills.

FACTORS THAT INFLUENCE THE COUNSELING PROCESS

A number of factors affect the counseling process for better or worse. Those covered here are the seriousness of the concern presented, structure, initiative, physical setting, client qualities, and counselor qualities.

Seriousness of the Presenting Problem

Counseling is impacted by the seriousness of the client's presenting problem. "Evidence has suggested a relationship between initial self-reported disturbance level and treatment course. Thus, clients reporting higher initial distress take more sessions to reach clinically significant improvement than clients reporting lower levels of distress" (Leibert, 2006, p. 109).

In addition, research suggests that the largest gains in improvement occur early in treatment but that seriously disturbed individuals benefit from longer term treatment. Furthermore, some conditions such as schizophrenia and clients who exhibit antisocial personality disorders are least likely to show improvement through traditional talk therapies.

Overall, clients who are in better shape at the onset of treatment seem to improve the most, in the least amount of time, and with the best long-term results. Research, as summarized by Leibert (2006), has found "50% of clients diagnosed with anxiety or depression had improved by Sessions 8–13" and "85% of clients improved after 1 year of weekly treatment" (p. 109).

Structure

Clients and counselors sometimes have different perceptions about the purpose and nature of counseling. Clients often do not know what to expect from the process or how to act. Seeing a counselor is a last resort for many individuals. They are likely to have already sought help from more familiar sources, such as friends, family members, ministers, or teachers (Hinson & Swanson, 1993). Therefore, many clients enter counseling reluctantly and hesitantly. This uncertainty can inhibit the counseling process unless some structure is provided (Ritchie, 1986). *Structure* **in counseling** is defined as "a joint understanding between the counselor and client regarding the characteristics, conditions, procedures, and parameters of counseling" (Day & Sparacio, 1980, p. 246). Structure helps clarify the counselor–client relationship and give it direction; protect the rights, roles, and obligations of both counselors and clients; and ensure the success of counseling (Brammer, Abrego, & Shostrom, 1993).

Practical guidelines are part of building structure. They include **time limits** (such as a 50-minute session), **action limits** (for the prevention of destructive behavior), **role limits** (what will be expected of each participant), and **procedural limits** (in which the client is given the responsibility to work on specific goals or needs) (Brammer & MacDonald, 2003). Guidelines also provide information on fee schedules and other important concerns of clients. In general, structure promotes the development of counseling by providing a framework in which the process can take place. "It is therapeutic in and of itself" (Day & Sparacio, 1980, p. 246).

Structure is provided throughout all stages of counseling but is especially important at the beginning. Dorn (1984) states that "clients usually seek counseling because they are in a static behavior state" (p. 342). That is, clients feel stuck and out of control to change behavior. To help clients gain new directions in their lives, counselors provide constructive guidelines. Their decisions on how to establish this structure are based on their theoretical orientation to counseling, the personalities of their clients, and the major problem areas with which they will deal. Too much structure can be just as detrimental as not enough (Welfel & Patterson, 2005). Therefore, counselors need to stay flexible and continually negotiate the nature of the structure with their clients.

The importance of structure is most obvious when clients arrive for counseling with unrealistic expectations (Welfel & Patterson, 2005). Counselors need to move quickly to establish structure at such times. One way is for counselors to provide information about the counseling process and themselves with **professional disclosure statements** that include details about the nature of counseling, expectations, responsibilities, methods, and ethics of counseling (Figure 6.1).

PERSONAL REFLECTION

When have you found structure helpful in your life? What did it provide for you that would not have been there otherwise?

Professional Disclosure Statement

Samuel T. Gladding, Ph.D.—Licensed Professional Counselor

I am glad you have selected me as your counselor. In considering our professional relationship, I have written this document to describe my background and my clinical approach.

Professional Background

I hold a Master of Arts degree in counseling from Wake Forest University, a Master of Arts degree in religion from Yale Divinity School, and a Ph.D. from the University of North Carolina in family relations with cognates in counseling and psychology. In addition, I did a post doctorate at UNCG (18 semester hours) in psychology. I have worked in a public mental health center (Rockingham County, North Carolina) and in a private clinical practice (Birmingham, Alabama). I have also taught counseling at the graduate level in Connecticut (Fairfield University), in Alabama (University of Alabama at Birmingham), and in North Carolina (Wake Forest University).

I am a Licensed Professional Counselor (#636) in the state of North Carolina, a National Certified Counselor (#334), and a Certified Clinical Mental Health Counselor (#351).

Counseling Services Offered

As a licensed professional counselor with a specialty in mental health, I am interested in the growth, development, and wellness of the whole person. I respect the uniqueness of each person and his/her life journey where applicable. My responsibility is to facilitate and empower your use of thoughts, feelings, and behaviors to achieve healing and wholeness in your life.

I have offered outpatient, fee-based counseling services since 1971, although not sequentially. I have worked with individuals, couples, families, and groups in areas such as depression, anxiety, grief, abuse, career exploration, situational adjustments, life development, and crises.

Counseling presents you with the opportunity to invest in your personal, emotional, cognitive, behavioral, and spiritual well-being and growth in the context of a helping relationship. Your goals for seeking counseling, which I will explore and update with you frequently, will give direction to our work together and will influence the therapeutic approaches that I will use. My style of counseling is based on person-centered, gestalt, existential, family systems, and cognitive-behavioral theories. Although some counseling changes may be easy and rapid, others are slow and deliberate. These latter changes will require considerable proactive commitment on your part. This commitment may involve work outside of our sessions such as reading, reflecting, journaling, and working on cognitive-behavioral assignments.

At the outset I will listen carefully to your story and take a history to learn the specific initial therapy goals that emerge. I will work closely with you to evaluate and fine-tune together these goals as the process unfolds. At any session each of us may evaluate how the process is unfolding and where we may need to make revisions. At the end of the counseling process, you will be provided with an evaluation form to reflect on our work together. Coming to know yourself in greater depth and make changes can be inspiring as well as painful. You may experience a myriad of thoughts and feelings during this process, including but not limited to, frustration, sadness, anxiety, guilt, and anger. I will typically make a diagnosis regarding your situation, which will become a part of your record.

Professional Ethics

For our relationship to be respectful and effective, confidentiality is a must. I will not discuss the content of our work outside of our sessions. State law and the ethical principles of my professional organizations (the American Counseling Association, the National Board for Certified Counselors,

FIGURE 6.1 Professional disclosure statement (*continued*)

and the North Carolina Board of Licensed Professional Counselors) mandate confidentiality except under two circumstances: (1) when I believe you intend to harm yourself or another person, or (2) when I believe a child or elderly person has been or will be abused or neglected. In rare circumstances, a court of law can mandate me to release information on you. Otherwise, I will not disclose anything about your history, diagnosis, or progress. I will not even acknowledge our professional relationship without your full knowledge and a signed Release of Information Form. Such a form must be signed to release information to your insurance carrier as well.

Ethical and legal standards mandate that even though our relationship might be intense and intimate in many ways, it must remain professional rather than social. You will be served best if our sessions and relationship concentrate exclusively on your concerns. Thus, I will not attend social events, receive gifts, or relate to you in any way other than in the professional context of our sessions.

Length of Sessions

My services will be rendered in a professional manner consistent with the accepted clinical standards of the American Counseling Association, National Board for Certified Counselors, and the North Carolina Board of Licensed Professional Counselors. Sessions will last fifty (50) minutes. We shall schedule sessions by mutual agreement. Often persons prefer to maintain a standard appointment time. A twenty-four (24)-hour notice is required for cancellation unless there is a sickness or emergency. Without these exceptions, payment for missed sessions is required. Every effort will be made to start and stop sessions on time. Each of us has the responsibility of being prompt.

Fees and Methods of Payment

The fee for initial intake sessions is $115.00 with each subsequent session being $95.00. Sessions are payable by personal check or in cash at the beginning of each appointment. Our office will provide you with a super bill for your records or to submit to your insurance carrier. Some insurance companies will pay for counseling services; others will not. Please remember that you and not your insurance company are responsible for paying in full the fees agreed upon.

Complaint Procedure

If you have difficulty with any aspect of our work, please inform me immediately so that we can discuss how we might work better together. This discussion is an important aspect of our continuous evaluation of this process.

Should you feel treated unfairly or unethically by me or another counselor, you may make a formal complaint to the following licensure board and associations.

North Carolina Board of Licensed Professional Counselors
PO Box 2105
Raleigh, NC 27619-1005
919-661-0820

National Board for Certified Counselors
3 Terrace Way
Greensboro, NC 27403
336-547-0607

FIGURE 6.1 Professional disclosure statement (*continued*)

American Counseling Association
5999 Stevenson Avenue
Alexandria, VA 22304
1-800-347-6647

Please sign and date both copies of this form. A copy for your records will be returned to you.
I shall keep a copy in my confidential records.

Signature of Client/Parent/Guardian	Date
Signature of Counselor	Date

FIGURE 6.1   *continued*

Initiative

Initiative can be thought of as the motivation to change. Most counselors and counseling theories assume that clients will be cooperative. Indeed, many clients come to counseling on a voluntary or self-referred basis. They experience tension and concern about themselves or others, but they are willing to work hard in counseling sessions. Other clients, however, are more reserved about participating in counseling. Vriend and Dyer (1973) estimate that the majority of clients who visit counselors are reluctant to some degree. When counselors meet clients who seem to lack initiative, they often do not know what to do with them, much less how to go about counseling. Therefore, some counselors are impatient, irritated, and may ultimately give up trying to work with such persons. The result is not only termination of the relationship but also *scapegoating*—blaming a person when the problem was not entirely his or her fault. Many counselors end up blaming themselves or their clients if counseling is not successful. Such recriminations need not occur if counselors understand the dynamics involved in working with difficult clients. Part of this understanding involves assuming the role of an involuntary client and imagining how it would feel to come for counseling. A **role-reversal exercise** can promote counselor empathy as well.

A *reluctant client* is one who has been referred by a third party and is frequently "unmotivated to seek help" (Ritchie, 1986, p. 516). Many schoolchildren and court-referred clients are good examples. They do not wish to be in counseling, let alone talk about themselves. Many reluctant clients terminate counseling prematurely and report dissatisfaction with the process.

CASE EXAMPLE

Rachel the Reluctant

Rachel was caught smoking marijuana in the girl's bathroom at her high school. The school had a zero tolerance policy on drugs and immediately suspended Rachel until she received counseling. Rachel was furious, but made an appointment with a counselor that the school recommended. Her first words to the counselor were, "You can make me come but you can't make me talk."

Sure enough, through the first two sessions Rachel said little and acted sullen. Her counselor, Rose, was both frustrated and angry with her attitude. Therefore, Rose decided that if Rachel did not act more cooperatively during the third session, she would terminate her.

What do you think the counselor might do, besides get angry, that could make a difference in the counseling process and in Rachel's life? Compare your ideas with the seven ideas for counseling reluctant and resistant clients given later in this chapter to see which of your suggestions overlap and which do not.

A *resistant client* is a person in counseling who is unwilling, unready, or opposed to change (Otani, 1989; Ritchie, 1986). Such an individual may actively seek counseling but does not wish to go through the emotional pain, change in perspective, or enhanced awareness that counseling demands (Cowan & Presbury, 2000). Instead, the client clings to the certainty of present behavior, even when such action is counterproductive and dysfunctional. Some resistant clients refuse to make decisions, are superficial in dealing with problems, and take any action to resolve a problem (i.e., do anything a counselor says). According to Sack (1988), "the most common form of resistance is the simple statement 'I don't know'" (p. 180). Such a response makes the counselor's next move difficult and protects the client from having to take any action.

Otani (1989) has proposed four broad categories of resistance: "amount of verbalization; content of message; style of communication; and attitude toward counselors and counseling sessions" (p. 459). They add up to 22 forms of resistance in these categories including silence, intellectual talk, emotional displays, last-minute disclosures, and payment delay/refusal.

Counselors can help clients win the battle for initiative and achieve success in counseling in several ways. One is to anticipate the anger, frustration, and defensiveness that some clients display. Counselors who realize that a percentage of their clients are reluctant or resistant can work with these individuals because they are not surprised by them or their behaviors.

A second way to deal with a lack of initiative is to show acceptance, patience, and understanding as well as a general nonjudgmental attitude. This stance promotes trust, which is the basis of an interpersonal relationship. Nonjudgmental behavior also helps clients better understand their thoughts and feelings about counseling. Thus, acceptance opens clients to others, themselves, and the counseling process.

A third way to win the battle for initiative is for counselors to use persuasion (Kerr, Claiborn, & Dixon, 1982; Senour, 1982). All counselors have some influence on clients, and vice versa (Dorn, 1984; Strong, 1982). How a counselor responds to the client, directly or indirectly, can make a significant difference in whether the client takes the initiative in working to produce change. Roloff and Miller (1980) mention **two direct persuasion techniques** employed in counseling: the *"foot in the door"* and the *"door in the face."* In the first technique, the counselor asks the client to comply with a minor request and then later follows with a larger request. For example, an initial request might be "Would you keep a journal of your thoughts and feelings for this week" followed the next week by "I'd like you to keep a journal of your thoughts and feelings from now on." In the second technique, the counselor asks the client to do a seemingly impossible task and then follows by requesting the client to do a more reasonable task. For instance, the initial request might be "I'd like you to talk briefly to 100 people a day between now and our next session" followed, after the client's refusal, by "Since that assignment seems to be more than you are comfortable in handling, I'd like you to say hello to just three new people each day."

A fourth way a counselor can assist clients in gaining initiative is through ***confrontation***. In this procedure the counselor simply points out to the client exactly what the client is doing, such as being inconsistent. For example, a parent might be disciplining children for misbehaving sometimes and then letting them act out at other times. In such situations, the client must take responsibility for responding to the confrontation. The three primary ways of responding are denying the behavior, accepting all or part of the confrontation as true, or developing a middle position that synthesizes the first two (Young, 2009). Doing something differently or gaining a new perception on a problem can be a beneficial result of confrontation, especially if what has previously been tried has not worked.

Counselors can also use language, especially **metaphors**, to soften resistance or reluctance. "Metaphors can be used to teach and reduce threat levels by providing stories, by painting images, by offering fresh insights, by challenging rigid thinking, by permitting tolerance for new beliefs, and by overcoming the tension often present between a counselor and the resistant [or reluctant] client" (James & Hazler, 1998, p. 122). For instance, in addressing a client who keeps repeating the same mistake, the counselor might say, "What does a fighter do when he gets badly beaten up every time he fights?" (p. 127).

The sixth way counselors can help reluctant and resistant clients, indeed all clients, and strengthen the counseling relationship is through "***mattering***," the perception that as human beings we are important and significant to the world around us and to others in our lives (Rayle, 2006). Research shows that mattering to others directly affects individuals' lives and relationships.

Finally, Sack (1988) recommends the use of pragmatic techniques, such as silence (or pause), reflection (or empathy), questioning, describing, assessing, pretending, and sharing the counselor's perspective, as ways to overcome client resistance. These techniques are especially helpful with individuals who respond to counselor initiatives with "I don't know." Depending on one's theoretical orientation, resistance can also be declared officially dead (deShazer, 1984). From such a perspective, change is inevitable and clients are seen as cooperative. The reason change has not occurred is that the counselor has yet to find a way to help stuck clients initiate a sufficient push to escape patterns that have been troubling them.

The Physical Setting

Counseling can occur almost anywhere, but some physical settings promote the process better than others. Among the most important factors that help or hurt the process is the place where the counseling occurs. Most counseling occurs in a room, although Benjamin (1987) tells of counseling in a tent. He says that there is no universal quality that a room should have "except [that] it should not be overwhelming, noisy, or distracting" (p. 3). Shertzer and Stone (1980) implicitly agree: "The room should be comfortable and attractive" (p. 252). Erdman and Lampe (1996) believe that certain features of a counseling office will improve its general appearance and probably facilitate counseling by not distracting the client. These features include soft lighting; quiet colors; an absence of clutter; harmonious, comfortable furniture; and diverse cultural artifacts. They go on to recommend that when working with families who have children or with children apart from families, counselors need to have furniture that is child size.

In an extensive review of the research on the physical environment and counseling, Pressly and Heesacker (2001, p. 156) looked at **eight common architectural characteristics of space and their potential impact** on counseling sessions. The factors they reviewed and their findings are as follows:

1. **Accessories** (i.e., artwork, objects, plants)—"people prefer texturally complex images of natural settings, rather than posters of people, urban life, and abstract compositions"; people feel "more comfortable in offices that are clean and have plants and artwork"
2. **Color** (i.e., hue, value, intensity)—"bright colors are associated with positive emotions and dark colors are linked with negative emotions"
3. **Furniture and room design** (i.e., form, line, color, texture, scale)—"clients prefer intermediate distance in counseling and . . . more protective furniture layouts . . . than do counselors"
4. **Lighting** (i.e., artificial, natural)—"general communication tends to occur in bright environments, whereas more intimate conversation tends to occur in softer light"; "full-spectrum lighting helps to decrease depression symptomatology" (In an experiment with 80 undergraduates in Japan, Miwa and Hanyu [2006] found that dim lighting yields more pleasant and relaxed feelings, more favorable impressions of the counselor, and more self-disclosure than bright lighting.)
5. **Smell** (i.e., plants, ambient fragrances, general odors)—"unpleasant smells elicit unhappy memories, whereas pleasant smells trigger happy memories"; "inhaled food and fruit fragrances have resulted in self-reported depressive symptoms"
6. **Sound** (i.e., loudness, frequency)—"sound may enhance or detract from task performance"; "music may enhance the healing process and affect muscle tone, blood pressure, heart rate, and the experience of pain"
7. **Texture** (i.e., floors, walls, ceilings, furniture)—"counselors should consider using soft, textured surfaces to absorb sound and to increase clients' feelings of privacy"
8. **Thermal conditions** (i.e., temperature, relative humidity, air velocity)—"most individuals feel comfortable in temperatures ranging from 69 to 80 degrees F and 30% to 60% relative humidity"

The distance between counselor and client (the spatial features of the environment or *proxemics*) can also affect the counseling relationship and has been studied. Individuals differ about the level of comfort experienced in interactions with others. Among other things, comfort level is influenced by cultural background, gender, and the nature of the relationship. A distance of 30 to 39 inches has been found to be the average range of comfort between counselors and clients of both genders in the United States (Haase, 1970). This optimum distance may vary because of room size and furniture arrangement (Haase & DiMattia, 1976).

The arrangement of furniture depends on the counselor. Some counselors prefer to sit behind a desk during sessions, but most do not. The reason desks are generally eschewed by counselors is that a desk can be a physical and symbolic barrier against the development of a close relationship. Benjamin (1987) suggests that counselors include two chairs and a nearby table in the setting. The chairs should be set at a 90-degree angle from one another so that clients can look either at their counselors or straight ahead. The table can be used for many purposes, such as a place to keep a box of tissues. Benjamin's ideas are strictly his own; each counselor must find a physical arrangement that is comfortable for him or her.

Regardless of the arrangement within the room, counselors should not be interrupted when conducting sessions. All phone calls, including cell phone calls, should be held. If necessary,

counselors should put "do not disturb" signs on the door to keep others from entering. Auditory and visual privacy are mandated by professional codes of ethics and ensure maximum client self-disclosure.

Client Qualities

Counseling relationships start with first impressions. The way that counselor and client perceive one another is vital to the establishment of a productive relationship. Warnath (1977) points out that "clients come in all shapes and sizes, personality characteristics, and degrees of attractiveness" (p. 85). Some clients are more likely to be successful in counseling than others. The most successful candidates for traditional approaches tend to be **YAVIS**: young, attractive, verbal, intelligent, and successful (Schofield, 1964). Less successful candidates are seen as **HOUNDs** (homely, old, unintelligent, nonverbal, and disadvantaged) or **DUDs** (dumb, unintelligent, and disadvantaged) (Allen, 1977). These acronyms are cruel (Lichtenberg, 1986), but counselors are influenced by the appearance and sophistication of the people with whom they work. Counselors most enjoy working with clients who they think have the potential to change.

A number of stereotypes have been built around the physical attractiveness of individuals, and these stereotypes generalize to clients. The **physically attractive** are perceived as healthiest and are responded to more positively than others. Goldstein (1973), for instance, found that clients who were seen by their counselors as most attractive talked more and were more spontaneous when compared with other clients. Most likely, counselors were more encouraging to and engaged with the attractive clients. Therefore, aging clients and those with physical disabilities may face invisible but powerful barriers in certain counseling situations. Ponzo (1985) suggests that counselors become aware of the importance of physical attractiveness in their own lives and monitor their behavioral reactions when working with attractive clients. Otherwise, stereotypes and unfounded assumptions may "lead to self-fulfilling prophecies" (p. 485).

The **nonverbal behaviors** of clients are also very important. Clients constantly send counselors unspoken messages about how they think or feel. Children are especially prone to use nonverbal means to convey their thoughts and feelings. Mehrabian (1971) and associates found that expressed like and dislike between individuals could be explained as follows:

> Total liking equals 7% verbal liking plus 38% vocal liking plus 55% facial liking. The impact of **facial expression** is greatest, then the impact of the tone of voice (or vocal expression), and finally that of the words. If the facial expression is inconsistent with the words, the degree of liking conveyed by the facial expression will dominate and determine the impact of the total message. (p. 43)

Thus, a client who reports that all is going well but who looks down at the ground and frowns while doing so is probably indicating just the opposite. A counselor must consider a client's body gestures, eye contact, facial expression, and vocal quality to be as important as verbal communication in a counseling relationship. It is also crucial to consider the cultural background of the person whose body language is being evaluated and interpret nonverbal messages cautiously (Sielski, 1979).

Counselor Qualities

The personal and professional qualities of counselors are very important in facilitating any helping relationship. Okun and Kantrowitz (2008) note that it is hard to separate the helper's personality characteristics from his or her levels and styles of functioning, as both are interrelated. They then list five important characteristics that helpers should possess: self-awareness, honesty, congruence, ability to communicate, and knowledge.

Counselors who continually develop their self-awareness skills are in touch with their values, thoughts, and feelings. They are likely to have a clear perception of their own and their clients' needs and accurately assess both. Such awareness can help them be honest with themselves and others. They are able to be more congruent and build trust simultaneously. Counselors who possess this type of knowledge are more likely to communicate clearly and accurately.

Three other characteristics that make counselors initially more influential are perceived expertness, attractiveness, and trustworthiness (Strong, 1968). *Expertness* is the degree to which a counselor is perceived as knowledgeable and informed about his or her specialty. Counselors who display evidential cues in their offices, such as certificates and diplomas, are usually perceived as more credible than those who do not and, as a result, are likely to be effective (Loesch, 1984; Siegal & Sell, 1978). Clients want to work with counselors who appear to know the profession well.

Attractiveness is a function of perceived similarity between a client and counselor as well as physical features. Counselors can make themselves attractive by speaking in clear, simple, jargon-free sentences and offering appropriate self-disclosure (Watkins & Schneider, 1989). The manner in which a counselor greets the client and maintains eye contact can also increase the attractiveness rating. Counselors who use nonverbal cues in responding to clients, such as head nodding and eye contact, are seen as more attractive than those who do not (Claiborn, 1979; LaCross, 1975). The attire of the counselor also makes a difference (Hubble & Gelso, 1978). Clothes should be clean, neat, and professional looking but not attract undue attention. Physical features make a difference, too, in that under controlled conditions, research suggests individuals are more willing to self-disclose to an attractive counselor than to an unattractive one (Harris & Busby, 1998).

Trustworthiness is related to the sincerity and consistency of the counselor. The counselor is genuinely concerned about the client and shows it over time by establishing a close relationship. "There is and can be no such thing as instant intimacy" or trustworthiness (Patterson, 1985, p. 124). Rather, both are generated through patterns of behavior that demonstrate care and concern. Most clients are neither completely distrusting nor given to blind trust. But, as Fong and Cox (1983) note, many clients test the trustworthiness of the counselor by requesting information, telling a secret, asking a favor, inconveniencing the counselor, deprecating themselves, or questioning the motives and dedication of the counselor. It is essential, therefore, that the counselor respond to the question of trust rather than the verbal content of the client in order to facilitate the counseling relationship.

Many beginning counselors make the mistake of dealing with surface issues instead of real concerns. For example, if a client asks a counselor, "Can I tell you anything?" a novice counselor might respond, "What do you mean by anything?" An experienced counselor might say, "It sounds as if you are uncertain about whether you can really trust me and this relationship. Tell me more." Trust with children, like adults, is built by listening first and allowing children the freedom to express themselves openly on a verbal or nonverbal level before the counselor responds (Erdman & Lampe, 1996).

CASE EXAMPLE

Brigit's Breakdown

Brigit was 48, bucktoothed, pock-faced, undereducated, and largely avoided by most people. To make matters worse, she was introverted and lonely. Her best friend on the weekend was her television. Therefore, when her sister suggested she try counseling, she agreed and thought "I have nothing to lose." However, she encountered problems from the beginning. Brigit's counselor, Channel, acted as if Brigit's bad looks were contagious and seemed to distance herself from Brigit and blame her for not being more extraverted. Brigit became furious and decided to do something about the situation.

During the second session, Brigit pointed out specific behaviors Channel was doing that made her feel rejected. Channel was embarrassed and admitted engaging in all the actions Brigit confronted her with, but then continued to criticize Brigit in a subtle fashion.

What else might Brigit do with this situation? What would you suggest Channel do to help correct her mistakes and make the counseling session productive?

TYPES OF INITIAL INTERVIEWS

The counseling process begins with the initial session. Levine (1983) points out authorities in the profession have observed that "the goals of counseling change over time and change according to the intimacy and effectiveness of the counseling relationship" (p. 431). How much change happens or whether there is a second session is usually determined by the results of the first session.

In the first session, both counselors and clients work to decide whether they want to or can continue the relationship. Counselors should quickly assess whether they are capable of handling and managing clients' problems through being honest, open, and appropriately confrontive

(Okun & Kantrowitz, 2008). However, clients must ask themselves whether they feel comfortable with and trust the counselor before they can enter the relationship wholeheartedly.

Client-versus Counselor-Initiated Interviews

Benjamin (1987) distinguishes between **two types of first interviews**: those **initiated by clients** and those **initiated by counselors**. When the initial interview is requested by a client, the counselor is often unsure of the client's purpose. This uncertainty may create anxiety in the counselor, especially if background information is not gathered before the session. Benjamin (1987) recommends that counselors work to overcome these feelings by listening as hard as possible to what clients have to say. In such situations, as with counseling in general, listening "requires a submersion of the self and immersion in the other" (Nichols, 1998, p. 1). There is no formula for beginning the session. The helping interview is as much an art as a science, and every counselor must work out a style based on experience, stimulation, and reflection. The counselor is probably prudent not to inquire initially about any problem the client may have because the client may not have a problem in the traditional sense of the word and may just be seeking information.

When the first session is requested by the counselor, Benjamin (1987) believes that the counselor should immediately state his or her reason for wanting to see the client. In the case of a school counselor, for instance, a session might be requested so that the counselor can introduce himself or herself to a student. If the counselor does not immediately give a reason for requesting the session, the client is kept guessing and tension is created.

Welfel and Patterson (2005) think that all clients enter counseling with some anxiety and resistance regardless of prior preparation. Benjamin (1987) hypothesizes that most counselors are also a bit frightened and uncertain when conducting a first interview. Uncertain feelings in both clients and counselors may result in behaviors such as seduction or aggression (Watkins, 1983). Counselors can prevent such occurrences by exchanging information with clients. Manthei (1983) advocates counselors' presentations about themselves and their functioning be *multimodal*: visual, auditory, written, spoken, and descriptive. Although such presentations may be difficult, they pay off by creating good counselor–client relationships. Overall, early exchanges of information increase the likelihood that clients and counselors will make meaningful choices and participate more fully in the counseling process.

Information-Oriented First Interview

Cormier and Hackney (2012) point out that the initial counseling interview can fulfill two functions: (a) It can be an intake interview to collect needed information about the client, or (b) it can signal the beginning of a relationship. Each type of interview is appropriate and certain tasks are common to both, though the skills emphasized in each differ.

If the purpose of the first interview is to gather information, the structure of the session will be counselor focused: The counselor wants the client to talk about certain subjects. The counselor will respond to the client predominantly through the use of probes, accents, closed questions, and requests for clarification (Cormier & Hackney, 2012). These responses are aimed at eliciting facts.

The *probe* is a question that usually begins with *who, what, where,* or *how*. It requires more than a one- or two-word response—for example, "What do you plan to do about getting a job?" Few probes ever begin with the word *why,* which usually connotes disapproval, places a client on the defensive (e.g., "Why are you doing that?"), and is often unanswerable (Benjamin, 1987).

An *accent* is highlighting the last few words of the client. For example:

> CLIENT: The situation I'm in now is driving me crazy!
> COUNSELOR: Driving you crazy?

A *closed question* is one that requires a specific and limited response, such as yes or no. It often begins with the word *is, do,* or *are*:

> COUNSELOR: Do you enjoy meeting other people?
> CLIENT: Yes.

The closed question is quite effective in eliciting a good deal of information in a short period of time, but it does not encourage elaboration that might also be helpful.

In contrast to the closed question is the *open question*, which typically begins with *what, how*, or *could* and allows the client more latitude to respond. Examples are "How does this affect you?" "Could you give me more information?" and "Tell me more about it." The major difference between a closed and open question "is whether or not the question encourages more client talk" (Galvin & Ivey, 1981, p. 539). It is the difference between a multiple-choice inquiry that checks the facts and an essay in which a deeper level of understanding and explanation is encouraged.

Finally, a *request for clarification* is a response the counselor uses to be sure he or she understands what the client is saying. These requests require the client to repeat or elaborate on material just covered. For example, a counselor might say, "Please help me understand this relationship" or "I don't see the connection here."

Counselors wish to obtain several facts in an information-oriented first interview. They often assume this information may be used as a part of a psychological, vocational, or psychosocial assessment. Counselors employed by medical, mental health, correctional, rehabilitation, and social agencies are particularly likely to conduct these types of interviews. Cormier and Hackney (2012) outline some of the data counselors gather in these initial sessions (Figure 6.2).

Relationship-Oriented First Interview

Interviews that focus on feelings or relationship dynamics differ markedly from information-oriented first sessions. They concentrate more on the client's attitudes and emotions. Common counselor responses include restatement, reflection of feeling, summary of feelings, request for clarification, and acknowledgment of nonverbal behavior (Cormier & Hackney, 2012).

A *restatement* is a simple mirror response to a client that lets the client know the counselor is actively listening. Used alone, it is relatively sterile and ineffective:

> CLIENT: I'm not sure if I'll ever find a suitable partner. My job keeps me on the road and isolated.
> COUNSELOR: You don't know if you will ever find a spouse because of the nature of your job.

Reflection of feeling is similar to a restatement, but it deals with verbal and nonverbal expression. Reflections may be on several levels; some convey more empathy than others. An

I. **Identifying data**
    A. Client's name, address, telephone number through which client can be reached. This information is important in the event the counselor needs to contact the client between sessions. The client's address also gives some hint about the conditions under which the client lives (e.g., large apartment complex, student dormitory, private home, etc.).
    B. Age, sex, marital status, occupation (or school class and year).Again, this is information that can be important.It lets you know when the client is still legally a minor and provides a basis for understanding information that will come out in later sessions.

II. **Presenting problems, both primary and secondary**
    It is best when these are presented in exactly the way the client reported them. If the problem has behavioral components, these should be recorded as well. Questions that help reveal this type of information include
    A. How much does the problem interfere with the client's every day functioning?
    B. How does the problem manifest itself? What are the thoughts, feelings, and so on that are associated with it? What observable behavior is associated with it?
    C. How often does the problem arise? How long has the problem existed?
    D. Can the client identify a pattern of events that surround the problem? When does it occur? With whom? What happens before and after its occurrence?
    E. What caused the client to decide to enter counseling at this time?

III. **Client's current life setting**
    How does the client spend a typical day or week? What social and religious activities, recreational activities, and so on are present? What is the nature of the client's vocational and/or educational situation?

IV. **Family history**
    A. Father's and mother's ages, occupations, descriptions of their personalities, relationships of each to the other and each to the client and other siblings.
    B. Names, ages, and order of brothers and sisters; relationship between client and siblings.
    C. Is there any history of mental disturbance in the family?
    D. Descriptions of family stability, including number of jobs held, number of family moves, and so on. (This information provides insights in later sessions when issues related to client stability and/or relationships emerge.)

V. **Personal history**
    A. Medical history: any unusual or relevant illness or injury from prenatal period to present.
    B. Educational history: academic progress through grade school, high school, and post-high school. This includes extracurricular interests and relationships with peers.
    C. Military service record.
    D. Vocational history: Where has the client worked, at what types of jobs, for what duration, and what were the relationships with fellow workers?
    E. Sexual and marital history: Where did the client receive sexual information? What was the client's dating history? Any engagements and/or marriages? Other serious emotional involvements prior to the present? Reasons that previous relationships terminated? What was the courtship like with present spouse? What were the reasons (spouse's characteristics, personal thoughts) that led to marriage? What has been the relationship with spouse since marriage? Are there any children?

FIGURE 6.2 An information-oriented first interview

F. What experience has the client had with counseling, and what were the client's reactions?

G. What are the client's personal goals in life?

VI. Description of the client during the interview

Here you might want to indicate the client's physical appearance, including dress, posture, gestures, facial expressions, voice quality, tensions; how the client seemed to relate to you in the session; client's readiness of response, motivation, warmth, distance, passivity, etc. Did there appear to be any perceptual or sensory functions that intruded upon the interaction? (Document with your observations.) What was the general level of information, vocabulary, judgment, and abstraction abilities displayed by the client? What was the stream of thought, regularity, and rate of talking? Were the client's remarks logical? Connected to one another?

VII. Summary and recommendations

In this section you will want to acknowledge any connections that appear to exist between the client's statement of a problem and other information collected in this session. What type of counselor do you think would best fit this client? If you are to be this client's counselor, which of your characteristics might be particularly helpful? Which might be particularly unhelpful? How realistic are the client's goals for counseling? How long do you think counseling might continue?

FIGURE 6.2   *continued*   *Source:* From *Counseling Strategies and Interventions* (pp. 66–68), by L. S. Cormier and H. Hackney, Boston: Allyn & Bacon, 2008. All rights reserved. Reprinted by permission of Allyn & Bacon.

example is this counselor response to a client who is silently sobbing over the loss of a parent: "You're still really feeling the pain."

Summary of feelings is the act of paraphrasing a number of feelings that the client has conveyed. For example, a counselor might say to a client, "John, if I understand you correctly, you are feeling depressed over the death of your father and discouraged that your friends have not helped you work through your grief. In addition, you feel your work is boring and that your wife is emotionally distant from you."

Acknowledgment of nonverbal behavior differs from the previous examples. For instance, acknowledgment comes when the counselor says to a client, "I notice that your arms are folded across your chest and you're looking at the floor." This type of response does not interpret the meaning of the behavior.

CONDUCTING THE INITIAL INTERVIEW

There is no one place to begin an initial interview, but experts recommend that counselors start by trying to make their clients feel comfortable (Cormier & Hackney, 2012). Counselors should set aside their own agendas and focus on the person of the client, including listening to the client's story and presenting issues (Myers, 2000; Wilcox-Matthew, Ottens, & Minor, 1997). This type of behavior, in which there is a genuine interest in and accepting of a client, is known as *rapport*.

Ivey, Ivey, and Zalaquett (2010) state that the **two most important microskills for rapport** building are basic **attending behavior** and **client-observation skills**. A counselor needs to tune in to what the client is thinking and feeling and how he or she is behaving. In this process, "counselor sensitivity to client-generated metaphors may help to convey understanding of the client's unique way of knowing and at the same time contribute to the development of a shared language and collaborative bond between the client and counselor" (Lyddon, Clay, & Sparks, 2001, p. 270). For instance, a client may describe herself as being treated by others as "yesterday's leftovers." This metaphor gives both the client and counselor information about the thinking and behavior going on in the client as she seeks to be seen "as the blue plate special." Regardless, establishing and maintaining rapport is vital for the disclosure of information, the initiation of change, and the ultimate success of counseling.

Inviting clients to focus on reasons for seeking help is one way in which counselors may initiate rapport. Such noncoercive invitations to talk are called *door openers* and contrast with judgmental or evaluative responses known as *door closers* (Bolton, 1979). Appropriate door openers include inquiries and observations such as "What brings you to see me?" "What would you like to talk about?" and "You look like you are in a lot of pain. Tell me about it." These unstructured, open-ended invitations allow clients to take the initiative (Cormier & Hackney, 2012; Young, 2009. In such situations, clients are most likely to talk about priority topics.

The amount of talking that clients engage in and the insight and benefits derived from the initial interview can be enhanced by the counselor who appropriately conveys empathy, encouragement, support, caring, attentiveness, acceptance, and genuineness. Of all of these qualities, empathy is the most important.

Empathy

Rogers (1961) describes *empathy* as the counselor's ability to "enter the client's phenomenal world, to experience the client's world as if it were your own without ever losing the 'as if' quality" (p. 284). Empathy involves two specific skills: perception and communication (Welfel & Patterson, 2005).

An effective counselor perceives the cultural frame of reference from which his or her client operates, including the client's perceptual and cognitive process (Weinrach, 1987). This type of sensitivity, if it bridges the cultural gap between the counselor and client, is known as *culturally sensitive empathy* and is a quality counselors may cultivate (Chung & Bemak, 2002). Nevertheless, a counselor who can accurately perceive what it is like to be the client but cannot communicate that experience is a limited helper. Such a counselor may be aware of client dynamics, but no one, including the client, knows of the counselor's awareness. The ability to communicate clearly plays a vital role in any counseling relationship (Okun & Kantrowitz, 2008).

In the initial interview, counselors must be able to convey primary empathy (Welfel & Patterson, 2005). *Primary empathy* is the ability to respond in such a way that it is apparent to both client and counselor that the counselor has understood the client's major themes. Primary empathy is conveyed through nonverbal communication and various verbal responses. For example, the counselor, leaning forward and speaking in a soft, understanding voice, may say to the client, "I hear that your life has been defined by a series of serious losses." *Advanced empathy* is a process of helping a client explore themes, issues, and emotions new to his or her awareness (Welfel & Patterson, 2005). This second level of empathy is usually inappropriate for an initial interview because it examines too much material too quickly. Clients must be developmentally ready for counseling to be beneficial.

PERSONAL REFLECTION

It has been said that a counselor who cannot convey empathy is like a tree in a forest that falls with no one around. What do you think of that analogy? What other analogies do you think are appropriate to describe this phenomenon?

Verbal and Nonverbal Behavior

Whatever its form, empathy may be fostered by ***attentiveness*** (the amount of verbal and nonverbal behavior shown to the client). Verbal behaviors include communications that show a desire to comprehend or discuss what is important to the client (Cormier, Nurius, & Osborn, 2009). These behaviors (which include probing, requesting clarification, restating, and summarizing feelings) indicate that the counselor is focusing on the person of the client. Equally important are the counselor's nonverbal behaviors. According to Mehrabian (1970), physically attending behaviors such as smiling, leaning forward, making eye contact, gesturing, and nodding one's head are effective nonverbal ways of conveying to clients that the counselor is interested in and open to them.

Egan (2010) summarizes five nonverbal skills involved in initial attending. They are best remembered in the acronym ***SOLER***. The *S* is a reminder to face the client ***squarely***, which can be understood literally or metaphorically depending on the situation. The important thing is that the counselor shows involvement and interest in the client. The *O* is a reminder to adopt an ***open posture***, free from crossed arms and legs and showing nondefensiveness. The *L* reminds the counselor to ***lean* toward** the client. However, leaning too far forward and being too close may be frightening, whereas leaning too far away indicates disinterest. The counselor needs to find a middle distance that is comfortable for both parties. The *E* represents ***eye contact***. Good eye contact with most clients is a sign that the counselor is attuned to the client. For other clients, less eye contact (or even no eye contact) is appropriate. The *R* is a reminder to the counselor to ***relax***. A counselor needs to be comfortable.

Okun and Kantrowitz (2008) list supportive verbal and nonverbal behavioral aids that counselors often display throughout counseling. Among the supportive verbal responses are using understandable words, summarizing, being nonjudgmental and respectful, and occasionally using humor to reduce tension. Among the nonverbal responses are such behaviors as occasionally smiling, talking at a moderate rate, and using occasional hand gestures.

One of the last nonverbal behaviors on Okun and Kantrowitz's list, occasional **touching**, is politically sensitive and somewhat controversial. Although Willison and Masson (1986), in agreement with Okun and Kantrowitz, point out that human touch may be therapeutic in counseling, Alyn (1988) emphasizes that "the wide range of individual motivations for, interpretations of, and responses to touch make it an extremely unclear and possibly a dangerous means of communication in therapy" (p. 433). As a general counseling principle, Young (2009) suggests that touch should be appropriately employed, applied briefly and sparingly, and used to communicate concern. Applying the "**Touch Test**," which simply asks, "Would you do this with a stranger?" is one way to implement Young's suggestions (Del Prete, 1998, p. 63). Thus, counselors who use touch in their work should do so cautiously and with the understanding that what they are doing can have adverse effects. This same critical scrutiny is suggested when using any verbal or nonverbal technique.

Nonhelpful Interview Behavior

When building a relationship, counselors must also realize what they should not do. Otherwise, nonhelpful behaviors may be included in their counseling repertoire. Welfel and Patterson (2005) list **four major action**s that usually **block counselor–client communication** and should be generally avoided: advice giving, lecturing, excessive questioning, and storytelling by the counselor.

Advice giving is the most controversial of these four behaviors. Knowles (1979) found that 70% to 90% of all responses from volunteer helpers on a crisis line consisted of giving advice. When a counselor gives advice, especially in the first session, it may in effect deny a client the chance to work through personal thoughts and feelings about a subject and ultimately curtail his or her ability to make difficult decisions. A response meant to be helpful ends up being hurtful by disempowering the client. For example, if a client is advised to break off a relationship he or she is ambivalent about, the client is denied the opportunity to become aware and work through the thoughts and feelings that initially led to the ambivalence.

Sack (1985) suggests that advice giving need not always be destructive. He notes that there are emergency situations (as in crisis counseling) when, for the client's immediate welfare and safety, some direct action must be taken, which includes giving advice. He cautions counselors, however, to listen carefully to make sure the client is really asking for advice or simply being reflective through self-questions. There is a big difference between "What should I do?" and "I wonder what I should do." In addition, Sack advocates the responses developed by Carkhuff (1969) as ways in which counselors can answer direct requests for advice. In this model, counselors respond using one of seven approaches: respect, empathy, genuineness, concreteness, self-disclosure, confrontation, and immediacy. Sack (1985) concludes that counselors must examine their roles in counseling to "free themselves of the limitations and pitfalls of giving advice and move toward employing a variety of responses that can more appropriately address their clients' needs" (p. 131).

Lecturing, or preaching, is really a disguised form of advice giving (Welfel & Patterson, 2005). It sets up a power struggle between the counselor and client that neither individual can win. For example, if a sexually active girl is told "Don't get involved with boys anymore," she may do just the opposite to assert her independence. In such a case, both the counselor and client fail in their desire to change behaviors. Counselors are probably lecturing when they say more than three consecutive sentences in a row to their clients. Instead of lecturing, counselors can be effective by following the client's lead (Evans, Hearn, Uhlemann, & Ivey, 2011).

PERSONAL REFLECTION

When have you found advice helpful? When have you found it harmful? What were the results of each?

Excessive questioning is a common mistake of many counselors. Verbal interaction with clients needs to include statements, observations, and encouragers as well as questions. When excessive questioning is used, the client feels as though he or she is being interrogated rather than counseled. The client has little chance to take the initiative and may become guarded. Children may especially respond in this way or make a game out of answering a question, waiting for the next one, answering it, waiting, and so on (Erdman & Lampe, 1996). Counseling relationships are more productive when counselors avoid asking more than two questions in a row and keep their questions open rather than closed.

Storytelling by the counselor is the final nonhelpful behavior. There are a few prominent professionals who can use stories to benefit clients. Milton Erickson, a legendary pioneer in family counseling, was one. His stories were always metaphorically tailored to his clients' situations. They were beneficial because they directed clients to think about their own situations in light of the stories he told. Most counselors, however, should stay away from storytelling because the story usually focuses attention on the counselor instead of the client and distracts from problem solving.

Okun and Kantrowitz (2008) list other nonhelpful verbal and nonverbal behaviors. Some of these behaviors, such as yawning or acting rushed, clearly show the counselor's disinterest. Others, such as interrupting, blaming, and directing, are dismissive or disempowering, which is just the opposite of what counseling should be.,

EXPLORATION AND THE IDENTIFICATION OF GOALS

In the final part of building a counseling relationship, the counselor helps the client explore specific areas and begin to identify goals that the client wants to achieve. Hill (2009) emphasizes that establishing goals is crucial in providing direction at any stage of counseling. Egan (2010) observes that exploring and ultimately identifying goals often occur when a client is given the opportunity to talk about situations or to tell personal stories. The counselor reinforces the client's focus on self by providing structure, actively listening (hearing both content and feelings), and helping identify and clarify goals.

Rule (1982) states that goals "are the energizing fabric of daily living" but are often elusive (p. 195). He describes some goals as unfocused, unrealistic, and uncoordinated. *Unfocused goals* are not identified, too broad, or not prioritized. Sometimes counselors and clients may leave unfocused goals alone because the time and expense of chasing them is not as productive as changing unwanted behaviors. In most cases, however, it is helpful to identify a client's goals, put them into a workable form, and decide which goals to pursue first.

Unrealistic goals, as defined by either counselor or client, include happiness, perfection, progress, being number one, and self-actualization. They have merit but are not easily obtained or sustained. For example, the client who has worked hard and is happy about being promoted will soon have to settle into the duties of the new job and the reality of future job progress. Unrealistic goals may best be dealt with by putting them into the context of broader life goals. Then the counselor may encourage the client to devise exploratory and homework strategies for dealing with them.

Uncoordinated goals, according to Rule (1982), are generally divided "into two groups: those probably really uncoordinated and those seemingly uncoordinated" (p. 196). Goals in the first group may be incompatible with one another or with the personality of the client. A person who seeks counseling but really does not wish to work on changing exemplifies an individual with incompatible goals. These clients are often labeled resistant. Into the second group, Rule places the goals of clients who appear to have uncoordinated goals but really do not. These individuals may be afraid to take personal responsibility and engage any helper in a "yes, but . . ." dialogue.

Dyer and Vriend (1977) emphasize **seven specific criteria for judging effective goals in counseling**:

1. *Goals are mutually agreed on by client and counselor.*   Without mutuality, neither party will invest much energy in working on the goals.
2. *Goals are specific.*   If goals are too broad, they will never be met.
3. *Goals are relevant to self-defeating behavior.*   There are many possible goals for clients to work on, but only those that are relevant to changing self-defeating action should be pursued.
4. *Goals are achievement and success oriented.*   Counseling goals need to be realistic and have both intrinsic and extrinsic payoffs for clients.
5. *Goals are quantifiable and measurable.*   It is important that both client and counselor know when goals are achieved. When goals are defined quantitatively, achievement is most easily recognized.
6. *Goals are behavioral and observable.*   This criterion relates to the previous one: An effective goal is one that can be seen when achieved.
7. *Goals are understandable and can be restated clearly.*   It is vital that client and counselor communicate clearly about goals. One way to assess how well this process is achieved is through restating goals in one's own words.

CASE EXAMPLE

Crossing the Goal Line

Benjamin has lived with an overlay of depression all his life. Now that he is in college, he has decided to do something about it. When he visited the College Counseling Center, his counselor, LaShonda, suggested that he set goals on how he was going to handle his depression. Benjamin listed the following:

1. Exercise every morning before class.
2. Eat healthy food.
3. Get engaged in at least one campus activity, such as playing an intramural sport.
4. Keep a journal of my thoughts and feelings and when they come.
5. Come to counseling for a month.

What do you think of Benjamin's goals? Are they realistic? What else do you think he should do (if anything)?

Egan (2010) cautions that in the exploratory and goal-setting stage of counseling, several problems may inhibit the building of a solid counselor–client relationship. The most notable include moving too fast, moving too slow, fear of intensity, client rambling, and excessive time and energy devoted to probing the past. Counselors who are forewarned about such potential problems are in a much better position to address them effectively. It is vital that counselors work with clients to build a mutually satisfying relationship from the start. When this process occurs, a more active working stage of counseling begins.

MyCounselingLab™

Go to Topic 1: *Assessment and Diagnosis* in the MyCounselingLab™ site (www .MyCounselingLab.com) for *Counseling: A Comprehensive Profession,* Seventh Edition, where you can:

- Find learning outcomes for *Assessment and Diagnosis* along with the national standards that connect to these outcomes.
- Complete Assignments and Activities that can help you more deeply understand the chapter content.
- Apply and practice your understanding of the core skills identified in the chapter with the Building Counseling Skills unit.
- Prepare yourself for professional certification with a Practice for Certification quiz.
- Connect to videos through the Video and Resource Library.

Summary and Conclusion

Building a relationship, the first stage in counseling, is a continuous process. It begins by having the counselor win the battle for structure and the client win the battle for initiative. In such situations, both parties are winners. The client wins by becoming more informed about the nature of counseling and learning what to expect. The counselor wins by creating an atmosphere in which the client is comfortable about sharing thoughts and feelings.

Counseling may occur in any setting, but some circumstances are more likely than others to promote its development. Counselors need to be aware of the physical setting in which the counseling takes place. Clients may adjust to any room, but certain qualities about an environment, such as the seating arrangement, make counseling more conducive. Other, less apparent qualities also affect the building of a relationship. For example, the perception that clients and counselors have about one another is important. Attractive clients who are young, verbal, intelligent, and social may be treated in a more

positive way than clients who are older, less intelligent, and seemingly unmotivated. Clients are likely to work best with counselors they perceive as trustworthy, attractive, and knowledgeable.

Regardless of the external circumstances and the initial perceptions, a counselor who attends to the verbal and nonverbal expressions of a client is more likely to establish rapport. The counselor's conveying of empathy and the use of other helpful microskills such as the use of the SOLER model may further enhance the relationship. When counselors are attuned to their own values and feelings, they are able to become even more effective. The initial counseling interview can be counselor or client initiated and can center on the gathering of information or on relationship dynamics. In any situation, it is vital for the counselor to explore with the client the reasons for the possibilities of counseling. Such disclosures can encourage clients to define goals and facilitate the setting of a mutually agreed-on agenda in counseling. When this step is accomplished, the work of reaching goals begins.

7 Working in a Counseling Relationship

Chapter Overview

From this chapter you will learn about

- The Johari Window of a client
- Counselor skills in the understanding and action phases of counseling, such as empathy, leading, immediacy, and confrontation
- Transference and countertransference
- The real relationship

As you read consider

- How you conceptualize change occurring
- Your ability to smoothly incorporate new skills into your interpersonal relationships
- When you have transferred thoughts and feelings onto someone else
- When you have had a genuine and deep relationship with someone and how it felt

I listen and you tell me how
    the feelings rage and toss within you.
A mother died, a child deserted,
    and you, that child, have not forgotten
        what it is to be alone.
I nod my head, your words continue
    rich in anger from early memories,
Feelings that you tap with care
    after years of shaky storage.
As you drink their bitter flavor,
    which you declined to taste at seven,
I mentally wince while watching you
    open your life to the dark overflow
        of pain that has grown strong with age.

From "Memory Traces," by S. T. Gladding, 1977, *North Carolina Personnel and Guidance Journal, 6*, p. 50. © S. T. Gladding.

MyCounselingLab™

The successful outcome of any counseling effort depends on a working alliance between counselor and client (Kottler, Sexton, & Whiston, 1994; Okun & Kantrowitz, 2008). A ***working alliance*** is a conscious and purposeful aspect of a counseling relationship and includes affective or bonding elements such as "liking, respect, and trust," along with a collaborative spirit between counselor and client in "establishing tasks and goals of treatment" (Fitzpatrick & Irannejad, 2008, p. 438). Building this relationship is a developmental process that involves exploring the situation that has motivated the client to seek help. "Research with adults has shown that to establish effective alliances, counselors need to constantly assess clients' commitment and deal with obstacles that impinge on this commitment" (p. 438). Establishing a working alliance with adolescents is more difficult yet because many of them do not seek counseling on a voluntary basis and do not think they need therapeutic services.

Regardless of age or stage in life, clients arrive in counseling with certain areas of their lives open or understood and other areas hidden or suppressed. The **Johari window**, shown in Figure 7.1, is a conceptual device used to represent the way in which most individuals enter the counseling relationship (Luft, 1970). This simple diagram depicts what clients know about themselves and what others know about them. Usually, clients have limited or distorted information about how others see them, and they have substantial hidden areas of themselves that they avoid exposing. They live a rather constricted life that is freely known to themselves and others but is not fulfilling, and they are often unaware (as are others) of their potential.

	Known to Self	Not Known to Self
Known to Others	I. Area of Free Activity	III. Blind Area—Blind to self, seen by others
Not Known to Others	II. Avoided or Hidden Area—Self hidden from others	IV. Area of Unknown Activity

FIGURE 7.1   The Johari window of the client   *Sources: From Of Human Interaction* (p. 13), by J. Luft, Palo Alto, CA: National Press Books, 1969; and *Group Processes: An Introduction to Group Dynamics* (3rd ed.), by J. Luft, Mountain View, CA: Mayfield Publishing Co., 1984. Copyright 1969 by Joseph Luft. Reprinted by permission of the author.

Successful counseling helps clients relax enough to tell their story and discover information located in the blind areas of themselves, two regions about which they have been unaware (Quadrants III & IV). Once they obtain a better understanding of these areas (either verbally or nonverbally), informed clients can decide how to proceed in expanding what is known to themselves and to others (Quadrant I). If they are successful in their work, they extend the dimensions of this area of free activity as represented in the Johari window while shrinking the dimensions of the more restrictive areas. Quadrant II (known to self but hidden from others) may expand a lot or a little depending on the sensitivity of the information within it (Figure 7.2).

It may appear that the counseling process described in this book and represented in the Johari window is linear, but such is not the case (Moursund & Kenny, 2002). Counseling is multifaceted, with various factors impacting each other continuously. Therefore, procedures overlap considerably, and progress is uneven (Egan, 2010). Because of the unevenness of counseling and times of regression, some techniques used in the involvement and exploration phases are also employed in the understanding and action phases. Yet as counseling progresses, new and different skills are regularly incorporated. Thus, counseling requires counselors to monitor in a sensitive but constant manner the status of the relationship and the client's development. Counselors must be alert to new needs and demands as they develop.

In this chapter, we explore the skills commonly associated with the understanding and action phases of counseling. These phases involve a number of counselor skills, including changing perceptions, leading, multifocused responding, accurate empathy, self-disclosure, immediacy, confrontation, contracting, and rehearsal. In addition, clients and counselors must work through any transference or countertransference issues that arise out of earlier situations or present circumstances (Gelso & Carter, 1985). There is, of course, a constant need to uncover real aspects of the counselor–client relationship (i.e., those not overlaid with defense mechanisms such as denial or projection) and use them therapeutically.

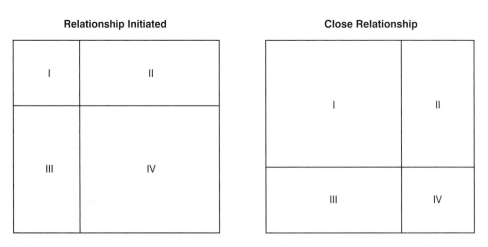

Relationship Initiated   **Close Relationship**

FIGURE 7.2 Johari window as modified through the relationship with the counselor   *Source: From Of Human Interaction* (p. 14), by J. Luft, Palo Alto, CA: National Press Books, 1969; and *Group Processes: An Introduction to Group Dynamics* (3rd ed.), by J. Luft, Mountain View, CA: Mayfield Publishing Co., 1984. Copyright 1969 by Joseph Luft. Reprinted by permission of the author.

COUNSELOR SKILLS IN THE UNDERSTANDING AND ACTION PHASES

Counselors must be active in helping clients change. "Counselors constantly and collaboratively negotiate with clients: goals, particular question and answer sequences, agreements on interventions, intended reformulations of client meaning, or client homework" (Strong & Zeman, 2010, p. 338). After rapport has been established, counselors need to employ skills that result in clients' viewing their lives differently and thinking, feeling, and behaving accordingly.

Changing Perceptions

Clients often come to counseling as a last resort, when they perceive that the situation is not only serious but hopeless (Watzlawick, 1983). People think their perceptions and interpretations are accurate. When they communicate their view of reality to others, it is commonly accepted as factual (Cavanagh & Levitov, 2002). This phenomenon, called *functional fixity*, means seeing things in only one way or from one perspective or being fixated on the idea that this particular situation or attribute is the issue (Cormier, Nurius, & Osborn, 2009).

For example, a middle-aged man is concerned about taking care of his elderly mother. He realizes that personal attention to this task will take him away from his family and put a strain on them and him. Furthermore, he is aware that his energy will be drained from his business and he might not receive the promotion he wants. He is torn between caring for two families and sees his situation as an either–or problem. Appropriate and realistic counseling objectives would include finding community and family resources the man could use to help take care of his mother, his family, and himself. In the process, the man would discover what he needs to do to relieve himself of sole responsibility in this case and uncover concrete ways he can increase his work efficiency but not his stress. The focus on taking care of self and others, as well as using community and family resources, gives the man a different perspective about his situation and may help him deal with it in a healthy manner.

Counselors can help clients change distorted or unrealistic objectives by offering them the opportunity to explore thoughts and desires within a safe, accepting, and nonjudgmental environment. Goals are refined or altered using cognitive, behavioral, or cognitive–behavioral strategies, such as

- redefining the problem,
- altering behavior in certain situations, or
- perceiving the problem in a more manageable way and acting accordingly (Okun & Kantrowitz, 2008).

By paying attention to both **verbal** (i.e., language) and **nonverbal** (i.e., behaviors) **metaphors**, counselors can help clients become more aware of both where they are and where they wish to be (Lyddon, Clay, & Sparks, 2001). They can also enhance counselor–client relationships and intervention strategies as well as improve their own competence in moving beyond jargon and fixed interpretations that may be less than accurate (Robert & Kelly, 2010; Sommer, Ward, & Scofield, 2010). Basically, metaphors (including similes) provide insight for clients and counselors and ways of conceptualizing the counseling process in a productive way, such as "life is a journey" (i.e., it takes time and effort) or "counseling is like baking a cake" (i.e., it requires a blending of the right ingredients).

Perceptions commonly change through the process of *reframing*, a technique that offers the client another probable and positive viewpoint or perspective on a situation. Such a changed point of view gives a client a different way of responding (Young, 2009). Effective counselors consistently reframe life experiences for both themselves and their clients. For instance, a person's rude behavior may be explained as the result of pressure from trying to complete a task quickly rather than dislike for the rudely treated person.

Reframing is used in almost all forms of counseling. For example, in family counseling reframing helps families change their focus from viewing one member of the family as the source of all their problems (i.e., the *scapegoat*) to seeing the whole family as responsible. In employment counseling, Amundson (1996) has developed 12 reframing strategies that deal with looking back, looking at the present, and looking ahead to help clients widen their perspective of themselves and the labor market. In cases concerning individuals, Cormier et al. (2009) point out that reframing can reduce resistance and mobilize the client's energy to do something differently by changing his or her perception of the problem. In short, reframing helps clients become more aware of situational factors associated with behavior. It shifts the focus from a simplistic attribution of traits, such as "I'm worthless," to a more complex and accurate view, such as "I have some days when things don't go very well and I put myself down" (Ellis, 1971). Through reframing, clients see themselves and their environments with greater accuracy and insight.

PERSONAL REFLECTION

When our third child was born, my wife, Claire, looked up at me and said, "The honeymoon is not over. There are just more people on it!"

When have you or someone close to you reframed a situation or circumstance? How did it influence your perception of the situation or circumstance?

Leading

Changing client perceptions requires a high degree of persuasive skill and some direction from the counselor. Such input is known as *leading*. The term was coined by Francis Robinson (1950) to describe certain deliberate behaviors counselors engage in for the benefit of their clients. Leads vary in length, and some are more appropriate at one stage of counseling than another. Robinson used the analogy of a football quarterback and receiver to describe a lead. A good quarterback anticipates where the receiver will be on the field and throws the ball to that spot. (By the way, Robinson worked at Ohio State, a university known for its football and counseling tradition.)

The same kind of analogy of quarterbacks and receivers is true for counselors and clients. Counselors anticipate where their clients are and where they are likely to go. Counselors then respond accordingly. If there is misjudgment and the lead is either too far ahead (i.e., too persuasive or direct) or not far enough (too uninvolved and nondirect), the counseling relationship suffers.

Welfel and Patterson (2005) list a number of leads that counselors can use with their clients (Figure 7.3). Some, such as silence, acceptance, and paraphrasing, are most appropriate at the beginning of the counseling process. Others, such as persuasion, are directive and more appropriate in the understanding and action phases.

The type of lead counselors use is determined in part by the theoretical approach they embrace and the current phase of counseling. *Minimal leads* (sometimes referred to as *minimal encouragers*) such as "hmmm," "yes," or "I hear you" are best used in the building phase of a relationship because they are low risk (Young, 2009). *Maximum leads*, however, such as confrontation, are more challenging and should be employed only after a solid relationship has been established.

Least leading response

Silence	When the counselor makes no verbal response at all, the client will ordinarily feel some pressure to continue and will choose how to continue with minimum input from the counselor.
Acceptance	The counselor simply acknowledges the client's previous statement with a response such as "yes" or "uhuh." The client is verbally encouraged to continue, but without content stimulus from the counselor.
Restatement (paraphrase)	The counselor restates the client's verbalization, including both content and affect, using nearly the same wording. The client is prompted to reexamine what has been said.
Clarification	The counselor states the meaning of the client's statement in his or her own words, seeking to clarify the client's meaning. Sometimes elements of several of the client's statements are brought into a single response. The counselor's ability to perceive accurately and communicate correctly is important, and the client must test the "fit" of the counselor's lead.
Approval (affirmation)	The counselor affirms the correctness of information or encourages the client's efforts at self-determination: "That's good new information," or "You seem to be gaining more control." The client may follow up with further exploration as he or she sees fit.
General leads	The counselor directs the client to talk more about a specific subject with statements such as "Tell me what you mean," or "Please say some more about that." The client is expected to follow the counselor's suggestion.
Interpretation	The counselor uses psychodiagnostic principles to suggest sources of the client's stress or explanations for the client's motivation and behavior. The counselor's statements are presented as hypotheses, and the client is confronted with potentially new ways of seeing self.
Rejection (persuasion)	The counselor tries to reverse the client's behavior or perceptions by actively advising different behavior or suggesting different interpretations of life events than those presented by the client.
Reassurance	The counselor states that, in his or her *judgment,* the client's concern is not unusual and that people with similar problems have succeeded in overcoming them. The client may feel that the reassurance is supportive but may also feel that his or her problem is discounted by the counselor as unimportant.
Introducing new information or a new idea	The counselor moves away from the client's last statement and prompts the client to consider new material.

Most leading response

FIGURE 7.3   Continuum of leads   *Source:* From *The Counseling Process* (3rd ed., pp. 126–127), by L. E. Patterson and S. Eisenberg, 1983, Boston: Houghton Mifflin. Copyright 1983 by Houghton Mifflin. Reprinted by permission of S. Eisenberg. All rights reserved.

Multifocused Responding

People have preferences for the way they process information through their senses. Counselors can enhance their effectiveness by remembering that individuals receive input from their worlds differently and that preferred styles influence perceptions and behaviors. Some clients experience the world visually: They see what is happening. Others are primarily auditory: They hear the world around them. Still others are kinesthetically oriented: They feel situations as though physically in touch with them. (Two of my three children are olfactory—they judge much of their environment through smell, which is especially important in restaurants.) Regardless, Ivey, Ivey, and Zalaquett (2010) and Lazarus (2008) think that tuning into clients' major modes of perceiving and learning is crucial to bringing about change. Because many clients have multiple ways of knowing the world, counselors should vary their responses and incorporate words that reflect an understanding of clients' worlds. For example, the counselor might say to a multimodal sensory person, "I see your point and hear your concern. I feel that you are really upset."

The importance of responding in a client's own language can be powerful, too. Counselors need to distinguish between the predominantly affective, behavioral, and cognitive nature of speech. *Affective responses* focus on a client's feelings, *behavioral responses* focus on actions, and *cognitive responses* focus on thought. Thus, counselors working with affectively oriented individuals select words accordingly. Table 7.1 shows some of the most common of these words, as identified by Carkhuff and Anthony (1979).

Accurate Empathy

There is near-universal agreement among practitioners and theorists that the use of empathy is one of the most vital elements in counseling, one that transcends counseling stages (Fiedler, 1950; Gladstein, 1983; Hackney, 1978; Rogers, 1975; Truax & Mitchell, 1971). In Chapter 6, two types of empathy were briefly noted. The basic type is called *primary empathy;* the second level is known as *advanced empathy* (Carkhuff, 1969). *Accurate empathy* on both levels is achieved when counselors see clients' worlds from the clients' point of view and are able to communicate this understanding back (Egan, 2010). Two factors that make empathy possible are (a) realizing that "an infinite number of feelings" does not exist and (b) having a personal security so that "you can let yourself go into the world of this other person and still know that you can return to your own world. Everything you are feeling is 'as if'" (Rogers, 1987, pp. 45–46).

Primary empathy, when it is accurate, involves communicating a basic understanding of what the client is feeling and the experiences and behaviors underlying these feelings. It helps establish the counseling relationship, gather data, and clarify problems. For example, a client might say, "I'm really feeling like I can't do anything for myself." The counselor replies, "You're feeling helpless."

Advanced empathy, when it is accurate, reflects not only what clients state overtly but also what they imply or state incompletely. For example, a counselor notes that a client says: ". . . and I hope everything will work out" while looking off into space. The counselor responds, "For if it doesn't, I'm not sure what I will do next."

Empathy involves three elements: perceptiveness, know-how, and assertiveness (Egan, 2010). Several levels of responses reflect different aspects of counselor empathy. A scale formulated by Carkhuff (1969), called *Empathic Understanding in Interpersonal Process*, is a

TABLE 7.1 Commonly Used Affect Words

Level of Intensity	Category of Feeling						
	Happiness	Sadness	Fear	Uncertainty	Anger	Strength, Potency	Weakness, Inadequacy
Strong	Excited	Despairing	Panicked	Bewildered	Outraged	Powerful	Ashamed
	Thrilled	Hopeless	Terrified	Disoriented	Hostile	Authoritative	Powerless
	Delighted	Depressed	Afraid	Mistrustful	Furious	Forceful	Vulnerable
	Overjoyed	Crushed	Frightened	Confused	Angry	Potent	Cowardly
	Ecstatic	Miserable	Scared		Harsh		Exhausted
	Elated	Abandoned	Overwhelmed		Hateful		Impotent
	Jubilant	Defeated			Mean		
		Desolate			Vindictive		
Moderate	"Up"	Dejected	Worried	Doubtful	Aggravated	Tough	Embarrassed
	Good	Dismayed	Shaky	Mixed up	Irritated	Important	Useless
	Happy	Disillusioned	Tense	Insecure	Offended	Confident	Demoralized
	Optimistic	Lonely	Anxious	Skeptical	Mad	Fearless	Helpless
	Cheerful	Bad	Threatened	Puzzled	Frustrated	Energetic	Wom out
	Enthusiastic	Unhappy	Agitated		Resentful	Brave	Inept
	Joyful	Pessimistic			"Sore"	Courageous	Incapable
	"Turned on"	Sad			Upset	Daring	Incompetent
		Hurt			Impatient	Assured	Inadequate
		Lost			Obstinate	Adequate	Shaken
					Self-confident		
					Skillful		
Weak	Pleased	"Down"	Jittery	Unsure	Perturbed	Determined	Frail
	Glad	Discouraged	Jumpy	Surprised	Annoyed	Firm	Meek
	Content	Disappointed	Nervous	Uncertain	Grouchy	Able	Unable
	Relaxed	"Blue"	Uncomfortable	Undecided	Hassled	Strong	Weak
	Satisfied	Alone	Uptight	Bothered	Bothered		
	Calm	Left out	Uneasy		Disagreeable		
			Defensive				
			Apprehensive				
			Hesitant				
			Edgy				

Source: Reprinted from *The Skills of Helping* written by Carkhuff, R. R. & Anthony, W. A., copyright 1979. Reprinted by permission of the publisher, HRD Press, Amherst Road, Amherst, MA, (413) 253–3488.

measure of these levels. Each of the five levels either adds to or subtracts from the meaning and feeling tone of a client's statement.

1. The verbal and behavioral expressions of the counselor either do not attend to or detract significantly from the verbal and behavioral expressions of the client.
2. Although the counselor responds to the expressed feelings of the client, he or she does so in a way that subtracts noticeable affect from the communications of the client.
3. The expressions of the counselor in response to the expressions of the client are essentially interchangeable.

4.   The responses of the counselor add noticeably to the expressions of the client in a way that expresses feelings a level deeper than the client was able to express.
5.   The counselor's responses add significantly to the feeling and meaning of the expressions of the client in a way that accurately expresses feeling levels below what the client is able to express.

Responses at the first two levels are not considered empathic; in fact, they inhibit the creation of an empathic environment. For example, if a client reveals that she is heartbroken over the loss of a lover, a counselor operating on either of the first two levels might reply, "Well, you want your former love to be happy, don't you?" Such a response misses the pain that the client is feeling.

At level 3 on the Carkhuff scale, a counselor's response is rated as "interchangeable" with that of a client. Such a response may well come in the form of a paraphrase such as follows:

CLIENT: "I am really feeling anxious."
COUNSELOR: "You are really feeling nervous."

On levels 4 and 5, a counselor either "adds noticeably" or "adds significantly" to what a client has said. This ability to go beyond what clients say distinguishes counseling from conversation or other less helpful forms of behavior (Carkhuff, 1972). The following interchange is an example of a higher level empathetic response:

CLIENT: I have been running around from activity to activity until I am so tired I feel like I could drop.
COUNSELOR: Your life has been a merry-go-round of activity, and you'd like to slow it down before you collapse. You'd like to be more in charge of your own life.

Means (1973) elaborates on levels 4 and 5 to show how counselors can add noticeably and significantly to their clients' perceptions of an emotional experience, an environmental stimulus, a behavior pattern, a self-evaluation, a self-expectation, and beliefs about self. Clients' statements are extremely varied, and counselors must therefore be flexible in responding to them (Hackney, 1978). Whether a counselor's response is empathic is determined by the reaction of clients (Turock, 1978). Regardless, in the understanding and action phases of counseling, it is important that counselors integrate the two levels of empathy they use in responding to clients seeking help.

CASE EXAMPLE

Edwina Attempts Empathy

Edwina still considered herself a novice, although she had worked as a counselor for 2 years. She seemed to have an especially hard time conveying empathy on any level.

One day a client, Andre, who was agonizing over the death of a recent relationship, made an appointment with Edwina. In the session he became tearful.

"I just feel like a hollow tree," he said. "The shell of the tree is standing but inside there is an emptiness. The outside of me does not reveal my interior feeling."

Edwina replied: "It's as if you were a robot. On the outside you look fine, but inside you lack all the necessary elements of life."

What do you think of Edwina's response? Is it empathetic? If so, on what level? If not, why not? What might you say to Andre?

Self-Disclosure

Self-disclosure is a complex, multifaceted phenomenon that has generated more than 200 studies (Watkins, 1990a). It may be succinctly defined as "a conscious, intentional technique in which clinicians share information about their lives outside the counseling relationship" (Simone, McCarthy, & Skay, 1998, p. 174). Sidney Jourard (1958, 1964) did the original work in this area. For him, self-disclosure referred to making oneself known to another person by revealing personal information. Jourard discovered that self-disclosure helped establish trust and facilitated the counseling relationship. He labeled reciprocal self-disclosure the *dyadic effect* (Jourard, 1968).

Client self-disclosure is necessary for successful counseling to occur. Yet it is not always necessary for counselors to be self-disclosing. "Each counselor-client relationship must be evaluated individually in regard to disclosure," and when it occurs, care must be taken to match disclosure "to the client's needs" (Hendrick, 1988, p. 423).

Clients are more likely to trust counselors who disclose personal information (up to a point) and are prone to make reciprocal disclosures (Curtis, 1981; Kottler et al., 1994). Adolescents especially seem to be more comfortable with counselors who are "fairly unguarded and personally available" (Simone et al., 1998, p. 174). Counselors employ self-disclosure on a formal basis at the initial interview by giving clients written statements about the counselor and the counseling process (the professional disclosure statement illustrated in Figure 6.1). They also use self-disclosure spontaneously in counseling sessions to reveal pertinent personal facts to their clients, especially during the understanding and action phases. Spontaneous self-disclosure is important in facilitating client movement (Doster & Nesbitt, 1979; Watkins, 1990a).

According to Egan (2010), counselor self-disclosure serves two principal functions: modeling and developing a new perspective. Clients learn to be more open by observing counselors who are open. Counselor self-disclosure can help clients see that counselors are not free of problems or devoid of feelings (Cormier & Hackney, 2012). Thus, while hearing about select aspects of counselors' personal lives, clients may examine aspects of their own lives, such as stubbornness or fear, and realize that some difficulties or experiences are universal and manageable. Egan (2010) stresses that **counselor self-disclosure**

- **should be brief and focused**,
- **should not add to the clients' problems**, and
- **should not be used frequently**.

The process is not linear, and more self-disclosure is not necessarily better. Before self-disclosing, counselors should ask themselves such questions as "Have I thought through why I am disclosing?" "Are there other more effective and less risky ways to reach the same goal?" and "Is my timing right?" (Simone et al., 1998, pp. 181–182).

Kline (1986) observes that clients perceive self-disclosure as risky and may be hesitant to take such a risk. *Hesitancy* may take the form of refusing to discuss issues, changing the subject, being silent, and talking excessively. Counselors can help clients overcome these fears by not only modeling and inviting self-disclosure but also exploring negative feelings that clients have about the counseling process, contracting with clients to talk about a certain subject area, and confronting clients with the avoidance of a specific issue.

CASE EXAMPLE

Della Discloses

Della's client, Candace, was reluctant to talk. She had been mandated to see Della because she was acting out sexually, and her mother could not handle her without some help. Della had tried everything she knew to invite Candace to talk. Finally, she self-disclosed by saying to Candace: "When I was 18, I could not stand my mother or any older adult. I thought they were all full of rules that were irrelevant to my life and what I wanted to do. I wonder if you might be feeling that way, too?"

Do you believe Della's self-disclosure to Candace might be helpful? Why or why not?

Immediacy

"Immediacy . . . is one of the most important skills" in counseling (Wheeler & D'Andrea, 2004, p. 117). It "focuses on the here and now and the therapeutic relationship" from the perspective of how both the client and the counselor feel (p. 117). At its core, *immediacy* involves a counselor's and a client's understanding and communicating at the moment what is going on between them in the helping relationship, particularly feelings, impressions, and expectations (Kasper, Hill, & Kivlighan, 2008; Turock, 1980).

There are basically **three kinds of immediacy**:

1. **Overall relationship** immediacy—"How are you and I doing?"
2. "Immediacy that **focuses on some particular event in a session**—'What's going on between you and me right now?'"
3. **Self-involving statements** (i.e., present-tense, personal responses to a client that are sometimes challenging)—"I like the way you took charge of your life in that situation" (Egan, 2010, pp. 180–181).

Egan (2010) believes that immediacy is difficult and demanding. It requires more courage or assertiveness than almost any other interpersonal communication skill.

Turock (1980) lists three fears many counselors have about immediacy. First, they may be afraid that clients will misinterpret their messages. Immediacy requires counselors to make a tentative guess or interpretation of what their clients are thinking or feeling, and a wrong guess can cause counselors to lose credibility with their clients.

Second, immediacy may produce an unexpected outcome. Many counseling skills, such as reflection, have predictable outcomes; immediacy does not. Its use may break down a familiar pattern between counselors and clients. In the process, relationships may suffer.

Third, immediacy may influence clients' decisions to terminate counseling sessions because they can no longer control or manipulate relationships. Some clients play games, such as "ain't it awful," and expect their counselors to respond accordingly (Berne, 1964). When clients receive an unexpected payoff, they may decide not to stay in the relationship. Egan (2010) states that immediacy is best used in the following situations:

- In a directionless relationship
- Where there is tension
- Where there is a question of trust
- When there is considerable social distance between counselor and client, such as in diversity
- Where there is client dependency
- Where there is counterdependency
- When there is an attraction between counselor and client

Hope

Clients do best in counseling when hope is engendered into the process. **Hope** is the feeling that something desirable, such as the achievement of a goal, is possible. Hope has multiple benefits, including increasing a client's motivation to work on a problem. It has been linked to academic success, athletic performance, psychological adjustment, and physical health (Pedrotti, Edwards, & Lopez, 2008). One way of conceptualizing hope is to realize that if it is realistic, it is an asset in the counseling process. Another way to think about hope is that if it is unrealistic, it is a liability.

Humor

Humor involves giving an incongruent or unexpected response to a question or situation to the amusement of those involved. It makes people laugh, and healthy humor requires both sensitivity and timing on the part of the counselor. Humor in counseling should never be aimed at demeaning anyone (Gladding, 1995). Instead, it should be used to build bridges between counselors and clients. If used properly, it is "a clinical tool that has many therapeutic applications" (Ness, 1989, p. 35). Humor can circumvent clients' resistance, build rapport, dispel tension, help clients distance themselves from psychological pain, and aid in the increase of a client's self-efficacy (Goldin et al., 2006; Vereen, Butler, Williams, Darg, & Downing, 2006). "Ha-ha" often leads to an awareness of "ah-ha" and a clearer perception of a situation (i.e., insight) (Kottler, 1991). For instance, when a counselor is working with a client who is unsure whether he or she wants to be in counseling, the counselor might initiate the following exchange:

COUNSELOR: Joan, how many counselors does it take to change a lightbulb?

CLIENT: *(hesitantly)* I'm not sure.

COUNSELOR: Just one, but the lightbulb has got to really want to be changed.

CLIENT: *(smiling)* I guess I'm a lightbulb that's undecided.

COUNSELOR: It's OK to be undecided. We can work on that. Our sessions will probably be more fruitful, however, if you can turn on to what you'd like to see different in your life and what it is we could jointly work on. That way we can focus more clearly.

Overall, humor can contribute to creative thinking; promote attachment; help keep things in perspective; and make it easier to explore difficult, awkward, or nonsensical aspects of life (Bergman, 1985; Goldin et al., 2006; Nelson, 2008; Piercy & Lobsenz, 1994). However, "counselors must remember that to use humor effectively they must understand what is humorous and under what circumstances it is humorous" (Erdman & Lampe, 1996, p. 376). Therefore, they need to realize before attempting humor in a counseling situation that both clients and counselors must be comfortable with it as an activity, that there should be a purpose to it, that trust and respect must have been established before humor is used, and that humor should be tailored or customized to a particular client's specific cultural orientation and uniqueness (Maples et al., 2001). Counselors can use humor to challenge a client's beliefs, magnify irrational beliefs to absurdity, or even to make a paradoxical intervention (Goldin & Bordan, 1999). When handled right, humor can open up counselor–client relationships.

PERSONAL REFLECTION

I have a counselor friend who was completely different in almost every way from a client he saw. Instead of saying to the client something like "We really appear to be different," he lightheartedly said, "If I didn't know better, I would say you must be the other half of me since we never seem to agree or see things the same way." What do you think of that as a humorous response (on a scale from 1 to 10)? What might you say in such a situation that would be more humorous (unless you rated the response a 10)?

Confrontation

Confrontation, like immediacy, is often misunderstood. Uninformed counselors sometimes think confrontation involves an attack on clients, a kind of "in your face" approach that is berating. Instead, confrontation is invitational and a dialogue (Strong & Zeman, 2010). At its best, **confrontation** challenges a client to examine, modify, or control an aspect of behavior that is currently nonexistent or improperly used. Sometimes confrontation involves giving meta-communication feedback that is at variance with what the client wants or expects. This type of response may be inconsistent with a client's perception of self or circumstances (Wilcox-Matthew, Ottens, & Minor, 1997).

Confrontation can help "people see more clearly what is happening, what the consequences are, and how they can assume responsibility for taking action to change in ways that can lead to a more effective life and better and fairer relationships with others" (Tamminen & Smaby, 1981, p. 42). A good, responsible, caring, and appropriate confrontation produces growth and encourages an honest examination of self. Sometimes it may actually be detrimental to the client if the counselor fails to confront. Avoiding confrontation of the client's behavior is known as the **MUM effect** and results in the counselor's being less effective than he or she otherwise would be (Rosen & Tesser, 1970).

However, there are certain boundaries to confrontation (Leaman, 1978). The counselor needs to be sure that the relationship with the client is strong enough to sustain a confrontation. The counselor also must time a confrontation appropriately and remain true to the motives that have led to the act of confronting. It is more productive in the long run to confront a client's strengths than a client's weaknesses (Berenson & Mitchell, 1974). The counselor should challenge the client to use resources he or she is failing to employ.

Regardless of whether confrontation involves strengths or weaknesses, counselors use a "you said . . . but look" structure to implement the confrontation process (Cormier & Hackney, 2012). For example, in the first part of the confrontation, a counselor might say, "You said you wanted to get out more and meet people." In the second part, the counselor highlights the discrepancy or contradiction in the client's words and actions—for instance, "But you are now watching television 4 to 6 hours a night."

Contracting

There are two aspects of contracting: One focuses on the processes involved in reaching a goal; the other concentrates on the final outcome. In goal setting, the counselor operates from a theoretical base that directs his or her actions. The client learns to change ways of thinking, feeling, and behaving to obtain goals. It is natural for counselors and clients to engage in contractual behavior. Goodyear and Bradley (1980) point out that all interpersonal relationships are contractual, but some are more explicit than others are. Because the median number of counseling sessions may be as few as five to six, it is useful and time saving for counselors and clients to work on goals through a contract system. Such a system lets both parties participate in determining direction in counseling and evaluating change. It helps them be more specific (Brammer, Abrego, & Shostrom, 1993).

Other **advantages to using contracts in counseling** are as follows:

- First, a contract provides a written record of goals the counselor and client have agreed to pursue and the course of action to be taken.
- Second, the formal nature of a contract and its time limits may act as motivators for a client who tends to procrastinate.
- Third, if the contract is broken down into definable sections, a client may get a clear feeling that problems can be solved.
- Fourth, a contract puts the responsibility for any change on the client and thereby has the potential to empower the client and make him or her more responsive to the environment and more responsible for his or her behaviors.
- Finally, the contract system, by specifically outlining the number of sessions to be held, ensures that clients will return to counseling regularly (Thomas & Ezell, 1972).

There are several approaches to setting up contracts. Goodyear and Bradley (1980) offer recommendations for promoting maximum effectiveness of contracts:

- It is essential that counselors indicate to their clients that the purpose of counseling is to work. It is important to begin by asking the client, "What would you like to work on?" as opposed to "What would you like to talk about?"
- It is vital that the contract for counseling concern change in the client rather than a person not present at the sessions. The counselor acts as a consultant when the client wishes to examine the behavior of another person, such as a child who throws temper tantrums, but work of this type is limited.
- The counselor must insist on setting up contracts that avoid the inclusion of *client con words* such as *try* or *maybe*—or any **words that are not specific**. Such words usually result in the client's failing to achieve a goal.
- The counselor must be wary of client **goals that are directed toward pleasing others** and include words such as *should* or *must*. Such statements embody **externally driven**

goals. For instance, a client who sets an initial goal that includes the statement "I should please my spouse more" may do so only temporarily because the goal is not internally driven. To avoid this kind of contract goal, the counselor needs to ask what the client really wants.

• It is vital to define concretely what clients wish to achieve through counseling. There is a great deal of difference between clients who state that they wish to be happy and clients who explain that they want to lose 10 pounds or talk to at least three new people a day. The latter goals are more concrete, and both counselors and clients are usually aware when they are achieved.

• The counselor must insist that contracts focus on change. Clients may wish to understand why they do something, but insight alone rarely produces action. Therefore, counselors must emphasize contracts that promote change in a client's behaviors, thoughts, or feelings.

Another briefer way to think of what to include in a contract is to use the acronym *SAFE*, where the *S* stands for **specificity** (i.e., treatment goals), *A* for **awareness** (i.e., knowledge of procedures, goals, and side effects of counseling), *F* for **fairness** (i.e., the relationship is balanced and both client and counselor have enough information to work), and *E* for **efficacy** (i.e., making sure the client is empowered in the areas of choice and decision making) (Moursund & Kenny, 2002).

Even though contracts are an important part of helping clients define, understand, and work on specific aspects of their lives, a contract system does have disadvantages. Okun and Kantrowitz (2008) stress that contracts need to be open to renegotiation by both parties. This process is often time-consuming and personally taxing. Thomas and Ezell (1972) list several other **weaknesses of a contract system**.

• First, a counselor cannot hold a client to a contract. The agreement has no external rewards or punishments that the counselor can use to force the client to fulfill the agreement.

• Second, some client problems may not lend themselves to the contract system. For example, the client who wants to make new friends may contract to visit places where there is a good opportunity to encounter the types of people with whom he or she wishes to be associated. There is no way, however, that a contract can ensure that the client will make new friends.

• Third, a contractual way of dealing with problems focuses on outward behavior. Even if the contract is fulfilled successfully, the client may not have achieved insight or altered perception.

• Finally, the initial appeal of a contract is limited. Clients who are motivated to change and who find the idea fresh and appealing may become bored with such a system in time.

In determining the formality of the contract, a counselor must consider the client's background and motivational levels, the nature of the presenting problems, and what resources are available to the client to ensure the successful completion of the contract. Goodyear and Bradley (1980) suggest that the counselor ask how the client might sabotage the contract. This question helps make the client aware of any resistance he or she harbors to fulfillment of the agreement.

Rehearsal

Once a contract is set up, the counselor can help the client maximize the chance of fulfilling it by getting him or her to rehearse or practice designated behavior. The old adage that practice makes perfect is as true for clients who wish to reach a goal as it is for athletes or artists. Clients can rehearse in two ways: overtly and covertly (Cormier et al., 2009). ***Overt rehearsal*** requires the client to verbalize or act out what he or she is going to do. For example, if a woman is going to ask a man out for a date, she will want to rehearse what she is going to say and how she is going to act before she actually encounters the man. ***Covert rehearsal*** is imagining or reflecting on the desired goal. For instance, a student giving a speech can first imagine the conditions under which he will perform and then reflect about how to organize the subject matter that he will present. Imagining the situation beforehand can alleviate unnecessary anxiety and help the student perform better.

Sometimes a client needs counselor coaching during the rehearsal period. Such coaching may take the form of providing temporary aids to help the client remember what to do next (Bandura, 1976). It may simply involve giving feedback to the client on how he or she is doing. Feedback means helping the client recognize and correct any problem areas that he or she has in mastering a behavior, such as overexaggerating a movement. Feedback works well as long as it is not overdone (Geis & Chapman, 1971). To maximize its effectiveness, feedback should be given both orally and in writing.

Counselors can also assign clients ***homework*** (sometimes called "**empowering assignments**" or "**between-session tasks**") to help them practice the skills learned in the counseling sessions and generalize such skills to relevant areas of their lives. Homework involves additional work on a particular skill or skills outside the counseling session and has numerous advantages, such as

- keeping clients focused on relevant behavior between sessions,
- helping them to see clearly the kind of progress they are making,
- motivating clients to change behaviors,
- helping them to evaluate and modify their activities,
- making clients more responsible for self-control, and
- celebrating a breakthrough achieved in counseling (Hay & Kinnier, 1998; Hutchins & Vaught, 1997).

Cognitive–behavioral counselors are most likely to emphasize homework assignments. For instance, counselors with this theoretical background may have clients use workbooks to augment cognitive–behavioral in-session work. **Workbooks** require active participation and provide a tangible record of what clients have done. Two excellent cognitive–behavioral workbook exercises geared toward children are Vernon's (2006) "*Decisions and Consequences*," in her book *Thinking, Feeling and Behaving*, which focuses on cause and effect by having the counselor do such things as drop an egg into a bowl, and Kendall's (1990) *Coping Cat Workbook*, which concentrates on the connections between thoughts and feelings by having children engage in such activities as viewing life from a cat's perspective.

However, counselors from all theoretical perspectives can use homework if they wish to help clients help themselves. For homework to be most effective, it needs to be specifically tied to some measurable behavior change (Okun & Kantrowitz, 2008). It must also be relevant to clients' situations if it is to be meaningful and helpful (Cormier et al., 2009; Young, 2009). Furthermore, clients need to complete homework assignments if they are to benefit from using a homework method.

"The kinds of homework that can be assigned are limited only by the creativity of the counselor and the client" (Hay & Kinnier, 1998, p. 126). **Types of homework** that are frequently given include those that are **paradoxical** (an attempt to create the opposite effect), **behavioral** (practicing a new skill), **risk taking** (doing something that is feared), **thinking** (mulling over select thoughts), **written** (keeping a log or journal), **bibliotherapeutic** (reading, listening, or viewing literature), and **not doing anything** (taking a break from one's usual habits).

CASE EXAMPLE

Conrad Undermines the Contract

Conrad went to see a counselor because he was socially inept. He did not pick up on nonverbal cues, and he was not able to sustain a conversation for any length of time. Conrad's counselor, Penelope, worked up a contract for him. First, he was to watch television without the sound and try to identify emotional expressions. Second, he was to ask three people each day in the park how they were doing and talk with them as long as he could.

Conrad fulfilled his contract for the first week but then gave it up. He said it was "too hard." If you were Penelope, what would you do to help Conrad get back on a contract?

TRANSFERENCE AND COUNTERTRANSFERENCE

Counselor skills that help promote development during the counseling process are essential if the counselor is to avoid *circular counseling*, in which the same ground is covered over and over again. There is an equally important aspect of counseling, however, that influences the quality of the outcome: the relationship between counselor and client. The ability of the counselor and client to work effectively with each other is influenced largely by the relationship they develop. Counseling can be an intensely emotional experience (Cormier et al., 2009; Sexton & Whiston, 1994). In a few instances, counselors and clients genuinely dislike each other or have incompatible personalities (Welfel & Patterson, 2005). Usually, however, they can and must work through transference and countertransference phenomena that result from the thoughts and emotions they think, feel, and express to one another. Although some counseling theories emphasize transference and countertransference more than others, these two concepts occur to some extent in almost all counseling relationships.

Transference

Transference is the client's projection of past or present feelings, attitudes, or desires onto the counselor (Brammer et al., 1993; Brammer & MacDonald, 2003). It can be used in two ways. Initially, transference reactions help counselors understand clients better. A second way to use transference is to employ it as a way of resolving the client's problems (Teyber, 2000). Transference as a concept comes from the literature of psychoanalysis. It originally emphasized the transference of earlier life emotions onto a therapist, where they would be worked through. Today, transference is not restricted to psychoanalytic therapy, and it may be based on current as well as past experiences (Corey, Corey, & Callanan, 2011).

All counselors have what Gelso and Carter (1985) describe as a *transference pull*, an image generated through the use of personality and a particular theoretical approach. A client reacts to the image of the counselor in terms of the client's personal background and current conditions. The way the counselor sits, speaks, gestures, or looks may trigger a client reaction. An example of such an occurrence is a client saying to a counselor, "You sound just like my mother." The statement in and of itself may be observational. But if the client starts behaving as if the counselor were the client's mother, transference has occurred.

Five patterns of transference behavior frequently appear **in counseling**: The client may perceive the counselor as ideal, seer, nurturer, frustrator, or nonentity (Watkins, 1983b, p. 207). The counselor may at first enjoy transference phenomena that hold him or her in a positive light. Such enjoyment soon wears thin. To overcome any of the effects associated with transference experiences, Watkins (1983b) advocates focusing on the client's needs and expectations as well as establishing trust.

Cavanagh and Levitov (2002) note that transference can be either direct or indirect. Direct transference is well represented by the example of the client who thinks of the counselor as his or her mother. Indirect transference is harder to recognize. It is usually revealed in client statements or actions that are not obviously directly related to the counselor (e.g., "Talk is cheap and ineffective" or "I think counseling is the experience I've always wanted").

Regardless of its degree of directness, transference is either negative or positive. *Negative transference* is when the client accuses the counselor of neglecting or acting negatively toward him or her. Although painful to handle initially, negative transference must be worked through for the counseling relationship to get back to reality and ultimately be productive. It has a direct impact on the quality of the relationship. *Positive transference*, especially a mild form such as client admiration for the counselor, may not be readily acknowledged because it appears at first to add something to the relationship (Watkins, 1983b). Indirect or mild forms of positive transference are least harmful to the work of the counselor and client.

Cavanagh and Levitov (2002) hold that both negative and positive transference are forms of resistance. As long as the client keeps the attention of the counselor on transference issues, little progress is made in setting or achieving goals. To resolve transference issues, the counselor may work directly and interpersonally rather than analytically. For example, if the client complains that a counselor cares only about being admired, the counselor can respond, "I agree that some counselors may have this need, and it is not very helpful. On the other hand, we have been focusing on your goals. Let's go back to them. If the needs of counselors, as you observe them, become relevant to your goals, we will explore that issue."

Corey and associates (2011) see a therapeutic value in working through transference. They believe that the counselor–client relationship improves once the client resolves distorted perceptions about the counselor. If the situation is handled sensitively, the improved relationship is reflected in the client's increased trust and confidence in the counselor. Furthermore, by resolving feelings of transference, a client may gain insight into the past and become free to act differently in the present and future.

Countertransference

Countertransference refers to the counselor's projected emotional reaction to or behavior toward the client (Fauth & Hayes, 2006; Hansen, Rossberg, & Cramer, 1994). This reaction may be irrational, interpersonally stressful, and neurotic—emanating from the counselor's own unresolved issues. Furthermore, countertransference is often "harmful to, threatening, challenging, and/or taxing" to the counselor's coping resources (Fauth & Hayes, 2006, p. 431).

Thus, managing countertransference successfully is related to better therapy outcomes (Hayes, Gelso, & Hummel, 2011). Two examples of countertransference are a counselor manifesting behaviors toward his client, as he did toward her sister when they were growing up, or a counselor overidentifying with her client who has an eating disorder (DeLucia-Waack, 1999). Such interaction can destroy the counselor's ability to be therapeutic, let alone objective. Unless resolved adequately, countertransference can be detrimental to the counseling relationship.

Kernberg (1975) takes **two major approaches to the problem of conceptualizing countertransference**. In the **classic approach**, countertransference is seen negatively and viewed as the direct or indirect unconscious reaction of the counselor to the client. The **total approach** sees countertransference as more positive. From this perspective, countertransference is a diagnostic tool for understanding aspects of the client's unconscious motivations. Blanck and Blanck (1979) describe a third approach. This approach sees countertransference as both positive and negative. Watkins (1985) considers this third approach more realistic than the first two.

The **manifestation of countertransference** takes several forms (Corey et al., 2011). The most prevalent are (a) feeling a constant desire to please the client, (b) identifying with the problems of the client so much that one loses objectivity, (c) developing sexual or romantic feelings toward the client, (d) giving advice compulsively, and (e) wanting to develop a social relationship with the client.

Watkins (1985) thinks that countertransference can be expressed in a myriad of ways. He views four forms as particularly noteworthy: overprotective, benign, rejecting, and hostile. The first two forms are examples of *overidentification*, in which the counselor loses his or her ability to remain emotionally distant from the client. The latter two forms are examples of *disidentification*, in which the counselor becomes emotionally removed from the client. Disidentification may express itself in counselor behavior that is aloof, nonempathetic, hostile, cold, or antagonistic.

It is vital that counselors work through any negative or nonproductive countertransference. Otherwise, the progress of the client will lessen, and both counselor and client will be hurt in the process (Brammer & MacDonald, 2003; Watkins, 1985). It is also important that a counselor recognize that he or she is experiencing countertransference feelings. Once aware of these feelings, a counselor needs to discover the reasons behind them. It is critical to develop some consistent way of monitoring this self-understanding, and one way is to undergo supervision (DeLucia-Waack, 1999). Counselors, like clients, have blind spots, hidden areas, and aspects of their lives that are unknown to them.

Supervision involves working in a professional relationship with a more experienced counselor so that the counselor being supervised can simultaneously monitor and enhance the services he or she offers to clients (Bernard & Goodyear, 2009). Among the procedures used in supervision are observing counselor–client interactions behind one-way mirrors, monitoring audiotapes of counseling sessions, and critiquing videotapes of counseling sessions

---

PERSONAL REFLECTION
_____

When have you met people you immediately seemed to like or dislike? How did you treat them? How did you feel when you interacted with them? How is that like countertransference? How is it different?

(Borders, 1994). Analyzing the roles a counselor plays in sessions is a crucial component of supervision.

THE REAL RELATIONSHIP

This chapter has emphasized the skills and interpersonal qualities that contribute to a working alliance between counselors and clients and ultimately result in clients' self-understanding and goal achievement. Using leads, levels of empathy, confrontation, encouragement, and contracts; recognizing transference and countertransference; and working through personal issues in professional ways all contribute to the counseling process. According to Gelso (2011), if helping skills have been used well, a *real relationship*—with its twin components of **genuineness** (the intent to avoid deception, including self-deception) and **realism** (perceiving or experiencing the other in ways that benefit the other)—will emerge. The real relationship begins as a two-way experience between counselors and clients from their first encounter. Counselors are real by being genuine (owning their thoughts and feelings), trying to facilitate genuineness in their clients, and attempting to see and understand clients in a realistic manner. Clients contribute to the realness of the relationship by being genuine and perceiving their own situations realistically.

The real relationship that exists in counseling has been written about mostly from counselors' viewpoints and has been misunderstood or incompletely defined. According to Gelso (2011), there are specific propositions about the nature of a real relationship. One is that the relationship increases and deepens during the counseling process. Another is that counselors and clients have different expectations and actualizations of what a real relationship is like. Counseling is a dynamic, interactional process, and the strength of relationships between counselors and clients varies over time.

Study of the real relationship has headed in a promising direction toward the *social construction perspective*—that is, "the process by which people come to describe, explain, or otherwise account for the world (including themselves) in which they live" (Sexton & Whiston, 1994, p. 60). Realness and growth, although not precisely defined at present, appear to be an important part of counseling relationships that will continue to attract attention and be important.

MyCounselingLab™

Go to Topic 3: *Characteristics of the Effective Counselor* in the MyCounselingLab™ site (www.MyCounselingLab.com) for *Counseling: A Comprehensive Profession,* Seventh Edition, where you can:

- Find learning outcomes for *Characteristics of the Effective Counselor* along with the national standards that connect to these outcomes.
- Complete Assignments and Activities that can help you more deeply understand the chapter content.
- Apply and practice your understanding of the core skills identified in the chapter with the Building Counseling Skills unit.
- Prepare yourself for professional certification with a Practice for Certification quiz.
- Connect to videos through the Video and Resource Library.

Summary and Conclusion

This chapter has emphasized the understanding and action phases of counseling, which occur after clients and counselors have established a relationship and explored possible goals toward which to work. These phases are facilitated by mutual interaction between the individuals involved. The counselor can help the client by appropriate leads, challenges to perception, multifocused responding, accurate empathy, self-disclosure, immediacy, confrontation, contracts, and rehearsal. These skills are focused on the client, but they also help the counselor gain self-insight.

Client and counselor must work through transference and countertransference, which can occur in several forms in a counseling relationship. Some clients and counselors will encounter less transference and countertransference than others, but it is important that each person recognize when he or she is engaged in such modes of communication. The more aware people are about these ways of relating, the less damage they are likely to do in their relationships with significant others and the more self-insight they are likely to achieve. A successful resolution of these issues promotes realness, and at the root of growth and goal attainment is the ability to experience the world realistically.

Closing Counseling Relationships

Active as I am in sessions
going with you to the marrow of emotions
our shared journey has an end.
Tonight, as you hesitantly leave my office
to the early darkness of winter days
and the coldness of December nights,
you do so on your own.
Yet, this season of crystallized rain
changes, if however slowly,
and our time and words together
can be a memory from which may grow
a new seed of life within you,
Not without knowledge of past years' traumas
but rather in the sobering realization
that in being heard a chance is created
to fill a time with different feelings,
And savor them in the silent hours
when you stand by yourself alone.

From "Memory Traces," by S. T. Gladding, 1977, *North Carolina Personnel and Guidance Journal, 6,* 51. © 1977 by S. T. Gladding.

MyCounselingLab™

Visit the MyCounselingLab™ site (www.MyCounselingLab.com) for *Counseling: A Comprehensive Profession,* Seventh Edition to enhance your understanding of chapter concepts. You'll have the opportunity to practice your skills through video- and case-based Assignments and Activities as well as Building Counseling Skills units and to prepare for your certification exam with Practice for Certification quizzes.

Closing a counseling relationship refers to the decision to end it. Sometimes this is called ***termination***. The decision may be made unilaterally or mutually. Regardless, closing is probably the least researched, most neglected aspect of counseling. Many theorists and counselors assume that closing will occur naturally and leave both clients and counselors pleased and satisfied with the results. Goodyear (1981) states that "it is almost as though we operate from a myth that closing is a process from which the counselor remains aloof and to which the client alone is responsive" (p. 347).

However, the closing of a counseling relationship has an impact on all involved, and it is often complex, difficult, and awkwardly done (Bulkeley, 2009). Closing may well produce mixed feelings on the part of both the counselor and the client (Kottler, Sexton, & Whiston, 1994). For example, a client may be both appreciative and regretful about a particular counseling experience. Unless it is handled properly, closing has the power to harm as well as heal.

This chapter addresses closing as a multidimensional process that can take any of several forms. Specifically, we will examine the general function of closing as well as closing of individual sessions and the entire counseling relationship. Closing strategies, resistance to closing, premature closing, counselor-initiated closing, and the importance of terminating a relationship on a positive note will also be discussed. The related areas of follow-up, referral, and recycling in counseling will be covered, too.

FUNCTION OF CLOSING A COUNSELING RELATIONSHIP

Historically, addressing the process of **closing a counseling relationship** directly has been **avoided** for a couple of reasons. Ward (1984) has suggested two of the most prominent. First, ending is associated with **loss**, a traditionally taboo subject in all parts of society, especially counseling, which is generally viewed as emphasizing growth and development unrelated to endings. Second, closing is **not directly related to** the **microskills** that facilitate counseling relationships. Therefore, closing is not a process usually highlighted in counseling. Its significance has begun to emerge, however, because of societal trends, such as the aging of the American population (Erber, 2010), the wide acceptance of the concept of life stages (Sheehy, 1976), an increased attention to death as a part of the life span (Kubler-Ross, 1969), and the fact that loss may be associated with re-creation, transcendence, greater self-understanding, and new discoveries such as **posttraumatic growth** (i.e., positive life changes that come about as a result of suffering or struggling with natural or human made traumatic events, such as hurricanes and wars) (Calhoun & Tedeschi, 2006; Hayes, 1993).

Closing serves several important functions. First, closing signals that something is finished. Life is a series of hellos and good-byes (Goldberg, 1975; Maholick & Turner, 1979; Meier &

Davis, 2011). Hellos begin at birth, and good-byes end at death. Between birth and death, individuals enter into and leave a succession of experiences, including jobs, relationships, and life stages. Growth and adjustment depend on an ability to make the most of these experiences and learn from them. To begin something new, a former experience must be completed and resolved (Perls, 1969). Closing is the opportunity to end a learning experience properly, whether on a personal or professional level (Hulse-Killacky, 1993). In counseling, **closing** is more than an act signifying the end of therapy; it is also **a motivator** (Yalom, 2005).

Both client and counselor are motivated by the knowledge that the **counseling experience is limited in time** (Young, 2009). This awareness is similar to that of a young adult who realizes that he or she cannot remain a promising young person forever—an event that often occurs on a person's 30th or 40th birthday. Such a realization may spur individuals on to hard work while there is still time to do something significant. Some counselors, such as those associated with strategic, systemic, and solution-focused family therapy, purposely limit the number of counseling sessions so that clients and counselors are more aware of time constraints and make the most of sessions (Gladding, 2011).

Second, **closing is a means of maintaining changes** already achieved and generalizing problem-solving skills acquired in counseling. Successful counseling results in significant changes in the way the client thinks, feels, or acts. These changes are rehearsed in counseling, but they must be practiced in the real world. Closing provides an opportunity for such practice. The client can always go back to the counselor for any needed follow-up, but closing is the natural point for the practice of independence to begin. It is a potentially empowering experience for the client and enables him or her to address the present in an entirely new or modified way. At closing, the opportunity to put "insights into actions" is created (Gladding, 1990a, p. 130). In other words, what seems like an exit becomes an entrance.

Third, **closing serves as a reminder that the client has matured** (Vickio, 1990). Besides offering the client new skills or different ways of thinking about himself or herself, effective counseling closing marks a time in the client's life when he or she is less absorbed by and preoccupied with personal problems and more able to deal with outside people and events. This ability to handle external situations may result in more interdependent relationships that are mutually supportive and consequently lead toward a "more independent and satisfying life" (Burke, 1989, p. 47). Having achieved a successful resolution to a problem, a client now has new insights and abilities that are stored in memory and may be recalled and used on occasions.

PERSONAL REFLECTION

Think about times you have voluntarily ended events or relationships. What did closing feel like for you? What did you learn from the experience? What value do you see in concluding an experience?

TIMING OF CLOSING

When to terminate a relationship is a question that has no definite answer. However, closing should be planned and deliberate, not hastily conceived and abrupt (Meier & Davis, 2011). If the relationship is ended too soon, clients may lose the ground they gained in counseling and regress to earlier behaviors. However, if closing is never addressed, clients can become dependent on the counselor and fail to resolve difficulties and grow as persons. There are several **pragmatic considerations in the timing of closing** (Cormier & Hackney, 2012; Young, 2009).

- *Have clients achieved behavioral, cognitive, or affective contract goals?*   When both clients and counselors have a clear idea about whether particular goals have been reached, the timing of closing is easier to figure out. The key to this consideration is setting up a mutually agreed-on contract before counseling begins.
- *Can clients concretely show where they have made progress in what they wanted to accomplish?*   In this situation, specific progress may be the basis for making a decision about closing.
- *Is the counseling relationship helpful?*   If either the client or the counselor senses that what is occurring in the counseling sessions is not helpful, closing is appropriate.
- *Has the context of the initial counseling arrangement changed?*   In cases where there is a move or a prolonged illness, closing (as well as a referral) should be considered.

Overall, there is no one right time to terminate a counseling relationship. The "when" of closing must be figured out in accordance with the uniqueness of the situation and overall ethical and professional guidelines.

ISSUES IN CLOSING

Closing of Individual Sessions

Closing is an issue during individual counseling sessions. Initial sessions should have clearly defined time limits (Brammer & MacDonald, 2003; Cormier & Hackney, 2012). A range of 45 to 50 minutes is generally considered adequate for an individual counseling session. It usually takes a counselor 5 to 10 minutes to adjust to the client and the client's concerns. Counseling sessions that terminate too quickly may be as unproductive as ones that last too long.

Benjamin (1987) proposes two important factors in closing an interview. First, both client and counselor should be aware that the session is ending. Second, no new material should be introduced or discussed during this ending. If the client introduces new material, the counselor needs to work to make it the anticipated focus of the next session. On rare occasions, the counselor has to deal with new material on an emergency basis.

A **counselor can close an interview effectively** in several ways. One is simply to **make a brief statement indicating that time is up** (Cormier & Hackney, 2012). For example, he or she might say, "It looks like our time is up for today." The simpler the statement, the better it is. If a client is discussing a number of subjects in an open-ended manner near the end of a session, the counselor should remind the client that there are only 5 or 10 minutes left. For example, the counselor can say: "Lily, it looks like we only have a few minutes left in our session. Would you like to summarize what you have learned today and tell me what you would like to focus on next time?" The client can then focus attention on important matters in the present as well as those that need to be addressed in the future. As an alternative or in addition to the direct statement, the **counselor can use nonverbal gestures to indicate that the session is ending**. These include looking at his or her watch or standing up. Nonverbal gestures are probably best used with verbal indicators. Each reinforces the other.

As indicated toward the end of the interview, it is usually helpful to summarize what has happened in the session. Either the counselor or the client may initiate this summation. A good **summary** ties together the main points of the session and should be brief, to the point, and without interpretation. If both the counselor and client summarize, they may gain insight into what each has gotten out of the session. Such a process provides a means for clearing up any misunderstandings.

An important part of terminating any individual session is setting up the next appointment. Most problems are resolved over time. Clients and counselors need to know when they will meet again to continue the work in progress. It is easier and more efficient to set up a next appointment at the end of a session than to do it later by phone.

CASE EXAMPLE

Tina Terminates a Session

Tina grew impatient with her client, Macheta, as Macheta seemed to drone on and on about the misery in her life. Tina was sympathetic and empathetic, but only up to a point. Then she became annoyed and realized she was not doing the kind of work as a counselor that was helpful to her or to her client. Therefore, even though only 35 out of 50 minutes had passed since they began, Tina decided to end the session. She told Macheta that she was having a difficult time following her, and she asked if Macheta would summarize what she was trying to convey. Macheta was startled but when she thought about it, she was able to convey the essence of the session in only a few sentences.

What do you think of Tina's tactic? What else might she have done to make the session with Macheta more productive?

Closing of a Counseling Relationship

Counseling relationships vary in length and purpose. It is vital to the health and well-being of everyone that the subject of closing be brought up early so that counselor and client can make the most of their time together (Cavanagh & Levitov, 2002). Individuals need time to prepare for the end of a meaningful relationship. There may be some sadness, even if the relationship ends in a positive way. Thus, closing should not necessarily be presented as the zenith of the counseling experience. Cormier and Hackney (2012) stress that it is better to play down the importance of closing rather than play it up.

The counselor and client must agree on when closing of the relationship is appropriate and helpful (Young, 2009). Generally, they give each other verbal messages about a readiness to terminate. For example, a client may say, "I really think I've made a lot of progress over the past few months." Or a counselor may state, "You appear to be well on your way to no longer needing my services." Such statements suggest the beginning of the end of the counseling relationship. They usually imply recognition of growth or resolution. A number of other **behaviors** may also **signal the end of counseling**. These include a decrease in the intensity of work; more humor; consistent reports of improved abilities to cope; verbal commitments to the future; and less denial, withdrawal, anger, mourning, or dependence (McGee, Schuman, & Racusen, 1972; Shulman, 2009; Welfel & Patterson, 2005).

Cormier and Hackney (2012) believe that, in a relationship that has lasted more than 3 months, the final 3 or 4 weeks should be spent discussing the impact of closing. For instance, counselors may inquire how their clients will cope without the support of the relationship. Counselors may also ask clients to talk about the meaning of the counseling relationship and how they will use what they have learned in the future. Shulman (2009) suggests that, as a general rule of thumb, one-sixth of the time spent in a counseling relationship should be devoted to focusing on closing.

Maholick and Turner (1979) discuss specific areas of concern when deciding whether to terminate counseling:

- An examination of whether the client's initial problem or symptoms have been reduced or eliminated
- A determination of whether the stress-producing feelings that led to counseling have been eliminated
- An assessment of the client's coping ability and degree of understanding of self and others
- A determination of whether the client can relate better to others and is able to love and be loved
- An examination of whether the client has acquired abilities to plan and work productively
- An evaluation of whether the client can better play and enjoy life

These areas are not equally important for all clients, but it is essential that, before the closing of counseling, clients feel confident to live effectively without the relationship (Huber, 1989; Ward, 1984; Young, 2009).

There are at least two other **ways to facilitate the ending of a counselor–client relationship**. One involves the use of fading. Dixon and Glover (1984) define *fading* as "a gradual decrease in the unnatural structures developed to create desired changes" (p. 165). In other words, clients gradually stop receiving reinforcement from counselors for behaving in certain ways, and appointments are spread out. A desired goal of all counseling is to help clients become less dependent on the counselor and the counseling sessions and more dependent on themselves and interdependent with others. From counseling, clients should also learn the positive reinforcement of natural contingencies. To promote fading, counseling sessions can be simply shortened (e.g., from 50 to 30 minutes) as well as spaced further apart (e.g., from every week to every 2 weeks) (Cormier, Nurius, & Osborn, 2009; MacCluskie & Ingersoll, 2001).

Another way to promote closing is to help clients **develop successful problem-solving skills**. Clients, like everyone else, are constantly faced with problems. If counselors can help their clients learn more effective ways to cope with these difficulties, clients will no longer need the counseling relationship. This is a process of **generalization** from counseling experience to life. At its best, this process includes an emphasis on education and prevention as well as decision-making skills for everyday life and crisis situations.

PERSONAL REFLECTION

When has education, either formal or self-taught, helped you stop doing something (e.g., smoking, biting your nails, displaying a nervous twitch, talking excessively)? How do you relate doing something new to closing?

RESISTANCE TO CLOSING

Resistance to closing may come from either the counselor or the client. Welfel and Patterson (2005) note that resistance is especially likely when the counseling relationship has lasted for a long time or has involved a high level of intimacy. Other factors that may promote resistance include the pain of earlier losses, loneliness, unresolved grief, need gratification, fear of rejection, and fear of having to be self-reliant. Some of these factors are more prevalent with clients, whereas others are more likely to characterize counselors.

Client Resistance

Clients resist closing in many ways. **Two easily recognized expressions of resistance are (a) asking for more time at the end of a session and (b) asking for more appointments once a goal has been reached**. Another more troublesome form of client resistance is the **development of new problems** that were not part of his or her original concerns, such as depression or anxiety. The manifestation of these symptoms makes closing more difficult; in such situations, a client may convince the counselor that only he or she can help. Thus, the counselor may feel obligated to continue working with the person for either personal or ethical reasons.

Regardless of the strategy employed, the closing process is best carried out gradually and slowly. Sessions can become less frequent over time, and client skills, abilities, and resources can be highlighted simultaneously. Sometimes when clients are especially hesitant to terminate, the counselor can "prescribe" a limited number of future sessions or concentrate with clients on how they will set themselves up for relapse (Anderson & Stewart, 1983). These procedures make the covert more overt and help counselors and clients identify what issues are involved in leaving a helping relationship.

Vickio (1990) has developed a unique way of implementing a concrete strategy for college students who are dealing with loss and closing. In *The Goodbye Brochure,* he describes what it means to say good-bye and why good-byes should be carried out. He then discusses five *D*s for successfully dealing with departure and loss and an equal number of *D*s for unsuccessfully dealing with them (Vickio, 1990, p. 576).

Successfully Dealing with Loss

1. Determine ways to make your transition a gradual process.
2. Discover the significance that different activities have had in your life.
3. Describe this significance to others.
4. Delight in what you have gained and in what lies ahead of you.
5. Define areas of continuity in your life.

Unsuccessfully Dealing with Loss

1. Deny the loss.
2. Distort your experience by overglorifying it.
3. Denigrate your activities and relationships.
4. Distract yourself from thinking about departure.
5. Detach yourself abruptly from your activities and relationships.

Lerner and Lerner (1983) believe that client resistance often results from a fear of change. If clients come to value a counseling relationship, they may fear that they cannot function well without it. For example, people who have grown up in unstable or chaotic environments involving the abuse of alcohol or an adversarial divorce may be especially prone to hold on to the stability of counseling and the relationship with the counselor. It is vital that the counselor recognize the special needs of these individuals and the difficulties they have in coping with loneliness and intimacy (Loewenstein, 1979; Weiss, 1973). It is even more critical that the counselor take steps to help such clients help themselves by exploring with them the advantages of working in other therapeutic settings, such as support or self-help groups. For such clients, counseling is potentially addictive. If they are to function in healthy ways, they must find alternative sources of support.

Counselor Resistance

Although the ultimate goal in counseling is for counselors to become obsolete and unnecessary to their clients, some counselors are reluctant to say good-bye at the appropriate time (Nystul, 2011). Clients who have special or unusual needs or those who are very productive may be especially attractive to counselors. Goodyear (1981) lists **eight conditions in which closing may be particularly difficult for counselors**:

1. When closing signals the end of a significant relationship
2. When closing arouses the counselor's anxieties about the client's ability to function independently
3. When closing arouses guilt in the counselor about not having been more effective with the client
4. When the counselor's professional self-concept is threatened by the client who leaves abruptly and angrily
5. When closing signals the end of a learning experience for the counselor (e.g., the counselor may have been relying on the client to learn more about the dynamics of a disorder or a particular culture)
6. When closing signals the end of a particularly exciting experience of living vicariously through the adventures of the client
7. When closing becomes a symbolic recapitulation of other (especially unresolved) farewells in the counselor's life
8. When closing arouses in the counselor conflicts about his or her own individuation (p. 348)

It is important that counselors recognize any difficulties they have in letting go of certain clients. A counselor may seek consultation with colleagues in dealing with this problem or undergo counseling to resolve the problem. The latter option is quite valuable if the counselor has a personal history of detachment, isolation, and excessive fear of intimacy. Kovacs (1965, 1976) and Guy (1987) report that some persons who enter the helping professions possess just such characteristics.

PERSONAL REFLECTION

Almost everyone has a situation in his or her life that ended too soon or that was less than ideal. You may want to explore some of those times in your own life.

Could acknowledging those feelings or behaviors help you in working with a client you may not want to terminate? How?

PREMATURE CLOSING

The question of whether clients terminate counseling prematurely is not one that can usually be measured by the number of sessions the client has completed. Rather, premature closing often has to do with how well clients believe they have achieved personal goals and how well they are functioning generally (Ward, 1984). A substantial minority of individuals reported terminating prematurely because of treatment dissatisfaction. Clients with weaker therapeutic alliance are more likely to drop out of counseling than those who bond well with their counselor (Sharf, Primavera, & Diener, 2010). Early termination seems to be more prevalent with lower income and less well educated clients who may not understand many of the subtleties of counseling and therefore perceive that therapy is not helping (Westmacott & Hunsley, 2010). Younger clients, those with greater dysfunctionality, and people of color are more likely to drop out of counseling as well (Lampropoulos, Schneider, & Spengler, 2009).

Regardless of socioeconomic class and other background factors, some clients show little, if any, commitment or motivation to change their present circumstances and request that counseling be terminated after the first session. Such a request is more likely to happen if these clients see an intake counselor first and are then transferred to another treatment counselor (Nielsen et al., 2009). Other clients express the desire to terminate early after realizing the work necessary for change. Still others make this wish known more indirectly by missing or being late for appointments.

Regardless of how clients express a wish for premature closing, it is likely to trigger thoughts and feelings within the counselor that must be dealt with. Hansen, Warner, and Smith (1980) suggest that the topic of premature closing be discussed openly between a counselor and client if the client expresses a desire to terminate before specified goals have been met or if the counselor suspects that premature closing may occur. With discussion, thoughts and feelings of both the client and counselor can be examined and a premature ending prevented.

Sometimes a client fails to keep an appointment and does not call to reschedule. In such cases, the counselor should attempt to reach the client by phone or mail. Sending a letter to a client allows him or her more "space" in which to consider the decision of whether to continue counseling or not (MacCluskie & Ingersoll, 2001). A model for a *"no show" letter* is as follows.

Dear _____:

I have missed you at our last scheduled sessions. I would like very much for us to continue to work together, yet the choice about whether to counsel is yours. If you do wish to reschedule, could you please do so in the next 30 days? Otherwise, I will close your chart and assume you are not interested in services at this time.

Sincerely,

Mary Counselor (p. 179)

If the counselor finds that the client wishes to quit, an **exit interview** may be set up. Ward (1984) reports four possible benefits from such an interview:

1. An exit interview may help the client resolve any negative feelings resulting from the counseling experience.
2. An exit interview serves as a way to invite the client to continue in counseling if he or she so wishes.
3. Another form of treatment or a different counselor can be considered in an exit interview if the client so desires.
4. An exit interview may increase the chance that the next time the client needs help, he or she will seek counseling.

In premature closing, a counselor often makes one of two mistakes. One is to blame either himself or herself or the client for what is happening. A counselor is more likely to blame the client. In either case, someone is berated, and the problem is compounded. It may be more productive for the counselor to think of the situation as one in which no one is at fault. Such a strategy is premised on the idea that some matches between clients and counselors work better than others do.

A second mistake on the counselor's part is to act in a cavalier manner about the situation. An example is the counselor who says, "It's too bad this client has chosen not to continue counseling, but I've got others." To avoid making either mistake, counselors need to find out why a **client terminated prematurely. Possible reasons** include the following:

- To see whether the counselor really cares
- To try to elicit positive feelings from the counselor
- To punish or try to hurt the counselor
- To eliminate anxiety
- To show the counselor that the client has found a cure elsewhere
- To express to the counselor that the client does not feel understood

Counselors need to understand that, regardless of what they do, some clients terminate counseling prematurely. Such a realization allows counselors to feel that they do not have to be perfect and frees them to be more authentic in the therapeutic relationship. It also enables them to acknowledge overtly that, no matter how talented and skillful they are, some clients find other counselors more helpful. Ideally, counselors are aware of the anatomy of closing. With such knowledge, they become empowered to deal realistically with situations concerning client closing.

Not all people who seek counseling are equally ready to work in such a relationship, and the readiness level may vary as the relationship continues. Some clients need to terminate prematurely for good reasons, and their action does not necessarily reflect on the counselor's competence. Counselors can control only a limited number of variables in a counseling relationship. The following list includes several of the variables most likely to be effective in **preventing premature closing** (Young, 2009):

- *Appointments.*   The less time between appointments and the more regularly they are scheduled, the better.
- *Orientation to counseling.*   The more clients know about the process of counseling, the more likely they are to stay with it.
- *Consistency of counselor.*   Clients do not like to be processed from counselor to counselor. Therefore, the counselor who does the initial intake should continue counseling the client if at all possible.
- *Reminders to motivate client attendance.*   Cards, telephone calls, texts, or e-mail can be effective reminders. Because of the sensitivity of counseling, however, a counselor should always have the client's permission to send an appointment reminder.

COUNSELOR-INITIATED CLOSING

Counselor-initiated closing is the opposite of premature closing. A counselor sometimes needs to end relationships with some or all clients. Reasons include illness, working through countertransference, relocation to another area, the end of an internship or practicum experience, an extended trip, or the realization that client needs could be better served by someone else. These are what Cavanagh and Levitov (2002) classify as **"good reasons" for the counselor to terminate**.

There are also **poor reasons for counselor-initiated terminations**. They include a counselor's feelings of anger, boredom, or anxiety. If a counselor ends a relationship because of such feelings, the client may feel rejected and even worse than he or she did in the beginning. It is one thing for a person to handle rejection from peers; it is another for that same person to handle rejection from a counselor. Although a counselor may have some negative feelings about a client, it is possible to acknowledge and work through those feelings without behaving in an extreme or detrimental way.

Both London (1982) and Seligman (1984) present models for helping clients deal with the temporary absence of the counselor. These researchers stress that clients and counselors should prepare as far in advance as possible for temporary closing by openly discussing the impending event and working through any strong feelings about the issue of separation. Clients may actually experience benefits from counselor-initiated closing by realizing that the counselor is human and replaceable. They may also come to understand that people have choices about how to deal with interpersonal relationships. Furthermore, they may explore previous feelings and major life decisions, learning more clearly that new behaviors carry over into other life experiences (London, 1982). Refocusing may also occur during the closing process and help clients see issues on which to work more clearly.

Seligman (1984) recommends a more structured way of preparing clients for counselor-initiated closing than London does, but both models can be effective. It is important in any situation like this to make sure clients have the names and numbers of a few other counselors to contact in case of an emergency.

There is also the matter of **permanent counselor-initiated closing**. In today's mobile society "more frequently than before, it is counselors who leave, certain they will not return" (Pearson, 1998, p. 55). In such cases, closing is more painful for clients and presents quite a challenge for counselors. The timing expected in the counseling process is off.

In permanent counselor-initiated closing, it is still vital to review clients' progress, end the relationship at a specific time, and make postcounseling plans. A number of other tasks also must be accomplished (Pearson, 1998); among these are counselors working through their own feelings about their closing, such as sadness, grief, anger, and fear. Furthermore, counselors need to put clients' losses in perspective and plan accordingly how each client will deal with the loss of the counseling relationship. Counselors must take care of their physical needs as well and seek professional and personal support where necessary.

In the process of their own closing preparations, counselors should be open with clients about where they are going and what they will be doing. They should make such announcements in a timely manner and allow clients to respond spontaneously. "Advanced empathy is a powerful means for helping clients express and work through the range of their emotions" (Pearson, 1998, p. 61). Arranging for transfers or referrals to other counselors is critical if clients' needs are such. Finally, there is the matter of saying good-bye and ending the relationship. This process may be facilitated through the use of immediacy and/or rituals.

CASE EXAMPLE

Miguel Moves

Miguel enjoyed his work as a counselor at family services. He was enthusiastic, energetic, and carried a full case load. However, when his wife received a promotion at work that required a move to another city, he realized he had to end his present counseling practice. Most troubling was the fact that he had only a month to do so, and as a child Miguel had had some trauma regarding loss. Thus, Miguel was not sure exactly what to do and how. He wanted to be professional and helpful to his clients, but he also wanted to take care of himself.

How would you prioritize the actions Miguel needs to take first in regard to his clients? Would a letter letting them know that he is leaving be unprofessional or crass? How would you suggest Miguel take care of himself?

ENDING ON A POSITIVE NOTE

The process of closing, like counseling itself, involves a series of checkpoints that counselors and clients can consult to evaluate the progress they are making and determine their readiness to move to another stage. It is important that closing be mutually agreed on, if at all possible, so that all involved can move on in ways deemed most productive. Nevertheless, this is not always possible. Welfel and Patterson (2005, pp. 124–125) present **four guidelines a counselor can use to end an intense counseling relationship in a positive way**:

1. *"Be aware of the client's needs and desires and allow the client time to express them."* At the end of a counseling relationship, the client may need time to express gratitude for the help received. Counselors should accept such expressions "without minimizing the value of their work."

2. *"Review the major events of the counseling experience and bring the review into the present."* The focus of this process is to help a client see where he or she is now as compared with the beginning of counseling and realize more fully the growth that has been accomplished. The procedure includes a review of significant past moments and turning points in the relationship with a focus on personalizing the summary.

3. *"Supportively acknowledge the changes the client has made."* At this point, the counselor lets the client know that he or she recognizes the progress that has been achieved and actively encourages the client to maintain it. "When a client has chosen not to implement action plans" for issues that emerged in counseling, "the process of closing should also include an inventory of such issues and a discussion of the option of future counseling."

4. *"Request follow-up contact."* Counseling relationships eventually end, but the caring, concern, and respect the counselor has for the client are not automatically terminated at the final session. Clients need to know that the counselor continues to be interested in what is happening in their lives. It is an additional incentive for clients to maintain the changes that counseling has produced.

ISSUES RELATED TO CLOSING: FOLLOW-UP AND REFERRAL

Follow-Up

Follow-up entails checking to see how the client is doing, with respect to whatever the problem was, sometime after closing has occurred (Okun & Kantrowitz, 2008). In essence, it is a **positive monitoring process** that encourages client growth (Egan, 2010). Follow-up is a step that some counselors neglect. It is important because it reinforces the gains clients have made in counseling and helps both the counselor and the client reevaluate the experience. It also emphasizes the counselor's genuine care and concern for the client.

Follow-up can be conducted on either a short- or long-term basis. **Short-term follow-up** is usually conducted 3 to 6 months after a counseling relationship terminates. **Long-term follow-up** is conducted at least 6 months after closing.

Follow-up may take many forms, but there are **four main ways** in which it is usually conducted (Cormier et al., 2009). The first is to **invite the client in for a session** to discuss any progress he or she has continued to make in achieving desired goals. A second way is through a **telephone call** to the client. A call allows the client to report to the counselor, although only verbal interaction is possible. A third way is for the counselor to send the client a **letter** asking about the client's current status. A fourth and more impersonal way is for the counselor to **mail or e-mail the client a questionnaire** dealing with his or her current levels of functioning. Many public agencies use this type of follow-up as a way of showing accountability. Such procedures do not preclude the use of more personal follow-up procedures by individual counselors. Although time-consuming, a personal follow-up is probably the most effective way of evaluating past counseling experiences. It helps assure clients that they are cared about as individuals and are more than just statistics.

Sometimes, regardless of the type of follow-up used, it is helpful if the client monitors his or her own progress through the use of graphs or charts. Then, when relating information to the counselor, the client can do so in a more concrete and objective way. If counselor and client agree at the end of the last session on a follow-up time, this type of self-monitoring may be especially meaningful and give the client concrete proof of progress and clearer insight into current needs.

CASE EXAMPLE

Follow-Up Flo

Flo was an excellent counselor, but she had one major fault: She never followed up with her clients. As far as she was concerned, they were doing fine unless proven otherwise. In her 20 years of counseling, Flo had had only a handful of clients ever return for more therapy. Therefore, Flo hypothesized that she had been able to see and help more people because she was not spending time interacting with those who were better.

Could Flo's philosophy be right? If not, why not? Would you adopt it?

Referral and Recycling

Counselors are not able to help everyone who seeks assistance. When a counselor realizes that a situation is unproductive, it is important to know whether to terminate the relationship or make a referral. A *referral* involves arranging other assistance for a client when the initial arrangement is not or cannot be helpful (Okun & Kantrowitz, 2008). There are **many reasons for referring**, including the following (Goldstein, 1971):

- The client has a problem the counselor does not know how to handle.
- The counselor is inexperienced in a particular area (e.g., substance abuse or mental disorders) and does not have the necessary skill to help the client.
- The counselor knows of a nearby expert who would be more helpful to the client.
- The counselor and client have incompatible personalities.
- The relationship between counselor and client is stuck in an initial phase of counseling.

Referrals involve a how, a when, and a who. The *how* involves knowing how to call on a helping resource and handle the client to maximize the chances that he or she will follow through with the referral process. A client may resist a referral if the client feels rejected by the counselor. Welfel and Patterson (2005) suggest that a counselor spend at least one session with the client in preparation for the referral. Some clients will need several sessions.

The *when* of making a referral involves timing. The longer a client works with a counselor, the more reluctant the client may be to see someone else. Thus, timing is crucial. If a counselor suspects an impasse with a certain client, he or she should refer that client as soon as possible. However, if the counselor has worked with the client for a while, he or she should be sensitive about giving the client enough time to get used to the idea of working with someone else.

The *who* of making a referral involves the person to whom you are sending a client. The interpersonal ability of that professional may be as important initially as his or her skills if the referral is going to work well. A good question to ask oneself when making a referral is whether the new counselor is someone you would feel comfortable sending a family member to see (MacCluskie & Ingersoll, 2001).

Recycling is an alternative when the counselor thinks the counseling process has not yet worked but can be made to do so. It means reexamining all phases of the therapeutic process. Perhaps the goals were not properly defined or an inappropriate strategy was chosen. Whatever the case, by reexamining the counseling process, counselor and client can decide how or whether to revise and reinvest in the counseling process. Counseling, like other experiences, is not always successful on the first attempt. Recycling gives both counselor and client a second chance to achieve what each wants: positive change.

MyCounselingLab™

Go to Topic 3: *Characteristics of the Effective Counselor* in the MyCounselingLab™ site (www.MyCounselingLab.com) for *Counseling: A Comprehensive Profession*, Seventh Edition, where you can:

- Find learning outcomes for *Characteristics of the Effective Counselor* along with the national standards that connect to these outcomes.
- Complete Assignments and Activities that can help you more deeply understand the chapter content.
- Apply and practice your understanding of the core skills identified in the chapter with the Building Counseling Skills unit.
- Prepare yourself for professional certification with a Practice for Certification quiz.
- Connect to videos through the Video and Resource Library.

Summary and Conclusion

Closing is an important but often neglected and misunderstood phase of counseling. The subjects of loss and ending are usually given less emphasis in counseling than those of growth and development. Thus, the subject of closing is frequently either ignored or taken for granted. Yet, successful closing is vital to the health and well-being of both counselors and clients. It is a phase of counseling that can determine the success of all previous phases and must be handled with skill. Otherwise, everyone in the counseling relationship will become stuck in reviewing data in areas that may be of little use. In addition, closing gives clients a chance to try new behaviors and serves as a motivator.

This chapter has emphasized the procedures involved in terminating an individual counseling session as well as the extended counseling relationship. These processes can be generalized to ending group or family counseling sessions. Both clients and counselors must be prepared for these endings. One way to facilitate this preparation is through the use of structure, such as time frames, and both verbal and nonverbal signals. Clients need to learn problem-solving skills before a counseling relationship is over so that they can depend on themselves rather than their counselors when they face difficult life situations. Nevertheless, it is important that a client be given permission to contact the counselor again if needed. An open policy does much to alleviate anxiety.

At times the counselor, client, or both resist terminating the relationship. Many times this resistance is related to unresolved feelings of grief and separation. When a client has such feelings, he or she may choose to terminate the relationship prematurely. A counselor may also initiate closing but usually does so for good reasons. Regardless of who initiates closing, it is vital that all involved know what is happening and prepare accordingly. If possible, it is best to end counseling on a positive note. Once closing is completed, it is helpful to conduct some type of follow-up within a year. Sometimes, referrals or recycling procedures are indicated to ensure that the client receives the type of help needed.

9

Psychoanalytic, Adlerian, and Humanistic Theories of Counseling

Chapter Overview

From this chapter you will learn about

- The nature of and importance of relatively early theories of counseling
- The premises, counselor roles, goals, techniques, and strengths/limitations of psychoanalytic theories
- The premises, counselor roles, goals, techniques, and strengths/limitations of Adlerian theory
- The premises, counselor roles, goals, techniques, and strengths/limitations of humanistic theories, specifically person-centered counseling, existential counseling, and Gestalt therapy

As you read consider

- How theories guide and direct what counselors do in sessions
- How theories influence each other and overlap while maintaining their distinctiveness
- Which theories appeal to you most and why

I know how the pressure can build sometimes
    in your own metallic tea-kettle world,
Sporadically you whistle to me,
    at other times you explode!
Somewhere beneath that noisy facade
    (in silence or stillness perhaps)
Feelings might flow with quickness and strength,
    like the Dan or the Shenandoah,
But now they incessantly boil in your mind
    steam-filling dark shadows and choking conversation.

Reprinted from "Tea-Kettle Song," by S. T. Gladding, 1974, *School Counselor, 21,* p. 209. © Samuel T. Gladding.

MyCounselingLab™

Counseling, by definition, is a process that involves interpersonal relationships (Patterson, 1985). Frequently it is conducted on an individual level in which an atmosphere of trust is fostered between counselor and client that ensures communication, exploration, planning, change, and growth. In counseling, a client gains the benefit of immediate feedback from the counselor about behaviors, feelings, plans, and progress.

The following **four variables determine the amount of growth and change that take place in any type of counseling**:

1. **counselor**,
2. **client**,
3. **setting**, and
4. **theoretical orientation**.

We have already examined some of the universal qualities of effective counselors and the counseling process. Certain characteristics seem to distinguish these aspects of counseling. For example, effective counselors have a good understanding of themselves and others, an appreciation for the influence of cultures, and a strong educational background. They understand and work with their clients using agreed-on goals and realizing that the personalities of counselors and clients have a powerful impact on each other and the counseling process. The setting in which counseling is conducted is also a critical variable. Counselors respond to client needs in different ways in various settings, such as schools, agencies, and mental health centers. The stages of counseling relationships likewise play a role in how counseling is conducted.

This chapter focuses on three theoretical orientations to counseling: psychoanalytic, Adlerian, and humanistic. These theories are grouped together because they were among the earliest counseling theories constructed. Psychoanalysis became popular in the 1910s and 1920s, Adlerian therapy in the 1930s and 1940s, and humanistic theories in the 1940s and early 1950s. Thus, there is a chronology in regard to these theories with some of the theorists actually meeting or knowing each other—for example Sigmund Freud, Alfred Adler, Fritz Perls, and Viktor Frankl (Alex Vesley, personal communication, June 4, 2011).

While there are variations and distinctions within and among these theories, some of their practices overlap with practitioners, such as Adlerians in Vienna, Austria, using a number of psychoanalytic methods including transference and countertransference. Even within the humanistic oriented theories—person-centered, existential, and Gestalt—there is some overlap with all the founders of these approaches having had a strong exposure to Freud or having practiced psychoanalysis before they formulated their distinct ways of working. Thus, the theories covered in this chapter are among the oldest and most overlapping—at least in their origin—among any that are used in the profession today. Before examining them, however, we will first focus on the nature of and importance of theory within the counseling process.

THEORY

A *theory* is a model that counselors use as a guide to hypothesize about the formation of possible solutions to a problem. "Theoretical understanding is an essential part of effective counseling practice. Theories help counselors organize clinical data, make complex processes coherent, and provide conceptual guidance for interventions" (Hansen, 2006, p. 291). Counselors decide which theory or theories to use on the basis of their educational background, philosophy, and the needs of clients. Not all approaches are appropriate for all counselors or clients. Exceptional practitioners who formulated their ideas on the basis of their experiences and observations have developed most counseling theories. Yet most theorists are somewhat tentative about their positions, realizing that no one theory fits all situations and clients (Tursi & Cochran, 2006). Indeed, one theory may not be adequate for the same client over an extended period. Counselors must choose their theoretical positions carefully and regularly reassess them.

Some theoretical models are more comprehensive than others are and "all theories are hopelessly entangled in culture, politics, and language" (Hansen, 2006, p. 293). Effective counselors realize this and are aware of which theories are most comprehensive and for what reasons. They know that theories determine what and how they see in counseling and that theories can be cataloged in a number of ways including modernism and postmodernism categories. Hansen, Stevic, and Warner (1986) list **five requirements of a good theory**:

1. *Clear, easily understood, and communicable.*   It is coherent and not contradictory.
2. *Comprehensive.*   It encompasses explanations for a wide variety of phenomena.
3. *Explicit and heuristic.*   It generates research because of its design.
4. *Specific in relating means to desired outcomes.*   It contains a way of achieving a desired end product (i.e., it is pragmatic).
5. *Useful to its intended practitioners.*   It provides guidelines for research and practice.

In addition to these five qualities, a good theory for counselors is one that matches their personal philosophies of helping. Shertzer and Stone (1974) suggest that a counseling theory must fit counselors like a suit of clothes. Some theories, like some suits, need tailoring. Therefore, effective counselors realize the importance of alterations. Counselors who wish to be versatile and effective should learn a wide variety of counseling theories and know how to apply each without violating its internal consistency (Auvenshine & Noffsinger, 1984).

PERSONAL REFLECTION

When have you received coaching or instruction on how to kick a ball or draw a figure so that you could improve as an athlete or an artist? How do you think that experience relates to a good counseling theory?

Importance of Theory

Theory is the foundation of good counseling. It challenges counselors to be caring and creative within the confines of a highly personal relationship that is structured for growth and insight (Gladding, 1990b). Theory has an impact on how client communication is conceptualized, how interpersonal relationships develop, how professional ethics are implemented, and how counselors view themselves as professionals. Without theoretical backing, counselors operate haphazardly in a trial-and-error manner and risk being both ineffective and harmful. Brammer, Abrego, and Shostrom (1993) stress the pragmatic value of a solidly formulated theory for counselors. Theory helps explain what happens in a counseling relationship and assists the counselor in predicting, evaluating, and improving results. Theory provides a framework for making scientific observations about counseling. Theorizing encourages the coherence of ideas about counseling and the production of new ideas. Hence, counseling theory can be practical by helping to make sense out of the counselor's observations.

Boy and Pine (1983) elaborate on the practical **value of theory** by suggesting that theory is the *why* **behind the** *how* **of counselors' roles**, providing a framework within which counselors can operate. Counselors guided by theory can meet the demands of their roles because they have reasons for what they do. Boy and Pine point out **six functions of theory** that help counselors in a practical way:

1. Theory helps counselors find unity and relatedness within the diversity of existence.
2. Theory compels counselors to examine relationships they would otherwise overlook.
3. Theory gives counselors operational guidelines by which to work and helps them evaluate their development as professionals.
4. Theory helps counselors focus on relevant data and tells them what to look for.
5. Theory helps counselors assist clients in the effective modification of their behavior.
6. Theory helps counselors evaluate both old and new approaches to the process of counseling. It is the base from which new counseling approaches are constructed.

"The ultimate criterion for all counseling theories is how well they provide explanations of what occurs in counseling" (Kelly, 1988, pp. 212–213). The value of theories as ways of organizing information "hinges on the degree to which they are grounded in the reality of people's lives" (Young, 1988, p. 336).

Theory into Practice

As of 2008, more than **400 systems of psychotherapy and counseling** were available worldwide (Corsini, 2008). Thus, counselors have a wide variety of theories from which to choose. Effective counselors scrutinize theories for proven effectiveness and match them to personal beliefs and realities about the nature of people and change.

However, as Okun (1990) states, the present emphasis in counseling is on connecting theories instead of creating them. This emphasis is built on the fundamental assumption that "no one theoretical viewpoint can provide all of the answers for the clients we see today" (p. xvi). Furthermore, counselors seem to be pragmatically flexible in adapting techniques and interventions from different theoretical approaches into their work without actually accepting the premises of some theoretical points of view. This practice seems to be of necessity because counselors must consider intrapersonal, interpersonal, and external factors when working with clients, and few theories blend all these dimensions together.

Most professional counselors today (approximately 60% to 70%) identify themselves as *eclectic* in the use of theory and techniques (Lazarus & Beutler, 1993). That is, they use various theories and techniques to match their clients' needs with "an average of 4.4 theories making up their therapeutic work with clients" (Cheston, 2000, p. 254). As needs change, counselors depart from a theory they are using to use another approach (a phenomenon called *style-shift counseling*). Changes counselors make are related to the **client's developmental level** (Ivey, Ivey, Myers, & Sweeney, 2005). To be effective, counselors must consider how far their clients have progressed in their structural development, as described by Jean Piaget. For example, a client who is not developmentally aware of his or her environment may need a therapeutic approach that focuses on "emotions, the body, and experience in the here and now," whereas a client who is at a more advanced level of development may respond best to a "consulting-formal operations" approach in which the emphasis is on thinking about actions (Ivey & Goncalves, 1988, p. 410). The point is that counselors and theories must start with where their clients are, helping them develop in a holistic manner.

Whereas a strength of eclecticism is its ability to draw on various theories, techniques, and practices to meet client needs, this approach has its drawbacks. For instance, an eclectic approach can be hazardous to the counseling process if the counselor is not thoroughly familiar with all aspects of the theories involved. In such situations, the counselor may become a technician without understanding why certain approaches work best with specific clients at certain times and certain ways (Cheston, 2000). This unexamined approach of undereducated counselors is sometimes sarcastically referred to as "electric"—that is, such counselors try any and all methods that "turn them on." The problem with an eclectic orientation is that counselors often do more harm than good if they have little or no understanding about what is helping the client.

To combat this problem, McBride and Martin (1990) advocate a **hierarchy of eclectic practices** and discuss the importance of having a sound theoretical base as a guide. The lowest or first level of eclecticism is really *syncretism*—a sloppy, unsystematic process of putting unrelated clinical concepts together. It is encouraged when graduate students are urged to formulate their own theories of counseling without first having experienced how tested models work. The second level of eclecticism is *traditional*. It incorporates "an orderly combination of compatible features from diverse sources [into a] harmonious whole" (English & English, 1956, p. 168). It is more thought out than syncretism, and theories are examined in greater depth.

On a third level, eclecticism is described as professional or theoretical or as *theoretical integrationism* (Lazarus & Beutler, 1993; Simon, 1989). This type of eclecticism requires that counselors master at least two theories before trying to make any combinations. The trouble with this approach is that it assumes a degree of equality between theories (which may not be true) and the existence of criteria "to determine what portions or pieces of each theory to preserve or expunge" (Lazarus & Beutler, 1993, p. 382). It differs from the traditional model in that no mastery of theory is expected in the traditional approach.

A fourth level of eclecticism is called *technical eclecticism*, exemplified in the work of Arnold Lazarus (2008) and his multimodal approach to counseling, which assesses what he describes as the seven elements of a client's experience. These vectors are summarized in the acronym *BASIC ID:*

Behavior

Affect

Sensations (e.g., seeing, hearing, smelling, touching, tasting)

Imagery

Cognitions (e.g., beliefs and values)

Interpersonal relationships

Drugs (i.e., any concerns about health, including drug use, fitness, or diet)

In this approach, procedures from different theories are selected and used in treatment "without necessarily subscribing to the theories that spawned them" (Lazarus & Beutler, 1993, p. 384). The idea is that techniques, not theories, are actually used in treating clients. Therefore, after properly assessing clients, counselors may use behavioral methods (such as assertiveness training) with existential techniques (such as confronting persons about the meaning in their lives) if the situations warrant.

This approach is in line with what Cavanagh and Levitov (2002) propose as a **healthy eclectic approach to counseling**. It requires counselors to have (a) a sound knowledge and understanding of the counseling theories used, (b) a basic integrative philosophy of human behavior that brings disparate parts of differing theories into a meaningful collage, and (c) a flexible means of fitting the approach to the client, not vice versa. Counselors who follow this model may operate pragmatically and effectively within an eclectic framework. The critical variables in being a healthy eclectic counselor are a mastery of theory and an acute sensitivity to knowing what approach to use when, where, and how (Harman, 1977).

A final type of eclectic approach is the *transtheoretical* **model** (TTM) of change (Norcross & Beutler, 2008; Prochaska & DiClemente, 1992). This model is developmentally based and has been empirically derived over time. It is "an alternative to technical eclectic approaches that tend to be inclusive to the point that various components are 'poorly' held together" (Petrocelli, 2002, p. 23). The model is direction focused and proposes **five stages of change** from precontemplation to maintenance. There are also five levels of change:

- **symptom/situation problems,**
- **maladaptive cognitions,**
- **current interpersonal conflicts,**
- **family system conflicts,** and
- **intrapersonal conflicts.**

"Counseling from a TTM perspective allows for a more *macroscopic approach* (involving a broad and comprehensive theoretical framework) and *personal adaptation* (involving an increase in critical, logical, accurate, and scientific-like thinking) rather than simple *personal adjustment*" (Petrocelli, 2002, p. 25). Its main drawbacks are its comprehensiveness and complexity and the fact that TTM has been tested only among limited groups (for example, addictions populations).

Past the pure theory views and eclectic approaches, **counseling theories are now entering a postmodernist perspective**. As such they are being seen as prepackaged narratives that help clients create new meaning systems, "not by objectively discovering old ones" (Hansen, 2006, p. 295). The essence of such a view is seen in **social constructive approaches**. For the rest of this chapter and the next, 13 mainline theories that have gained popularity over time will be explained.

CASE EXAMPLE

Tim's Theories

Tim was a newly minted counselor. As such, he was observant and quick to pick up nuances in various forms of related therapeutic approaches. However, Tim was troubled. He liked most of the theories he read about and had a hard time deciding which ones he would master. He really began to waffle when he found out that most of the theories worked well when implemented by a **master therapist—one who had practiced counseling diligently for at least 10 years**.

Knowing Tim's plight and the fact that he did not want to use only techniques, what might you advise him to do in deciding on a theoretical approach? Would eclecticism work for someone as undecided as Tim? Why or why not?

PSYCHOANALYTIC THEORIES

From a historical point of view alone, psychoanalytic theories are important and in briefer as well as classic forms are still practiced today. They were among the first to gain public recognition and acceptance. Psychoanalysis in its classic form, as developed by Sigmund Freud, is examined in this section. Freud's conceptualization and implementation of psychoanalysis is the basis from which many other theories developed, either by modifying parts of this approach or reacting against it.

Psychoanalysis

FOUNDERS/DEVELOPERS.   Sigmund Freud, a Viennese psychiatrist (1856–1939), is the person primarily associated with psychoanalysis. His genius created the original ideas. His daughter, Anna Freud, further elaborated the theory, especially as it relates to children and development of defense mechanisms. In more recent times, Heinz Kohut has extended the theory to developmental issues, especially attachment, through his conceptualization of object relations theory.

VIEW OF HUMAN NATURE.   Freud's view of human nature is dynamic with the transformation and exchange of energy within the personality (Hall, 1954). People have a *conscious mind* (attuned to an awareness of the outside world), a *preconscious mind* (that contains hidden memories or forgotten experiences that can be remembered), and an *unconscious mind* (containing the instinctual, repressed, and powerful forces). According to Freud, the personality consists of three parts:

1. *Id* (comprised of amoral basic instincts, which operates according to the pleasure principle)
2. *Ego* (the conscious, decision-making "executive of the mind," which operates according to the reality principle)
3. *Superego* (the conscience of the mind that contains the values of parental figures and that operates according to the moral principle)

The id and the superego are confined to the unconscious; the ego operates primarily in the conscious but also in the preconscious and unconscious.

Psychoanalysis is also built on what Freud referred to as *psychosexual developmental stages*. Each of the stages focuses on a zone of pleasure that is dominant at a particular time:

the *oral stage*, where the mouth is the chief pleasure zone and basic gratification is from sucking and biting;

the *anal stage*, where delight is in either withholding or eliminating feces;

the *phallic stage*, where the chief zone of pleasure is the sex organs, and members of both sexes must work through their sexual desires;

latency, where energy is focused on peer activities and personal mastery of cognitive learning and physical skills; and

the *genital stage*, where if all has gone well previously, each gender takes more interest in the other and normal heterosexual patterns of interaction appear.

Excessive frustration or overindulgence in the first three stages are the main difficulties that can arise going through these stages, in which case the person could become *fixated* (or arrested) at that level of development and/or overly dependent on the use of immature *defense mechanisms* (i.e., ways of coping with anxiety on an unconscious level by denying or distorting reality) (Table 9.1).

TABLE 9.1 Psychoanalytic defense mechanisms

• Repression	The most basic of the defense mechanisms, repression is the unconscious exclusion of distressing or painful thoughts and memories. All other defense mechanisms make some use of repression.
• Denial	In this process, a person refuses to see or accept any problem or troublesome aspect of life. Denial operates at the preconscious or conscious level.
• Regression	When individuals are under stress, they often return to a less mature way of behaving.
• Projection	Instead of stating what one really thinks or feels, he or she attributes an unacceptable thought, feeling, or motive onto another.
• Rationalization	This defense mechanism involves giving an "intellectual reason" to justify a certain action. The reason and the action are connected only in the person's mind after the behavior has been completed.
• Reaction Formation	When an individual behaves in a manner that is just the opposite of how he or she feels, it is known as a "reaction formation." This type of behavior is usually quite exaggerated, such as acting especially nice to someone whom one dislikes intensely.
• Displacement	This defense is a redirection of an emotional response onto a "safe target." The substitute person or object receives the feeling instead of the person directly connected with it.

Source: Gladding, S. T. (2008). *Group work: A counseling specialty.* Upper Saddle River, NJ: Prentice Hall.

ROLE OF THE COUNSELOR.   Professionals who practice classical psychoanalysis function as experts. They encourage their clients to talk about whatever comes to mind, especially childhood experiences. To create an atmosphere in which the client feels free to express difficult thoughts, psychoanalysts, after a few face-to-face sessions, often have the client lie down on a couch while the analyst remains out of view (usually seated behind the client's head). The analyst's role is to let clients gain insight by reliving and working through the unresolved past experiences that come into focus during sessions. The development of transference is encouraged to help clients deal realistically with unconscious material. Unlike some other approaches, psychoanalysis encourages the counselor to interpret for the client.

GOALS.   The goals of psychoanalysis vary according to the client, but they focus mainly on personal adjustment, usually inducing a reorganization of internal forces within the person. In most cases, a primary goal is to help the client become more aware of the unconscious aspects of his or her personality and to work through current reactions that may be dysfunctional (Tursi & Cochran, 2006).

A second major goal, often tied to the first, is to help a client work through a developmental stage not previously resolved. If accomplished, clients become unstuck and are able to live more productively. Working through unresolved developmental stages may require a major reconstruction of the personality.

A final goal of psychoanalysis is helping clients cope with the demands of the society in which they live. Unhappy people, according to this theory, are not in tune with themselves or society. Psychoanalysis stresses environmental adjustment, especially in the areas of work and intimacy. The focus is on strengthening the ego so that perceptions and plans become more realistic.

TECHNIQUES. **Psychoanalytic techniques** are most often applied within a specific setting, such as a counselor's office or a hospital's interview room. Among the most prominent of these techniques are free association, dream analysis, analysis of transference, analysis of resistance, and interpretation. Although each technique is examined separately here, in practice they are integrated.

- *Free Association.* In free association, the client abandons the normal way of censoring thoughts by consciously repressing them and instead says whatever comes to mind, even if the thoughts seem silly, irrational, suggestive, or painful. In this way, the id is requested to speak and the ego remains silent (Freud, 1936). Unconscious material enters the conscious mind, and there the counselor interprets it.
- *Dream Analysis.* Freud believed that dreams were a main avenue to understanding the unconscious, even calling them "the royal road to the unconscious." He thought dreams were an attempt to fulfill a childhood wish or express unacknowledged sexual desires. In dream analysis, clients are encouraged to dream and remember dreams. The counselor is especially sensitive to two aspects of dreams: the *manifest content* (obvious meaning) and the *latent content* (hidden but true meaning) (Jones, 1979). The analyst helps interpret both aspects to the client.
- *Analysis of Transference.* *Transference* is the client's response to a counselor as if the counselor were some significant figure in the client's past, usually a parent figure. The analyst encourages this transference and interprets the positive or negative feelings expressed. The release of feelings is therapeutic, an emotional catharsis. But the real value of these experiences lies in the client's increased self-knowledge, which comes through the counselor's analysis of the transference. Those who experience transference and understand what is happening are then freed to move on to another developmental stage.
- *Analysis of Resistance.* Sometimes clients initially make progress while undergoing psychoanalysis and then slow down or stop. Their resistance to the therapeutic process may take many forms, such as missing appointments, being late for appointments, not paying fees, persisting in transference, blocking thoughts during free association, or refusing to recall dreams or early memories. A counselor's analysis of resistance can help clients gain insight into it as well as other behaviors. If resistance is not dealt with, the therapeutic process will probably come to a halt.
- *Interpretation.* Interpretation should be considered part of the techniques we have already examined and complementary to them. When interpreting, the counselor helps the client understand the meaning of past and present personal events. Interpretation encompasses explanations and analysis of a client's thoughts, feelings, and actions. Counselors must carefully time the use of interpretation. If it comes too soon in the relationship, it can drive the client away. However, if it is not employed at all or used infrequently, the client may fail to develop insight.

STRENGTHS AND CONTRIBUTIONS. Classical psychoanalysis has several unique emphases:

- The approach emphasizes the importance of **sexuality** and the **unconscious** in human behavior. Before this theory came into being, sexuality (especially childhood sexuality) was denied, and little attention was paid to unconscious forces.
- The approach lends itself to empirical studies; it is **heuristic**. Freud's proposals have generated a tremendous amount of research.

- The approach provides a theoretical base of support for a number of **diagnostic instruments**. Some psychological tests, such as the Thematic Apperception Test or the Rorschach Ink Blots, are rooted in psychoanalytic theory.
- Psychoanalysis continues to evolve and most recently has emphasized adaptive processes and social relations.
- The approach appears to be **effective** for those who suffer from a **wide variety of disorders**, including hysteria, narcissism, obsessive-compulsive reactions, character disorders, anxiety, phobias, and sexual difficulties (Luborsky, O'Reilly-Landry, & Arlow, 2008).
- The approach stresses the importance of developmental growth stages.

LIMITATIONS. The following limiting factors are a part of psychoanalysis:

- The classical psychoanalytic approach is **time-consuming** and **expensive**. A person who undergoes psychoanalysis is usually seen three to five times a week over a period of years (Bankart, 1997; Nye, 2000).
- The approach does not seem to lend itself to working with older clients or even a large variety of clients. "Patients benefiting most from analysis" are mainly "middle-aged men and women oppressed by a sense of futility and searching for meaning in life" (Bradley & Cox, 2001, p. 35).
- The approach has been **claimed almost exclusively by psychiatry**, despite Freud's wishes (Vandenbos, Cummings, & Deleon, 1992). Counselors and psychologists without medical degrees have had a difficult time getting extensive training in psychoanalysis.
- The approach is based on many concepts that are **not easily communicated or understood**—the id, ego, and superego, for instance. Psychoanalytical terminology seems overly complicated.
- The approach is **deterministic**. For instance, Freud attributed certain limitations in women to be a result of gender—that is, of being female.
- The approach does not lend itself to the needs of most individuals who seek professional counseling. The psychoanalytic model has become associated with people who have **major adjustment difficulties** or want or need to explore the unconscious.

PERSONAL REFLECTION

Sometimes classic psychoanalysis is characterized this way: Too much superego, you're a cabbage; too much id, you're a savage.

How does such a characterization do justice or injustice to achieving a healthy ego within a person? What does it say about the therapeutic challenge in implementing the psychoanalytic approach in counseling? What does it say about the strength of the ego?

ADLERIAN THEORY

Adlerian theory focuses on social interests as well as the purposefulness of behavior and the importance of developing a healthy style of life. The therapeutic approach that has grown out of this theory is internationally popular.

Adlerian Counseling

FOUNDERS/DEVELOPERS.   Alfred Adler (1870–1937) was the founder of the Adlerian approach to counseling, also known as *Individual Psychology* (to emphasize the holistic and indivisible nature of people). He was a contemporary of Sigmund Freud and even a member of his Vienna Psychoanalytic Society. However, Adler differed from Freud about the importance of biological drives as the primary motivating force of life and stressed the importance of subjective feelings and social interests. His theory is more hopeful. Individual psychology waned in popularity after his death but was revitalized by Rudolph Dreikurs, Manford Sonstegard, Oscar Christensen, Raymond Corsini, Donald Dinkmeyer, and Thomas Sweeney, among others.

VIEW OF HUMAN NATURE.   A central idea for Adler in regard to human nature is that people are primarily motivated by *social interest*, that is, a feeling of being connected to society as a part of the social whole, an active interest in and empathy with others, as well as a need and will-ingness to contribute to the general social good (Mosak & Maniacci, 2008; Overholser, 2010). Those with social interest take responsibility for themselves and others and are cooperative and positive in regard to their mental health. "Those who are failures, including neurotics, psychot-ics, and criminally oriented individuals are failures because they are lacking in social interest" (Daugherty, Murphy, & Paugh, 2001, p. 466).

Adler's theory holds that conscious aspects of behavior, rather than the unconscious, are central to the development of personality. A major Adlerian tenet is that people strive to become successful (i.e., the best they can be); a process he called *striving for perfection* or complete-ness (Adler, 1964). There is also a tendency for each person initially to feel inferior to others. If this feeling is not overcome, the person develops an *inferiority complex*. Such a complex, if not changed, becomes the basis by which one's personality is defined. In contrast, a person who overcompensates for feelings of inferiority develops a *superiority complex*, which is what Adler also described as a *neurotic fiction* that is unproductive.

Adler believed that people are as influenced by future (teleological) goals as by past causes. His theory also places considerable emphasis on *birth order*: those who share ordinal birth positions (e.g., firstborns) may have more in common with one another than siblings from the same family (Dreikurs, 1950). **Five ordinal positions** are emphasized in Adlerian literature on the family constellation: **firstborns, secondborns, middle children, youngest children**, and **only children** (Dreikurs, 1967; Dreikurs & Soltz, 1964; Sweeney, 2009).

In addition to birth order, the family environment is important to a person's development, particularly in the first 5 years of life. Adlerian theory stresses that each person creates a *style of life* (an individual's methods of relating to others, viewing the world, and governing behavior) by age 5. This is done by the child primarily through interacting with other family members. A **negative family atmosphere** might be authoritarian, rejecting, suppressive, materialistic, over-protective, or pitying (Dreikurs & Soltz, 1964), whereas a **positive family atmosphere** might be democratic, accepting, open, and social. Nevertheless, perception of the family atmosphere, rather than any events themselves, is crucial to the development of a style of life (Adler, 1964). Individuals behave as if the world were a certain way and are guided by their *fictions*—that is, their subjective evaluations of themselves and their environments.

Overall, Adlerians believe there are **three main life tasks: society, work, and sexuality**. As mentioned previously, Adlerian theory places strong emphasis on developing social interest and contributing to society. The theory holds that work is essential for human survival and that we must learn to be interdependent. Furthermore, a person must define his or her sexuality in regard to self and others, in a spirit of cooperation rather than competition. Adler also mentions **two other challenges of life**, although he does not fully develop them: **spirituality and coping with self** (Dreikurs & Mosak, 1966). According to Adlerian theory, it is crucial to emphasize that, when facing any life task, *courage* (a willingness to take risks without knowing what the consequences may be) is required.

ROLE OF THE COUNSELOR.   Adlerian counselors function primarily as diagnosticians, teachers, and models in the equalitarian relationships they establish with their clients. They try to assess why clients are oriented to a certain way of thinking and behaving. The counselor makes an assessment by gathering information on the family constellation and a client's earliest memories. The counselor then shares impressions, opinions, and feelings with the client and concentrates on promoting the therapeutic relationship. The client is encouraged to examine and change a faulty lifestyle by developing social interest (Adler, 1927, 1931).

Adlerians are frequently active in sharing hunches or guesses with clients and are often directive when assigning clients homework, such as to act "as if" the client were the person he or she wants to be. Adlerian counselors employ a variety of techniques, some of which are borrowed from other approaches.

GOALS.   The goals of Adlerian counseling revolve around helping people develop healthy, holistic lifestyles. This may mean educating or reeducating clients about what such lifestyles are as well as helping them overcome feelings of inferiority. One of the major goals of Adlerian counseling is to help clients overcome a *faulty style of life*—that is, a life that is self-centered and based on mistaken goals and incorrect assumptions associated with feelings of inferiority. These feelings might stem from being born with a physical or mental defect, being pampered by parents, or being neglected. The feelings must be corrected, and inappropriate forms of behavior must be stopped. To do so, the counselor assumes the role of teacher and interpreter of events. Adlerian counseling deals with the whole person (Kern & Watts, 1993). The client is ultimately in charge of deciding whether to pursue social or self-interests.

TECHNIQUES.   The establishment of a counseling relationship is crucial if the goals of Adlerian counseling are to be achieved. Certain techniques help enhance this process. Adlerian counselors try to develop a warm, supportive, empathic, friendly, and equalitarian relationship with clients. Counseling is seen as a collaborative effort (Adler, 1956). Counselors actively listen and respond in much the same way that person-centered counselors do (James & Gilliland, 2003).

After a relationship has been established, the counselor concentrates on an analysis of the client's lifestyle, including examination of the family constellation, early memories, dreams, and priorities. As previously noted, the family constellation and the atmosphere in which children grow greatly influence both self-perception and the perceptions of others. No two children are born into the same environment, but a child's ordinal position and assessment of the family atmosphere have a major impact on development and behavior. Often, a client is able to gain insight by recalling early memories, especially events before the age of 10. Adler (1931) contended that a person remembers childhood events that are consistent with his or her present view of self, others, and the world in general. Adlerian counselors look both for themes and specific details within these early recollections (Slavik, 1991; Statton & Wilborn, 1991; Watkins, 1985). Figures from the past are treated as prototypes rather than specific individuals. Recent and past dreams are also a part of lifestyle analysis. Adlerian theory holds that dreams are a possible rehearsal for future courses of action. Recurrent dreams are especially important. A look at the client's priorities is helpful in understanding his or her style of life. A client may persist in one predominant lifestyle, such as always trying to please, unless challenged to change.

Counselors next try to help clients develop insight, especially by asking open-ended questions and making interpretations. Open-ended questions allow clients to explore patterns in their lives that have gone unnoticed. Interpretation often takes the form of intuitive guesses. The ability to empathize is especially important in this process, for the counselor must be able to feel what it is like to be the client before zeroing in on the reasons for the client's present behaviors. At other times, interpretations are based on the counselor's general knowledge of ordinal position and family constellation.

To foster behavioral change, the Adlerian counselor uses specific techniques:

- *Confrontation.*   The counselor challenges clients to consider their own private logic. When clients examine this logic, they often realize they can change it and their behavior.
- *Asking "the question."*   The counselor asks, "What would be different if you were well?" Clients are often asked the question during the initial interview, but it is appropriate at any time.
- *Encouragement.*   Encouragement implies faith in a person (Dinkmeyer & Losoncy, 1980; Dreikurs & Soltz, 1964). Counselors encourage their clients to feel good about themselves and others (Adler, 1931). They state their belief that behavior change is possible for clients. Encouragement is the key to making productive lifestyle choices in learning and living.
- *Acting "as if."*   Clients are instructed to act "as if" they are the persons they want to be—for instance, the ideal persons they see in their dreams (Gold, 1979). Adler originally got the idea of acting "as if" from Hans Vaihinger (1911), who wrote that people create the worlds they live in by the assumptions they make about the world.
- *Spitting in the client's soup.*   A counselor points out certain behaviors to clients and thus ruins the payoff for the behavior. For example, a mother who always acts superior to her daughter by showing her up may continue to do so after the behavior has been pointed out, but the reward for doing so is now gone.
- *Catching oneself.*   Clients learn to become aware of self-destructive behaviors or thoughts. At first, the counselor may help in the process, but eventually this responsibility is taken over by clients.
- *Task setting.*   Clients initially set short-range, attainable goals and eventually work up to long-term, realistic objectives. Once clients make behavioral changes and realize some control over their lives, counseling ends.
- *Push button.*   Clients are encouraged to realize they have choices about what stimuli in their lives they pay attention to. They are taught to create the feelings they want by concentrating on their thoughts. The technique is like pushing a button because clients can choose to remember negative or positive experiences (Mosak & Maniacci, 2008).

STRENGTHS AND CONTRIBUTIONS.   The Adlerian approach to counseling has a number of unique contributions and emphases:

- The approach fosters an **equalitarian atmosphere** through the positive techniques that counselors promote. Rapport and commitment are enhanced by its processes, and the chances for change are increased. Counselor encouragement and support are valued commodities. Adlerian counselors approach their clients with an educational orientation and take an optimistic outlook on life.

- The approach is **versatile** over the life span. "Adlerian theorists have developed counseling models for working with children, adolescents, parents, entire families, teacher groups, and other segments of society" (Purkey & Schmidt, 1987, p. 115). Play therapy for children ages 4 to 9 seems to be especially effective.
- The approach is useful in the treatment of a **variety of disorders**, including conduct disorders, antisocial disorders, anxiety disorders of childhood and adolescence, some affective disorders, and personality disorders (Seligman, 2004).
- The approach has contributed to other helping theories and to the public's knowledge and understanding of human interactions. Many of Adler's ideas have been integrated into other counseling approaches.
- The approach can be **employed selectively in different cultural contexts** (Brown, 1997). For instance, the concept of "encouragement" is appropriately emphasized in working with groups that have traditionally emphasized collaboration such as Hispanics and Asian Americans, whereas the concept "sibling rivalry" may be highlighted with traditional European North Americans who stress competition.

LIMITATIONS.   Adlerian theory is limited in the following ways:

- The approach **lacks a firm, supportive research base**. Relatively few empirical studies clearly outline Adlerian counseling's effectiveness.
- The approach is **vague in regard to some of its terms and concepts**.
- The approach **may be too optimistic about human nature**, especially social cooperation and interest. Some critics consider this view neglectful of other life dimensions, such as the power and place of the unconscious.
- The approach's basic principles, such as a democratic family structure, may not fit well in working with clients whose **cultural context** stresses the idea of a lineal social relationship, such as with traditional Arab Americans (Brown, 1997).
- The approach, which **relies heavily on verbal erudition, logic, and insight**, may be limited in its applicability to clients who are not intellectually bright (James & Gilliland, 2003).

CASE EXAMPLE

Ansley Acts "As If"

Ansley had always been verbally aggressive. She had a sharp tongue and an exceptional vocabulary. She could put other girls in their place quickly. Thus, she was both admired and hated.

On the suggestion of a friend, Ansley saw an Adlerian counselor. She liked the social emphasis that she learned, so she decided to change her ways. Ansley thought the quickest way to become the person she wanted to be was to act "as if."

Was Ansley naive to think that acting as if would help her become her ideal? From an Adlerian perspective, what else would you suggest she do or try?

HUMANISTIC THEORIES

The term *humanistic*, as a descriptor of counseling, focuses on the potential of individuals to actively choose and purposefully decide about matters related to themselves and their environments. Professionals who embrace humanistic counseling approaches help people increase self-understanding through experiencing their feelings. The term is broad and encompasses counseling theories that are focused on people as decision makers and initiators of their own growth and development. Three of these theories are covered here: person-centered, existential, and Gestalt.

Person-Centered Counseling

FOUNDERS/DEVELOPERS.   Carl Rogers (1902–1987) is the person most identified with person-centered counseling. Indeed, it was Rogers who first formulated the theory in the form of nondirective psychotherapy in his 1942 book, *Counseling and Psychotherapy*. The theory later evolved into client-centered and person-centered counseling with multiple applications to groups, families, and communities as well as individuals.

VIEW OF HUMAN NATURE.   Implicit in person-centered counseling is a particular view of human nature: People are essentially good (Rogers, 1961). Humans are characteristically "positive, forward-moving, constructive, realistic, and trustworthy" (Rogers, 1957, p. 199). Each person is aware, inner directed, and moving toward self-actualization from infancy on.

According to Rogers, self-actualization is the most prevalent and motivating drive of existence and encompasses actions that influence the total person. "The organism has one basic tendency and striving, to actualize, maintain, and enhance the experiencing organism" (Rogers, 1951, p. 487). Person-centered theorists believe that each person is capable of finding a personal meaning and purpose in life. Dysfunctionality is really a failure to learn and change (Bohart & Watson, 2011).

Rogers views the individual from a *phenomenological perspective*: What is important is the person's perception of reality rather than an event itself (Rogers, 1955). This way of seeing the person is similar to Adler's. The concept of self is another idea that Rogers and Adler share. But for Rogers the concept is so central to his theory that his ideas are often referred to as *self theory*. The self is an outgrowth of what a person experiences, and an awareness of self helps a person differentiate himself or herself from others (Nye, 2000).

For a healthy self to emerge, a person needs *positive regard*—love, warmth, care, respect, and acceptance. But in childhood, as well as later in life, a person often receives *conditional regard* from parents and others. Feelings of worth develop if the person behaves in certain ways because conditional acceptance teaches the person to feel valued only when conforming to others' wishes. Thus, a person may have to deny or distort a perception when someone on whom the person depends for approval sees a situation differently. An individual who is caught in such a dilemma becomes aware of incongruities between self-perception and experience. If a person does not do as others wish, he or she will not be accepted and valued. Yet if a person conforms, he or she opens up a gap between the *ideal self* (what the person is striving to become) and the *real self* (what the person is). The further the ideal self is from the real self, the more alienated and maladjusted a person becomes.

ROLE OF THE COUNSELOR.   The counselor's role is a holistic one. He or she sets up and promotes a climate in which the client is free and encouraged to explore all aspects of self (Rogers,

1951, 1980). This atmosphere focuses on the counselor–client relationship, which Rogers describes as one with a special "I-Thou" personal quality. The counselor is aware of the client's verbal and nonverbal language, and the counselor reflects back what he or she is hearing or observing (Braaten, 1986). Neither the client nor the counselor knows what direction the sessions will take or what goals will emerge in the process. The client is a person in process who is "entitled to direct his or her own therapy" (Moon, 2007, p. 277). Thus, the counselor trusts the client to develop an agenda on which he or she wishes to work. The counselor's job is to work as a facilitator rather than a director. In the person-centered approach, the counselor is the process expert and expert learner (of the client). Patience is essential (Miller, 1996).

GOALS.   The goals of person-centered counseling center around the client as a person, not his or her problem. Rogers (1977) emphasizes that people need to be assisted in learning how to cope with situations. One of the main ways to accomplish this is by helping a client become a fully functioning person who has no need to apply defense mechanisms to everyday experiences. Such an individual becomes increasingly willing to change and grow. He or she is more open to experience, more trusting of self-perception, and engaged in self-exploration and evaluation (Rogers, 1961). Furthermore, a fully functioning person develops a greater acceptance of self and others and becomes a better decision maker in the here and now. Ultimately, a client is helped to identify, use, and integrate his or her own resources and potential (Boy & Pine, 1983; Miller, 1996).

TECHNIQUES.   For person-centered therapists, the quality of the counseling relationship is much more important than techniques (Glauser & Bozarth, 2001). Rogers (1957) believed there are **three necessary and sufficient (i.e., core) conditions of counseling**:

1. **empathy**,
2. **unconditional positive regard** (acceptance, prizing), and
3. **congruence** (genuineness, openness, authenticity, transparency).

Empathy may be subjective, interpersonal, or objective (Clark, 2004; Rogers, 1964). "**Subjective empathy** enables a counselor to momentarily experience what it is like to be a client, **interpersonal empathy** relates to understanding a client's phenomenological experiencing, and **objective empathy** uses reputable knowledge sources outside of a client's frame of reference" (Clark, 2010a, p. 348).

In therapeutic situations, empathy is primarily the counselor's ability to feel with clients and convey this understanding back to them. This may be done in multiple ways but, essentially, **empathy** is an attempt to **think with**, rather than for or about, **the client** and to grasp the client's communications, intentions, and meanings (Brammer et al., 1993; Clark, 2007; Moon, 2007). Rogers (1975) noted, "The research keeps piling up and it points strongly to the conclusion that a high degree of empathy in a relationship is possibly the most potent and certainly one of the most potent factors in bringing about change and learning" (p. 3).

Unconditional positive regard, also known as **acceptance**, is a deep and genuine caring for the client as a person—that is, prizing the person just for being (Rogers, 1961, 1980). *Congruence* is the condition of being transparent in the therapeutic relationship by giving up roles and facades (Rogers, 1980). It is the "counselor's readiness for setting aside concerns and personal preoccupations and for being available and open in relationship with the client" (Moon, 2007, p. 278).

Since 1980, person-centered counselors have tried a number of other procedures for working with clients, such as limited self-disclosure of feelings, thoughts, and values (Corey, 2009). **Motivational interviewing (MI)** has also grown out of the person-centered approach and has been used to help ambivalent clients more clearly assess their thoughts and feelings as they contemplate making changes. "Typically MI is differentiated from Rogers's style in that MI is directive, attending to and reinforcing selective change talk regarding the presenting behavioral problem" (Mason, 2009, p. 357). At the heart of person-centered counseling, regardless of procedures, is that clients grow by experiencing themselves and others in relationships (Cormier, Nurius, & Osborn, 2009). Therefore, Rogers (1967) and person-centered counselors of today believe that "significant positive personality change" cannot occur except in relationships (p. 73).

Methods that help promote the counselor–client relationship include, but are not limited to, active and passive listening, accurate reflection of thoughts and feelings, clarification, summarization, confrontation, and general or open-ended leads. Questions are avoided whenever possible (Tursi & Cochran, 2006).

STRENGTHS AND CONTRIBUTIONS.   Person-centered counseling's unique aspects include the following:

- The approach revolutionized the counseling profession by linking counseling with psychotherapy and demystifying it by making audiotapes of actual sessions and publishing actual transcripts of counseling sessions (Goodyear, 1987; Sommers-Flanagan, 2007).
- The person-centered approach to counseling is applicable to a wide range of human problems, including institutional changes, labor–management relationships, leadership development, career decision making, and international diplomacy. For instance, Cornelius-White (2005) has found the person-centered approach can be effective in promoting multicultural counseling. Likewise, Lemoire and Chen (2005) have argued that "the person-centered approach seems to have the potential to create the necessary conditions that counteract stigmatization, allowing adolescents who are associated with a stigmatized sexual minority group to cope with their sexual identity in a manner that is more constructive for them" (p. 146).
- The approach has generated extensive research (Tursi & Cochran, 2006). It initially set the standard for doing research on counseling variables, especially those that Rogers (1957) deemed "necessary and sufficient" to bring about therapeutic change.
- The approach is effective in a number of settings. Person-centered counseling helps improve psychological adjustment, learning, and frustration tolerance and decrease defensiveness. It is appropriate in treating mild to moderate anxiety states, adjustment disorders, and conditions not attributable to mental disorders, such as uncomplicated bereavement or interpersonal relations (Seligman, 2004).
- The person-centered approach may be especially helpful in working with clients who have experienced tragedies since it allows them "to struggle through emotions and actually become less affected in time by fully realizing feelings related to the tragedies" (Tursi & Cochran, 2006, p. 395).
- The approach focuses on the open and accepting relationship established by counselors and clients and the short-term nature of the helping process.
- The basics of the approach take a relatively short time to learn. With its emphasis on mastering listening skills, person-centered counseling is a foundation for training many paraprofessional helpers. Furthermore, it is the basis for several new and emerging

approaches to treatment, and it is frequently combined with other theoretical orientations to counseling such as cognitive and behavioral (Prochaska & Norcross, 2010; Seligman & Reichenberg, 2010).

- The approach has a positive view of human nature and it continues to evolve.

LIMITATIONS.   The limitations of person-centered theory are also noteworthy:

- The approach may be too simplistic, optimistic, leisurely, and unfocused for clients in crisis or who need more structure and direction (Seligman & Reichenberg, 2010; Tursi & Cochran, 2006).
- The approach depends on bright, insightful, hard-working clients for best results. It has limited applicability and is seldom employed with the severely disabled or young children (Henderson & Thompson 2011).
- The approach ignores diagnosis, the unconscious, developmental theories, and innately generated sexual and aggressive drives. Many critics think it is overly optimistic.
- The approach deals only with surface issues and does not challenge the client to explore deeper areas. Because person-centered counseling is short term, it may not make a permanent impact on the person.
- The approach is more attitudinal than technique-based. It is void of specific techniques to bring about client change (Moon, 2007).

PERSONAL REFLECTION

What do you find most appealing about the person-centered approach? Why? What do you find least appealing? Why?

Existential Counseling

FOUNDERS/DEVELOPERS.   Rollo May (1909–1994) and Viktor Frankl (1905–1997) are two of the most influential professionals in the field of existential counseling. May dealt extensively with anxiety, especially in regard to his life and death struggle with tuberculosis, whereas Frankl, who was interred in Nazi concentration camps during World War II, focused on the meaning of life even under the most horrendous death camp conditions.

VIEW OF HUMAN NATURE.   "The existential approach disclaims the deterministic view of human nature and emphasizes the freedom that human beings have to choose what to make of their circumstances" (Fernando, 2007, p. 226). As a group, existentialists believe that people form their lives by the **choices** they make. Even in the worst situations, such as the Nazi death camps, there is an opportunity to make important life-and-death decisions, such as whether to struggle to stay alive (Frankl, 1969). Existentialists focus on this free will of choice and the action that goes with it. They view people as the authors of their lives. They contend that people are responsible for any decision in life they make and that some choices are healthier and more meaningful than others.

According to Frankl (1962), the "meaning of life always changes but it never ceases to be" (p. 113). His theory, known as *logotherapy*, states that **meaning goes beyond self-actualization** and exists at **three levels**: (a) *ultimate meanings* (e.g., there is an order to the universe);

(b) **meaning of the moment**; and (c) **common, day-to-day meaning** (Das, 1998). We can **discover life's meaning in three ways**:

1. *by doing a deed,* that is, by achieving or accomplishing something,
2. *by experiencing a value,* such as a work of nature, culture, or love, and
3. *by suffering,* that is, by finding a proper attitude toward unalterable fate.

Existentialists believe that psychopathology is a failure to make meaningful choices and maximize one's potential (McIllroy, 1979). Choices may be avoided and potentials not realized because of the anxiety that is involved in action. Anxiety is often associated with paralysis, but May (1977) argues that normal anxiety may be healthy and motivational and can help people change.

ROLE OF THE COUNSELOR.   There are no uniform roles that existential counselors follow. Every client is considered unique. Therefore, counselors are sensitive to all aspects of their clients' character, "such as voice, posture, facial expression, even dress and apparently accidental movements of the body" (May, 1939, p. 101). Basically, **counselors concentrate on being authentic** with their clients and entering into deep and personal relationships with them. "The counselor strives to be with the client in the here-and-now, and to understand and experience the ongoing emotional and mental state of the client. In order to do this, the counselor needs to express his or her own feelings" (Fernando, 2007, p. 231). Therefore, it is not unusual for an existential counselor to share personal experiences with a client to deepen the relationship and help the client realize a shared humanness and struggle. Buhler and Allen (1972) suggest that existential counselors focus on person-to-person relationships that emphasize mutuality, wholeness, and growth. Counselors who practice from Frankl's logotherapy perspective are Socratic in engaging their clients in dialogue (Alex Vesley, June 3, 2011, personal communication).

However, all existential counselors serve as a model of how to achieve individual potential and make decisions. They concentrate on helping the client experience subjective feelings, gain clearer self-understanding, and move toward the establishment of a new way of being in the world. The focus is living productively in the present, not recovering a personal past. They also focus on ultimate human concerns such as death, freedom, isolation, and meaninglessness (Yalom, & Josselson, 2011).

GOALS.   The goals of existentialists include helping clients realize the importance of meaning, responsibility, awareness, freedom, and potential. Existentialists hope that during the course of counseling, clients will take more responsibility for their lives. "The aim of therapy is that the patient experience his existence as real" (May, Angel, & Ellenberger, 1958, p. 85). In the process, the client is freed from being an observer of events and becomes a shaper of meaningful personal activity and an embracer of personal values that lead to a meaningful lifestyle.

TECHNIQUES.   "Existential theory does not limit the counselor to specific techniques and interventions" (Fernando, 2007, p. 230). The existential approach has fewer techniques available than almost any other model of counseling. Yet this apparent weakness (i.e., a lack of therapeutic tricks and psychological jargon) is paradoxically a strength because it allows existential counselors to borrow ideas as well as use a wide range of personal and professional skills. "Approaching human beings merely in terms of techniques necessarily implies manipulating them," and manipulation is opposed to what existentialists espouse (Frankl, 1967, p. 139). Thus, existentialists are free to use techniques as widely diversified as desensitization and free association or to disassociate themselves from these practices entirely. For instance, Southwick, Gilmartin, Mcdonough, and Morrissey (2006) used logotherapy as part of a group educational treatment in working with chronic combat-related PTSD veterans by having those in the group focus on meaning combined with having them perform community service such as tutoring children and delivering Meals-on-Wheels. The result for the majority of the participants was an increase in selfless acts and more motivation for intentional living.

The most effective and powerful technique existential counselors have is the relationship with the client. Ideally, the counselor transcends his or her own needs and focuses on the client. In the process, the counselor is open and self-revealing in an attempt to help the client become more in touch with personal feelings and experiences. The emphasis in the relationship is on authenticity, honesty, and spontaneity (Mendelowitz & Schneider, 2008).

Existential counselors also make use of confrontation. Clients are confronted with the idea that everyone is responsible for his or her own life (Blair, 2004). Existential counselors borrow some techniques from other models of counseling such as the employment of awareness exercises, imagery, paradox, deflection, and goal-setting activities.

STRENGTHS AND CONTRIBUTIONS.   The existential approach to counseling has a number of strengths:

- The approach emphasizes the uniqueness of each individual and the importance of meaningfulness in their lives. It is a very humanistic way of working with others (Alex Vesley, June 3, 2011, personal communication).
- The approach recognizes that anxiety is not necessarily a negative condition. Anxiety is a part of human life and can motivate some individuals to make healthy and productive decisions (Fernando, 2007).
- The approach gives counselors access to a tremendous amount of philosophy and literature that is both informative and enlightening about human nature (Mendelowitz & Schneider, 2008).
- The approach stresses continued human growth and development and offers hope to clients through directed readings and therapeutic encounters with the counselor.
- The approach is effective in multicultural counseling situations because its global view of human existence allows counselors to focus on the person of the client in an "I-Thou" manner without regard to ethnic or social background (Epp, 1998; Jackson, 1987).
- The approach helps connect individuals to universal problems faced by humankind, such as the search for peace and the absence of caring (Baldwin, 1989).
- The approach may be combined with other perspectives and methods (such as those based on learning principles and behaviorism) to treat extremely difficult problems, such as addiction (Fernando, 2007).

LIMITATIONS.   Professionals who embrace different and more structured approaches have noted several limitations in the existential approach:

- The approach has not produced a fully developed model of counseling. Professionals who stress developmental stages of counseling are particularly vehement in this criticism.
- The approach lacks educational and training programs. Each practitioner is unique. Although uniqueness is valued, it prohibits the systematic teaching of theory.
- The approach is difficult to implement beyond an individual level because of its subjective nature. Existentialism lacks the type of methodology and validation processes prevalent in

most other approaches. In short, it lacks the uniformity that beginning counselors can readily understand.
- The approach is closer to existential philosophy than to other theories of counseling. This distinction limits its usefulness in some cases.

CASE EXAMPLE

Ned's Nothingness

Ned was an existentialist who believed in nothingness. He did not think there was any meaning or logic to life and that those who took such a position were naive. His strong stance at times alienated him from others, but generally Ned was respected for his philosophical reasoning.

One day, seeking support for his views, Ned called a local private practice group and made an appointment to see Jim, a counselor who had a reputation for being an existentialist. Ned expected Jim to discuss philosophy with him and to support his nihilism. Instead, Jim told Ned that he found great meaning every day in all that he did. Ned was surprised.

How could Ned have been so inaccurate in his assessment of Jim? How could the gulf between Ned and Jim be broached constructively?

Gestalt Therapy

Gestalt therapy is associated with Gestalt psychology, a school of thought that stresses perception of completeness and wholeness. The term *gestalt* means whole figure. Gestalt psychology and therapy arose as a reaction to the reductionist emphasis in other schools of psychology and counseling, such as psychoanalysis and behaviorism. Thus, Gestalt therapy emphasizes how people function in their totality.

FOUNDERS/DEVELOPERS. Frederick (Fritz) Perls (1893–1970) is credited with establishing Gestalt therapy and popularizing it both through his flamboyant personality and his writings. Laura Perls (his wife) and Paul Goodman helped Perls develop and refine his original ideas. A number of other theorists, particularly Joen Fagan and Irma Lee Shepherd (1970), developed the model further.

VIEW OF HUMAN NATURE. Gestaltists believe that human beings work for wholeness and completeness in life. Each person has a self-actualizing tendency that emerges through personal interaction with the environment and the beginning of self-awareness. *Self-actualization* is centered in the present; it "is the process of being what one is and not a process of striving to become" (Kempler, 1973, p. 262). The Gestalt view of human nature places trust on the inner wisdom of people, much as person-centered counseling does. Each person seeks to live integratively and productively, striving to coordinate the various parts of the person into a healthy, unified whole. From a Gestalt perspective, persons are more than a sum of their parts (Perls, 1969).

The **Gestalt view is antideterministic**: Each person is able to change and become responsible (Hatcher & Himelstein, 1997). Individuals are actors in the events around them, not just reactors to events. Overall, the Gestalt point of view takes a position that is existential, experiential, and phenomenological: The **now is what really matters**. One discovers different aspects of oneself through experience, not talk, and a person's own assessment and interpretation of his or her life at a given moment in time are what is most important.

According to Gestalt therapy, many troubled individuals have an overdependency on intellectual experience (Simkin, 1975). Such an emphasis diminishes the importance of emotions and the senses, limiting a person's ability to respond to various situations. Another common problem is the inability to identify and resolve **unfinished business**—that is, earlier thoughts, feelings, and reactions that still affect personal functioning and interfere with living life in the present. The most typical unfinished business in life is not forgiving one's parents for their mistakes. Gestaltists do not attribute either of these difficulties to any unconscious forces within persons. Rather, the focus is on awareness, "the ability of the client to be in full mental and sensory" contact of "experiencing the now" (James & Gilliland, 2003, p. 49). Every person operates on some conscious level, from being very aware to being very unaware. Healthy individuals are those who are most aware.

According to Gestaltists, a person may experience difficulty in several ways. First, he or she may lose contact with the environment and the resources in it. Second, the person may become overinvolved with the environment and out of touch with the self. Third, he or she may fail to put aside unfinished business. Fourth, he or she may become fragmented or scattered in many directions. Fifth, the person may experience conflict between the *top dog* (what one thinks one should do) and the *underdog* (what one wants to do). Finally, the person may have difficulty handling the **dichotomies of life**, such as love/hate, masculinity/femininity, and pleasure/pain.

ROLE OF THE COUNSELOR. The role of the Gestalt counselor is to create an atmosphere that promotes a client's exploration of what is needed to grow. The counselor provides such an atmosphere by being intensely and personally involved with clients and being honest. Polster and Polster (1973) stress that counselors must be exciting, energetic, and fully human. Involvement occurs in the now, which is a continuing process (Perls, 1969). The now often involves having the counselor help a client focus on blocking energy and using that energy in positive and adaptive ways (Zinker, 1978). The now also entails the counselor's helping the client recognize patterns in his or her life (Fagan, 1970).

GOALS. The goals of Gestalt therapy are well defined. They include an emphasis on the **here and now** and a recognition of the immediacy of experience (Bankart, 1997). Further goals include a focus on both nonverbal and verbal expression, and a focus on the concept that life includes **making choices** (Fagan & Shepherd, 1970). The Gestalt approach concentrates on helping a client resolve the past to become integrated. This goal includes the **completion of mentally growing up**. It emphasizes the coalescence of the emotional, cognitive, and behavioral aspects of the person. A primary focus is the **acceptance of polarities within the person** (Gelso & Carter, 1985).

As a group, Gestalt therapists emphasize action, pushing their clients to experience feelings and behaviors. They also stress the meaning of the word *now*. Perls (1969) developed a formula that expresses the word's essence: **"Now = experience = awareness = reality**. The past is no more and the future not yet. Only the now exists" (p. 14).

TECHNIQUES. Some of the most innovative counseling techniques ever developed are found in Gestalt therapy (Harman, 1997). These techniques take two forms: exercises and experiments. *Exercises* are ready-made techniques, such as the enactment of fantasies, role-playing, and psychodrama (Coven, 1977). They are employed to evoke a certain response from the client, such as anger or exploration. ***Experiments***, on the other hand, are activities that grow out of the interaction between counselor and client. They are not planned, and what is learned is often a surprise to both the client and the counselor. Many of the techniques of Gestalt therapy take the form of unplanned experiments (Zinker, 1978). The concentration here, however, is on exercise-oriented counseling techniques.

One common exercise is **dream work**. Perls describes dreams as messages that represent a person's place at a certain time (Bernard, 1986). Unlike psychoanalysts, Gestalt counselors do not interpret. Rather, clients present dreams and are then directed to experience what it is like to be each part of the dream—a type of dramatized free association. In this way, a client can get more in touch with the multiple aspects of the self.

Another effective technique is **the empty chair** (Figure 9.1). In this procedure, clients talk to the various parts of their personality, such as the part that is dominant and the part that is passive. An empty chair is the focus. A client may simply talk to the chair as a representative of one part of the self, or the client may switch from chair to chair and have each chair represent a different part. In this dialogue, both rational and irrational parts of the client come into focus; the client not only sees these sides but also becomes able to deal with the dichotomies within the self. This method is not recommended for those who are severely emotionally disturbed (Bernard, 1986).

One of the most powerful Gestalt exercises is confrontation. Counselors point out to a client incongruent behaviors and feelings, such as a client's smiling when admitting to nervousness. Truly nervous people do not smile. **Confrontation involves asking clients *what* and *how* questions. *Why* questions are avoided** because they lead to intellectualization.

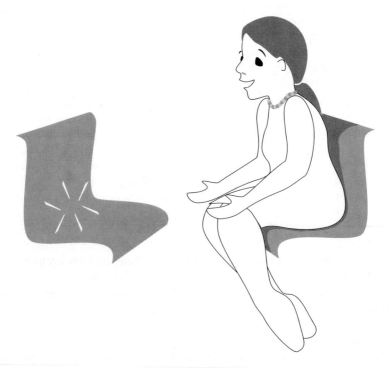

FIGURE 9.1 The empty chair

Some **other powerful Gestalt exercises** that are individually oriented are often used in groups (Harman, 1997).

- *Making the rounds.*   This exercise is employed when the counselor feels that a particular theme or feeling expressed by a client should be faced by every person in the group. The client may say, for instance, "I can't stand anyone." The client is then instructed to say this sentence to each person in the group, adding some remarks about each group member. The rounds exercise is flexible and may include nonverbal and positive feelings, too. By participating in it, clients become more aware of inner feelings.
- *I take responsibility.*   In this exercise, clients make statements about perceptions and close each statement with the phrase "and I take responsibility for it." The exercise helps clients integrate and own perceptions and behaviors.
- *Exaggeration.*   Clients accentuate unwitting movement or gestures. In doing so, the inner meaning of these behaviors becomes more apparent.
- *May I feed you a sentence?*   The counselor, who is aware that implicit attitudes or messages are implied in what the client is saying, asks whether the client will say a certain sentence (provided by the counselor) that makes the client's thoughts explicit. If the counselor is correct about the underlying message, the client will gain insight as the sentence is repeated.

STRENGTHS AND CONTRIBUTIONS.   Gestalt therapy strengths and contributions include the following:

- The approach emphasizes helping people incorporate and accept all aspects of life. An individual cannot be understood outside the context of a whole person who is choosing to act on the environment in the present.
- The approach helps a client focus on resolving areas of unfinished business. When a client is able to make these resolutions, life can be lived productively.
- The approach places primary emphasis on doing rather than talking. Activity helps individuals experience what the process of change is about and make more rapid progress.
- The approach is flexible and not limited to a few techniques. Any activity that helps clients become more integrative can be employed in Gestalt therapy.
- The approach is appropriate for certain affective disorders, anxiety states, somatoform disorders, adjustment disorders, and DSM diagnoses such as occupational problem and interpersonal problem (Seligman, 2004). In short, Gestalt therapy is versatile.

LIMITATIONS.   Gestalt therapy also has some limitations:

- The approach lacks a strong theoretical base. Some critics view Gestalt counseling as all experience and technique—that is, as too gimmicky (Corey, 2009). They maintain that it is antitheoretical.
- The approach deals strictly with the now and how of experience (Perls, 1969). This two-pronged principle does not allow for passive insight and change, which some clients are more likely to use.
- The approach eschews diagnosis and testing.
- The approach is too concerned with individual development and is criticized for its self-centeredness. The focus is entirely on feeling and personal discovery.

PERSONAL REFLECTION

What is something in your life that is greater than the sum of its parts? How do you know this?

MyCounselingLab™

Go to Topic 6: *Current Trends in Counseling* in the MyCounselingLab™ site (www .MyCounselingLab.com) for *Counseling: A Comprehensive Profession,* Seventh Edition, where you can:

- Find learning outcomes for *Current Trends in Counseling* along with the national standards that connect to these outcomes.
- Complete Assignments and Activities that can help you more deeply understand the chapter content.
- Apply and practice your understanding of the core skills identified in the chapter with the Building Counseling Skills unit.
- Prepare yourself for professional certification with a Practice for Certification quiz.
- Connect to videos through the Video and Resource and Library.

Summary and Conclusion

This chapter has covered the nature of and importance of theory in counseling. In addition, it has focused on the practice of theory in counseling today, especially different forms of eclecticism.

Three orientations to counseling—psychoanalytic, Adlerian, and humanistic—were also described and discussed. There are some variations in the practice of psychoanalytic and Adlerian counseling, but the core of these approaches remains basically the same regardless of what aspects of the theories are emphasized. In the humanistic orientation, however, there are three distinct theories: person-centered, existential, and Gestalt. Each of these theories, while helping and empowering clients to make choices and be in touch with their feelings, differs significantly from the others. Therefore, the humanistic orientation to counseling is more diverse than the psychoanalytic and Adlerian. Regardless, with each of the five counseling theories covered, a brief overview was given in a uniform manner on

- the founders/developers of the approach,
- the theory's view of human nature,
- the role of the counselor,
- therapeutic goals,
- primary techniques,
- strengths/contributions, and
- limitations of the approach.

Behavioral, Cognitive, Systemic, Brief, and Crisis Theories of Counseling

10

She stands
      leaning on his outstretched arm
            sobbing awkwardly
Almost suspended between
      the air and his shoulder
            like a leaf being blown
                  in the wind from a branch of a tree
                  at the end of summer.
He tries to give her comfort
      quietly offering up soft words
            and patting her head sporadically.
"It's okay," he whispers
      realizing that as the words leave his mouth
            he is lying
And that their life together has collapsed
      like the South Tower of the World Trade Center
            that killed their only son.

Reprinted from "Reflections on Counseling After the Crisis," by S. T. Gladding. In G. R. Walz & C. J. Kirkman (Eds.), (2002). *Helping People Cope with Tragedy & Grief* (p. 9). Greensboro, NC: CAPS Publication. Reprinted with permission. No further reproduction authorized without written permission of the ERIC Counseling and Student Services Clearinghouse and the National Board for Certified Counselors.

Chapter Overview

From this chapter you will learn about

- Behavioral, cognitive–behavioral, systemic, and brief theories of counseling
- The strengths and limitations of each of the theories covered
- The distinct and universal nature of crisis counseling

As you read consider

- The role of the counselor in promoting each theory
- The major goals and most frequently used techniques in each theory
- The differences and similarities in linear versus systems counseling approaches

MyCounselingLab™

Visit the MyCounselingLab™ site (www.MyCounselingLab.com) for *Counseling: A Comprehensive Profession,* Seventh Edition to enhance your understanding of chapter concepts. You'll have the opportunity to practice your skills through video- and case-based Assignments and Activities as well as Building Counseling Skills units and to prepare for your certification exam with Practice for Certification quizzes.

This chapter covers a plethora of theories that are currently in vogue in counseling. These theories fall under five main orientations: behavioral counseling, cognitive counseling, systemic counseling, brief counseling, and crisis counseling. Within each orientation are several theoretical ways of working with clients that emphasize different aspects of the orientation. For this chapter, behavioral counseling will be treated as an entity even though those who are more cognitively based and professionals who are more action oriented also appear within this approach. Under cognitive counseling, rational emotive behavioral therapy (REBT), a theory that started out much more cognitive than it is today, will be described along with reality therapy (RT) and Aaron Beck's cognitive therapy (CT). Sometimes these theories are described as cognitive–behavioral. Following this material is a presentation on system and brief counseling approaches as well as a description of crisis theory and the unique ways it is used in counseling.

In all these theories, a uniformed descriptive method will be used, as in the previous chapter. Specifically, the sections describing these theories will focus on founders/developers, the view of human nature, the role of the counselor, goals, techniques, strengths and contributions, and limitations.

BEHAVIORAL COUNSELING

Behavioral theories of counseling focus on a broad range of client behaviors. Often, a person has difficulties because of a deficit or an excess of behavior. Counselors who take a behavioral approach seek to help clients learn new, appropriate ways of acting, or help them modify or eliminate excessive actions. In such cases, adaptive behaviors replace those that were maladaptive, and the counselor functions as a learning specialist for the client (Krumboltz, 1966a). Also, "behavioral change opens doors to perceptual change" (Shadley, 2010, p.17)

Behavioral counseling approaches are especially popular in institutional settings, such as mental hospitals or sheltered workshops. They are the approaches of choice in working with clients who have specific problems such as eating disorders, substance abuse, and psychosexual dysfunction. Behavioral approaches are also useful in addressing difficulties associated with anxiety, stress, assertiveness, parenting, and social interaction (Cormier & Hackney, 2008; Seligman & Reichenberg, 2010).

Behavioral Therapy

FOUNDERS/DEVELOPERS. B. F. (Burrhus Frederick) Skinner (1904–1990) is the person most responsible for the popularization of behavioral treatment methods. Applied behavior analysis is "a direct extension of Skinner's (1953) radical behaviorism" (Wilson, 2008, p. 224), which is based on operant conditioning. Other notables in the behavioral therapy camp are historical figures, such as Ivan Pavlov, John B. Watson, and Mary Cover Jones. Contemporary figures, such as Albert Bandura, John Krumboltz, Neil Jacobson, Steven Hayes, and Marsha Linehan, have also greatly added to this way of working with clients.

VIEW OF HUMAN NATURE. Behaviorists, as a group, share the following ideas about human nature (Rimm & Cunningham, 1985; Seligman & Reichenberg, 2010):

- A concentration on *behavioral processes*—that is, processes closely associated with overt behavior (except for cognitive–behaviorists)
- A focus on the here and now as opposed to the then and there of behavior
- An assumption that all behavior is learned, whether it be adaptive or maladaptive
- A belief that learning can be effective in changing maladaptive behavior
- A focus on setting up well-defined therapy goals with their clients
- A rejection of the idea that the human personality is composed of traits

In addition, behaviorists stress the importance of obtaining empirical evidence and scientific support for any techniques they use. Some behaviorists, who embrace the **social-cognitive form of learning**, stress that people acquire new knowledge and behavior by observing other people and events without engaging in the behavior themselves and without any direct consequences to themselves (i.e., *modeling*). This type of learning does not require active participation.

ROLE OF THE COUNSELOR. A counselor may take one of several roles, depending on his or her behavioral orientation and the client's goal(s). Generally, however, a behaviorally based counselor is active in counseling sessions. As a result, the client learns, unlearns, or relearns specific ways of behaving. In the process, the counselor functions as a consultant, teacher, adviser, reinforcer, and facilitator (James & Gilliland, 2003). He or she may even instruct or supervise support people in the client's environment who are assisting in the change process. An effective behavioral counselor operates from a broad perspective and involves the client in every phase of the counseling.

GOALS. The goals of behaviorists are similar to those of many other counselors. Basically, behavioral counselors want to help clients make good adjustments to life circumstances and achieve personal and professional objectives. Thus, the focus is on modifying or eliminating the maladaptive behaviors that clients' display, while helping them acquire healthy, constructive ways of acting. Just to eliminate a behavior is not enough; unproductive actions must be replaced with productive ways of responding. A major step in the behavioral approach is for counselors and clients to reach mutually agreed-on goals.

TECHNIQUES. Behavioral counselors have at their disposal some of the best-researched and most effective counseling techniques available.

General Behavioral Techniques. General techniques are applicable in all behavioral theories, although a given technique may be more applicable to a particular approach at a given time or in a specific circumstance. Some of the most general behavioral techniques are briefly explained here.

Use of reinforcers. *Reinforcers* are those events that, when they follow a behavior, increase the probability of the behavior repeating. A reinforcer may be either positive or negative.

Schedules of reinforcement.   When a behavior is first being learned, it should be reinforced every time it occurs—in other words, by continuous reinforcement. After a behavior is established, however, it should be reinforced less frequently—in other words, by intermittent reinforcement. Schedules of reinforcement operate according to either the number of responses (*ratio*) or the length of time (*interval*) between reinforcers. Both ratio and interval schedules may be either fixed or variable.

PERSONAL REFLECTION

Reflect back on times when you have been on the various schedules just described. Which did you prefer? Why?

Shaping.   Behavior learned gradually in steps through successive approximation is known as *shaping*. When clients are learning new skills, counselors may help break down behavior into manageable units.

Generalization.   Generalization involves the display of behaviors in environments outside where they were originally learned (e.g., at home, at work). It indicates that transference into another setting has occurred.

Maintenance.   Maintenance is defined as being consistent in performing the actions desired without depending on anyone else for support. In maintenance, an emphasis is placed on increasing a client's self-control and self-management. One way this may be done is through *self-monitoring*, when clients learn to modify their own behaviors. It involves two processes related to self-monitoring: self-observation and self-recording (Goldiamond, 1976). *Self-observation* requires that a person notice particular behaviors he or she does; *self-recording* focuses on recording these behaviors.

Extinction.   Extinction is the elimination of a behavior because of a withdrawal of its reinforcement. Few individuals will continue doing something that is not rewarding.

Punishment.   Punishment involves presenting an aversive stimulus to a situation to suppress or eliminate a behavior.

Specific Behavioral Techniques.   Specific behavioral techniques are refined behavioral methods that combine general techniques in precise ways. They are found in different behavioral approaches.

Behavioral rehearsal.   Behavioral rehearsal consists of practicing a desired behavior until it is performed the way a client wishes (Lazarus, 1985).

Environmental planning.   Environmental planning involves a client's setting up part of the environment to promote or limit certain behaviors.

Systematic desensitization.   Systematic desensitization is designed to help clients overcome anxiety in particular situations. A client is asked to describe the situation that causes anxiety and then to rank this situation and related events on a hierarchical scale (Table 10.1), from aspects that cause no concern (0) to those that are most troublesome (100). To help the client avoid anxiety and face the situation, the counselor teaches him or her to relax physically or mentally. The hierarchy is then reviewed, starting with low-anxiety items. When the client's

TABLE 10.1   Joe's Anxiety Hierarchy

Amount of Anxiety (%)	Event
90	Marriage relationship
85	In-law relationship
80	Relating to my newborn child
75	Relating to my dad
70	Relating to my mother
65	General family relations and responsibilities
60	Being a project manager at work
50	Work in general
40	Coming to counseling
35	Personal finances
20	Having fun (being spontaneous)
10	Going to sleep

anxiety begins to mount, the client is helped to relax again, and the procedures then start anew until the client is able to be calm even when thinking about or imagining the event that used to create the most anxiety.

Assertiveness training.   The major tenet of assertiveness training is that a person should be free to express thoughts and feelings appropriately without feeling undue anxiety (Alberti & Emmons, 2008). The technique consists of counterconditioning anxiety and reinforcing assertiveness. A client is taught that everyone has the right (not the obligation) of self-expression. The client then learns the differences among aggressive, passive, and assertive actions.

Contingency contracts.   Contingency contracts spell out the behaviors to be performed, changed, or discontinued; the rewards associated with the achievement of these goals; and the conditions under which rewards are to be received (Corey, 2009).

Implosion and flooding.   *Implosive therapy* is an advanced technique that involves desensitizing a client to a situation by having him or her imagine an anxiety-producing situation that may have dire consequences. The client is not taught to relax first (as in systematic desensitization). *Flooding* is less traumatic, as the imagined anxiety-producing scene does not have dire consequences.

Time-out.   Time-out is a mild aversive technique in which a client is separated from the opportunity to receive positive reinforcement. It is most effective when employed for short periods of time, such as 5 minutes.

Overcorrection.   Overcorrection is a technique in which a client first restores the environment to its natural state and then makes it "better than normal."

Covert sensitization.   Covert sensitization is a technique in which undesired behavior is eliminated by associating it with unpleasantness.

STRENGTHS AND CONTRIBUTIONS. Among the unique and strong aspects of the behavioral approach are the following:

- The approach deals directly with symptoms. Because most clients seek help for specific problems, counselors who work directly with symptoms are often able to assist clients immediately.
- The approach focuses on the here and now. A client does not have to examine the past to obtain help in the present. A behavioral approach saves both time and money.
- The approach offers numerous techniques for counselors to use.
- The approach is based on learning theory, which is a well-formulated way of documenting how new behaviors are acquired (Krumboltz & Thoresen, 1969, 1976).
- The approach is buttressed by the Association for Behavioral and Cognitive Therapies (ABCT), which promotes the practice of behavioral counseling methods.
- The approach is supported by exceptionally good research on how behavioral techniques affect the process of counseling.
- The approach is objective in defining and dealing with problems and demystifies the process of counseling.

LIMITATIONS. The behavioral approach has several limitations, among which are the following:

- The approach does not deal with the total person, just explicit behavior. Critics contend that many behaviorists have taken the person out of personality.
- The approach is sometimes applied mechanically.
- The approach is best demonstrated under controlled conditions that may be difficult to replicate in normal counseling situations.
- The approach ignores the client's past history and unconscious forces.
- The approach does not consider developmental stages.
- The approach programs the client toward minimum or tolerable levels of behaving, reinforces conformity, stifles creativity, and ignores client needs for self-fulfillment, self-actualization, and feelings of self-worth (James & Gilliland, 2003).

CASE EXAMPLE

Bill Becomes a Behaviorist

Bill liked counseling theories. He especially liked behaviorism because he identified it as an "action" approach. Bill was not a counselor but a fifth-grade teacher, and he applied the theory well in his classroom to the point that he was recognized as having an orderly and achievement-oriented class.

Bill rewarded students for promptness and polite behavior, for turning in their homework on time, and for using proper table manners in the lunchroom. No one complained.

Do you think that a teacher, other than one in an elementary school like Bill, could apply behavior theory so extensively and effectively? Why or why not?

COGNITIVE AND COGNITIVE–BEHAVIORAL COUNSELING

Cognitions are thoughts, beliefs, and internal images that people have about events in their lives (Holden, 1993, 2001). Cognitive counseling theories focus on mental processes and their influences on mental health and behavior. A common premise of all cognitive approaches is that how people think largely determines how they feel and behave (Beck & Weishaar, 2008).

As a rule, cognitive theories are successful with clients who have the following characteristics (Cormier & Hackney, 2008):

- They are average to above-average in intelligence.
- They have moderate to high levels of functional distress.
- They are able to identify thoughts and feelings.
- They are not psychotic or disabled by present problems.
- They are willing and able to complete systematic homework assignments.
- They possess a repertoire of behavioral skills and responses.
- They process information on a visual and auditory level.
- They frequently have inhibited mental functioning, such as depression.

Three theories that have a cognitive base, rational emotive behavioral therapy (REBT), reality therapy (RT), and cognitive therapy (CT) are discussed here under the cognitive umbrella. In practice, these theories are cognitive–behavioral in nature because they emphasize both cognitions and behaviors. They are humanistic as well.

Rational Emotive Behaviorial Therapy (REBT)

FOUNDERS/DEVELOPERS.   The founder of rational emotive behavioral therapy (REBT) is Albert Ellis (1913–2007). His theory has similarities to Aaron Beck's cognitive therapy (which was formulated independently at about the same time) and David Burns's new mood therapy. An interesting variation on REBT is rational behavior therapy (RBT), which was formulated by Maxie Maultsby, and is more behavioral.

VIEW OF HUMAN NATURE.   Ellis (2008) believes that people have both self-interest and social interest. However, REBT also assumes that people are "inherently rational and irrational, sensible and crazy" (Weinrach, 1980, p. 154). According to Ellis (2008), this latter duality is biologically inherent and perpetuated unless a new way of thinking is learned (Dryden, 1994). *Irrational thinking*, or as Ellis defines it, *irrational Beliefs* (**iBs**), may include the invention of upsetting and disturbing thoughts.

Although Ellis does not deal with the developmental stages of individuals, he thinks that children are more vulnerable to outside influences and irrational thinking than adults are. By nature, he believes human beings are gullible, highly suggestible, and are easily disturbed. Overall, people have within themselves the means to control their thoughts, feelings, and actions, but they must first realize what they are telling themselves (*self-talk*) to gain command of their lives (Ellis, 1962; Weinrach, et al., 2001). This is a matter of personal, conscious awareness. The unconscious mind is not included in Ellis's conception of human nature. Furthermore, Ellis believes it is a mistake for people to evaluate or rate themselves beyond the idea that everyone is a **fallible human being**.

ROLE OF THE COUNSELOR. In the REBT approach, counselors are active and direct. They are instructors who teach and correct the client's cognitions. "Countering a deeply ingrained belief requires more than logic. It requires consistent repetition" (Krumboltz, 1992). Therefore, counselors must listen carefully for illogical or faulty statements from their clients and challenge beliefs. Ellis (1980) and Walen, DiGuiseppe, and Dryden (1992) have identified several characteristics desirable for REBT counselors. They need to be bright, knowledgeable, empathetic, respectful, genuine, concrete, persistent, scientific, interested in helping others, and users themselves of REBT.

GOALS. The primary goals of REBT focus on helping people realize that they can live more rational and productive lives. REBT helps clients stop making demands and becoming upset through "*catastrophizing*." Clients in REBT may express some negative feelings, but a major goal is to help them avoid having more of an emotional response to an event than is warranted (Weinrach et al., 2001).

Another goal of REBT is to help people change self-defeating habits of thought or behavior. One way this is accomplished is through teaching clients the *A-B-C-D-E model of REBT*:

A signifies the **activating experience**;

B represents **how the person thinks about the experience**;

C is the **emotional reaction to *B***.

D **is disputing irrational thoughts**, usually with the help of a REBT counselor, and replacing them with

E **effective thoughts** and hopefully a new personal philosophy that will help clients achieve great life satisfaction (Ellis, 2008).

Through this process, REBT helps people learn how to recognize an *emotional anatomy*—that is, to learn how feelings are attached to thoughts. **Thoughts about experiences may be characterized in four ways: positive, negative, neutral, or mixed**.

REBT also encourages clients to be more tolerant of themselves and others and urges them to achieve personal goals. These goals are accomplished by having people learn to think rationally to change self-defeating behavior and by helping them learn new ways of acting.

CASE EXAMPLE

Delores Gets Drunk

Delores went wild one night at a sorority party and became noticeably drunk. The president of the sorority, Kissa, approached her, took the beer from her hand, and told her she had too much to drink and that she would not be allowed to have another drink that night. Being a follower of the REBT philosophy, Delores knew she could think one of four ways. The easiest was negative: "Kissa should have minded her own business and not taken my drink or scolded me!"

What might Delores have said to herself that was positive? What mixed message could she have given herself? How would those messages have affected her feelings?

TECHNIQUES. REBT encompasses a number of diverse techniques. Two primary ones are teaching and disputing. **Teaching** involves having clients learn the basic ideas of REBT and understand how thoughts are linked with emotions and behaviors. This procedure is didactic and directive and is generally known as **rational emotive education (REE)**.

Disputing thoughts and beliefs takes one of **three forms**: cognitive, imaginal, and behavioral. The process is most effective when all three forms are used (Walen et al., 1992). *Cognitive disputation* involves the use of direct questions, logical reasoning, and persuasion. *Imaginal disputation* uses a client's ability to imagine and employs a technique known as **rational emotive imagery (REI)** (Maultsby, 1984). *Behavioral disputation* involves behaving in a way that is the opposite of the client's usual way, including role-playing and the completion of a homework assignment in which a client actually does activities previously thought impossible to do. Sometimes behavioral disputation may take the form of bibliotherapy, in which clients read self-help books such as *A Guide to Rational Living* or *Staying Rational in an Irrational World.*

Two other powerful REBT techniques are confrontation and encouragement. REBT counselors explicitly encourage clients to abandon thought processes that are not working and try REBT. Counselors will also challenge a client who claims to be thinking rationally but in truth is not.

STRENGTHS AND CONTRIBUTIONS.   REBT has a number of unique dimensions and special emphases:

- The approach is clear, easily learned, and effective. Most clients have few problems in understanding the principles or terminology of REBT.
- The approach can easily be combined with other behavioral techniques to help clients more fully experience what they are learning.
- The approach is relatively short term, and clients may continue to use the approach on a self-help basis.
- The approach has generated a great deal of literature and research for clients and counselors. Few other theories have developed as much bibliotherapeutic material.
- The approach has continued to evolve over the years as techniques have been refined.
- The approach has been found effective in treating major mental health disorders such as depression and anxiety (Puterbaugh, 2006).

LIMITATIONS.   The limitations of the REBT approach are few but significant:

- The approach cannot be used effectively with individuals who have mental problems or limitations, such as schizophrenics and those with severe thought disorders.
- The approach may be too closely associated with its founder, Albert Ellis. Many individuals have difficulty separating the theory from Ellis's eccentricities.
- The approach is direct, and the potential for the counselor being overzealous and not as therapeutic as would be ideal is a real possibility (James & Gilliland, 2003).
- The approach's emphasis on changing thinking may not be the simplest way of helping clients change their emotions.

Reality Therapy (RT)

FOUNDERS/DEVELOPERS.   William Glasser (1925–) developed reality therapy in the mid-1960s. Robert Wubbolding has advanced this approach both through his explanation of it and his research into it.

VIEW OF HUMAN NATURE.   Reality therapy does not include a comprehensive explanation of human development, as Freud's system does. Yet it offers practitioners a focused view of some important aspects of human life and human nature. A **major tenet of reality therapy is its focus on consciousness**: Human beings operate on a conscious level; they are not driven by unconscious forces or instincts (Glasser, 1965, 1988, 2005).

A **second belief about human nature is that everyone has a health/growth force** (Glasser & Wubbolding, 1995) manifested on **two levels**: the **physical** and the **psychological**. Physically, there is the need to obtain life-sustaining necessities such as food, water, and shelter and use them. According to Glasser, human behavior was once controlled by the physical need for survival (e.g., behaviors such as breathing, digesting, and sweating). He associates these behaviors with *physical, or old-brain, needs* because they are automatically controlled by the body. In modern times, most important behavior is associated with *psychological, or new-brain, needs*. The *four primary psychological needs* are the following:

1. *Belonging*—the need for friends, family, and love
2. *Power*—the need for self-esteem, recognition, and competition
3. *Freedom*—the need to make choices and decisions
4. *Fun*—the need for play, laughter, learning, and recreation

Associated with meeting psychological needs is the need for *identity*—that is, the **development of a psychologically healthy sense of self**. Identity needs are met by being accepted as a person by others.

Reality therapy proposes that **human learning** is a life-long process **based on choice**. When people realize this fact, they are more likely to choose to focus on controlling those things they have power over, such as themselves, than to center on something or someone they cannot control, such as their partner (Oliver, 2010). If individuals do not learn they have choices early in life, such as how to relate to others, they can choose to learn it later. In the process they may change their identity and the way they behave (Glasser, 2000, 2005; Glasser & Wubbolding, 1995).

ROLE OF THE COUNSELOR.   The counselor serves primarily as a teacher and model, accepting the client in a warm, involved way and creating an environment in which counseling can take place. The counselor immediately seeks to build a relationship with the client by developing trust through friendliness, firmness, and fairness (Wubbolding, 1998). **Counselors use -*ing verbs***, such as *angering* or *bullying,* to describe client thoughts and actions. Thus, there is an emphasis on choice, on what the client chooses to do. Counselor–client interaction focuses on behaviors that the client would like to change and ways to go about making these desires a reality. It emphasizes positive, constructive actions (Glasser, 1988, 2005). Special attention is paid to metaphors and themes clients verbalize.

GOALS.   The **primary goal of reality therapy** is to **help clients become psychologically strong and rational** and **realize they have choices** in the ways they treat themselves and others. Related to this first goal is a **second** one: **to help clients clarify what they want in life**. It is vital for persons to be aware of life goals if they are to act responsibly. In assessing goals, reality therapists help their clients examine personal assets as well as environmental supports and hindrances. It is the client's responsibility to choose behaviors that fulfill personal needs. A **third goal** of reality therapy is **to help the client formulate a realistic plan to achieve personal needs and wishes**.

An **additional goal of reality therapy** is **to have the counselor become involved with the client in a meaningful relationship** (Glasser, 1980, 1981, 2000). This relationship is based on understanding, acceptance, empathy, and the counselor's willingness to express faith in the client's ability to change. A **fifth goal** of reality therapy is **to focus on behavior and the present**. Glasser (1988) believes that behavior (i.e., thought and action) is interrelated with feeling and physiology. Thus, a change in behavior also brings about other positive changes.

Finally, **reality therapy aims to eliminate punishment and excuses from the client's life**. Often, a client uses the excuse that he or she cannot carry out a plan because of punishment for failure by either the counselor or people in the outside environment. Reality therapy helps the client formulate a new plan if the old one does not work.

PERSONAL REFLECTION

When have you made a new plan when your old plan did not work? When have you abandoned your plan altogether? What made the difference?

TECHNIQUES. Basically, **reality therapy uses action-oriented techniques** that help clients realize they have choices in how they respond to events and people and that others do not control them any more than they control others (Glasser, 1998; Onedera & Greenwalt, 2007). Reality therapy **eschews external control psychology** and what Glasser (2000) calls its *seven deadly habits (i.e., "criticizing, blaming, complaining, nagging, threatening, punishing, and bribing")* (p. 79). Some of reality therapy's more effective and active techniques are teaching, employing humor, confronting, role-playing, offering feedback, formulating specific plans, and composing contracts.

Reality therapy uses the ***WDEP system*** as a way of helping counselors and clients make progress and employ techniques. In this system the ***W*** stands for ***wants***; at the beginning of the counseling process counselors find out what clients want and what they have been doing (Wubbolding, 1988, 1991). Counselors in turn share their wants for and perceptions of clients' situations. The ***D*** in WDEP involves clients further exploring the ***direction*** of their lives. Effective and ineffective self-talk that they use is discussed and even confronted. Basic steps strategically incorporated in these two stages include establishing a relationship and focusing on present behavior.

The ***E*** in the WDEP procedure stands for ***evaluation*** and is the cornerstone of reality therapy. Clients are helped to evaluate their behaviors and how responsible their personal behaviors are. Behaviors that do not contribute to helping clients meet their needs often alienate them from self and significant others. If clients recognize a behavior as unproductive, they may be motivated to change. If there is no recognition, the therapeutic process may break down. It is therefore crucial that clients, not the counselor, do the evaluation. The use of humor, role-playing, and offering feedback can help at this juncture.

After evaluation, the final letter of the WDEP system, ***P***, for ***plan***, comes into focus. A client concentrates on making a plan for changing behaviors. The plan stresses actions that the client will take, not behaviors that he or she will eliminate. The best plans are simple, attainable, measurable, immediate, and consistent (Wubbolding, 1998). They are also controlled by clients and sometimes committed to the form of a written contract in which responsible alternatives are spelled out. Clients are then requested to make a commitment to the plan of action.

STRENGTHS AND CONTRIBUTIONS.   Reality therapy has a number of strengths and has made contributions to counseling as follows:

- The approach is versatile and can be applied to many different populations, such as in schools (Mason & Duba, 2009). It is especially appropriate in the treatment of conduct disorders, substance abuse disorders, impulse control disorders, personality disorders, and antisocial behavior. It can be employed in individual counseling with children, adolescents, adults, and the aged and in group, marriage, and family counseling.
- The approach is concrete. Both counselor and client are able to assess how much progress is being made and in what areas, especially if a goal-specific contract is drawn up.
- The approach emphasizes short-term treatment. Reality therapy is usually limited to relatively few sessions that focus on present behaviors.
- The approach has national training centers and is taught internationally.
- The approach promotes responsibility and freedom within individuals without blame or criticism or an attempt to restructure the entire personality.
- The approach has successfully challenged the medical model of client treatment. Its rationale and positive emphasis are refreshing alternatives to pathology-centered models (James & Gilliland, 2003).
- The approach addresses conflict resolution.
- The approach stresses the present because current behavior is most amenable to client control. Like behaviorists, Gestaltists, and rational emotive behavior therapists, reality therapists are not interested in the past (Wubbolding, 2000).

LIMITATIONS.   Reality therapy also has limitations, among which are the following:

- The approach emphasizes the here and now of behavior so much that it sometimes ignores other concepts, such as the unconscious and personal history.
- The approach holds that all forms of mental illness are attempts to deal with external events (Glasser, 1984).
- The approach has few theoretical constructs, although it is now tied to choice theory, which means that it is becoming more sophisticated.
- The approach does not deal with the full complexity of human life, preferring to ignore developmental stages.
- The approach is susceptible to becoming overly moralistic.
- The approach is dependent on establishing a good counselor–client relationship.
- The approach depends on verbal interaction and two-way communication. It has limitations in helping clients who, for any reason, cannot adequately express their needs, options, and plans (James & Gilliland, 2003).
- The approach keeps changing its focus (Corey, 2009).

Cognitive Therapy (CT)

FOUNDER/DEVELOPER.   Aaron Beck (1921–), a psychiatrist, is credited as the founder of cognitive therapy (CT). His daughter, Judith Beck, is the leading proponent of CT today. Beck's early work began about the same time as that of Ellis. Like Ellis, he was initially trained to be psychoanalytic and formulated his ideas about CT only after conducting research into the effectiveness of using psychoanalytic theories in the treatment of depression, which he found were not adequate.

VIEW OF HUMAN NATURE.   Beck proposes that perception and experience are "active processes that involve both inspective and introspective data" (Tursi & Cochran, 2006, p. 388). Furthermore, how a person "apprises a situation is generally evident in his cognitions (thoughts and visual images)" (p. 388). Therefore, dysfunctional behavior is caused by dysfunctional thinking. If beliefs do not change, there is no improvement in a person's behaviors or symptoms. If beliefs change, symptoms and behaviors change.

ROLE OF THE COUNSELOR.   The CT counselor is active in sessions. He or she works with the client to make covert thoughts more overt. This process is especially important in examining cognitions that have become automatic, such as "Everyone thinks I'm boring."

GOALS.   The goals of CT center on examining and modifying unexamined and negative thoughts. CT counselors especially home in on **excessive cognitive distortions**, such as all-or-nothing thinking, negative prediction, overgeneralization, labeling of oneself, self-criticism, and personalization (i.e., taking an event unrelated to the individual and making it meaningful to the person; "It always rains when I want to play tennis").

Simultaneously counselors work with clients on overcoming their lack of motivation, which is often linked with the tendency that clients have to view problems as insurmountable.

TECHNIQUES.   There are a number of *techniques associated with CT:*

- *Challenging the way individuals process information*
- *Countering mistaken belief systems (i.e., faulty reasoning)*
- *Doing self-monitoring exercises designed to stop negative "automatic thoughts"*
- *Improving communication skills*
- *Increasing positive self-statements and exercises*
- *Doing homework, including disputing irrational thoughts*

STRENGTHS AND CONTRIBUTIONS

- CT has been adapted to a wide range of disorders, including depression and anxiety (Puterbaugh, 2006).
- CT has spawned, in conjunction with cognitive–behavioral therapy, *dialectical behavior therapy*, an intensive psychosocial treatment for individuals who are at risk for self-harm such as people diagnosed with borderline personality disorder (BPD). The objective is to help clients be more mindful and accepting of things that cannot be easily changed and live lives worth living (Day, 2008).
- CT is applicable in a number of cultural settings. For instance, Beck's model of cognitive therapy was introduced in China in 1989 and a variation of it has been popular there since (Chang, Tong, Shi, & Zeng, 2005).
- CT is a well-researched, evidence-based therapy that has proven effective for clients from multiple backgrounds.
- CT has spawned a number of useful and important clinical instruments including the Beck Anxiety Inventory, the Beck Hopelessness Scale, and the Beck Depression Scale (Beck & Weishaar, 2008).
- CT has a number of training centers around the United States and Europe including the Beck Institute in Bala Cynwyd, Pennsylvania (Beck & Weishaar, 2008).

LIMITATIONS. The CT approach has several limitations, among which are the following:

- CT is structured and requires clients to be active, which often means completing homework assignments.
- CT is not an appropriate therapy for people seeking a more unstructured, insight-oriented approach that does not require their strong participation (Seligman & Reichenberg, 2010).
- CT is primarily cognitive in nature and not usually the best approach for people who are intellectually limited or who are unmotivated to change.
- CT is demanding. Clinicians as well as clients must be active and innovative. The approach is more complex than it would appear on the surface.

SYSTEMS THEORIES

Systems theory is a generic term for conceptualizing a group of related elements (e.g., people) that interact as a whole entity (e.g., a family or a group). As a concept systems theory "is more of a way of thinking than a coherent, standardized theory" (Worden, 2003, p. 8). The originator of general systems theory was Ludwig von Bertalanffy (1968), a biologist. According to the theory, any living organism is composed of interacting components mutually affecting one another. **Three basic assumptions distinguish systems theory** from other counseling approaches:

1. **causality is interpersonal,**
2. **"psychosocial systems are best understood as repeated patterns of interpersonal interaction,"** and
3. **"symptomatic behaviors must . . . be understood from an interactional viewpoint"** (Sexton, 1994, p. 250).

Thus, the focus in general systems theory is on how the interaction of parts influences the operation of the system as a whole.

Circular causality is one of the main concepts introduced by this theory: the idea that events are related through a series of interacting feedback loops. *Scapegoating* (in which one person is singled out as the cause of a problem) and *linear causality* (in which one action is seen as the cause of another) are eliminated.

There are a number of approaches to counseling that are based on systems theory. One is Bowen systems theory, which was developed to help persons differentiate themselves from their families of origin. Structural family therapy is a second theory and one that focuses on creating healthy boundaries. A third approach, strategic therapy, originated from the work of Milton Erickson and has a variety of forms, which can be employed in a variety of ways.

Bowen Systems Theory

FOUNDERS/DEVELOPERS. One of the earliest systems approaches to working with clients, especially in regard to family members, was created by Murray Bowen (1913–1990). According to Bowen, who had personal difficulty with his own family of origin, individuals who do not examine and rectify patterns passed down from previous generations are likely to repeat them in their own families (Kerr, 1988). Therefore, it is important to examine the past so as to be informed in the present. Michael Kerr is the successor to Bowen at the Georgetown Family Center. Edwin Friedman also made major contributions to Bowen systems work.

VIEW OF HUMAN NATURE.   Bowen believed that there is **chronic anxiety in all life** that is both **emotional and physical**. Some individuals are more affected than others by this anxiety "because of the way previous generations in their families have channeled the transmission" of it to them (Friedman, 1991, p. 139). If anxiety remains low, few problems exist for people or families. However, if anxiety becomes high, people are much more "prone to illness" and they may become chronically dysfunctional (Greene, Hamilton, & Rolling, 1986, p. 189). Thus, the focus of Bowen systems theory is on *differentiation*, or distinguishing one's thoughts from one's emotions and oneself from others (Kerr & Bowen, 1988; Kim-Appel, Appel, Newman, & Parr, 2007).

For example, couples marry at the same level of emotional maturity, with those who are less mature being prone to have a more difficult time in their marriage relationships than those who are more mature. When a great deal of friction exists in a marriage, the less mature partners tend to display a high degree of *fusion* (undifferentiated emotional togetherness) or *cutoff* (physical or psychological avoidance) because they have not separated themselves from their families of origin in a healthy way, nor have they formed a stable self-concept. When they are stressed as persons within the marriage, these individuals tend to *triangulate* (focus on a third party) (Papero, 1996). The third party can be the marriage itself, a child, an institution (such as a church or school), or a somatic complaint like a headache. It leads to unproductive couple interactions.

ROLE OF THE COUNSELOR.   The role of the counselor is to coach and teach the client to be more cognitive in his or her dealings with others. At its best the process of counseling is "just like a **Socratic dialogue**, with the teacher or 'coach' calmly asking questions, until the student learns to think for him- or herself" (Wylie, 1991, p. 27). The counselor may construct a multigenerational genogram with the client to aid in this process (Figure 10.1).

GOALS.   If counseling is successful, clients will understand and modify the coping strategies and patterns of coping with stress that have been passed on from generation to generation. They will display a nonanxious presence in their daily lives and will be able to separate their thoughts from their feelings and themselves from others.

TECHNIQUES.   Techniques in this approach focus on ways to create an individuated person with a healthy self-concept who can interact with others and not experience undue anxiety every time the relationship becomes stressful. Ways of achieving this goal include assessment of self and family in a number of ways. One of them is through the construction of a multigenerational *genogram*, which is a visual representation of a person's family tree depicted in geometric figures, lines, and words (Sherman, 1993). Genograms include information related to a family and its members' relationships with each other over at least three generations. A genogram helps people gather information, hypothesize, and track relationship changes in the context of historic and contemporary events (Gladding, 2011).

Another technique is to focus on cognitive processes, such as *asking content-based questions* of one's family (Bowen, 1976). The objective is to understand what happened in one's family without any emotional overlay. A client may also *go home again* and visit with his or her family in order to get to know them better. Such a procedure promotes *person-to-person relationships* on a dyadic level and the *asking of questions* about pivotal events that had an impact on the family such as deaths, births, and marriages. Asking questions is an especially important tool in Bowen's work.

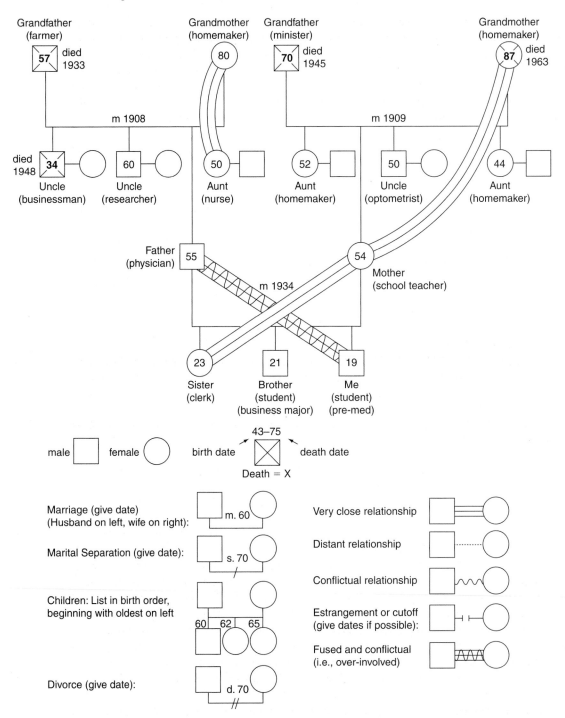

FIGURE 10.1 Genogram: Three generations of the Smith family (as of 1965) *Source: Community and Agency Counseling*, by Samuel T. Gladding (p. 132). © 1997 by Prentice-Hall, Inc. Reprinted by permission of Pearson Education, Inc., Upper Saddle River, NJ.

In addition, there is a focus on **detriangulation**, which involves "the process of being in contact and emotionally separate" with others (Kerr, 1988, p. 55). Detriangulation operates on two levels. One is to resolve anxiety over family situations and not project feelings onto others. The second is to avoid becoming a target or scapegoat for people who may be overcome with anxiety. Finally, there is the **differentiation of self**, which is the ability of a person to distinguish between subjective feelings and objective thinking. Becoming differentiated involves most, if not all, of the techniques previously mentioned plus some confrontation between the client and counselor.

STRENGTHS AND CONTRIBUTIONS.   There are a number of unique aspects surrounding Bowen systems theory:

- The approach focuses on multigenerational family history and the importance of noticing and dealing with past patterns in order to avoid repeating these behaviors in interpersonal relationships.
- The approach uses genograms in plotting historical links, which is a specific tool that was originated with the Bowen approach. It has now become an instrument borrowed by many approaches.
- The cognitive emphasis of this approach and its focus on differentiation of self and detriangulation are unique, too.

LIMITATIONS.   Bowen systems theory, however, is limited in these ways:

- The approach is extensive and complex. The theory is inseparable from the therapy and the intertwine makes the approach more involved than many other therapeutic approaches.
- Clients who benefit most from Bowen work are those who are severely dysfunctional or have a low differentiation of self.
- This approach may require considerable investment on multiple levels, which some clients may not be willing or able to do.

Structural Family Counseling

FOUNDERS/DEVELOPERS.   Salvador Minuchin (1921–) is the founder of structural family counseling. Minuchin formulated the theory while director of the Philadelphia Child Guidance Clinic in the 1960s. Braulio Montalvo and Jay Haley are also notable contributors to this approach.

VIEW OF HUMAN NATURE.   Every family has a structure according to Minuchin (1974). A **structure** is the informal way in which a family organizes itself and interacts. Structure influences people in families for better or worse. If there is a hierarchical structure, people relate well to each other. However, if there is no such structure or little structure, developmental or situational events increase family stress, rigidity, chaos, and dysfunctionality, throwing the family into crisis. In such circumstances, **coalitions** (i.e., alliances between specific members against a third member) or **cross-generational alliances** (alliances between family members of two different generations) arise. Neither works well in the healthy growth of individuals or a family.

ROLE OF THE COUNSELOR.   Structural family counseling practitioners are both observers and experts in making interventions to modify and change the underlying structure of a family. They advocate for structural changes in the organization of the family unit, with particular attention on changing interactional patterns in subsystems of the family such as in the marital dyad. They also work at establishing clear boundaries among family members (Minuchin, Montalvo, Guerney, Rosman, & Schumer, 1967).

In working with families, structural family counselors join with the family in a position of leadership. They map within their minds the structure of a family, determining how it is stuck in a dysfunctional pattern, and how to help it change.

GOALS.   In structural family therapy, **action is emphasized over insight** in order to alter and reorganize a family into a more functional and productive unit. Dated and outgrown rules are replaced with ones that are more related to the family's current realities. Distinctions and differentiation between subsystems are stressed with a special focus on parents being in charge of their children. If all works well, the cultural context of a family is changed.

TECHNIQUES.   Structuralists employ a number of techniques aimed at getting a family to change the way it operates (Minuchin & Fishman, 1981). One primary technique is to work with *family interaction*. When family members repeat nonproductive sequences of behavior or demonstrate a disengaged or enmeshed position in the family structure, the counselor will rearrange the physical environment so they have to act in a different way. The technique may be as simple as having people face each other when they talk.

Structural family counselors also use *reframing*, a technique that involves helping the family see its problem from a different and more positive perspective. For example, if a child is misbehaving, the behavior may be labeled "naughty" instead of "crazy." As a consequence, the child and his or her actions will be viewed as less pathological.

Other structural techniques are:

- *Punctuation*—"the selective description of a transaction" (Colapinto, 2000, p. 158)—for instance, declaring a person competent at a specific moment in time.
- *Unbalancing*—a procedure wherein the counselor supports an individual or subsystem against the rest of the family (e.g., a daughter who is lobbying for a later curfew against her parents).
- *Enactment*—a process that consists of a family bringing their problematic behaviors, such as making decisions, into treatment sessions and demonstrating them. In the process, the counselor challenges their existing patterns and rules as the family gains heightened awareness of the way they function.
- *Boundary making*—the process of creating lines that separate people or subsystems from each other psychologically in order to maximize individual and group development and functioning.
- *Intensity*—the structural method of changing maladaptive transactions by using strong affect, repeated intervention, or prolonged pressure in order to help an individual or family reach a goal by doing something differently (Minuchin & Fishman, 1981).
- *Restructuring*—changing the structure of a family by altering existing hierarchies or interaction patterns so that problems are not maintained (e.g., uniformly refusing to obey a certain request or to act in a specific way).
- *Adding cognitive constructions*—the verbal component of what is a primarily action-oriented approach that includes advice, information, *pragmatic fictions* (i.e., pronouncements that help people change, such as "you are capable"), and *paradox* (a confusing message, such as "don't change," meant to frustrate and motivate an individual or group to seek alternative actions).

STRENGTHS AND CONTRIBUTIONS. Structural family therapy is unique in its contribution to counseling in the following ways:

- The approach is quite versatile, being an approach that is appropriate for low-socioeconomic-level families as well as for other families (Minuchin, Colapinto, & Minuchin, 1999).
- The approach is effective, having been used in treating juvenile delinquents, alcoholics, and anorexics (Fishman, 1988).
- The approach is culturally sensitive and appropriate for use in multicultural settings.
- The approach is clear in its definition of terms and procedures and is easily applicable.
- The approach emphasizes symptom removal and a reorganization of the family in a pragmatic way.

LIMITATIONS. The structural approach's main limitations include the following:

- Critics have charged that structural work is not complex enough, may be sexist at times, and focuses too much on the present.
- The accusation that structural therapy has been influenced by strategic family therapy and the charge that it is difficult to distinguish it from strategic therapy at times is problematic.
- Since the counselor is in charge of the process of change, families may not become empowered enough, which may limit their overall adjustment and change in the future (Friesen, 1985).

PERSONAL REFLECTION

Every family has a *"family dance,"* a sequence of actions within the family that repeat themselves when certain situations arise, such as yelling and then withdrawing from each other during stress.

What was one of the dances your family-of-origin engaged in when you were growing up? Was your family ever able to structure it differently (i.e., create a new pattern)?

Strategic (Brief) Counseling

FOUNDERS/DEVELOPERS. John Weakland, Paul Watzlawick, Jay Haley, and Cloe Madanes are prominent leaders in the strategic school of counseling. This school and the individuals who are proponents of it are subdivided into a couple of branches—the Mental Research Institute (California) and the Family Therapy Institute (Washington, DC). Nevertheless, there are some common threads that weave the strategic counseling approach together so that it is recognizable as an entity with a number of subgroup emphases.

VIEW OF HUMAN NATURE. Strategic theory is based on the belief that when dysfunctional symptoms occur, they are an attempt to help people adapt. This **approach sees problems as occurring within a developmental framework of the family life cycle**. For instance, marital difficulties are generated by the system the couple is in. Consequently, the symptoms that emerge help maintain the marital system in which they operate (Todd, 1986).

As a group, strategic counselors focus on several dimensions of family life that are developmentally significant, such as

- *family rules*—the overt and covert rules families use to govern themselves,
- *family homeostasis*—the tendency of families to remain in their same pattern of functioning unless challenged to do otherwise,

- *quid pro quo*—the responsiveness of family members to treat each other in the ways they are treated (i.e., something for something), and
- *circular causality*—the idea that events are interconnected and that factors behind a behavior are multiple.

ROLE OF THE COUNSELOR.   Strategic counselors take a systemic view of problem behaviors and focus on the process rather than the content of dysfunctional interactions. The job of a strategic counselor is to get people to try new behaviors because their old behaviors are not working. Usually, a specific behavior is targeted for change. If this behavior can be modified, a ***spillover effect*** is hypothesized; that is, the results will help individuals make other behavior changes as well.

Thus, strategic counselors strive to resolve presenting problems and pay little attention to instilling insight. To bring about change, counselors are active, direct, and goal oriented as well as problem focused, pragmatic, and brief (Snider, 1992; Todd, 1986). They usually limit the number of times they see families to 10 visits or less.

GOALS.   The idea behind the strategic approach is to resolve, remove, or ameliorate a problematic behavior brought to counseling. In the process, new functional behaviors are generated that will help individuals, couples, and families achieve a specific goal. By limiting the number of sessions available for treatment, strategic counselors hope to increase the motivation and determination of the client to be successful. Another goal of the approach is for the persons involved in the process to learn new skills for resolving future conflicts.

TECHNIQUES.   As a group, strategic family counselors are quite innovative. Each intervention is tailored to the specifics of persons and problems. This customization makes strategic counseling one of the most technique-driven approaches to helping within systems theory. Strategic family counselors are nonblaming, avoid pathological labels, ***accept the presenting problems*** of families, and view symptoms as serving the positive purpose of communication.

Relabeling (giving a new perspective to a behavior) is frequently used. (For example, in regard to asking for a second helping of pie several times, Johnny's behavior might be relabeled "assertive" rather than "rude.") ***Paradoxing*** (insisting on just the opposite of what one wants) and ***prescribing the symptom*** (having the couple or family display voluntarily what they had previously manifested involuntarily, such as fighting) are employed, too. In addition, the counselor may use ***pretend*** to have the client make changes or carry out homework assignments that would not be completed otherwise (Madanes, 1984; Minuchin, 1974).

Individuals or families are sometimes asked to go through ***ordeals***, such as traveling or suffering, during the treatment process. The idea is that if people have to make sacrifices to get better, then the long-term improvements of treatment are enhanced. A major aspect of strategic family counseling is the assignment of original ***homework*** tasks (often given in the form of prescriptions or directives) that are to be completed between sessions.

STRENGTHS AND CONTRIBUTIONS.   Like other approaches, strategic counselors have unique aspects to what they do and how. Among the most prominent of these emphases are the following:

- Many of these therapists work in teams.
- The nature of the approach is pragmatic and flexible.
- The focus of practitioners is on innovation and creativity, which is in the lineage of Milton Erickson who was especially good at devising novel ways to help his clients.

- The emphasis within the approach is to change the perceptions within people as a way of fostering new behaviors.
- A deliberate attempt is made to work on one problem at a time and limit the number of sessions clients can be seen so that the focus and motivation for doing things differently is enhanced.
- The approach may be modified and carried over into settings, such as schools, where it may be systemically applied to serve a total population, as well as individuals and families in them (Nelson, 2006).

LIMITATIONS.   The limitations of the strategic approach are few in number but significant:

- First, some of its underlying foundation and techniques overlap with other system and brief therapy theories. Therefore, there is sometimes confusion as to whether a counselor is using the strategic approach or another approach, such as the structural.
- Second, some of the stands taken by leading strategic practitioners are controversial, such as Jay Haley's view that schizophrenia is not biologically based.
- Finally, the emphasis within strategic camps on the expertise and power of the counselor may mean that clients do not attain as much independence or ability as they might otherwise.

BRIEF COUNSELING APPROACHES

Brief counseling has grown in scope and influence in recent years. Some older systemic approaches, like the **Mental Research Institute (MRI)** approach to strategic therapy in Palo Alto, California (Watzlawick, Weakland, & Fisch, 1974), are brief in nature and have been designated as brief therapy. Likewise, some newer approaches to counseling, specifically solution-focused counseling and narrative therapy, have been explicitly designed to be brief in regard to treatment. Regardless, brief therapies are particularly important in an age where people and institutions are demanding quick and effective mental health services. The skills employed in these approaches are vital for counselors working in managed care settings and for counselors in public settings who are expected to do more in less time (Presbury, Echterling, & McKee, 2008).

Brief counseling approaches are characterized by both their foci and time-limited emphasis. Most brief counseling is not systemic in nature. However, as has been previously mentioned, strategic counseling is both systemic and time limited. Techniques used in brief counseling are concrete and goal oriented. In addition, counselors are active in helping foster change and in bringing it about. The emphasis in brief counseling is to identify solutions and resources rather than to focus on etiology, pathology, or dysfunction. Therefore, the number of sessions conducted is limited to increase client focus and motivation.

Solution-Focused Counseling

FOUNDERS/DEVELOPERS.   Solution-focused counseling, also commonly known as **solution-focused brief therapy (SFBT)**, is a midwestern phenomenon, having been originated in its present form in the 1980s by Steve deShazer and Bill O'Hanlon, both of whom were influenced directly by Milton Erickson, the creator of brief therapy in the 1940s. Other prominent practitioners and theorists connected with solution-focused counseling are Michele Weiner-Davis and Insoo Kim Berg.

VIEW OF HUMAN NATURE.   Solution-focused counseling does not have a comprehensive view regarding human nature but it focuses on client health and strength (Fernando, 2007). It traces its roots, as do some of the other theories in this chapter, to the work of Milton Erickson (1954), particularly Erickson's idea that people have within themselves the resources and abilities to solve their own problems even if they do not have a causal understanding of them. Erickson also "believed that a small change in one's behavior is often all that is necessary to lead to more profound changes in a problem context" (Lawson, 1994, p. 244).

In addition to its Ericksonian heritage, solution-focused counseling sees people as being *constructivist* in nature, meaning that reality is a reflection of observation and experience. Finally, solution-focused counseling is based on the **assumption** that **people really want to change** and that **change is inevitable**.

ROLE OF THE COUNSELOR.   The solution-focused counselor's first role is to determine how active and committed a client is to the process of change. Clients usually fall into three categories:

1. *visitors,* who are not involved in the problem and are not a part of the solution,
2. *complainants,* who complain about situations but can be observant and describe problems even if they are not invested in resolving them, and
3. *customers,* who are not only able to describe problems and how they are involved in them, but are willing to work on finding solutions (Fleming & Rickord, 1997).

In addition to determining commitment, solution-focused counselors act as facilitators of change to help clients "access the resources and strengths they already have but are not aware of or are not utilizing" (Cleveland & Lindsey, 1995, p. 145). They encourage, challenge, and set up expectations for change. They do not blame or ask "why?" They are not particularly interested in how a problem arose. Rather they are concerned with working together with the client to arrive at a solution to the problem. Basically, they allow the client to be the expert on his or her life (Helwig, 2002).

GOALS.   A major goal of solution-focused counseling is to help clients tap inner resources and to notice *exceptions* to the times when they are distressed. The goal is then to direct them toward solutions to situations that already exist in these exceptions (West, Bubenzer, Smith, & Hamm, 1997). Thus, the focus of sessions and homework is on positives and possibilities either now or in the future (Walter & Peller, 1992).

TECHNIQUES.   Solution-focused counseling is a **collaborative process** between the counselor and client. Besides encouraging the client to examine exceptions to times when there are problems, several other techniques are commonly used. One is the *miracle question*, which basically focuses on a hypothetical situation where a problem has disappeared. One form of it goes as follows: "Let's suppose tonight while you were sleeping a miracle happened that solved all the problems that brought you here. How would you know it? What would be different?" (deShazer, 1991).

Another technique is *scaling*, where the client is asked to use a scale from 1 (low) to 10 (high) to evaluate how severe a problem is. Scaling helps clients understand both where they are in regard to a problem and where they need to move in order to realistically achieve their goals.

Another intervention is to give clients *compliments*, which are written messages designed to praise clients for their strengths and build a "*yes set*" within them (i.e., a belief that they can resolve difficulties). Compliments are usually given right before clients are given tasks or assignments.

Two final techniques are:

1. *clues,* which are intended to alert clients to the idea that some behaviors they are doing now are likely to continue and they should not worry about them; and
2. *skeleton keys,* which are procedures that have worked before and that have universal applications in regard to unlocking a variety of problems.

STRENGTHS AND CONTRIBUTIONS. Unique strengths of solution-focused family counseling include the following:

- The approach emphasizes brevity and its empowerment of client families (Fleming & Rickord, 1997).
- The approach displays flexibility and excellent research in support of its effectiveness.
- The approach reveals a positive nature to working with a variety of clients in various settings, including school children (Murphy, 2008; Paterson, 2009).
- The approach focuses on change and its premise that emphasizes small change in behaviors.
- The approach can be combined with other counseling approaches, such as existentialism (Fernando, 2007).

LIMITATIONS. Solution-focused counseling has its limitations. These include the following:

- The approach pays almost no attention to client history.
- The approach has a lack of focus on insight.
- The approach uses teams, at least by some practitioners, to make the cost of this treatment high.

CASE EXAMPLE

Saul Becomes Solution Focused

Saul read and studied solution-focused therapy. He even took advanced continuing education seminars in it. He liked its philosophy and, most important, he liked the empowerment it gave clients and its overall effectiveness.

One day a family came to see Saul because of a daughter who was constantly running away. When Saul asked about exceptions to her behavior, everyone agreed there were none. Saul was shocked.

How could Saul counsel therapeutically besides continuing to probe and ask for exceptions? (Hint: Think about the miracle question or scaling.)

Narrative Counseling

FOUNDERS/DEVELOPERS. Michael White and David Epston (1990), practitioners from Australia and New Zealand, respectively, created narrative counseling, **a postmodern and social constructionist approach**. Other prominent practitioners and theorists in the field include Michael Durrant and Gerald Monk.

VIEW OF HUMAN NATURE. Narrative counselors emphasize "that meaning or knowledge is constructed through social interaction" (Worden, 2003, p. 8). There is **no absolute reality**

except as a social product. People are seen as internalizing and judging themselves through creating stories of their lives. Many of these stories highlight negative qualities about individuals or situations in their lives and are troublesome or depressing. Through treatment, clients can reauthor their lives and change their outlooks in a positive way.

ROLE OF THE COUNSELOR. The narrative approach to change sees **counselors as collaborators and masters of asking questions** (Lambie & Milsom, 2010; Walsh & Keenan, 1997). Like counselors in other traditions, those who take a narrative orientation engage their clients and use basic relationship skills such as attending, paraphrasing, clarifying, summarizing, and checking to make sure they hear the client's story or problem correctly (Monk, 1998). They assume that symptoms do not serve a function and are, in fact, oppressive. Therefore, an effort is made by the counselor to address and eliminate problems as rapidly as possible. Overall, the counselor uses *narrative reasoning*, which is characterized by stories, meaningfulness, and liveliness, in an effort to help clients redefine their lives and relationships through new narratives.

GOALS. According to the narrative viewpoint, "people live their lives by stories" (Kurtz & Tandy, 1995, p. 177). Therefore, the emphasis in this approach is shifted to a narrative way of conceptualizing and interpreting the world that is more expansive and filled with more possibilities. Clients who undergo narrative therapy learn to value their own life experiences and stories if they are successful. They will also learn how to construct new stories and meaning in their lives and, in the process, create new realities for themselves.

TECHNIQUES. The narrative approach seeks to empower clients and play to their strengths (Lambie & Milsom, 2010). It emphasizes developing unique and alternative stories of one's life in the hope that a client will come up with novel options and strategies for living. In order to do so, the problem that is brought to counseling is externalized. In externalization, the problem is the problem. Furthermore, *externalization of the problem* separates a person from a problem and objectifies difficulties so that the resources of a client can be focused on how a situation, such as chaos, or a feeling, such as depression, can be dealt with. Awareness and objectivity are also raised through asking *how the problem affects the person and how the person affects the problem.*

Other ways narrative therapists work are *raising dilemmas*, so that a client examines possible aspects of a problem before the need arises, and *predicting setbacks*, so the client will think about what to do in the face of adversity. *Reauthoring* lives is one of the main foci for the treatment, though. By refining one's life and relationships through a new narrative, change becomes possible (White, 1995). In changing their stories, clients perceive the world differently and are freed up to think and behave differently.

Counselors send *letters* to families about their progress. They also hold formal *celebrations* at the termination of treatment and give out *certificates* of accomplishment when clients overcome an externalized problem such as apathy or depression.

STRENGTHS AND CONTRIBUTIONS. In the narrative approach a number of unique qualities have contributed to counseling. Among them are the following:

- Blame is alleviated and dialogue is generated as everyone works to solve a common problem (Walsh & Keenan, 1997).
- Clients create a new story and new possibilities for action. Stories can be used even as early as the elementary school counseling level (Eppler, Olsen, & Hidano, 2009).

- Exceptions to problems are highlighted as in solution-focused therapy.
- Clients are prepared ahead of time for setbacks or dilemmas through counselor questions.

LIMITATIONS. Narrative counseling is not without its limitations, however.

- This approach is quite cerebral and does not work well with clients who are not intellectually astute.
- There are no norms regarding who clients should become.
- The history of a difficulty is not dealt with at all.

CRISIS AND TRAUMA COUNSELING APPROACHES

A *crisis* is "a perception or experiencing of an event or situation as an intolerable difficulty that exceeds the person's current resources and coping mechanisms" (James, 2008, p. 3). *Crisis counseling* is the employment of a variety of direct and action-oriented approaches to help individuals find resources within themselves and/or deal externally with crisis. In all forms of crisis counseling, quick and efficient services are provided in specialized ways.

A *trauma* is an exposure to an event in which a person is confronted with actual or threatened death or serious injury, or a threat to self or others' physical well-being (American Psychiatric Association, 2000). Definitions of trauma have been broadened to include hearing about trauma, direct exposure to the aftereffects of trauma (such as in rescue workers), indirect exposure to the effects of trauma (such as mental health counselors and court workers), and even observation at a safe distance from the trauma (as in the television coverage of the terrorist attacks of September 11) (Dreisbach, 2003; Kroll, 2003; North & Pfefferbaum, 2002). *Trauma counseling* refers to the kind of counseling that people participate in when they have perceived a threat to their life (Briere & Scott, 2006). It can take many forms, from a cognitive–behavioral approach to psychodrama. It is important to deal with traumas as soon as possible lest they become chronic and incapacitate.

Crisis Counseling

FOUNDERS/DEVELOPERS. Erich Lindemann (1944, 1956) and Gerald Caplan (1964) are considered two of the most prominent pioneers in the field of crisis counseling. Lindemann helped professionals recognize normal grief due to loss and the stages that individuals go through in resolving grief. Caplan expanded Lindemann's concepts to the total field of traumatic events. He viewed crisis as a state resulting from impediments to life's goals that are both situational and developmental.

VIEW OF HUMAN NATURE. Loss is an inevitable part of life. Developmentally and situationally, healthy people grow and move on, leaving some things behind, whether intentionally, by accident, or because of growth. In leaving, there may be **grieving**, which is a natural reaction to loss. The extent of the grief and its depth are associated with the value of what has been lost and how. In some cases, the pain may be small because the person was not attached to or invested in the object left behind, or the person had adequate time to prepare. In other cases, an individual may feel overwhelmed because of the value the person, possession, or position had in his or her life or because of the sudden and/or traumatic way the loss occurred. In such cases, there is a crisis.

People can have a variety of crises. **Four of the most common types of crises** include the following:

1. *Developmental,* which takes place in the normal flow of human growth and development under circumstances that are considered normal (e.g., birth of a child, retirement)
2. *Situational,* in which uncommon and extraordinary events occur that an individual has no way of predicting or controlling (e.g., automobile accident, kidnapping, loss of job)
3. *Existential,* which includes "inner conflicts and anxieties that accompany important human issues of purpose, responsibility, independence, freedom, and commitment" (James, 2008, p. 13) (e.g., realizing at age 50 that one has wasted one's life and cannot relive past years)
4. *Ecosystemic,* in which "some natural or human-caused disaster overtakes a person or a . . . group of people who find themselves, through no fault or action of their own, inundated in the aftermath of an event that may adversely affect virtually every member of the environment in which they live" (James, 2008, p. 14) (e.g., a hurricane, such as Katrina, a blizzard, an act of terrorism)

GOALS.   Many, but not all, crises are time limited and last somewhere between 6 and 8 weeks. Goals within crisis counseling revolve around getting those who are suffering immediate help in a variety of forms (e.g., psychological, financial, legal). "What occurs during the immediate aftermath of the crisis event determines whether or not the crisis will become a disease reservoir that will be transformed into a chronic and long-term state" (James, 2008, p. 5). Initially, counselors use basic crisis theory to help "people in crisis recognize and correct temporary affective, behavioral, and cognitive distortions brought on by traumatic events" (p. 11). This service is different from brief counseling approaches that try to help individuals find remediation for more ongoing problems. Long-term adjustment and health may require considerable follow-up on the part of the crisis counselor or another helping specialist.

ROLE OF THE COUNSELOR.   Counselors who work in crises need to be mature individuals with a variety of life experiences with which they have successfully dealt. They need to also have a good command of basic helping skills, high energy, and quick mental reflexes, and yet be poised, calm, creative, and flexible in the midst of highly charged situations.

Counselors are often direct and active in crisis situations. The role is quite different from that of ordinary counseling. Crisis counseling has three stages that those who participate in it must realize and be ready for: **precrisis preparation, in-crisis action**, and **postcrisis recovery** (McAdams III & Keener, 2008).

TECHNIQUES.   Techniques used in crisis counseling vary according to the type of crisis as mentioned earlier, and the potential for harm. However, according to James (2008), what a crisis worker does and when he or she does it is dependent on assessing the individuals experiencing crisis in a continuous and fluid manner.

After assessment, there are three essential listening activities that need to be implemented:

1. *defining the problem,* especially from the client's viewpoint;
2. *ensuring client safety,* which means minimizing physical and psychological danger to the client or others; and
3. *providing support,* which means communicating to the client genuine and unconditional caring.

After, and sometimes during, the middle of listening skills come *acting strategies*, or in-crisis actions, which include:

1. *examining alternatives* (i.e., recognizing alternatives that are available and realizing some choices are better than others);
2. *making plans,* where clients feel a sense of control and autonomy in the process so they do not become dependent; and
3. *obtaining commitment* from the client to take actions that have been planned.

Where possible, counselors should follow up with clients to make sure they have been able to complete their plan and to further assess whether they have had delayed reactions to the crisis they have experienced, such as posttraumatic stress disorder.

After a crisis has past, counselors need to debrief. Two approaches to debriefing are ***Critical Incident Stress Debriefing (CISD)*** and **one-on-one crisis counseling** (Jordan, 2002). In CISD a seven-stage group approach is used that helps individuals deal with their thoughts and feelings in a controlled environment using two counselors (Roberts, 2005). This approach evolves through an emphasis on introduction, facts, thoughts, reactions, symptoms, teaching, and reentry. The CISD group ranges from 1 to 3 hours and is generally provided 1 to 10 days after an acute crisis and 3 to 4 weeks after the disaster in mass disasters (Roberts, 2005). One-to-one counseling uses some of the same techniques as in CISD but the treatment lasts from 15 minutes to 2 hours and for only one to three sessions (Everly, Lating, & Mitchell, 2000).

STRENGTHS AND CONTRIBUTIONS.   As a specialty, crisis counseling is unique and has contributed to the profession of counseling in the following ways:

- The approach benefits from its brevity and its directness.
- The approach uses modest goals and objectives because of the sudden and/or traumatic nature of crises.
- The approach relies on its intensity, which is greater than regular forms of counseling.
- The approach utilizes a more transitional nature.

LIMITATIONS.   Crisis counseling is limited in these ways:

- The approach deals with situations of an immediate nature.
- The approach does not go into the same depth in regard to resolution that most counseling approaches do.
- The approach is more time limited and trauma oriented than most forms of therapeutic interventions.

MyCounselingLab™

Go to Topic 6: *Current Trends in Counseling* in the MyCounselingLab™ site (www .MyCounselingLab.com) for *Counseling: A Comprehensive Profession,* Seventh Edition, where you can:

- Find learning outcomes for *Current Trends in Counseling* along with the national standards that connect to these outcomes.
- Complete Assignments and Activities that can help you more deeply understand the chapter content.
- Apply and practice your understanding of the core skills identified in the chapter with the Building Counseling Skills unit.
- Prepare yourself for professional certification with a Practice for Certification quiz.
- Connect to videos through the Video and Resource Library.

Summary and Conclusion

This chapter has covered a wealth of counseling theories, specifically

- behavioral counseling;
- three cognitive–behavioral theories: rational emotive behavioral therapy (REBT), reality therapy (RT), and cognitive therapy (CT);
- three systems theories: Bowen systems theory, structural family counseling, and strategic (brief) counseling;
- two brief counseling approaches: solution-focused counseling and narrative counseling; and
- crisis counseling.

All of these approaches are widely used and in demand because of the premises on which they are based and their effectiveness in practice. The fact that none of them are extensive in regard to a time commitment, except possibly the Bowen approach, is a positive factor influencing their popularity. As in the preceding chapter, these theories were examined by briefly discussing their founders/developers, the view of human nature, the role of the counselor, goals, techniques, strengths and contributions, and limitations.

Counselors may well find a theory or theories in this chapter that will serve them and their client(s) well. There is continued research being conducted on all of them.

PART III

Core Counseling Activities in Various Settings

11 Groups in Counseling

Chapter Overview

From this chapter you will learn about

- The place of groups in counseling
- The four major types of groups counselors use: psychoeducational, task/work, psychotherapy, and counseling
- Stages of and issues in groups
- Qualities of effective group leaders

As you read consider

- What groups have worked well for you in the past and the dynamics that made such groups successful
- Issues you have seen arise in groups and how they were settled successfully or not
- What skills you may need to develop if you are to become a group leader
- The differences you notice in group work compared with individual counseling

Who am I in this pilgrim group
   whose members differ so in perception?
Am I timid like a Miles Standish,
   letting others speak for me
      because the experience of failure is softened
         if a risk is never personally taken?
Or am I more like a John Alden
   speaking boldly for others in the courting of beauty
      but not seeking such for myself?
Perhaps I am more than either man
   or maybe I'm both at different times!
In the silence and before others, I ponder the question anew.

Reprinted from "A Restless Presence: Group Process as a Pilgrimage," by S. T. Gladding, 1979, *School Counselor, 27*, p. 126. © S. T. Gladding.

MyCounselingLab™

Working in groups is a counseling activity that is often effective in helping individuals resolve personal and interpersonal concerns. Organized groups make use of people's natural tendency to gather and share thoughts and feelings as well as work and play cooperatively. "Groups are valuable because they allow members to experience a sense of belonging, to share common problems, to observe behaviors and consequences of behaviors in others, and to find support during self-exploration and change" (Nims, 1998, p. 134). By participating in a group, people develop social relationships and emotional bonds, and often become enlightened (Posthuma, 2002).

This chapter examines the following aspects of groups: their history; their place in counseling, including the types of groups most often used; their theoretical basis; issues and stages in groups; and qualities of effective group leaders. Both national and local organizations have been established for professionals engaged primarily in leading groups. One of the most comprehensive (and the one to which most professional counselors belong) is the **Association for Specialists in Group Work** (ASGW; http://www.asgw.org/), a national division of the American Counseling Association (ACA). This organization, which has a diverse membership, was chartered by ACA in 1974 (Carroll & Levo, 1985). It has been a leader in the field of group work in establishing best practice guidelines, training standards, and principles for diversity-competent group workers. ASGW also publishes a quarterly periodical, *The Journal for Specialists in Group Work*. Other prominent group organizations are the American Group Psychotherapy Association (AGPA), the American Society of Group Psychotherapy and Psychodrama (ASGPP), and the Group Psychology and Group Psychotherapy division of the American Psychological Association (APA) (Division 49).

A BRIEF HISTORY OF GROUPS

Groups have a long and distinguished history in the service of counseling. Joseph Hersey Pratt, a Boston physician, is generally credited with starting the first psychotherapy/counseling group in 1905. Pratt's group members were tubercular outpatients at Massachusetts General Hospital who found the time they regularly spent together informative, supportive, and therapeutic. Although this group was successful, the spread of groups to other settings and the development of different types of groups were uneven and sporadic until the 1970s. The following people were pioneers in the group movement along with Pratt:

- Jacob L. Moreno, who introduced the term *group psychotherapy* into the counseling literature in the 1920s;
- Kurt Lewin, whose field theory concepts in the 1930s and 1940s became the basis for the Tavistock small study groups in Great Britain and the T-group movement in the United States;

- Fritz Perls, whose Gestalt approach to groups attracted new interest in the field by stressing the importance of awareness and obtaining congruence within oneself;
- W. Edwards Deming, who conceptualized and implemented the idea of **quality work groups** to improve the processes and products people produced and to build morale among workers in businesses;
- William Schutz and Jack Gibb, who emphasized a humanistic aspect to T-groups that focused on personal growth as a legitimate goal; and
- Carl Rogers, who devised the basic encounter group in the 1960s that became the model for growth-oriented group approaches.

Besides influential individuals, a number of types of groups, some of which have just been mentioned, developed before groups were classified as they are today. Chronologically, psychodrama was the first, followed by T-groups, encounter groups, group marathons, and self-help/support groups. We will briefly look at each type of group because each has had an influence on what groups are now.

Psychodrama

Jacob L. Moreno, a Viennese psychiatrist, is credited as the originator of *psychodrama*. This type of group experience, employed for decades with mental patients at Saint Elizabeth's Hospital in Washington, DC, was initially used with ordinary citizens in Vienna, Austria (Moreno's original home), at the beginning of the 20th century. In psychodrama, members enact unrehearsed role-plays, with the group leader serving as the director. Other group members are actors in the protagonist's play, give feedback to the protagonist as members of the audience, or do both (Blatner, 2004). This type of group is popular today with a number of behaviorists, Gestaltists, and affective-oriented group leaders who have adapted it as a way of helping clients experience the emotional qualities of an event (Baim, Burmeister, & Manuela, 2007).

T-Groups

The first *T-group* (the *T* stands for *training*) was conducted at the National Training Laboratories (NTL) in Bethel, Maine, in 1946. These groups appeared at a time when neither group counseling nor group psychotherapy had evolved. In fact, they may be considered the beginning of modern group work (Ward, 2002). Kurt Lewin's ideas about group dynamics formed the basis for the original groups. Since that time, T-groups have evolved from a focus on task accomplishment to a primary emphasis on interpersonal relationships. Although it is difficult to classify T-groups in just one way, members of such groups are likely to learn from the experience how one's behavior in a group influences others' behavior and vice versa. In this respect, T-groups are similar to some forms of family counseling in which the emphasis is on both how the system operates and how an individual within the system functions.

Encounter Groups

Encounter groups emerged from T-groups in an attempt to focus on the growth of individual group members rather than the group itself. They were intended for "normally functioning" people who wanted to grow, change, and develop (Lieberman, 1991). These groups took many forms in their heyday (the 1970s), from the minimally structured groups of Carl Rogers (1970) to the highly structured, open-ended groups of William Schutz (1971). Regardless of the structure, the primary emphasis of such groups was on individual expression and recognition of affect.

Group Marathons

A *group marathon* is an extended, one-session group experience that breaks down defensive barriers that individuals may otherwise use. It usually lasts for a minimum of 24 hours. Frederick Stoller and George Bach pioneered the concept in the 1960s. Group marathons have been used successfully in working with substance abusers in rehabilitation programs and well-functioning individuals in other group counseling settings. Often labor and peace negotiations are held in a group marathon setting to achieve breakthroughs.

Self-Help/Support Groups

Self-help groups and *mutual help groups* are synonymous (Klaw & Humphreys, 2004, p. 630). They take two forms: those that are organized by an established, professional helping organization or individual (*support groups*) and those that originate spontaneously and stress their autonomy and internal group resources (*self-help groups* in the truest sense). Self-help groups usually develop spontaneously, center on a single topic, and are led by a layperson with little formal group training but with experience in the stressful event that brought the group together (Riordan & Beggs, 1987). For example, residents in a neighborhood may meet to help each other make repairs and clean up after a natural disaster, or they may assemble to focus government attention on an issue, such as toxic waste, that directly affects the quality of their lives. Self-help groups can be either short or long term, but they basically work to help their members gain greater control of their lives. Over 10 million people are involved in approximately 500,000 such groups in the United States, and the number continues to increase.

Support groups, as noted, are similar to self-help groups in their focus on a particular concern or problem, but established professional helping organizations or individuals (such as Alcoholics Anonymous, Lamplighters, or Weight Watchers) organize them (Gladding, 2012). Some support groups charge fees; others do not. The involvement of laypeople as group leaders varies. Like self-help groups, support groups center around topics that are physical, emotional, or social (L'Abate & Thaxton, 1981).

Self-help and support groups partly fill the needs of populations who can best be served through groups and that might otherwise not receive services. They meet in churches, recreation centers, schools, and other community buildings as well as in mental health facilities.

Lieberman (1994) sees self-help and support groups as healthy for the general public, and Corey (2012) thinks such groups are complementary to other mental health services. Like other group experiences, however, "cohesion is always a vital characteristic for success," and proper guidelines must be set up to ensure the group will be a positive, not a destructive, event (Riordan & Beggs, 1987, p. 428).

PERSONAL REFLECTION

What self-help groups have you been a part of or watched develop? Do you think most self-help groups are successful? Why or why not?

MISPERCEPTIONS AND REALITIES ABOUT GROUPS

Because the history of groups is uneven, certain misperceptions about groups have sprung up. Some of the reasons for these misperceptions occurred in the 1960s when groups were unregulated and yet a popular part of the culture, with the *New York Times* even declaring 1968 as the

"Year of the Group." It was during this time that a number of inappropriate behaviors happened in groups, with the stories generated from the actions taking on a life of their own after being passed on by word of mouth. It is the remnants of these stories that make some people skeptical about groups or keep them from joining groups (Gladding, 2012). The majority of misperceptions involve counseling and psychotherapy groups (as opposed to psychoeducational and task/ work groups). Some prevalent myths about groups are as follows (Childers & Couch, 1989):

- They are artificial and unreal.
- They are second-rate structures for dealing with problems.
- They force people to lose their identity by tearing down psychological defenses.
- They require people to become emotional and spill their guts.
- They are touchy-feely, confrontational, and hostile; they brainwash participants.

The reality is that none of these myths are true, at least in well-run groups. Indeed, the opposite is normally true. Therefore, it is important that individuals who are unsure about groups ask questions before they consider becoming members. Doubts and misperceptions they may have can be addressed and their anxiety may be lessened. Therefore, they may be able to benefit significantly within a group environment.

THE PLACE OF GROUPS IN COUNSELING

A *group* is defined as two or more people interacting together to achieve a goal for their mutual benefit. Everyone typically spends some time in group activities each day (for example, with schoolmates or business associates). Gregariousness is part of human nature, and many personal and professional skills are learned through group interactions. It is only natural, then, for counselors to make use of this primary way of human interaction.

Most counselors have to make major decisions about when, where, and with whom to use groups. In some situations groups are not appropriate ways of helping. For instance, a counselor employed by a company would be unwise to use groups to counsel employees with personal problems who are unequal in rank and seniority in the corporate network. Likewise, a school counselor would be foolish to use a group setting as a way of working with children who are all behaviorally disruptive. But a group may be ideal for helping people who are not too disruptive or unequal in status and who have common concerns. In such cases, counselors generally schedule a regular time for people to meet in a quiet, uninterrupted setting and interact together.

Groups differ in purpose, composition, and length. Basically, however, they all involve work, which Gazda (1989) describes as "the dynamic interaction between collections of individuals for prevention or remediation of difficulties or for the enhancement of personal growth/ enrichment" (p. 297). Hence, the term "group work" is often used to describe what goes on within groups. The ASGW (2000) defines *group work* as

> a broad professional practice involving the application of knowledge and skill in group facilitation to assist an independent collection of people to reach their mutual goals, which may be intrapersonal, interpersonal, or work related. The goals of the group may include the accomplishment of tasks related to work, education, personal development, personal and interpersonal problem solving, or remediation of mental and emotional disorders. (pp. 329–330)

Groups have a number of general advantages in helping individuals. Yalom (2005) has characterized these positive forces as ***therapeutic factors*** within groups. For counseling and psychotherapy groups, these factors include the following:

- ***Instillation of hope***   (i.e., assurance that treatment will work)
- ***Universality***   (i.e., the realization that one is not alone, unique, or abnormal)
- ***Imparting of information***   (i.e., instruction about mental health, mental illness, and how to deal with life problems)
- ***Altruism***   (i.e., sharing experiences and thoughts with others, helping them by giving of oneself, working for the common good)
- ***Corrective recapitulation of the primary family group***   (i.e., reliving early family conflicts and resolving them)
- ***Development of socializing techniques***   (i.e., interacting with others and learning social skills as well as more about oneself in social situations)
- ***Imitative behavior***   (i.e., modeling positive actions of other group members)
- ***Interpersonal learning***   (i.e., gaining insight and correctively working through past experiences)
- ***Group cohesiveness***   (i.e., bonding with other members of the group)
- ***Catharsis***   (i.e., experiencing and expressing feelings)
- ***Existential factors***   (i.e., accepting responsibility for one's life in basic isolation from others, recognizing one's own mortality and the capriciousness of existence)

The group may also serve as a catalyst to help persons realize a want or a need for individual counseling or the accomplishment of a personal goal.

CASE EXAMPLE

Gerard Joins a Group

Gerard moved to a large city where he did not know anyone. He worked in isolation at his job in computer programming. Therefore, when he saw that a local church was starting a series of small-group studies, he decided to join. He found his particular group, which focused on social issues, to be stimulating and he looked forward to the weekly meetings. The group even worked with the city to improve a neighborhood project. Members actively talked to one another in between meetings. After about a month, Gerard reported to his friends back home that he was now feeling better and more a part of his new environment.

Although this group was not one devoted to counseling, how do you think it helped Gerard? Which of Yalom's factors may have been important in the process?

BENEFITS AND DRAWBACKS OF GROUPS

Groups have specific advantages that can be beneficial in helping individuals with a variety of problems and concerns. Literally hundreds of studies describe group approaches and statistically support the effectiveness of various forms of groups. Documentation of group experiences is occurring at such a fast rate, however, that it is difficult to stay abreast of the latest developments. Some researchers in the field regularly write comprehensive reviews on select group activities that help practitioners become better informed.

Some recent findings about groups reveal the following:

- Group counseling can help increase the achievement of African American high school students who are first-time-test-takers on end-of-year high-stakes tests (Bruce, Getch, & Ziomek-Daigle, 2009).
- Group counseling can help third-grade students with social skill deficits reduce loneliness and social anxiety as well as improved academic achievement (Bostick & Anderson, 2009).
- Groups can promote career development in general (Pyle, 2000) and can be used effectively in vocational planning with some underserved populations, such as battered and abused women (Peterson & Priour, 2000).
- Group treatment, under the right conditions, can help adult women improve their functioning and general subjective well-being (Marotta & Asner, 1999).
- Group counseling and psychoeducational programs can help persons who have sustained heart attacks deal better with stressors in their lives (Livneh & Sherwood-Hawes, 1993).
- Group intervention with adolescent offenders can help them increase their maturational processes, especially the ability to work in a sustained way and to achieve a sense of relationship with others (Viney, Henry, & Campbell, 2001).

Yet groups are not a panacea for all people and problems. They have definite limitations and disadvantages. For example, some client concerns and personalities are not well-suited for groups. Likewise, the problems of some individuals may not be dealt with in enough depth within groups. In addition, group pressure may force a client to take action, such as self-disclosure, before being ready. Groups may also lapse into a *groupthink* mentality, in which stereotypical, defensive, and stale thought processes become the norm and creativity and problem solving are squelched. Another drawback to groups is that individuals may try to use them for escape or selfish purposes and disrupt the group process. Furthermore, groups may not reflect the social milieu in which individual members normally operate. Therefore, what is learned from the group experience may not be relevant. Finally, if groups do not work through their conflicts or developmental stages successfully, they may become regressive and engage in nonproductive and even destructive behaviors such as scapegoating, group narcissism, and projection (McClure, 1994).

PERSONAL REFLECTION

There are a number of horrific examples of dysfunctional groups, many of which ended in loss of life (e.g., the Charles Manson family commune that resulted in the death of Sharon Tate and others). On the other hand, there are a number of exemplary groups that have made a difference in the lives of others and society (e.g., the firefighters and police officers during 9/11). Make a list of groups you are aware of historically and on a scale of 1 (being lowest) to 10 (being highest) rate them in regard to their functionality.

TYPES OF GROUPS

Groups come in many forms: "there seems to be a group experience tailored to suit the interests and needs of virtually anyone who seeks psychotherapy, personal growth, or simply support and companionship from others" (Lynn & Frauman, 1985, p. 423). There are a number of group models appropriate for a wide variety of situations. Although lively debate persists about how groups should be categorized, especially in regard to goals and process (Waldo & Bauman, 1998), the following types of groups have training standards developed by the ASGW (2000).

Psychoeducational Groups

Psychoeducational groups, sometimes known as *guidance groups* or *educational groups*, are preventive and instructional (Brown, 2011; Pence, Paymar, Ritmeester, & Shepard, 1998). Their purpose is to teach group participants how to deal with a potential threat (such as catching the flu), a developmental life event (such as growing older), or an immediate life crisis (such as the death of a loved one). These types of groups are often found in educational settings, such as schools, but are increasingly being used in other settings such as hospitals, mental health centers, social service agencies, and universities (Jones & Robinson, 2000).

One of the most important parts of the process in such groups revolves around group discussions of how members will personalize the information presented in the group context (Ohlsen, 1977). In school settings, instructional materials such as unfinished stories, puppet plays, films, audio interviews, and guest speakers are employed in psychoeducational groups. In adult settings, other age-appropriate means, using written materials or guest lecturers, are used.

An example of a psychoeducational group is the promotion of student development on college and university campuses. During the traditional college-age years, "students grow and change in complexity along a variety of dimensions" (Taub, 1998, p. 197). Their development can be enhanced through psychoeducational groups that address issues important to them such as control of anger, dating relationships, and study skills. These groups are relatively brief in duration and meet for only a limited time. Yet, they prepare those who attend more adequately for the issues that are covered.

Counseling Groups

Counseling groups, sometimes known as *interpersonal problem-solving groups*, seek "to help group participants to resolve the usual, yet often difficult, problems of living through interpersonal support and problem solving. An additional goal is to help participants develop their existing interpersonal problem-solving competencies so they may be better able to handle future problems. Non-severe career, educational, personal, social, and developmental concerns are frequently addressed" (ASGW, 1992, p. 143).

Distinguishing between a group counseling and a psychoeducational group is sometimes difficult to do. Generally, group counseling is more direct than a psychoeducational group in attempting to modify attitudes and behaviors. For instance, group counseling stresses the affective involvement of participants, whereas a psychoeducational group concentrates more on the cognitive understanding of its members. A second difference is that group counseling is conducted in a small, intimate setting, whereas a psychoeducational group is more applicable to room-size environments (Gazda, Ginter, & Horne, 2001).

At times, a counseling group and a psychoeducational group may overlap (Pérusse, Goodnough, & Lee, 2009; Waldo & Bauman, 1998). An example of a brief but effective group counseling approach that overlaps some with a psychoeducational group is a structured group for high school seniors making the transition to college and to military service (Goodnough & Ripley, 1997). These groups are held for soon-to-be high school graduates. They give the students an opportunity to deal with the complex set of emotions they are experiencing while providing them with information that will assist them in gaining a helpful cognitive perspective on what they are about to do. In group counseling such as this, participants get *"airtime"* (an opportunity to speak) to discuss their own concerns. The interaction of group members and the personalizing of the information are greater than in a psychoeducational group.

Psychotherapy Groups

Psychotherapy groups, sometimes known as *personality reconstruction groups*, are set up to help individual group members remediate in-depth psychological problems. "Because the depth and extent of the psychological disturbance is significant, the goal is to aid each individual to reconstruct major personality dimensions" (ASGW, 1992, p. 13).

Sometimes there is overlap in group counseling and group psychotherapy, but the emphasis on major reconstruction of personality dimensions usually distinguishes the two. Group psychotherapy often takes place in *inpatient facilities*, such as psychiatric hospitals or other mental health facilities that are residential in nature, because it may be necessary to keep close control over the people involved. Certain types of individuals are **poor candidates for outpatient, intensive group psychotherapy**: depressives, incessant talkers, paranoids, schizoid and sociopathic personalities, suicidals, and extreme narcissists (Yalom, 2005). It may be easier to identify group psychotherapy candidates who should be excluded than choose those who should be included. Regardless, group psychotherapy is an American form of treatment and has provided much of the rationale for group counseling.

Task/Work Groups

Task/work groups help members apply the principles and processes of group dynamics to improve practices and accomplish identified work goals. "The task/work group specialist is able to assist groups such as task forces, committees, planning groups, community organizations, discussion groups, study circles, learning groups, and other similar groups to correct or develop their functioning" (ASGW, 1992, p. 13).

Like other types of groups, task/work groups run best when the following factors are in place:

- the purpose of the group is clear to all participants,
- process (dynamics) and content (information) are balanced,
- time is taken for culture building and learning about each other,
- conflict is addressed,
- feedback between members is exchanged,
- leaders pay attention to the here-and-now, and
- time is taken by leaders and members to reflect on what is happening (Hulse-Killacky, Killacky, & Donigian, 2001).

The classic example of a task/work group is a team. In athletics, art, and employment settings, teams are often formed to accomplish objectives that would be impossible for an individual to achieve alone. The *quality circle*, an employee-run group of workers who meet weekly to examine the processes they are using in their jobs and devise ways to improve them, is a business example of a task/work group (Johnson & Johnson, 2009). However, counselors often work in teams to resolve internal and external situations as well as to plan and implement ideas, so these groups have broad applicability.

Another type of task/work group that counselors may employ is a *focus group* (Kress & Shoffner, 2007). These groups "can be defined broadly as a technique wherein 8 to 12 individuals discuss a particular topic of interest for 1–2 hours under the direction of a group moderator" (p. 190). The moderator promotes interaction by asking group members open-ended questions and ideally elicits "a synergistic effect that cannot be obtained through individual interviews" (p. 192). Themes are delineated in the process and the group facilitator may gain valuable information in the process about group members' preferences as well as be able to describe, evaluate, and assess programs, such as mental health services.

CASE EXAMPLE

Thomas the Taskmaster

Thomas was in charge of his office's innovation team. The purpose of the team was to think of ideas that would help streamline work and promote a more cooperative spirit. The task was challenging and after a few good ideas, nothing new came out of the weekly meetings of the team. Therefore, Thomas decided to hold a team retreat away from the office to help his members focus more and come up with new ideas.

When the team met for the morning in a lovely setting, Thomas made sure that everyone was warmly welcomed and had refreshments. Then, he divided team members into groups of three and assigned each a task.

What do you think of Thomas's plan? Are there other ways the group could have tackled the task at hand? What might they be? Do you think that having the group work together as a whole would be more productive than having small groups concentrate on a particular task? Why or why not?

THEORETICAL APPROACHES IN CONDUCTING GROUPS

Theoretical approaches to counseling in groups vary as much as individual counseling approaches. In many cases, the theories are the same. For instance, within group work there are approaches based on psychoanalytic, Gestalt, person-centered, rational emotive behavior, cognitive, and behavioral theories. Because the basic positions of these theories are examined elsewhere in this text, they will not be reviewed here. Yet the implementation of any theoretical approach differs when employed with a group because of **group dynamics** (the interaction of members within the group).

In an evaluation of seven major theoretical approaches to groups, Ward (1982) analyzed the degree to which each approach paid attention to the individual, interpersonal, and group levels of the process. For instance, psychoanalytic, Gestalt, and behavioral approaches were strong in focusing on the individual but weak on interpersonal and group-level components of the group process. However, the person-centered approach was strong on the individual level and medium on the interpersonal and group level. Ward pointed out the limiting aspects of each approach and the importance of considering other factors, such as the group task and membership maturity, in conducting comprehensive group assignments.

Similarly, Frey (1972) outlined how eight approaches to group work can be conceptualized on a continuum from insight to action and rational to affective; whereas Hansen, Warner, and Smith (1980) conceptualized group approaches on a continuum from process to outcome and leader centered to member centered. Group leaders and potential group members must know how theories differ to make wise choices. Overall, multiple theoretical models provide richness and diversity for conducting groups.

Three factors, in addition to the ones already mentioned, are useful for group leaders to consider when deciding on what theoretical approach to take:

1. Do I need a theoretical base for conducting the group?
2. What uses will the theory best serve?
3. What criteria will be employed in the selection process?

A theory is a lot like a map. In a group, it provides direction and guidance in examining basic assumptions about human beings. It is also useful in determining goals for the group, clarifying one's role and functions as a leader, and explaining the group interactions. Finally, a theory can help in evaluating the outcomes of the group. Trying to lead a group without an explicit theoretical rationale is similar to attempting to fly an airplane without a map and knowledge of instruments. Either procedure is foolish, dangerous, and likely to lead to injury.

A good theory also serves practical functions. For example, it gives meaning to and a framework for experiences and facts that occur within a setting. Good theory helps make logical sense out of what is happening and leads to productive research. With so many theories from which to choose, the potential group leader is wise to be careful in selecting an approach.

Ford and Urban (1998) believe counselors should consider **four main factors when selecting a theory: personal experience, consensus of experts, prestige, and a verified body of knowledge**. All these criteria contain liabilities and advantages. Therefore, it is crucial for beginning counselors to listen to others and read the professional literature critically to evaluate the theories that are most verifiable and that fit in with their personality styles.

STAGES IN GROUPS

Groups, like other living systems, go through stages. If an individual or group leader is not aware of these stages, the changes that occur within the group may appear confusing rather than meaningful, and the benefits may be few. Leaders can maximize learning by either setting up conditions that facilitate the development of the group or "using developmentally based interventions, at both individual and group levels" (Saidla, 1990, p. 15). In either case, group members and leaders benefit.

There is debate in the professional literature about what and when groups go through stages. Developmental stages have been identified in various types of groups, such as learning groups and training groups, yet much of the debate about stages centers around group counseling. Group counseling is most often broken into four or five stages, but some models depict as few as three stages and others as many as six. Tuckman's stage model is considered mainstream.

Tuckman (1965) was one of the first theorists to design a stage process for group counseling. He believed there were four stages of group development: forming, storming, norming, and performing. This concept was later expanded to include a fifth stage: adjourning (Tuckman & Jensen, 1977) or mourning/morning (Waldo, 1985). In each stage certain tasks are performed. For example, in the *forming stage*, the foundation is usually laid down for what is to come and who will be considered in or out of group deliberations. In this stage (the group's infancy), members express anxiety and dependency and talk about nonproblematic issues. One way to ease the transition into the group at this stage is to structure it so that members are relaxed and sure of what is expected of them. For example, before the first meeting, members may be told they will be expected to spend 3 minutes telling others who they are (McCoy, 1994).

In the second stage, *storming*, considerable turmoil and conflict usually occur, as they do in adolescence. Conflict within the group at this and other times "forces group members to make some basic decisions about the degree of independence and interdependence in their relationship with one another" (Rybak & Brown, 1997, p. 31). Group members seek to establish themselves in the hierarchy of the group and deal successfully with issues concerning anxiety, power, and future expectations. Sometimes the group leader is attacked at this stage.

The third stage, *norming*, is similar to young adulthood, in which "having survived the storm the group often generates enthusiasm and cohesion. Goals and ways of working together are decided on" (Saidla, 1990, p. 16). This stage is sometimes combined with the storming stage, but whether it is combined or not, it is followed by *performing/working*, which parallels adulthood in a developmental sense. In the performing stage, group members become involved with each other and their individual and collective goals. This is the time when the group, if it works well, is productive.

Finally, in the *mourning/termination* stage, the group comes to an end, and members say good-bye to one another and the group experience. In termination, members feel either fulfilled or bitter. Sometimes there is a celebration experience at this point of the group; at a minimum, a closure ceremony almost always takes place.

Table 11.1 offers a brief breakdown and summary of the characteristics of each of the five stages discussed here.

TABLE 11.1   Characteristics of the Five Group Stages

Forming	Storming	Norming	Performing/ Working	Mourning/ Termination
Characterized by initial caution associated with any new experience; attempt to avoid being rejected by others.	**Characterized** by a time of conflict and anxiety; group moves from primary to secondary tension; attempt to balance between too much and too little tension.	**Characterized** by a feeling of "Weness" that comes when individuals feel that they belong to the group; often enthusiasm and cooperation at this time.	**Characterized** by a focus on the achievement of individual and group goals and the movement of the group into a more unified and productive system.	**Characterized** by participants coming to know themselves on a deeper level; primary activities in termination—reflect on past experiences, process memories, evaluate what was learned, acknowledge ambivalent feelings, engage in cognitive decision making
Peer relationships: group members tend to be superficial and center conversion around historical or future events that do not have a direct impact on the group.	**Peer relationships:** group members tend to be more anxious in their interactions with one another; concern for power is prevalent.	**Peer relationships:** identification with others in the group; hope, cooperation, collaboration, cohesion.	**Peer relationships:** genuine concern on a deep, personal level by members for one another; greater willingness to self-disclose on the part of members; increased awareness in the group about individual participants and the world of each person.	**Peer relationships:** feelings of empathy, compassion, and care abound; participants relate to one another on a deep and sometimes emotional level; feelings of warmth and sorrow often occur simultaneously.

(continued)

TABLE 11.1   Characteristics of the Five Group Stages (*Continued*)

Forming	Storming	Norming	Performing/ Working	Mourning/ Termination
Task processing: dealing with apprehension; reviewing members' goals and contracts; specifying more clearly or reiterating group rules; setting limits; promoting positive interchange among members so they will want to continue.	**Task processing:** concentration on direct objectives diminishes; a healthy "pause" takes place; scapegoating might take place.	**Task processing:** members must agree on the establishment of norms from which to operate the group; groups accept both prescriptive and proscriptive norms; importance of commitment is stressed during this time.	**Task processing:** major emphasis on productivity whether the results are tangibly visible or not; maintenance of interpersonal relationships must be attended to and balanced with productivity.	**Task processing:** major emphasis on promoting a successful end to the group and relationships in the group; consolidation of gains; finding of meaning in group, making decisions for new ways of behaving; prepare for a new beginning after group ends.
Useful procedures: joining, linking, cutting off, drawing out and clarifying purpose.	**Useful procedures:** leveling, feedback, informal and formal feedback.	**Useful procedures:** supporting, empathizing, facilitating, self-disclosure.	**Useful procedures:** modeling, exercises, group observing group, brainstorming, nominal-group technique, synectics, written projections, group processing, teaching skills.	**Useful procedures:** summarization, rounds, dyads, written reactions, rating sheets, homework, time limits, capping skills, and modeling.

Overall, the developmental stages of a group are not always easily differentiated at any one point in time. "A group does not necessarily move step by step through life stages, but may move backward and forward as a part of its general development" (Hansen et al., 1980, p. 476). The question of what stage a group is in and where it is heading can best be answered through retrospection or insightful perception.

ISSUES IN GROUPS

Conducting successful groups entails a number of issues. Some deal with procedures for running groups; others deal with training and ethics. Before a group is set up, the leader of the group needs to have a clear idea of why the group is being established and what its intermediate as well as ultimate goals are. It is only from such a process that a successful group will emerge.

Selection and Preparation of Group Members

Screening and preparation are essential for conducting a successful group (Couch, 1995) because the maturity, readiness, and composition of membership plays a major role in whether the group will be a success or not (Riva, Lippert, & Tackett, 2000). Some individuals who wish to be members of groups are not appropriate candidates for them. If such persons are allowed to join a group, they may end up being difficult group members (e.g., by monopolizing or manipulating) and cause the group leader considerable trouble (Kottler, 1994b). They may also join with others who are at an equally low level of functioning and contribute to the regression of the group. When this happens, members become psychologically damaged, and the group is unable to accomplish its goals (McClure, 1990).

Screening and preparation are usually accomplished through pregroup interviews and training, which take place between the group leader and prospective members. During a *pregroup interview* group members should be selected whose needs and goals are compatible with the established goals of the group. These are members who will not impede the group process, and whose well-being will not be jeopardized by the group experience. Research indicates that *pregroup training*, in which members learn more about a group and what is expected of them, provides important information for participants and gives them a chance to lower their anxiety (Sklare, Petrosko, & Howell, 1993).

In following ethical guidelines and best practices for group counselors (ASGW, 1998), certain individuals may need to be screened out or may elect to screen themselves out of the group. Screening is a two-way process. Potential group members may not be appropriate for a certain group at a particular time with a designated leader. They should be advised of their options if they are not selected for a group, such as joining another group or waiting for a group to form that is better able to address their situation. In selecting group members, a group leader should heed Gazda's (1989) advice that individuals in the group be able to identify with other group members at least on some issues. In essence, the screening interview "lays the foundation upon which the group process will rest" (McCoy, 1994, p. 18).

PERSONAL REFLECTION

Not being selected for a group may be painful for many people. How might you tell someone he or she was not chosen for a particular group in a diplomatic but truthful way?

Before the group begins, group members and leaders need to be informed as much as possible about *group process* (how group member interactions influence the development of the group). For instance, in *homogeneous groups* (in which members are more alike than unalike), there is usually less conflict and risk taking, more cohesion and support, and better attendance. In contrast, in *heterogeneous groups* (in which members are more unalike than alike), there is more conflict initially and greater risk taking, but support and cohesion may lag and members may drop out (Merta, 1995). It is the process of the group, not the content, focus, or purpose, that will eventually determine whether a group succeeds. In successful groups, the process is balanced with content (Donigian & Malnati, 1997; Kraus & Hulse-Killacky, 1996).

"When either the content or the process of . . . groups becomes disproportionate, the group may experience difficulty accomplishing work" (Nelligan, 1994, p. 8). Veterans of group experiences usually need minimal information about how a group will be conducted, whereas novice participants may require extensive preparation. Members who are informed about the procedures and focus of a group before they begin will do better in the group once it starts.

In joining a group, it is important to check first with the group organizer and become clear about what possibilities and outcomes are expected in a group experience. Corey (2012) lists **issues that potential participants should clarify before they enroll in a group**. The following are among the most important:

- A clear statement of the group's purpose
- A description of the group format, ground rules, and basic procedures
- A statement about the educational and training qualifications of the group leader(s)
- A pregroup interview to determine whether the potential group leader and members are suited for one's needs at the time

- A disclosure about the risks involved in being in a group and the members' rights and responsibilities
- A discussion about the limitations of confidentiality and the roles group leaders and participants are expected to play within the group setting

Regardless of the perceived need for information, research supports the idea that "providing a set of expectations for participants prior to their initiation into a group improves the possibility of members having a successful group . . . experience" (Sklare, Keener, & Mas, 1990, p. 145). Specifically, group leaders can facilitate "here and now group counseling . . . by discouraging 'you' and 'we' language, questioning, speaking in the third person, seeking approval, rescuing, and analyzing.

Finally, group leaders must know how to handle challenges to their leadership and resistance from individual group members or the group as a whole.

Group Size and Duration

A group's size is determined by its purpose and preference. Large groups are less likely to spotlight the needs of individual members. Therefore, outside of group guidance there is an optimal number of people that should be involved. A generally agreed-on number is 6 to 8 group members, although Gazda (1989) notes that if groups run as long as 6 months, up to 10 people may productively be included. Group size and duration affect each other. Corey (2012) states, "For ongoing groups with adults, about eight members with one leader seems to be a good size. Groups with children may be as small as three or four. In general, the group should have enough people to afford ample interaction so it doesn't drag and yet be small enough to give everyone a chance to participate frequently without . . . losing the sense of 'group'" (p. 72).

Open-Ended versus Closed Groups

Open-ended groups admit new members after they have started; *closed groups* do not. Lynn and Frauman (1985) point out that open-ended groups are able to replace lost members rather quickly and maintain an optimal size. Many long-term outpatient groups are open ended. Closed-ended groups, although not as flexible in size, promote more cohesiveness among group members and may be productive in helping members achieve stated goals.

Confidentiality

Groups function best when members feel a sense of *confidentiality*—that is, what has been said within the group setting will not be revealed outside. To promote a sense of confidentiality and build trust, a group leader must be active. In the prescreening interview the subject of confidentiality should be raised. The importance of confidentiality needs to be stressed during the first meeting of the group and on a regular basis thereafter (Corey, Corey, & Callanan, 2011).

Furthermore, it is the group leader's role to protect his or her members by clearly defining what confidentiality is and the importance and difficulty of enforcing it. Whenever any question arises about the betrayal of confidentiality within a group, it should be dealt with immediately. Otherwise, the problem grows and the cohesiveness of the group breaks down. Olsen (1971) points out that counselors must realize they can only guarantee their own adherence to the principles of confidentiality. Still, they must strive to ensure the rights of all group members.

Physical Structure

The setting where a group is conducted is either an asset or a liability. Terres and Larrabee (1985) emphasize the need for a physical structure (a room or a setting) that ensures the safety and growth of group members. Groups within schools and community agencies need to be conducted in places that promote the well-being of the group. The furnishings of the space (attractive) and the way the group is assembled (preferably in a circle) can facilitate the functioning of the group.

Co-Leaders

It is not necessary for groups to have *co-leaders* (two leaders), but such an arrangement can be beneficial to the group and the leaders, especially if the group is large (over 10 members). With co-leaders, one leader can work with the group while the other monitors the group process. A co-leader arrangement may also be beneficial when an inexperienced leader and experienced leader are working together. In such a setup, the inexperienced leader can learn from the experienced one. Many group specialists advocate that an inexperienced leader co-lead a group first before attempting the process alone.

Dinkmeyer and Muro (1979) suggest that successful, experienced co-leaders (a) possess a similar philosophical and operational style, (b) have similar experience and competence, (c) establish a model relationship for effective human interaction, (d) be aware of splitting and member loyalty ties to one leader or the other and help the group deal with this, and (e) agree on counseling goals and the processes to achieve them so that power struggles are avoided.

Pietrofesa, Hoffman, and Splete (1984) recommend that co-leaders sit opposite each other in a group so that leader responsibility and observation are maximized. They point out that it is not necessary for group co-leaders to be of the opposite sex; skills, not gender, matter most.

Self-Disclosure

Shertzer and Stone (1981) define *self-disclosure* as "here and now feelings, attitudes, and beliefs" (p. 206). The process of self-disclosure is dependent on the trust that group members have for one another. If there is high trust, greater self-disclosure will ensue. An interesting aspect of this phenomenon is that self-disclosure builds on itself. During the first stages of the group, it may have to be encouraged. Morran (1982) suggests that leaders, in the beginning sessions of a group, use self-disclosure often to serve as a model for others and promote the process. As Stockton, Barr, and Klein (1981) document, group members who make few verbal self-disclosures are more likely than others to drop out of a group.

Feedback

Feedback is a multidimensional process that consists of group members' responding to the verbal messages and nonverbal behaviors of one another. It is one of the most important and abused parts of any group experience. When feedback is given honestly and with care, group members can gauge the impact of their actions on others and attempt new behaviors.

Corey (2012) distinguishes between group feedback given at the end of a session and that given at the termination of a group. During the latter process, Corey encourages group members to be clear, concise, and concrete with one another. Group members should give themselves feedback about how they have changed during the group experience. After processing feedback information, group members should record some of the things said during final feedback sessions so they will not forget and can make use of the experience in evaluating progress toward their goals.

To promote helpful feedback, Pietrofesa et al. (1984) list **criteria for feedback evaluation**. Here are some important recommendations:

- Feedback should be beneficial to the receiver and not serve the needs of the giver.
- Feedback is more effective when it is based on describable behavior.
- In the early stages of group development, positive feedback is more beneficial and more readily accepted than negative feedback.
- Feedback is most effective when it immediately follows a stimulus behavior and is validated by others.
- Feedback is of greater benefit when the receiver is open and trusts the giver (p. 376).

Follow-Up

Follow-up is keeping in touch with members after the group has terminated to determine how well they are progressing on personal or group goals. Often group leaders fail to conduct proper follow-up. This failure is especially prevalent in short-term counseling groups or groups led by an outside leader (Gazda, 1989). ASGW's *Best Practice Guidelines* (1998) (which clarify the application of the ACA's Code of Ethics to the field of group work) states that group workers provide for follow-up after the termination of a group as appropriate to assess outcomes or when requested by a group member(s). Follow-up helps group members and leaders assess what they gained in the group experience and allows the leader to refer a group member for help, if appropriate (Gladding, 2012). Follow-up sessions maximize the effects of a group experience and encourage members to keep pursuing original goals (Jacobs, Masson, Harvill, & Schimmel, 2012).

Corey (2012) suggests that a follow-up session for a short-term group be conducted about 3 months after termination. He points out that the process of mutual feedback and support from other group members at this time can be very valuable. If group members are aware during the termination stage of their group that they will meet again for a follow-up, they are more likely than not to continue pursuing their goals. In addition to a whole-group follow-up, individual follow-up between leaders and group members is important, even if these sessions are conducted by phone.

QUALITIES OF EFFECTIVE GROUP LEADERS

There are distinguishing qualities of effective and ineffective group leaders. For instance, group leaders who are authoritarian, aggressive, confrontational, or emotionally removed from the group are ineffective and produce *group casualties* (members who drop out or are worse after the group experience) (Yalom & Lieberman, 1971). However, **four leadership qualities** have a **positive effect on the outcome of groups**, if they are not used excessively (Yalom, 2005):

1. *Caring*—the more, the better
2. *Meaning attribution*—includes clarifying, explaining, and providing a cognitive framework for change
3. *Emotional stimulation*—involves activity, challenging, risk taking, self-disclosure
4. *Executive function*—entails developing norms, structuring, and suggesting procedures

It is vital that group leaders find a position between the two extremes of emotional stimulation and executive function for the group's well-being. Leaders should not allow members to experience so much emotion that they are unable to process the material being discovered in the group or structure the situation so rigidly that no emotion is expressed.

Kottler (1994a) states that effective leaders understand the forces operating within a group, recognize whether these forces are therapeutic, and, if they are not, take steps to better manage the group with the assistance of its members. His assessment of leadership comple-ments that of Yalom's (2005) and Osborne's (1982), who believe that good group leaders behave with intentionality because they are able to anticipate where the group process is mov-ing and recognize group needs. An example of this phenomenon is the ability of group leaders to treat the group homogeneously when there is a need to manage group tensions and protect members and to emphasize heterogeneous qualities when the group has become too comfort-able and is not working.

In addition, Corey (2012) maintains that effective group leaders are committed to self-improvement to become effective as human beings. He lists a number of personal qualities that are related to effective group leadership. Among them are presence, personal power, courage, willingness to confront oneself, sincerity, authenticity, enthusiasm, sense of identity, and inventiveness/creativity.

A final quality of effective group leaders is that they are well educated in group theory, practice, and techniques. For instance, in group counseling and psychotherapy, "the group leader's task is to translate symptoms into interpersonal issues" (Pistole, 1997a, p. 7). By so doing, the leader helps participants in groups learn how to develop distortion-free and gratifying relationships. Regardless of the type of group, leaders employ a number of techniques such as active listening, clarifying, summarizing, questioning, supporting, empathizing, evaluating, giving feedback, modeling, blocking, and terminating.

CASE EXAMPLE

Lydia as a Leader

Lydia was a caring and energetic counselor. She loved what she did and had much success working with individuals.

One day Lydia's supervisor, Susan, asked her to lead a group of clients who were all ex-periencing trauma of various kinds. Lydia wanted to be helpful, but she had never experienced trauma and was not sure what to do. When she expressed her reservations to Susan, Susan's reply was: "Use the skills you already have as a counselor of individuals. The group will work well if you do."

Is Susan's advice to Lydia very helpful? What other skills and abilities might Lydia need in order to lead the group she has been assigned?

THE FUTURE OF GROUP WORK

The future of group work is filled with possibilities. It is headed in many directions. One focus of group work is the development of new ways of working in groups that are theory driven. For ex-ample, solution-focused counseling and brief therapy groups appear to be gaining popularity and have been found through research to be effective (Cooley, 2009; LaFountain, Garner, & Eliason, 1996; Shapiro, Peltz, & Bernadett-Shapiro, 1998). These groups differ from problem-solving groups in their "focus on beliefs about change, beliefs about complaints, and creating solutions" (LaFountain et al., 1996, p. 256).

Groups are also becoming more preventive. Life-skill training in groups is one example of the prevention emphasis. Four areas of this approach are (a) interpersonal communication and human relations, (b) problem solving and decision making, (c) physical fitness and health maintenance, and (d) development of identity and purpose of life. But the biggest manifestation of prevention in groups is in managed health care, where financial premiums are attached to helping individuals stay well or prevent future difficulties.

Overall, the future of group work seems robust and headed toward more diversity in both its theory and practice (DeLucia-Waack, 1996). Multicultural issues, especially in regard to awareness of others, self, training, and research, are receiving more attention (Merta, 1995). For example, Conyne (1998) has developed a set of "multicultural sensitizers" that can be used along with Hanson's (1972) original group process observation guidelines to help students and other trainees become more aware of multicultural issues in group work. Likewise, guidelines for groups that focus on working with specific cultural minorities have been devised. For instance, ways of working with African American women in groups have been formulated and published (Pack-Brown, Whittington-Clark, & Parker, 1998). More such developments should occur in the 21st century.

MyCounselingLab™

Go to Topic 9: *Group Counseling* in the MyCounselingLab™ site (www.MyCounselingLab .com) for *Counseling: A Comprehensive Profession,* Seventh Edition, where you can:

- Find learning outcomes for *Group Counseling* along with the national standards that connect to these outcomes.
- Complete Assignments and Activities that can help you more deeply understand the chapter content.
- Apply and practice your understanding of the core skills identified in the chapter with the Building Counseling Skills unit.
- Prepare yourself for professional certification with a Practice for Certification quiz.
- Connect to videos through the Video and Resource Library.

Summary and Conclusion

Groups are an exciting, necessary, and effective way to help people. They can take an educational, preventive, or remedial form. The ASGW has formulated standards for psychoeducational groups, counseling groups, psychotherapy groups, and task groups. The theories and some of the techniques used in groups are often the same as those employed in working with individuals. There are differences in application, however.

To be maximally effective, group leaders must be competent in dealing with individual as well as group issues. Learning how to do this is a developmental process. Effective group leaders know what type of groups they are leading and share this information with potential members. Leaders follow ethical, legal, and procedural guidelines of professional organizations. They are concerned with the general well-being of their groups and the people in them. They anticipate problems before they occur and take proactive steps to correct them. They systematically follow up with group members after the group has terminated, and they keep up with the professional literature about groups and are constantly striving to improve their personal and professional levels of functioning.

Overall, groups are a stage-based and expanding way of working with people to achieve individual and collective goals. Professional counselors must acquire group skills if they are to be well-rounded and versatile.

Consultation

Chapter Overview

From this chapter you will learn about

- The multifaceted nature of consultation
- The differences and similarities between consultation and counseling
- Direct and indirect consultation
- Stages in the consultation process
- Specific areas of consultation (e.g., individual, educational, agency)

As you read consider

- How important consultation is to counseling
- Different models of consultation and how comfortable you feel with them
- When you have sought consultation directly or indirectly and the outcome of the process
- What level of consultation you think you might be best at
- How comfortable you feel in the role as a consultant as opposed to the role of a counselor

She went about kissing frogs
for in her once-upon-a time mind
that's what she had learned to do.
With each kiss came expectations
of slimy green changing to Ajax white.
With each day came realizations
that quick-tongued, fly-eating, croaking creatures
Don't magically turn to instant princes
from the after effects of a fast-smooching,
smooth-talking helping beauty.
So with regret she came back from a lively lily-pond
to the sobering stacks of the village library
To page through the well-worn stories again
and find in print what she knew in fact
that even loved frogs sometimes stay frogs
no matter how pretty the damsel or how high the hope.

From "Of Frogs, Princes and Lily Pond Changes," by S. T. Gladding, 1976, in *Reality Sits in a Green Cushioned Chair* (p. 17). Atlanta: Collegiate Press. © Samuel T. Gladding.

251

MyCounselingLab

Visit the MyCounselingLab™ site (www.MyCounselingLab) for *Counseling: A Comprehensive Profession,* Seventh Edition to enhance your understanding of chapter concepts. You'll have the opportunity to practice your skills through video- and case-based Assignments and Activities as well as Building Counseling Skills units and to prepare for your certification exam with Practice for Certification quizzes.

Although counselors in a variety of work settings provide "some consulting services as part of their professional responsibilities, the formal literature on consultation as a function of counselors did not emerge until the late 1960s and early 1970s" (Randolph & Graun, 1988, p. 182). Initially, consultant was defined as an expert with special knowledge to share with the consultee. Therefore, certain theoretical approaches to counseling (such as Adlerian, cognitive, and behavioral) were considered to be best suited for this activity because of their emphases on teaching and pragmatic application. Affective and humanistic theories, such as person-centered or existential, were considered to be less desirable because of their focus on close personal relationships and their generally less precise structure. However, as time has shown, consultation can be premised on a variety of theoretical concepts depending on the need of the client or the group.

Regardless of the orientation, consultation is a function expected of all counselors and one that is receiving increased attention. Sometimes counselors who function in this capacity are referred to as ***counselor–consultants*** (Randolph & Graun, 1988); at other times, only the word consultant is used. "First and foremost, [consultation is] a human relationship" process (Dougherty, 2009, p. v). It requires a personal touch as well as professional input if it is to be effective. It also requires an acute sensitivity to cultural nuances and multicultural issues (Jackson & Hayes, 1993).

CONSULTATION: DEFINING A MULTIFACETED ACTIVITY

Many attempts have been made through the years to define consultation, although there is still no universal agreement on the definition. As early as 1970, Caplan defined it as "a process between two professional persons, the consultant, who is a specialist, and the consultee, who invokes the consultant's help in regard to current work problems" (p. 19). In the late 1970s, two special issues of the *Personnel and Guidance Journal* (now the *Journal for Counseling and Development)* (February and March 1978) were published on consultation, which were followed 7 years later by a special issue of *The Counseling Psychologist* (July 1985) devoted exclusively to the same topic. Eight years later, two additional issues of the *Journal for Counseling and Development* (July/August and November/December 1993) addressed the subject of consultation again in multiple ways. All five publications, and others like them, brought consultation to the forefront of counseling and helped professionals delineate **common aspects of the consultation process**:

- it has a problem-solving focus,
- it is tripartite in nature, and
- it emphasizes improvement (Dougherty, 2009).

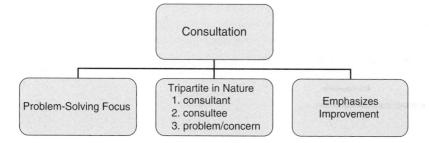

BASIC ASPECTS OF CONSULTATION

In spite of all the attention it has received, consultation is not well conceptualized by many counselors, who often do not understand its exact nature (Drapela, 1983). Consequently, some counselors misinterpret the concept, feel uncomfortable about engaging in consultative activities, or both (Goodyear, 1976). Brown (1983) relates the story of a man whose image of a consultant was "someone who blows in, blows off, and blows out" (p. 124). As inaccurate as this idea is, it may well reflect the impreciseness implied by the term.

Consultation has "proliferated wildly" since the early 1970s. However, the "theory and research lag far behind" actual practice (Gallessich, 1985, p. 336). The reasons for this lag include the following:

- There is an atheoretical attitude toward consultation that inhibits its development. Consultation originated in many different settings with various groups and has multiple forms, thereby making it hard to organize (Gallessich, 1982). In addition, many counseling consultants do not conceptualize or practice consultation as a specialized professional process.
- Consultation is not the primary activity of all professionals or of any professional group. It lacks "the organizational support, leadership, and resources necessary for theory-building and research" (Gallessich, 1985, p. 342).
- Consultation practices have changed rapidly. Unlike most other forms of helping, consultation reacts quickly to social, political, or technical changes. For example, the humanistic consultation practices of the late 1960s were not widely employed in the more conservative 1980s.

Other factors inhibiting the growth and development of consultation involve difficulties in (a) defining variables and obtaining permission to do specialized research in organizational settings and (b) understanding the changing nature of goals in the consultation process. In other words, initial goals may change.

PERSONAL REFLECTION

Why do you think it might be important to be a practicing counselor first if an individual aspires to be a consultant to counselors? What would be the drawback of a lack of experience?

Some debate still persists about the exact definition of consultation (Kurpius & Fuqua, 1993). One of the best definitions of consultation (that elaborates on the one given previously by

Caplan) has been crafted by Kurpius (1978), who defines *consultation* as "a voluntary relationship between a professional helper and help-needing individual, group, or social unit in which the consultant is providing help to the client(s) in defining and solving a work-related problem or potential problem with a client or client system."

An important word Kurpius has added to the definition of Caplan (1970) mentioned earlier in this chapter is "voluntary." In a consultation activity, help is sought from a professional but it may be cancelled at any time. It is not mandatory such as an inspection from an accrediting body might be. In addition Kurpius has delineated even further who a consultee may be, that is, "an individual, group, or social unit." Thus, a counseling unit (i.e., a group) at a college might seek consultation in striving to be more efficient or collegial. Community organizations as well as individuals might do the same. In other words, consultee is broad-based and inclusive. Finally, Kurpius's definition includes the words "defining" and "potential problem." These words are important because before solving a situation, it must be defined clearly and accurately. Secondly, consultants do not just make recommendations for resolving current concerns. Rather, they focus on potential problems as well and strive to prevent difficulties from occurring in the first place.

In general, **consulting approaches** have the **following characteristics in common** (Gallessich, 1985; Kurpius & Fuqua, 1993; Newman, 1993):

- Consultation is **content based** (supported by a recognized body of knowledge).
- Consultation is **goal oriented**; it has an objective, often a work-related one.
- Consultation is **governed by variable roles and relationship rules**.
- Consultation is **process oriented**; it involves gathering data, recommending solutions, and offering support.
- Consultation is **triadic**.
- Consultation is **based on ideologies, value systems, and ethics**.

Kurpius (1986a, 1988) also stresses that consultation is systems oriented. It aims to help change aspects of the system, such as its structure or people and to change the system itself. Forces within systems either facilitate or inhibit their receptivity to the consultation process (Kurpius, Fuqua, & Rozecki, 1993).

Because of its importance to the overall role of counselors, "a generic consultation course is required in many counselor training programs, and consultation experiences have been included in the Council for Accreditation of Counseling and Related Programs (CACREP) . . . standards for accreditation of such programs" (Randolph & Graun, 1988, p. 182).

CONSULTATION VERSUS COUNSELING

Schmidt and Osborne (1981) found that in actual practice most counselors they surveyed did not distinguish between consultation and counseling activities. These researchers concluded "the ultimate goals of both are so similar that it is difficult to differentiate between the two when studying them as general processes" (p. 170). Indeed, many of the principles and processes are similar. For example, consultation and counseling may be offered on a primary (preventive) level, and both are interpersonal processes. Yet there are distinctions.

One of the differences between consultation and counseling is that "the content of the consulting interview, unlike counseling, is a unit external to the counseltee" (Stum, 1982, p. 297). Most consultation takes place in a natural setting (often the consultee's work environment), whereas most counseling occurs at the designated center where a counselor is employed (Kurpius, 1986b). It is often informal and even indirect where peers discuss a matter that one has had difficulty with. Indeed, informal consultation happens frequently often without those involved in the process even realizing they are involved in the process.

Skill in communication is another area in which there are contrasts between these two activities. Communication skills employed in consultation do not differ much from those used in counseling (Kurpius, 1988; Schmidt, 2007). Both counselors and consultants listen, attend, question, clarify, confront, and summarize. But consultants initially focus more on content than feeling because the process concentrates primarily on problems and issues.

Another difference between consultation and counseling is in the role of practitioners. Professionals who operate from either position try to initiate change in the people with whom they work. Yet consultants play more of a catalyst role than do counselors because they do not have "direct control over the consultee or the consultee's client" (Kurpius, 1986a, p. 58).

Finally, even though the goals of counseling and consulting are similar (i.e., to help consultees become more efficient, effective, independent, and resourceful in their abilities to solve the problems that they face), consultation activities work indirectly rather than directly (Nelson & Shifron, 1985, p. 298). Often consultants teach consultees a skill that can be applied to a third party, whereas counseling skills are usually focused on and directly applicable to a specific individual, group, or system with which counselors work.

CASE EXAMPLE

Katie's Consultation

Katie has been a counselor for a number of years. She finds the work highly rewarding. However, she wants to do more on a global society level. A friend, Shawn, suggested she become a consultant. Katie is not sure if such work will really make a difference or that she can transition into such a role.

From what you have read so far, how hard do you think transitioning into the role of a consultant is? Do you think a consultant's impact is as great as a counselor's? What makes you think so? How might Kate combine counseling and consultation?

FOUR CONCEPTUAL MODELS

Many different models of consultation exist, but only a few of them are comprehensive and useful in counseling. **Four of the most comprehensive models of consultation** elaborated on by a number of experts (Keys, Bemak, Carpenter, & King-Sears, 1998; Kurpius, 1978; Kurpius & Brubaker, 1976; Schein, 1978) follow:

1. *Expert or provision model.*   In the expert model, consultants provide a direct service to consultees who do not have the time, inclination, or perceived skills to deal with a particular problem area. This model of consultation was the first to develop (Kurpius & Robinson, 1978). It was used extensively in the 1940s and early 1950s. The advantage of the model is that experts can handle difficult problems and leave consultees free to manage their other duties without work conflicts. The major disadvantage is that consultants are blamed if a particular problem does not get better.

2. *Doctor–patient or prescription model.*   In the prescription model, consultants advise consultees about what is wrong with the targeted third party and what should be done about it. A good way to conceptualize this method is to compare it with the traditional

medical model in which patients' problems are diagnosed and a prescription to rectify their situations is given. This model is usually implemented when consultees lack confidence in their own intervention strategies. It does not require consultants to bring about a change or a cure, as the provision model does.

3. *Mediation model.*   Consultants act as coordinators in the mediation model. Their main function is to unify the services of a variety of people who are trying to solve a problem (Baker & Gerler, 2008). They accomplish this goal by (a) coordinating the services already being provided or (b) creating an alternative plan of services that represents a mutually acceptable synthesis of several solutions. A consultant might work this way in a school system in which a child with a disability is receiving a variety of different services that are disruptive to both the child and school. Through mediation, the consultant would seek to have services offered in a systematic way with less disruption.

4. *Process consultation or collaboration model.*   Consultants are facilitators of the problem-solving process in the collaboration model. Their main task is to get consultees actively involved in finding solutions to the present difficulties they have with clients. Thus, in a school situation, consultees (i.e., parents, educators, youth, counselors, and community agency professionals) would define their problems clearly, analyze them thoroughly, design workable solutions, and then implement and evaluate their own plans of action. This approach does not assume that any one person has sufficient knowledge to develop and implement solutions and that the group assembled must work as an interdependent team (Keys et al., 1998).

Setting up an atmosphere in which this process can happen is a major task for collaboration consultants. It requires the use of a number of interpersonal counseling skills, such as empathy, active listening, and structuring (Baker & Gerler, 2008). In addition, counselors who work as consultants in these situations must be highly intelligent and analytical thinkers who are able to generate enthusiasm, optimism, and self-confidence in others. They must also be able to integrate and use affective, behavioral, and cognitive dimensions of problem solving.

Four-Stage Model of Consultation	
1. Expert	Consultant provides direct services, handles difficult problems
2. Prescriptive	Traditional medical model, problem diagnosis and prescription
3. Meditation	Consultant coordinates existing services, creates alternative plans
4. Collaborator	Consultant is a facilitator, gets others involved finding solutions

PERSONAL REFLECTION

Of the four models of consultation just presented, which do you like the most or feel most drawn toward? Try to assess your reason for being attracted to a particular model, drawing on events or experiences you have had.

LEVELS OF CONSULTATION

Consultation services may be delivered on several levels. Three of the most common ways to implement the process involve working at the individual, group, and organizational/community level (Kurpius, 1988).

Individual Consultation

Kisch (1977) has discussed aspects of one-to-one consultation. He employs a ***role-reversal process***, in which a client role-plays either an active or passive consultant while the counselor role-plays the client. The client sits in different chairs when playing the separate roles. When passive, the client gives only familiar, safe, nonthreatening advice in response to the presented problem, and there is no confrontation. When active, the client reflects "thoughts, feelings, and strategies that are assertive, confrontive, and may be novel and frightening" (p. 494). In each case, counselors ask clients about the payoffs and risks of the client-consultant ideas for change.

Another form of individual consultation involves ***teaching self-management skills***. Kahn (1976) points out that externally maintained treatment modalities are not very effective. To replace them, he proposes a four-part interdependent component model with the following requirements:

- ***Self-monitoring:*** persons observe their own behavior
- ***Self-measurement:*** persons validate the degree to which the problem exists
- ***Self-mediation:*** persons develop and implement strategies of change
- ***Self-maintenance:*** persons continually monitor and measure the desired effects of the self-management process

Kahn gives examples of excessive and deficit behaviors that can be managed through this model, including cigarette smoking, obesity, assertiveness, and depression. He points out that when individuals learn the steps of self-management, they can take preventive and remedial actions on their own.

Kurpius (1986a) emphasizes that "mutual trust and respect are essential" on an individual consultation level (p. 61). For example, Fogle (1979) suggests that teaching individuals a **constructive negative-thinking process** can sometimes alleviate anxiety, restore motivation, promote risk-taking behaviors, and shift attention to the present. In this process, clients are instructed to think negatively about future-oriented events and make contingency plans if the worst possible situation occurs. They are instructed to follow the instructions of the consultant only if they believe what is being suggested will work.

Overall, at the individual consultation level, a consultant is often required to model a skill or prescribe a solution. Working on an individual level is appropriate if the consultee clearly has an individual problem, a systems intervention is inappropriate or impossible, or individual change would be more beneficial and efficient (Fuqua & Newman, 1985). One recent form of individual consultation that has become increasingly popular, especially in business, is an activity known as ***coaching, life coaching,*** or ***executive coaching*** (Center for Credentialing and Education, 2011; Sears, Rudisill, & Mason-Sears, 2006). In the coaching process, outside experts in human services or the helping professions, such as counselors, work with individuals, often in business, to assist them in becoming more insightful and aware of what they are doing and what they could do better. The Center for Credentialing and Education (CCE), an affiliate of NBCC, has recently introduced a certificate credential in this area under the title ***Board Certified Coach***. In addition, there are numerous other organizations that train individuals in coaching.

Group Consultation

Group consultation is employed when several individuals share a similar problem (e.g., in a work setting). Kurpius (1986a) states that in work situations in which group consultation is employed the group may be either focused on problem-solving or person-focused. In problem-solving groups, the consultant acts as a catalyst and facilitator. In person-focused groups, the consultant may help group members build teams to understand and resolve person problems (Sears et al., 2006).

The *C group* was one of the first effective collaborative consultation models (Dinkmeyer, 1971, 1973b; Dinkmeyer & Carlson, 1973, 2006). All aspects of the approach begin with a *C*: collaboration, consultation, clarification, confrontation, concern, confidentiality, and commitment. Its primary purpose is to present new knowledge about human behavior to members of the group. It encourages group members to work together as equals (collaboration); give and receive input from each other (consultation); understand the relationship among beliefs, feelings, and actions (clarification); share openly with each other (confrontation); empathize with one another (concern); keep information within the group (confidentiality); and make plans for specific changes (commitment). Although the C group has the potential to influence parent–child interactions dramatically, the group is always composed of adults because its Adlerian orientation assumes that adults control parent–child interactions for better or worse. Furthermore, it is never used for counseling purposes—only for sharing information and mutual support.

Voight, Lawler, and Fulkerson (1980) have developed a consultation program that assists women who are making midlife decisions. It has some parallels to C groups because it is directed toward promoting self-help and providing information in a group setting. The program makes use of women's existing social networks to help them become psychologically stronger and more informed about community resources and opportunities. A lasting advantage is that participants not only become better educated and self-directed, but continue to live in an environment where they can receive support and input from others who have gone through the same experience. Similarly, a self-help center for adolescents has been designed to function as a form of group consultation (O'Brien & Lewis, 1975). At the center, which was originally set up for substance abusers, clients are empowered with information and methods of helping themselves and each other.

Organization/Community Consultation

Because organization and community consultations are much larger in scope than individual or group consultations, consultants must possess sophisticated knowledge of systems to operate effectively on this level. Unlike individual or group consultants, organization or community consultants are external to the project, although most of their activities involve individuals or groups (Sears et al., 2006). For example, counselors may function as political consultants because they are "in a pivotal position to effectively communicate the concerns of people they serve to policy makers at local, state, and national levels of government" (Solomon, 1982, p. 580). Such activities involve lobbying with individual representatives as well as testifying before and making recommendations to special committees.

Conyne (1975) mentions other ways of consulting on a community or on an organizational level. He emphasizes the individual within the environment, stressing *environmental mapping*. In other words, he believes that when counselors find individuals who exist in less-than-optimal mental health settings, they can work as change agents to improve the situation of the target population. Focusing on social action and social justice improves clients' conditions and their mental health while lessening their need sometimes for counseling (Lee, 2006a; Lee & Walz, 1998).

Barrow and Prosen (1981) also address the importance of working as consultants on environmental factors, but they advocate a global-change process. In addition to helping clients find coping techniques to deal with stress, counselors must help clients change stress-producing environments. This process is best achieved by working to change the structure of the system rather than the person within it.

CASE STUDY

Rebecca's Recommendation

Rebecca was called in as a consultant to help the executive director of a mental health center, Ramon, become more efficient in his job. As she worked with him, she realized he did not follow through on the recommendations she made. Instead, he told her one thing and then did another. Ramon rationalized this behavior by telling himself that he knew more about the organization than Rebecca ever would.

As time went by, it became obvious that Ramon was not changing and that morale was slipping among center employees. Ramon was stuck in his ways, Rebecca was frustrated, and the efficiency of the center was deteriorating rapidly.

What do you think should be the next action taken by Rebecca? Why?

STAGES AND ATTITUDES IN CONSULTATION

Developmental stages are an important part of many consultation activities (Wallace & Hall, 1996). Two well-known theories propose distinct **consultation stages**. The first is Splete's (1982a) **nine-stage process** based on the premise that clients collaborate with consultants to work on predetermined concerns. The order of the stages in this approach is as follows:

1. *Precontract.* The consultant clarifies personal skill and areas of expertise that can be used in the consultation process.
2. *Contract and exploration of relationship.* The consultant discusses a more formal arrangement between himself or herself and the consultee. The consultee's readiness and the consultant's ability to respond must be determined.
3. *Contracting.* A mutual agreement is set up that defines what services are to be offered and how.
4. *Problem identification.* Both the consultant and consultee determine and define the precise problem to be worked on and the desired outcome.
5. *Problem analysis.* The focus is on reviewing pertinent information and generating possible solutions.
6. *Feedback and planning.* Here the alternative solutions generated in stage 5 are evaluated and the probabilities of success are determined. One or more solution plans are then systematically implemented.
7. *Implementation of the plan.* The consultee carries out the proposed plan with the consultant's support.
8. *Evaluation of the plan.* Both the consultant and consultee determine how well the plan worked in relationship to the desired outcome.
9. *Conclusion and termination of relationship.* Both parties in the process review what has happened and plan for any follow-up, either independently or with the consultant.

Although Splete's plan is detailed and useful, it does not elaborate on counselor skills contained within the process. A second model that does has been proposed by Dustin and Ehly (1984). It outlines a **five-stage process of consultation** along with counselor techniques and behaviors that accompany each stage. The model assumes that the consultant is working in a school setting with either a parent or teacher, but it has potential usefulness outside the school environment—for example, in business, government, corrections, and rehabilitation. Its stages are as follows:

1. ***Phasing in.*** The focus is on relationship building and can be compared with Splete's (1982a) precontract stage. The consultant uses skills such as active listening, self-disclosure, and empathy and promotes a sense of trust.

2. ***Problem identification.*** Comparable to stages 2 through 4 in the Splete model, this step focuses on determining whether a suspected third-party problem really exists. Consultants employ focusing skills as well as other counseling techniques, such as paraphrasing, restatement, genuineness, and goal setting.

3. ***Implementation.*** Similar to stages 5 through 7 of Splete's scheme, this stage defines strategies and sets up a time frame. Feedback is an important part of this process. Flexibility, dealing with resistance and negative feelings, and patience are other counselor skills involved.

4. ***Follow-up and evaluation.*** This stage merges with stage 3 at times, but its focus is distinct. It concentrates on the results gained from the consultation process, especially if the consultee is satisfied with the outcome of changes. Counselor skills include risk taking, openness, and persistence. These skills are especially important if the consultee is dissatisfied or frustrated.

5. ***Termination.*** The consultant helps bring closure to previous activities. Relationship skills such as empathy and genuineness are again employed. Giving and asking for feedback time are important. It is vital that the consultant and consultee evaluate what was most profitable for each and what aspects of the procedure were less effective.

Five Stage Model of Consultation

Phasing In → Problem Identification → Implementation → Follow-up and Evaluation → Termination

---

Splete (1982a) also lists **four attitude** areas that are important for consultants. First, they must display an attitude of **professionalism**. They must take responsibility for helping their clients deal with immediate and long-term problems. Second, consultants must show **maturity**. They have to be willing to stand up for their own views, take risks, and deal with hostility or rejection. Third, consultants need to demonstrate **open-mindedness** and not close off ideas and input into the problem-solving process too soon. Finally, they need to believe in the importance of individuals and **place people above technology**.

SPECIFIC AREAS OF CONSULTATION

Consultation often takes place in schools and community agencies, but the process may take place in almost any environment. In this section, some of the work conducted in schools and agencies will be examined as examples of the kinds of consultation programs that can be set up.

School Consultation

Kahnweiler (1979) has traced the concept of school counselors as consultants from its beginnings in the late 1950s. As he points out, the accompanying literature has evolved in theory and practice. The development of school consultation has been summarized by Bundy and Poppen (1986), who surveyed articles from *Elementary School Guidance and Counseling* and *The School Counselor* over 28 years, and found that consultation was effective in prevention and intervention in schools. Consultation by school counselors enhances overall school achievement, improves student self-concept, reduces stress in certain populations, leads to better classroom management skills, and facilitates the moral growth of students (Carlson & Dinkmeyer, 2006; Conoley & Conoley, 1992; Kampwirth & Powers, 2012; Van Veisor, 2009). As a process, "consultation is an efficient method of impacting the well-being and personal development of many more students than can be seen directly by a counselor" (Otwell & Mullis, 1997, p. 25).

Generally, school counselors are in the perfect position to act as consultants and change agents (Baker & Gerler, 2008; Erchul & Martens, 2010). On most school organizational charts, the counselor is positioned as a staff authority rather than a line authority. Persons in **staff authority positions** are expected to have specialized knowledge, such as familiarity with local, state, and federal laws (McCarthy & Sorenson, 1993). Therefore, they can act in an advisory and supportive way for others. By functioning in this manner, school counselors help bring about environmental and systemic changes (Schmidt, 2007; Van Veisor, 2009). They advise persons in positions of power about what conditions need modifying and then support efforts to make improvements (Dollarhide & Saginak, 2012).

Umansky and Holloway (1984) view the many aspects of consultation as a way of serving students and the larger population of the school community without increasing expenditures. They advocate **four approaches to consultation in the schools**: Adlerian, behavioral, mental health, and organizational development.

The *Adlerian-based approach* is a psychological education model that assumes individuals, groups, and communities lack information. The consultant teaches within the organizational structure of the school and emphasizes ways to promote positive behavior in children (Carlson, Watts, & Maniacci, 2006).

The *behavioral approach*, also geared to teaching, concentrates on instructing consultees how to use behavioral principles in working with students and collect empirical data to validate each intervention strategy (Kampwirth & Powers, 2012).

The *mental health approach* is based on the broader community mental health approach developed by Caplan (1970). Psychodynamic theory underlies mental health consultation. The goal of this approach is to help teachers and other powerful personnel in the school gain new insight into themselves and their students.

Finally, the *organizational development approach* emphasizes the context in which problems arise. Thus, if students and teachers have problems, the climate of the school becomes the focus of concern. To be most helpful, the consultant has to work on changing the school's atmosphere and structure (Baker & Gerler, 2008). Sometimes the task requires the support of administrators who may not favor such an objective. In other cases, it involves asking school counselors to set up an environment in which other school personnel, mainly teachers, feel "that it is natural to consult and work with counselors" (Edgemon, Remley, & Snoddy, 1985, p. 298).

Consultation with teachers is an effective way to provide services for them and the school in general. In this systemic process, school counselors can use a developmental counseling and therapy-based model to access how teachers are conceptualizing students' behaviors. Furthermore, they can respond to the stress teachers may feel in connection with certain behaviors. Just as importantly, if not more so, through their consultation efforts, they may indirectly effect change in classroom systems (Clemens, 2007; Dollarhide & Saginak, 2012; Kampwirth & Powers, 2012).

Offering consultation for curriculum developers and community organizations is yet another way school counselors can provide services. This broader type of consultation takes time and effort but is worth it. Theoretical bases for this group consultation process include those that are person-centered, Adlerian, and behavioral.

School counselors can also work from a **parent–counselor consulting model**, which aims to solve student problems (behavioral, attitudinal, or social) and educate parents on how to help their children with particular situations (Campbell, 1993a; Holcomb-McCoy & Bryan,

2010; Ritchie & Partin, 1994). In offering consultation services to parents, counselors may face **resistance**, such as

- **excuses** ("I can't come during the day"),
- **negative mindsets** ("My child is doing well; why bother me?"), and
- **denial** ("There is nothing wrong with my child's relationship to the school").

To overcome resistance, school counselors can be empathetic, arrange for parental observations of a child, help the parent refocus or reframe situations, and share parables (i.e., stories of similar situations). They may also use one of the **three main theoretical models of parent consultation** described in the literature as prevalent since 2000 (Holcomb-McCoy & Bryan, 2010). These are **conjoint behavioral consultation (CBC), Adlerian consultation**, and **values-based consultation**.

- **CBC** is an extension of behavioral consultation that combines the resources of home and school to create change in a child (i.e., the client)" (p. 259). Like other behavioral approaches it relies on empirical evidence throughout the process and has shown considerable promise as a way to make change happen.
- In **Adlerian consultation** parents are encouraged to recognize the part they play in exacerbating counterproductive behavior in children and to alter these actions. They are also taught how to encourage their children as well as formulate logical consequences when children misbehave.
- **Value-based consultation** is based on recognizing the expertise and knowledge parents have. "Often, parents possess the wisdom and experience to solve complex school-related issues, whereas school-based consultants have an understanding of the consultation process but very limited understanding of the community and community dynamics" (p. 260). Unfortunately, there is little research to support the effectiveness of this approach.

Regardless of what model is used, Holcomb-McCoy and Bryan state that it is critical for consultants to understand how the cultural background of a parent may affect the consultation process. They therefore recommend the use of empowerment and advocacy theories for consultation especially with cultural groups that have been oppressed. **Empowerment** is a process that empowers (i.e., helps people implement actions to improve their situations). "**Advocacy** consists of organized actions to highlight critical issues that have been ignored and submerged, to influence public attitudes, and to enact and implement laws and public policies so that visions of 'what should be' in a just, decent society become a reality" (p. 263). "By applying an advocacy and empowerment perspective to parent consultation, counselors may be able to develop a new theory related to parent consultation that includes "power status," environmental factors (e.g., community, racism, sexism), and the personal responsibility of parents to guide their children and to take charge of their schools and communities" (p. 265).

PERSONAL REFLECTION

The rock singer Bruce Springsteen has a lyric that says: "You can't go the distance with too much resistance." Obviously, as just mentioned, there is resistance in consultation settings. What are some things you could say to address excuses, negative mindsets, and denial?

One aspect of school consultation (which can be used in agency consultation, too) is the use of peers. A **peer consultant** group can "provide appropriate supervision and feedback for school counselors" (Logan, 1997, p. 4) while increasing self-confidence, self-direction, and independence for counselors. Peer consultation also is time efficient. It can be organized to provide "(a) case consultation; (b) solution-focused problem solving; (c) peer support; (d) constructive feedback without concern for evaluation or necessity for change unless the member chooses to do so; and (e) access to needed materials and resources" (p. 4). In the Structured Peer Consultation Model for School Counselors (SPCM-SC), a total of nine 90-minute sessions are held every other week in which counselors "use their basic helping skills" to help one another progress in their growth as professionals (Benshoff & Paisley, 1996, p. 314). Such a model makes use of talent within a group of similarly employed counselors and can be as useful and productive as more formalized supervision sessions.

A final model for school consultation is to have an outside professional, a **collaborative consultant**, work with the school community in an action research approach (Lusky & Hayes, 2001). Such an approach is global in scope and premised on the fact that many school counselors cannot for various reasons provide overall consultation services for their schools. However, they can participate with others in the school environment in such research and evaluation and help implement outcomes that are generated from the process. This type of collaborative consultation involves five major phases: planning, analyzing, designing, implementing, and evaluating. At the genesis of this process an outside consultant meets with the school program stakeholders including the superintendent and school board in order to get a buy in for the consultation intervention that reexamines current practices within a school and future goals. School personnel, parents, and students help shape and own the process by contributing ideas, giving feedback along the way, and working in teams with the consultant. Such a procedure, when successful, takes time and effort but is focused at the uniqueness of the school and results in a school climate that is ready and willing to implement needed changes on a continuous basis.

Agency Consultation

According to Werner (1978), agency consultation resulted from the passage of the **Community Mental Health Centers Act of 1963**. Implicit within the act is the philosophy that mental health should be viewed from a local community perspective with an emphasis on prevention.

Caplan (1964) sets forth a **three-level definition of prevention**. The first level consists of *primary prevention*, a reduction in the incidence of mental disorders. This goal is achieved within the general population "by actively changing environments and settings and by teaching life skills" (Goodyear, 1976, p. 513). One of the primary activities at this level of intervention is consultation. *Secondary prevention*, a reduction in the duration of mental disorders, is the

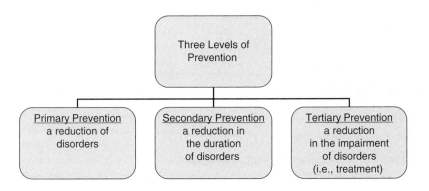

next focus. This goal is achieved by working with individuals to forestall or alleviate problem areas and attempting early detection and reversal of acute psychological crises. Finally, ***tertiary prevention*** is a reduction in the impairment that may result from psychological disorders. One way to conceptualize this level of prevention is as treatment. The more successful primary and secondary prevention are, the less need there is for tertiary prevention.

Examples abound of primary prevention in agency settings. Werner (1978) and Caplan and Caplan (1993) propose six levels of community mental health consultation:

1. ***Client-centered case consultation.***   The goal is to enable the consultee to deal more effectively with the current situation and similar situations in the future.
2. ***Consultee-centered case consultation.***   The goal is collaboratively to identify consultee difficulties in working with certain types of clients and help the consultee develop the skills to deal effectively with this and similar situations in the future.
3. ***Program-centered administrative consultation.***   The goal is to help the consultee deal more effectively with specific parts of a mental health program and improve his or her abilities to function with similar program problems in the future.
4. ***Consultee-centered administrative consultation.***   The goal is to identify consultee problems generated by implementing a mental health program and develop collaboratively the consultee's skills in dealing with similar problems.
5. ***Community-centered ad hoc consultation.***   The goal is to enable an ad hoc consultee to deal more effectively with community problems encountered while developing a temporary program of mental health services.
6. ***Consultee-centered ad hoc consultation.***   The goal is to identify collaboratively the ad hoc consultee's problems generated in providing temporary mental health services and take steps to help the consultee develop skills in dealing with these problems.

Aplin (1985) points out consultants who work with agencies such as public corporations, governments, or universities must be aware of trends that affect the process of consultation itself. He lists **five trends that have continued to influence agency consultation**:

1. **Downsizing** of organizations
2. Creation of **semiautonomous work units** brought about by mergers
3. Rebirth of **commitment leadership** by managers
4. **Process-based technologies** (such as robotics and computers) in manufacturing
5. **Egalitarian social and organizational values**

Because of the rapid changes in agencies, consultation skills are in great demand, but "the key to successfully implementing systems change programs is to increase the basic skills the consultant brings to the change process." Aplin (1985) stresses that the demands on consultants "will grow in direct proportion to growth in organizational complexity and turbulence associated with underlying social and economic change" (p. 401).

CASE EXAMPLE

Preston's Prevention

Preston had worked for a counseling agency for several years when one day he had an epiphany. He realized that he was continually seeing clients with the same kind of problems. He recognized that he was stuck on treatment—tertiary prevention. Therefore, he went to his supervisor, Fredrica, to ask how the agency might move to a secondary and primary, as well as tertiary prevention, model. Fredrica was sympathetic and open to the idea, but extremely busy. She told him that if he could come up with a plan, she would consider it.

What are some global strategies you think Preston might use to bring his agency more into secondary and primary prevention? How would such a change impact the center's staff? Could people be terminated if the center became too effective in its consultant activities? Should that consequence be considered when making up a plan?

TRAINING IN CONSULTATION

Since the late 1970s, a number of models for training individuals in consultation skills have been proposed and developed (Brown, 1993; Brown, Pryzwansky, & Schulte, 2011; Conoley, 1981; Kampwirth & Powers, 2012; Sears et al., 2006). Most models are competency based and emphasize various modes of training consultants, such as didactic, laboratory, field placement, and supervision (Gallessich, 1974).

Stum's (1982) **Directed Individual Response Educational Consulting Technique (DIRECT)** is an excellent example of a model that has attempted to synthesize previous knowledge and help students learn what they are supposed to do in a consulting interview and how they are supposed to do it. Stum views consulting as a systematic process with sequential steps. The model is structured so that beginning students can conceptualize the consultation process developmentally. It includes the following steps: (a) establish the consulting relationship, (b) identify and clarify the problem situation, (c) determine the desired outcome, (d) develop ideas and strategies, (e) develop a plan, (f) specify the plan, and (g) confirm the consulting relationship. The DIRECT model also specifies four sequential leads for each of the seven developmental steps. Based on systematic human relations training, these leads provide guidelines for the consultant and consultee to enter, initiate, educate, and evaluate each step in the consulting process. Cue words are provided for the consultant trainee at each step and level of the process. An evaluation chart, the Technique and Relationship Evaluation Chart (TREC), is available to assess the degree of competency that the consultant trainee achieves.

Brown (1985, 1993) also proposes developmental stages for training human services consultants. He stresses didactic, laboratory, and field placement competencies that must be mastered. In addition, he elaborates on problems (e.g., resistance) and strategies to overcome these problems (e.g., ways to select proper interventions). His model requires instructors to help trainees master consultation skills by analyzing case histories, modeling cognitive strategies by talking through cases, and employing a Socratic method of inquiry. Brown emphasizes that the well-trained consultant should master conceptual and relationship skills at **five discernable stages of consultation**: (a) **relationship or entry**, (b) **assessment or problem identification**, (c) **goal setting**, (d) **choosing and implementing change strategies**, and (e) **evaluation and termination**.

Gallessich (1985) advocates that future consultation models and training be based on one of three models, which are not mutually exclusive. They are as follows:

1. *Scientific/technological consultation.* In this model, which focuses on knowledge deficits, the consultant's primary role is that of an expert on information and technique.
2. *Human-development consultation.* The consultant's primary role, according to this model, is to be an educator and facilitator in affective and cognitive processes that influence professional and personal relationships in an organization.
3. *Social/political consultation.* In this model, the consultant takes a partisan role to help change organizations so that they conform with particular values, such as democracy. Methods of training consultants in this model are still being developed.

In addition to training consultants, Zins (1993) emphasizes the need to educate consultees in skills such as problem solving, communication, and intervention techniques before the actual consultation process. If consultees have these skills, they can make better use of consultation services within specific environments.

MyCounselingLab™

Go to Topic 2: *Career/Individual/Development Counseling* in the MyCounselingLab™ site (www.MyCounselingLab.com) for *Counseling: A Comprehensive Profession,* Seventh Edition, where you can:

- Find learning outcomes for *Career/Individual/Development Counseling* along with the national standards that connect to these outcomes.
- Complete Assignments and Activities that can help you more deeply understand the chapter content.
- Apply and practice your understanding of the core skills identified in the chapter with the Building Counseling Skills unit.
- Prepare yourself for professional certification with a Practice for Certification quiz.
- Connect to videos through the Video and Resource Library.

Summary and Conclusion

Consultation is a systematic concept with a set of skills (Parsons, 1996). Although it is growing in importance, it is still in the process of being defined. Several definitions of **consultation** emphasize that it is primarily an indirect service; usually triadic; voluntary; and based on roles, rules, values, and goals. Consultation and counseling have distinct differences, such as the directness of the activity, the setting in which it is conducted, and the way communications are focused. Counselors are in an ideal position to function as human service consultants, but they must receive specialized training to do so.

The four models of comprehensive consultation found in the literature (i.e., expert [provision], doctor–patient [prescription], mediation, and process/collaboration) emphasize the multidimensional aspects of consultation. There are distinct consultation levels (individual, group, and organizational) and definite stages that the process goes through (e.g., phasing in, identifying problems, implementing, following up, terminating). Important skills and attitudes make up the complete process. Consultation is implemented in schools and agencies, and training models are being used to teach consultation skills. The concept and implementation of counselor as consultant are ideas that are still developing.

Evaluation and Research

Chapter Overview

From this chapter you will learn about

- The difference between evaluation and research
- Proper steps in evaluation
- Crucial steps in the research process
- Major research methods
- Statistics and statistical methods

As you read consider

- Whether you find evaluation or research more attractive and why
- The importance of evaluation
- The similarities between counseling and outcome research
- Which major research method you like most
- Your reaction to the word "statistics" before and after you read the section in this chapter on statistics

There you sit Alice Average
  midway back in the long-windowed classroom
    in the middle of Wednesday's noontime blahs,
Adjusting yourself to the sound of a lecture
  and the cold of the blue plastic desk that supports you.
In a world full of light words, hard rock,
  Madonnas, long hair, short memories, and change
Dreams fade like blue jeans
  and "knowing" goes beyond the books
    that are bound in semester days
      and studied until the start of summer. . . .

"Thoughts on Alice Average Midway through the Mid-day Class on Wednesday," by S. T. Gladding, 1980/1986, *Humanist Educator, 18*, p. 203. © Samuel T. Gladding.

MyCounselingLab™

Visit the MyCounselingLab™ site (www.MyCounselingLab.com) for *Counseling: A Comprehensive Profession,* Seventh Edition to enhance your understanding of chapter concepts. You'll have the opportunity to practice your skills through video- and case-based Assignments and Activities as well as Building Counseling Skills units and to prepare for your certification exam with Practice for Certification quizzes.

Evaluation and research are essential parts of counseling and counseling-related activities (LaFountain & Bartos, 2002). It is not enough for counselors to be warm, caring, and empathetic persons trained in the theories, methods, and techniques of counseling. In addition, counselors must be evaluators and researchers, for it is through evaluation and research that they come to understand and improve their practices (Hadley & Mitchell, 1995; May, 1996). Counselors who lack research and evaluation abilities place themselves and the counseling profession in jeopardy with the general public, third-party payers, and specific clients who rightfully demand accountability. A failure to evaluate and research counseling methods also puts counselors in danger of being unethical because they cannot prove that the counseling services they offer have reasonable promise of success required by the ethical codes of the professional counseling associations (Heppner, Wampold, & Kivlighan, 2008; Sexton & Whiston, 1996).

Thus, evaluation and research are ways counselors can ensure quality client care and positive outcomes (Herman, 1993). These counseling procedures also help counselors pause and examine their practices. At such times, counselors may "think differently about, and even behave differently in counseling," thereby improving themselves and the profession (Watkins & Schneider, 1991, p. 288).

Being an evaluator, a researcher, and a consumer of evaluations and research demands time and a thorough understanding of the commonly used methods in these domains (Sexton, 1996). This chapter explores the processes of evaluation and research in counseling, with the assumption that counselors can cultivate skills in these areas.

THE NATURE OF EVALUATION AND RESEARCH

Evaluation and research are different, yet they have much in common. Wheeler and Loesch (1981) note that the two terms have often been paired conceptually and are frequently used interchangeably. Krauskopf (1982) asserts that there is "essentially no difference between the two. The same empirical attitude is there, and the same tools are needed" (p. 71). However, Van Brunt and Manley (2009) distinguish between the two stating "evaluation differs from research in that it assesses the quality, worth, or merit of the object or program being considered" (p. 455). Gold (2009) agrees stating "**evaluation** involves the process of applying judgments to or making decisions based on the results of measurement" (p. 39). Thus evaluation "is more mission-oriented, may be less subject to control, is more concerned with providing information for decision makers, tends to be less rigorous or sophisticated, and is concerned primarily with explaining events and their relationship to established goals and objectives" (Burck & Peterson, 1975, p. 564). For example, in counselor preparation programs, students may prepare a ***counseling portfolio*** (a collection of papers and projects they have completed during their graduate studies) as a capstone project. Based on an evaluation of the portfolio, faculty and students decide how much progress has been made and whether there is a need for additional work or training.

Thus, *research* is "more theory-oriented and discipline-bound, exerts greater control over the activity, produces more results that may not be immediately applicable, is more sophisticated in terms of complexity and exactness of design, involves the use of judgment on the part of the researcher, and is more concerned with explaining and predicting phenomena" (Burck & Peterson, 1975, p. 564). For example, counselors may conduct research to assess which of several theoretical techniques has the most positive results when applied to a client population all suffering from the same disorder. In such a setting, variables, such as age, gender, and cultural background, are controlled as tightly as possible so that the researcher can be accurate in gaining a clear picture of what works and on whom so that the results can be reported and the findings translated appropriately.

Cross-cultural research is especially important because it "increases contextual understanding, shows sensitivity to language and culture, and takes a collaborative and flexible stance" in regard to findings (Sullivan & Cottone, 2010, p. 357). In counseling research, most counselors are *applied researchers*: They use knowledge from research studies in their own work settings.

In the following sections, we will explore how evaluation and research are commonly employed in the practical world of professional counseling.

PERSONAL REFLECTION

What do you think about the differences between evaluation and research? How are they complementary? How are they distinct?

EVALUATION

Evaluation usually involves gathering meaningful information on various aspects of a counseling program to guide decisions about the allocation of resources and ensure maximum program effectiveness (Gay, Mills, & Airasian, 2009; Wheeler & Loesch, 1981). Evaluation has a quality of immediate utility. In clinical settings, it gives counselors direct feedback on the services they provide and insight into what new services they need to offer. It also enables clients to have systematic, positive input into a counseling program.

Incorrect Evaluation Methods

Although many solid models of evaluation are available, there are a number of incorrect evaluation procedures used by the uninformed (Daniels, Mines, & Gressard, 1981). These ill-conceived methods, which produce invalid and unreliable results, have some or all of the following defects:

- They **restrict opinion sampling**.
- They make **comparisons between nonequivalent groups**.
- They **promote services rather than evaluate**.
- They try to **assess a program without any clear goals**.

Steps in Evaluation

Program evaluation should be systematic and follow a sequential step-by-step process. The steps may vary in different evaluations, but a procedure that Burck and Peterson (1975) have laid out for implementing an evaluation program is an excellent one to follow.

According to these authors, the first step in formulating an evaluation program involves a *needs assessment*. If counselors are to be accountable, they must first identify problems or concerns within their programs. A *need* is "a condition among members of a specific group . . . that reflects an actual lack of something or an awareness (perception) that something is lacking" (Collison, 1982, p. 115). Needs are assumed to exist based on a number of factors, such as institutional or personal philosophy, government mandate, available resources, history or tradition, and expert opinion. "Need assessment techniques include clearly identifying the target of the survey, specifying a method of contact, and resolving measurement-related issues" (Cook, 1989, p. 463).

The second step in evaluation is "stating goals and performance objectives." Here, both *terminal program outcomes* (those that are most immediately recognizable) and *ultimate program outcomes* (those that are most enduring) are described in terms of measurable performance objectives. There are normally several performance objectives for each goal statement.

The third step in evaluation is designing a program. When a program is developed to meet stated objectives, activities that focus on the stated goals can be precisely designed. The fourth step is revising and improving a program. Specific activities and the adequacy of communication patterns are both evaluated at this point.

The fifth and final step is "noting and reporting program outcome" (Burck & Peterson, 1975, p. 567). This task is performed primarily by disseminating the findings of the program evaluation to the general public. Such consumer information is vital for potential clients if they are to make informed decisions, and counselors within a clinical program need this kind of feedback to improve their skills and services.

Evaluators must get others involved in the evaluation process for the results of the study to have any direct impact on a program. Individuals who have an investment in conducting a needs assessment are more likely to help counselors meet identified needs and establish program goals than those people who are not involved.

Selecting an Evaluation Model

Because evaluation is a continual part of their profession, counselors must prepare accordingly. Part of this preparation includes setting aside time to conduct evaluations and raising questions about what is to be evaluated and how. Questions raised before an evaluation (i.e., *a priori questions*) are more likely to be answered satisfactorily than those brought up after an evaluation is complete (*ex post facto questions*). In some cases, such as investigations into clients' perspectives on suicide behavior, researchers have little choice but to ask survivors of suicide attempts to give them insights into their thoughts after they have displayed their behaviors (Paulson & Worth, 2002).

Regardless, evaluators must ask themselves at the outset what they wish to evaluate and how they are going to do it (Davidson, 1986). **Three models** incorporate these concerns: the program plus personnel equal results model (P + P = R) (Gysbers & Henderson, 2006b); the planning, programming, budgeting systems (PPBS); and the context-input-process-product (CIPP) model (Humes, 1972; Stufflebeam et al., 1971).

CASE EXAMPLE

Edward's Evaluation

Edward was in a new position as director of student life at his college. The former director had been terminated because he was not providing services students wanted. Edward did not want to make that mistake, and he sincerely wished to do a good job. So, he decided to do a needs evaluation. His plan was to have students vote on a list of activities a nearby large state university offered to its students. Even though he was working at a small, liberal arts college, he thought programs that were popular could be added to the student life curriculum if there was a demand for them. He also imagined he might eliminate some less popular programs at his college in the process and use that money for implementing other activities.

What is solid about Edward's plan? What are its flaws?

The *P + P = R evaluation* is one that Gysbers and Henderson (2006b) devised for school counselors and a school example will be given here. However, this evaluation model can be modified to work in a number of institutional environments. According to Gysbers and Henderson, counselors in schools are increasingly being asked to demonstrate that their work contributes to student success, particularly student academic achievement, as a result of the passage of the No Child Left Behind Act (PL 107–110) in 2001 (McGannon, Carey, & Dimmitt, 2005). School counselors can do this through using three kinds of evaluation to demonstrate how the counseling program they administer contributes to overall student success. *Personnel evaluation* is the first kind of measure and describes the way counselors in a school are supervised and evaluated. *Program evaluation* is the second kind of assessment. It benchmarks the status of a particular program against established program standards to ascertain the degree to which the program is being implemented. Finally, *results evaluation* focuses on the impact that the activities and services of a program are having on students, the school, and the community. Although each type of evaluation is important, it is crucial that all the evaluations relate to and interact with each other. Personnel evaluation plus program evaluation equals results evaluation.

The *PPBS model* emphasizes planning programs with specifically stated goals, objectives, and evaluation criteria. The situation, population, and treatment involved are all major concerns of this model. Humes (1972) points out that information derived from a PPBS model is *criterion referenced* (related directly to the dimension being measured) rather than *normative referenced* (related to other members of a group, as is the case when standardized tests are used). Therefore, if proper planning and programming are carried out, the evaluator is able to demonstrate that effective counseling is an important variable in a client's progress. Moreover, when budgeting decisions are being made, the impact of counseling and its cost-effectiveness can be clearly shown, and program strengths and weaknesses can be documented. Counseling services administrators are in a better position at such times to justify requests for funds for developing and delivering services not currently being provided. This aspect of program analysis is vital.

The *CIPP model* presents four types of evaluation. In the first, *context evaluation*, a comparison is made between what the program set out to do and what it actually accomplished. In the second, *input evaluation*, information is gathered about what resources are needed and which are available to meet program objectives. This part of the evaluation demonstrates cost-effectiveness and points out the need for additional resources as well. The third type of evaluation, *process evaluation*, focuses on the strengths and weaknesses of the program's design. If there are weaknesses, such as the design of communication flow, corrective measures may be taken. The fourth type of evaluation, ***product evaluation***, focuses on the final results of the entire program. At this stage evaluators ask how effective the program really was. Plans can be made to continue, reuse, expand, or eliminate the program. Regardless of the type of evaluation used, most evaluation processes employ research in reaching their conclusions.

COUNSELORS AND RESEARCH

The profession of counseling has had "a long and ambivalent relationship" with research (Sprinthall, 1981, p. 465). The word "research" has a certain mystique about it (Leedy & Ormrod 2010). It suggests an activity that is exclusive, elusive, and removed from everyday life. Some counselors are drawn to research because of its mystique and their own general interests in investigation. However, "research typically evokes emotional reactions of fear, anxiety, and even disdain" among other counselors (Fall & VanZandt, 1997, p. 2). These counselors feel that the majority of research studies are poorly related to their practical needs (Murray, 2009). Furthermore, they perceive research as cold and impersonal (Krauskopf, 1982).

Some practitioners find that the demands of daily work with clients leaves them little time to be investigative, let alone keep up with the latest findings and outcome studies (Sexton, 1993). Therefore, most counselors do not engage in research activities, and there appears to be a serious gap in the integration of research into the practice of counseling (Murray, 2009; Sexton & Whiston, 1996). Indeed, a number of counselor practitioners have even "shown evidence of hostility and resentment toward researchers" and research (Robinson, 1994, p. 339).

Counselors' negative feelings about research and their reluctance to spend time and energy on it are related to a number of factors. Chief among them are:

- a **lack of knowledge** about research methods,
- an **absence of clear goals** and objectives for the programs in which they work,
- a **lack of awareness** of the importance of research in planning effective treatment procedures,
- a **fear of finding negative results**,
- a **discouragement** from peers or supervisors,
- a **lack of financial support**, and
- **low aptitudes and limited abilities** for conducting investigative studies (Heppner & Anderson, 1985; Sexton, 1993).

In addition, some counseling theories deemphasize the importance of empirical investigations.

Yet, despite the strain between some counselors and research, there are similarities between the activities of counseling practice and outcome research. Both involve a six-stage process (Whiston, 1996).

For instance, the first stage in both processes involves identification. In counseling, the identification is of a client's problem or difficulty, whereas in research the focus is on **identifying a question or questions to investigate**. Similarly, in the second stage, there is an analogy in formulating treatment goals and **formulating a research design**. Then a **determining stage** follows in which counseling interventions are selected; in research, methods **for ensuring treatment integrity** are chosen. In the fourth stage, action occurs in the form of either implementing counseling or **collecting data**, followed by an appraisal and evaluation of progress in counseling or **data analysis** in research. Finally, both processes end with either the completion of counseling or the **interpretation and conclusions** from research.

RESEARCH

There are many definitions of research, but Barkley (1982) gives one of the best: "***Research*** is the systematic collection, organization, and interpretation of observations in order to answer questions as unambiguously as possible" (p. 329). The challenge of research is to answer questions that do not yield truths easily. The quality of research depends on the degree to which resistance can be overcome, and ways can be devised to answer questions with maximum confidence by minimizing contaminating influences.

Steps in the Research Process

Good research is scientific in the broadest definition of the word. As alluded to before, it begins with systematic observations that concentrate on a particular population, variable, or question (Gay et al., 2009; Heppner et al., 2008). Such complete and systematic observation attempts to explain relations among variables and why certain events happen. Explanation leads to understanding and eventually to some degree of prediction and control.

Some guidelines for conducting research investigations are available. Campbell and Katona (1953), for instance, developed a flowchart to indicate the sequence of steps involved in carrying out surveys. More recently, Ary, Jacobs, Sorensen, & Razavieh (2010) devised an **eight-step process for conducting research**. It is ideally suited for clinical work but is also applicable to other areas of counseling research.

1. *Statement of the problem.*   This statement must be clear and concise. If there is confusion at this step, the investigative endeavor will probably produce little of value. An example of a clear problem statement is, "The purpose of this research is to test the hypothesis that eye contact between counselor and client is related to the effectiveness of the counseling process."
2. *Identification of information needed to solve the problem.*   This step may include a variety of information derived from sources such as psychological or educational tests or systematic observations, including experiments. Some data that investigators need may be impossible to collect. They must then decide whether to modify the problem statement or end the research.
3. *Selection or development of measures for gathering data.*   Common measures for gathering data are surveys, tests, and observational report sheets. If researchers cannot find an existing appropriate measure, they must develop one and test its reliability and validity.
4. *Identification of the target population and sampling procedures.*   If a group is small enough, an entire population may be studied. Otherwise, a sample is selected by careful standard sampling procedures.
5. *Design of the procedure for data collection.*   This step involves determining how, when, where, and by whom information will be collected.
6. *Collection of data.*   A systematic procedure is implemented to obtain the desired information. Usually this process involves careful monitoring and a substantial investment of time.

7. *Analysis of data.* Select procedures are employed at this step to organize the data in a meaningful fashion and determine whether they provide an answer to the problem being investigated.

8. *Preparation of a report.* Research results should be made available to others in some meaningful form, such as a journal article or a professional presentation.

The Relevance of Research

One primary question raised by readers of counseling research focuses on the relevance of a study's results for practitioners. Much research does not produce results relevant to practical issues and is not useful (Goldman, 1976, 1977, 1978, 1979, 1986, 1992). Many research efforts lack vision, concentrating instead on small details. Researchers who conduct their work in such a way have too readily accepted the experimental research designs of the physical and biological sciences and, in the process, have failed to develop research methods appropriate for counseling. What they pass on as research is often sterile and trivial.

The argument for **research relevancy** centers on the fact that not all knowledge is equally useful for counselors (Krumboltz & Mitchell, 1979). Therefore, limited funds and energy should be directed toward studies that are likely to make a difference in the way in which counselors function. One way to define relevance in research is to emphasize studies that focus on the reasons individuals seek counseling, such as their goals, intentions, and purposes (Howard, 1985). Another important way to assess relevance is to determine "how closely the research approximates what is done in the counseling office" (Gelso, 1985, p. 552). Such research is called *experience-near research*. Because it is applicable to counselors, it is likely to be read and used.

Action research is a form of experience-near research. It focuses on resolving practical problems that counselors routinely encounter, such as how to help manage a child with learning disabilities, evaluate the effects of a self-esteem program on a group of children, or provide evidence that school counselors can initiate, develop, lead, and coordinate programs that can contribute to systemic change and improved learning success for every student. (Dahir & Stone, 2009; Gillies, 1993). Action research includes studies aimed at diagnostic action, participant action, empirical action, and experimental action. Some of this research is likely to be less controlled and not as easily generalized as more rigorous research. To help solve the problem of relevancy in research, Gelso (1985) suggests reading all research studies with certain questions in mind—for example, "How was this research conducted?" and "How will it influence the way I practice counseling?"

Choosing a Research Method

Despite problems inherent in counseling research, counselors regularly employ a number of investigative methodologies. Kaplan (1964) defines a *method* as a procedure that is applicable to many disciplines. In contrast, a *technique* is a discipline-specific procedure. Most counseling research uses procedures, such as controlled observations, that are common to other disciplines. Therefore, the term "method" rather than "technique" is appropriate when referring to ways of doing counseling research. None of these methods is considered "best to test the counseling process" (Hill, 1982, p. 16). Rather, different research methods address different research questions (Watkins & Schneider, 1991). Ultimately, research methods provide answers to research questions by controlling select variables that have an impact on the counseling process (Kerlinger & Lee, 2000).

All research methods have what Gelso (1979) describes as ***bubbles***, or flaws. Gelso says that selecting research methods is like putting a sticker on a car windshield. Bubbles always appear; even though one may try to eliminate as many bubbles as possible, some remain. The only way to eliminate the bubbles totally is to remove the sticker. In research, the only way to avoid all flaws is not to do research. Yet as imperfect as research methods are, they are necessary for professional edification and development. The alternative is to remain uninformed about the effects of counseling and forego the development of newer methods and techniques.

CASE EXAMPLE

Oscar's Observation

Oscar noticed that in his agency many clients were tearful when they set up a return appointment before leaving the premises. His observation made him wonder if there was a better way for such appointments to be made. One way might be to have clients schedule return visits before they went into counseling. That way they could exit the building with seemingly less embarrassment or stress.

He proposed his idea to other clinicians and to the agency staff. They were skeptical, but agreed to give his idea a trial run.

What do you think Oscar might have to do to make sure his research yielded valuable and useful results?

Emphases of Research

Counseling research has several different emphases. Four of the most prominent can be represented as contrasts:

1. **Laboratory versus field research**
2. **Basic versus applied research**
3. **Process versus outcome research**
4. **Quantitative (group) versus qualitative (individual) research**

Each of these emphases is concerned with the contrast between two investigative dimensions. The various dimensions are not mutually exclusive (Leech & Onwuegbuzie, 2010); many research studies, such as those that quantitatively report the outcome of counseling techniques in a laboratory setting, include more than one of them (Creswell, 2012).

The first emphasis is on laboratory research versus field research. ***Laboratory research*** concentrates on conducting the investigation within a confined environment, such as a counseling lab, where as many extraneous variables as possible may be controlled (Dobson & Campbell, 1986). Under such conditions, some researchers think they can obtain the most reliable information. Indeed, researcher John Gottman found his "love lab" yielding extremely pertinent information about the quality of couple relationships. Practitioners of ***field research***, however, see most laboratory investigations as artificial and believe that counseling theories and techniques are best observed and recorded in actual counseling situations, such as counseling centers and clinics. They argue that these settings are realistic and that the results are likely to be applicable to other practitioners.

FIGURE 13.1 Relation of basic research, applied research, and practice *Source:* From "Counseling Research as an Applied Science," by T. J. Tracey, 1991, in C. E. Watkins, Jr., and L. J. Schneider (Eds.), *Research in Counseling* (p. 27), Hillsdale, NJ: Erlbaum. © 1991 by Lawrence Erlbaum Associates, Inc. Used with permission.

The second emphasis is basic research versus applied research. ***Basic research*** is oriented to theory, and those who practice it are "interested in investigating some puzzle or problem that is suggested by theory" (Forsyth & Strong, 1986, p. 113). An example is research that focuses on the number of times Rogerian-based counselors use reflective versus confrontive clinical methods. In contrast, ***applied research*** focuses on examining practical problems and applying their findings to existing problems. An example of applied research is a program evaluation where information about services at a counseling center is collected from recipients and analyzed as to the efficiency, effectiveness, and impact on the community served (Astramovich & Coker, 2007). Tracey (1991) offers one way of distinguishing basic and applied research (Figure 13.1).

The third emphasis is process research versus outcome research. According to Hill (1991), ***process research*** focuses on what "happens in counseling and therapy sessions" (p. 85). She states that identifying the changes in counseling "can be quite overwhelming and frustrating" (Hill, 1982, p. 7). It demands a concentrated amount of time and energy focused on a few variables, such as the reactions of the counselor to the client. The burnout rate among process-oriented researchers is high. Yet such research is indispensable in enlightening counselors about the dynamics of the counseling relationship itself. An example of process research is the work of Allen Ivey (1980) in assessing the importance of counselor skills in select stages of counseling. ***Outcome research***, however, is "the experimental investigation of the impact of counseling on clients" (Lambert, Masters, & Ogles, 1991, p. 51). It is "typified by measurement before and after treatment on specified dependent variables" (Hill, 1982, p. 7). An example of outcome research would be the effect of person-centered counseling with depressed persons. Outcome research emphasizes results rather than the factors producing them.

The fourth emphasis is quantitative research versus qualitative research (i.e., naturalistic inquiry). ***Quantitative research*** is deductive and objective, usually involving numbers and subordinating subjective understanding to clarity, precision, and reproducibility of objective phenomena. A quantitative approach is based on a positive-reductive conceptual system that "values objectivity, linearity, cause and effect, repeatability, and reproductivity, predictability, and the quantification of data" (Merchant & Dupuy, 1996, p. 538). Two basic quantitative research designs are the experimental and the survey (Rosenthal, 2001). An example of quantitative research that also yielded practical outcomes in regard to what counselors actually do is the nationwide Practice Research Network (PRN) that, through a survey, investigated the daily practice of mental health workers (Smith, Sexton, & Bradley, 2005).

In contrast, ***qualitative research*** is inductive, naturalistic, cybernetic, and phenomenological. It places primary emphasis on understanding the unique frameworks within which persons make sense of themselves and their environments. It is useful in situations where theory and research are lacking (Merriam, 2002). It focuses on understanding a complex social situation without previously defined parameters (Creswell, 2012; Jencius & Rotter, 1998). Furthermore, "qualitative research examines what people are doing and how they interpret what is occurring rather than pursuing patterns of cause and effect in a controlled setting" (Merchant & Dupuy, 1996, p. 537).

In many ways qualitative research is especially appropriate for counseling "because the centrality of interpersonal relations defines its [counseling's] domain" (Berrios & Lucca, 2006, p. 175). Overall, "qualitative research in counseling requires a dual commitment both to service delivery and to a scientific investigation of that delivery" (p. 181). It has grown in recent years as a proportion of research studies being published in the flagship journal of the ACA, *Journal of Counseling and Development* (Erford et al., 2011).

Frequently used qualitative methods are field research, case studies, narratives, in-depth interviews, and life histories. Mark Savickas (2005) has proven to be a master of qualitative research in using narrative counseling method for helping clients to fit work into their lives, rather than fit themselves to jobs. His approach looks at a client's life as a novel being written. It emphasizes recurring themes that reveal how the client uses work to advance his or her life projects.

Thus, the emphasis of these two approaches differs because of the purposes of each and the different assumptions each makes about the goals of research (May, 1996; Merchant & Dupuy, 1996). Neither quantitative nor qualitative research is superior to the other per se. Rather, the use of each depends on what question is being asked and for what reason. The major strength of quantitative research is its emphasis on analyzing large amounts of data in a clear, mathematical fashion. The major strength of qualitative research is the way it picks up subtle, individually focused, developmental, and experientially reported aspects of counseling (Creswell, 2012; Denzin & Lincoln, 2011; Mertens, 2005).

Counseling is slowly moving toward espousing research that is both qualitative (versus quantitative) and more field oriented (versus laboratory) (Goldman, 1992; Watkins & Schneider, 1991). Clients are seen as active rather than passive in the counseling process (Gelso, 1985; Howard, 1985). Overall, a more holistic emphasis within counseling research is being proposed with *mixed research* (combining qualitative and quantitative research) as a growing phenomenon (Leech & Onwuegbuzie, 2010). "Combining or mixing quantitative and qualitative research approaches enables researchers, including researchers from the field of counseling, to be more flexible, integrative, holistic, and rigorous in their investigative techniques as they attempt to address a range of complex research questions that come to the fore. More specifically, mixed research helps counseling researchers to attain participant enrichment, instrument fidelity, treatment integrity, and significance enhancement" (p. 66).

Major Research Methods

The research methods that counselors choose are determined by the questions they are trying to answer, their special interests, and the amount of time and resources they have available for the study (Heppner et al., 2008). Methods should be the slaves of research, not the masters (Smith, 1981). No method is suitable for all research attempts. Indeed, as Ohlsen (1983) states, "developing and clarifying a research question is a slow, painstaking process" (p. 361). A *research question* provides the context in which one begins to consider a method. In most cases, a research question is about the state of affairs in the field of counseling (LaFountain & Bartos, 2002). Once a question has been decided on, a quantitative or qualitative method may be chosen.

Methods and ways of obtaining data may differ for research conducted in personal, group, or couple/family counseling. A research strategy, which is "the guiding or underlying force that directs" a research project, is intended to place the investigator "in the most advantageous position" possible (Husband & Foster, 1987, p. 53). The primary research method can be chosen from among those that present data from historical, descriptive, or experimental points of view

(Galfo & Miller, 1976; Vacc & Loesch, 2001). The procedures used in these methods are not mutually exclusive. For example, Tracey (1983) reports that *N of 1 research*, which focuses on the study of a single qualitative entity (such as a person), may be employed in historical studies, case studies, and intensive design studies. Such research may be either associational or experimental. The fact that this and other research methods are so flexible gives investigators more latitude in planning their strategies and carrying out their studies.

PERSONAL REFLECTION

From what you know about counseling now, what questions are you most interested in finding out answers to? Do you think your questions might best be answered through qualitative or quantitative research methods?

HISTORICAL METHODS. Historical research has been largely neglected in counseling (Goldman, 1977). The reasons are numerous, but among the most salient is the association of historical research with psychohistory (Frey, 1978). **Psychohistory** has been closely linked to the theory of psychoanalysis, and its usefulness as a way of understanding persons and events has been questioned (Thoresen, 1978). Yet as Frey (1978) reports, psychohistory as practiced by Erik Erikson (1958) and the Wellfleet group (whose members included Kenneth Keniston and Robert Coles) involves two aspects:

1. experiencing and reporting events and procedures from earlier times that have influenced the development of the profession, and
2. embellishing current theories and generating new research hypotheses.

For the most part, counseling journals limit their dealings with historical research to printing obituaries of prominent counselors and featuring interviews with pioneers in the profession (Heppner, 1990a, 1990b). Although the methods used in historical research are usually less rigorous and more qualitative than those employed in other research, they produce both interesting and enlightening results. They have an important place in the understanding of persons, as exemplified in Gordon Allport's idiographic studies of traits and personality. This approach to research is clearly open to further development.

DESCRIPTIVE METHODS.   Descriptive research concentrates on depicting present factors in a profession. It has three subcategories: surveys, case studies, and comparative studies.

Surveys.   Surveys are one of the most popular and widely used methods for gathering information about the occurrence of behaviors and describing the characteristics of those that are not well understood (Fong, 1992; Heppner et al., 2008). Surveys are similar to other methods of research: They begin with the formation of a research question, then generate hypotheses, select a research design, and collect and analyze data (Kerlinger & Lee, 2000). **Survey data can be collected in five ways: personal interviews, mailed questionnaires, online questionnaires, telephone interviews, and nonreactive measures such as existing records or archives** (Fowler, 2009). Data are gathered in either a structured or nonstructured way with either a *cross section* of people (many people at one point in time) or *longitudinally* (the same people at two or more points in time).

If conducted properly, survey research can provide counselors with a great deal of information about how clients perceive them and their programs. Surveys can also offer information about clients' needs or trends in the field of counseling (Heppner et al., 2008; Hosie, 1994).

Online questionnaires, especially the use of **SurveyMonkey** (http://www.surveymonkey.com) and **Zoomerang** (http://www.zoomerang.com), have become increasing popular in recent years and most likely will continue. They are convenient, relatively inexpensive, and provide quick and easy-to-understand data analysis.

Nevertheless, **four major problems often plague survey research**.

- First, survey instruments may be **poorly constructed**.
- Second, they **may not generate a very high rate of return**.
- Third, the **sample surveyed is sometimes nonrandom and unrepresentative** of the population. In any of these three cases, the results are essentially useless because the design and methodology of the survey research lack rigor (Fong, 1992).
- A final problem of survey research (or almost any research, for that matter) is that it **can be expensive** (Robinson, 1994), especially if it involves a large number of people.

The social impact of well-conceived and well-conducted survey research is apparent in the work of Kinsey on the sexual practices of men and women. The NBCC survey of counselor education programs that was originally started by Joe Hollis is an example of the usefulness of this method for counseling. Every few years Hollis, and now NBCC, gathers information for a published directory of counselor education programs. This survey is quantitative in emphasis and yields relevant data about national program trends in counseling.

Case Studies.   A *case study* is an attempt to understand one unit, such as a person, group, or program, through an intense and systematic investigation of that unit longitudinally. Almost any phenomenon can be examined by means of the case study method (Leedy & Ormrod, 2010). Some case studies rely on self-report methods that are not very reliable; others involve naturalistic inquiry in which the study extends over a period of time (Smith, 1981). The difficulties involved in naturalistic research are many and include issues such as what constitutes good research, the high cost of labor, the problems of establishing causality, and restrictions on generalizing results. In addition, they often demonstrate problems of observed bias and the *halo effect* (a favorable observation generalized to a person or situation as a whole) (Goldman, 1977). To help minimize such problems, Anton (1978) and Huber (1980) describe several intensive experimental designs suitable for case studies. Counselors with limited time and resources may find them useful in tracing changes over time. These designs will be discussed in a later section on experimental methods.

Comparative Studies.   Comparative research studies (also called *correlational studies*) form a link between historical/case study methods and experimental and quasi-experimental designs. They make directional and quantitative comparisons between sets of data. Such studies are nonmanipulative (Cozby, 2009). They simply note similarities in variations among factors with no effort to discern cause-and-effect relationships. An example of such a study is the relationship of scores on a test of religiosity with scores on instruments measuring various aspects of mental health (Gladding, Lewis, & Adkins, 1981). A major finding of this study was that people who scored high on the religiosity test also scored high on the mental health instruments. The results do not suggest that religiosity causes a person to have better mental health; rather, it simply compares the direction of the scores. Any study that compares measures in this manner is an example of comparative research.

EXPERIMENTAL METHODS.   *Experimental research* methods are employed to describe, compare, and analyze data under controlled conditions (Galfo & Miller, 1976; Heppner et al., 2008; McLeod, 2003). Experimental methods used in counseling research have their origin in the natural sciences. The purpose of using these methods is to determine the effect of one variable on another by controlling for other factors that might explain the effect. In other words, researchers who use this method are seeking to determine causation. To do this, they define independent and dependent variables. The *independent variable* is the one manipulated by the researcher, such as treatment. The *dependent variable* is the one in which the potential effect is recorded, such as the client's behavior. The researcher assumes that if the effect of other factors is eliminated, then any change in the dependent variable will be a result of the independent variable. Examples of independent variables in counseling might be the age, gender, personal attractiveness, or physical appearance of the counselor. Examples of dependent variables are a client's reactions to these counselor traits, such as degree of relaxation, cooperation, and overall responsiveness in the counseling setting. The reactions could be measured by a variety of procedures, including an analysis of an audio- or videotape or a postcounseling interview or questionnaire.

Cohen (1990) recommends **two general principles** for those who are **conducting research with independent and dependent variables: Less is more, and simple is better**. The fewer variables there are to keep track of and the more clearly they can be reported (e.g., through graphs), the easier it is for researchers and consumers to understand the significance of counseling research studies.

It is imperative in conducting experimental research that the counselor be sure to control for *contaminating variables* (variables that invalidate a study, such as one group of clients that is healthier than another). One of the most common ways of controlling for potentially contaminating variables is by establishing equivalent experimental and control groups. When the independent variable is manipulated for the experimental group while being held constant for the control group, the effect of the independent variable can be determined by comparing the postexperimental data for the two groups. Campbell and Stanley (1963) describe in detail the problems involved in experimental and quasi-experimental research; their work is recommended to readers who wish to pursue the issue further.

Traditional experimental research has involved group comparison studies. Since the 1970s, *single-subject research*, commonly known as **N of 1** (i.e., $n = 1$) **research**, has become increasingly accepted in the field of counseling but underutilized by counselors (Sharpley, 2007). "Essentially, an $n = 1$ research study is one in which the data from a single participant (rather than a group) are the focus of the research design" (p. 350). There are a **number of advantages to single-case research designs**. Among these are the following:

- They are theory free, thus allowing counselors of any persuasion to use them.
- They are flexible and appropriate for use in practice settings.
- They may improve counseling effectiveness.
- They do not require the use of statistical methods.
- They produce scientifically effective evidence that leads to professional credibility.
- They are "consistent with CACREP standards that call for increased emphasis on research, accountability, and diverse research methodologies in the scientist-practitioner model of counselor preparation" (Lundervold & Belwood, 2000, p. 100).

Miller (1985, p. 491) summarizes **six major advantages that single-subject research** has over traditional group studies. (His study is derived from Hill, Carter, & O'Farrell [1983] and Sue [1978b].)

1. It allows a **more adequate description** of what happens between a counselor and client.
2. Positive and negative outcomes can be understood in terms of **process** data.
3. Outcome measures can be tailored to the client's **specific problems**.

4. It allows for the **study of a rare or unusual phenomenon**.
5. It is **flexible** enough to allow for novel procedures in diagnosis and treatment.
6. It can be used in evaluating the **effectiveness of an intervention strategy on a single client**.

A potential problem in single-subject studies is "when they are used following a period of standard treatment that has not worked." Some general improvement may occur that has nothing to do with the treatment being used but is a *regression toward the mean* (i.e., "the tendency of an extreme value when it is remeasured to be closer to the mean"; Aldridge, 1994, p. 337). To overcome this problem, especially if medication is involved, the researcher may allow for a *washout period*: a time when no treatment occurs and there is an opportunity for previous effects (such as medication) to leave the body by natural means.

Three intense experimental designs that focus on individuals are simple time series, reversal design, and multiple baseline design.

Simple Time Series.   A simple time series, the most common intense experimental design method, is referred to as an *AB design* (Sharpley, 2007). First, a baseline (A) is established by having the client observe and record the occurrence of the targeted behavior every day. Then an intervention strategy (B) is introduced. The client continues to record the targeted behavior in the same way as before. The manifestation of the targeted behavior is compared during these two periods and trends are noted. By graphing results, counselors can determine what, if any, effect the intervention strategy had.

Reversal Design.   A reversal design is more complex than a simple time series. It involves a reversal—an *ABAB design*. The first part is executed as it is in the simple time series, but the intervention strategy (B) is discontinued after a time, and a second baseline and intervention follow. "If the second intervention period produces proportionately the same results as the first intervention period, then it can be safely assumed that it is the strategy itself that is causing the changes in the level of interactions made" (Huber, 1980, p. 212).

Multiple Baseline Design.   The multiple baseline design, the most complex of these experimental designs, permits greater generalization of the results. There are **three types of multiple baseline research designs: across individuals, across situations, and across behaviors** (Schmidt, 1974). Each emphasizes a different focus. The common trait of all three is that intervention is initially employed with a select individual, situation, or behavior while the researcher continues to gather baseline data on other persons, situations, or behaviors. When intervention strategies are extended to the baseline populations, counselors are able to see more clearly the power of the intervention. As with other designs, it is important to graph the results.

Overall, there are **five steps in intensive experimental designs** on individuals:

1. **identify an observable problem** that can be monitored for change,
2. **gather baseline data**,
3. **decide on the intervention** to be studied,
4. **carry out the intervention strategy** within one of the three research designs, and
5. **evaluate the changes**, if any, in the targeted behavior.

Guidelines for Using Research

Counselors who use research as a base for their practices can follow certain guidelines. They include recognizing the flaws and strengths of research methods, taking care to define terms

CASE EXAMPLE

Shannon and Her Single-Subject Research

Shannon was fascinated by the idea of doing single-subject research. She thought it would be easier and simpler than any type of quantitative method. She was particularly interested in how clients and counselors perceive what is happening in a counseling session, especially after having read some of Irvin Yalom's novels about people in therapy.

Shannon wondered if she could be her own subject. After all, she was sensitive, perceptive, smart, and willing. She knew she could produce a good written report of the experiment as well.

Would it be unethical for Shannon to become her own subject? Would it be wise? What are the pluses and minuses?

carefully, and not overgeneralizing beyond the scope of particular findings. Such procedures help consumers evaluate studies as objectively as possible so that they can employ the results more skillfully and ethically.

Several writers have been concerned about the **fair assessment of gender differences** (McHugh, Koeske, & Frieze, 1986; Wakefield, 1992). Altmaier, Greiner, and Griffin-Pierson (1988, p. 346) offer some of the most salient advice on this issue.

- Readers should note the values on which particular research studies are based.
- Counselors should look for findings that are in accord with their experiences and findings that converge across settings and studies.
- Consumers of research should not overlook topics of importance to women, such as childbearing.
- The assumption should not be made that differences between men and women fall along one continuum in a bipolar fashion.
- The magnitude of effects should be considered in reading research about gender differences. In other words, the reader should note how much variance in the observed behavior is accounted for by the significance of gender difference.

In the final analysis, counselors who use research should do so in relation to the skills they acquired in their graduate and continuing education programs. Clinicians must study research methodology well so that their practices reflect only the best professional knowledge available. In addition, they must refrain from *questionable research practices* such as practices being sloppy or careless, making avoidable statistical errors, inappropriately allocating authorship, and being inaccurate with their references (Davis, Wester, & King, 2008).

STATISTICS

Statistics and statistical testing first became prominent in the early 1900s (Thompson, 2002). They have been the lifeblood and bane of helping professionals, such as counselors, ever since. Whether counselors are drawn to do statistically significant research or not, all counselors should be aware of several research tools, such as libraries and their resources, computers and their software, techniques of measurement, and statistics. Statistics are not a fixed part of evaluation and research, and using statistics is not what "makes" or "breaks" a good study (Leedy & Ormrod, 2010). Rather, statistics are simply a means for researchers to use in analyzing and interpreting findings and communicating those findings to others (Wilson & Yager, 1981). As Barkley (1982) emphasizes, "it is possible to be a good researcher and know nothing about sophisticated statistical techniques. It is also possible to know a great deal about statistics and be a mediocre or poor researcher" (p. 327). The distinction between research and statistics is important.

Statistical Concepts

There are some statistical concepts that every counselor must know to read and evaluate research reports intelligently. One is **measures of the central tendency**—that is, the median, the mean, and the mode. All these measures encompass different meanings of the term **average** (LaFountain & Bartos, 2002). The **median** is the midpoint of a distribution of scores ranked highest to lowest. The **mean** is the arithmetic average of scores. The **mode** is the score or measure that occurs most often in a distribution. In a true normally distributed population (which can be graphed as a **bell-shaped or normal curve**), the median, mean, and mode are the same. In actuality, however, this situation rarely occurs.

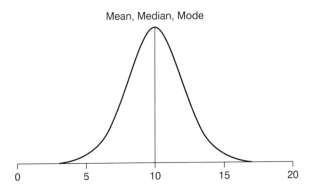

Normal curve

Mean, Median, Mode

Two other important statistical concepts are standard deviation and sampling procedure. A **standard deviation** is a measure of the dispersion of scores about their mean. It indicates how much response variability is reflected in a set of scores; that is, it is a measure of how homogeneous a group is. The larger the standard deviation, the greater the variability among the individuals (Thorndike & Thorndike-Christ, 2010). The standard deviation on a normal curve, which is rare, is as follows.

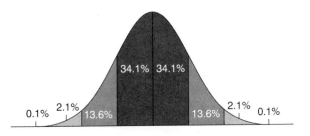

Sampling is important because it determines how applicable research findings are. If a sample does not adequately represent the population on which it is based, the results cannot be considered applicable to the population. When samples are chosen in a representative, random way, results can be generalized to the population with confidence.

Statistical Methods

Descriptive, correlational, and inferential statistics are the three most widely used statistical methods in research (Mertens, 2005).

- *Descriptive statistics* literally describe characteristics of a sample. These devices, which are used to organize and summarize data, are also used in analyzing single-subject research and simply describing populations (Miller, 1985). Mean and standard deviation are examples of descriptive statistics.
- *Correlational statistics* describe the strength and connection of relationships—for example, the strength of a relationship between one's attitude toward drugs and one actually using drugs (Creswell, 2012).
- *Inferential statistics* allow for group comparisons or make predictions about an entire population from a given sample. They determine whether research results are due to chance or the treatment of variables in a study (Cozby, 2009).

A number of statistical tests have been devised to measure the probability of change occurring by chance in an experimental research design. **Two broad categories of tests** are used for this purpose: **parametric** and **nonparametric**.

- *Parametric tests* are usually more powerful. Parametric tests are used when it is thought that the population being described has evenly distributed characteristics that could be represented by a bell-shaped curve. Examples of parametric tests are the Pearson product moment correlation and *t* tests.
- *Nonparametric tests* are used when no normal curve distribution can be assumed but sharp dichotomies can. Nonparametric tests require larger sample sizes to yield a level of significance similar to parametric tests. Examples of nonparametric tests are the Spearman rank-order correlation and chi-square (Leedy & Ormrod, 2010).

In addition, statistics can be used to compare research findings across studies. One prominent approach of doing this is through an empirically based method known as *meta-analysis* (Glass, 1976; Wilson, 1981). Before the conceptualization of meta-analysis, researchers were forced to compare studies through narrative methods that were often filled with errors. With meta-analysis, large amounts of data can be compared and contrasted across studies (Baker, Swisher, Nadenichek, & Popowicz, 1984).

Statistics are invaluable to the counselor who wants to understand, organize, communicate, and evaluate data (Remer, 1981). Consumers of research should expect that authors of research reports will provide them with indices of practical and clinical significance of their works (e.g., effect size) for "statistical significance is not sufficiently useful to be invoked as the sole criterion for evaluating the noteworthiness of counseling research" (Thompson, 2002, p. 66).

MyCounselingLab™

Go to Topic 14: *Research and Evaluation* in the MyCounselingLab™ site (www .MyCounselingLab) for *Counseling: A Comprehensive Profession,* Seventh Edition, where you can:

- Find learning outcomes for *Research and Evaluation* along with the national standards that connect to these outcomes.
- Complete Assignments and Activities that can help you more deeply understand the chapter content.
- Apply and practice your understanding of the core skills identified in the chapter with the Building Counseling Skills unit.
- Prepare yourself for professional certification with a Practice for Certification quiz.
- Connect to videos through the Video and Resource Library.

Summary and Conclusion

This chapter focused on the relationship between evaluation and research. Although the terms are sometimes defined identically, each is unique. Evaluation aims at helping counselors decide how programs are meeting the goals and objectives of staff and clients. A major first step in conducting an evaluation is to do a needs assessment. Several excellent models are available for counselors to use in completing this task.

Research scares many counselors. Yet this fear may diminish as counselors become more aware that there are many ways to conduct investigative studies. Three main research methods are historical, descriptive, and experimental. For years, experimental research has been valued most highly, but this emphasis is changing. Case studies and intensive experimental designs are gaining popularity. In addition, the difference between understanding research methods and statistical concepts is growing; that is, people are realizing that the two approaches are not the same. Both are important, but it is possible for researchers to be stronger in one area than the other.

Counselors must constantly strive to update their research and evaluation skills and stay current. The life span of knowledge is brief, and counselors who do not exercise their minds and find areas of needed change will become statistics instead of an influence.

Testing, Assessment, and Diagnosis in Counseling

Chapter Overview

From this chapter you will learn about

- How testing and tests have evolved over the years
- The problems and potential of using tests in counseling
- Qualities of good tests
- Classifications of tests
- Administration and interpretation of tests

As you read consider

- Your reaction to tests you have taken and the concept of testing
- Advantages and disadvantages in using tests
- What tests you like or dislike and why
- How you like being assessed
- The problems and benefits of diagnosis

I read the test data like a ticker tape
    from the New York Stock Exchange.
Your "neurotic" scales are slightly up
    with a large discrepancy in your Wechsler scores.
Myers-Briggs extroversion is in the moderate range
    with an artistic interest expressed in your Strong profile.
At first, like a Wall Street wizard,
    I try to assess and predict your future,
But in talking about expected yields
    I find the unexpected. . . .
Alone, you long for the warmth of relationships
    as well as for the factual information at hand.
In the process of discussion,
    a fellow human being emerges.
Behind what has been revealed on paper
    is the uniqueness of a person.

Reprinted from "Thoughts of a Wall Street Counselor," by S. T. Gladding, 1986/1995,
Journal of Humanistic Education and Development, 24, p. 176. © by Samuel T. Gladding.

MyCounselingLab™

"From the very beginning of professional counseling, counseling professionals have applied the use of testing and assessment to the assistance of individuals and society" (Ponton & Duba, 2009, p. 120). Testing, assessment, and diagnosis "are integral components of the counseling process" that are used in all stages of counseling from referral to follow-up (Hohenshil, 1996, p. 65). According to Hood and Johnson (2007), "During the early days, counseling and testing were virtually synonymous. Many of the counseling centers established during the 1930s and 1940s were called Counseling and Testing Centers" (p. 3). Today, virtually all counselors are involved in testing, assessment, and diagnosis. The amount they do of each is dependent on their theoretical backgrounds, education, values, and settings. Therefore, it is essential for counselors to understand the procedures connected with each process.

Counselors interested in activities that require the use of measurement and associated procedures usually belong to the **Association for Assessment in Counseling and Education** (AACE; www.theaaceonline.com), if they are members of the ACA. This division, originally named the Association for Measurement and Evaluation in Guidance (AMEG), was chartered as the seventh division of the ACA in 1965 (Sheeley & Eberly, 1985). It publishes a quarterly journal, *Measurement and Evaluation in Counseling and Development.* Several American Psychological Association (APA) divisions are involved with tests, assessment, and diagnosis, as well. Clinical Psychology (Division 12), School Psychology (Division 16), and Counseling Psychology (Division 17) are among the most prominent.

In addition to these associations, a multiprofessional group has drawn up *Standards for Psychological and Educational Testing* (American Educational Research Association, American Psychological Association, and National Council on Measurement in Education, 1999). "The Standards provide a strong ethical imperative as a criterion for the evaluation and development of tests, testing practices, and effects of test use as they affect professional practice. They can be viewed as addressing three audiences: **test developers** (i.e., those who create and validate tests), **test users** (i.e., those who administer tests), and **test takers** (i.e., those to whom tests are administered)" (Vacc, Juhnke, & Nilsen, 2001, p. 218). In addition, the Joint Committee on Testing Practices (www.apa.org/science/jctpweb. html#about) has developed and revised *The Code of Fair Testing Practices in Education.*

This chapter examines the nature of tests, assessment, and diagnosis and how each activity fits into the counseling profession. It covers basic concepts associated with testing, such as validity, reliability, and standardization. In addition, it reviews some of the major tests that counselors use and are expected to understand. Finally, it examines the nature of assessment and diagnosis and their usefulness.

A BRIEF HISTORY OF THE USE OF TESTS IN COUNSELING

The employment of tests by counselors has a long, paradoxical, and controversial history. The origin of present-day tests developed and "grew out of the late 19th century study of individual differences" (Bradley, 1994, p. 224). Since the early years of the 20th century, when Frank Parsons (1909) asserted that vocational guidance should be based on formal assessment, counselors have been part of the testing movement.

During World War I, the army hired a group of psychologists to construct paper-and-pencil intelligence tests to screen inductees (Cohen & Swerdik, 2009). These test pioneers, led by Arthur Otis and Robert Yerkes, built on the work of Alfred Binet (an originator of an early intelligence test), Charles Spearman (an important early contributor to test theory), Sir Francis Galton (an inventor of early techniques for measuring abilities), and James M. Cattell (an early researcher into the relationship of scores to achievement) (Anastasi & Urbina, 1997; Urbina, 2005). The testing movement, which gained impetus in the 1920s, gave counselors a new identity and respectability and gave them an expanded theoretical rationale on which to base their job descriptions, especially in schools and in career service agencies.

As a group, counselors have varied in their degree of involvement with tests. The 1930s and 1960s are two distinct periods of high counselor involvement with assessment and testing. Vocational testing was emphasized in the 1930s because of the Great Depression. The University of Minnesota's **Employment Stabilization Research Institute** led the vocational testing movement during those years. Its personnel assembled and administered batteries of tests in an effort to help the unemployed find suitable work. Paterson and Darley (1936) estimated that up to 30% of unemployed workers in the 1930s were mismatched with their stated job preferences and training. In 1957 the Soviet Union's launch of *Sputnik* raised U.S. interest in testing because many Americans believed that the United States had fallen behind in science. Congress subsequently passed the **National Defense Education Act (NDEA)**, which contained a provision, Title V, for funding testing in the secondary schools to identify students with outstanding talents and encourage them to continue their education, especially in the sciences.

In 1959, the *Journal of Counseling and Development*, then known as the *Personnel and Guidance Journal*, began to publish test reviews to supplement the *Mental Measurements Yearbook* (*MMY*; Watkins, 1990b). These reviews were discontinued in 1966, but they were revived in 1984 and continued to be published occasionally until the 1990s. *Measurement and Evaluation in Counseling and Development* is now the leading professional periodical in counseling that regularly publishes test reviews.

The 1970s and 1980s brought greater criticism of testing. Goldman (1972b) set this tone in an article that declared that the marriage between counseling and testing had failed. In the same year, the **National Education Association (NEA)** passed **Resolution 72–44**, which called for a moratorium on the use of standardized intelligence, aptitude, and achievement tests (Engen, Lamb, & Prediger, 1982). Since that time, many court suits have been filed to challenge the use of tests, and several bills have been introduced in state legislatures to prohibit the administration of certain tests. Jepsen (1982) has observed that the trends of the 1970s make it more challenging than ever to select tests and interpret scores carefully. His observations on testing can be generalized to other areas of counseling. As Tyler (1984) notes, "the antitesting movement has become a force to be reckoned with" (p. 48). Ironically, the use of tests in schools is more popular now than ever, and many school counselors on all levels consider it either important or very important to their work (Elmore, Ekstrom, Diamond, & Whittaker, 1993). Assessment devices, such as intelligence and achievement tests, substance abuse screening instruments, and career inventories, are frequently employed in working with school-age children (Giordano, Schwiebert, & Brotherton, 1997).

Most of the problems with testing in schools and other settings are being addressed through the revision of problematic instruments (Hogan, 2007). Indeed, Anastasi (1982) once made an observation that "psychological testing today does not stand still long enough to have its picture taken" (p. v). Thus careful attention is paid to the education of counseling students and the continuing education of counselors in the use and abuse of psychoeducational tests (Chew, 1984). However, more needs to be done. According to Goldman (1994b), we need a "large decrease in the number of standardized tests bought for use by counselors, a great increase in the use of qualitative assessment, and . . . [more dedication to the AACE] being a consumer organization" (p. 218). In other words, the AACE should inform counselors about the strengths and limitations of standardized tests.

PERSONAL REFLECTION

What tests or assessment instruments have you taken in your life? What do you remember about taking them? What do you remember about the results you were given? How could the feedback have been improved?

TESTS AND TEST SCORES

Anastasi (1982) defines a ***psychological test*** (or ***test***, for short) as "essentially an objective and standardized measure of behavior" (p. 22). Most often test results are reported as ***test scores***, statistics that have meaning only in relation to a person. A *score* is a reflection of a particular behavior at a moment in time. Test scores are important in counseling despite their limitations, for they provide information that might not be obtained in any other way and do so with comparatively small investments of time and effort. Although tests and test scores have been criticized for a number of reasons, testing is an indispensable part of an evaluation process. How tests and test scores are used depends on the user (Anastasi & Urbina, 1997; Urbina, 2005). As Loesch (1977) observes, "we usually don't have a choice about whether we will be involved with testing" (p. 74). There is a choice, however, about whether counselors will be informed and responsible.

To **understand a test**, counselors must know

- the characteristics of its standardization **sample**,
- the types and degree of its **reliability** and **validity**,
- the reliability and validity of **comparable tests**,
- the **scoring procedures**,
- the **method of administration**,
- the **limitations**, and
- the **strengths** (Kaplan & Saccuzzo, 2009).

Much of this information is contained in the test manuals that accompany standardized tests, but acquiring a thorough knowledge of a particular test takes years of study and practice. Because it is important that counselors use tests to the fullest extent possible, they are wise to "prepare local experience tables" so they can give test takers more specific information about what their scores mean in relation to a particular community or situation (Goldman, 1994a, p. 216).

Today, in the United States approximately 10 million "counselees each year complete 'tests,' 'inventories,' and other 'assessments' and that estimate does not include school achievement tests or college entrance exams" (Prediger, 1994, p. 228). Some counseling professionals specialize in the administration and interpretation of tests. Those employed as testing and appraisal specialists are known as *psychometrists* and their discipline of comparing the test scores of a person to a norm-referenced group is known as *psychometrics*. (The opposite of psychometrics is *edumetrics*, based on a constructivist trend in education, where client achievement is compared to the client's previous and best results [Tymofievich & Leroux, 2000].) Regardless, most professionals who administer and interpret tests do not do so on a full-time basis. Usually they are counselors and other helping professionals who are sometimes surprisingly uncomfortable with testing instruments and the negative connotation of the word "test." A test is often linked to "a heavy emphasis on objectivity" (Loesch, 1977, p. 74), and the process of testing can be mechanical, creating psychological distance between the examiner and client. To overcome such barriers, counselors who test need to be well trained in good test practice and the use of the most frequently given tests, as well as other standardized instruments.

While many periodicals review standardized tests, including *Measurement and Evaluation in Counseling and Development* and the *Review of Educational Research*, a number of authoritative reference books on tests are also available. O. K. Buros originated a series of reference books on personality tests, vocational tests, and other similar instruments. His most well-known reference was titled *Tests in Print*. It continues to be updated periodically by the institute he established, the **Buros Institute of Mental Measurements**, and is now in its eighth edition. Buros also edited eight editions of the *Mental Measurements Yearbook*, which is considered his best work in this area and is now in its 18th edition (www.unl.edu/buros/bimm/index.html).

PROBLEMS AND POTENTIAL OF USING TESTS

There are similarities between the tests administered by counselors and those used by psychologists (Bubenzer, Zimpfer, & Mahrle, 1990). However, the ways in which tests are given is more crucial for their success in serving the welfare of clients and the general public than the professional identity of who administers them (Harris, 1994).

Tests may be used alone or as part of a group (a *test battery*). Cronbach (1979) asserts that test batteries have little value unless competent, well-educated counselors are available to interpret them. The same is true for individual tests. Many of the problems associated with testing are usually the result of the way in which instruments are employed and interpreted rather than problems with the tests themselves (Hood & Johnson, 2007).

Shertzer and Stone (1980) maintain that opponents of tests generally object to them for the following reasons:

- Testing encourages client dependency on both the counselor and an external source of information for problem resolution.
- Test data prejudice the counselor's picture of an individual.
- Test data are invalid and unreliable enough so that their value is severely limited (p. 311).

Other critics conclude that tests are culturally biased and discriminatory, measure irrelevant skills, obscure talent, are used mechanically, invade privacy, can be faked, and foster undesirable competition (Hood & Johnson, 2007; Shertzer & Linden, 1979; Talbutt, 1983). "Over reliance on test results, especially in isolation from other information about an individual, is one of the most serious test misuse problems" (Elmore et al., 1993, p. 76). Another criticism is that tests are regressive and used for predictability rather than screening or self-exploration (Goldman, 1994b).

The use of tests with cultural minorities has been an especially controversial area and one in which abuse has occurred (Suzuki & Kugler, 1995; Suzuki, Meller, & Ponterotto, 2001). Assessment instruments must take into consideration the influences and experiences of persons from diverse cultural and ethnic backgrounds if they are going to have any meaning. Oakland (1982) points out that testing can be a dehumanizing experience, and minority culture students may spend years in ineffective or inappropriate programs as a result of test scores. To avoid cultural bias, the AACE has developed *Standards for Multicultural Assessment* (Prediger, 1993). Ethical guidelines for test use are also contained in the *American Counseling Association Code of Ethics (2005)*. These standards, as well as those drawn up by other professional associations, should be consulted when trying to prevent test abuse with minority populations (Hansen, 1994). In assessing bias, it should be recognized that prejudicial acts may result from omission as well as acts of commission (Chernin, Holden, & Chandler, 1997).

Success or failure with tests is related to the sensitivity, ability, and knowledge of the counselors who select, administer, and interpret them. "Counselors have a general obligation to take an empirical approach to their instruments, especially those for which there are not complete norms and substantial validation" (Carlson, 1989, p. 489). If they do not consider multiple criteria in the selection process, counselors are likely to make mistakes that are costly to clients and themselves. To avoid these situations, some counselors include clients in the process of test selection.

CASE EXAMPLE

Susan Makes a Selective Decision

Michael was referred to Susan, the school counselor, because he was acting out in class. According to his teacher, he did not seem capable of sitting still. Sure enough, when he arrived at Susan's office he immediately became fidgety and began squirming in his chair.

Instead of talking with him, Susan decided she needed to have him assessed. She looked up tests for behavioral disorders in Buros's *Tests in Print*. Then she asked that the school psychologist do an evaluation.

What was wrong with Susan's strategy? What was right with it? What would you do before asking for a formal evaluation of anyone who was referred to you?

Learner (1981) and Oakland (1982) report that the general public's attitude toward testing is positive, even among minority cultures, perhaps because people believe that tests serve many useful purposes. From the public's perspective, the **primary function of tests** is to **help clients make better decisions about their futures**. Tests may also accomplish the following:

- Help clients **gain self-understanding**
- Help counselors **decide if clients' needs are within their range of expertise**
- Help counselors **better understand clients**
- Help counselors **determine which counseling methods might be most appropriately employed**
- Help counselors **predict the future performance of clients in select areas**, such as mechanics, art, or graduate school

- Help counselors **stimulate new interests within their clients**
- Help counselors **evaluate the outcome of their counseling efforts** (Shertzer & Stone, 1980)

QUALITIES OF GOOD TESTS

All tests are not created equal, but those that do the job best have certain qualities in common. Among the most important qualities are validity, reliability, standardization, and norms, which facilitate the interpretation of scores (Cohen & Swerdik, 2009; Hogan, 2007).

Validity

Validity is unquestionably the most important test quality and is "the degree to which a test measures what it is supposed to measure, and consequently permits appropriate interpretation of scores" (Gay, Mills, & Airasian, 2009, p. 134). If a test does not fulfill this function, it is basically useless. The validity of a test is determined by comparing its results with measures of a separate and independent criterion. Thus, if a test purports to measure an individual's probability of succeeding in a professional field (such as medicine, law, or counseling), the test scores are correlated with measures of success (such as grades and ratings of instructors) once the tested individual completes his or her education. Examples of such tests would be the MCAT, LSAT, GRE, and the Miller's Analogies Test (MAT), all of which are used as screening devices in admitting students to professional and graduate programs of study. If scores on the testing instrument correlate highly and positively with these independent measures of success, then the instrument is said to possess a high degree of validity.

There are **four types of validity**: content, construct, criterion, and consequential (Anastasi & Urbina, 1997; Kaplan & Saccuzzo, 2009; Tymofievich & Leroux, 2000; Urbina, 2005). *Content validity*, sometimes referred to as *face validity*, is an indication of the degree to which a test appears to measure what it is supposed to measure (Cohen & Swerdik, 2009). More important, content validity is concerned with whether the test includes a fair sample of the universe of factors it is supposed to assess. As a general rule, content validity is associated with achievement, aptitude, and ability tests.

Construct validity is the most important type of validity "because it asks the fundamental validity question: What is the test really measuring?" (Gay et al., 2009, p. 137). Simply defined, construct validity is "the degree to which a test measures an intended hypothetical construct" (p. 137) such as empathy or intelligence. Much depends on the test maker's definition of the construct, but generally construct validity is applied to personality and interest inventories.

Criterion validity refers to the comparison of test scores with a person's actual performance of a certain skill across time and situations. For example, a test that measures a person's fine-motor skills may be validated against that person's ability to type. When the criterion is available at the time of testing, then the concurrent validity of the test is being measured. When the criterion is not available until after the test is administered, then the predictive validity of the test is being measured (Cohen & Swerdik, 2009). Two well-known criterion-based instruments are frequently used in counseling environments: the Minnesota Multiphasic Personality Inventory-2 (MMPI-2), a test with concurrent validity (Nichols & Kaufman, 2011), and the revised Strong Interest Inventory (SII), a test with predictive validity (Osborne, Brown, Niles, & Miner, 1997).

Finally, the newest type of validity is *consequential validity*, the social implications or consequences of test use and interpretation (Tymofievich & Leroux, 2000). Test score interpretations have both long-term and short-term effects on clients. Counselors must consider the client's perspective and position in using tests of any sort regardless of the age of the clients.

Tests are just one technique in counselors' repertoires and, in interpreting results, counselors should not be too dogmatic or authoritarian (Meier & Davis, 2011).

Overall, validity appears strong for most standardized tests. In a comprehensive review of the research literature based on more than 125 meta-analysis of psychological test validities, Meyer et al. (2001) found evidence that psychological tests are comparable with the validity of most medical tests and have "strong and compelling" validity for use in counseling practice, especially if multimethod assessment procedures are used.

Reliability

"In everyday English, *reliability* means dependability or trustworthiness. The term means the same thing when describing measurement" (Gay et al., 2009, p. 139). Thus, reliability is a measure of the degree to which a test produces consistency of test scores when people are retested with the same or an equivalent instrument (Anastasi & Urbina, 1997; Hogan, 2007; Urbina, 2005). Although reliability is related to validity, a test score may be reliable but not valid. There are three traditional ways of **determining reliability**:

1. *test-retest,* in which the same test is given again after a period of time;
2. *parallel-form or alternate-form,* in which two equivalent forms of the same test are administered; and
3. *internal consistency analysis,* in which the scores of two arbitrarily selected halves of a test are compared.

PERSONAL REFLECTION

When have you questioned the reliability of a test score? How do you think that outside variables, such as your general health at a particular time, influence test results? If you question the reliability of test results, what are some things you can do?

Standardization and Norms

Standardization refers to the uniform conditions under which a test is administered and scored (Cohen & Swerdik, 2009). Standardization makes possible the comparison of an individual's successive scores over time as well as the comparison of scores of different individuals. *Norms,* or average performance scores for specified groups, make possible meaningful comparisons among people in regard to what can be expected (Kaplan & Saccuzzo, 2009). Test norms have their limitations and may be misused. For example, a major criticism of some tests is that their norms were established on members of the majority population; therefore, they may discriminate against cultural minorities and people who are disadvantaged and disabled. Counselors must carefully examine the norming procedures of tests, and they should also establish their own local norms. In this way, prejudice and the inappropriate use of tests can be minimized.

CLASSIFICATION OF TESTS

There are many **classifications of tests**. Shertzer and Stone (1981) list seven:

1. *Standardized versus nonstandardized*—tests that are administered and scored according to specific directions (e.g., the Self-Directed Search) as opposed to those that are not (e.g., an experimental projective test)

2. *Individual versus group*—tests that are designed to be given to one person at a time (e.g., the Kaufman Assessment Battery for Children [Kamphaus, Beres, Kaufman, & Kaufman, 1996]) as opposed to those that are given to groups (e.g., Minnesota School Attitude Survey [Callis, 1985])

3. *Speed versus power*—tests that must be completed within a specified period of time (e.g., most achievement tests) as opposed to those that allow for the demonstration of knowledge within generous time boundaries (e.g., many individually administered intelligence tests)

4. *Performance versus paper and pencil*—tests that require the manipulation of objects (e.g., the Object Assembly subtest of the Wechsler Intelligence Scale for Children-IV [WISC-IV]) as opposed to those in which subjects mark answers or give written responses (e.g., the Adjective Check List)

5. *Objective versus subjective*—tests that require the scorer not to make a judgment (e.g., short answer, true–false, matching, multiple-choice [Cohen & Swerdik, 2009]) as opposed to those that require the scorer to exercise a judgment (e.g., the Vocabulary subtest of the Wechsler Adult Intelligence Scale-IV [WAIS-IV; Wechsler, 2008])

6. *Maximum versus typical performance*—tests that require the examinees to do their best (e.g., tests of intelligence and special abilities) as opposed to those that measure what a person is most likely to do or usually does (e.g., tests that indicate interests or attitudes)

7. *Norm versus criterion based*—tests that compare an individual's score with scores within a group (e.g., intelligence or achievement test) as opposed to those that measure a person's score compared to a desirable level or standard (e.g., a reading test; Cohen & Swerdik, 2009; Hogan, 2007)

Another way in which tests may be classified, and one that is even more important for counselors, is "by the purpose for which they are designed or by the aspects of behavior they sample" (Shertzer & Stone, 1981, p. 242). In this classification Shertzer and Stone list six categories of tests: mental ability, aptitude, achievement, interests, career development, and personality. Yet another system of classification includes the following categories: educational, vocational, or personal aspects of counseling (Elmore & Roberge, 1982). A third classification scheme, originated by Sylvania (1956), groups tests according to their frequency of use: intelligence/scholastic aptitude, vocational (and other aptitude), and achievement/diagnostic. All these classification systems have their merits and limitations. Counselors are usually involved in dealing with **four distinct but sometimes overlapping categories of tests: intelligence/ aptitude, interest/career, personality**, and **achievement**.

CASE EXAMPLE

Carl's Code

Carl had a difficult time finding tests that he wanted to use. He realized he could alphabetize them, but he wanted a better system so Carl decided to use color codes like those found in doctors' offices. He color-coded all intelligence tests with a green tag, all personality tests with a blue tag, and so on. He then put the color-coded tests in order of most used to least used. After testing clients, Carl added a color or colors to their files, with some being only one hue and some being many.

What do you think of Carl's system? How would you go about coding test instruments that you might use?

Intelligence/Aptitude

Among the most controversial but popular types of tests are those that attempt to measure general intelligence and special aptitude. *Intelligence* is defined in many different ways, and there are **multiple forms of intelligence**, such as musical, athletic, spatial, logical-mathematical, and so on (Gardner, 2011). However, when intelligence is usually discussed, it is done so related to **linguistic and problem-solving capabilities** (Gottfredson, & Saklofske, 2009). Indeed, Anastasi (1982) reports that most intelligence tests "are usually overloaded with certain functions, such as verbal ability, and completely omit others" (p. 228). She notes that many intelligence tests are "validated against measures of academic achievement" and "are often designated as tests of scholastic aptitude" (Anastasi, 1982, p. 228). Such tests are designed to measure an individual's aptitude for scholastic work or other kinds of occupations requiring reasoning and verbal ability. Thus they are used primarily as screening devices for overall ability and are followed by more specialized aptitude tests that assess aptitude in particular areas, such as music or mechanics.

Most modern intelligence tests are descendants of the original scales developed in France by Alfred Binet in the early 1900s. The **Stanford-Binet Intelligence Scale**, a revision of the Binet-Simon scales, was prepared by L. M. Terman and published in 1916; it is the grandparent of American intelligence tests. The test is individually administered and has traditionally been used more with children than with adults. In 2000, it underwent a fifth revision (SB5) and now has a more modern look as well as appropriateness for adults and those who are less verbally fluent. Another popular series of individually administered intelligence tests are those originated by David Wechsler. They are the **Wechsler Preschool and Primary Scale of Intelligence-III (WPPSI-III)**, designed for ages 2 years, 6 months to 7 years, 3 months; the **Wechsler Intelligence Scale for Children-Fourth Edition (WISC-IV)**, designed for ages 6 years through 16 years 11 months; and the **Wechsler Adult Intelligence Scale-Fourth Edition (WAIS-IV)**, designed for ages 16 years to 89 years. The Wechsler intelligence tests provide a verbal IQ, performance IQ, and full-scale IQ score. Extensive research has been done on all the Wechsler scales, and they are often the instruments of choice in the evaluation of intelligence (Piotrowski & Keller, 1989; Thorndike & Thorndike-Christ, 2010).

There are a number of other widely respected individually administered intelligence tests. Among them are the Bayley Scales of Infant Development, the Vineland Social Maturity Scale, the Kaufman Assessment Battery for Children (K-ABC), the McCarthy Scales of Children's Abilities, the Peabody Picture Vocabulary Test (PPVT-IV), and the Kaufman Adolescent and Adult Intelligence Test (KAIT).

Also available are numerous intelligence scales intended to be administered to groups. These instruments were first developed during **World War I** when the United States Army created its **Alpha and Beta intelligence tests**, the best-known forerunners of today's group intelligence instruments. These tests were initially employed to screen army inductees and classify them for training according to ability level. Among the most widely used and respected group intelligence tests are the Otis-Lennon School Ability Test, the Cognitive Abilities Test, and the Test of Cognitive Skills.

Aptitude tests are similar in many ways to intelligence tests, but they are designed to tap a narrower range of ability. An *aptitude* is a capability for a task or type of skill, and an *aptitude test* measures a person's ability to profit from further training or experience in an occupation or skill. Aptitude tests are usually divided into two categories: (a) *multiaptitude batteries*, which test a number of skills by administering a variety of tests; and (b) *component ability tests*, which assess a single ability or skill, such as music or mechanical ability (Bradley, 1984). Some of the best-known multiaptitude batteries are the Scholastic Aptitude Test (SAT), the American College Testing (ACT) Assessment, the Miller Analogies Test (MAT), the Differential Aptitude Test (DAT), and the Armed Services Vocational Aptitude Battery (ASVAB) (Anastasi & Urbina, 1997; Hood & Johnson, 2007; Urbina, 2005).

Interest/Career

Although there is an expected relationship between ability and an interest in exercising that ability, tests that best measure interests are those designed specifically for the purpose. An *interest inventory* is a test or checklist that assesses a person's preferences for activities and topics. Responses derived from such tests are compared with the scores of others at either a similar developmental level (e.g., in an educational setting) or with people already working in a particular area (e.g., in a vocational setting). Anastasi (1982) notes that "the study of interests has probably received its strongest impetus from educational and career counseling" because a person's achievement in a learning situation or a career is greatly influenced by his or her interests (p. 534). Indeed, "interest inventory interpretation is one of the most frequently used interventions in career counseling" (Savickas, 1998, p. 307).

Instruments that measure career interests began in a systematic and standardized way with the 1927 publication of the **Strong Vocational Interest Blank (SVIB)**. The test has been revised and expanded half a dozen times since its inception, with the latest edition of this instrument, the **Strong Interest Inventory (SII)**, encompassing over 200 occupational scales that indicate the similarity between the respondent's interests to those of satisfied workers in each of these occupations. The test's founder, E. K. Strong, Jr., devised only 10 Occupational Scales for the original test (Donnay, 1997). **SII test results are explained in three forms: General Occupational Themes, Basic Interest Scales, and Occupational Scales**. Thus, they help clients examine themselves in both a general and specific way. Another attractive feature of the instrument is its link to **John Holland's theory of career development**, which proposes **six major types of people and environments: realistic (R), investigative (I), artistic (A), social (S), enterprising (E), and conventional (C) (RIASEC**; Holland, 1997). The closer the correlation between people and environment types, the more satisfying the relationship (Spokane & Catalano, 2000). Overall, the SII offers a breadth and depth in the measurement of occupational interests that are unmatched by any other single instrument. The accompanying user's guide suggests ways of employing the test with adults, cross-cultural groups, and special populations (Drummond & Jones, 2010). In addition, strong theoretical underpinnings, empirical construction, and a long history are major benefits of this inventory.

Another popular career inventory, also based on Holland's six personality/environmental types, is the **Self-Directed Search** (SDS; Holland, 1994). This instrument is self-administered, self-scored, and sometimes self-interpreted. It comprises 228 items divided into three sets: activities, competencies, and occupations (Krieshok, 1987). After scoring, clients examine a three-letter *Occupational Code Finder* (a booklet that accompanies the SDS), comparing it with career codes found in the *Dictionary of Occupational Titles (DOT)*. The inventory has four versions, including Form E, which is designed for poor readers. Test takers from ages 15 to 70 report that the SDS is enjoyable and useful.

A third popular interest/career inventory is the **Kuder Occupational Interest Survey (KOIS)**, which was first published in 1939 and continues to evolve (Kuder, 1939, 1977). The latest revision of the KOIS was in 1991 (Betsworth & Fouad, 1997). There are six forms of this activity preference, item-type, untimed instrument, but each form has a forced-choice, triad-response format (Zytowski, 1992). Some forms of the test are computer scored, while others are self-scored. Clients respond to each triad by selecting the most and least preferred activity. Scores on the Kuder correlate highly with commonly expressed interests of select career groups and college majors (Zytowski & Holmberg, 1988). The test's **10 broad career areas** include the following (Zytowski, 1992, pp. 245–246):

1. *Social services*—"preference of helping people"—comparable to the Holland "social" scale
2. *Persuasive*—"preference for meeting and dealing with people and promoting projects or selling things and ideas"—comparable to the Holland "enterprising" scale
3. *Clerical*—"preference for tasks that require precision and accuracy"—comparable to the Holland "conventional" scale
4. *Computational*—"preference for working with numbers"—comparable also to the Holland "conventional" scale
5. *Musical*—"preference for going to concerts, playing musical instruments, singing, and reading about music and musicians"—comparable to the Holland "artistic" scale
6. *Artistic*—"preference for creative work involving attractive design, color, form, and materials"—comparable to the Holland "artistic" scale
7. *Literary*—"preference for reading and writing"—comparable to the Holland "artistic" scale
8. *Mechanical*—"preference for working with machines and tools"—comparable to the Holland "realistic" scale
9. *Outdoor*—"preference for activities that keep you outside most of the time, and usually deal with animals and plants"—comparable to the Holland "realistic" scale
10. *Scientific*—"preference for discovering new facts and solving problems"—comparable to the Holland "investigative" scale

A fourth instrument, primarily career focused, is the **Career Beliefs Inventory** (CBI; Krumboltz, 1991). "The CBI is an instrument which, when used sensitively by a qualified professional, can help people identify the beliefs that might be blocking them" (Krumboltz, 1992, p. 1). It is most usefully employed at the beginning of a career-counseling session. It makes possible the exploration of deep-seated attitudes and assumptions.

Other well-known interest/career tests include the California Occupational Preference System, the Jackson Vocational Interest Survey, the Ohio Vocational Interest Survey, the Unisex Edition of the ACT Interest Inventory, and the Vocational Preference Inventory.

For **non-college-bound students**, Bradley (1984) reports three interest inventories designed to "measure interests in occupations that do not require college training" (p. 7). These include (a) the **Minnesota Vocational Interest Inventory**, (b) the **Career Assessment Inventory**, and (c) the **Career Guidance Inventory in Trades, Services, and Technologies**. Interest tests designed for more specialized use are the Bem Sex-Role Inventory, the Jenkins Activity Survey, the Personal Orientation Inventory, the Survey of Values, and the Survey of School Attitudes.

In selecting appropriate interest/career instruments, "you [must] know what you are looking for and . . . what you are getting" (Westbrook, 1988, p. 186). Two excellent resource books describe career decision-making and assessment measures: *Handbook of Vocational Psychology* (Walsh & Savickas, 2005) and *A Counselor's Guide to Career Assessment Instruments*

(Whitfield, Feller, & Wood, 2009). The latter text reviews 52 major career assessment instruments, annotates 250 others, and describes their intended populations.

Personality

Personality can be defined in many ways; what is considered normal in one culture may be perceived as abnormal in another. Nevertheless, there are a number of personality theories that examine the biological, social, and environmental aspects of human beings. The most popular 20th-century theorist of personality assessment was Henry A. Murray. He was especially cognizant of needs (or environmental forces/presses) and how they determined behavior (Drummond & Jones, 2010).

A *personality test* may be defined as any of several methods of analyzing personality, such as checklists, personality inventories, and projective techniques (Cohen & Swerdik, 2009). Such tests may be divided into **two main categories: objective and projective**. Some of the best-known objective tests are the Minnesota Multiphasic Personality Inventory-2 (MMPI-2), the Myers-Briggs Type Indicator (MBTI), and the Edwards Personal Preference Schedule (EPPS). These tests yield scores that are independent of any opinion or judgment of the scorer, as are all objective tests. Projective tests include the Rorschach, the Thematic Apperception Test (TAT), and the House-Tree-Person (HTP) Test. These types of tests yield measures that, in varying degrees, depend on the judgments and interpretations of administrators/scorers. They may be especially valuable and appropriate in multicultural counseling settings because many of them require a minimal amount of words and thereby decrease the chance for cultural bias.

The prototype of the personality test was a self-report inventory, known as the **Personal Data Sheet**, developed during World War I by R. S. Woodworth (Kaplan & Saccuzzo, 2009). However, the first significant projective test was the **Rorschach Inkblot Test**, published in 1921 (Exner, 2003). The Rorschach is still widely used in personality evaluations in the United States. It consists of a series of 10 ink blots, which are presented to individuals one at a time. Test takers are asked what they see in the ink blots, and their answers are recorded. Later their answers are evaluated and interpreted to diagnose psychotic versus nonpsychotic thoughts and general themes they have generated. An overall assessment of personality and emotional functioning are included in reports produced from those responding to this instrument. Projective tests, such as the Rorschach, are not used extensively in counseling. However, objectively scored personality tests are, so we will begin our discussion with a review of them.

The **Minnesota Multiphasic Personality Inventory-2 (MMPI-2)** is one of the most widely used psychological tests in the world (Nichols & Kaufman, 2011). It is a revision of the original MMPI. Instead of being normed on a limited population, however, this version uses a geographically and ethnically diverse reference group representative of the population of the United States. The restandardized MMPI-2 is also on tape for individuals who are blind, illiterate, semiliterate, or disabled (Drummond & Jones, 2010). It has several forms, including one for adolescents (the MMPI-A), but the most popular form consists of 567 affirmative statements that clients respond to in one of three ways: true, false, or cannot say. There are 10 clinical scales on the MMPI-2 (Table 14.1) and three major validity scales: Lie (L), Infrequency (F), and Correction (K). In addition, there is a "?" scale, which is a compilation of unanswered questions throughout the test. In addition to distinguishing individuals who are experiencing psychiatric problems, the MMPI-2 is able to discern important characteristics such as anger, alienation, Type A behavior, and even marital distress. Extensive training and experience are necessary for counselors to use this instrument accurately and appropriately. Overall, uses of the MMPI-2 are still being refined (Austin, 1994).

TABLE 14.1   Clinical scales on the Minnesota Multiphasic Personality Inventory–2

Scale	Item Total	Item Content
Hypochondriasis (Hs)	(32)	Undue concern with physical health
Depression (D)	(57)	Depression, denial of happiness and personal worth, lack of interest, withdrawal
Hysteria (Hy)	(60)	Specific somatic complaints, denial of psychological or emotional problems, discomfort in social situations
Psychopathic deviate (Pd)	(50)	Antisocial acting-out impulses, constricted social conformity
Masculinity–femininity (Mf)	(56)	Identification with culturally conventional masculine and feminine choices, aesthetic interests, activity–passivity
Paranoia (Pa)	(40)	Delusions of persecution and ideas of reference, interpersonal sensitivity, suspiciousness, moral self-righteousness
Psychasthenia (Pt)	(48)	General dissatisfaction with life, difficulty with concentration, indecisiveness, self-doubt, obsessional aspects
Schizophrenia (Sc)	(78)	Feeling of being different, feelings of isolation, bizarre thought processes, poor family relationships, sexual identity concerns, tendency to withdraw
Hypomania (Ma)	(46)	Elevated energy level, flight of ideas, elevated mood, increased motor activity, expansiveness, grandiosity
Social introversion–extroversion	(69)	Introversion–extroversion; social insecurity

Source: From *Appraisal Procedures for Counselors and Other Helping Professionals* (2nd ed., p. 181), by R. J. Drummond, Upper Saddle River, NJ: Prentice Hall. © 1992. Reprinted by permission of Prentice Hall, Inc., Upper Saddle River, NJ.

The **Myers-Briggs Type Indicator (MBTI)** is a test that reflects Carl Jung's theory of personality type (Myers, 1962, 1980). The inventory "has been widely used in various contexts including career counseling, marital and family therapy, and team building" (Vacha-Haase & Thompson, 2002, p. 173). The MBTI contains 166 two-choice items concerning preferences or inclinations in feelings and behaviors (Cohen & Swerdik, 2009). It yields **four indexes**: extroversion versus introversion (EI), sensing versus intuition (SN), thinking versus feeling (TF), and judgment versus perception (JP). The MBTI consists of four bipolar scales:

1. *Extroversion or introversion (EI)*—whether perception and judgment are directed to the outer (E) or inner (I) world
2. *Sensing or intuitive (SN)*—which kind of perception is preferred when one needs to perceive
3. *Thinking or feeling (TF)*—which kind of judgment is trusted when a decision needs to be made
4. *Judgment or perception (JP)*—whether to deal with the world in the judgment attitude (using thinking or feeling) or in the perceptual attitude (using sensing or intuition)

Combinations of these four indexes result in **16 possible personality types**. A clear understanding of personality type provides counselors with constructive information on how clients perceive and interact with their environments (Lynch, 1985). Research indicates that different MBTI types appear to be attracted to certain occupations and lifestyles (Healy & Woodward, 1998). For example, 76% of tested counseling students score high on the intuitive/feeling scales of the MBTI and are described as insightful, enthusiastic, and able to handle challenging situations with personal warmth (Myers, 1980). Alternative tests to the MBTI that also yield Jungian psychological-type preferences include the Keirsey Temperament Sorter (Keirsey & Bates, 1984) and the Personal Preferences Self-Description Questionnaire (PPSDQ; Thompson, 1996).

The **Edwards Personal Preference Schedule (EPPS)** is based on the need-press theory of personality developed by Henry Murray (1938). It consists of 225 forced-choice questions that examine the strength of 15 individual needs in relation to a person's other needs (Anastasi & Urbina, 1997; Urbina, 2005). The scores are plotted on a percentile chart based on group norms for college students or adults in general. Other objectively scored, self-report personality tests are the California Psychological Inventory (CPI), the Guilford-Zimmerman Temperament Survey, the Mooney Problem Check List, the Sixteen Personality Factor Questionnaire (16 PF), and the State-Trait Anxiety Inventory (STAI).

Projective personality tests are much less structured and far more difficult to score, but they are harder for the client to fake. Advocates claim that these tests measure deeper aspects of a client's personality than do other instruments. Some researchers and clinicians, such as Exner (2003), have tried to standardize the methods by which projectives are administered and scored. Although there has been success for some instruments, the scoring of many other projectives, such as the Thematic Apperception Test, is questionable. In addition to the tests already mentioned in this section, projective tests include the Holtzman Inkblot Technique, the Draw-a-Person Test, the Children's Apperception Test, and the Rotter Incomplete Sentences Blank.

Achievement

An *achievement test* is a measure of an individual's degree of accomplishment or learning in a subject or task (Cohen & Swerdik, 2009). Achievement tests are much more direct as measurement instruments than any other type of test. Their results give clients a good idea of what they have learned in a certain area as compared with what others have learned. The tests give clients the type of information they need to make sound educational and career decisions (Bradley, 1984). If a client has aptitudes, interests, or personality dispositions suitable for select career areas but has little knowledge or skill, he or she can take positive steps to correct these deficiencies.

Achievement tests may be either teacher made or standardized. The advantages of **teacher-made tests** are that they measure specific units of study emphasized in an educational setting, are easy to keep up-to-date, and reflect current emphases and information. **Standardized tests**, however, measure more general educational objectives, are usually more carefully constructed, and give the test taker a good idea about how he or she compares with a wider sample of others in a particular subject. Teacher-made and standardized tests complement each other, and both may be used profitably in the helping process.

Various achievement tests are employed for distinct purposes. In a school setting, a combination of teacher-made and standardized tests are linked to age and grade levels. General achievement batteries used in elementary and secondary schools measure basic skills. They include the TerraNova Tests, the Iowa Tests of Basic Skills, the SRA Achievement Series, the Metropolitan Achievement Tests, the Wide Range Achievement Test, and the Stanford Achievement Test (Anastasi & Urbina, 1997; Urbina, 2005). School counselors must become especially knowledgeable about these instruments to converse intelligently and efficiently with teachers, parents, administrators, students, and educational specialists.

Instruments are also available that measure adult achievement such as the Adult Basic Learning Examination and the Tests of General Education Development (GED). Professionally oriented achievement tests include the National Teacher Examination, Law School Admissions Test, and the National Counselor Examination (NCE). These latter tests help protect the public and the professions they represent by ensuring that individuals who pass them have achieved a minimum level of informational competence.

PERSONAL REFLECTION

To be nationally certified and licensed in most states, a counselor must pass the National Counselor Examination (NCE). What do you think you need to do in order to pass this test (besides reading this textbook)? How do you perceive this test will be similar and different from other types of tests you have taken before? Hint: You may want to consult the NBCC website at www.nbcc.org.

ADMINISTRATION AND INTERPRETATION OF TESTS

A major criticism of test use in counseling focuses on administration and interpretation. The process of administering a test is described in the manual that accompanies each one, and most tests specify uniform procedures to be followed at each step, from preparing the room to giving instructions. Some tests have specialized instructions, and counselors must follow these procedures if they expect to obtain valid test results.

One question usually not addressed in manuals is whether a test taker should be involved in selecting the test and, if so, how much he or she should be involved. In some cases, such as the administration of achievement tests in elementary schools, it is inappropriate for test takers to be involved in test selection. But on other occasions participation is beneficial. Goldman (1971) lists several **advantages of involving test takers in test selection**. Among the reasons for involving test takers in test selection are

- the willingness of the tested population to **accept test results**,
- the **promotion of independence**,
- the **value of the decision-making experience** that might generalize to other decision-making opportunities,
- the **opportunity for diagnosis** based on the test taker's reactions to various tests, and
- the selection of tests that **best fit** the needs of the tested population.

After tests are selected, administered, and scored, counselors need to interpret the results for the tested population in an understandable way (Tymofievich & Leroux, 2000). **Four basic interpretations** can be **helpful to test takers**, depending on the test (Goldman, 1971; Hanna, 1988):

1. *Descriptive interpretation,* which provides information on the current status of the test taker
2. *Genetic interpretation,* which focuses on how the tested person got to be the way he or she is now
3. *Predictive interpretation,* which concentrates on forecasting the future
4. *Evaluative interpretation,* which includes recommendations by the test interpreter

Unfortunately, some counselors fail to learn how to administer or interpret tests. "Misuse occurs in all three basic testing areas, employment, educational, and clinical" (Azar, 1994, p. 16). Misuse can result from administering and interpreting a good test in the wrong way or giving it to the wrong person for the wrong reason. In any case, when tests are misused, clients may not understand the meaning of "the numbers, charts, graphs or diagrams presented to them" (Miller, 1982, p. 87) and may leave counseling as uninformed and unenlightened as when they began.

By maintaining conditions of standardization when tests are administered, by knowing the strengths and limitations of the norms, reliability and validity of particular instruments, and by translating raw test data into meaningful descriptions of current or predicted behavior, counselors ensure that tests are used to promote the welfare of their clients (Harris, 1994, p. 10).

Several ways have been suggested to correct deficiencies associated with test interpretation. For example, besides making sure that those who give tests are well educated and sensitive, Hanna (1988, p. 477) recommends using a person's ***percentile rank*** ("the percentage of persons in a reference group who scored lower than the person") as one way to provide descriptive interpretation clearly and concisely (Figure 14.1).

Another way of rectifying deficiencies in interpretive skills depends on counselor–client preparation for the process of interpretation. First, counselors should be educated in test theory and construction. Counselors cannot explain test results unless they are well-informed about the instruments with which they are dealing.

Second, Tyler (1984) points out that scores are only clues and should be seen as such. Scores must be considered in light of what else is known about a client. The total combination of information can form the basis for a more meaningful and productive dialogue between counselor and client. Goldman (1971) points out that if a test is given on an individual basis, counselors notice many things about clients that otherwise would be missed. This extra information, when combined with the test scores, often allows for a more complete assessment of the client.

Third, Tinsley and Bradley (1986), Miller (1982), and Strahan and Kelly (1994) advocate concrete ways of dealing with test results. Tinsley and Bradley believe that, before meeting with a client, the counselor must be prepared to make a clear and accurate interpretation of test results. They advise against interpreting off the cuff. A reasonable plan is to begin the interpretation with concrete information, such as interest or achievement scores, and then move to abstract information, such as personality or ability results. If the interpretation of information is to be meaningful, the emotional needs of the client must be considered and the information must be fresh in the counselor's mind. One way to achieve both goals is to ***interpret test results on an as-needed basis***—that is, interpret the scores the client needs to know only at a point in time (Goldman, 1971). There is less information to deal with when this approach is followed, and both counselor and client are likely to remember results better. The major disadvantage of this approach is that it may become fragmented.

Tinsley and Bradley (1986) propose that when interpretation occurs, a client should be prepared through the establishment of rapport between counselor and client. Test information can then be delivered in a way that focuses on what the client wants to know. Client feedback is promoted, and dialogue is encouraged.

Miller (1982) makes similar remarks in his five-point plan for interpreting test results to clients. First, he has his client remember feelings on the test day and give impressions of the test or tests. He then reviews with the client the purpose of testing and how test scores are presented (e.g., by percentiles). Next, he and the client actually examine the test results together and discuss what the scores mean. Meaning is elicited by asking the client open-ended questions. The client can then integrate scores with other aspects of self-knowledge. The final stage

FIGURE 14.1 Percentile rank band for a percentile range of 60 to 70 on a standardized test of 0 to 100

involves incorporating all knowledge into a client-originated plan for continuing self-study. Counselors can help clients formulate a plan, but the plan itself should come from the client.

A final way of making test results concrete is to present them in simple **graph displays** (Strahan & Kelly, 1994). Graphical data help clients see test results in a simple, clear, and interesting way.

Overall, test interpretation may be the most sensitive part of any assessment process. "When done properly . . . test results—may enhance the counseling process and facilitate client change. Research has shown that many clients benefit from receiving feedback about their test results" (Hanson & Claiborn, 2006, p. 349).

CASE EXAMPLE

Inez Attempts Interpretation

The first time Inez attempted to give her client, Henrico, feedback on tests he had taken, she stumbled. She was used to being reflective, and she was very dedicated to empowering her clients. Therefore, she initially gave Henrico his test results and asked him to give her feedback on what they meant. Needless to say, Henrico, who was unsophisticated in test interpretation, had real questions about aspects of some of the instruments used, such as whether the lie scale meant he was not telling the truth or what exactly was indicated when his score on the masculine/feminine scale was high. To her credit, Inez became more direct and interactive with Henrico.

What does Henrico's experience tell you about your role as an interpreter of tests? What is your style in conveying information, and does it need to be modified if you are going to give clients feedback about their test results?

ASSESSMENT

In addition to, and supplementing, testing is *assessment*, the procedures and processes of collecting information and measures of human behavior apart from test data. According to Cormier, Nurius, and Osborn (2009, p. 151) **assessment has six purposes**:

1. "To **obtain information** on a client's presenting problem and on other, related problems."
2. "To i**dentify** the controlling or contributing **variables** associated with the problem."
3. "To **determine the client's goals/expectations** for counseling outcomes."
4. "To **gather baseline data** that will be compared to subsequent data to assess and evaluate client progress and the effects of treatment strategies."
5. "To **educate and motivate the client**" by sharing the counselor's view of the situation, increasing client receptivity to treatment, and contributing to therapeutic change.
6. "To use the information obtained from the client to **plan effective treatment inventions and strategies**. The information obtained during the assessment process should help to answer this well-thought-out question: '*What* treatment, by *whom*, is most effective for *this* individual with *that* specific problem and under *which* set of circumstances?'" (Paul, 1967, p. 111)

Assessment can be obtained "through a variety of formal and informal techniques including standardized tests, diagnostic interviews, projective personality measures, questionnaires, mental status examinations, checklists, behavioral observation, and reports by significant others (medical, educational, social, legal, etc.)" (Hohenshil, 1996, p. 65). Usually it involves a combination of procedures and not just one method (Hood & Johnson, 2007; Wall & Walz, 2004). The word "assessment" emphasizes the humanness of counseling. Included in "humanness" is a total picture of the person being evaluated. According to Anastasi (1992b), "the term assessment is being used increasingly to refer to the intensive study of an individual, leading to recommendations for action in solving a particular problem" (p. 611).

As stated previously, the **goal of the assessment process** is a comprehensive evaluation of individuals, usually in the present. Often it includes a formulation of a treatment plan that will result in positive and predictable outcomes (Groth-Marnat, 2010; Kaplan & Saccuzzo, 2009). To help counselors formulate such treatment plans, commercial as well as local treatment planners are available. For instance, Jongsma and Peterson (1995) have produced a manual that includes definitions of problematic behaviors along with long- and short-term goals. In addition, therapeutic interventions as well as bibliotherapy suggestions are given.

One way of conducting assessment is through the use of biographical and behavioral measures. Numerous ***structured clinical interviews*** are available for collecting this type of information. "In general, a structured clinical interview consists of a list of relevant behaviors, symptoms, and events to be addressed during an interview, guidelines for conducting the interview, and procedures for recording and analyzing the data" (Vacc & Juhnke, 1997, p. 471). The questions are asked in an ordered sequence; from the results of the interview, an assessment is made that is either diagnostic (specifically related to the *Diagnostic and Statistical Manual* [DSM]) or descriptive (indicating the degree of psychopathology that is present or giving a non-DSM dysfunctional descriptor).

Although not a formal psychometric instrument, the ***mental status examination (MSE)*** is being "increasingly used by counselors in work settings requiring assessment, diagnosis, and treatment of mental disorders" (Polanski & Hinkle, 2000, p. 357). The MSE is organized under the following categories:

- **appearance** (i.e., physical characteristics of client), **attitude** (i.e., client's approach to the interview and interaction with examiner), and **activity** (i.e., physical or motor movement)
- **mood** (i.e., predominant internal feeling state) and **affect** (i.e., outward expression of a client's emotional state)
- **speech and language** (i.e., the ability to express oneself and to comprehend word meaning)
- **thought process** (i.e., the organization, flow, and production of thought), **thought content**, and **perception** (i.e., delusions, hallucinations, anxiety symptoms, phobias)
- **cognition** (i.e., ability to think, use logic, intellect, reasoning, and memory)
- **insight and judgment** (i.e., awareness of one's own personality traits and behaviors, insight, and the ability to consider long-term effects and possible outcomes)

The MSE "provides counselors with a format for organizing objective (observations of clients) and subjective (data provided by clients)" (Polanski & Hinkle, 2000, p. 357). It is included in many managed care treatment plans as well as plans used in mental health centers and psychiatric hospitals. There are even computer-assisted MSE programs to aid counselors in report writing.

Overall, assessment (whether one uses the MSE or not) is crucial because it allows counselors not only to determine what a client's problem is but to learn the client's orientation to problem solving. Such a procedure helps counselors and clients avoid blaming and work collaboratively in finding solutions that bring about positive change rather than repeating past patterns. Assessment then makes sense to the degree that it contributes to learning and to formulating interventions in counseling that work (Egan, 2010). In clinical settings, assessment is a continuous process because, once initial difficulties are resolved, new ones sometimes arise or come more into focus.

DIAGNOSIS

"*Diagnosis* . . . is the meaning or interpretation that is derived from assessment information and is usually translated in the form of some type of classification system" (Hohenshil, 1993, p. 7). Thus, a diagnosis is a description of a person's condition and not a judgment of a person's worth (Rueth, Demmitt, & Burger, 1998). For instance, the DSM, which provides the standard nomenclature for describing most symptomatology and dysfunctionality in the United States, recommends referring to clients as

> people with particular types of mental disorders . . . Using labeling in this way emphasizes that the mental disorder is only one characteristic of the individual, not a descriptor of the whole person. (Hohenshil, 1996, p. 65)

"All clients experiencing symptoms of illness also possess basic strengths and complex coping skills" (Harris, Thoresen, & Lopez, 2007, p. 5). Therefore, a diagnosis is a measure in time and not a fixed entity.

Like test interpretation, some diagnostic categories are appropriately shared with clients. However, most diagnoses from the DSM categories are withheld from clients because they may prove frightening or misleading (Moursund & Kenny, 2002). In addition, negative diagnoses may set up **self-fulfilling prophesies** for clients where they begin to behave as they were diagnosed. Instead, diagnoses may be used to guide the counselor in formulating a treatment plan for helping. **When used appropriately, diagnoses do the following**:

- Describe a person's **current functioning**
- **Provide a common language** for clinicians to use in discussing the client
- Lead to a **consistent and continual type of care**
- Help direct and **focus treatment planning**
- Help counselors fit clients within their **scope of treatment** (Rueth et al., 1998)

Diagnoses are important for at least two other reasons. First, some insurance companies will reimburse for counseling services only if clients are diagnosed. Second, to work with psychiatrists, psychologists, and some medical specialists, as well as managed care specialists and some governmental agencies, counselors must be able to speak about, understand, or report a client diagnosis (Hamann, 1994; Hinkle, 1999).

To make proper diagnoses, counselors must receive extensive training and supervision. They should know diagnostic categories, particularly those in the DSM. They should also realize that diagnostic decisions are an evolving process and not a static event (Hohenshil, 1996). "Diagnosis and treatment planning are now such standard components of counseling practice" that a failure to diagnose on some level or a lack of professional diagnostic training may be construed as unethical (Sommers-Flanagan & Sommers-Flanagan, 1998, p. 189).

In making a diagnosis, a counselor must observe a client for signs of symptoms, listen for complaints, and look for functional disturbances (Lopez et al., 2006). In doing so, a counselor must take into account cultural, developmental, gender, sexual orientation, socioeconomic, and spiritual aspects of a client's life as well as coping mechanisms, stressors, and learned behavior (Eriksen & Kress, 2008; Rueth et al., 1998). Sometimes a behavior in a client's life is merely a symptom of a situational problem in living, whereas at other times it is due to the manifestation of a severe disorder. Therefore, difficulties are best represented as occurring on a continuum and counselors must be careful to neither overdiagnose nor underdiagnose. After all, a diagnosis is only as helpful as it is reliable and valid (Sherry, Lyddon, & Henson, 2007). "When a formal diagnosis is made, certain symptoms must exist; [and] they must be severe enough to interfere significantly with the client's life" (Hohenshil, 1996, p. 65). In some cases, a ***dual diagnosis*** will be made, which basically means that an individual is perceived to be carrying both a substance abuse and mental health diagnosis. Such a situation is said to be ***comorbid*** (the two conditions existing simultaneous but independently).

To properly diagnose, a counselor must learn clinical decision-making skills and cultural sensitivity. ***Clinical decision making*** refers to "the intricate decisions professional counselors make when they assess the degree of severity of a client's symptoms, identify a client's level of functioning, and make decisions about a client's prognosis" (Hays, Prosek, & McLeod, 2010). Cultural sensitivity enables counselors to consider behaviors on a broader level. Such a process is important and prevents mislabeling that has often occurred especially in regard to African Americans and other cultural minority groups (Schwartz & Feisthamel, 2009). Unfortunately, in the past, "individuals belonging to typically oppressed groups (e.g., racial/ethnic minorities, women, sexual minorities) [have been] diagnosed with more severe diagnoses" (Hays, Prosek, & McLeod, 2010, p. 114).

It is wise to **delay making a decision initially if a counselor is unsure** of how severe a symptom is. In delaying, a counselor is able to consult with colleagues and think more thoroughly so as to assess as many factors as possible in the client's life (Hill & Ridley, 2001). Cultural sensitivity, sound clinical judgment, and decision making take time, knowledge, and reflection. As a group, accurate clinicians arrive at their final diagnosis later than those who are less accurate (Elstein, Shulman, & Sprafka, 1978).

Finally, in making a diagnosis, a **counselor should consider alternative conceptualizations of behavior**, including developmental meaning (Ivey, Ivey, Myers, & Sweeney, 2005), a continuum of personality dimensions (Oldham & Morris, 1995), and levels of well-being (i.e., whether a person is "flourishing" or "languishing"; Keyes & Lopez, 2002). Substitutes for the DSM have not been widely accepted at this point in time but they hold promise, especially those that expand the DSM by

- including good health and optimal functioning as well as impaired functioning (Lopez et al., 2006),
- including personal strengths and facilitators of growth, so that a more comprehensive picture of a client could be created (Lopez et al., 2006), and
- developing a system of new diagnostic classification based on psychological strengths, such as the VIA Classification of Strengths system (Peterson & Seligman, 2004).

MyCounselingLab™

Go to Topic 1: *Assessment and Diagnosis* in the site (www.MyCounselingLab.com) for *Counseling: A Comprehensive Profession,* Seventh Edition, where you can:

- Find learning outcomes for *Assessment and Diagnosis* along with the national standards that connect to these outcomes.
- Complete Assignments and Activities that can help you more deeply understand the chapter content.
- Apply and practice your understanding of the core skills identified in the chapter with the Building Counseling Skills unit.
- Prepare yourself for professional certification with a Practice for Certification quiz.
- Connect to videos through the Video and Resource Library.

Summary and Conclusion

This chapter has covered the intricacies of testing, assessment, and diagnosis in counseling, with a particular emphasis on the qualities of useful test instruments and the types of tests counselors use. Testing is almost as old as the profession of counseling itself, but the popularity of test use in counseling has varied over the years. Nevertheless, testing will most likely remain an essential part of counseling. Therefore, counselors must be well versed in the types of tests available and their appropriate use in counseling. With this knowledge they can attain greater professional competence and help clients live healthier, more productive lives. Being well informed involves an awareness of the validity, reliability, standardization, and norms of the instruments used. A test that is reliable but not valid is inappropriate. Similarly, an instrument that discriminates against cultural minorities because it has been normed only on the majority population has no value; in fact, it can be quite harmful.

Counselors usually encounter four main types of tests: intelligence/aptitude tests, interest/career tests, personality tests, and achievement tests. A wide variety of instruments are available in each category. Counselors who work with tests must constantly examine current research results to ensure that various instruments are appropriate. They also need to consult with clients to be certain that the tests give clients the type of information they want.

Finally, counselors must be sensitively involved with the interpretation of test data. From the interpretation of tests and other analysis of data, such as behaviors and verbal complaints, counselors make assessments and diagnoses. It is on their assessments and diagnoses that counselors base treatment plans. Such plans should help their clients change unwanted, destructive, or unproductive behaviors, thoughts, or feelings. Therefore, to be accountable and competent, counselors must master all three processes so that they provide the best services possible and their clients benefit.

Counseling Specialties

15 Career Counseling over the Life Span

Chapter Overview

From reading this chapter you will learn about

- The importance of career counseling and the scope of career counseling

- Major career counseling theories and techniques, (e.g., developmental, social–cognitive)

- Career counseling with diverse populations, (e.g., children, adolescents, adults, women, GLBTs, and cultural minorities)

As you read consider

- How career counseling is similar to and different from personal counseling

- What career theory or theories appeal to you most and why

- The challenges of career counseling with populations you are not as familiar with and what you can do to help make yourself more prepared

Far in the back of his mind he harbors thoughts
    like small boats in a quiet cove
        ready to set sail at a moment's notice.
I, seated on his starboard side,
    listen for the winds of change
        ready to lift anchor with him
        and explore the choppy waves of life ahead.
Counseling requires a special patience
    best known to seamen and navigators—
        courses are only charted for times
        when the tide is high and the breezes steady.

Reprinted from "Harbor Thoughts," by S. T. Gladding, 1985, *Journal of Humanistic Education and Development, 23,* p. 68. © 1985 by Samuel T. Gladding.

MyCounselingLab™

Visit the MyCounselingLab™ site (www.MyCounselingLab.com) for *Counseling: A Comprehensive Profession,* Seventh Edition to enhance your understanding of chapter concepts. You'll have the opportunity to practice your skills through video- and case-based Assignments and Activities as well as Building Counseling Skills units and to prepare for your certification exam with Practice for Certification quizzes.

The counseling profession began charting its course when Frank Parsons (1909) outlined a process for choosing a career and initiated the vocational guidance movement. According to Parsons, it is better to choose a vocation than merely to hunt for a job. Since his ideas first came into prominence, a voluminous amount of research and theory has been generated in the field of career development and counseling.

Choosing a career is more than simply deciding what one will do to earn a living. Occupations influence a person's whole way of life, including physical and mental health. "There are interconnections between work roles and other life roles" (Imbimbo, 1994, p. 50). Thus, income, stress, social identity, meaning, education, clothes, hobbies, interests, friends, lifestyle, place of residence, and even personality characteristics are tied to one's work life (Herr, Cramer, & Niles, 2004). Qualitative research indicates that individuals who appear most happy in their work are committed to following their interests, exhibit a breadth of personal competencies and strengths, and function in work environments that are characterized by freedom, challenge, meaning, and a positive social atmosphere (Henderson, 2000).

Yet despite the evidence of the importance of a person's work, systematically exploring and choosing careers often does not happen. Nearly one in five American workers reports getting his or her current job by chance, and more than 60% of workers in the United States would investigate job choices more thoroughly if they could plan their work lives again (Hoyt, 1989). Therefore, it is important that individuals obtain career information early and enter the job market with knowledge and flexibility in regard to their plans.

The process of selecting a career is unique to each individual. It is influenced by a variety of factors. For instance, personality styles, developmental stages, and life roles come into play (Drummond & Ryan, 1995). Happenstance and serendipity (Guindon & Hanna, 2002), family background (Chope, 2006), gender (Watt & Eccles, 2008), giftedness (Maxwell, 2007), and age (Canaff, 1997) may also influence the selection of a career. In addition, the global economy at the time one decides on a career is a factor (Andersen & Vandehey, 2012). In the industrial age, punctuality, obedience, and rote work performance were the skills needed to be successful; in the present technological-service economy, emphasis is on "competitive teamwork, customer satisfaction, continual learning, and innovation" (Staley & Carey, 1997, p. 379).

Because an enormous amount of literature on careers is available, this chapter can provide only an overview of the area. It will concentrate on career development and counseling from a holistic, life-span perspective (as first proposed by Norman Gysbers). In the process, theories and tasks appropriate for working with a variety of clients will be examined.

THE IMPORTANCE OF CAREER COUNSELING

Despite its long history and the formulation of many models, career counseling has not enjoyed the same degree of prestige that other forms of counseling or psychotherapy have. This is unfortunate for both the counseling profession and the many people who need these services. Surveys of high school juniors and seniors and college undergraduates show that one of the counseling services they most prefer is career counseling. Brown (1985) also posits that career counseling may be a viable intervention for some clients who have emotional problems related to nonsupportive, stress-producing environments. The contribution of career counseling to personal and relational growth and development is well documented (Krumboltz, 1994; Schultheiss, 2003). In fact, Herr and colleagues (2004) contend that a variety of life difficulties and mental problems ensue when one's career or work life is unsatisfactory.

Crites (1981, pp. 14–15) lists **important aspects of career counseling**, which include the following:

1. *"The need for career counseling is greater than the need for psychotherapy."* Career counseling deals with the inner and outer world of individuals, whereas most other counseling approaches deal only with internal events.
2. *"Career counseling can be therapeutic."* A positive correlation exists between career and personal adjustment (Crites, 1969; Hinkelman & Luzzo, 2007; Krumboltz, 1994; Super, 1957). Clients who successfully cope with career decisions may gain skill and confidence in the ability to tackle other problem areas. They may invest more energy into resolving noncareer problems because they have clarified career objectives. Although Brown (1985) provides a set of assessment strategies that are useful in determining whether a client needs personal or career counseling first, Krumboltz (1994) asserts that career and personal counseling are inextricably intertwined and often must be treated together. Indeed, research data refute the perspective "that career help seekers are different from non-career help seekers" (Dollarhide, 1997, p. 180). For example, people who lose jobs and fear they will never find other positions have both a career problem and a personal anxiety problem. It is imperative to treat such people in a holistic manner by offering information on the intellectual aspects of finding a career and working with them to face and overcome their emotional concerns about seeking a new job or direction in life.
3. *"Career counseling is more difficult than psychotherapy."* Crites states that, to be an effective career counselor, a person must deal with both personal and work variables and know how the two interact. "Being knowledgeable and proficient in career counseling requires that counselors draw from a variety of both personality and career development theories and techniques and that they continuously be able to gather and provide current information about the world of work" (Imbimbo, 1994, p. 51). The same is not equally true for counseling, which often focuses on the inner world of the client.

PERSONAL REFLECTION

How did you become interested in the career you are pursuing? Did you receive any career counseling? If so, was it helpful? If not, what use might you have made of career counseling?

CAREER COUNSELING ASSOCIATIONS AND CREDENTIALS

The **National Career Development Association, or NCDA** (formerly the National Vocational Guidance Association, or NVGA; http://ncda.org/), and the **National Employment Counselors Association, or NECA** (http://geocities.com/employmentcounseling/neca.html), are the two divisions within the American Counseling Association (ACA) primarily devoted to career development and counseling. The NCDA, the oldest division within the ACA, traces its roots back to 1913 (Sheeley, 1978, 1988; Stephens, 1988). The association comprises professionals in business and industry, rehabilitation agencies, government, private practice, and educational settings who affiliate with the NCDA's special-interest groups, such as Work and Mental Health, Substance Abuse in the Workplace, and Employee Assistance Programs (Parker, 1994; Smith, Engels, & Bonk, 1985). The NECA's membership is also diverse but more focused. Until 1966, it was an interest group of the NCDA (Meyer, Helwig, Gjernes, & Chickering, 1985). Both divisions publish quarterly journals: the *Career Development Quarterly* (formerly the *Vocational Guidance Quarterly*) and the *Journal of Employment Counseling*, respectively.

THE SCOPE OF CAREER COUNSELING AND CAREERS

Career counseling is a hybrid discipline, often misunderstood and not always fully appreciated by many helping professionals, businesspeople, the public, or the government (Hoyt, 2005). The NCDA defines *career counseling* as a "process of assisting individuals in the development of a life-career with a focus on the definition of the worker role and how that role interacts with other life roles" (p. 2).

Throughout its history, career counseling has been known by a number of different names, including *vocational guidance, occupational counseling*, and *vocational counseling*. Crites (1981) emphasizes that the word *career* is more modern and inclusive than the word *vocation*. *Career* is also broader than the word *occupation*, which Herr et al. (2004) define as a group of similar jobs found in different industries or organizations. A *job* is merely an activity undertaken for economic returns (Fox, 1994).

Career counselors clearly must consider many factors when helping persons make career decisions. Among these factors are avocational interests, age or stage in life, maturity, gender, familial obligations, and civic roles (Shallcross, 2009a). Some of these factors are represented in various ways. For example, the integration and interaction of work and leisure in one's career over the life span according to McDaniels (1984) is expressed in the formula $C = W + L$, where *C* equals *career*; *W*, *work*; and *L*, *leisure* (Gale, 1998, p. 206).

All theories of counseling are potentially applicable and useful in working with individuals on career choices, but people gain understanding and insight about themselves and how they fit into the world of work through educational means as well as counseling relationships. Well-informed persons may need fewer counseling services than others and respond more positively to this form of helping.

CAREER INFORMATION

The NCDA (then the NVGA) has defined *career information* as "information related to the world of work that can be useful in the process of career development, including educational, occupational, and psychosocial information related to working, e.g., availability of training, the nature of work, and status of workers in different occupations" (Sears, 1982, p. 139). A more modern term for career information is *career data* meaning "a collection of facts about occupational and educational opportunities" (Niles & Harris-Bowlsbey, 2009, p. 176). Data become information only when they are "understood by clients and used to inform decision making, that is, to assist them to choose one alternative over another" (p. 177).

As has been discussed in previous chapters, the word *guidance* is usually reserved for activities that are primarily educational. *Career guidance* involves all activities that seek to disseminate information about present or future vocations in such a way that individuals become more knowledgeable and aware about who they are in relation to the world of work. Guidance activities can take the form of

- *career fairs* (inviting practitioners in a number of fields to explain their jobs),
- library assignments,
- outside interviews,
- computer-assisted information experiences,
- *career shadowing* (following someone around on his or her daily work routine),
- didactic lectures, and
- experiential exercises such as role-playing.

Career guidance and the dissemination of career information is traditionally pictured as an educational activity. However, this process is often conducted outside a classroom environment—for example, at governmental agencies, industries, libraries, and homes or with a private practitioner (Harris-Bowlsbey, 1992). According to C. H. Patterson, career guidance is "for people who are pretty normal and have no emotional problems that would interfere with developing a rational approach to making a vocational or career choice" (Freeman, 1990, p. 292). Many government and educational agencies (such as the National Career Information System [NCIS] in Eugene, Oregon) computerize information about occupations and disseminate it through libraries. Overall, the ways of becoming informed about careers are extensive.

Not all ways of learning are as effective as others are, however, and those who fail to personalize career information to specific situations often have difficulty making vocational decisions. The result may be **unrealistic aspirations**, goals beyond a person's capabilities (Salomone & McKenna, 1982). Therefore, it is vital to provide qualitative and quantitative information to individuals who are deciding about careers including the nature of the career decision process, such as mentioning that "career decidedness develops over time" and "the decision-making process is complex, not simple" (Krieshok, 1998). Knowledge of career information and the processes associated with it does not guarantee self-exploration in career development, but good career decisions cannot be made without these data. A lack of enough information or up-to-date information is one reason that individuals fail to make decisions or make unwise choices.

Several publications are considered classic references for finding in-depth and current information on careers and trends. They include the government-published *Dictionary of Occupational Titles (DOT)* which has now been transformed into the Occupational Information Network (O*Net) and put online (www.doleta.gov/programs/onet) by the U.S. Department of Labor as a replacement for the *DOT*. *O*Net* is a comprehensive database that provides information about approximately 975 occupations, worker skills, and job training requirements. It is updated regularly. Likewise, the *Occupational Outlook Handbook* (www.bls.gov/oco/home.htm) and other major publications of the Department of Labor have been put on the Web. Career counselors can also make use of applied technology outside the government, especially the use of electronic career searches.

CASE EXAMPLE

Mugsy Bogues and Basketball

On a good day Mugsy Bogues stood 5 foot 3 inches tall and weighed 136 pounds. Yet he went on to play college basketball and then to play 14 years in the National Basketball Association (NBA).

He was an exceptional passer, a ball stealer, and one of the fastest men on the court. He came from an impoverished background and yet attained fame and fortune at the end of the 20th century.

How does a case like Mugsy Bogues reflect on the value of career counseling? (Would any career counselor have advised him in high school or college to try to play professional basketball?)

A number of *computer-based career planning systems (CBCPSs)* and *computer-assisted career guidance systems (CACGS)* offer career information and help individuals sort through their values and interests or find job information. One of the beauties of computer-based and computer-assisted career planning and guidance systems is their accessibility: They are available in many settings and with diverse people across cultures and the life span (Niles & Harris-Bowlsbey, 2009; Sampson & Bloom, 2001). Some of the top programs include *SIGI³* (*System of Interactive Guidance and Information*, with "*3*" indicating a refinement of the system), *DISCOVER*, and the Kuder Career Planning System (Maples & Luzzo, 2005).

SIGI³ (www.valparint.com/sigi.htm; Katz, 1975, 1993) contains **five components** with a focal point on

1. **self-assessment (Values),**
2. **identification of occupational alternatives (Locate),**
3. **review of occupational information (Compare),**
4. **review of information on preparation programs (Planning),** and
5. **making tentative occupational choices (Strategy).**

By using SIGI³, searchers are able to clarify their values, locate and identify occupational options, compare choices, learn planning skills, and develop rational career decision-making skills.

DISCOVER (www.act.org; ACT, 1998) contains **nine modules**:

1. **Beginning the career journey**
2. **Learning about the world of work**
3. **Learning about yourself**
4. **Finding occupations**
5. **Learning about occupations**
6. **Making educational choices**
7. **Planning next steps**
8. **Planning your career**
9. **Making transitions**

Most users of DISCOVER proceed through the modules in a sequential order, but the modules may be accessed on demand depending on need.

The *Kuder Career Planning System* (www.kuder.com) offers a comprehensive solution for career planners at all stages of career development. It includes, among other things, the Kuder Online Career Portfolio and Research-Based Assessments. The **Online Career Portfolio** provides lifelong career planning that allows individuals to store personal and academic information, search and save educational and occupational data, build resumes, and access assessment progress and results from any Internet connection. The **Research-Based Assessments**, which are available in either English or Spanish, help system users discover their interests, skills, and work values and how those characteristics relate to the world of work.

Ways of enhancing computer-based career planning systems and computer-assisted career guidance systems are constantly being implemented, including interactive programs (Niles & Harris-Bowlsbey, 2009; Zunker, 2012). No matter how sophisticated the programs, however, it is wise to have trained career counselors available to assist those individuals who may make use of this technology but still have questions about its applicability to their lives (Walker-Staggs, 2000).

In addition to these instruments, there are career choices curriculums developed by the ***National Occupational Information Coordinating Committee (NOICC)*** that can be used in educational settings such as high schools to provide career information that is relevant to students in English, math, and social science classes.

Furthermore, some self-help books, such as Bolles (2012) *What Color Is Your Parachute?* and Kay's (2006) *Life's a Bitch and Then You Change Careers: 9 Steps to Get Out of Your Funk and on to Your Future*, are still available in print form. These books outline practical steps most individuals, from late adolescence on, can follow to define personal values and successfully complete career-seeking tasks, such as writing a resume. These texts also provide a wealth of information on how to locate positions of specific interest.

CAREER DEVELOPMENT THEORIES AND COUNSELING

Career development theories try to explain why individuals choose careers. They also deal with the career adjustments people make over time. Modern theories, which are broad and comprehensive in regard to individual and occupational development, began appearing in the literature in the 1950s (Gysbers, Heppner, & Johnstone, 2003). The theories described here (i.e., trait-and-factor, developmental, and social–cognitive) and the counseling procedures that go with them are among the most prominent and widely used in the field of career counseling.

Trait-and-Factor Theory

The origin of ***trait-and-factor theory*** can be traced back to Frank Parsons. It stresses that the traits of clients should first be assessed and then systematically matched with factors inherent in various occupations. Its most widespread influence occurred during the Great Depression when E. G. Williamson (1939) championed its use. It was out of favor during the 1950s and 1960s but has resurfaced in a more modern form, which is best characterized as "structural" and is reflected in the work of researchers such as John Holland (1997). The trait-and-factor approach has always stressed the uniqueness of persons. Original advocates of the theory assumed that a person's abilities and traits could be measured objectively and quantified. Personal motivation was considered relatively stable. Thus, satisfaction in a particular occupation depended on a proper fit between one's abilities and the job requirements.

In its modern form, trait-and-factor theory stresses the interpersonal nature of careers and associated lifestyles as well as the performance requirements of a work position. Holland (1997) identifies **six categories in which personality types and occupational environments can be classified: realistic, investigative, artistic, social, enterprising, and conventional (RIASEC)** (Figure 15.1). Ranked according to prestige, investigative (I) occupations rank highest, followed by enterprising (E), artistic (A), and social (S) occupations, which have roughly the same level of prestige. The lowest levels of prestige are realistic (R) and conventional (C) occupations (Gottfredson, 1981).

In an analysis of census data using the Holland codes, Reardon, Bullock, and Meyer (2007) confirmed that the distribution across Holland's types is asymmetrical. They found that from

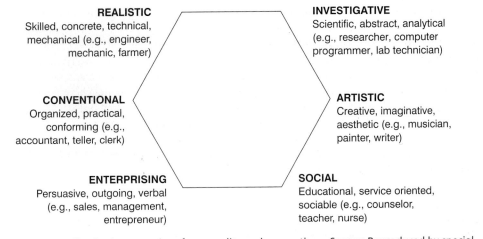

REALISTIC
Skilled, concrete, technical, mechanical (e.g., engineer, mechanic, farmer)

INVESTIGATIVE
Scientific, abstract, analytical (e.g., researcher, computer programmer, lab technician)

CONVENTIONAL
Organized, practical, conforming (e.g., accountant, teller, clerk)

ARTISTIC
Creative, imaginative, aesthetic (e.g., musician, painter, writer)

ENTERPRISING
Persuasive, outgoing, verbal (e.g., sales, management, entrepreneur)

SOCIAL
Educational, service oriented, sociable (e.g., counselor, teacher, nurse)

FIGURE 15.1   Holland's six categories of personality and occupation   *Source:* Reproduced by special permission of the Publisher, Psychological Assessment Resources, Inc., from *Making Vocational Choices: A Theory of Careers, Third Edition*, copyright 1973, 1985, 1992, 1997 by Psychological Assessment Resources, Inc. All rights reserved.

1960 to 2000 "the Realistic area had the largest number of individuals employed and that the Artistic area had the fewest number employed" (p. 266). The gap between the number of people employed in the Realistic and Enterprising areas shrank during the five decades to where in 2000 there were approximately equal numbers of people employed in both areas. Interestingly, the Investigative area more than doubled during this time whereas the other four areas remained relatively stable. Regardless of age, between 75% and 85% of male workers were employed in the Realistic and Enterprising areas; women were more varied and concentrated in Conventional, Realistic, Social, and (more recently) Enterprising areas.

Personal satisfaction in a work setting depends on a number of factors, but among the most important are the degree of congruence between personality type, work environment, and social class (Gade, Fuqua, & Hurlburt, 1988; Holland & Gottfredson, 1976; Savickas, 2012; Trusty, Robinson, Plata, & Ng, 2000). Also as a general rule, with notable exceptions, "women value language-related tasks more, and men value mathematics-related tasks more" (Trusty et al., 2000, p. 470). Some nonpsychological factors, such as economic or cultural influences, account for why many professional and nonprofessional workers accept and keep their jobs (Brown, 2012; Salomone & Sheehan, 1985).

Nevertheless, as Holland emphasizes, it is vital for persons to have adequate knowledge of themselves and occupational requirements to make informed career decisions. According to Holland, a three-letter code represents a client's overall personality, which can be matched with a type of work environment. Three-letter codes tend to remain relatively stable over the life span beginning as early as high school (Miller, 2002). A profile of SAE would suggest a person is most similar to a social type, then an artistic type, and finally an enterprising type. However, it is the interaction of letter codes that influences the makeup of the person and his or her fit in an occupational environment. Miller (1998) suggests that, instead of using the three highest scores on Holland's hexagon for such a purpose, the top two, middle two, and lowest two scores should be paired and presented to give the client a fuller picture of his or her personality profile and similarity to others in a given career. Given the first criteria, Donald Super's profile would be

S/I/R, whereas John Holland's would be A/E/IRS. The second criteria would yield a profile for Super of SI/RA/EC, with Holland's profile being AE/IR/SC (Weinrach, 1996).

Trait-and-factor career counseling is sometimes inappropriately caricatured as "three interviews and a cloud of dust." The first interview session is spent getting to know a client's background and assigning tests. The client then takes a battery of tests and returns for the second interview to have the counselor interpret the results of the tests. In the third session, the client reviews career choices in light of the data presented and is sent out by the counselor to find further information on specific careers. Williamson (1972) originally implemented this theory to help clients learn self-management skills. But as Crites (1969, 1981) notes, trait-and-factor career counselors may ignore the psychological realities of decision making and fail to promote self-help skills in their clients. Such counselors may overemphasize test information, which clients either forget or distort.

CASE STUDY

Hannah and the Hammer

Hannah loved tools from the time she was a little girl. Now as an 11th grader, she wondered whether she should go to a liberal arts college or a trade school. She saw advantages to both. Her dad was a carpenter and her mother a teacher. They simply told her they would help her regardless of what she decided to do. Her Holland profile was a bit unusual: SR/CA/IE. She was ambivalent.

What advice might you give to Hannah about her upcoming decision if you were a trait-and-factor career counselor?

Developmental Theories

Two of the most widely known career theories are those associated with Donald Super and Eli Ginzberg. They are both based on personal development. The original developmental theory proposed by Ginzberg and associates (Ginzberg, Ginsburg, Axelrad, & Herma, 1951) has had considerable influence and has been revised (Ginzberg, 1972). However, Super's theory is examined in detail here because more extensive work has been done with it and it has overshadowed other developmental approaches to career counseling.

Compared with other theoretical propositions, **developmental theories** are generally more inclusive, more concerned with longitudinal expression of career behavior, and more inclined to highlight the importance of self-concept. Super (1957, 1990) believed that making a career choice is "linked with implementing one's vocational self-concept" (Hinkelman & Luzzo, 2007, p. 143). People's views of themselves are reflected in what they do. He suggested that vocational development unfolds in **five stages**, each of which contains a developmental task to be completed (Table 15.1). The first stage is *growth* (from birth to age 14). During this stage, with its substages of fantasy (ages 4–10), interest (ages 11–12), and capacity (ages 13–14), children form a mental picture of themselves in relation to others. Support affirming the multiple dimensions of this stage in Super's theory has been substantiated (Palladino Schultheiss, Palma, & Manzi, 2005). During the process of growth, children become oriented to the world of work in many ways (e.g., exploration, information, interests, etc.).

The second stage, *exploration* (ages 14–24), has three substages: tentative (ages 14–17), transition (ages 18–21), and trial (ages 22–24). The major task of this stage is a general exploration of the world of work and the specification of a career preference.

TABLE 15.1 Super's Stages

Growth	Exploration	Establishment	Maintenance	Decline
Birth to Age 14	**Ages 14 to 24**	**Ages 24 to 44**	**Ages 44 to 64**	**Ages 64 and Beyond**
Self-concept develops through identification with key figures in family and school; needs and fantasy are dominant early in this stage; interest and capacity become more important with increasing social participation and reality testing; learn behaviors associated with self-help, social interaction, self-direction, industrialness, goal setting, persistence.	Self-examination, role tryouts, and occupational exploration take place in school, leisure activities, and part-time work.	Having found an appropriate field, an effort is made to establish a permanent place in it. Thereafter changes that occur are changes of position, job, or employer, not of occupation.	Having made a place in the world of work, the concern is how to hold on to it. Little new ground is broken, continuation of established pattern. Concerned about maintaining present status while being forced by competition from younger workers in the advancement stage.	As physical and mental powers decline, work activity changes and in due course ceases. New roles must be developed: first, selective participant and then observer. Individual must find other sources of satisfaction to replace those lost through retirement.
Substages	**Substages**	**Substages**		**Substages**
Fantasy (4–10) Needs are dominant; role-playing in fantasy is important.	*Tentative* (15–17) Needs, interests, capacities, values and opportunities are all considered; tentative choices are made and tried out in fantasy, discussion, courses, work, and so on. Possible appropriate fields and levels of work are identified.	*Trial-Commitment and Stabilization* (25–30) Settling down. Securing a permanent place in the chosen occupation. May prove unsatisfactory resulting in one or two changes before the life work is found or before it becomes clear that the life work will be a succession of unrelated jobs.		*Deceleration* (65–70) The pace of work slackens, duties are shifted, or the nature of work is changed to suit declining capacities. Many find part-time jobs to replace their full-time occupations.
Interest (11–12) Likes are the major determinant of aspirations and activities.				*Retirement* (71 on) Variation on complete cessation of work or shift to part-time, volunteer, or leisure activities.
Capacity (13–14) Abilities are given more weight and job requirements (including training) are considered.		*Advancement* (31–44) Effort is put forth to stabilize, to make a secure place in the world of work. For most persons these are the creative years. Seniority is acquired; clientele are developed; superior performance is demonstrated; qualifications are improved.		

(continued)

TABLE 15.1 Super's Stages *(Continued)*

Growth	Exploration	Establishment	Maintenance	Decline
Tasks	**Task—Crystallizing a Vocational Preference**	**Tasks**	**Tasks**	**Tasks**
Developing a picture of the kind of person one is. Developing an orientation to the world of work and an understanding of the meaning of work.	*Transition* (18–21) Reality considerations are given more weight as the person enters the labor market or professional training and attempts to implement a self-concept. Generalized choice is converted to specific choice.	Finding opportunity to do desired work. Learning to relate to others. Consolidation and advancement. Making occupational position secure. Settling down in a permanent position.	Accepting one's limitations. Identifying new problems to work on. Developing new skills. Focusing on essential activities. Preservation of achieved status and gains.	Developing nonoccupational roles. Finding a good retirement spot. Doing things one has always wanted to do. Reducing working hours.
	Task—Specifying a Vocational Preference *Trial-Little Commitment* (22–24) A seemingly appropriate occupation having been found, a first job is located and is tried out as a potential life work. Commitment is still provisional, and if the job is not appropriate, the person may reinstitute the process of crystallizing, specifying, and implementing a preference. Implementing a vocational preference. Developing a realistic self-concept. Learning more about more opportunities.			

Source: From Edwin L. Herr, Stanley H. Cramer, and Spencer Niles, *Career Guidance and Counseling Through the Life Span: Systematic Approaches, 6/e.* Published by Allyn and Bacon, Boston, MA. Copyright © 2004 by Pearson Education. Reprinted by permission of the publisher.

The third stage is known as *establishment* (ages 24–44). Its two substages, trial (ages 24–30) and advancement (ages 31–44), constitute the major task of becoming established in a preferred and appropriate field of work. Once established, persons can concentrate on advancement until they tire of their job or reach the top of the profession.

The fourth stage, *maintenance* (ages 44–64), has the major task of preserving what one has already achieved. The final stage, *decline* (age 65 to death), is a time for disengagement from work and alignment with other sources of satisfaction. It has two substages: deceleration (ages 65–70) and retirement (age 71 to death).

The major contributions of developmental career counseling are its emphases on the importance of the life span in career decision making and on career decisions that are influenced by other processes and events in a person's life. This "life pattern paradigm for career counseling encourages counselors to consider a client's aptitudes and interests in a matrix of life experiences, not just in comparison to some normative group" (Savickas, 1989, p. 127).

The developmental approach can be conceptualized as *career-pattern counseling* (Super, 1954a). Although this method has been criticized for its historical and descriptive emphases, these features, along with the conceptual depth of the theory, have also been considered strengths (Herr, 1997). Overall, developmental career counseling as conceptualized by Super has a number of applications. "For example, it has been used as the framework for career development programs for children and adolescents" (Brown, 2012, p. 54). In addition, the comprehensive *rainbow theory* that Super conceptualized toward the end of his life continues to attract research interest (Super, 1990; Super, Thompson, & Lindeman, 1988) (Figure 15.2). Finally, the theory has been used not only as the basis for career counseling but also for attempts at understanding

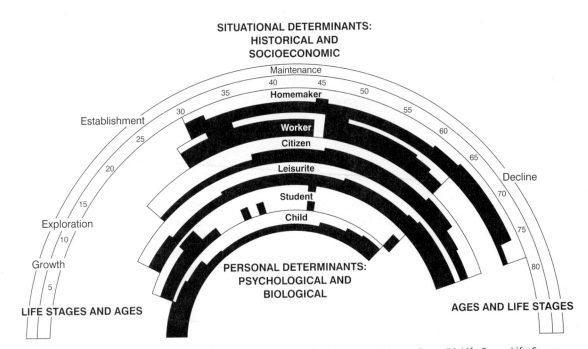

FIGURE 15.2 Super's rainbow theory: Six life roles in schematic life space   *Source:* From "A Life-Span, Life-Space Approach to Career Development," by D. E. Super, 1980, *Journal of Vocational Behavior, 16*, pp. 282–298. Copyright 1980 by Academic Press. Reprinted by permission.

the development of career maturity. One of the drawbacks to Super's approach, however, is its applicability to groups other than those with a Eurocentric background, such as Asian Americans who subscribe to more collaborative social values.

Social–Cognitive Career Theory

Social–cognitive career theory (SCCT) was first published in 1994 and has had a tremendous impact on research regarding career choice. It stems from the initial work of Albert Bandura and his emphasis on the "triadic reciprocal model of causality, which assumes that personal attributes, the environment, and overt behavior" operate with each other in an interlocking bidirectional way (Niles & Harris-Bowlsbey, 2009, p. 87). The most important part of this triad is *self-efficacy*—that is, "a person's beliefs regarding her or his ability to successfully perform a particular task" (Maples & Luzzo, 2005, p. 275).

Among other central propositions of SCCT are the following:

1. "The interaction between people and their environments is highly dynamic" (i.e., they influence each other)
2. "Career-related behavior is influenced by four aspects of the person: behavior, self-efficacy, outcome expectations, and goals in addition to genetically determined characteristics"
3. "Self-efficacy beliefs and expectations of outcomes interact directly to influence interest development"
4. In addition to expectations of outcome, factors such as "gender, race, physical health, disabilities, and environmental variables influence self-efficacy development"
5. "Actual career choice and implementation are influenced by a number of direct and indirect variables other than self-efficacy, expectations, and goals" (e.g., discrimination, economic variables, and chance happenings)
6. "All things being equal, people with the highest levels of ability and the strongest self-efficacy beliefs perform at the highest level" (Brown, 2012, p. 69).

One other important assumption of SCCT is that "self-efficacy and interests are linked" and interests "can be developed or strengthened using modeling, encouragement, and most powerfully, by performance enactment. Therefore, groups of clients, such as women [and minorities] who may have little opportunity to engage in certain activities because of sex-typing [or discrimination], can benefit from the application of this theory" (Brown, 2007, p. 70).

Social–cognitive career theory can be used in a number of settings. For instance, it can be used with rural Appalachian youth to help them develop, change, and go after career interests (Ali & Saunders, 2006). It can also be used with first-generation college students who need information that will counteract incorrect beliefs they may have (Gibbons & Shoffner, 2004). Overall, SCCT-based interventions can be used with diverse groups. "An additional strength of SCCT is that it addresses both intra-individual and contextual variables in career development" (Niles & Harris-Bowlsbey, 2009, p. 91).

Krumboltz (1979, 1996) has formulated an equally comprehensive but less developmental social–cognitive approach to career development. He takes the position that **four factors influence a person's career choice:**

- genetic endowment,
- conditions and events in the environment,
- learning experiences, and
- task-approach skills (e.g., values, work habits).

According to Krumboltz, career decisions are controlled by both internal and external processes. There is continuous learning that results in what Krumboltz labels

- *self-observation generalizations,* an overt or covert self-statement of evaluation that may or may not be true;
- *task-approach skills,* an effort by people to project their self-observation generalizations into the future in order to predict future events; and
- *actions,* implementations of behaviors, such as applying for a job.

Overall, a strength of Krumboltz's theory is that it views people as having some control over events they find reinforcing. Whereas individuals and the world change, persons can learn to take advantage of learning opportunities and make career decisions accordingly. "In summary, Krumboltz outlines a dynamic approach to career counseling that can be applied to males and females, as well as to racial and ethnic minorities who have individualistic perspectives" (Brown, 2012, p. 68).

CAREER COUNSELING WITH DIVERSE POPULATIONS

Career counseling and education are conducted with a wide variety of individuals in diverse settings. Brown (1985) observes that career counseling typically is offered in college counseling centers, rehabilitation facilities, employment offices, and public schools. He thinks it could be applied with great advantage in many other places as well, including mental health centers and private practice offices. Jesser (1983) agrees, asserting that there is a need to provide career information and counseling to potential users, such as people who are unemployed, learning disabled, in prison, and those released from mental hospitals who seek to reenter the job market. Reimbursement is a drawback to offering career counseling outside its traditional populations and settings. Career concerns are not covered in the DSM, and most health care coverage excludes this service from reimbursement.

This lack of coverage is unfortunate because many people have **difficulties making career decisions**. These difficulties are related to three factors present both prior to and during the decision-making process. These factors are:

- **lack of readiness,**
- **lack of information**, and
- **inconsistent information**.

Because the concept of careers encompasses the life span, counselors who specialize in this area find themselves working with a full age range of clients, from young children to octogenarians. Consequently, many different approaches and techniques have been developed for working effectively with select groups.

Career Counseling with Children

The process of career development begins in the preschool years and becomes more direct in elementary schools. Herr and colleagues (2004) cite numerous studies to show that during the first 6 years of school, many children develop a relatively stable self-perception and make a tentative commitment to a vocation. These processes are observed whether career counseling and guidance activities are offered or not. Nevertheless, it is beneficial for children, especially those who live in areas with limited employment opportunities, to have a broad, systematic program of career counseling and guidance in the schools. Such programs should focus on awareness rather than firm decision making. They should provide as many experiential activities as possible and should help children realize that they have career choices. As children progress in the elementary school grades, they should receive more detailed information about careers and become acquainted with career opportunities that might transcend socioeconomic levels and gender (Bobo, Hildreth, & Durodoye, 1998).

Jesser (1983) suggests that levels of career awareness in elementary schoolchildren may be raised through activities such as field trips to local industries, bakeries, manufacturing plants, or banks. For example, "because pizza is an immediate attention getter with elementary school children, a field trip to a pizza restaurant can provide an entertaining learning experience" (Beale & Nugent, 1996, p. 294). When such trips are carefully preplanned, implemented, and followed up with appropriate classroom learning exercises (e.g., class discussions), children become aware of a wider spectrum of related occupations, the value of work, and the importance of teams in carrying out tasks. For instance, for a pizza parlor to run efficiency there have to be dishwashers, cashiers, managers, and waitressing staff as well as pizza makers.

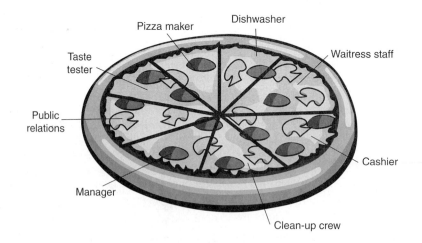

Other ways of expanding children's awareness of careers are through "inviting parents into the elementary classroom and encouraging parents to invite students into their work environments" (Wahl & Blackhurst, 2000, p. 372). Such a process capitalizes on parents' influence as role models and may be especially helpful for children whose parents are unemployed or underemployed. To break down children's stereotypes connected with careers, persons who hold nontraditional occupations may be invited to speak. Reading stories about or seeing videos about persons and their typical activities on jobs may likewise be helpful. For example, the *Children's Dictionary of Occupations* (Paramore, Hopke, & Drier, 2004) and other publications like it that contain student activity packages are excellent sources of accurate information.

Splete (1982b) outlines a comprehensive program for working with children that includes parent education and classroom discussions jointly planned by the teacher and counselor. He emphasizes that there are three key career development areas at the elementary school level: self-awareness (i.e., one's uniqueness), career awareness and exploration, and decision making. Well-designed career guidance and counseling programs that are implemented at an early age and coordinated with programs across all levels of the educational system can go a long way toward dispelling irrational and decision-hindering career development myths, such as "a career decision is an event that should occur at a specific point in time" (Lewis & Gilhousen, 1981, p. 297).

PERSONAL REFLECTION

Think about careers that you aspired to during childhood (before the age of 12). List as many as you can think of but at least five. How similar are they to each other according to John Holland's code? How similar are they to the profession of counseling?

Career Counseling with Adolescents

In working with adolescents in regard to career matters, the American School Counselor Association (ASCA) National Model (2005) emphasizes that school counselors should provide career counseling on a school-wide basis. This service should involve others, both inside and outside the school, in its delivery.

Cole (1982) stresses that in middle school, career guidance activities should include the exploration of work opportunities and students' evaluation of their own strengths and weaknesses in regard to possible future careers. Assets that students should become aware of and begin to evaluate include talents and skills, general intelligence, motivation level, friends, family, life experience, appearance, and health (Campbell, 1974). "Applied arts curriculum such as industrial arts (applied technology), home economics (family life education) and computer literacy classes . . . offer ideal opportunities for integrated career education. Libraries and/or career centers may have special middle level computerized *career information delivery systems (CIDS)* for student use" (NOICC, 1994, p. 9). The four components common to most CIDS are "assessment, occupational search, occupational information, and educational information" (Gysbers et al., 2003, p. 135). Overall, "career exploration is an important complement to the intellectual and social development" of middle school students (Craig, Contreras, & Peterson, 2000, p. 24).

At the senior high school, career guidance and counseling activities are related to students' maturity. Some students know themselves better than others. Regardless, many high school students benefit from using self-knowledge as a beginning point for exploring careers (Roudebush, 2011). The greatest challenge and need for career development programs occur on this level, especially in the area of acquiring basic skills (Bynner, 1997). In general, career counseling at the high school level has three emphases: stimulating career development, providing treatment, and aiding placement. More specifically, counselors provide students with reassurance, information, emotional support, reality testing, planning strategies, attitude clarification, and work experiences, depending on a student's needs and level of functioning (Herr et al., 2004).

Several techniques have proven quite effective in helping adolescents crystallize ideas about careers. Some are mainly cognitive whereas others are more experiential and comprehensive. Among the cognitive techniques is the use of guided fantasies, such as imagining a typical day in the future, an awards ceremony, a midcareer change, or retirement (Morgan & Skovholt, 1977). Another cognitive technique involves the providing of fundamental information about career entry and development. For example, a career day or a career fair "featuring employers and professionals from a variety of occupations allows students to make a realistic comparison of each occupation's primary duties, day-to-day activities, and training needs" (Wahl & Blackhurst, 2000, p. 372). Completing an occupational family tree to find out how present interests compare with the careers of family members is a final cognitive approach that may be useful (Dickson & Parmerlee, 1980).

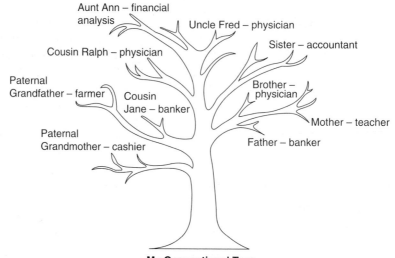

Aunt Ann – financial analysis

Uncle Fred – physician

Cousin Ralph – physician

Sister – accountant

Paternal Grandfather – farmer

Cousin Jane – banker

Brother – physician

Mother – teacher

Paternal Grandmother – cashier

Father – banker

My Occupational Tree

More experiential and comprehensive techniques include offering youth apprenticeships. These apprenticeships are a popular approach that provides work-based learning for adolescents. Apprenticeships also help students who are not college-bound make a smooth transition from high school to the primary work environment. Although apprenticeships hold much promise, they pose several challenges for career counselors such as

> (a) helping clients learn adaptive skills that will enable them to change with change, (b) helping clients find ways to acquire the kinds of work [identified in government reports], and (c) helping clients to develop a personally meaningful set of work values that will enable them to humanize the workplace for themselves and thus receive the personal satisfaction that comes from true work. (Hoyt, 1994, p. 222)

In addition to helping youth in school, career counselors must make special efforts to help high school students who leave school before graduation (Rumberger, 1987). These young people are at risk of unemployment or underemployment for the rest of their lives. **Educational and experiential programs**, such as Mann's (1986) *four Cs* (**cash, care, computers, and coalitions**), can help at-risk students become involved in career exploration and development.

According to Bloch (1988, 1989), successful **educational counseling programs for students at risk of dropping out should follow six guidelines**:

1. They make a **connection** between a **student's present and future status** (i.e., cash—students are paid for attending).
2. They **individualize programs** and communicate caring.
3. They form successful **coalitions** with **community institutions and businesses**.
4. They **integrate sequencing of career development activities**.
5. They **offer age- and stage-appropriate career development activities**.
6. They **use a wide variety of media and career development resources**, including computers.

Career Counseling with College Students

"Committing to a career choice is one of the main psychosocial tasks that college students face" (Osborn, Howard, & Leierer, 2007, p. 365). Approximately half of all college students experience career-related problems (Herr et al., 2004). Part of the reason is that despite appearances "most college students are rarely the informed consumers that they are assumed to be" (Laker, 2002, p. 61). Therefore, college students need and value career counseling services, such as undergraduate career exploration courses (Osborn et al., 2007). Even students who have already decided on their college majors and careers seek such services both to validate their choices and seek additional information. As Erikson (1963) stated: "it is primarily the inability to settle on an occupational identity which disturbs young people" (p. 252).

In responding to student needs, comprehensive career guidance and counseling programs in institutions of higher education attempt to provide a number of services. Among these services are

- helping with the selection of a major field of study;
- offering self-assessment and self-analysis through psychological testing;
- helping students understand the world of work;
- facilitating access to employment opportunities through career fairs, internships, and campus interviews;
- teaching decision-making skills; and
- meeting the needs of special populations (Herr et al., 2004).

Besides offering these options, students need "**life-career developmental counseling**," too (Engels, Jacobs, & Kern, 2000). This broader approach seeks to help people plan for future careers while "balancing and integrating life-work roles and responsibilities" in an appropriate way, for example, being a worker and a family member, parent, and citizen" (p. 192). Anticipating problems related to work, intimate relationships, and responsibilities is an important career-related counseling service counselors can offer college students. Counselors can often be the bridge that connects college students to school and work (Murphy, Blustein, Bohlig, & Platt, 2010). By sharing information pertinent to their intended career field and knowledge about the emerging adulthood transition, counselors can help prepare these students for their first work experience and beyond (Kennedy, 2008). Such knowledge can help prevent, *work-family conflicts (WFC)* that might otherwise arise and negatively affect a person's behavior, emotions, and health (Frone, 2003).

A way that college students can avoid problems and create *realistic job previews (RJPs)* of a specific job is to contact and interview people with knowledge about the careers they are considering. RJPs ultimately benefit potential job seekers in an occupation by both decreasing employee turnover and by increasing employee satisfaction (Laker, 2002). Students should supplement these types of interviews by completing computer-based career planning systems (CBCPSs) such as DISCOVER. The reason is that the completion of such systems is active, immediate, empowering, and rewarded with a printed result that promotes self-efficacy and the likelihood that individuals will complete other career-exploratory behaviors (Maples & Luzzo, 2005).

Despite preparation, economic factors, such as a recession, can impact the initial career decision of college graduates. Thus while many college graduates in 2008 were whisked off to high-paying jobs in consulting and finance, the graduates of the barren years of 2009 and 2010 were not. The result was more young people were employed in public service positions, such as government and nonprofits. Applications for AmeriCorps positions nearly tripled to 258,829 in 2010 from 91,399 in 2008 and the number of applicants for Teach for America climbed 32 percent during the same time to a record 46,359 (Rampell, 2010).

Career Counseling with Adults

Career interest patterns tend to be more stable after college than during college. *Emerging adults* (young adults up to age 30) are especially in need of relationship support and space to develop autonomy and competence as they transition from college to career (Murphy et al., 2010). However, many older adults continue to need and seek career counseling even into *late adulthood* (adults 65 years and older) (AARP, www.aarp.org; Swanson & Hansen, 1988). Indeed, adults experience cyclical periods of stability and transition throughout their lives, and career change is a developmental as well as situational expectation at the adult stage of life (Kerka, 1991).

Developmentally, some adults have a midlife career change that occurs as they enter their 40s and what Erik Erikson described as a stage of generativity versus stagnation. At this time, adults may change careers as they become more introspective and seek to put more meaning in their lives. Situationally, adults may seek career changes after a trauma such as a death, layoff, or divorce (Marino, 1996).

Adults may have particularly difficult times with their careers and career decisions when they find "themselves unhappy in their work yet feel appropriately ambivalent about switching directions" (Lowman, 1993, p. 549). In such situations they may create illogical or troublesome career beliefs that become self-fulfilling and self-defeating (Krumboltz, 1992). An example of such a belief is "I'll never find a job I really like." It is crucial in such cases to help people change their ways of thinking and become more realistic.

There are **two dominant ways of working with adults in career counseling**: the differential approach and the developmental approach. The *differential approach* stresses that "the typology of persons and environments is more useful than any life stage strategies for coping with career problems" (Holland & Gottfredson, 1976, p. 23). It avoids age-related stereotypes, gender and minority group issues, and the scientific and practical difficulties of dealing with life-span problems. "At any age, the level and quality of a person's vocational coping is a function of the interaction of personality type and type of environment plus the consistency and differentiation of each" (Holland & Gottfredson, 1976, p. 23).

According to this view, a career counselor who is aware of typological formulations such as Holland's can predict the characteristic ways a given person may cope with career problems. For example, a person with a well-defined social/artistic personality (typical of many individuals employed as counselors) would be expected to have high educational and vocational aspirations, to have good decision-making ability, to have a strong and lifelong interest in learning, to have moderate personal competency, and to have a marked interest in creative and high-level performance rather than in leadership (Holland, 1997). A person with such a profile would also have a tendency to remold or leave an environment in the face of adversity. A major advantage of working from this approach is the ease with which it explains career shifts at any age. People who shift careers, at any point in life, seek to find more consistency between personality and environment.

The ***developmental approach*** examines a greater number of individual and environmental variables. "The experiences people have with events, situations and other people play a large part in determining their identities (i.e., what they believe and value, how they respond to others, and what their own self images are)" (Gladstein & Apfel, 1987, p. 181). **Developmental life-span career theory** proposes that adults are always in the process of evaluating themselves in regard to how they are affected by outside environmental influences (e.g., spouse, family, friends) and how they impact these variables. Okun (1984) and Gladstein and Apfel (1987) believe the interplay of other people and events strongly influences career decisions in adulthood.

Gladstein and Apfel's (1987) approach to **adult career counseling** focuses on a combination of six elements: developmental, comprehensive, self-in-group, longitudinal, mutual commitment, and multimethodological. These elements work together in the process of change at this stage of life. This model, which has been implemented on a practical level at the University of Rochester Adult Counseling Center, considers the person's total identity over time. In a related model, Chusmir (1990) stresses the interaction of multiple factors in the process that men undergo when choosing ***nontraditional careers*** (careers in which people of one gender are not usually employed). Whether or not careers are nontraditional, the fact is that many forces enter into career decisions.

CASE EXAMPLE

Dick Becomes Differentiated

Dick had struggled with holding a job for years. He moved from one position to another as a cook, a sanitation engineer, a security officer, and a landscaper. Not being satisfied with any of his work, at 29 he went to see Susan, a career counselor.

Susan gave Dick several inventories, including those on O*Net. She noted from Dick's results that he had a predominant artistic and social theme, which was just the opposite of the realistic and conventional jobs he had been dissatisfied with. Susan then explored with Dick what he could do at various levels of education with this predominant theme and, through the use of the *Occupational Outlook Handbook,* what job growth was expected in each area.

Dick decided to enroll in a local community college and further his education so that he could pursue a career in the entertainment industry. He was pleased. As he said to Susan in leaving: "This type of career just feels right for me."

Career Counseling with Women and Ethnic Minorities

"Many of the assumptions inherent in traditional theories of career development fall short in their application to women and ethnic minorities" (Luzzo & McWhirter, 2001, p. 61). Women and ethnic minorities historically have received less adequate career counseling than European American males have and have faced more barriers in pursuit of their careers (Brown, 2002).

The reason has often involved stereotypical beliefs and practices connected with these two groups (Herr, Cramer, & Niles, 2004). For example, society has generally assumed that women will have discontinuous career patterns to accommodate their families' needs. Likewise, ethnic minorities have often been viewed as interested in only a limited number of occupations. The growing social activism among women and ethnic minority groups, combined with a growing body of research, are helping challenge constraining negative forces and create models of career counseling for these populations (Peterson & Gonzalez, 2000). That is why, among other reasons, career counselors should promote social justice in the workplace.

WOMEN.   Gender-based career patterns for women have changed for several reasons. For one thing, more than 70 percent of women in the United States now work for wages (Greenstone & Looney, 2011). Furthermore, "children are being exposed to greater and more varied career choices. Additionally, women have moved into careers previously reserved for men, thereby creating a broader range in the role models they provide girls" (Bobo et al., 1998, pp. 40–41).

Since 1970, there has been a dramatic rise in research on and interest in the career development of women (King & Knight, 2011; Luzzo & McWhirter, 2001; Whitmarsh, Brown, Cooper, Hawkins-Rodgers, & Wentworth, 2007). "Research on women's career development has identified both internal and external barriers associated with women's career development, documenting that the process of career decision making and maintaining a career are more complex and restricted for women than for men" (Sullivan & Mahalik, 2000, p. 54). One aspect of the complexity of career development for women is what is known as the **work/family conflict**, where there is a clash between work responsibilities such as working late and family responsibilities such as picking up children at day care (Slan-Jerusalim & Chen, 2009). This conflict may result in *role overload* (competing and sometimes conflicting demands for multiple roles expected of a person, such as breadwinner, breadmaker, parent, community service) (Pearson, 2008). In such a situation there is little to no time left over for leisure, which has an impact on a person's sense of "psychological health and overall well-being" (p. 57). Complicating matters even further, many theories of career development cannot be appropriately applied to women because they were formulated for men or are incomplete (Cook et al., 2002; Gottfredson, 2005; Jackson & Scharman, 2002).

Therefore, in working with women, counselors need to realize they are often entering new territory and must watch out for and resist *occupational sex-role stereotyping*, even at the elementary school level (McMahon & Patton, 1997). Common stereotypes include viewing women as primarily mothers (nurturing), children (dependent), iron maidens (hard driving), and sex objects (Gysbers et al., 2003) or mistakenly assuming that, as a group, females prefer social, artistic, and conventional occupations as opposed to realistic, investigative, and enterprising occupations (Tomlinson & Evans-Hughes, 1991).

In addition, there is the *"glass ceiling" phenomenon* in which women are seen as able to rise only so far in a corporation because they are not viewed as being able to perform top-level executive duties. When these myths are accepted, girls and women are not challenged to explore their abilities and possibilities and, as a result, some women fail to develop their abilities or gifts to the fullest. Consequently, they never work; develop a low or moderate commitment to work; or focus on "safe," traditional, female-dominated occupations such as teaching, clerical work, nursing, or social services (Betz & Fitzgerald, 1987; Brown, 2002; Walsh & Heppner, 2006).

In addition, other barriers outside these myths must be considered in career counseling for women. For instance, a company culture may revolve around the expectation of working far more hours than may be described in a job, in attending certain events, or being "one of the guys." Thus, women must overcome these realities, as well as the myths that surround them, in order to achieve career goals (Luzzo & McWhirter, 2001). Counselors may advise them that they may more readily find a job that is not in a female-dominated occupational field by socially contacting men rather than women (Mencken & Winfield, 2000). Overcoming barriers and misperceptions and finding balance is an essential part of the counseling process.

To understand how women may combine a career and a family, Jackson and Scharman (2002) studied a national sample of "26 women identified as having creatively constructed their careers to maximize time with their families" (p. 181). Eight different themes emerged as to how these women managed to construct family-friendly careers. Their strategies ranged from "peaceful trade-offs" to "partner career flexibility." However, "each participant found satisfying solutions to combining career and family that did not require an either/or choice" (p. 184). Overall, these women demonstrated remarkable self-efficacy (i.e., confidence in themselves to cope with or manage complex or difficult situations). This ability is becoming an increasingly important factor in the career development of women. Career self-efficacy is one that can be increased through working with women in groups to address factors that compose it, such as performance accomplishments, vicarious experiences, emotional arousal, and verbal persuasion (Sullivan & Mahalik, 2000).

Another helpful career counseling strategy in working with women, especially if they are depressed and indecisive about a career, is to offer "*career plus life counseling*, meaning that in counseling they [the women] focus on personal and relationship issues in addition to explicit career issues" (Lucas, Skokowski, & Ancis, 2000, p. 325). An ecological perspective, where career counselors work with women on career development issues in the context and complexity of the environment in which they live, is increasingly gaining recognition as a way of helping women become more empowered and shape their futures (Cook et al., 2002).

An area that warrants counselors' attention in career counseling with women in the future is demographics and trends. The labor market has shifted from goods-producing to service-producing industries (Van Buren, Kelly, & Hall, 1993). Service jobs are those such as sales clerk and computer operator. When young women take these jobs when they are qualified to pursue higher paying, nontraditional careers in skilled trades, they become more subjected to economic forces such as poverty, social welfare, and dependence on men that are not in their or society's best interest. Therefore, there is "an urgent need for career counseling interventions" offered through live or video modeling "that will persuade young women to consider the economic benefits of nontraditional career choices" or choices that are in line with their real interests (Van Buren et al., 1993, p. 101). Interestingly, more women are beginning to pursue their career interests and in recent years have been turning to enterprising occupations where they may earn more and be more in charge of their lives (Reardon et al., 2007).

PERSONAL REFLECTION

From all you have read in this chapter, as well as your own observations, why is it important to have different theories and approaches for career counseling with women? Do you think some theories and approaches apply equally to both sexes?

CULTURAL MINORITIES. "Career counseling must incorporate different variables and different processes to be effective for clients from different cultural contexts" (Fouad & Byars-Winston, 2005, p. 223). Yet cultural minorities are so diverse that it is almost impossible to focus on all the factors that career counselors must deal with in working with them individually or collectively.

Many cultural minorities have difficulty obtaining meaningful employment because of employers' discrimination practices, lack of marketable skills, and limited access to informal networks that lead to good jobs (Leong, 1995; Turner & Conkel, 2010). Therefore, many racial/ethnic minorities are "concentrated in lower level positions and unskilled occupations"

(Fouad & Byars-Winston, 2005, p. 223). In addition, the interest patterns of cultural minorities (as a group) have tended not to necessarily fall within Holland's (1997) circular RIASEC ordering in the same way European Americans have, thus presenting challenges for many career counselors in regard to helping them (Osipow & Fitzgerald, 1996). Whereas about 27% of adults in the United States express a need for assistance in finding information about work, the rate is much higher among specific minority populations: African Americans, 44%; Asian/Pacific Islanders, 36%; and Hispanics/Latinos, 35% (National Career Development Association [NCDA], 1990).

Counselors must remember that cultural minorities have special needs in regard to establishing themselves in careers. Thus, counselors need to be sensitive to such issues and at the same time help individuals overcome artificial and real barriers that prohibit them from maximizing their potential. For instance, compared to White students, Black college students are more attracted to future income and future status when making a career choice (Daire, LaMothe, & Fuller, 2007). Likewise, some Black youths who have lived in poverty all their lives are characterized as vocationally handicapped because "they have few positive work-related experiences, limited educational opportunities, and frequently lack positive work role models" (Dunn & Veltman, 1989, pp. 156–157). Structured programs for these individuals use positive role models and experiences to affirm cultural or ethnic heritage and abilities, thus working to address and overcome traditional restrictions (Drummond & Ryan, 1995; Locke & Faubert, 1993). In the process, counselors help these youths, as they do others, to distinguish between barriers over which they have control and responsibility for transcending those which they may not have the capacity to overcome (Albert & Luzzo, 1999).

Career awareness programs for Chinese American and Korean American parents have also proven beneficial (Evanoski & Tse, 1989). In these Asian cultures, parents traditionally make career decisions for their children, regardless of the children's interests. By staging neighborhood workshops to introduce parents to American career opportunities, a greater variety of choices is opened to all concerned. The success of such workshops is due to bilingual role models and career guidance materials written in the participants' language.

Finally, when working with inner city youth in the area of careers, counselors need to realize that traditional theories of career development may not work well. In essence many of these theories are middle class and are not a good fit for the environment in which these young people grow up in because inner city youth face the challenge of overcoming the effects of poverty, minority status, and lack of opportunity. To gain adaptive advantages in the current and future labor markets, young people need to acquire an integrated set of vocational development skills (Turner & Conkel, 2010, p. 463). Career development gains can be increased by using the **Integrative Contextual Model of Career Development (ICM).** ICM is a career model, drawn from different theoretical perspectives, that includes the skills of self- and career-exploration; person-environment fit; goal setting; social, prosocial, and work readiness skills; self-regulated learning; and the utilization of social support. Although this approach still needs more empirical research, it has been found to be effective with middle school students.

Career Counseling with Gays, Lesbians, Bisexuals, and Transgenders

Special diverse groups not often considered in career counseling are gays, lesbians, bisexuals, and transgenders (GLBT). These individuals face unique concerns as well as many that are common to other groups. Of special concern to many GLBTs is whether to be overt or covert in disclosing their sexual orientation at work (Chojnacki & Gelberg, 1994). Persons with minority sexual orientations face personal and professional developmental concerns, including discrimination, if they openly acknowledge their beliefs and practices (Degges-White & Shoffner, 2002; O'Ryan & McFarland, 2010). This may be especially true if gay members of this population are in male-dominated occupations, which tend to be more homophobic than other occupational groups (Jome, Surething, & Taylor, 2005). To overcome the difficulties they face, O'Ryan & McFarland (2010) found that dual-career lesbian and gay couples use three primary strategies: planfulness, creating positive social networks, and shifting from marginalization to consolidation and integration.

Although traditional career-counseling methods are usually appropriate with individuals of all sexual orientations, special attention should be given to helping GLBTs assess the fit between their lifestyle preferences and specific work environments. Sexual orientation cannot be ignored as an important variable in career counseling if the process is to be constructive (Croteau & Thiel, 1993; Degges-White & Shoffner, 2002).

In working with members of this population, career counselors must evaluate both theirs and the surrounding community's stereotyping of GLBTs. In such an appraisal, they must gauge personal, professional, and environmental bias toward people who are not heterosexual. In addition, they need to use gender-free language and become familiar with support networks that are within their communities for members of these groups. Furthermore, they need to become informed about overt and covert discrimination in the workplace, such as blackmail, ostracism, harassment, exclusion, and termination. The *"lavender ceiling"* also needs to be discussed with gays, lesbians, bisexuals, and transgenders. This barrier to advancement in a career is the equivalent to the **glass ceiling** for women, where a career plateaus early due to discreet prejudice by upper management against persons because of beliefs about them related to their sexuality (Friskopp & Silverstein, 1995; Zunker, 2012).

CASE EXAMPLE

David and His Career Decision

David struggled. He was a gay African American man who was just finishing college and had no idea what to do with his life. He was accepted in his neighborhood but he wondered about how well he would be accepted in a work environment. He was particularly interested in business and the culinary arts. His Holland code was AS/ER/CI.

After working with a career counselor at his college, David decided to set up a catering service. He was a good cook and had a flare for organization as well as a disciplined style with his money. He thought by starting such a business, he could be successful, meet people, and avoid blatant prejudice outside his neighborhood. His career counselor was not as sure as David that his choice was a good one.

What do you think about David's career choice? What other options might he have?

MyCounselingLab™

Go to Topic 2: *Career/Individual/Development Counseling* in the MyCounselingLab™ site (www.MyCounselingLab.com) for *Counseling: A Comprehensive Profession,* Seventh Edition, where you can:

* Find learning outcomes for *Career/Individual/Development Counseling* along with the national standards that connect to these outcomes.
* Complete Assignments and Activities that can help you more deeply understand the chapter content.
* Apply and practice your understanding of the core skills identified in the chapter with the Building Counseling Skills unit.
* Prepare yourself for professional certification with a Practice for Certification quiz.
* Connect to videos through the Video and Resource Library.

Summary and Conclusion

This chapter has covered information on various aspects of career counseling including its importance and the associations within counseling, such as the NCDA and NECA, which are particularly concerned with its development. Major theories of career counseling—trait-and-factor, developmental, and social–cognitive—were reviewed. Career counseling with particular populations—especially individuals at different developmental ages and stages in life, women, cultural minorities, and those with distinct sexual orientation—were examined, too.

Overall, multiple factors, including inner needs and drives and external circumstances such as the economy, gender, educational attainment, ethnicity, and the social milieu, combine to influence career decisions. Developments around the world, especially in technology, are impacting the field of careers as well. "The information age continues to alter the number of job openings as well as the way in which a wide variety of jobs are done" (Walls &

Fullmer, 1996, p. 154). As advancing technology creates new or modifies old kinds of jobs, previously valued skills and entire occupations may diminish or vanish. Therefore, career counseling is becoming ever more important, and counselors who are going to be relevant to their clients must be knowledgeable about procedures and practices in this field across the life span.

Among the many functions that career and employment counselors perform are:

* administering and interpreting tests and inventories;
* conducting personal counseling sessions;
* developing individualized career plans;
* helping clients integrate vocational and avocational life roles;
* facilitating decision-making skills; and
* providing support for persons experiencing job stress, job loss, or career transitions.

Marriage, Couple, and Family Counseling

16

Chapter Overview

From this chapter you will learn about

- Family life, the family life cycle, and the changing forms of families
- The nature of marital, couple, and family counseling
- The process of marital, couple, and family counseling

As you read consider

- How you might treat different family types and why
- The research associated with the various forms of family counseling
- The difference between working with families and groups or individuals

At thirty-five, with wife and child
  a Ph.D.
    and hopes as bright as a full moon
      on a warm August night,
He took a role as a healing man
  blending it with imagination,
    necessary change and common sense
To make more than an image on an eye lens
  of a small figure running quickly up steps;
Quietly he traveled
  like one who holds a candle to darkness
    and questions its power
So that with heavy years, long walks,
  shared love, and additional births
He became as a seasoned actor,
  who, forgetting his lines in the silence,
    stepped upstage and without prompting
      lived them.

Reprinted from "Without Applause," by S. T. Gladding, 1974, *Personnel and Guidance Journal, 52*, p. 586. © S. T. Gladding.

MyCounselingLab™

Visit the **MyCounselingLab™** site (www.MyCounselingLab.com) for *Counseling: A Comprehensive Profession,* Seventh Edition to enhance your understanding of chapter concepts. You'll have the opportunity to practice your skills through video- and case-based Assignments and Activities as well as Building Counseling Skills units and to prepare for your certification exam with Practice for Certification quizzes.

This chapter examines the genesis and development of marriage, couple, and family counseling along with an overview of marriage, couple, and family counseling organizations and research. It also describes the family life cycle and addresses how family counseling differs from individual and group counseling. The process of marriage, couple, and family counseling from beginning to closure is looked at as well.

Marital relations and family life are rooted in antiquity. Whether arranged by a family or the couple themselves, men and women have paired together in unions sanctioned by religion and society for economic, societal, and procreation reasons for millennia. The terms marriage, couple, and family have distinct connotations in different societies. Marriage is generally seen as a socially or religiously sanctioned union between two adults for economic and/or procreational reasons. The term couple is more informal and broader. It simply denotes two people in a relationship together. They may be married or not, intimate or not. Nevertheless, they are seen as linked together in one or more ways. A family, on the other hand, consists of "those persons who are biologically and/or psychologically related . . . [through] historical, emotional, or economic bonds . . . and who perceive themselves as a part of a household" (Gladding, 2011, p. 6). These definitions of marriage, couple, and family allow for maximum flexibility and can encompass a wide variety of forms.

Marriage, couple, and family counseling is a popular pursuit of counselors. There are at least **three reasons** why.

First is the realization that **persons are directly affected by how their families function** (Goldenberg & Goldenberg, 2002). For instance, chaotic families frequently produce offspring who have difficulty relating to others because of a lack of order or even knowledge of what to do, whereas enmeshed families have children who often have difficulty leaving home because they are overdependent on parents or other family members.

A second reason couple and family counseling is attractive is a **financial consideration**. Problems can often be addressed **more economically when a couple or family is seen together**.

Finally, the **encompassing nature of marriage, couple, and family counseling work** makes it intrinsically appealing. There are **multiple factors to be aware of and to address**. Counselors who are engaged in helping marital units, couples, and families must constantly be active mentally and even sometimes physically. The process itself can be exciting as well as rewarding when change takes place. Marriage, couple, and family counseling attracts many clinicians who wish to work on complex, multifaceted levels in the most effective way possible.

THE CHANGING FORMS OF FAMILY LIFE

The strong interest in marriage, couple, and family counseling today is partly due to the rapid change in American family life since World War II. In 1950, two types of families, which still exist, dominated American cultural life:

- the **nuclear family**, a core unit of husband, wife, and their children; and
- the **multigenerational family**, households that include at least three generations, such as a child/children, parent(s), and grandparent(s). This type of family sometimes includes unmarried relatives, such as aunts and uncles.

After the war, a rising divorce rate made two more family types prevalent:

- the **single-parent family**, which includes one parent, either biological or adoptive, who is solely responsible for the care of self and a child/children; and
- the **blended** (i.e., remarried, step) **family**, a household created when two people marry and at least one of them has been previously married and has a child/children.

In addition, changes in societal norms and demographics since the 1950s have fostered the development and recognition of several other family forms besides those already mentioned, specifically,

- the **dual-career family**, in which both marital partners are engaged in work that is developmental in sequence and to which they have a high commitment;
- the **childless family**, which consists of couples who consciously decide not to have children or who remain childless as a result of chance or biological factors;
- the **aging family**, in which the head or heads of the household are age 65 or above;
- the **gay/lesbian family**, which is made up of same-sex couples with or without a child/children from either a previous union or as a result of artificial insemination or adoption; and
- the **multicultural family**, in which individuals from two different cultures unite and form a household that may or may not have children.

Couples and families in the 21st century are quite varied. Those who choose to enter such relationships face a host of economic, social, and developmental challenges that demand their attention daily. They also find a number of rewards in such unions including physical, financial, and psychological support. The drawbacks and impacts of marriage, couple, and family life are great and sometimes complicated. Professional counselors who work with the married, couples, and families must be attuned to a host of difficulties as well as possibilities. They must be ready to deal with extremely intricate and unsettling changes that developmentally or situationally may face these units (Napier, 1988).

PERSONAL REFLECTION

What type of family did you grow up in? What were its strengths? What were its weaknesses? What type of family listed previously would you prefer, if you could choose? Why?

THE BEGINNINGS OF MARRIAGE, COUPLE, AND FAMILY COUNSELING

The profession of marriage, couple, and family counseling is relatively new (Framo, 1996). Its substantial beginnings are traced to the 1940s and early 1950s, but its real growth occurred in the late 1970s and the 1980s (Nichols, 1993). It is interesting to note that the rise in popularity of marriage, couple, and family counseling closely followed dramatic changes in the form, composition, structure, and emphasis of the American family noted earlier (Markowitz, 1994). In this section, trends and personalities that influenced the development of the field will be noted, including some contemporary leaders.

Trends

At the end of World War II, the United States experienced an unsettling readjustment from war to peace that manifested itself in three trends that had an impact on the family, other than a rise in different types of family forms (Walsh, 1993). One was a sharp rise in the **divorce rate**, which took place almost simultaneously with the **baby boom** beginning in 1946. Whereas divorce had been fairly uncommon up to that point, it rose dramatically thereafter and did not level out until the 1990s. The impact of this phenomenon was unsettling. Today, a large percentage (around 50%) of couples who marry eventually dissolve their unions (Maples & Abney, 2006; Whitehead, 1997). However, new Census data shows the divorce rate for most age groups dropped in the 1996–2009 period by an average of 5% (Kreider & Ellis, 2011). The reason for the drop in divorce rates in recent years can be attributed to a number of factors but perhaps the most significant one is that couples in the United States are waiting longer to get married and are therefore more mature when they do marry (U.S. Census, 2010).

A second trend that influenced the rise of marriage, couple, and family counseling was the **changing role of women**. After World War II, more women sought employment outside the home. Many women became the breadwinners of their families as well as the bread makers. The women's rights movement of the 1960s also fostered the development of new opportunities for women. Thus, traditions and expectations fell and/or were expanded for women. The results were unsettling, as any major social change is, and both men and women in families and marriages needed help in making adequate adjustments. In 2010, 51% of women in the United States were unmarried and most women, including those who were married, worked outside the home.

The **expansion of the life span** was the third event that had an impact on family life and made marriage, couple, and family counseling more relevant to the American public. Couples found themselves living with the same partners longer than at any previous time in history (Maples & Abney, 2006). Many were not sure exactly how to relate to their spouses, partners, or children over time because there were few previous models.

Thus, the need to work with families, couples, and individuals who were affected by these changes brought researchers, practitioners, and theorists together. They set the stage for an entirely new way of conceptualizing and working with married people, couples, and families.

Family Therapy Pioneers and Contemporary Leaders

A number of helping specialists advanced the field of marriage, couple, and family counseling after World War II and up to the present—more than can be mentioned here. Some, like Nathan Ackerman and Virginia Satir, did it using the persuasive nature of their personalities. Others, such as Salvador Minuchin and John Gottman, became important and notable because of the research they conducted.

The work of Nathan Ackerman (1958), a New York City psychoanalyst, was especially critical in focusing the attention of a well-established form of therapy, psychoanalysis, on families. Before Ackerman, psychoanalysts had purposely excluded family members from the treatment of individual clients for fear that family involvement would be disruptive. Ackerman applied psychoanalytic practices to the treatment of families and made family therapy respected in the profession of psychiatry.

Two other pioneers that emerged on a national level about the time of Ackerman were experiential in nature: Virginia Satir and Carl Whitaker. Both of these individuals had engaging personalities and a presence that commanded attention. Satir was an especially clear writer and presenter, whereas Whitaker was a maverick whose unorthodox style and creativity, such as falling asleep during a session and having a dream, provoked considerable thought and discussion in the marriage and family field and in the couples and families with whom he worked.

gathered Jay Haley was probably the dominant figure of the early family therapists, however. Haley culled ideas from Milton Erickson, blended them with his own thoughts, and through persistence kept early family counselors in touch with each other and with developing ideas in the field. Haley also had a major role in developing strategic family therapy and influencing structural family therapy.

Other pioneers worked in teams as researchers conducting exploratory studies in the area of family dynamics and the etiology of schizophrenia. Among the teams were the Gregory Bateson group (Bateson, Jackson, Haley, & Weakland, 1956) in Palo Alto, California, and the Murray Bowen and Lyman Wynne groups (Bowen, 1960; Wynne, Ryckoff, Day, & Hirsch, 1958) at the National Institute of Mental Health (NIMH). They observed how couples and families functioned when a family member was diagnosed as schizophrenic. The Bateson group came up with a number of interesting concepts, such as the **double bind**, where a person receives two contradictory messages at the same time and, unable to follow both, develops physical and psychological symptoms as a way to lessen tension and escape. Bowen went on to develop his own systemic form of treatment based on multigenerational considerations and originate a now widely popular clinical tool, the **genogram** (a three-generational visual representation of one's family tree depicted in geometric figures, lines, and words).

The group movement, especially in the 1960s, also had an impact on the emergence of couple and family counseling. Some practitioners, such as John Bell (e.g., Bell, 1975, 1976), even started treating families as a group and began the practice of couple/family group counseling (Ohlsen, 1979, 1982). Foreign-born therapists have had a major influence on marriage, couple, and family therapy since the 1960s. These include Salvador Minuchin, the originator of Structural Family Therapy; Mara Selvini Palazzoli, a creator of a form of strategic family therapy known as the Milan Approach; as well as (more recently) Michael White and David Epston, the founders of Narrative Therapy.

Most recently there has been a Midwestern influx into the field led by Steve deShazer and Bill O'Hanlon, who developed brief therapeutic therapies that emphasize solutions and possibilities. In addition, Monica McGoldrick (McGoldrick, Giordano, & Garcia-Preto, 2005) has emphasized the importance of multicultural factors and cultural background in treating couples and families. Included in the idea of culture today are **inherited cultures** (e.g., ethnicity, nationality, religion, groupings such as baby boomers) and **acquired cultures** (learned habits, such as those of being a counselor) (Markowitz, 1994). Betty Carter and a host of others have also focused on an awakening in the marriage, couple, and family counseling field to gender-sensitive issues, such as the overriding importance of power structures. Finally, exemplary researchers, such as John Gottman and Neil Jacobson, have helped practitioners understand better the dynamics within marriages, couples, and families, especially factors related to domestic violence and higher functioning marriage relationships (Peterson, 2002).

ASSOCIATIONS, EDUCATION, AND RESEARCH

Associations

Four major professional associations attract marriage, couple, and family clinicians.

- The largest and oldest, which was established in 1942, is the **American Association for Marriage and Family Therapy (AAMFT)**.
- The second group, the **International Association of Marriage and Family Counselors (IAMFC)**, a division within the American Counseling Association (ACA), was chartered in 1986.
- The third association, **Division 43 (Family Psychology)**, a division within the American Psychological Association (APA), was formed in 1984 and comprises psychologists who work with couples and families.
- The fourth association is the **American Family Therapy Association (AFTA)**, formed in 1977. It is identified as an academy of advanced professionals interested in the exchange of ideas.

Education

Both the AAMFT and IAMFC have established guidelines for training professionals in working with couples and families. AAMFT standards are drawn up and administered by the Commission on Accreditation for Marriage and Family Therapy Education (CAMFTE); those for IAMFC are handled through the Council for Accreditation of Counseling and Related Educational Programs (CACREP). A minimum of a 60-semester-hour master's degree is required for becoming a marriage, couple, and family counselor through a CACREP-accredited program. The exact content and sequencing of courses will vary from program to program but the courses in Table 16.1 are almost always included.

Research

Regardless of professional affiliation and curriculum background, professionals are attracted to marriage, couple, and family counseling largely due to a societal need for the specialty and its growing research base. Gurman and Kniskern (1981) reported that approximately **50% of all problems brought to counselors are related to marriage and family issues**. Unemployment, poor school performance, spouse abuse, depression, rebellion, and self-concept issues are just a few of the many situations that can be dealt with from this perspective. Individual development dovetails with family and career issues (Cavanaugh & Blanchard-Fields, 2011; Okun, 1984). Each one impacts the resolution of the other in a systemic manner. Bratcher (1982) comments on the interrelatedness of career and family development, recommending the use of family systems theory for experienced counselors working with individuals seeking career counseling.

TABLE 16.1 Example of Coursework Areas Required for a Master's Degree in AAMFT-Accredited and CACREP-Accredited Programs

CACREP Curriculum	AAMFT Curriculum
Human Growth and Development	Introduction Family/Child Development
Social and Cultural Foundations	Marital and Family Systems
Helping Relationships	Introduction to Family/Child Development
Groups	Dysfunctions in Marriage/Family
Lifestyle and Career Development	Advanced Child Development
Appraisal/Assessment	Assessment in Marital/Family
Research and Evaluation	Research Methods Child/Family
Professional Orientation	Professional Issues Family
Theoretical Foundation MFT	Theories of MFT
Techniques/Treatment MFT	Marriage/Family Pre-Practicum
Clinical Practicum/Internship	Clinical Practicum
Substance Abuse Treatment	Human Sexual Behavior
Human Sexuality	Thesis
Electives	Electives

Source: From "The Training of Marriage and Family Counselors/Therapists: A 'Systemic' Controversy among Disciplines," by Michael Baltimore, 1993, *Alabama Counseling Association Journal, 19*, p. 40. Copyright 1993, Alabama Counseling Association. Reprinted with permission.

Research studies summarized by Doherty and Simmons (1996), Gurman and Kniskern (1981), Haber (1983), Pinsof and Wynne (1995), and Wohlman and Stricker (1983) report a number of interesting findings:

- First, **family counseling interventions are at least as effective as individual interventions** for most client complaints and lead to significantly greater durability of change.
- Second, **some forms of family counseling (e.g., using structural-strategic family therapy with substance abusers) are more effective in treating problems than other counseling approaches.**
- Third, **the presence of both parents, especially noncompliant fathers, in family counseling situations greatly improves the chances for success.** Similarly, **the effectiveness of marriage counseling when both partners meet conjointly with the counselor is** nearly twice that of counselors working with just one spouse.
- Fourth, **when marriage and family counseling services are not offered to couples conjointly or to families systemically, the results of the intervention may be negative and problems may worsen.**
- Finally, there is **high client satisfaction from those who receive marital, couple, and family counseling services**, with over 97% rating the services they received from good to excellent. Overall, the basic argument for employing marriage and family counseling is its proven efficiency. This form of treatment is logical, fast, satisfactory, and economical.

CASE EXAMPLE

Shasta Seeks Out a Marriage Counselor

Shasta grew up in a single-parent family that was often strapped for money. Therefore Shasta learned to hoard food and to hide any valuables she might obtain. Later, she married Marcus who was financially quite successful. Still, she hoarded and hid items around the house to the point that it caused tension in the relationship.

Shasta finally realized she needed help and sought out a marriage and family counselor. Do you think such a counselor could help her resolve her problem? If so, how? If not, why not?

FAMILY LIFE AND THE FAMILY LIFE CYCLE

Family life and the growth and developments that take place within it are at the heart of marriage, couple, and family counseling. The *family life cycle* is the name given to the stages a family goes through as it evolves over the years. These stages sometimes parallel and complement those in the individual life cycle, but often they are unique because of the number of people involved and the diversity of tasks to be accomplished. Becvar and Becvar (2009) outline a nine-stage cycle that begins with the unattached adult and continues through retirement (Table 16.2).

Some families and family members are more "on time" in achieving **stage-critical tasks** that go with the family life cycle and their own personal cycle of growth. In such cases, a better sense of well-being is achieved (McGoldrick, Carter, & Garcia-Preto, 2011). Other families, such as those that are dysfunctional, never achieve stage-critical tasks, for instance, **substance abuse families**. In these families substance abuse behavior is promoted or enabled. Thus, children "from homes in which parents are chemically dependent or abuse alcohol or other drugs (CDs) are at risk for a wide range of developmental problems" (Buelow, 1995, p. 327). Many families that abuse alcohol, for example, tend to be isolated and children within them consequently suffer from a lack of positive role models. As children get older, they seem to be particularly affected for the worse from growing up in these families.

Substance abuse is used by these young people as a way to relieve stress, reduce anxiety, and structure time (Robinson, 1995). It is also an attempt by young adults to protect and stabilize dysfunctional families by keeping their attention off overall dynamics and on predictable problematic behaviors (Stanton & Todd, 1982). Substance abuse may serve as a substitute for sex as well and promote *pseudo-individuation* (a false sense of self). These complex and interrelated factors make it difficult to help families caught up in substance abuse patterns to change behaviors without an intensive social action approach designed to change dysfunctional systems (Lee & Walz, 1998; Margolis & Zweben, 2011).

Families often organize themselves around substance abuse in a systemic way and enable family members to drink excessively (Bateson, 1971; Steinglass, 1979). In the alcoholic family system, there is an *overresponsible–underresponsible phenomenon*, with the overresponsible person(s) being a so-called *codependent* (Berenson, 1992). "An essential characteristic of someone who is codependent is that they continually invest their self-esteem in the ability to control and influence behavior and feelings in others as well as in

TABLE 16.2 Stages of the Family Life Cycle

Stage	Emotion	Stage-Critical Tasks
1. Unattached adult	Accepting parent-offspring separation	a. Differentiation from family of origin b. Development of peer relations c. Initiation of career
2. Newly married	Commitment to the marriage	a. Formation of marital system b. Making room for spouse with family and friends c. Adjusting career demands
3. Childbearing	Accepting new members into the system	a. Adjusting marriage to make room for child b. Taking on parenting roles
4. Preschool-age child	Accepting the new personality	a. Adjusting family to the needs of specific child(ren) b. Coping with energy drain and lack of privacy c. Taking time out to be a couple
5. School-age child	Allowing child to establish relationships outside the family	a. Extending family/society interactions b. Encouraging the child's educational progress c. Dealing with increased activities and time demands
6. Teenage child	Increasing flexibility of family boundaries to allow independence	a. Shifting the balance in the parent-child relationship b. Refocusing on mid-life career and marital issues c. Dealing with increasing concerns for older generation
7. Launching center	Accepting exits from and entries into the family	a. Releasing adult children into work, college, marriage b. Maintaining supportive home base c. Accepting occasional returns of adult children
8. Middle-age adult	Letting go of children and facing each other	a. Rebuilding the marriage b. Welcoming children's spouses, grandchildren into family c. Dealing with aging of one's own parents
9. Retirement	Accepting retirement and old age	a. Maintaining individual and couple functioning b. Supporting middle generation c. Coping with death of parents, spouse d. Closing or adapting family home

Source: From *Family Therapy: A Systematic Integration* (pp. 128–129), by Dorothy Stroh Becvar and Raphael J. Becvar. © 1993 by Allyn & Bacon. All rights reserved. Reprinted with permission.

themselves, even when faced with adverse consequences such as feelings of inadequacy after failure" (Springer, Britt, & Schlenker, 1998, p. 141). In such a situation, it is easier and more productive to work with the overfunctioning person(s) and modify that phenomenon than to try to get the underfunctioning person(s) to change.

Regardless of functionality, all families have to deal with *family cohesion* (emotional bonding) and *family adaptability* (ability to be flexible and change). These two dimensions each have four levels, represented by Olson (1986) in the **circumplex model of marital and family systems** (Figure 16.1). "The two dimensions are curvilinear in that families that apparently are very high or very low on both dimensions seem dysfunctional, whereas families that are balanced seem to function more adequately" (Maynard & Olson, 1987, p. 502). For instance, a family that is high in cohesion is enmeshed (extremely close sometimes to the point of not being well differentiated). If the same family is also high in adaptability they will also be chaotic (disorganized). This combination results in a family that is chaotically enmeshed, very close but not able to function effectively, with the result being they are unbalanced. In examining the circumplex model, ideals for family functioning are close to the center with less functional ways

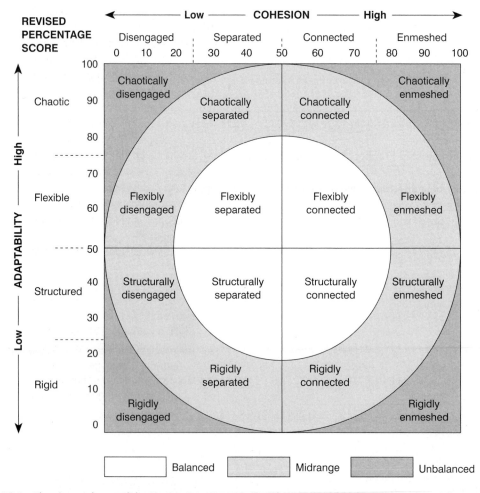

FIGURE 16.1 The circumplex model *Source:* From Prepare/Enrich, Inc., David H. Olson, president, Minneapolis, MN. © 1979 (rev. 1986). Reprinted with permission.

of working closest to the outside. In reality, even the most dysfunctional families execute well at times and vice versa. Also, families move around on the circumplex model during their life cycles. For instance, the death of a family member may send a family that is flexibly separated into one that is rigidly disengaged as individuals drift apart and grieve separately.

Families that are most successful, functional, happy, and strong are not only balanced but

- committed to one another,
- appreciate each other,
- spend time together (both qualitatively and quantitatively),
- have good communication patterns,
- have a high degree of religious/spiritual orientation, and
- are able to deal with crisis in a positive manner (Gladding, 2011; Stinnett, 1998; Stinnett & DeFrain, 1985).

According to Wilcoxon (1985), marriage, couple, and family counselors need to be aware of the different stages within the family while staying attuned to the developmental tasks of individual members. When counselors are sensitive to individual family members and the family as a whole, they are able to realize that some individual manifestations, such as depression (Stevenson, 2007), career indecisiveness (Kinnier, Brigman, & Noble, 1990), and substance abuse (Edwards, 2012), are related to family structure and functioning. Consequently, they are able to be more inclusive in their treatment plans.

When evaluating family patterns and the mental health of everyone involved, it is crucial that an assessment be based on the form and developmental stage of the family constellation. To facilitate this process, McGoldrick et al. (2011) propose sets of developmental tasks for traditional and nontraditional families, such as those headed by single parents or blended families. It is important to note that nontraditional families are not pathological because of their differences; they are merely on a different schedule of growth and development.

Today, more than four-in-ten American adults have at least one step relative in their family—either a stepparent, a step or half sibling, or a stepchild. People with step relatives are just as likely as others to say that family is the most important element of their life. Seven-in-ten adults who have at least one step relative say they are very satisfied with their family life. Those who do not have any step relatives register slightly higher levels of family satisfaction (78% very satisfied) (Parker, 2011).

Bowen (1978) suggests terms such as "enmeshment" and "triangulation" to describe family dysfunctionality regardless of the family form. (**Enmeshment** refers to family environments in which members are overly dependent on each other or are undifferentiated. **Triangulation** describes family fusion situations in which the other members of the triangle pull a person in two different directions.) Counselors who effectively work with couples and families have guidelines for determining how, where, when, or whether to intervene in the family process. They do not fail to act (e.g., neglect to engage everyone in the therapeutic process), nor do they overreact (perhaps place too much emphasis on verbal expression).

PERSONAL REFLECTION

Who were you closest to in your family of origin? Who were you most distant from? What factors or events brought you together? What factors or events distanced you from one another?

COUPLE/FAMILY COUNSELING VERSUS INDIVIDUAL/GROUP COUNSELING

There are similarities and differences in the approaches to couple or family counseling and individual or group counseling (Gladding, 2011; Hines, 1988; Trotzer, 1988). A major similarity centers on theories. Some theories used in individual or group counseling (e.g., person-centered, Adlerian, reality therapy, behavioral) are used with couples and families (Horne, 2000). Other approaches (e.g., structural, strategic, solution-focused family therapy) are unique to couple and family counseling and are systemic in nature. Counselors must learn about these additional theories as well as new applications of previous theories to become skilled at working with couples or families.

Couple or family counseling and individual counseling share a number of assumptions. For instance, both recognize the importance the family plays in the individual's life, both focus on problem behaviors and conflicts between the individual and the environment, and both are developmental. A difference is that individual counseling usually treats the person outside his or her family, whereas couple or family counseling generally includes the involvement of others, usually family members. Further, couple and family counseling works at resolving issues within the family as a way of helping individual members better cope with the environment (Nichols, 2010).

Couple and family counseling sessions are similar to group counseling sessions in organization, basic dynamics, and stage development. Furthermore, both types of counseling have an interpersonal emphasis. However, the family is not like a typical group, although knowledge of the group process may be useful. For example, family members are not equal in status and power. In addition, families may perpetuate myths, whereas groups are initially more objective in dealing with events. More emotional baggage is also carried among family members than members of another type of group because the arrangement in a family is not limited in time and is related to sex roles and affective bonds that have a long history (Becvar, 1982). Although the family may be a group, it is not well suited to work that takes place only through group theory.

Finally, the emphasis of couple and family counseling is generally on dynamics as opposed to linear causality as in much individual and some group counseling. In other words, the dynamics behind couple and family counseling generally differ from the other two types of counseling. In making the transition from an individual perspective to a family orientation, Resnikoff (1981) stresses specific questions that counselors should ask themselves to understand family functioning and dynamics. By asking the right questions, the counselor becomes more attuned to the family as a client and how best to work with it.

- What is the outward appearance of the family?
- What repetitive, nonproductive sequences are noticeable; that is, what is the family's dance?
- What is the basic feeling state in the family, and who carries it?
- What individual roles reinforce family resistance, and what are the most prevalent family defenses?
- How are family members differentiated from one another, and what are the subgroup boundaries?
- What part of the life cycle is the family experiencing, and what are its problem-solving methods?

Whether working with families or with couples, counselors ask many of these same questions.

OVERVIEW OF MARRIAGE, COUPLE, AND FAMILY COUNSELING

Marriage and Couple Counseling

Early pioneers in marriage and couple counseling focused on the marriage or couple relation-ship, rather than just the individuals involved. The new emphasis meant that three entities were considered in such relationships: two individuals and one couple. Thus, from its beginning mar-riage and couple counselors set a precedent for seeing couples together in conjoint sessions, a practice that continues today.

Couples seek marriage or relationship counseling for a wide variety of reasons, including finances, children, fidelity, communication, and compatibility (Long & Young, 2007). Almost any situation can serve as the impetus to seek help. Regardless of who initiates the request, it is crucial that the counselor see both members of the couple from the beginning if at all possible. Whitaker (1977) notes that if a counselor is not able to structure the situation in this way, he or she will probably not help the couple and may do harm. Trying to treat one spouse or partner alone for even one or two sessions increases the other's resistance to counseling and his or her anxiety. Moreover, if one member of a couple tries to change without the other's knowledge or support, conflict is bound to ensue.

If both partners decide to enter marriage and couple counseling, the counselor may take a variety of approaches. Seven of the main approaches are object relational, behavioral, cognitive–behavioral, Bowen systems (i.e., transgenerational), structural, emotionally focused, and narrative (Gurman, 2008). All of these theoretical perspectives have their strengths. The two strongest, however, are the emotionally focused approach of Susan Johnson and the behavioral approach of John Gottman. The reason is that both are heavily research based.

Family Counseling

Families enter counseling for a number of reasons. Usually, there is an ***identified patient (IP)***—an individual who is seen as the cause of trouble within the family structure—whom family members use as their ticket of entry. Most family counseling practitioners do not view one mem-ber of a family as the problem but instead work with the whole family system. Occasionally, family therapy is done from an individual perspective but with the hope that changes in the person will have a **ripple effect** (an influence generated from the center outward) and positively impact a family (Nichols, 1988).

Family counseling has expanded rapidly since the mid-1970s and encompasses many as-pects of couples counseling. Although a few family counselors, such as behaviorist, narrative, or solution-focused therapists, are linearly based and work on a cause-and-effect or a constructiv-ist perspective, most are not. Rather, the majority of counselors operate from a general systems framework and conceptualize the family as an open system that evolves over the family life cycle in a sociocultural context. Functional families follow rules and are flexible in meeting the demands of family members and outside agencies. Family systems counselors stress the idea of circular causality. They also emphasize the following concepts:

- ***Nonsummativity.***   The family is greater than the sum of its parts. It is necessary to exam-ine the patterns within a family rather than the actions of any specific member alone.
- ***Equifinality.***   The same origin may lead to different outcomes, and the same outcome may result from different origins. Thus, the family that experiences a natural disaster may become stronger or weaker as a result. Likewise, healthy families may have quite dissimilar

backgrounds. Therefore, treatment focuses on interactional family patterns rather than particular conditions or events.

- *Communication.* All behavior is seen as communicative. It is important to attend to the two functions of interpersonal messages: *content* (factual information) and *relationship* (how the message is to be understood). **The *what* of a message** is conveyed by how it is delivered.

- *Family rules.* A family's functioning is based on explicit and implicit rules. Family rules provide expectations about roles and actions that govern family life. Most families operate on a small set of predictable rules, a pattern known as the *redundancy principle*. To help families change dysfunctional ways of working, family counselors have to help them define or expand the rules under which they operate.

- *Morphogenesis.* The ability of the family to modify its functioning to meet the changing demands of internal and external factors is known as morphogenesis. Morphogenesis usually requires a *second-order change* (the ability to make an entirely new response) rather than a *first-order change* (continuing to do more of the same things that have worked previously) (Watzlawick, Weakland, & Fisch, 1974). Instead of just talking, family members may need to try new ways of behaving.

- *Homeostasis.* Like biological organisms, families have a tendency to remain in a steady, stable state of equilibrium unless otherwise forced to change. When a family member unbalances the family through his or her actions, other members quickly try to rectify the situation through negative feedback. The model of functioning can be compared to a furnace, which comes on when a house falls below a set temperature and cuts off once the temperature is reached. Sometimes homeostasis can be advantageous in helping a family achieve life-cycle goals, but often it prevents the family from moving on to another stage in its development.

Counselors who operate from a family systems approach work according to the concepts just listed. For instance, if family rules are covert and cause confusion, the counselor helps the family make these regulations overt and clear. All members of the family are engaged in the process so that communication channels are opened. Often, a genogram is constructed to help family members and the counselor detect intergenerational patterns of family functioning that have an impact on the present (McGoldrick, Gerson, & Petry, 2008).

For a **genogram**, three generations of the family should be drawn. Names, dates of birth, marriage, separation, and divorce should be indicated, along with basic information such as current age and occupation. A genogram can also be used in a multicultural context to assess the worldview and cultural factors that often influence family members' behaviors (Thomas, 1998). Overall, "the genogram appears to provide an effective and personally meaningful strategy to facilitate systems thinking," especially by new client families and counselors who are just beginning to work with families (Pistole, 1997b, p. 339).

THE PROCESS OF MARRIAGE, COUPLE, AND FAMILY COUNSELING

The process of marriage, couple, and family counseling is based on several premises. One is that persons conducting the counseling are psychologically healthy and understand their own families of origin well. When such is the case, counselors are able to clearly focus on their client families and not contaminate sessions with material from their own family life that they have not resolved.

A second premise of working with families is that counselors will not overemphasize or underemphasize possible aspects or interventions in the therapeutic process (Gladding, 2011). In other words, counselors will balance what they do. Such a process means not being overly concerned about making family members happy but at the same time engaging members in a personable way.

A third component of conducting marriage, couple, and family counseling is for the counselor to win the ***battle for structure*** (i.e., establish the parameters under which counseling is conducted) while letting the family win the ***battle for initiative*** (i.e., motivation to make needed changes) (Napier & Whitaker, 1978). The battle for structure is won when counselors inform clients about ways they will work with them, including important but mundane facts about how often they will meet, for how long, and who is to be involved. A good part of structure can be included in a disclosure statement that the counselor has the couple or family read and sign. Initiative in the therapeutic process must come from couples and families themselves; however, once counselors listen and outline what they see as possibilities, couple or family members often pull together toward common goals.

Fourth, marriage, couple, and family counselors need to be able to see the couple or family difficulties in the context in which they are occurring. Thus, the counselor needs to be developmentally sophisticated on multiple levels of life and have some life experiences including resolving toxic or adversarial conditions in less than ideal conditions. Such skills and insights bring to counselors an understanding of how couples and families become either more together or apart when faced with different life stages, cultural norms, or situational circumstances.

Presession Planning

Before a couple or family is seen for counseling, several matters should be addressed. One is the expectation(s) the caller has for an initial session or for treatment in general. The person who calls gives a rationale for seeking therapy that may or may not be the reason anyone else in the couple or family relationship has for wanting or not wanting counseling. Nevertheless, the counselor must listen carefully and obtain essential clinical information—such as a concise description of the problem—and factual information—such as the caller's name, address, and phone number. In gathering this information, the counselor should listen for what is conveyed as well as what is not said. In doing so, the counselor can begin to hypothesize about issues that are prevalent in certain family life stages and cultural traditions as they may relate to the caller's family. For example, a family with adolescents may expect to have boundary problems; however, the way they are handled in a traditional Italian family versus a traditional British family may be quite different. Regardless, by the end of the initial phone call, an appointment should be scheduled.

Initial Session(s)

Research indicates that the first few sessions are the most critical in regard to whether counselors have success therapeutically with couples and families (Odell & Quinn, 1998). Therefore, getting off to a good start is essential. One way a good beginning can be fostered is for the counselor to **establish rapport** with each person attending and the couple or family unit as a whole. This type of bonding, in which trust, a working relationship, and a shared agenda evolve, is known as a ***therapeutic alliance***. It can be created through a number of means such as

- *Maintenance*—as the counselor confirms or supports a couple's or family member's position;

- **Tracking**—when a counselor, through a series of clarifying questions, tracks or follows a sequence of events; and
- **Mimesis**—when a counselor adopts a couple's or family's style or tempo of communication, such as being jovial with a light-hearted couple or family or serious with a couple or family that is somber.

In establishing a therapeutic alliance, it is important for the counselor to engage the couple or family and its members enough to gain a perspective on how individuals view the presenting problem, person, or situation. This perspective is called a **frame**. The counselor may challenge the frame of the couple or family members to gain a clearer perspective of what is happening in the relationship or to give the couple or family another option by which they can perceive their situation (i.e., reframe).

In the initial session or sessions, the counselor is also an observer. He or she looks for a phenomenon called the couple or **family dance**, which is the way a couple or family typically interacts on either a verbal or nonverbal level (Napier & Whitaker, 1978). If the counselor misses this interaction at first, he or she need not worry, for the pattern will repeat itself. It is important in observing the family dance to see whether some member or members of the family are being **scapegoated** (i.e., blamed for the family's problems). For instance, a family may accuse its teenage son of being a lazy troublemaker because the adolescent sleeps late whenever possible and gets into mischief when he is out on the town with his friends. Although it may be true that the son has some problems, it is more likely that he is not the main cause of the family's problems. Thus, again, the counselor will need to probe and even challenge the family members' perceptions of where difficulties are located.

One way of broadly defining or clarifying what is happening in the couple or family is to ask **circular questions**—that is, questions that focus attention on couple or family connections and highlight differences among members. For instance, in a family the father might be asked how his daughter responds when verbally attacked by his wife and how other members of the family react as well, including himself. Such a strategy helps counselors and the families they work with see more of the dynamics involved in family life and may well take pressure off the person who has been seen as the problem. This type of questioning may also help the counselor and family see if **triangulation** is taking place (i.e., the drawing in of a third person or party into a dyadic conflict, such as the mother enlisting the father's support whenever she has an argument with the daughter).

In addition to these aspects of engaging the couple or family, it is crucial that the counselor develop the capacity to draw some initial conclusions in regard to the way the couple or family behaves (e.g., in a family, who talks to whom and who sits next to whom). In this way the counselor can gauge the dimensions of boundaries (i.e., those that allow closeness and caregiving versus ones that may be intrusive, such as a parent speaking for a child who is capable of speaking for himself or herself) (Worden, 2003). Intimacy and power can also be determined in this way. Essentially, through observation and engagement of the couple or family in conversation, the counselor becomes attuned to the dynamics within the couple or family, which in the long run are usually as important as, if not more important than, the content of conversations that occur within the counseling process.

Overall, a first session(s) usually is one in which a counselor evaluates how the couple or family is functioning and what may need to be done to help the relationship run more smoothly. Tentative goals are set as well, and a return appointment is made.

CASE EXAMPLE

Cleo Takes the Intake Call

Cleo had worked at family services for some time, but the call she received from a distraught mother at 2 a.m. confirmed the importance of listening to details. Helena, the mother, who was sobbing told Cleo that she would like to make an appointment for her family because of abuses occurring within it. Cleo carefully probed and found out there was no immediate danger, but still something felt wrong. She then took the names and addresses of family members and their relationship to one another as well as other details. Finally, she said to Helena, "I can see your family in my office at 9 a.m. tomorrow morning," to which Helena responded, "I hope you can straighten them out for me."

Cleo then realized what was happening. Helena was not planning to come to the session but instead was going to send her family to the therapist to be "fixed."

What would be your response to Helena at this point? What would you hope to accomplish by responding to her in this way? What difficulties might arise if the referring members of a family did not come to a session?

The Middle Phase of Marriage, Couple, and Family Counseling

The middle phase of marriage, couple, and family counseling consists of those sessions between the initial session(s) and termination. This part of treatment is where the couple or family will most likely make needed changes in themselves, if they change at all.

During this time, couples or families and the counselor explore new behaviors and take chances. Couples and families that are not sure if they wish to change will often make only superficial alterations in what they do. This type of change is known as a *first-order change*. An example is parents setting a curfew back by an hour without any real discussion about it or the importance of a teenage daughter accepting responsibility for her actions. *Second-order change*, where structured rules are altered, is quite different and is the type of change that is hoped for in a couple or family undergoing therapy. An example of second-order change is a rigid, authoritarian family becoming more democratic by adopting new rules regarding family interactions after everyone has had a chance to make suggestions and give input in regard to them (Watzlawick et al., 1974).

In fostering change within the couple or family, the counselor stays active mentally, verbally, and behaviorally (Friedlander, Wildman, Heatherington, & Skowron, 1994). The counselor also makes sure the couple or family goes beyond merely understanding what they need to do because cognitive knowledge alone seldom produces change. In addition, during the middle phase of counseling, the counselor links the couple or family with appropriate outside agencies, if possible. For example, in working with a family that has one or more members who are alcohol abusers, the counselor makes sure they find out information about *Alcoholics Anonymous (AA)* (an organization of individuals who help one another stay sober), *Al-Anon* (a self-help organization for adult relatives and friends of people with drinking problems), and/or *Alateen* (a similar program to Al-Anon but for younger people, usually ages 12 to 19).

Throughout the middle phase of treatment, there is a continuous focus on the process of what is happening within the couple or family. In many cases, couples and families make the easiest changes first. Consequently, counselors must press the couple or family for greater change if treatment is going to have any significance for them. The press is manifested in concentrating on cognitions, as well as their affective responses and behaviors (Worden, 2003). Sometimes this action is done in a straightforward manner whereas at other times it is accomplished through injecting humor into the therapeutic process, a right that a counselor has to earn through first showing care and developing trust. An example of using humor in treatment to promote change can be seen in the following mother and daughter interaction:

MOTHER TO DAUGHTER:	I will just die if you repeat that behavior again.
DAUGHTER TO MOTHER:	You will not. You're just trying to make me feel guilty.
COUNSELOR:	Sounds like this plan has worked before.
DAUGHTER:	It has. But she never dies and I just get mad and frustrated.
MOTHER:	I tell you, if you do it one more time, I will die!
COUNSELOR TO MOTHER:	So your daughter is pretty powerful. She can end your life with an action?
MOTHER (DRAMATICALLY):	Yes.
COUNSELOR TO DAUGHTER:	And you have said before that you love your mother.
DAUGHTER:	I do. But I'm tired of her reactions to what I do. They are just so overdone.
COUNSELOR TO DAUGHTER:	But your mother says you are powerful and could kill her. Since you love her, I know you wouldn't do that. However, since you have so much power I wonder if you would ever consider paralyzing one of her arms with a lesser behavior?
MOTHER:	What?!
DAUGHTER (LAUGHING):	Well, it might get her to stop harping at me and give us a chance to talk.
COUNSELOR (TO MOTHER AND DAUGHTER):	Maybe that chance is now and no one has to suffer physically if we do it right.

The counselor in this case addressed a pressing issue of power and drama in a serious but somewhat humorous way that got the attention of the two individuals most involved in the struggle, broke a dysfunctional pattern, and set up an opportunity for real dialogue and new interactions to emerge.

In addition to the previous ways of working, the counselor must look for evidence of stability of change such as a couple or family accommodating more to one another through subtle as well as obvious means. For instance, seating patterns, the names family members call each other, or even the tone individuals use when addressing one another are all signs that somewhat permanent change has occurred in the couple or family if they differ greatly from where they were when the therapeutic process began. In the case of a couple or family that is changing, the tone of addressing one another might go from harsh to inviting.

PERSONAL REFLECTION

Many people today carry cell phones. What do you notice about their ring tones? Are some more appealing than others? Could the same kind of linkage be made in regard to the tones family members use with each other? How would you react if your ring tone always conveyed a harsh sound?

In the middle phase of marriage, couple, and family counseling, it is crucial that the counselor not get ahead of the couple or family members. Should that happen, therapeutic progress will end because the couple or family will not be invested. Therefore, staying on task and on target requires the counselor to keep balanced and push only so far. A way to help couples and families stay engaged and make progress is to give them ***homework*** (i.e., tasks to complete outside the counseling sessions such as setting aside time for a conversation) and ***psychoeducational assignments*** (i.e., reading a book or viewing a video) to complete together so that they are literally learning more and interacting together. For example, the family might watch some episodes from the comedy television show of the 1960s *The Addams Family*. They could then come back and talk about how they are like and unlike in regard to the macabre family they viewed. Such a way of working gives family members even more in common than would otherwise be the case, may draw them closer psychologically, and helps them clarify who they are and what they do.

Termination/Closure

Termination can be considered to be a misnomer in couple or family counseling since "from a family systems perspective, the therapist-family therapeutic system has reached an end point, but the family system certainly continues" (Worden, 2003, p. 187). Regardless, termination (including follow-up) is the final phase of treatment in working with couples and families.

The couple or family, the counselor, or both may initiate termination. There is no one person who should start the process or one single way that closure should be conducted. However, termination should not be sudden and should not be seen as the highlight of counseling (Gladding, 2011). Rather, termination is designed to provide a counselor and a couple or family with closure. It should be a means to assess whether couple or family goals have been reached.

Thus, in beginning termination, the counselor and couple or family should ask themselves why they are entering this phase. One reason may be that enough progress has been made that the couple or family is now able to function on its own better than ever before. Likewise, everyone involved may agree that the couple or family has accomplished what it set out to do and that to continue would not be a wise investment in time and effort.

Whatever the reason for terminating, the counselor should make sure that the work the couple or family has done is summarized and celebrated (if appropriate) so that the couple or family leaves counseling more aware and feeling stronger in realizing what they accomplished. In addition to summarization, another aspect of termination is deciding on ***long-term goals***, such as creating a calm household where members are open to one another. This projective process gives couple and family members something to think about and plan out (sometimes with the counselor's input). A part of many termination sessions involves ***predicting setbacks*** as well, so that couples and families do not become too upset when they fail to achieve their goals as planned.

A final part of termination is ***follow-up*** (i.e., checking up on the couple or family following treatment after a period of time). Follow-up conveys care and lets couples and families know that they can return to counseling to finish anything they began there or to work on other issues. Client couples and families often do better when they have follow-up because they become aware that their progress is being monitored both within and outside the context in which they live.

MyCounselingLab™

Go to Topic 8: *Family Counseling* in the MyCounselingLab™ site (www.MyCounselingLab .com) for *Counseling: A Comprehensive Profession,* Seventh Edition, where you can:

- Find learning outcomes for *Family Counseling* along with the national standards that connect to these outcomes.
- Complete Assignments and Activities that can help you more deeply understand the chapter content.
- Apply and practice your understanding of the core skills identified in the chapter with the Building Counseling Skills unit.
- Prepare yourself for professional certification with a Practice for Certification quiz.
- Connect to videos through the Video and Resource Library.

Summary and Conclusion

American families have changed over the years from a few dominant forms to a great many varieties. These changes were brought about by a number of forces within society such as the women's movement, global and regional wars, and federal legislation. With these changes has come a greater need for working with married and unmarried couples as well as families. The professions of marriage, couple, and family counseling have grown rapidly since the 1950s for a number of reasons, including theory development and proven research effectiveness. It has prospered also because it has had strong advocates and has generated a number of unique and effective approaches for a variety of couple and family forms.

Professionals who enter the marriage, couple, and family counseling field align with at least four associations, depending on their background. Most counselors join the International Association for Marriage and Family Counseling (IAMFC) because of its affiliation with the ACA, but some affiliate with the American Association for Marriage and Family Therapy (AAMFT), the largest marriage and family therapy association. Regardless of affiliation, those who work with couples and families need to know the life cycle of families in order to assess whether a marriage or family problem is developmental or situational. Marriage, couple, and family counselors also need to be aware of systems theories and the ways that couples and families work systemically.

The field of marriage counseling is sometimes incorporated into family counseling models, but professionals in this specialty need to be aware of the theories and processes that are used in each area. They must also realize how individual or group theories may complement or detract from work with families. Finally, marriage, couple, and family counselors need to be well schooled in the stages that family counseling entails—preplanning, initial session(s), the middle phase, and termination—and the general techniques and emphasis within each.

Overall, working with couples and families is a dynamic and exciting way of helping people. Because of its complexity and the intricacies of the process, it is not for everyone but it is an entity that many counselors seem to enjoy and from which many people in society benefit.

Professional School Counseling

I skip down the hall like a boy of seven
   before the last bell of school
      and the first day of summer,
My ivy-league tie flying through the stagnant air
   that I break into small breezes as I bobbingly pass.
At my side, within fingertip touch,
   a first grade child with a large cowlick
      roughly traces my every step
         filling in spaces with moves of his own
            on the custodian's just waxed floor.
"Draw me a man"
   I ask as we stop,
And with no thought of crayons and paper
   he shyly comes with open arms
      to quietly take me in with a hug.

From "Portraits," by S. T. Gladding, 1974, *Personnel and Guidance Journal, 53*, p. 110. © Samuel T. Gladding.

MyCounselingLab™

Visit the MyCounselingLab™ site (www.MyCounselingLab.com) for *Counseling: A Comprehensive Profession,* Seventh Edition to enhance your understanding of chapter concepts. You'll have the opportunity to practice your skills through video- and case-based Assignments and Activities as well as Building Counseling Skills units and to prepare for your certification exam with Practice for Certification quizzes.

The field of school counseling involves a wide range of ages, developmental stages, background experiences, and types of problems (Baker & Gerler, 2008; Cobia & Henderson, 2007). In the United States almost four million children begin their formal education each year, while millions more continue their schooling. Within this population, some children are developmentally ready, eager, and able, whereas others are disadvantaged because of physical, mental, cultural, or socioeconomic factors (Bemak & Chung, 2008). Yet a third group carries the burden of traumas, such as various forms of abuse, through no fault of their own (Fontes, 2002; Richardson & Norman, 1997).

Like children in other countries, American schoolchildren face a barrage of complex events and processes that have temporary and permanent impacts on them. Alcohol and other drug abuse, changing family patterns, poor self-esteem, hopelessness, AIDS, racial and ethnic tensions, crime and violence, teenage pregnancy, sexism, and the explosion of knowledge have negative influence on these children regardless of their age or environment (Keys & Bemak, 1997; McGowan, 1995). It is little wonder then that 1 in 5 children have a diagnosable mental disorder and 1 in 10 has a serious emotional disturbance that significantly impairs functioning at school, at home, and in the community (Mellin, 2009, p. 501). That is where school counselors come in.

Years of research have concluded that, in school environments, "counseling interventions have a substantial impact on students' educational and personal development" (Borders & Drury, 1992, p. 495). Indeed, outcome research has indicated that school counselors make a positive difference in children's lives and in educational environments (Gysbers, 2001; Whiston & Sexton, 1998). Counseling interventions tend to be particularly effective in increasing students' problem-solving behaviors and reducing disciplinary referrals (Whiston, Wendi Lee, Rahardja, & Eder, 2011). School counselors contribute "to student academic achievement through school counseling programs that address the personal/social, career, and academic development of all students" (Barna & Brott, 2011, p. 243).

Overall, school counselors and comprehensive guidance and counseling programs help children and adolescents become better adjusted academically and developmentally while

- feeling safer,
- having better relationships with teachers and peers,
- believing their education is relevant to their futures,
- having fewer problems in school, and
- earning higher grades (Lapan, Gysbers, & Petroski, 2001).

In 2008–2009, the U.S. student-to-counselor ratio was 457:1, far above the American Counseling Association's recommended maximum average student-to-counselor ratio of 250:1. The lower figure recommended is to ensure that students have adequate access to counseling services.

This chapter examines the roles of professional school counselors in general and the unique and overlapping roles they have at the elementary, middle, and secondary levels. It addresses the special situational and developmental aspects of dealing with each school-age population and the importance of being sensitive to children's cultural backgrounds and differing worldviews (Baker & Gerler, 2008; Hobson & Kanitz, 1996; Lee, 2001). Particular attention is given to prevention and treatment issues associated with children in schools and to the American School Counselor Association (ASCA) National Model.

THE ASCA NATIONAL MODEL

Historically, professional school counseling grew out of vocational guidance and character development initiatives. However, **school counseling** is now widely considered to be a comprehensive, developmental, programmatic component of K-12 public education (Falco, Bauman, Sumnicht, & Engelstad, 2011). Because of some identity problems and perceptions both within and outside the profession, school counselors have been asked to perform multiple duties as part of their daily work (Bemak & Chung, 2008; Gysbers, 2011). "Some of these duties match the descriptions set forth by national standards for school counseling programs, whereas others do not" (Wilkerson & Bellini, 2006, p. 440). Thus, some school counselors have struggled to prove their worth to superintendents, principals, teachers, students, and parents who sometimes have misunderstood what they do (Guerra, 1998). In order to overcome this confusion and to focus on what activities school counselors should be engaged in, the **American School Counselor Association** (**ASCA**; 801 N. Fairfax Street, Suite 310, Alexandria, VA 22314) published a national model for school counseling (ASCA, 2005). It defines what a school counselor is and clarifies the roles of school counselors for the profession and for the public. At its core, the ASCA National Model "encourages school counselors to think in terms of the expected results of what students should know and be able to do as a result of implementing a standards-based comprehensive **school counseling program**" (Dahir & Stone, 2009, p. 12). It does this through an **interlocking lineage of four components** (Scarborough, & Culbreth, 2008):

- **foundation (beliefs and philosophy, mission),**
- **delivery system (guidance curriculum, individual student planning, responsive services, systems support),**
- **management systems (agreements, advisory council, use of data, action plans, use of time, use of calendar),** and
- **accountability (results reports, school counselor performance standards, program audit).**

The **ASCA National Model** supports the mission of schools by promoting **three main areas** in the delivery system (see next page). They can be conceptualized as follows:

- **academic achievement,**
- **career planning,** and
- **personal and social development.**

The ASCA National Model recommends that school counselors collaborate with parents, students, teachers, and support staff to focus on the development of all students—not just those who are high achievers or at high risk. Furthermore, this national model recommends that 80% of school counselors' time be spent in direct contact with students. Inappropriate duties assigned to school counselors should be jettisoned in favor of appropriate responsibilities (Table 17.1).

ASCA National Model

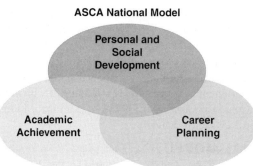

TABLE 17.1 Appropriate and Inappropriate Counseling Responsibilities

Inappropriate (Noncounseling) Activities:	Appropriate (Counseling) Responsibilities:
Registering and scheduling all new students	Designing individual student academic programs
Administering cognitive, aptitude and achievement tests	Interpreting cognitive, aptitude and achievement tests
Signing excuses for students who are tardy or absent	Counseling students with excessive tardiness or absenteeism
Performing disciplinary actions	Counseling students with disciplinary problems
Sending home students who are not appropriately dressed	Counseling students about appropriate school dress
Teaching classes when teachers are absent	Collaborating with teachers to present guidance curriculum lessons
Computing grade-point averages	Analyzing grade-point averages in relationship to achievement
Maintaining student records	Interpreting student records
Supervising study halls	Providing teachers with suggestions for better study hall management
Clerical record keeping	Ensuring student records are maintained in accordance with state and federal regulations
Assisting with duties in the principal's office	Assisting the school principal with identifying and resolving student issues, need, and problems
Working with one student at a time in a therapeutic, clinical mode	Collaborating with teachers to present proactive, prevention-based guidance curriculum lessons

Source: American School Counselor Association (2002). Executive Summary, ASCA National Model. Alexandria, VA: Author. p. 4.

Overall, the ASCA National Model embodies what is known as **strength-based school counseling (SBSC)** (Galassi, Griffin, & Akos, 2008). In SBSC the emphasis is on promoting evidence-based interventions and practices that are proactive on the individual, group, and school levels. Activities in SBSC include a focus on student strengths, advocacy for students who lack resources, and the forming of partnerships with other professionals and families of children. This approach differs from **deficit-based counseling**, where the focus is on fixing a problem.

School Counselors at Various Levels

Within the field of school counseling, the professional literature focuses on three distinct school-age populations: **elementary school children (Grades K–5), middle school children (Grades 6–8),** and **secondary school children (Grades 9–12).** Each of these populations has particular concerns and universal needs. How needs are addressed depends on many variables, including school level of employment (i.e., elementary, middle, high), years of experience as a school counselor, number of students per caseload, amount of time spent in non-guidance-related activities, professional identity and development, as well as the organizational culture in the school (Scarborough, & Culbreth, 2008). However, at the very heart of school counseling on any level is the enhancement of student personal/social development (Van Veisor, 2009).

PERSONAL REFLECTION

What do you remember most about the school counselors you had growing up? What duties did they perform? Was there a difference in their focus at various levels? How do you think the ASCA National Model might have helped them and your school(s)?

ELEMENTARY SCHOOL COUNSELING

Elementary school counseling is a relatively recent development. The first book on this subject was published in the 1950s, and the discipline was virtually nonexistent before 1965 (Dinkmeyer, 1973a, 1989). In fact, fewer than 10 universities offered coursework in elementary school counseling in 1964 (Muro, 1981).

The development of elementary school counseling was slow for three reasons (Peters, 1980; Schmidt, 2007). First, many people believed that elementary school teachers should serve as counselors for their students because they worked with them all day and were in an ideal position to identify specific problems. Second, counseling at the time was primarily concerned with vocational development, which is not a major focus of elementary school children. Finally, many people did not recognize a need for counseling on the elementary school level. Psychologists and social workers were employed by some secondary schools to diagnose emotional and learning problems in older children and offer advice in difficult family situations, but full-time counseling on the elementary level was not considered.

Although the first elementary school counselors were employed in the late 1950s, elementary school counseling did not gain momentum until the 1960s (Faust, 1968). In 1964, Congress passed the **National Defense Education Act (NDEA) Title V-A**, and counseling services were extended to include elementary school children (Herr, 2002). Two years later, the Joint Committee on the Elementary School Counselor (a cooperative effort between the Association for Counselor Education and Supervision [ACES] and ASCA) issued a report defining the roles and functions of the elementary school counselor, which emphasized counseling, consultation, and coordination (ACES-ASCA, 1966). Government grants to establish training institutes for elementary school counselors were authorized in 1968; by 1972, more than 10,000 elementary school counselors were employed (Dinkmeyer, 1973a).

During the 1970s, the number of counselors entering the elementary school counseling specialty leveled off and then fell temporarily due to declining school enrollments and economic problems (Baker & Gerler, 2008). In the late 1980s, however, accrediting agencies and state departments of public instruction began mandating that schools provide counseling services on the elementary level, and a surge in demand for elementary school counselors ensued. This renewed interest in the specialty was a result of publications such as *A Nation at Risk*, which was released by the National Commission of Excellence in Education (Schmidt, 2007). Although it does not refer to elementary school counseling, the report emphasizes accountability and effectiveness within schools at all levels.

Emphases and Roles

Elementary school counselors are a vanguard in the mental health movement at educational settings (Gysbers & Henderson, 2006b). No other profession has ever been organized to work with individuals from a purely preventive and developmental perspective. Among the **tasks that elementary school counselors regularly perform** are the following:

- implement effective classroom guidance,
- provide individual and small-group counseling,
- assist students in identifying their skills and abilities,
- work with special populations,
- develop students' career awareness,
- coordinate school, community, and business resources,
- consult with teachers and other professionals,
- communicate and exchange information with parents/guardians, and
- participate in school improvement and interdisciplinary teams (Campbell & Dahir, 1997).

A study in California of the perceived, actual, and ideal roles of elementary school counselors found that the majority of counselors who were surveyed spent a large portion of their time in counseling, consultation, and parental-help activities (Furlong, Atkinson, & Janoff, 1979). Their actual and ideal roles were nearly identical. Schmidt and Osborne (1982) found similar results in a study of North Carolina elementary school counselors, whose top activities were counseling with individuals and groups and consulting with teachers. Morse and Russell (1988) also found preferences involving consultation, counseling, and group work when they analyzed the roles of Pacific Northwest elementary school counselors in K–5 settings. Three of the five highest ranked actual roles of these counselors involved consultation activities, whereas two of the five included individual counseling with students. These counselors ranked four of their top five ideal activities as those that involved working with groups of students. Indeed, it appears that elementary school counselors desire to spend time in group activities with children.

The lowest ranked and most inappropriate tasks that other school personnel try to assign elementary school counselors include substitute teaching, monitoring lunchrooms or playgrounds, and acting as school disciplinarian or student records clerk. The emphases that elementary school counselors place on such noncounseling services have important consequences for them and the children and schools they serve. If counselors are used in such ways, they lose their effectiveness and everyone suffers.

CASE EXAMPLE

Pat and the Promotion

Pat was an elementary school counselor and loved his job even though at times it was stressful and he was economically stretched. One day his principal, Daniel, came by to see him and announced he was considering retirement. During the conversation Daniel mentioned that he thought Pat would make a great principal. To get Pat ready for taking on such a responsibility and to make him an attractive candidate, Daniel suggested shifting some of his administrative duties to Pat. "It won't take much time" he said, "and it is important. Besides, you'll make a lot more money."

Put yourself in Pat's shoes. How would you respond and why?

In an important and well-investigated article on the effectiveness of elementary school counseling, Gerler (1985) reviewed research reports published in *Elementary School Guidance and Counseling* from 1974 to 1984. He focused on studies designed to help children from behavioral, affective, social, and mental image/sensory awareness perspectives. Gerler found strong evidence that elementary school counseling programs "can positively influence the affective, behavioral, and inter-personal domains of children's lives and, as a result, can affect children's achievement positively" (p. 45). In another article, Keat (1990) detailed how elementary school counselors can use a multimodal approach called *HELPING* (an acronym for **health; emotions; learning; personal relationships; imagery; need to know; and guidance of actions, behaviors, and consequences**) to help children grow and develop.

The fact that elementary school counselors have, can, and do make a difference in the lives of the children they serve is a strong rationale for keeping and increasing their services. That is one reason ASCA initiated its model. It is easier to handle difficulties during the younger years than at later times (Bailey, Deery, Gehrke, Perry, & Whitledge, 1989; Campbell & Dahir, 1997). Elementary school counselors who have vision (for example, that children can be problem solvers) and follow through (such as Claudia Vangstad in Oregon) can transform the culture of a school (Littrell & Peterson, 2001). In Vangstad's case, she used ten core values (Table 17.2) to build an exemplary elementary school counseling program and helped transform a school culture. She utilized her power as a person and a counselor in the interest of creatively conceiving a program that others could and did buy into.

Activities

Elementary school counselors engage in a number of activities. Some of these are prescribed by law, such as the reporting of child abuse. "In the United States, all 50 states and the District of Columbia have laws that require schools and their agents to report suspicions or allegations of child abuse and neglect to a local agency mandated to protect children" (Barrett-Kruse, Martinez, & Carll, 1998, p. 57). Most activities of elementary school counselors are not so legally mandated, however, and include a plethora of preventive and remedial activities. Prevention is preferred because of its psychological payoff in time invested and results.

PREVENTION.   Elementary school counseling programs strive to create a positive school environment for students. They emphasize the **four Cs: counseling services, coordination of activities, consultation with others, and curriculum development**. The last activity, curriculum development, is both developmental and educational. It focuses on formulating "guidance classes [on]

TABLE 17.2   A Comparison of the Old and New School Culture

Old School Culture

1. Adult-driven
2. Punishment
3. Externally imposed discipline
4. Focus on problems
5. Competitive, non-collaborative
6. Unit expected to change: the individual
7. Peer isolation
8. Problems approached by adults using discipline, threats, paddle, and behavior modification
9. Children try to solve problems by swearing, hitting, and threats
10. Children not empowered to change themselves and to help others change

New School Culture

1. Student-driven
2. Learning new skills
3. Self-imposed discipline
4. Focus on problem solving
5. Cooperative, collaborative
6. Unit expected to change: the individual, the group, and the community
7. Peer support
8. Problems resolved by adults using dialogue, positive interactions, cooperation, and a problem-solving model
9. Children try to solve problems by the problem-solving model and peer support
10. Children are empowered to change themselves and to help others change

life skills and in preventing . . . difficulties" that might otherwise occur (Bailey et al., 1989, p. 9). The ASCA National Model (American School Counselor Association [ASCA], 2005) suggests that elementary school counselors spend up to 45% of their time delivering classroom guidance. "**Classroom guidance** lessons are an efficient way for school counselors to inform students about school-wide opportunities (e.g., counseling department services), distribute information (e.g., educational resources, postsecondary opportunities), and address student needs (e.g., preparing for school transitions, learning skills to eliminate bullying)" (Akos, Cockman, & Strickland, 2007, p. 455).

At their best, classroom guidance lessons are proactive and focus on prevention (e.g., school violence) as well as promotion (e.g., a positive body image). As an example of proactive classroom guidance, Magnuson (1996) developed a lesson for fourth graders that compared the web that Charlotte, the spider, spins for physical nutrition in the book *Charlotte's Web* (White, 1952) with the webs that human beings spin for personal nurturing. Just as Charlotte needed a variety of insects to stay healthy, the lesson stressed that people need to attract a variety of friends and support to live life to the fullest. The lesson ended with children not only discussing the parallels between Charlotte and themselves but also drawing a "personal web" filled with significant and important persons in their lives.

A first priority for elementary school counselors is making themselves known and establishing links with others. "School personnel are not usually viewed by young children as the first source of help" (Bachman, 1975, p. 108). Therefore, elementary school counselors need to publicize who they are, what they do, and how and when they can help. This process is usually handled best through orientation programs, classroom visits, or both. The important point is to let children, parents, teachers, and administrators know what counseling and guidance services are available and how they are a vital part of the total school environment.

For instance, in situations in which very young children (3- to 5-year-olds) are part of the school environment, elementary school counselors can make themselves known by offering special assistance to these children and their families, such as monitoring developmental aspects of the children's lives (Hohenshil & Hohenshil, 1989). Many children in this age range face a multitude of detrimental conditions including poverty, family/community violence, and neglect (Carnegie Task Force on Meeting the Needs of Young Children, 1994). The efforts of elementary school counselors with these children may include offering prosocial classroom guidance lessons centered around socialization skills (Paisley & Hubbard, 1994; Smead, 1995). Furthermore, elementary school counselors can consult with teachers and other mental health professionals to be sure that efforts at helping these young children are maximized.

It is especially important to work with parents and the community when children, regardless of age, are at risk for developing either low self-concepts or antisocial attitudes (Capuzzi, 2008). Having lunch with parents where they work, even at odd hours, is one way for counselors to reach out and support families in the education of their children (Evans & Hines, 1997). Family counseling interventions by school counselors is another way to focus on **three primary subsystems: the family, the school, and the subsystem formed by the family and school interactions** (Lewis, 1996). Elementary school counselors (and for that matter middle and secondary school counselors) avoid assuming that most student problems are a result of dysfunctional families and instead focus on constructively addressing all three subsystems as needed.

Yet a third way of combating potential destructiveness is known as ***multiple concurrent actions***. In this approach, counselors access more than one set of services within the community at a time—for example, social services and learning disabilities specialists. This type of coordinated action between school and community agencies is collaborative and integrative, and it requires energy and commitment on the part of the counselor (Keys et al., 1998).

Simultaneous with publicizing their services and establishing relationships with others in the community, elementary school counselors must be active in their schools in a variety of ways, especially in guidance activities. Myrick (2003) recommends a proactive, developmental, comprehensive approach to guidance programs: two to three large classroom meetings each week and twice as many small-group sessions. These activities focus on structured learning, such as understanding oneself, decision making, problem solving, establishing healthy girl-boy relations, and how to get along with teachers and make friends (Coppock, 1993; Snyder & Daly, 1993). Classroom guidance should also address conflict resolution and peer mediation in which students learn peaceful and constructive ways of settling differences and preventing violence (Carruthers, Sweeney, Kmitta, & Harris, 1996).

Other preventive services offered by elementary school counselors include setting up peer mediation programs and consultation/education activities. ***Peer mediators*** are specially selected and trained students who serve the school and the counselor in positive and unique ways. They may help students get to know one another, create an atmosphere of sharing and acceptance, provide opportunities for other students to resolve personal difficulties, and enhance the problem-solving skills of the students (Garner, Martin, & Martin, 1989). Peer mediators assist elementary school counselors in reaching a number of individuals they might otherwise miss.

Peer mediators also may enhance the overall cooperative atmosphere in a school (Joynt, 1993). The effectiveness of peer mediation on the elementary school level can be seen in preventing and reducing school-wide violence. For example, Schellenberg, Parks-Savage, and Rehfuss (2007) found in a 3-year longitudinal study that a school-wide peer mediation program reduced out-of-school suspensions and resulted in "significant mediator knowledge gains pertaining to conflict, conflict resolution, and mediation" (p. 475). In another similar type of situation, Scarborough (1997) found that she could foster the social, emotional, and cognitive skills of fifth graders through a peer helper program she called the Serve Our School (SOS) Club. Students in the club served as assistants working with school staff as they carried out their responsibilities. Members also provided cross-age tutoring. Everyone benefited and learned.

By implementing consultation/education sessions for teachers, administrators, and parents, counselors address common concerns and teach new ways of handling old problems by getting many people committed to working in a cooperative manner (Dougherty, 1986). For example, helping establish culturally compatible classrooms in which student diversity is recognized, appreciated, and used is a service elementary school counselors can provide constituents (Herring & White, 1995; Lee, 2001). Promoting communication skills between teachers and students is another crucial cooperative service elementary school counselors can set up (Hawes, 1989). Yet a third cooperative service that elementary school counselors can provide is a class on parenting skills that emphasizes effective communication procedures and behavior management (Ritchie & Partin, 1994).

Skilled elementary school counselors can even use their counseling role in a preventive way. For instance, by meeting regularly in individual sessions with **at-risk children** (those most likely to develop problems because of their backgrounds or present behaviors), counselors can assess how well these children are functioning and what interventions, if any, might be helpful to them or significant others (Webb, 1992).

Bullying behavior may be one place where preventive interventions can also take place. "**Bullying** is a subset of aggression with three components: (*a*) intent to harm, (*b*) repetition, and (*c*) a power imbalance between the bully and the target or victim. Bullying is distinguished from conflict by unequal power between the persons involved" (Bauman, 2008, p. 363). Although bullying is usually thought of "as one person threatening or actually physically assaulting another person for no apparent reason," it can include "name-calling, teasing, writing hurtful statements, intentional exclusion, stealing, and defacing personal property" (Beale & Scott, 2001, p. 300). Elementary school children are twice as likely to be bullied as secondary school children, with grades 5–8 consistently found to be the grades where bullying is most likely to take place (Janson, Carney, Hazler, & Insoo, 2009). Contrary to expectations, most bullying occurs in schools such as playgrounds, hallways, and bathrooms, where there is a minimum of adult supervision (Bauman, 2008). Surprisingly, bystanders experienced significant traumatic reactions as a result of witnessing common forms of repetitive abuse between their peers, thus signaling another reason not to let such behavior continue (Janson et al., 2009).

Regardless, bullying behavior can be addressed in a preventive fashion through a number of means. Probably the most effective is for the elementary school counselor to take a leadership role as an advocate in **antibullying efforts** for a school. In such a role, the counselor can serve as a catalyst, a consultant, and a change agent (Bauman, 2008). An important step in this process is the forming of a **steering committee** (composed of teachers, administrators, and students) that works as a team to combat bullying.

Other techniques used to prevent bullying can be found in several forms. One is a peer-performed **psychoeducational drama** that "allows students to indirectly experience many of the negative consequences of bullying in an impersonal, non-threatening way" (Beale & Scott, 2001, p. 302). Providing **positive adult role models** for children to emulate may be helpful too as a preventive measure along with **systemically addressing negative influences** such as parental physical discipline, negative peer models, lack of adult supervision, and neighborhood safety concerns (Espelage, Bosworth, & Simon, 2000).

Besides obvious problems, such as bullying, preventive counseling services are needed for less obvious groups and behaviors. For example, **gifted and talented students** may need special help from a prevention perspective. Although this subgroup of students usually appears to function well, in reality these individuals may have some concerns, such as underachiev-ing, overextending, and handling stress (Greene, 2006). Helping them learn to manage stress, plan ahead, and not be overcritical of themselves or their abilities are just some of the ways elementary school counselors can help these talented students stay balanced and develop healthy self-concepts.

In working with children and the topic of **divorce**, elementary school counselors can do much good on the preventive level (Crosbie-Burnett & Newcomer, 1989). Preventively, they can address divorce as a topic in classroom guidance classes. Such classes should be information-ally humane in intent and aimed at alleviating much of the negative stereotyping and myths that surround divorce. Elementary school counselors can use small groups to concentrate on specific children's needs regarding divorce as well, thereby preventing further problems. Groups for chil-dren experiencing divorce have been found effective in reducing dysfunctional behaviors, espe-cially if both the custodial and noncustodial parents are involved (Frieman, 1994).

Small-group counseling programs on the elementary level can also help students increase learning behaviors and narrow the gap between poor students, students of color, and students who have material and psychological advantages (Steen & Kaffenberger, 2007). Integrating aca-demic interventions and group counseling improves students' behaviors (e.g., asking questions, completing assignments, and staying on task) related to school achievement. At the same time, it can address personal/social concerns as well, such as "changing families, friendships, and/or anger management" (p. 516).

Overall, elementary school counselors can work with others in the school to design and implement a comprehensive prevention program, the best known of which is the ***school-wide positive behavioral support (SWPBS) program*** (Curtis, Van Horne, Robertson, & Karvonen, 2010). The SWPBS is composed of "five basic components: (a) a leadership team; (b) a brief, overriding school-wide philosophy; (c) specific behavioral guidelines for each area of the school (e.g., playground, buses, cafeteria); (d) individual classroom guidelines; and (e) specific strate-gies for students who need extra attention. Another key component of SWPBS is collecting and monitoring data to determine where further action is needed. This way, if problems persist on the buses or in the restrooms, for instance, the leadership team can target strategies for those two specific areas" (Curtis et al., 2010).

A specific form of a SWPBS is to use **a positive behavior support approach** on a school-wide basis (Sherrod, Getch, & Ziomek-Daigle, 2009). In this type of approach, school counselors help school administrators define, teach, and acknowledge expected behaviors while applying clear consequences to inappropriate behaviors in specific areas of the school, such as the hall-ways and in classrooms. Individualized plans used to address the specific problem behaviors of the students who have chronic behavior problems and those at risk of developing behavior prob-lems are used as well. Basically, this approach is systematic. Because it is so comprehensive, it has proven more effective than "tough love" approaches such as suspension and expulsion.

PERSONAL REFLECTION

As you have read, elementary school counselors work hard at providing preventive mental health services. How do you think they might present their work to the public, especially since many indi-viduals are skeptical of prevention programs?

REMEDIATION. *Remediation* is the act of trying to make a situation right. The word implies that something is wrong and that it will take work to implement correction. In elementary school counseling, a number of activities come under the remediation heading. One example is children's self-esteem.

Children's self-esteem is related to their *self-concept*, how they perceive themselves in a variety of areas, academically, physically, socially, and so forth (McWhirter, McWhirter, McWhirter, & McWhirter, 2007). *Self-esteem* results from the comparison of oneself to others in a peer group. Although it may be situational or characterological, self-esteem is basically how well individuals like what they see—how people evaluate themselves (Street & Isaacs, 1998). It is always evolving (Duys & Hobson, 2004). To enhance self-esteem is an arduous process. For such a task, counselors need an understanding of developmental theory, such as that of Robert Kegan. Such a theory can help them conceptualize the evolution of self-esteem, especially since Kegan incorporates cognitive, moral, and psychosocial development into his assumptions about the evolution of self-esteem. Pragmatically, counselors must focus on helping low-self-esteem children, who are at risk for failure, improve in the following areas: **critical school academic competencies, self-concept, communication skills, coping ability,** and **control**. McWhirter, McWhirter, McWhirter, and McWhirter (1994) call these the **"Five Cs of Competency"** (p. 188). Counselors can enhance self-esteem in these areas by skill building, such as improving social skills, problem-solving skills, and coping skills (Street & Isaacs, 1998). In working in remediation, elementary school counselors must rely on their individual and group counseling skills, as well as their social action abilities, in making environmental changes and modifications.

One way of determining what needs to be remediated and at what level is to use a needs assessment. *Needs assessments* are structured surveys that focus on the systematic appraisal of the types, depths, and scope of problems in particular populations (Cook, 1989; Rossi, Lipsey & Freeman, 2004). Needs assessments may be purchased commercially, borrowed and modified from others, or originated by an institution's staff. In school settings, counselors can gain a great deal of useful information if they regularly take the time to survey students, teachers, parents, and support personnel. This knowledge helps them address specific problems. Typically, concerns uncovered through needs assessments fall into **four main areas: school, family relations, relationships with others, and the self** (Berube & Berube, 1997; Dinkmeyer & Caldwell, 1970).

Example of Needs Assessment: Evaluation of Self

Please circle the number of your concern about the following statements as they pertain to you.

Not Concerned	Somewhat Concerned	Concerned	Very Concerned
1	2	3	4

1. My ability to relate well to other students.   1 2 3 4
2. My ability to learn.   1 2 3 4
3. My ability to keep quiet or still in class.   1 2 3 4
4. My looks and appearance.   1 2 3 4
5. My eating habits.   1 2 3 4

A second way of determining what needs to be remediated is through evidence-based or *data-based decision making* where the school counselor uses institutional data about student performance and behavior to identify problems that need to be addressed (Carey & Dimmitt, 2008). The collection of such information is followed up using multidisciplinary teams to identify and implement research-based interventions. The interventions and programs are evaluated to demonstrate their effectiveness. The result of this three-step process is better outcomes for students and enhanced professional status for the counselor.

Three-Step Process of Evidence-Based or Data-Based Decision Making
1. Collect institutional data to identify or describe problems that need to be addressed
2. Use multidisciplinary evidence-based teams led by the school counselor to implement research-based interventions
3. Evaluate interventions used to assess their effectiveness

In remediation sessions, young children often respond best to counseling strategies built around techniques that require active participation. Play therapy, bibliotherapy, and the use of games are three strategic interventions that help counselors establish rapport with young children and facilitate their self-understanding.

Play therapy is a specialized way of working with children that requires skill and training. It, along with art therapy, is "less limited by cultural differences" between counselors and clients "than are other forms of interventions" (Cochran, 1996, p. 287). Therefore, this form of counseling is covered more and more frequently in counselor education programs (Landreth, 2002). Basically, children express emotions by manipulating play media such as toys. "In what might be called '**play reconstruction**,' children symbolically reenact traumatic or puzzling experiences by repeating a significant pattern in play" (Chesley, Gillett, & Wagner, 2008, p. 401). When counselors participate with children in the play process—that is, communicate by acknowledging children's thoughts and feelings—they establish rapport and a helping relationship (Campbell, 1993b). By expressing their feelings in a natural way, children are more able to recognize and constructively deal with volatile affect (Henderson & Thompson, 2011; Janson et al., 2009). A number of approaches can be used in play therapy, but Jungian and person centered are two of the most popular.

When conducting play sessions with children, it is ideal to have a well-equipped playroom. However, most schools do not, so counselors usually need a tote bag in which to store their materials. **Play materials** fall into one of **three broad categories**: **real-life toys, acting-out or aggressive toys,** and **toys for creative expression or release** (Landreth, 2002). Items frequently include puppets, masks, drawing materials, and clay. Sand play has been effective in working with children who have low self-esteem, poor academic progress, high anxiety, and mild depression (Allan & Brown, 1993; Carmichael, 1994). In some situations, counselors may work with parents to continue play therapy sessions at home (Guerney, 1983); in other cases, counselors may hold counseling sessions for students who are involved in play therapy. Child-centered group play therapy is a culturally sensitive counseling approach that Baggerly and Parker (2005) have found effective with African American boys. This approach honors the **African worldview** (emotional vitality, interdependence, collective survival, and harmonious blending; Parham, White, & Ajamu, 2000) and builds self-confidence. It helps African American boys "develop an internal strength to buffer racism" (Baggerly & Parker, 2005, p. 393).

Bibliotherapy can be used, too, in counseling and guidance activities with elementary school children (Borders & Paisley, 1992; Gladding & Gladding, 1991). **Bibliotherapy** is "the use of books [or media] as aids to help children gain insight into their problems and find appropriate solutions" (Hollander, 1989, pp. 184–185). For example, books and videos that emphasize diversity, such as *Babe, Pocahontas, The Lion King,* or *The Little Mermaid,* may be used to promote acceptance and tolerance (Richardson & Norman, 1997). These counseling tools are especially helpful if counselors summarize stories for children, openly discuss characters' feelings, explore consequences of a character's action, and sometimes draw conclusions (Schrank, 1982).

School counselors who work directly with children who have been abused may also choose to use bibliotherapy because of the way media promote nonthreatening relationships. A number of books can be used therapeutically with children who have been sexually abused. Two of the best are *I Can't Talk About It,* a book about how a young girl deals with her father touching her private parts, and *My Body Is Private,* a book about a young girl's awareness of her body and her discussion with her mother about keeping one's body private.

Games are yet a third way to work with elementary school children in counseling. Games "offer a safe, relatively non-threatening connection to children's problems" (Friedberg, 1996, p. 17). They are also familiar to children and valued by them. What's more, games are considered fun and enhance the counseling relationship. For example, playing with a Nerf ball may relax a nervous child and lead to the child revealing some troublesome behaviors.

A number of games have been professionally developed to deal with such common elementary school child problems as assertiveness, anger, self-control, anxiety, and depression (Berg, 1986, 1989, 1990a, 1990b, 1990c; Erford, 2008). In addition, counselors can make up games, the best of which are simple, flexible, and connected with the difficulties the child is experiencing (Friedberg, 1996). *Game!*

MIDDLE SCHOOL COUNSELING

Emphasis on middle school counseling is an even more recent phenomenon than elementary school counseling. It came into prominence in the 1970s as a hybrid way to offer services for students who did not fit the emphases given by either elementary school or high school counselors (Cole, 1988; Stamm & Nissman, 1979). That may be why school counseling articles that focus specifically on middle school populations have been the least frequently published in mainstream periodicals such as *Professional School Counseling* (Falco et al., 2011).

The idea of a special curriculum and environment for preadolescents and early adolescents was first implemented as a junior high concept—an attempt to group younger adolescents (ages 12–14 and Grades 7–9) from older adolescents. However, middle schools typically enroll children between the ages of 10 and 14 and encompass Grades 6 through 9. Children at this age and grade level are often referred to as **transescents** (Cole, 1988) or **bubblegummers** (Thornburg, 1978). "In addition to experiencing the normal problems that exist in the family, school, and community, middle school boys and girls adjust to changes in the body, pressure from peers, demands by the school for excellence, conflicting attitudes of parents, and other problems with establishing self-identity" (Matthews & Burnett, 1989, p. 122). There is little homogeneity about them, and their most common characteristic is unlikeness.

According to Dougherty (1986), we know less about this age group than any other. Part of the reason is that few middle school counselors conduct research or publish their findings about this population (St. Clair, 1989). Yet the Gesell Institute of Child Development and other child study centers offer a description of cognitive, physical, and emotional factors that can be *Problem* expected during this time (Johnson & Kottman, 1992). Furthermore, there has been a concerted effort in recent years by counselor educators and practitioners to present relevant research on early adolescent development and middle school counseling (e.g., Hughey & Akos, 2005). Too few counselors avail themselves of these data.

On a general level, however, most middle school counselors are aware of the major physical, intellectual, and social developmental tasks that middle school children must accomplish. Thornburg (1986) outlines them:

- Becoming aware of increased physical changes
- Organizing knowledge and concepts into problem-solving strategies
- Making the transition from concrete to abstract symbols
- Learning new social and sex roles
- Identifying with stereotypical role models
- Developing friendships
- Gaining a sense of independence
- Developing a sense of responsibility (pp. 170–171)

CASE EXAMPLE

Marge and Middle School Research

Marge wanted to know she was making a difference in the lives of middle schoolers as their counselor. Therefore, she thought she would set up a research study. She was not sure where to begin, but she thought a before and after design would be helpful.

She distributed a survey at the beginning of the school year asking students to check off problems or concerns they had. At the end of the year, she did the same thing and compared results. To her surprise and delight, some problems were checked fewer times. To her dismay, some were checked more often.

What did Marge do right in regard to her research with middle schoolers? What did she do wrong? What could she do, if anything, to fix the flaws in her approach?

Elkind (1986) notes that, in addition to developmental tasks, middle graders also must deal successfully with three basic stress situations. A *Type A stress situation* is one that is foreseeable and avoidable, such as not walking in a dangerous area at night. A *Type B stress situation* is neither foreseeable nor avoidable, such as an unexpected death. A *Type C stress situation* is foreseeable but not avoidable, such as going to the dentist.

Overall, middle school children tend to experience more anxiety than either elementary or high school students. Therefore, they are at risk for not achieving or successfully resolving developmental tasks (Matthews & Burnett, 1989; Schmidt, 2007). Middle school counselors can be most helpful during times of stress because they can provide opportunities for children to experience themselves and their worlds in different and creative ways (Schmidt, 2010). Counselors can also help middle schoolers foster a sense of uniqueness as well as identify with universal common concerns. In such a process, counselors help middle schoolers overcome their restlessness and moodiness and counter influences by peers and the popular culture that suggest violence or other destructive behaviors are an acceptable solution to complex, perplexing problems (Peterson & O'Neal, 1998).

Emphases and Roles

Schools often neglect the physical and social development of the child while stimulating intellectual growth (Thornburg, 1986; Van Veisor, 2009). Middle school counseling and guidance, like elementary school counseling and guidance, seeks to correct this imbalance by focusing on the child's total development. The emphasis is holistic: Counselors stress not only growth and development but also the process of transition involved in leaving childhood and entering adolescence (Cobia & Henderson, 2007; Schmidt, 2007). Their activities include

- working with students individually and in groups;
- working with teachers and administrators;
- working in the community with education agencies, social services, and businesses; and
- partnering with parents to address unique needs of specific children (Campbell & Dahir, 1997).

These roles may be fulfilled more easily if counselors develop capacities and programs in certain ways. The necessary capacities, according to Thornburg (1986), include general information about developmental characteristics of middle schoolers and specific tasks students are expected to achieve. In addition, middle school counselors must understand the specific child with whom they are interacting and his or her perspective on a problem. Finally, middle school counselors need to know how to help students make decisions so that students can help themselves in the future.

The **ideal role of middle school counselors** includes providing individual counseling, group experiences, peer support systems, teacher consultation, student assessment, parent consultation, and evaluation of guidance services (Schmidt, 2007, 2010). In a survey of Kansas principals and counselors, Bonebrake and Borgers (1984) found that participants agreed on not only the ideal role of the middle school counselor but also a counselor's lowest priorities: serving as principal, supervising lunchroom discipline, and teaching nonguidance classes. This survey is encouraging because it shows the close agreement between principals and counselors concerning ideal roles. After all, principals usually "determine the role and function of counselors within the school" (Ribak-Rosenthal, 1994, p. 158). Yet outside the school, various groups have different perceptions and priorities about the purpose of middle school counselors. To ease the tension that may arise from such evaluations, Bonebrake and Borgers (1984) recommend that counselors document their functions and run "a visible, well-defined, and carefully evaluated program" (p. 198). Middle school counselors also need to be in constant communication with their various publics about what they do and when. Publicity as well as delivery of services is as crucial at this level as it is in elementary schools (Ribak-Rosenthal, 1994).

Activities

Working with middle school children requires both a preventive and a remedial approach. It is similar to dealing with elementary school children except that counselors must penetrate more barriers if they are to be truly helpful in a holistic way.

PREVENTION. One of the most promising prevention programs for middle schoolers is the *Succeeding in School* approach (Gerler & Anderson, 1986). Composed of ten 50-minute classroom guidance units, this program is geared toward helping children become comfortable with themselves, their teachers, and their schools (Gerler, 1987). Furthermore, the approach is "designed to help students focus on behaviors, attitudes, and human relations skills that lead to improved academic success" (Baker & Gerler, 2008, p. 22). Each lesson plan focuses on a prosocial aspect of personal and institutional living, such as identifying with successful people, being comfortable in school, cooperating with peers and teachers, and recognizing the bright side of life events (Baker & Gerler, 2008; Gerler, Drew, & Mohr, 1990). *Succeeding in School* is now online and can be accessed through the website http://genesislight.com/succeedinginschool/. Its interactive program activities allow for students to complete pre- and postprogram measures of school success online.

A complement to the *Succeeding in School* program is Rosemarie Smead's (1995) group counseling activities for children and adolescents. These activities develop skills for living. Because her exercises for small groups can be used in various ways, middle school counselors have flexibility in helping students deal with sensitive areas such as anger, grief, stress, divorce, assertiveness, and friendship. As Akos, Hamm, Mack, and Dunaway (2007) have pointed out, group work is particularly appropriate for working with middle schoolers because they "naturally coalesce into peer groups" (p. 53).

In addition to classroom guidance and group work, middle school counselors (like elementary school counselors) can use individual counseling, peer counseling, and consultation activities to foster problem prevention (Henderson & Thompson, 2011). One theoretical approach that helps in this process is **Developmental Counseling and Therapy (DCT)** (Ivey, Ivey, Myers, & Sweeney, 2005). DCT incorporates developmental concepts from individual theories such as those by Kohlberg, Gilligan, Kegan, and Erikson, along with family theories and multicultural theories (Myers, Shoffner, & Briggs, 2002). It provides a systematic way for counselors to relate to middle schoolers in their preferred developmental orientation—sensorimotor, concrete, formal operations, and dialetic/systemic. Most middle schoolers will relate on the first two levels, with the third occasionally coming into play.

Another preventive type of program is **peer mentoring**. In this arrangement, an older student, usually high school age, is paired with a younger student, typically a seventh grader or younger (Karcher, 2008). The older student both accepts and teaches the younger student through a cooperative learning arrangement and both students learn and benefit from the experience. Noll (1997) reports that in a cross-age mentoring program she set up to help younger students with learning disabilities acquire social skills, the arrangement worked well. The younger students made significant gains in their social development, and the older students achieved an increase in their "ability to relate better to parents, an increase in self-esteem, better conflict resolution skills, and enhanced organization skills" (p. 241).

I was a peer mentor!

PERSONAL REFLECTION

Think of your middle school experience and what you learned from peers. How do you think a peer mentor could have helped you (assuming you did not have one)? How do you think being a peer mentor is helpful (whether you were one or not)?

Middle school counselors may also set up **teacher-advisor programs (TAPs)**, which are based on the premises that "guidance is everybody's responsibility, that there are not enough trained counselors to handle all of a school's guidance needs, and that teacher-based guidance is an important supplement to school counseling" (Galassi & Gulledge, 1997, p. 56). Through such programs, teachers become more involved with counselors and with the nonacademic lives of their students. The beneficiaries of these programs are middle schoolers and the schools in which they study.

REMEDIATION. One of the best ways to work remedially with middle school students is to combine it with a preventive approach. According to Stamm and Nissman (1979), the activities of middle school counselors are best viewed as services that revolve around "a **Human Development Center (HDC)** that deals with sensitive human beings (students, teachers, parents, and the community as a whole)" (p. 52). They recommend developing a rapport with these persons and coordinating middle school counseling and guidance services with others to provide the most productive program possible. Stamm and Nissman outline eight service areas that they believe are vital to a comprehensive middle school counseling and guidance program. Their model is based on service clusters. It is comprehensive like the ASCA National Model and is aimed at providing services to all students (although not necessarily by the school counselor).

Each service cluster is linked with the others. However, middle school counselors cannot perform all the recommended functions alone, so they must delegate responsibility and solicit the help of other school personnel, parents, and community volunteers. A counselor's job, then, entails coordinating service activities as well as delivering direct services when able.

The *communication service cluster* is primarily concerned with public relations. It is the counselor's outreach arm and is critical for informing the general public about what the school counseling program is doing. *Curriculum service*, however, concentrates on facilitating course placements and academic adjustment. Middle school counselors need to help teachers "psychologize" the curriculum so that students can deal with significant issues in their lives, such as peer relationships and values (Beane, 1986). If the curriculum is not relevant to children at this age, they often divert their energy to nonproductive activities. The *assessment service cluster* provides testing and evaluation services and is often linked to the *career resource cluster*, which focuses on the student's future goals and vocation.

The *counseling service cluster* and the *crisis center cluster* are also closely connected. Counseling services are provided on an individual, peer, and group level and are offered during off-school and in-school hours. Sometimes counseling activities are aimed at *self-counseling*, which is "when people (including middle graders) think the ideas that they believe, then react to those ideas with logical emotional reactions and logical physical behaviors" (Maultsby, 1986, p. 207). Rational self-counseling is one research-based way to help students help themselves deal effectively with their emotions. At other times, peer facilitators help middle schoolers make friends and learn about their environments and schoolwork (Bowman, 1986; Sprinthall, Hall, & Gerler, 1992).

There is also someone designated in the Stamm and Nissman model as a *crisis person* during the school day. This individual deals with emergencies and, with the help of the counselor, finds an appropriate way to assist the child who is experiencing sudden distress. On an individual level, a crisis and the resulting distress may be connected with loss or internal or external pressures that result in a child acting out or withdrawing. On a group level, a crisis and the resulting distress may involve "cases of trauma that affect large numbers of students such as homicide, suicide, accidental death, or severe accident" (Lockhart & Keys, 1998, p. 4). (It is vital that elementary and secondary school counselors have a crisis plan as well as a crisis person or better yet, a crisis team, in their school counseling programs.)

The *community contact cluster* focuses on working with parents and other interested people to open the lines of communication between the school and other agencies. The *professional growth cluster* provides programs for school staff and paraprofessionals. This last task is critical to the counselor's success. If the total school environment is to be positively affected, middle school counselors must help "teachers develop skills related to enhancing the students' self-concept and self-esteem" (Beane, 1986, p. 192).

SECONDARY SCHOOL COUNSELING

"There are few situations in life more difficult to cope with than an adolescent son or daughter during their attempt to liberate themselves" (Freud, 1958, p. 278). Liberation variables among adolescents include "relating to parents with new independence, relating to friends with new intimacy, and relating to oneself with new understanding" (Coll, Thobro, & Hass, 2004, p. 41). *Mattering* (the internal perception that an individual is recognized as important to those people who are significant in his or her life and matters to them) is a crucial element in liberating oneself as well as forming a positive identity (Dixon, Scheidegger, & McWhirter, 2009). It is negatively correlated with anxiety and depression.

Although most adolescents make it through this period of their lives by addressing these variables and the tasks that go with them in a healthy way, some experience great difficulty. Secondary school counselors must deal with this thorny population and the problems unique to it. They may take some comfort in the fact that some problems in adolescence are more cyclical than others. For example, "delinquent behaviors are rare in early adolescence, almost universal by midadolescence (ages 15 to 17), and decrease thereafter" (McCarthy, Brack, Lambert, Brack, & Orr, 1996, p. 277). However, many other concerns connected with this population are situational and unpredictable.

Secondary school counseling and guidance began in the early 1900s when its primary emphasis was on guidance activities that would help build better citizens (Gysbers & Guidance Program Field Writers, 1990) (see Chapter 1). Frank Parsons influenced the early growth of the profession, although John Brewer really pushed for the establishment of secondary school guidance in the 1930s (Aubrey, 1979). Brewer believed that both guidance and education meant assisting young people in living. His ideas did not gain wide acceptance at the time, but under the name *life skills training* they have become increasingly popular, and there is much more emphasis on this type of training and character education today.

The growth of secondary school counseling was particularly dramatic during the 1960s. Counselor employment in this specialty more than tripled from about 12,000 in 1958–1959 to more than 40,000 in 1969–1970 (Shertzer & Stone, 1981). According to the *Occupational Outlook Handbook*, an estimated 63,000 people worked as public school counselors during 2000, with a ratio of 3 to 1 in favor of secondary school counselors over elementary school counselors. Several thousand more counselors worked in private schools. Furthermore, the number of employment opportunities for school counselors began increasing in the late 1980s as many counselors who had trained in NDEA institutes began to retire and more states mandated better counseling services in the schools at all levels (Baker & Gerler, 2008). Today, there are an estimated 100,000 counselors in schools, many of them working on the secondary level.

Emphases and Roles

Counselors in high school environments concentrate on the following tasks:

- Providing direct counseling services individually, in groups, and to the school as a whole
- Providing educational and support services to parents
- Offering consultation and in-service programs to teachers and staff
- Delivering classroom guidance (up to 25% of their time as suggested by the ASCA National Model)
- Facilitating referrals to outside agencies
- Networking to postsecondary schools and businesses
- Advising academically (Campbell & Dahir, 1997)

Aubrey (1979) argues that a real conflict exists for secondary school counselors, who are faced with two needs: (a) engaging in student counseling and (b) doing academic and administrative tasks, such as scheduling, which school administrative personnel often require. He contends that school counselors, especially on the high school level, frequently get bogged down in nonprofessional activities. Brown (1989) states that dysfunctional counselors are frequently misunderstood or misdirected by their principals, are poorly educated, lack a plan of action, are not engaged in public relations, and violate ethical standards. To combat attempts to cast them into inappropriate roles, secondary school counselors need to develop and publicize what they do and how they do it, not only to students but to teachers, principals, and administrators as well (Guerra, 1998). They can do this by "writing monthly newsletters, posting the counselor's schedule, distributing the American School Counselor Association (ASCA) role statement, developing a guidance service handbook, making presentations at faculty meetings," and pointing out to others the cost efficiency of allowing counselors to do their jobs correctly (Ribak-Rosenthal, 1994, p. 163).

Peer (1985) elicited the opinions of state directors of guidance and counseling and others in regard to views about the role of secondary school counselors. He found mixed opinions. Those who held secondary school programs in highest regard were principals, superintendents, students, college and university personnel, other secondary school counselors, and counselor educators. Teachers, parents, community leaders, and business leaders were less positive. State directors overwhelmingly reported that secondary school counselors are "probably" or "definitely" heavily involved in nonprofessional activities. If this is true, it is understandable why secondary school counselors have come under heavy criticism from people outside the school environment.

The Peer survey also discovered that secondary school counselors are not seen as being actively involved in group counseling or group guidance, not serving as consultants, and not making an impact on the majority of students. Overall, programs at this level are not viewed as favorably as those in elementary schools in the same district. On a positive note, however, respondents perceived secondary counselors as avoiding disciplinarian roles, well qualified, and helpful to individual students, especially those bound for college. Significantly, respondents thought counselors could effect changes in counseling programs.

Ways of improving the perception and behavior of the secondary school counselor include an emphasis on roles that meet real needs. For instance, school counselors must be facilitators of healthy learning environments, which should include facilitating problem solving within regular classrooms, developing professional growth groups, and improving staff communications. All these roles give counselors maximum exposure among groups who have traditionally held them in low esteem. By functioning as facilitators in student–adult interactions and adult–adult transactions, counselors provide the means for a productive exchange between divergent and often isolated groups of people.

An important function for any school counselor is the **constant remodeling of the counseling program** (Gysbers, 2011; Gysbers & Henderson, 2006b). A systematic plan is crucial to this process. It includes not only implementation of services but also evaluation of these activities. Some stress can be expected in setting up and restructuring guidance and counseling activities within the school, but a great deal of satisfaction also results. Secondary school counselors must be in constant touch with their constituents if they are to keep their services and roles appropriate and current.

Activities

The activities of secondary school counselors can be divided into several areas. In addition to evaluating their own activities, they are involved in prevention, remediation and intervention, and cooperation and facilitation. These categories are not mutually exclusive, and there are a multitude of concerns under each heading.

PREVENTION. Secondary school counselors, like elementary and middle school counselors, stress preventive services. These efforts "need to be comprehensive, multifaceted, and integrated" (Keys & Bemak, 1997, p. 257). The reason is that adolescent problems outside the classroom and school problems are interrelated (McCarthy et al., 1996). Therefore, to address one situation and neglect the other usually will not work.

Sprinthall (1984) notes that *primary prevention* in the secondary school creates "classroom educative experiences that affect students' intellectual and personal development simultaneously" (p. 494). Through primary prevention, students become more self-reliant and less dominated by their peer group. They also become less egocentric, more attuned to principles as guidelines in making decisions, and more empathic. Relationships between the teacher and counselor and the student and counselor are enhanced in this process, too.

There are **multiple ways to build primary prevention programs**. One way for secondary school counselors to practice prevention is for them to become familiar with current **popular songs** (Ostlund & Kinnier, 1997). By listening attentively to the lyrics of these songs, secondary school counselors become "more knowledgeable about adolescent subcultures and may be better able to help many teenagers cope with typical adolescent problems" (pp. 87–88).

A second way for counselors to practice prevention is to run groups (Paisley & Milsom, 2007). **Thematic groups**, which "bring together students experiencing similar problems and allow counselors to make effective use of their time and skills," are particularly important (Zinck & Littrell, 2000, p. 51). Research indicates that group counseling has been especially effective in addressing and/or preventing adolescent problems in a number of areas. For instance, a 10-week group for at-risk adolescent girls was found to foster effective, positive, and lasting change (Zinck & Littrell, 2000).

Another way for counselors to be proactive in secondary school environments is occasionally to **teach prevention-based curriculum offerings** in classes. Anxieties about school and tests, study skills, interpersonal relationships, self-control, and career planning may be dealt with in this way. Such an approach has two major advantages: Less time needs to be devoted to remediation and intervention activities, and the counselor maintains a positive high profile with teachers and students. As an adjunct or an integrated part of curriculum offerings, counselors can have class members participate in an **interactive bibliotherapy** process in which they read either fiction or nonfiction books on specific subjects and discuss their reactions with the counselor. (This process may be individualized in personal counseling as well.) Books dealing with illness and death, family relations, self-destructive behaviors, identity, abuse, race and prejudice, and sex and sexuality are readily available. Christenbury, Beale, and Patch (1996) suggest several of them. Other works are easily attainable through *Books for You* (Christenbury, 1995).

CASE EXAMPLE

Leslie's Lessons Through Songs

Leslie realized that students in her high school listened to music all day. They not only listened, but they also talked about lyrics, and occasionally a student would saunter down the halls singing. Therefore, Leslie decided to use music and lyrics in her guidance lessons and to promote interpersonal skills.

She created the "Song Olympics" where students had to either fill in original lyrics or make up prosocial lyrics. Everyone was enthused, but the activity soon became very competitive.

How might Leslie modify the activity to make it more of a learning experience for everyone?

Five examples of **problem areas** in which **prevention can make a major difference** are **bullying, substance abuse, adolescent suicide/homicide, prevention of HIV infection, and abusive relationships**.

According to the Josephson Institute of Ethics 2010 survey of 43,000 high school students, half admitted they bullied someone in the past year, and nearly as many, 47%, said they were bullied, teased, or taunted in a way that seriously upset them (charactercounts.org). "Bullying can be face to face or through electronic media such as texting, e-mailing, social networking or postings on the Internet" (Pinjala & Pierce, 2010, p. 32). This latter type of bullying, known as **cyberbullying**, is particularly troublesome because it can be done in an anonymous and constant way with no place for the target of this abuse to hide. "Effective prevention programs strive to create a sense of shared ownership and responsibility of bully prevention among targets, bullies, bystanders, school staff, caregivers and the community. Together, standardized and clear policies and procedures must be created and implemented" (p. 35).

"A small proportion of students who experiment and regularly use substances will go on to develop more severe substance abuse problems that significantly affect their lives" (Burrow-Sanchez, & Lopez, 2009, p. 72). Programs for preventing substance abuse work best when they are started early in students' lives, based on social influence models, tailored to the age and stage of different student groups, and involve students, parents, teachers, and community members in the planning process (Mohai, 1991). A specific effective model is one in which counselors work with potentially susceptible at-risk students in a multidimensional way (Gloria & Kurpius Robinson, 2000). In general, multidimensional approaches increase self-esteem, reduce negative peer influence, and provide drug information. *Student assistance programs (SAPs)* set up by counselors in schools are also effective (Moore & Forster, 1993). SAP teams are composed of school personnel from a variety of backgrounds and function in ways similar to multidisciplinary special education teams in schools. They may be specific or general in nature but are aimed at being informative and helping students to cope with their problems (Rainey, Hensley, & Crutchfield, 1997).

Suicide and homicide prevention programs follow broad-based approaches that stress the seriousness of such violence and alternatives. Suicide is estimated to be attempted by 8% of American adolescents each year and is the third leading cause of death among them. It is the second leading cause of death among Canadian youth (ages 15 to 19 years) (Everall, Altrows, & Paulson, 2006). There is a suicide attempt by an adolescent almost every minute, making approximately 775,000 attempts annually (Carson, Butcher, & Mineka, 2000). Although more girls attempt suicides than boys, boys are more successful in carrying them out. Boys also tend to be the almost exclusive perpetrators of adolescent homicides. The number of youth homicides, especially those involving multiple deaths in schools, has increased dramatically in recent years, too. The word "Columbine" is tragically linked to mass killings in school settings.

Because antisocial behaviors like suicide and homicide are multidetermined phenomena, a variety of interventions are needed to prevent them (Dykeman, Daehlin, Doyle, & Flamer, 1996). Some ways to prevent suicides and homicides are to help students, parents, and school personnel become aware of their danger signs and alert counselors and other mental health helpers to the professional and legal standards that deal with breaking confidentiality (Peach & Reddick, 1991; Remley & Sparkman, 1993; Sheeley & Herlihy, 1989). Involving school peers, families, and significant others in the community is also vital (Cashwell & Vacc, 1996; Ritchie, 1989). It is important that suicide and homicide prevention programs in schools be proactive rather than reactive as well as systematically designed. One approach to such aggression is a concept known as *wraparound programs* (Cautilli & Skinner, 1996). These programs have multiple services provided by a team of many mental health professionals, including counselors, who work together to provide direct assistance to the youth at risk of violence as well as his or her family and community/school personnel who come in contact with the youth.

A common factor among suicidal and homicidal youth is feelings of depression and anger. Therefore, preventive programs, such as support or psychoeducational groups, that deal with improving self-esteem, social competence, and coping with loss and rejection are important. Such programs help youth use their intelligence wisely in a wide range of situations and assist them in developing *resilience*: "an adaptive process whereby the individual willingly makes use of internal and external resources to overcome adversity or threats to development" (Everall et al., 2006). Likewise, programs aimed at preventing copycat and cluster suicides and at providing community awareness are vital (Popenhagen & Qualley, 1998). Individual identification of youth at risk for either suicide or homicide is crucial, too. Youth intervention programs tailored to the needs and circumstances of potential suicide victims and homicide perpetrators are essential. A plan of action for dealing with suicide and homicide potential should be as broad-based as possible (Capuzzi, 2009).

When working to prevent HIV, counselors may or may not persuade students to change their sexual activity. However, they can help them avoid contracting HIV and other sexually transmitted diseases by employing both an informational and skills-based intervention system (Stevens-Smith & Remley, 1994). For instance, the school counselor can make sure students know how HIV is spread and what behaviors, such as sharing intravenous needles and unprotected casual sex, put them into greatest danger (Keeling, 1993). In addition, counselors can offer students opportunities for interpersonal skill building by simulating situations that are potentially hazardous. They can also support teenagers who decide to try new and positive behaviors such as changing their habits or environments. Support groups, workshops for parents and administrators, and peer education programs can also be used. Peer education is one of the strongest means of dissuading adolescents from engaging in destructive behaviors and helping them focus on productive action (Wittmer & Adorno, 2000).

Finally, *interpersonal violence* (i.e., abusive relationships) can be prevented through school counselor interventions (Becky & Farren, 1997; Bemak & Keys, 2000). In such programs, counselors work with students in groups to emphasize to them that slapping, pushing, and emotionally threatening language are not a normal or necessary part of interpersonal relationships. Furthermore, they focus on teaching students violence-prevention strategies such as anger management, assertiveness, and responsible verbal and nonverbal communication. "Dating Safely" is one model available in a programmed format that is easy to follow.

Overall, as these examples show, school counselors are in a strong position because of their skills, training, and knowledge "to be leaders in the development of . . . school- and community-based intervention" programs (Stevens-Smith & Remley, 1994, p. 182). They can help students master *coping skills*, that is, "an ability to adapt to stress and adversity" (Compass, Connor-Smith, Saltzman, Thomsen, & Wadsworth, 2001, p. 87). This mastery can take place through either active or passive means, such as through consequential thinking or simply observing (Balkin & Roland, 2007).

REMEDIATION.   Secondary school counselors initiate remediation and intervention programs to help students with specific problems that are not amenable to prevention techniques. Some common mental disorders of childhood and adolescence manifest themselves clearly at this time, such as problems centering around adjustment, behavior, anxiety, substance abuse, and eating (Geroski, Rodgers, & Breen, 1997). The identification, assessment, referral, and in some cases treatment of these disorders found in the *Diagnostic and Statistical Manual of Mental Disorders* are among the most valuable services a secondary school counselor, or any school counselor, can render (often in consultation with other mental health providers). Because of time and resources, secondary school counselors usually do not deal directly in treating severe mental disorders but rather focus on other specific problematic behaviors that occur in their settings. Four of the most prevalent of these problems are depression, parental divorce, teenage parenting, and substance abuse.

Depression is related in adolescence to negative life stress (Benson & Deeter, 1992). Forrest (1983) states that about 15% of all schoolchildren may be depressed because of external stressors and inadequate individual response abilities. He lists common emotional, physical, intellectual, and behavioral indicators of depression. Furthermore, he emphasizes the need for school counselors to use a variety of approaches in dealing with the problem. Among the most prominent are using Lazarus's multimodal model; teaching the student how to develop self-esteem; helping the student become aware of depression and the stress factors that influence it; and teaching relaxation procedures, new coping skills, and ways of modifying negative self-messages. All these approaches require a significant investment of time and energy.

Approximately one million children experience **parental divorces** each year, and it is estimated 45% of all American children can expect their families to break up before they reach the age of 18 (Whitehead, 1997). Secondary school counselors can help children, parents, and teachers adjust to divorce through both direct and indirect services. Interventions that directly address the problems of divorce include individual and group counseling services within the school for the children. Structured, short-term group work can make a positive impact in helping secondary school students sort out and resolve their feelings about the divorce experience (Smead, 1995). More indirect services can also be implemented, such as consulting with teachers and parents about the children's feelings. Teachers and parents need information about what to expect from children of divorce and what useful interventions they might employ in the process of helping.

Teenage parenting is filled with emotional issues for both society and teens. When parenting results from an out-of-wedlock pregnancy, feelings run high. The challenge for school counselors is to develop outreach strategies for working with members of this population. In addition, counselors must address personal and career concerns of young parents and make necessary referrals. Usually the process is accomplished best through collaborative efforts between school counselors and community mental health workers (Kiselica & Pfaller, 1993). One essential task is to prevent teenage parents from having a second child. Another crucial aspect is keeping unwed mothers (and fathers) in school and increasing their success in academic, personal, and interpersonal arenas (DeRidder, 1993).

Experimentation with various substances, from alcohol to hard drugs, is typical for teens. "Approximately 34% of 10th-grade students and 45% of 12th-grade students report the use of alcohol . . . , and almost 18% of 10th-grade students and 22% of 12th-grade students report using an illicit substance . . ." (Burrow-Sanchez, Jenson, & Clark, 2008, p. 238). Unfortunately, some adolescents develop **substance abuse** problems that substantially affect their lives. These problems are often paired with other mental health difficulties such as depression, ADHD, conduct disorders, anxiety disorders, bipolar disorders, and academic failure, which make them hard to treat. Thus, successfully intervening with students who abuse substances is a challenge for secondary school counselors because there are so many complexities to the problem. Treatment is even more difficult because most teens are reluctant to talk openly about substance abuse with adults.

Treatment can vary but may include individual interventions, such as a counselor trained to deal with substance abuse and motivational interviewing, as well as group interventions, such as psychoeducational groups and support (or after care) groups if the student has received community-based help. The process is time consuming, but results have been positive when these strategies have been implemented.

COOPERATION AND FACILITATION. Cooperation and facilitation involve the counselor in a variety of community and school activities beyond that of caregiver. Counselors who are not aware of or involved in community and school groups are not as effective as they could otherwise be. Part of a counselor's responsibility is becoming involved with others in ways outside direct counseling services (Lee & Walz, 1998). Thus, secondary school counselors often have to take the initiative in working with teachers and other school personnel. By becoming more involved with teachers, administrators, and sponsors of extracurricular activities, counselors integrate their views into the total life of schools and "help create the kind of school environments that stimulate growth and learning" (Glosoff & Koprowicz, 1990, p. 10).

In a very practical article on the role of the school counselor as service coordinator, DeVoe and McClam (1982) stress the importance of counselors' being accountable for performing three roles. The first role is *information retriever*. Here, the counselor either collects information or works with other professionals to collect information about particularly complex situations, such as the abused and drug-dependent pregnant teenager. The second role is related to *service coordination*. The counselor determines whether he or she has the expertise to meet particular students' needs. If the counselor does not have the expertise, an appropriate referral is made. The third role is *information administrator*. The counselor coordinates a plan in which individuals or agencies in nonschool counseling settings deliver student services. This activity involves planning and implementing continuous communication among service providers.

A less involved but important way in which counselors can cooperate with others in the school and community is through participation in *individualized education programs (IEPs)*— that is, educational programs tailored to the specialized needs of certain children. Counselors engage in either direct interventions or support services with students for whom IEPs are drawn up. Regardless of special considerations, counselors can work closely with other school and community personnel to ensure that atypical students receive appropriate educational and support services. Thus, fewer students drop out of school or are lost to the communities in which they live (Kushman, Sieber, & Heariold-Kinney, 2000).

21st-CENTURY SCHOOL COUNSELING

As an examination of school counseling in this chapter has indicated, "school counselors are frontline mental health professionals for students and families who present the gamut from normal developmental issues to serious dysfunctional problems" (Borders, 2002, p. 184). As such, school counselors are encouraged to be involved in a variety of both educational and mental health initiatives that are intentionally and collaboratively designed with other stakeholders in their school system and community such as teachers, principals, and families (Colbert, Vernon-Jones, & Pransky, 2006; Green & Keys, 2001; Paisley & McMahon, 2001). One innovative step in this direction has been the establishment of *school-based health centers (SBHCs)*, which are coordinated efforts to meet physical and mental health needs of students and include professionals from health education, nursing, nutrition, school counseling, and school psychology (Brown, 2006). In such a setting, school counselors work in partnership with other professionals and with consumers.

In the 21st century, school counselors' roles within schools and society are both evolving and being debated. "Changes in student populations may hold the equivalent impact of the National Defense Education Act of 1958 or the No Child Left Behind Act of 2001 (2002) on education and school counseling" (Portman, 2009, p. 26). By 2020, distribution for school-age persons between 5 and 17 years old is projected to be "30 million White; 9 million African American; 13 million Latino/a; 3 million Asian/Pacific Islander; and 4 million other" (p. 22).

A major task for school counselors is not forsaking or abandoning roles that are vital for the academic and environmental health of the schools they serve while simultaneously envisioning and making changes that increase their influence and service in educational settings (Dahir, 2009). This task most likely will include serving as cultural mediators by "engaging in prevention, intervention, and/or remediation activities that facilitate communication and understanding between culturally diverse human systems (e.g., school, family, community, and federal and state agencies) that aid the educational progress of all students" (Portman, 2009, p. 23).

In 1997 the ***Education Trust***, a social advocacy organization with the goal of improving schools, proposed a vision of school counseling that had counselors engaging in change-oriented activities that were empowering for schools, their students, and professional school counselors (Colbert et al., 2006; Sears & Granello, 2002). In addition, it chose 10 colleges and universities around the United States to make suggestions about revamping the school counselor education curriculum at institutions of higher education. The resulting work of those involved in this effort calls for school counselors "to work as leaders and advocates to remove systemic barriers that impede the academic success of all students" (House & Hayes, 2002, p. 255). It has been charted by the Educational Trust as "a new vision for school counselors" (Table 17.3). To what extent this vision will influence school counseling in the 21st century remains to be seen. However, "as with other pupil service professions, school counseling is going through a period of extensive reform and restructuring" (Adelman & Taylor, 2002, p. 235). In the 21st century, school counselors will need to define who they are more definitively as well as deal with external forces that wish to define or confine them. Documenting the effectiveness of school counseling programs will be crucial in this process (Whiston, 2002). Devising and implementing school counseling programs that are comprehensive and developmental will be essential as well (Gysbers, 2001).

In addition to the leadership provided by the Educational Trust, ASCA, as discussed earlier, formulated its National Model for School Counseling Programs (ASCA, 2005). This model "was written to define stable guidelines for school counselors to construct programs and to define a common language of practice for school counselors" (Lewis & Borunda, 2006, p. 411). Implementing this national model–based program will help school counselors switch their emphasis from a service-centered approach for some students to a program-centered approach for all students.

Both the Educational Trust and the ASCA National Model emphasize that in the transitional roles school counselors are now in, they as professionals must make three major shifts:

- From "service delivery for individuals, students and their families . . . to a focus on school-wide concerns"
- From "primarily responsive service orientation to school counseling partnerships that are proactive and developmental"
- From "working primarily as individuals to developing professional teams or 'communities'" (Colbert et al., 2006, p. 74)

Furthermore, the University of Massachusetts has moved toward serving as a resource for disseminating quality, evidence-based practices in schools in such pertinent areas as bullying, career intervention, violence, group counseling, and building social skills. It has established the **Center for School Counseling Outcome Research & Evaluation** (http://www.umass.edu/schoolcounseling) to provide research briefs on these and other subjects germane to school counselors. Through its work, the center gives "practicing school counselors ready access to relevant research in order for them to make effective program decisions" (Carey & Dimmitt, 2006, p. 416). Since its founding in 2003, the center has also provided training to develop counselor expertise in research, program evaluation, and data use.

TABLE 17.3 A New Vision for School Counselors	
Present Focus	**New Vision**
• Mental health providers	• Academic/student achievement focus
• Individual students' concerns/issues	• Whole school and system concerns/issues
• Clinical model focused on student deficits	• Academic focus, building on student strengths
• Service provider, 1–1, and small groups	• Leader, planner, program developer
• Primary focus on personal/social	• Focus on academic counseling, learning and achievement, supporting student success
• Ancillary support personnel	• Integral members of educational team
• Loosely defined role and responsibility	• Focused mission and role identification
• Gatekeepers	• Use of data to effect change
• Sorters, selectors in course placement process	• Advocates for inclusion in rigorous preparation for all—especially poor students and students of color
• Work in isolation or with other counselors	• Teaming and collaboration with all educators in school in resolving issues involving the whole school and community
• Guardians of the status quo	• Agents for change, especially for educational equity for all students
• Involvement primarily with students	• Involvement with students, parents, education professionals, community, community agencies
• Dependence on the use of system's resources for helping students and families	• Brokers of services for parents and students from community resources/agencies as well as school system's resources
• Postsecondary planners with interested students	• Champions for creating pathways for all students to achieve high aspirations

Source: © The Education Trust, Inc./Washington, DC.

MyCounselingLab™

Go to Topic 15: *School Counseling* in the MyCounselingLab™ site (www.MyCounselingLab
.com) for *Counseling: A Comprehensive Profession,* **Seventh Edition,** where you can:

- Find learning outcomes for *School Counseling* along with the national standards that connect to these outcomes.
- Complete Assignments and Activities that can help you more deeply understand the chapter content.
- Apply and practice your understanding of the core skills identified in the chapter with the Building Counseling Skills unit.
- Prepare yourself for professional certification with a Practice for Certification quiz.
- Connect to videos through the Video and Resource Library.

Summary and Conclusion

This chapter has covered professional school counseling. It has highlighted the roles of school counselors and the transitions school counselors and schools are now experiencing as the ASCA National Model is implemented and as the recommendations of the Educational Trust come to the forefront.

Various aspects of counseling in elementary, middle, and secondary schools have also been covered along with a brief history of how practices in these settings are carried out. The tasks of school counselors at each level are uniquely developmental and preventative, yet all focus on intrapersonal and interpersonal relationships and remediation. Counselors who work in schools must be flexible and skilled in knowing how to work with children, parents, and other school personnel who come from many different environments and have various worldviews. They must know what situations are best handled in what manner (through counseling, consultation, curriculum development, and so on).

Elementary school counselors focus on offering preventive services and increasing student awareness of individual needs and ways of meeting them in a healthy, prosocial manner. Much work on this level is the result of emphasizing curriculum issues (i.e., classroom guidance), conducting small groups, and providing consultation to others. Middle school counselors are more focused on helping students make the smoothest possible transition from childhood to adolescence. They offer many activities that parallel those on the elementary school level, and they especially focus on situations of major concern to children in this age range, such as how to handle anxiety and develop good peer relationships.

Secondary school counseling has traditionally emphasized individual counseling services with high-risk and high-achieving individuals. Now, however, counselors at this level have become more multidimensional thanks to new models and initiatives being set forth by ASCA and the Educational Trust. Secondary school counselors today are more involved in making an impact on the whole-school environment and implementing both prevention and remediation programs. They assist students in making a transition from a school environment into the world of work or further study. Resolving developmental and situational factors associated with this transition are equally important to them.

Overall, school counselors have multiple tasks and responsibilities. There is a new awareness that passive or poorly educated school counselors have not and will not work for the good of children and society (Guerra, 1998; House & Hayes, 2002). Most likely, improvements in school counseling at all levels will occur over the decades to come in the 21st century as grassroots school counselors and communities become more involved in the process, and leaders of associations and institutions take up the cause of school counseling on a national level (Baker & Gerler, 2008).

College Counseling
and Student-Life Services

18

Chapter Overview

From this chapter you will learn about

- The development of student life services and college counseling
- The emphases, roles, and activities of college counselors
- The emphases, roles, and activities of student-life services with traditional and nontraditional students

As you read consider

- How college is both a joy and a stressor to students and those who work with them
- What student life services are most valued by college students and why
- How students change during their college experience if programs are geared to meet their developmental needs

Just like fall foliage
  we watch what you bring forth each September.
Your changes are not as dramatic as the red of Maples,
  or as warm as the orange of twilight fires;
But your presence, both individually and collectively,
  like leaves adds color to a campus
    that would otherwise be bland
      in the shades of administration gray.
We celebrate your coming
  much as we look forward to the crisp cool air
    at the end of summer.
We welcome your spirit
  for it enlivens us to the metaphors and ideals
    that live unchanging lives. . . .

"Through the Seasons to New Life," by S. T. Gladding, 1982, *Humanist Educator*, 20,122. © Samuel T. Gladding.

MyCounselingLab™

Visit the **MyCounselingLab™** site (www.MyCounselingLab.com) for *Counseling: A Comprehensive Profession,* Seventh Edition to enhance your understanding of chapter concepts. You'll have the opportunity to practice your skills through video- and case-based Assignments and Activities as well as Building Counseling Skills units and to prepare for your certification exam with Practice for Certification quizzes.

Higher education is one of the most valued experiences in the United States, enrolling around 14 million people annually. At the start of the 21st century, approximately 27% of the United States population held a bachelor's degree or higher (U.S. Census Bureau, 2010) compared to 5% in 1940. "For many students, particularly those of traditional age, college marks the beginning of increased independence, of decision making, and of managing shifting roles" (Hinkelman & Luzzo, 2007, p. 144). It is "a critical period developmentally because students are actively exploring their identities and attempting to define themselves" (Jourdan, 2006, p. 328). Thus, college is not just about studying. It is about learning to live independently and successfully especially for those between ages 18 and 29 as they experiment with different lifestyles and careers and prepare for the critical tasks of adulthood—a phase of life now known as *emerging adulthood* (Arnett, 2007). That is why student-life services are offered on college campuses in addition to course work. These services are primarily in the form of cocurricular activities, support programs, and counseling (Schuh, Jones, Harper, & Associates, 2011) and are essential in helping members of this age group make successful transitions.

Student-life services and counseling on U.S. college and university campuses first emerged at the beginning of the 20th century. E. G. Williamson, dean of students at the University of Minnesota in the 1930s and 1940s, articulated what would later be called the *student personnel point of view* (Williamson, 1939). His model of student personnel services set the standard for the time. It was largely a **directed and counselor-centered approach**. The emphasis was "It is not enough to help counselees become what they want to become; rather it is more important to help them become what they ought to want to become" (Ewing, 1990, p. 104). The student personnel point of view, sometimes called the *Minnesota point of view*, remained in place until after World War II. At that time the federal government began pouring money into higher education for diverse services, and competing points of view emerged.

Ideas about the importance of student-life services, student development, and counseling have increasingly been accepted since the 1940s. They have been a part of what is known as the field of *student affairs* since the 1970s (Canon, 1988; Schuh et al., 2011; Winston & Creamer, 1997). Sometimes student-life services and college counseling are connected in specific ways (Evans, Carr, & Stone, 1982); sometimes they are not. Regardless, they share much common ground (e.g., emphasis on the **health and development of the whole person**) and are included together in this chapter because of the way they dovetail and influence the total campus life of students, faculty, staff, and administrators.

Professionals who work with college students outside the classroom vary in background and training (Bloland, 1992; Schuh et al., 2011). They include those employed in financial aid, admissions, career planning and placement, health education, campus unions, registration, residence life, advising, and international activities. The services they offer include the following (Kuh, 1996; Kuh, Bean, Bradley, & Coomes, 1986):

- Services connected with **student behaviors** (e.g., attrition, campus activities)
- Services associated with describing **student characteristics** (e.g., aptitudes, aspirations)
- Services concerned with **student growth** (e.g., cognitive, moral, social/emotional)
- Services connected with **student academic performance** (e.g., study skills, grades)

Counselors and student services personnel emphasize a common concern about the total development of the persons they serve (Brown & Helms, 1986; Johnson, 1985; Schuh et al., 2011). Many hold multiple memberships in professional organizations. One of the most diverse professional groups is the **American College Personnel Association (ACPA),** which was an affiliate of the ACA until 1992. This association, which was officially organized in 1924, has undergone three name changes. Its members are employed in a number of areas related to student services. Another important professional group is the **American College Counseling Association (ACCA)**, a division of the ACA since 1992. The ACCA's members are professionals who primarily work in colleges and universities and identify themselves as counselors (Davis, 1998; Dean, 1994). Other organizations in the student-life services field include the National Association of Student Personnel Administrators (NASPA), Division 17 (Society of Counseling Psychology) of the APA, and the postsecondary division of the American School Counselor Association (ASCA).

Several attempts have been made through the years to form a united organization of professionals who work in various college student-life services, but none has completely succeeded (Sheeley, 1983). This failure is partly attributable to different backgrounds and training (Bloland, 1992). Because college professionals who work with students are employed in different areas, they tend to concentrate their services on specific issues and people. Institutional focus also makes a difference. Some universities emphasize research and scholarship (known as the *German university tradition*), some the education of the whole person (the *English residential liberal arts tradition*), and some vocational or professional preparation (the *U.S. paradigm*) (Rodgers, 1989; Rubin, 1990). Quite often, student-life specialists have their perceptions, opinions, and values about programs shaped or directed by the institutions that employ them (Canon, 1985).

Moreover, publications in student-life services tend to be diverse. The leading periodicals are the *Journal of College Student Development,* the *National Association of Student Personnel Administrators Journal,* and the *Journal of College Counseling.* The theme-oriented quarterly series, *New Directions for Student Services* (published by Jossey-Bass), is also influential and popular.

THE BEGINNING OF STUDENT-LIFE SERVICES AND COLLEGE COUNSELING

Student-life services in higher education, including counseling, began largely by default. "Historically, the participation of faculty in what are now called student services functions gradually changed from total involvement to detachment" (Fenske, 1989, p. 16). This change was the result of significant developmental factors in the growth of American higher education over time, including the following:

- The passage of the **Morrill Land Grant Act in 1862**, which influenced the establishment and eventual dominance of state universities in American higher education
- The growth of pluralistic opinions and populations among U.S. college students

- A change in faculty role: professors and teachers no longer fostered students' moral character, took charge of character development, or adhered to a policy of *in loco parentis* (in place of parents)
- An increase in faculty interest in research and intellectual development (e.g., Hutchins, 1936)
- Lack of faculty interest in the daily implementation of institutional governance
- The emergence of counseling and other helping professions
- The documentation by Sanford (1962, 1979) that **student development during the college years can be promoted** by challenge and support and that curriculum and cocurriculum activities can "initiate, accelerate, or inhibit developmental change" (Canon, 1988, p. 451)

Student-life services as a profession grew rapidly in higher education between the end of World War I and the depression of the 1930s (Fenske, 1989; Schuh et al., 2011). During this period, many hoped that student-life professionals would be integrated into the mainstream of academic programs. But they were not, and a strong theoretical rationale for implementing student-life programs was not formulated. In addition, many student-life professionals were terminated during the Great Depression because of a lack of money and the failure of employed practitioners to define themselves adequately. Then as now, student-life services occupy the paradoxical position "of being both indispensable and peripheral" (Fenske, 1989, p. 6).

College counseling as a profession did not begin until the late 1940s. Before that time faculty and college presidents served as students' counselors (Pace, Stamler, Yarris, & June, 1996). The delay of college counseling was due to the prevailing cultural view that most students who entered college were well adjusted and that the only professionals helpful to mentally distressed college students were psychiatrists. It was not until after World War II that counseling psychologists and counselors were allowed to work with students in newly formed campus counseling centers, which were set up because large numbers of veterans returned to colleges and needed more help than could otherwise be provided. Furthermore, during and immediately after World War II, counseling psychologists won the right to work clinically with clients just as psychiatrists did (Ewing, 1990).

THE THEORETICAL BASES AND PROFESSIONAL PREPARATION FOR WORKING WITH COLLEGE STUDENTS

College counseling and student-life services involve understanding how college students of all ages learn, grow, and develop. Yet, as Bloland (1986) points out, some "entry-level and not a few seasoned professionals know little of student development theory or practice" (p. 1). This fact is unfortunate because working with students effectively requires this specialized knowledge. It is important that college counselors in particular distinguish between problems students have tied to **expected developmental struggles**, such as **autonomy, identity, and intimacy**, and more serious or chronic forms of psychological disturbance (Sharkin, 1997). Even among professionals with the best of intentions, ethically or legally questionable behavior may cause harm if one is not closely attuned to both the developmental and disordered aspect of the college population (Canon, 1989; Kitchener, 1985).

Theoretical Bases

Professionals in college counseling and student-life services can and do use a number of **theoretical models** as guides in working with students experiencing predictable developmental situations. From an ideological viewpoint, **three traditions dominate**: in loco parentis, student services, and student development (Rodgers, 1989). *In loco parentis* gives faculty and staff the parental role of teaching moral values. *The student services model* emphasizes students as consumers and mandates services that facilitate development. This approach stresses a cafeteria-style manner of program offerings that students select according to what they think they need. *Student development* focuses on creating research-based environments that "help college students learn and develop" (Rodgers, 1989, p. 120). Student development is proactive because it makes opportunities available for special groups of students.

Within **student development**, at least **four kinds of developmental theories** guide professionals' activities: psychosocial, cognitive-structural, person–environment interaction, and typological. *Psychosocial theories* are embodied most thoroughly in the writings of **Arthur Chickering** (e.g., Chickering & Reisser, 1993). Chickering contends that there are **seven specific developmental tasks of college students: competence, autonomy, managing emotions, identity, purpose, integrity,** and **relationships.** These tasks are in line with Erik Erikson's (1968) ideas about the developmental processes of youth. A major strength of Chickering is that he elaborates and specifies Erikson's concepts in such a way that college counselors and student-life professionals can plan and evaluate their practices and programs around **three key issues**: **career development, intimacy, and formulation of an adult philosophy of life.** For example, first-year students and seniors differ in their specific levels of development, with first-year students being more preoccupied than seniors with establishing competence, managing emotions, and developing autonomy. Seniors, however, concentrate more on issues such as establishing identity, freeing interpersonal relationships, developing purpose, and establishing integrity (Rodgers, 1989).

Cognitive-structural theories focus on how individuals develop a sense of meaning in the world. They deal with perception and evaluation and are best described in the moral and intellectual models of Perry (1970) and Kohlberg (1984). These models are process oriented, hierarchical, and sequential. For example, Perry's model assumes growth from "simple dualism (positions 1 and 2) through multiplicity (positions 3 and 4) and relativism (positions 5 and 6) to commitment within a relativistic framework (positions 7 through 9)." Kohlberg's model "outlines three levels of moral development: the preconventional, the conventional, and the postconventional" (Delve, Mintz, & Stewart, 1990, p. 8). According to these theories, each new stage contains the previous one and is a building block for the next one. *Cognitive discomfort* or *cognitive dissonance* (the feeling of uncomfortable tension that comes from holding two conflicting thoughts in the mind at the same time) is the **impetus for change.** Explicit in this approach is the idea that "people need the opportunity to learn how to think and act responsibly in order to control their own behavior in a democratic society" (Herman, 1997, p. 147).

The *person–environment interaction model* "refers to various conceptualizations of the college student and the college environment and the degree of congruence that occurs when they interact" (Rodgers, 1989, p. 121). Congruence is believed to lead to "satisfaction, stability, and perhaps, development" (Rodgers, 1980, p. 77). The theories in this model stress that development is a holistic process that involves all parts of the person with the environment in an interacting way. It is similar to the psychosocial approach in assuming that development in one area of life can facilitate growth in another. For example, when students participate and take leadership positions in student organizations, their life management skills develop more positively than those of students who are more passive (Cooper, Healy, & Simpson, 1994). Likewise, students who volunteer in community service initiatives (also known as "*service learning*") become more informed about environmental needs, less egocentric, and more empathetic (Butin, 2010; Delve, Mintz, & Stewart, 1990). Unlike psychosocial theories, person–environment theories "are not developmental per se" (Rodgers, 1980, p. 77). In many ways, they are rooted in Kurt Lewin's (1936) formula: $B = f(P, E)$, **where behavior (B) is a function (f) of person (P) and environment (E).**

Typological theories focus on individual differences, such as temperament, personality type, and patterns of socialization. These differences are assumed to persist over time, and most often individuals are combinations of types. Patterns of personality influence individuals to vary in their developmental growth patterns and are related to their motivation, effort, and achievement. This approach is exemplified in the writings of John Holland (1997), which study how personalities fit with work environments.

PERSONAL REFLECTION

There are a number of developmental theories that college student workers use as the basis for their interactions with college students. Which of the four theories covered here appeals to you most? Why?

Professional Preparation

Proper preparation is one of the difficulties in the field of college counseling and student-life services. Because there is such diversity in the functions of student-life professionals, no single professional preparation program can meet the needs of all graduate students. Those who enter this specialty "do not need the same kind of graduate work" (Sandeen, 1988, p. 21). Therefore, the Council for Accreditation of Counseling and Related Educational Programs (CACREP) provides different specialty standards for the field. CACREP accreditation in the student affairs area includes programs in **student affairs with college counseling** and **student affairs with professional practice.** Specific coursework and experiences needed for graduation have also been outlined by the **Council for the Advancement of Standards for Higher Education (CAS; 2009).** It is vital that specialization decisions be made as soon as possible in one's graduate career because the outcomes of each course of study vary considerably.

COLLEGE COUNSELING

Emphases and Roles

The emphases and roles of college counselors vary from campus to campus depending on the types of students particular institutions attract and the support for services that are funded. The work of college counselors is influenced by the models under which they operate, too. Traditionally, there have been **four main models that college/university counseling centers have followed** (Westbrook et al., 1993).

1. *Counseling as psychotherapy.* This model emphasizes long-term counseling with a small percentage of students. The counselor deals with personality change and refers other vocational and educational concerns to student academic advisers. The premise behind this approach is that "identity development is a core therapeutic issue in counseling traditional-age college students" (Hinkelman & Luzzo, 2007, p. 144).
2. *Counseling as vocational guidance.* This model emphasizes helping students productively relate academic and career matters. The counselor deals with academic or vocationally undecided students and refers those with personal or emotional problems to other agencies.

3. *Counseling as traditionally defined.* This model emphasizes a broad range of counseling services, including short- or long-term relationships and those that deal with personal, academic, and career concerns (Hinkelman & Luzzo, 2007). The counselor's role is diverse.

4. *Counseling as consultation.* This model emphasizes working with the various organizations and personnel who have a direct impact on student mental health. The counselor offers indirect services to students through strategic interventions.

A fifth model, *counseling as global* (i.e., an interactive, interdependent, community system), has been advocated, too (Pace, Stamler, Yarris, & June, 1996). This model is dynamic and fluid. It proposes that the counseling center staff work interactively with other members of a college/university community to create a mentally healthy environment and use personnel and other resources within a campus. The idea is an evolution of the **"Cube" concept** of counseling (a three-sided multidimensional conceptualization of counseling) first proposed by Morrill, Oetting, and Hurst (1974). Like the cube, this model focuses on three main areas as places for counselors to intervene in one or more ways: *target* (individual, primary group, associational group, and institution or community), *purposes* (remedial, preventive, or developmental), and *methods* (direct, consultation and training, or media). The global model changes the role of the counselor and the focus of the college counseling center by having center staff be more flexible and interactive. In reality, most college counseling centers offer a variety of services to help their diverse client populations and meet local campus needs.

CASE EXAMPLE

Debra Directs Services

Debra had worked long and hard to become a director of a college counseling center. She loved working with students, and she quickly assembled a fine staff. There was just one problem: Debra was not sure what services would be most in demand. However, her intuition told her she could not go wrong by offering counseling as traditionally defined, so that is how the center operated.

What other types of services should Debra have considered when deciding what the counseling center would offer? What model do you think would work best at your institution? Why?

Activities

The activities of college counselors are similar to those of student-life professionals in being comprehensive and varied. Some services of these two groups even overlap. Lewing and Cowger (1982) identified **nine counseling functions that generally dictate the agendas of college counselors.**

1. **Academic and educational counseling**
2. **Vocational counseling**
3. **Personal counseling**
4. **Testing**
5. **Supervision and training**
6. **Research**
7. **Teaching**
8. **Professional development**
9. **Administration**

In truth, three of these activities—personal, vocational, and educational counseling—account for more than 50% of college counselors' time.

Most of the counseling theories covered in this book are implemented in college counseling centers. For instance, Thurman (1983) found that rational emotive behavior therapy, including the use of rational emotive imagery, can be effective in reducing *Type A behavior* (time-urgent, competitive, and hostile) among college students and help them become healthier achievers. Likewise, Watkins (1983) found a person-centered approach to be most effective in helping students evaluate present and future plans and decide whether to stay in college. Even systems theory, most often used in marriage and family counseling, has proven effective in helping students understand family dynamics and patterns of interaction and how family patterns continue to influence important decisions about education (Gladding, 2011; Openlander & Searight, 1983). Similarly, brief therapy, a form of systems theory, has been employed in college counseling centers to help expand the "therapeutic framework to include nonfamilial members [who] can affect therapeutic progress" for better or worse (Terry, 1989, p. 352). In this treatment, conflictual nonfamily members within a campus community are brought together to form meaningful relationships and make changes in problematic situations. The idea behind the treatment is that students within a campus can help each other problem-solve and make their environments healthier through the resolution of problem behaviors. In the process, blaming and scapegoating cease.

A difficulty college counselors have faced in offering services has been dealing effectively with **mandated referrals**, which over 88% of campus counseling centers accept (Kiracofe & Wells, 2007). These cases are challenging because judicial boards and administrators who make referrals are more concerned with external behavioral changes than anything else. To further aggravate the situation, there is virtually no theoretical literature for dealing with involuntary students. Kiracofe and Wells suggest a readiness for change strategy be used with mandated clients based on Prochaska's (1999) readiness model.

Students at the **precontemplative stage of readiness** to change have no motivation to act differently and may well respond best to punishment and sanctions. However, if there is time, students can be brought along through **motivational interviewing** (semi-directive interviews that engage students by establishing rapport and helping them explore discrepancies in their lives so that they become intrinsically motivated and change their behaviors). Psychoeducational awareness activities may also be used to get students to commit to changes and actions that enhance their lives. Overall, clients to college counseling centers should be accepted only when there is an indication that they have reached or are in the preparation and action stages of readiness to change.

Another challenge that college counselors face is a constantly changing student culture (Bishop, 1992). For example, "with approximately 24% of college students having a body modification . . . tattoos and body piercings may represent an emerging cultural norm" (Roberti & Storch, 2005, p. 15). Behaviors among college students change with each generation The culture of the current student population is not the same as its predecessors. Indeed, college counseling center practitioners in recent years "have been expressing a sense of urgency about increasing numbers of students who present with serious psychological problems as well as an overall increase in the severity of presenting problems" (Sharkin, 1997, p. 275).

When services are varied and numerous at the professional level, everyone benefits. The *College Adjustment Scales* is a means of screening college students for common developmental and psychological problems (Anton & Reed, 1991). These nine scales measure psychological distress in the following areas: anxiety, depression, suicidal ideation, substance abuse, self-esteem problems, interpersonal problems, family problems, academic problems, and career problems. It is an important assessment instrument for college counseling centers to use in deciding what services and programs they will emphasize.

Peer counselors are also an effective way of reaching students beyond the traditional college counseling center. As a rule, students turn first to friends for help, then to close relatives, before finally turning to faculty and counseling services. Ragle and Krone (1985) found that first-year students who had previously undergone a summer orientation program at the University of Texas at Austin were, as a result, overwhelmingly at ease in talking with peer advisers over the telephone about various concerns. Furthermore, they felt that contact with peer counselors was helpful and indicated that it made the university seem less impersonal.

Sometimes peer counselors take the role of **resident assistants (RAs)** (Foubert, 2007). In this arrangement, RAs are assigned to live in selected residence halls. Their services, which include dealing with remedial, preventive, and developmental issues, are given high exposure (Schuh, Shipton, & Edman, 1986). RAs provide crisis intervention, short-term counseling, conflict mediation, and referral services (Blimling, 2003). They help students keep favorable attitudes toward counseling and counseling-related services and, at the same time, become more aware of opportunities offered by college counseling centers (Johnson, Nelson, & Wooden, 1985). In addition, RAs sponsor programs for residents on mental and physical health topics, bringing in faculty and staff from across the campus to give presentations. RAs usually receive ongoing professional training and supervision from the campus counseling center. This arrangement benefits the RAs, students in the residence halls, and the campus as a whole because of its integrative and preventive focus.

College counselors can also offer services and programs in conjunction with other student-life professionals. **Four of the most needed services** on most college campuses are those directed toward **alcohol consumption, sexual abuse and violence, eating disorders,** and **depression**.

"Alcohol use is a serious problem on college campuses" (Laux, Salyers, & Kotova, 2005, p. 41). Nearly 90% of students drink alcohol sometime during an academic year, and approximately 20% qualify as heavy drinkers, averaging one ounce of alcohol per day per month (Steenbarger, 1998). Thus, it is not surprising that alcohol-related problems, including the abuse of alcohol and its concomitant disorders, are prevalent (Kadison & DiGeronimo, 2004).

Binge drinking (having five or more drinks at a time for men and four or more drinks for women) appears to be increasing, and one in three college students drinks primarily to get drunk (Commission on Substance Abuse at Colleges and Universities, 1994; Marczinski, Grant, & Grant, 2009). Binge drinking hurts academic performance especially in the first year of college when students have not acclimated to the rigors of their new environment. In addition, irresponsible drinking may lead to violence in the form of date rape, unsafe sex, academic difficulties, and suicide. Riots on or near college campuses may occur when college administrators ban alcohol at certain campus events or areas (Lively, 1998).

Thus, alcohol abuse is likely to bring students in contact with counselors and other student-life professionals (Gill-Wigal, Heaton, Burke, & Gleason, 1988; Kadison & DiGeronimo, 2004). Systematic steps are usually implemented to help students get through denial they may have connected with alcohol abuse because before effective treatment can take place, students need to realize their need for help in correcting out-of-control behavior. Intervention is sometimes done individually, but often it involves a group and usually a wide variety of treatments, including insight and behavioral change.

Many students who abuse alcohol have grown up in dysfunctional families. They frequently experience problems related to growing up in such environments (e.g., workaholism, depression, dependency, antisocial tendencies, food addictions). Specific interventions counselors use with these students include helping them define more clearly the roles they played in their family-life dramas and then helping them break nonproductive patterns of interaction (Crawford & Phyfer, 1988). One way counselors can break nonproductive patterns is to respond to these students in functionally healthy ways that contrast with the behaviors they have experienced before. Peer counseling may also be helpful to an extent in this process.

Sexual assault and violence, including incest and rape, are matters that many students, primarily women, must deal with during their college experience. The dynamics surrounding sexual crimes have similarities and differences. A common denominator in many cases is alcohol abuse: Most campus rapes are alcohol-related, as are assaults (National Center on Addiction and Substance Abuse at Columbia University, 2007). There are at least **two stages in the recovery process**: (a) the **acute**, which is characterized by disorganization, and (b) **long-term** reorganization, which includes dealing with the pain of trauma and rebuilding one's life through support (Burgess & Holstrom, 1974; Scrignar, 1997).

CASE EXAMPLE

Al and His Alcohol

Al had heard stories from his relatives about how much fun he would have in college. Most of the stories revolved around alcohol-related incidents. Thus, Al was determined to make sure he had access to beer and before too long he had found the right connections.

Instead of applying himself to his studies, Al focused on his suds. He played "thumper" and other drinking games almost nightly. However, one night he was stopped by the campus police while driving in a less-than-sober state. When he was mandated to go to the campus counseling center, Al did so reluctantly. His first words to Charlotte, his counselor, were, "Can't a guy have a little fun without everyone getting upset with him? Geeee!"

Put yourself in Charlotte's position. How would you reply to engage Al and yet let him know that he had a problem that needed to be worked on?

Eating disorders, especially bulimia and anorexia nervosa, are a third area in which college counselors can team up with other student-life professionals, such as health educators, in offering services. Between 5% and 17% of college students have an eating disorder (Hackler, Vogel, & Wade, 2010). "Characterized by a preoccupation with and distorted attitude toward weight, food, and dieting, eating disorders are found more typically in White, middle- to upper-class females but appear to be on the rise in other ethnic and social groups" (Peck & Lightsey, 2008, p. 184). However, African Americans are becoming more affected due to acculturation, racism, and socioeconomic status (Talleyrand, 2010).

There is a great need to address eating disorders in universities, although many women with such disorders do not believe their behaviors warrant therapy (Meyer, 2005). Research indicates these disorders occur along a continuum of degree. Women who are caught up in them usually have maladaptive cognitions or faulty information concerning weight control techniques (Tylka & Subich, 2002). Regardless, it is estimated that up to 65% of women in their first year of college display "some behavioral and psychological characteristics of disturbed eating" (Meyer & Russell, 1998, p. 166) and less than 45% of those with a diagnosed eating disorder, regardless of their stage in life, ever receive treatment (Hackler et al., 2010). The reasons for the lack of treatment have to do with **stigma** (being negatively labeled) as well as anticipated risks and anticipated benefits. Thus, to help those with eating disorders, counselors must be proactive rather than reactive.

One way to address the needs of those with eating disorders is to consider them "within a developmental framework" (Sharkin, 1997, p. 275). Programs that emphasize the characteristics of eating disorders as well as highlight ways of combating such tendencies before they become full blown can do much to educate those most likely to experience them. Furthermore, such programming can give participants sources to which they can turn if either they or someone they know becomes caught up in a bulimic cycle. One key factor in education and prevention is the use of adaptive coping strategies (VanBoven & Espelage, 2006). There are a number of other symptoms eating disorder individuals have including perfectionism, body dissatisfaction, poor emotional insight, and ineffectiveness, so focusing on these signs of distress is important in any educational or preventive program.

A fourth area of concern for college counselors is **depression** (Kadison & DiGeronimo, 2004). "It is estimated that college students are twice as likely to have clinical depression and dysthymia as are people of similar ages and backgrounds in the workforce" (Dixon & Reid, 2000, p. 343). The excitement of attending college is often followed by the stress brought on by new challenges, from academic to social, resulting in depressive episodes. As many as 25% of students seeking help are diagnosed for depression problems each year in college health care centers (Mackenzie et al., 2011). Therefore, both educational and preventive programs must regularly be modified to help students handle current issues.

Depression and depressive symptoms are devastating in a college environment because they interfere with learning and lead to a lack of success. Counselors can treat depression through cognitive approaches, such as Beck's thought modification process; through behavioral approaches, such as helping clients engage in activities in which they have success; and cognitive–behavioral approaches such as rational emotive behavior therapy. It appears that **depression is modified through positive life experiences** (Dixon & Reid, 2000), so working with others in the college environment to assist depressed college students in finding successful experiences may be good not only as therapeutic practice but also for the college itself in retaining students and creating a more socially hospitable atmosphere.

In addressing issues pertinent to college students, counselors in cooperation with student-life professionals can take preventive action on tertiary, secondary, and primary levels. "*Tertiary prevention* is akin to remediation and includes direct services to victims" (Roark, 1987, p. 369; my emphasis). It includes encouraging the reporting of aggression and helping the victim use available resources. *Secondary prevention* is geared toward problems, such as date rape, already in existence on campus and is aimed at raising consciousness among poten-tial victims and perpetrators and setting policies to stop known abuses. *Primary prevention* focuses on stopping problems from ever developing. It involves modifying the physical envi-ronment as well as addressing causes and providing training to create awareness and change values. For example, to help students **manage stress**, a program referred to by the acronym *BRIMS* (breathing, relaxing, imagery, message, and signs) might be offered (Carrese, 1998). This program is **a type of cognitive self-hypnosis** that helps students relax both physically and mentally while giving themselves positive messages and physical signs that help them recall constructive ways of feeling and viewing a situation. In the process, students "transform nega-tive thoughts into constructive energy, allowing control over situations that produce unneces-sary anxiety" (p. 140).

STUDENT-LIFE PROFESSIONALS

Emphases and Roles

Initially, college/university student-life services concentrated on helping new students adjust to campus life (Williamson, 1961). This focus still exists but now includes an emphasis on older returning students, nontraditional students, and an increased concern for all persons in the college/university community, such as working with minority culture students and students with learning disabilities (Boesch & Cimbolic, 1994; Lynch & Gussel, 1996; Tate & Schwartz, 1993). There is a humanistic quality among individuals who choose student-life services as a profession: They try to maximize, personalize, and individualize the higher education of students, helping them fully use the environment to promote their development. An important by-product of this process is that students are greatly assisted in making successful transitions from their communities to institutional life and back again (Brown, 1986; McClellan & Stringer, 2009). Thus, student-life professionals are institutional integrators who facilitate the accomplishment of student and college/university goals.

At times during the college year (orientation, midterm examinations, and the end of the term) the work of student-life professionals increases dramatically. Although certain problems are universal regardless of one's developmental age or stage (including health, anxiety, and depression), other concerns are related directly to specific college student populations. For instance, dealing with a family member's illness when a college student is away from home may require student-life professionals to provide more support to a student than would otherwise be the case and work with professors on the student's behalf until matters are resolved (Schmidt & Welsh, 2010).

PERSONAL REFLECTION

What did you lose when you went to college? How did that loss affect you? What did you gain when you went to college? How did that additive impact your life?

Another unique problem is Greek life and rush. The rush system of fraternities and sororities, though exciting and fulfilling for many students, may also produce feelings of depression among students who are not offered bids. In helping students during these times, student-life professionals must be sensitive to individual needs, offer support, and try to help rejected students find a fulfilling peer group (Atlas & Morier, 1994).

In line with transitional problems, Grites (1979) found that 12 of the 43 items on the *Social Readjustment Rating Scale* (Holmes & Rahe, 1967) almost exclusively apply to first-year college students in their adjustment to a new environment. When translated into life-change units, these factors yield a combined score of 250, which the authors of this instrument consider to be in the "moderate life crisis" category. As a group, individuals in this category have a 51% greater risk of a deteriorating health change than those who score 150 or below.

Grites further observes that new students who face other changes outside the college/university environment (e.g., the death of a family member or friend) are likely to move into the "**major life crisis**" category, becoming an even greater risk for a detrimental health change. Therefore, many colleges and universities now employ special student-life staff to work with each incoming class to enhance the **first-year experience** and initially promote positive individual development as well as a sense of community (Loxley & Whiteley, 1986; Whiteley, 1982). Part of this effort may include helping students who are perfectionists assess the impact of these tendencies on their self-development and social well-being (Ashby & Rice, 2002; Rice & Dellwo, 2002). Such a process is complex and requires delicate handling, but it can be helpful in assisting students achieve greater self-esteem and social integration during their college careers.

Regardless of such attempts at prevention, approximately 10% of all students encounter an emotional difficulty during their years in college that is serious enough to impair academic performance (Mathiasen, 1984). In addition, stress on college students to pass examinations or get into a professional school increases the incidents of major depression in this population (Clay, Anderson, & Dixon, 1993). If appropriate intervention is not offered (e.g., training in appropriate anger expression or stress management), students experience emotional, social, or academic problems to such a degree that they drop out of school. Unfortunately, between 40% and 60% of students who begin 4-year institutions do not graduate (Gerdes & Mallinckrodt, 1994; Orfield, 2005). Even more tragically, students may take their own lives. Every year, approximately 6 of every 100,000 college students in the United States commit suicide (Chisolm, 1998).

Some of the strongest predictors of staying in school and maintaining good mental health are amenable to student-life services (Polansky, Horan, & Hanish, 1993). To help students have a successful and productive college experience, student-life professionals offer **campus-wide programs and individual assistance**. The goal of **comprehensive programs** is to make a positive impact on students and help them identify problems or concerns at strategic points where intervention strategies may be most beneficial. The emphases and roles of student-life professionals are aimed at helping sensitize students to the multiple issues that face them and constructively deal with these unfolding issues and themselves (Creamer & Associates, 1990; McClellan & Stringer, 2009). For example, many college students face the challenge of maintaining some form of separation from their parents and families while establishing their own identity through individuation. There is a correlation between student adjustment to college and attachment to parents (Rice & Whaley, 1994). "Research suggests that college students benefit from (a) secure attachment to parents in which there is mutual trust, communication, and little conflict or alienation, and (b) relationships with parents in which their separateness and individuality are mirrored, acknowledged, and supported" (Quintana & Kerr, 1993, p. 349). By helping students separate positively and yet stay connected with their families, student-life professionals assist students in their overall adjustment and achievement at college and beyond.

Activities

The activities of **student-life professionals** are related to the **specialty area** in which they work: administration, development, or counseling. "The ***administrative model*** . . . is based on the premise that the student services profession is an administrative, service-oriented unit in higher education that provides many facilitating and development activities and programs for students" (Ambler, 1989, p. 247; my emphasis). Examples of these services include admissions, records, food, health, and financial aid. The ***developmental model*** is one that stresses education, such as helping students learn decision-making skills by offering leadership seminars or facilitating increased autonomy in residence-life activities. Finally, the ***counseling model*** is one that emphasizes social and emotional growth in interpersonal and vocational decisions and includes conducting highly personalized seminars around a topic of interest, such as dating, careers, or stress (Forrest, 1989).

Not all student-life specialists follow these models, and not all student-life activities are conducted by professionals. Indeed, a national survey found that 72% of college/university student affairs divisions use **student paraprofessionals** to supplement and implement their offerings (Winston & Ender, 1988). These paraprofessionals are "undergraduate students who have been selected and trained to offer services or programs to their peers. These services are intentionally designed to assist in the adjustment, satisfaction, and/or persistence of students" (p. 466). Student paraprofessionals are frequently employed in residence halls and orientation programs; they also work with crisis lines, student judiciaries, academic advising, financial aid, international student programs, and student activities.

By involving student paraprofessionals in structured programs, student-life specialists directly and indirectly offer them leadership opportunities, improve the quality of life on campus, and accomplish critical tasks. Hundreds of U.S. colleges and universities offer students some type of formal leadership training, and the number is growing (Freeman, Knott, & Schwartz, 1996; Komives et al., 2011). Yet, certain core beliefs, underlying principles, and necessary curriculum topics must be dealt with before any such activity can be effective (Roberts & Ullom, 1989). Student-life professionals have become increasingly interested in improving their leadership abilities at the same time that they have devoted additional time and effort to helping students in this area. This dual focus may help colleges take more initiative overall and promote a greater sense of community.

COUNSELING AND STUDENT-LIFE SERVICES WITH FIRST-YEAR AND NONTRADITIONAL STUDENTS

In addition to working with mainstream groups, college counselors and student-life professionals also address the needs of first-year and nontraditional students. These may be older students, first-generation college students, minority culture students, or even student athletes. While first-year students at traditional 4-year colleges are relatively young and inexperienced, common characteristics of nontraditional students are factors such as financial independence (51%), part-time attendance (48%), and delayed enrollment (46%) (Evelyn, 2002). Nontraditional students, age 25 years and older, now number more than 6 million (about 40% of the total U.S. undergraduate population) (Chao & Good, 2004). Many of them are enrolled in public 2-year colleges and a growing number take courses online.

First-Year Students

Going to college for many students is their first full taste of freedom and being on their own. It is analogous somewhat to being a kid in a candy store and having to decide from an array of sweets from which to pick and enjoy. All look tempting! For some students, the transition is easy. They are mature and ready to make decisions about their lives. Thus, their entry into college appears almost seamless. However, for most students college is a challenge. In 2010 a survey by the Cooperative Institutional Research Program (CIRP) at UCLA of students at 4-year colleges and universities found that the emotional well-being of first-time freshmen was at a record low. Barely half of respondents—51.9%—described their emotional health as being in the "highest 10%" or "above average."

First-year college students may especially need help during their initial months in college. Graduation from high school involves a loss of identity and a need for reevaluation and goal commitment that is often unavailable to entering students before they matriculate (Hayes, 1981). In addition, first-year college students face the challenges of managing time effectively, making choices about what courses to take, taking academic tests, and coping with fellow students while simultaneously handling finances, as well as family and personal problems (Carrese, 1998). "Some of the most commonly reported crises in the first year involve difficulties in social adjustment manifested as feelings of homesickness and loneliness" (Gerdes & Mallinckrodt, 1994, p. 281). There is often the experience of psychological pain because of the disruption in established friendship networks (i.e., "*friendsickness*") and the silent grief that follows (Paul & Brier, 2001; Ponzetti & Cate, 1988).

In focusing on the first-year experience, colleges help students deal with these universal variables that are often developmental in nature. For instance, some students feel a strained or conflicted relationships with their parents. Such feelings may contribute to troubled ruminations about them and lead to a paralysis or immobility on the part of the new student (Schwartz & Finley, 2010). Others need assistance in learning how to study, getting along with roommates, and establishing a routine. College counselors and student-life professionals can best help in these situations by playing to students' strengths and providing needed information or guidelines for students to follow. Variables that have been linked to college adjustment include attachment separation, individuation, social support, spiritual well-being, particular coping styles, and negative life stress (Schmidt & Welsh, 2010).

Older Students

As a group, older nontraditional students are highly motivated, prefer interactive learning, have family and financial concerns, view education as an investment, and have multiple commitments and responsibilities that are not related to school (Richter-Antion, 1986). Within this large group, there are two basic subgroups: students ages 25–50 and those ages 50–80.

The first subgroup is usually motivated to return to college because of changing job or career requirements or opportunities that include family life transitions (e.g., marriage, divorce) (Aslanian & Brickell, 1980; Chao & Good, 2004). Building up self-esteem and providing academic and social support are particularly important for these younger nontraditional students. The latter subgroup, called *senior students*, come to campus for many purposes, which include obtaining degrees and finding personal enrichment. When working with senior students, college counselors and student-life professionals must take several factors into consideration, such as modifications to the environment (perhaps brighter lighting or warmer room temperatures), the clients' developmental stage (e.g., dealing with issues of generativity or integration), the pace of the counseling sessions (slower may be better), potentially difficult areas (such as transference), and the use of counseling techniques (e.g., bibliotherapy, journal writing) (Huskey, 1994). With an increase in the number of older people, the numbers of senior students will most likely continue to grow.

Regardless of how fast the number of senior students grows, the overall number of nontraditional students will increase because of business downsizing, the rapid advance of technology, and increased opportunities for professional development. Community and technical colleges and public universities are most likely to enroll the majority of these nontraditional students. As is the case with traditional students, more females than males will enroll, there will be an increase in the number of part-time students, and more cultural and racial minorities will seek a college education (McGlynn, 2007). All these events will test the limits of counseling and other student-life services.

Part-Time Students

Part-time undergraduates, especially exclusively part-time students, comprise almost 40% of students in higher education. As a group they are at a distinct disadvantage relative to those who are enrolled full time because

- they come from minority and low-income family backgrounds,
- they are not as well-prepared for college as their full-time peers,
- they are highly concentrated in 2-year colleges and nondegree/certificate programs, and
- many of them work full time while enrolled and are not enrolled continuously.

Thus, part-time enrollment is negatively associated with persistence and degree completion 6 years after beginning postsecondary education even after controlling for a wide range of factors related to these outcomes (Chen, 2007).

To help part-time students, college counselors and student personnel professionals must make special efforts to stay in contact with or reconnect with students as they transition in and out of classes. If part-time students know there is someone to whom they can go to talk with or find out information, they are more likely to persevere in their studies. Providing special programming for these students on overcoming barriers to part-time enrollment may also be helpful, especially if it is kept brief and factual.

First-Generation Students

Another group of nontraditional students is ***first-generation college students***—that is, students who are the first in their family to enter college. The individuals in this category come from a wide variety of backgrounds, including second-generation immigrants and upwardly mobile poor. They represent 27% of all graduating high school students and have special needs, one of which is family support (Gibbons & Shoffner, 2004). "Family support for education is the key difference between first-generation and second-generation students. Family support is also a fundamental variable in the decision to attend college and in the successful completion of college" (Fallon, 1997, p. 385).

Thus, first-generation college students have numerous needs. They must master knowledge of the college environment, including its specific vocabulary, for example, "credit hours," "GPA," and "dean" (Fallon, 1997). They must also become committed to the role of being a student, decipher the value systems of second-generation college students, as well as learn to understand student-life services and study skills. Language barriers and social or cultural customs must also be addressed.

Minority Culture Students

Minority culture students in the United States are predominantly African American, Native American, Asian American, Hispanic/Latino, or multiethnic individuals. They face a number of challenges different from other students, such as "a lack of support and an unwelcoming academic climate" (Ancis, Sedlacek, & Mohr, 2000, p. 180). In many cases, minority students fall into categories besides being minorities, such as being first-generation students, older students, or student athletes. They also may be more interdependent and relational oriented than majority students (Berkel & Constantine, 2005).

"Advisers, advocates, staff, administration, counselors, and higher education programming initiatives supporting diversity are, therefore, essential to meet the needs of students of color and Anglo-Americans alike" (Singley, & Sedlacek, 2009, p. 408). In helping minority culture students adjust to college and/or do well overall, these professionals can offer minority culture students encouragement and social support. They can also provide them tangible means by which to foster ethnic pride. For example, with African American college students, ethnic pride may become a part of the learning environment through official sponsorship in universities of programs such as Kwanzaa celebrations and Black History Month (Phelps, Tranakos-Howe, Dagley, & Lyn, 2001). Furthermore, they can offer them support services outside of student counseling centers, such as at informal gatherings, and realize that for some groups—for example, Korean undergraduates—the need for support differs considerably between men and women (Gloria, Castellanos, Park & Kim, 2008).

Another helpful activity college counseling and student-life professionals can do is to address the roles of race-ethnicity and gender in university student orientation sessions. White men as a group tend to be less oriented toward diversity and in many cases it is "off their radar" while women and minority groups are attuned to diversity and its importance much more (Singley & Sedlacek, 2009). Therefore, helping White men as a group to be more open to and engaged in diversity efforts on campus can improve the lives of everyone on campus.

Small- or large-group events that promote and enhance ethnic identity and one's self-concept may also prove useful and positive, as does mentoring. For example, "research indicates that Latino students who have a mentor who takes personal and academic interest in their educational experiences are more likely to succeed" (Gloria & Rodriguez, 2000, p. 151). In addition, some students, such as African American and Asian American women, may respond best to counseling that appreciates a relational-interdependent perspective (Berkel & Constantine, 2005). Overall, helping that promotes and protects "strong ethnic identity" fosters "minority students' self-esteem and allows them to feel more integrated with the college environment" (Jourdan, 2006, p. 328).

In order to offer minority students encouragement, specialized attention, and customized events, both counselors and student-life professionals need to understand the campus environments in which they work and the perception of it by minority groups. Racism and stereotyping are frequently a part of the climate (Guiffrida & Douthit, 2010). Therefore, counseling and life-skill strategies that effectively respond to these degrading influences need to be fostered and self-efficacy promoted. For instance, counselors who understand culturally specific humor can empower minority students to address issues they may face in a productive manner through seeing the absurdity of situations and laughing instead of feeling hopeless and becoming angry (Vereen, Butler, Williams, Darg, & Downing 2006).

To make an even wider impact and bring about needed changes, counselors and student-life personnel can work on campus-wide programming that impacts all aspects of the campus (i.e., faculty, staff, and students). Such programming can take the form of presentations to specific groups (such as academic classes, residence hall groups, and fraternities/sororities), or it can be in the form of sponsoring or cosponsoring campus wellness fairs or student services expos (Marks & McLaughlin, 2005).

By being proactive in such venues, college counselors and student-life personnel can challenge biases and promote understanding and appreciation of others (Ancis et al., 2000). They can also recognize that, in some cultures—for example, Mexican-American—as individuals lose their culture of origin and increase their generational status, their attitudes toward help seeking become less favorable. Therefore, "adherence to traditional Mexican culture and cultural values may actually encourage help seeking" (Ramos-Sánchez & Atkinson, 2009,

p. 62). Likewise, in working with African American students on predominantly White campuses, three themes have emerged in regard to helping them succeed. These themes include (a) adopting expanded definitions of student centeredness that are consistent with African American expectations, (b) remaining mindful of the complexities inherent in maintaining strong ties to family and friends at home, and (c) encouraging participation in student organizations that provide support for the shared concerns of African American students (Guiffrida & Douthit, 2010).

CASE EXAMPLE

Part-Time Patricia

Patricia was raised in a first-generation Guatemalan household. Her parents spoke broken English and worked in minimum-wage jobs, but they had great ambition for their daughter. Patricia was ambitious as well, and at the end of high school, she was offered a scholarship to a predominantly White university, where at first glance she looked like everyone else.

However, near the end of her sophomore year, Patricia was feeling isolated and alone. Her parents did not understand what she was feeling, and her fellow students did not relate well to a Latina.

When she sought counseling, Patricia's counselor, Ibby, suggested that Patricia's family come with her to the next session so that they could discuss the situation together. In the meantime, she referred Patricia to the dean of Student Services to see if she could get more involved with an activity on campus.

What do you think of the counselor's strategy in addressing Patricia's situation? What might you do?

Student Athletes

A final group of nontraditional students consists of student athletes. These students are less likely than others to seek help through counseling (Watson, 2005). Yet, many of them have "problems in relating to the university system and the larger society" (Engstrom & Sedlacek, 1991, p. 189). They are often seen by others as problem students who have trouble relating either socially or academically (Burke, 1993). In addition, many are from minority cultural groups and are the first within their families to attend college (Kirk & Kirk, 1993). A sports-oriented environment may foster dependence on a coach or a team. Therefore, these students may become isolated and alienated from the mainstream of college life and find stress as well as challenges in their dual roles of being students and athletes (Watson, 2005). Teaching time management and social skills are areas where counselors and student-life specialists can help.

In addition, when student athletes lose their athletic identity through loss of eligibility or because of injury, they need assistance in making an integrative transition back to college life (Wooten, 1994). Counselors and student-life professionals need to work with student athletes on both an emotional and cognitive basis by helping them identify and express their feelings and confront and correct irrational thoughts. Student athletes also need help in learning to see themselves beyond the college years, most likely as nonprofessional athletes. Therefore, career counseling and life-planning skills are important services to provide.

MyCounselingLab™

Go to Topic 15: *School Counseling* in the MyCounselingLab™ site (www.MyCounselingLab .com) for *Counseling: A Comprehensive Profession*, Seventh Edition, where you can:

- Find learning outcomes for *School Counseling* along with the national standards that connect to these outcomes.
- Complete Assignments and Activities that can help you more deeply understand the chapter content.
- Apply and practice your understanding of the core skills identified in the chapter with the Building Counseling Skills unit.
- Prepare yourself for professional certification with a Practice for Certification quiz.
- Connect to videos through the Video and Resource Library.

Summary and Conclusion

The professions of college counseling and student-life services have much in common. Both emphasize the total growth and maturation of students in college/university environments, and each has an optimistic outlook, focusing on the benefits of certain environments and events as catalysts to make students more self-aware and use their abilities fully. These specialties also share a common historical parallel: Their influence at colleges and universities has ebbed and flowed over time. In the 21st century, however, both specialties are well established and contributing positively to the overall functioning of institutions of higher education.

This chapter has covered the historical, philosophical, and pragmatic qualities of college student development and growth as they relate to counseling and student-life services. The quality and variety of activities associated with these specialties are strong. In college counseling centers, emphasis is increasingly placed on global outreach and interaction and a proactive stance in the delivery of services (Bishop, 1990; Marks & McLaughlin, 2005; Pace et al., 1996). These services include consultation, career counseling, crisis management, retention, personalization and humanization of the campus environment, establishment of self-help programs, and cooperation with other campus units. Student-life services are also becoming more fluid and dynamic. As the dialogue between professionals in each aspect of student life becomes more open, the ability to serve students and the systems in which they operate will continue to increase.

19 Abuse, Addiction, Disability, and Counseling

Chapter Overview

From this chapter you will learn about

- The nature of and treatment for interpersonal and intrapersonal abuse
- The nature of and treatment for various forms of addiction (e.g., physiological and process)
- Various aspects of disabilities including those linked to intellectual, physical, and traumatic sources
- Dynamics surrounding the work of being an addiction, offender, or rehabilitation counselor

As you read consider

- How interpersonal and intrapersonal abuse begin and why they continue
- What types of addiction are most prevalent, what types are most difficult to treat, and what treatments are the best for addiction
- What disabilities are like and what interventions are most successful in working with those who are disabled
- What the work of addiction, offender, and rehabilitation counselors is like

As our sessions go on you speak of your scars
   and show me the places where you have been burned.
Sadly, I hear your fiery stories
   reliving with you, through your memories and words,
     all of the tension-filled blows and events
      that have beaten and shaped your life.
"I wish I were molten steel," you say,
   "and you were a blacksmith's hammer.
Maybe then, on time's anvil, we could structure together
   a whole new person, with soft smooth sounds,
     inner strength and glowing warmth."

Reprinted from "Scars," by S. T. Gladding, 1977, *Personnel and Guidance Journal*, 56, p. 246. © 1977 S. T. Gladding.

MyCounselingLab™

Visit the MyCounselingLab™ site (www.MyCounselingLab.com) for *Counseling: A Comprehensive Profession,* Seventh Edition to enhance your understanding of chapter concepts. You'll have the opportunity to practice your skills through video- and case-based Assignments and Activities as well as Building Counseling Skills units and to prepare for your certification exam with Practice for Certification quizzes.

Counselors from varied backgrounds work with clients who have abuse, addictions, and disability concerns and problems. Counselors who specialize in these areas of treatment focus on a number of areas including the promotion of healthy lifestyles, the identification and elimination of stressors, the modification of toxic environments, the preservation or restoration of physical and mental health, and wellness. Specific ways in which clients are served depend on the counselors' skills and the needs of client populations. Throughout the years, counselors who work in abuse and addiction recovery and disability services have aligned themselves with the counseling specialties of addiction and offender counseling and rehabilitation counseling.

In this chapter we will examine the nature of abuse, addiction, and disability. A primary focus will be on how counselors can make a difference in the lives of those with these conditions.

THE CYCLE OF ABUSE

Abuse is the misuse or maltreatment of people, places, or things. It can be active as in physically or mentally punishing someone or passive in nature as in neglect. However, the end result is damaging. Often, abuse is cyclical with a predictable series of events and actions taking place as represented in the diagram below.

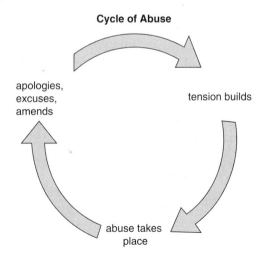

Cycle of Abuse

apologies, excuses, amends

tension builds

abuse takes place

People abuse for a number of reasons; however, that does not diminish the results of their actions or neglect. Abuse continues until there are interventions or insights that result in behavioral changes between the buildup of tension and the abuse that follows. Such changes can come through counseling if counselors recognize what is happening and use appropriate methods to break the cycle.

The two primary areas of abuse most prevalently seen in counseling are interpersonal abuse (e.g., violence or neglect of children, spouses, siblings, older adults) and intrapersonal abuse (e.g., overuse of substances, gambling, work, Internet). The latter often results in addiction. Both forms of abuse as well as addictions that come with intrapersonal abuse will be covered here.

INTERPERSONAL ABUSE

Interpersonal abuse involves violent or neglectful actions against others, especially those within one's family (i.e., siblings, spouses/partners, children, older adults) or those with whom one works or with whom one has daily contact. Interpersonal abuse can take a number of forms, but the two most prevalent are *emotional abuse* (e.g., verbal insults, yelling, ignoring, constant criticism), and *physical abuse* (e.g., punching, beating, slapping, biting, shaking, burning). Of all the types of abuse, emotional abuse is probably the most common. It is more subtle at times than physical abuse and is not confined to an age, stage, gender, or setting. For example, one place emotional abuse may occur that is seldom discussed is in school classrooms (McEachern, Aluede, & Kenny, 2008). "Teacher behaviors (e.g., excessive screaming at students . . . making degrading comments and labeling students as stupid and dumb, threatening students, and using homework as punishment)" are considered emotional abuse (p. 4). However, definitions of emotional abuse are culturally driven and interpersonal abuse is usually much more sinister and damaging than that found in classrooms. Four forms of interpersonal abuse: child, sibling, spouse/partner, and older adult will be covered in this section along with ways of treating such abuse.

PERSONAL REFLECTION

Because emotional abuse is so common, you have likely seen it expressed in a number of ways on various occasions. Describe the signs of abuse you have seen from those previously listed. What has been your reaction to witnessing emotional abuse?

Child Abuse

Child abuse (which involves acts of commission such as hitting) and *child neglect* (which involves acts of omission such as failure to provide necessities) are major concerns in American family life. Each year somewhere between 2 and 10 million children are victims of child abuse and neglect (American Academy of Pediatrics, 2007; Lawson, 2009; Skowron & Platt, 2005). Included in this category of abuse are physical, sexual, and psychological abuse, as well as neglect and abandonment. It should be stressed that abuse is seldom of one type and that families who engage in abuse are usually chaotic in nature and have relationship deficits (Mullen, Martin, Anderson, Romans, & Herbison, 1995).

The effects of child abuse, especially emotional and psychological abuse, include aggression, delinquency, and suicide, as well as cognitive, academic, and psychological impairment in children (McWey, 2004). Child abuse may also have a powerful influence on adult behavior that is lifelong (Elam & Kleist, 1999; Lawson, 2009). Adults who were abused as children appear to be less satisfied with their lives and prone to suffer from a number of disorders including those that are behavioral, cognitive, and affective such as depression and low self-esteem (May, 2005). However, there is not necessarily a direct causal relationship between abuse and adult symptoms (Mullen et al., 1995).

Child physical abuse resides on a continuum from physical contact that is mild, such as a swipe at a child's bottom, to that which is severe, such as a beating (Kemp, 1998). Severe physical child abuse is manifested in everything from skin injuries to death. In between are physical traumas such as broken bones, soft-tissue swelling, and bleeding. In addition to physical marks, psychological consequences result from physical abuse that range from fearfulness of others to posttraumatic stress disorder (PTSD) responses. Many children who are physically abused become distrustful of others, delinquent, and even depressed. In addition, a number of these children have difficulty forming close, lasting relationships with peers, let alone adults. Finally, physical child abuse can lead to serious cognitive problems including cognitive impairment, poor school performance, and later substance abuse (Skowron & Platt, 2005).

One of the most insidious forms of child abuse is *childhood sexual abuse (CSA)*. This type of abuse includes unwanted touching (i.e., fondling), sexual remarks, voyeurism, intercourse, oral sex, and pornography (Cobia, Sobansky, & Ingram, 2004; Elam & Kleist, 1999). Sexual abuse is tragically an all too common occurrence with cases reported in educational and even religious settings. Its long-term effects are almost always damaging regardless of whether the sexually abused person is male or female, heterosexual or homosexual (Hunter, 2006). When sexual abuse occurs in childhood, it often leads to distress, acute trauma, and even posttraumatic stress disorder (PTSD) (Putman, 2009).

"It is generally believed that sexual abuse of all children is significantly underreported, with sexual abuse of boys being reported least" (Tomes, 1996, p. 55). In sexual abuse situations, "most abuse of boys is done by perpetrators outside the family; girls' abuse is predominantly intrafamilial" (Hutchins, 1995, p. 21). Almost 1 in 3 girls is sexually abused by age 18 (Crespi & Howe, 2000) and 12% to 18% of boys are sexually abused during childhood or adolescence (Cobia et al., 2004; Tomes, 1996). It is difficult to detect and determine sexual abuse in families because, in many cases, all involved deny such actions and do not report them.

Sibling Abuse

Siblings may be abused and indeed "*sibling abuse* is pandemic and can have fatal results" (Kiselica & Morrill-Richards, 2007, p. 148). It is estimated that as many as 40% of children in the United States "engage in physical aggression against siblings, and as many as 85% engage in verbal aggression against siblings on a regular basis" (p. 148). Reasons for sibling abuse are complicated, but they include rivalry for dominance and power struggles for resources. Regardless, across cultures it has been found that when individuals experience sibling abuse the chances increase during their lifetimes of becoming either victims or perpetrators in abusive relationships (Cunradi, Caetano, & Schafer, 2002).

Sibling abuse takes three dominant forms: sexual, physical, and psychological. *Sexual abuse* is almost always perpetrated on sisters by brothers and includes acts that are incestuous. It may be a one-time act, but often it is continued over years. *Physical abuse* is inflicting harm by physical actions such as hitting, kicking, biting, scratching, or using objects such as hoses, coat hangers, belts, knives, and even guns. *Psychological abuse* includes constant, intense, or exaggerated teasing; contempt; or downgrading and may be a part of the other two types of abuse. Whereas sibling abuse usually declines with age, it leaves its mark on those who experience it. The victims may become more violent with those less powerful than they are as time goes by.

Spouse and Partner Abuse

Spouse and partner abuse is frequently referred to as "*domestic violence ,*" or " *marital/partner violence*"—that is, the "aggression that takes place in intimate relationships, usually between adults" (Kemp, 1998, p. 225). It is the attempt by one individual to "control the thoughts, beliefs, or behaviors of an intimate partner or to punish the partner for resisting one's control" (Peterman & Dixon, 2003, p. 41).

Although spouse abuse may be perpetrated on either men or women, in reality many more women than men are victims of its horrors. It is estimated that during adulthood 21% to 39% of all women will experience such abuse (Hage, 2006). Furthermore, "20% of emergency room visits for trauma and 25% of homicides of women involve intimate partner violence" (p. 83).

"Spouse and partner abuse can take many forms, including physical, sexual, psychological, and economic" (Schecter & Ganley, 1995). It is not confined to a particular economic class, family structure, sexual orientation, or ethnic group. The worst form of spouse and partner abuse is known as *battering*, "violence which includes severe physical assault or risk of serious injury" (Kemp, 1998, p. 225). However, other forms of domestic violence include grabbing, slapping, pushing, and throwing things at one another (O'Leary & Murphy, 1999).

Berg-Cross (2002) suggests that there are **12 signs of emotional abuse between partners**:

- Jealousy
- Controlling behavior
- Unrealistic expectations
- Isolation
- Blaming for problems and for feelings
- Hypersensitivity
- Verbal abuse
- Rigid sex roles
- Sudden changes in personality and mood
- Threats of violence
- Breaking or striking objects
- Use of force during arguments

Not surprisingly, there is a well-documented association between alcohol consumption and the violence that may accompany spouse/partner abuse. For instance, Fals-Stewart (2003) found severe aggression was 19 times higher when a male partner in a heterosexual relationship had become intoxicated.

CASE EXAMPLE

Cover-Up Charlene

Charlene always wore long-sleeve blouses and long, flowing skirts to her job every day at school. They were trendy clothes in some ways and antiquated in other ways. Every now and then she would wear a scarf around her neck and on occasion she sported sunglasses.

Madge, Charlene's best friend, noticed one day that Charlene had a bruise below her scarf. She noticed other physical marks as the months passed. Finally, she confronted Charlene about whether she was being abused. Charlene denied the accusation.

What do you think Madge should do now? Would confronting Charlene be helpful? Would encouraging here to enter counseling or going with her to see someone at social services be more helpful? Why or why not?

Older Adult Abuse

Older adult abuse or *elder abuse* can take a number of forms. Some of the most prevalent are infliction of physical injuries, dehydration, confinement (e.g., tied to furniture, locked in a room), and lack of cleanliness (Nerenberg, 2008; Sandell & Hudson, 2010). In recent years, well-known personalities, such as the actor Mickey Rooney, have spoken out about the abusive treatment they have received.

With a growing population of older adults from the Baby Boom Generation (1946–1964) aging into retirement, the prevalence of elder abuse will most likely increase. It is often hidden due to the immobility and living arrangements of older adults who are dependent on others to take care of their needs.

Preventing and Treating Interpersonal Abuse

Prevention programs in the interpersonal abuse arena are mainly educational and behavioral in nature. They focus on teaching listening skills and appropriate behavioral interactions. A number have an Adlerian base to them. Although they may take multiple forms, prevention programs usually stress cooperation, collaboration, and self-esteem.

Treatment for interpersonal abuse is prevalent. Four of the most common treatments for spouse/partner abuse are marital therapy, anger management training, individual counseling, and domestic conflict containment programs (Hammel, 2008). Marital therapy and domestic conflict programs may take the form of conjoint or couples therapy, but usually in abuse cases they do not because of the potential danger of violence. Anger management, like individual counseling, is conducted on a one-to-one basis. Recommended services are often gender-specific.

There are also a number of counseling approaches for dealing with sibling abuse. Most involve the direct participation of parents/guardians, children, and others involved and stress the importance of providing good supervision for children, giving children appropriate sexual education, and making sure homes are as violence proof as possible (Wiehe, 2000).

Prevention and treatment of child abuse and neglect is complicated because it involves legal, developmental, and psychological issues (Pistorello & Follette, 1998; Wilcoxon, Remley, & Gladding, 2012). All states require mental health workers and other professional helpers to report child abuse and neglect. "Failure to report child abuse usually constitutes unprofessional conduct that can lead to disciplinary action by a regulation board, possible conviction of a crime, and a civil lawsuit for damages" (Leslie, 2004, p. 48). Thus, before treatment can begin in most cases, legal issues must be resolved. In addition, developmental and psychological matters must be dealt with. For instance, when child sexual abuse occurs early in a person's life, the child may blame herself or himself for the abuse just as children of divorce often first find themselves at fault before they come to realize they have been victimized. In addition, child sexual abuse may not be treated until adulthood when other complications, such as couple intimacy, overlay the original problems.

Therefore, counselors must deal with a plethora of current and historical issues in working with child abuse. Anger and feelings of betrayal on the part of the abuser must be dealt with before working with the family as a whole in correcting the problem and preventing it from happening again. Furthermore, because of legal issues involved, the abuser in the family may be separated from the family, which makes the job of working with the family even more difficult and challenging. There are specific organizations, such as Prevent Child Abuse America and Parents Anonymous, which have local chapters that focus on promoting healthy family relationships.

Overall, those who have been abused physically or sexually, regardless of age, status, or gender, do not have one treatment modality that works best in helping them resolve the traumas of their experiences and make adequate and necessary adjustments (Hyde, Bentovim, & Monck, 1995; Oates & Bross, 1995; Roberts, 2007). Rather, a variety of treatments have been used with members of varied populations.

INTRAPERSONAL ABUSE AND ADDICTION

Intrapersonal abuse involves the misuse of objects or substances that were produced for one purpose, such as healing (prescriptive medication) or entertainment (video games), but are exploited excessively to the detriment of the person involved. The result is that often an ***addiction*** (a state of physiological or psychological dependence) occurs with excessive amounts of time and effort being devoted to the object or substance. There are **three C's of addiction** that conceptualize some of its core characteristics: "loss of control over addictive behaviors, despite the client's aim to stop; compulsive use; and continued use regardless of negative consequences" (Shallcross, 2011c, p. 31).

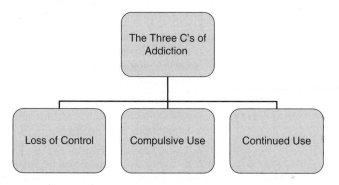

Almost any object or substance can become an addiction and the field of addictions has expanded and "now incorporates other compulsive behaviors including gambling, eating, shopping, working, exercising, as well as Internet and sexual compulsions" (Shadley, 2010, p. 19). As indicated earlier, excessive involvement with these objects or substances to the neglect of other aspects of life is a primary characteristic of intrapersonal addiction. Intrapersonal addictions have a physiological quality to them. Alcohol, nicotine, and illegal as well as prescriptive drugs will be highlighted here followed by two process addictive activities: compulsive gambling and workaholism.

Physiological Abuse and Addiction

Physiological abuse is to use substances, such as alcohol or drugs, to excess so that a person is not able to function (e.g., getting drunk or "high"). To be ***physiologically addicted*** is to have a physiological dependence on substances characterized by withdrawal symptoms should the substances be stopped suddenly. Physiological addiction usually starts with the habitual misuse of intoxicating and addicting substances, such as alcohol, drugs, tobacco (i.e., nicotine), and prescriptive medications, that is, ***substance abuse***.

The General Nature of Substance Abuse and Addiction

Whether people are addicted or not, abuse of substances and addiction to them results in mental, physical, emotional, social, and spiritual damages. For example, the abuse of alcohol and addiction to it are frequently involved in disorderly or heinous behavior such as public drunkenness, emergency department admissions, motor vehicle crashes, date rape, and suicide (Fagan, 2006; Griswold, Aronoff, Kernan, & Kahn, 2008). Indeed, substance abuse and addiction are "major public health issues in today's society" and cut across "gender, socioeconomic levels, ethnicity, age, religion, profession, geography, and most dimensions of human existence and background" (Stevens & Smith, 2009, p. iii). Alcohol and drug issues, including abuse and addiction, among the aged, adults, and adolescents are treated every day by counselors in nursing and retirement homes, mental health clinics, colleges and universities, and public schools (Hinkle, 1999). According to data from the Substance Abuse and Mental Health Services Administration "nearly a quarter of all Americans have participated in binge drinking, and 8.4% have used illicit drugs" (Shorman, 2011, 3D).

Indeed, abuse of and addiction to substances is one of the most frequently occurring mental health problems in the United States. The term *abuse* here refers to the use of a drug for the sole purpose of euphoria or recreation (Weigel, Donovan, Krug, & Dixon, 2007). For instance, in regard to alcohol "1 in 10 American adults in the general population has significant problems" (Miller & Brown, 1997, p. 1269) and in some cultural and diversity groups, such as Native Americans or gay and lesbian communities, the problem, especially in regard to addiction, is greater (Garrett & Carroll, 2000; Matthews, Lorah, & Fenton, 2006). Between "12% to 30% of all hospitalized patients abuse alcohol," and "health care costs among alcoholic families are twice as great as those of nonalcoholic families" (Steenbarger, 1998, p. 81). In addition, alcohol abuse and particularly addiction among some populations, such as older adults, is often unrecognized, misdiagnosed, or attributed to the aging process (Williams, Ballard, & Alessi, 2005).

Often people who abuse or are addicted to one substance also abuse or are addicted to other substances. *Polysubstance abuse and addiction* (the abuse of or addiction to two or more substances simultaneously) is a growing phenomenon. In addition, abuse of or addiction to substances is *comorbid* with a number of other disorders including depression, anxiety, conduct disorders, and attention deficit/hyperactivity. Often the abuse of or addiction to substances becomes a way of life related to social conditions. For example, many people begin smoking as adolescents in response to an unsatisfactory life rooted in poverty and hopelessness. Peer pressure, poor school performance, parental smoking, minority ethnic status, and an external locus of control make smoking more likely with the end result being addiction (Hilts, 1996).

Among the most prevalent factors affecting treatment for intrapersonal abuses and addiction are "motivation, denial, dual diagnosis, matching, control, and relapse" (L'Abate, 1992, p. 11). *Motivation* has to do with an internal desire to change, which most substance abusers do not wish to do because of their self-centeredness and comfort. *Denial* is basically minimizing the effects of substance abuse on either oneself or others. It plays down the harm that is being done. A *dual diagnosis* is one in which an abuser or addicted person has more than one aspect of personality that is open to treatment. For instance, a substance abuser may be impulsive or depressed in addition to being abusive. *Matching* concerns the right treatment for a disorder. Some substance abuses or addictions, such as overdosing with cocaine, require specialized treatment. *Control* has to do with the regulation of behavior, which substance abusers and addicted persons tend to disregard. Finally, *relapse* is the recidivism or reoccurrence of dysfunctional behaviors once they have been treated. It is discouraging to have substance abusers and those addicted to substances go through structured programs and end up acting the way they did before.

Treating Substance Abuse and Addiction

Treatment strategies for substance abusers may be aimed at prevention as well as remediation and may be individually, group, or society based. For example, to lower resistance in substance abuse cases involving individuals, *motivational interviewing (MI)* (Brooks & McHenry, 2009;

Miller & Rollnick, 2002) may be tried. "MI is a brief counseling intervention designed to reduce a client's ambivalence toward change while increasing his or her motivation to engage in the behavior-change process" (Burrow-Sanchez, 2006, p. 286). In this approach, counselors meet clients at their current level of motivation and work toward increasing it to the highest level possible. MI techniques are largely drawn from person-centered counseling and include skills such as active listening, reflection, and reframing in order to help clients feel understood and to reinforce client "behaviors that are congruent with the desired behavior change" (p. 286).

In addition to using MI as a treatment modality, a *solution-focused approach* may be used. In such an approach, the emphasis is to get the client to think about what an improved life would look like and what changes would be needed to live such a life (Juhnke, 2002; Juhnke & Hagedorn, 2006; Juhnke & Kelly, 2005). Narrative therapy may be used as well to cast addiction as an external force and devise an active strategy for attacking it (Shallcross, 2011c). A **bibliotherapeutic approach** is a fourth strategy that may work with some individuals (Hipple, Comer, & Boren, 1997). Using this strategy, counselors have those who are addicted read books or view/listen to media and discuss ideas related to what they have experienced. For example, in working with adolescent counselors, members might be asked to read *Go Ask Alice* by Anonymous, a nonfiction novel about teen drug abuse, or *Imitate the Tiger* by Jan Cheripko, a novel on teenage alcohol abuse. Clients then discuss their reactions with a counselor including how they are like or unlike the main characters of the book and what insights they gleaned from the reading.

A common element in approaches to substance abuse prevention involves group pressure and dynamics such as group support. In setting up preventive programs, counselors are wise to use their knowledge of groups. The reason is that most people, especially adolescents, who get involved in the use of substances, do so because their friends use drugs, they are bored, or they are under considerable stress (National Center on Addiction and Substance Abuse at Columbia University, 2003). Therefore, when a group perceives drugs as hazardous to their health or dangerous, members of such a group are less likely to engage in experimenting with these substances. The group norm becomes one of discouraging members from trying substances. Thus, educational and support groups are a valuable tool for counselors to employ in warding off abuse behaviors in preventive programs (Gladding, 2012).

PERSONAL REFLECTION

With so many types of prevention programs set up locally and nationally, why do you think there is still a major problem in the United States with substance abuse? What do you think could be done in addition to these prevention programs to decrease substance abuse?

Treatment for Alcohol Abuse and Addiction

Alcohol is a drug. However, it will be highlighted separately from other drug treatments because it is the most prevalent form of drug abuse and addiction. There are a number of treatment approaches for working with adults who abuse or are addicted to alcohol. However, in providing treatment for alcohol abuse it is important to remember that it is helpful, and sometimes necessary, that someone who is an abuser be *"dry,"* or not currently drinking, before any effective treatment can be started. Being dried out for a period of 28 or more days gives the person a "clean" body and mind to use in doing something different and positive. The difficulty of such a process can be seen graphically in Sandra Bullock's performance in the movie *28 Days*.

Regardless, counselors work to help alcohol abusers and addicts in a number of ways, but three are most dominant: outpatient, residential, and inpatient (Burrow-Sanchez, 2006).

The most well-known approach to working with those who abuse or who are addicted to alcohol is **Alcoholics Anonymous (AA).** AA is the oldest successful treatment program in the world, having been founded in the 1930s (AA World Services, 2002). It is "both a fellowship and a rehabilitation program" (Warfield & Goldstein, 1996, p. 196). Alcohol abusers and addicts suffer from what AA describes as "character defects" (AA World Services, 2002). "These are feelings, beliefs, and behaviors that dispose them to seek a sense of well-being by abusing alcohol" (Warfield & Goldstein, 1996, p. 197). AA meetings are conducted in small-group settings where literature—for example, *The Big Book* (AA World Services, 2002)—is used along with group discussion. AA also has meetings for family members in **Al-Anon** and **Alateen.**

A key component in AA is the use of a **12-step program** that has at its basis a spiritual foundation. Group discussions in AA meetings center on helping members realize they need and have the support of others and a dependence on a higher power. The spiritual dimension in AA results in an emphasis on members admitting their powerlessness over alcohol (or other substances). Members who abstain from the use and abuse of alcohol are never "cured"; rather, they are "in recovery." There is also an emphasis within AA on responsibility, forgiveness, restitution (when possible), affirmation, ritual, and fellowship.

AA, as a treatment model, has been adapted to treat many other addiction problems such as those involving the abuse of narcotics, cocaine, and food, (James & Hazler, 1998). However, some counselors are uncomfortable with the spiritual qualities of AA and prefer to discuss needed recovery qualities in cognitive–behavioral or humanistic language. Rational emotive behavior therapy has led the way in setting up recovery groups that are nonspiritual in nature.

Along with treating the person who is abusing alcohol or addicted to it, the counselor also needs to work with his or her family and community. The support or scapegoating that abusers of and addicts of alcohol receive from family and community systems in which they live makes a tremendous difference in their ability to abstain from the use of alcohol. AA and other recovery programs, such as Women for Sobriety, have special groups and programs for family members of persons who are substance abusers. Other groups outside Al-Anon and Alateen include national chapters of *S.A.D.D.* **(Students against Drunk Driving)** and *M.A.D.D.* **(Mothers against Drunk Driving)**. Both of these associations, plus those found on college and university campuses, help educate and orient young people about the hazards of alcohol in a sophisticated and proactive way.

In the gay and lesbian communities, individuals are "at risk" for abuse or addiction because alcohol is seen as a way of coping with stigmatization. In addition, one of the most accepting social places for gays and lesbians to meet is a bar (Matthews et al., 2006). Therefore, when working with members of these groups in any setting, counselors need to be sure to draw others into the conversation and even into the treatment plan.

In working with adolescents, especially in regard to alcohol, Pollock (2006) cautions that counselors need to remember the following:

- Working with adolescents is a treatment specialty.
- For counseling to be effective with adolescents, family and other significant people in the adolescent's life should be included.
- Adolescents need to be educated as to what counseling is.
- Because adolescents do not respond well to many adult treatments, therapeutic techniques need to be specifically tailored to them.

- Although relationship skills are important, the counselor cannot function well trying to be the adolescent's friend.
- Counseling works best with adolescents if it is centered around "problem solving, skill building, and just being heard" (p. 331).
- "Therapeutic moments" are much more uneven with adolescents than with adults.

Treating Nicotine Abuse and Addiction

In addition to methods used to treat alcohol abuse or addiction, there are unique approaches to working with individuals with *nicotine abuse or addiction*. In 2011 over 43 million Americans smoked cigarettes (WebMD, www.webmd.com/smoking-cessation/news/20081113/smoking-rate-is-declining-in-us).

Counselors can help improve the success rate of nicotine-addicted individuals in a number of ways (Singleton & Pope, 2000) such as the use of *telephone counseling*, which has a success rate comparable to group smoking-cessation programs. Telephone counseling consists of a 15- to 30-minute phone call where counselors give positive, nonjudgmental feedback to those who are trying to quit smoking. The idea behind the strategy is to promote self-efficacy. Another approach is *rapid smoking*, where smokers, after counseling, go through a series of six 1-hour sessions where they inhale a cigarette every 6 seconds until they feel too sick to continue. The goal is to "produce a conditioned negative response to the taste of cigarettes" (p. 452).

Skills training is a third technique. In this approach coping skills are taught, such as reframing and thought stopping, after clients have learned to recognize the cognitive, emotional, and environmental triggers that tend to produce the urge to smoke. Among the most successful skills are the use of self-statements concerned with the financial and health benefits of discontinuing smoking as well as oral substitutes, increased physical activity, and the buddy system.

Finally, self-help materials, such as brief and factual informational booklets related to smoking, can be useful. Two examples of these booklets are "Clearing the Air" (National Institute of Health Publication #95-1467, call 1-800-4-CANCER) and "Smart Move" (American Cancer Society). Booklets of this nature guide the smoker through the process of quitting and maintaining nonsmoking behavior.

There are also effective educational programs for teens who use tobacco and more potent substances (Mudore, 1997; Sunich & Doster, 1995). These programs focus on both external and internal factors important to individuals in this age bracket. For example, external factors include the impact of smoking on one's breath, teeth, and clothes, as well as monetary costs. Internal factors include such variables as lifestyle choices, time management, and nutrition. For younger individuals, external factors may be more effective in influencing their decisions to never begin smoking or doing drugs, whereas for older adolescents internal factors are more powerful.

CASE EXAMPLE

Nicholas Gives Up Nicotine

Nicholas had been a heavy smoker for 25 years. He went through a pack of cigarettes every day. Although he was not in the best of health, he felt healthy and was surprised that in a routine physical exam his doctor discovered a blood clot in his leg and ordered him to stay in bed for the next 6 weeks.

Nicholas complied with the request at first. His carton of cigarettes lasted him about 10 days. He then asked his wife, Lucy, to get him more. She refused, even though he begged. Later, Nicholas began to sweat and shake. He begged Lucy to go to the store to buy him more smokes. She again held her ground and continued to refuse to buy Nicholas any more cigarettes during the next month he was in bed. Nicholas eventually lost his strong craving for a smoke.

What do you think about Lucy's strategy? Do you think it continued to work once Nicholas got back on his feet?

Treating Drug Abuse and Addiction

Drugs are any substance other than food, including stimulants, depressants, and hallucinogens, that can affect the way a person's mind and body work. Americans consume a lot of drugs, both legal and illegal. Approximately half a million Americans are heroin addicts, and 4 million are regular users of marijuana, with up to 10% of Americans using marijuana in a year (Shorman, 2011).

Drug abuse and addiction are treated in two ways: prevention and remediation. **Prevention programs** usually are tied into a community effort to thwart abuse on a community or global level. In preventing abuse, there are two factors that must be considered. The first is a *risk factor*, which is "typically defined as anything that increases the probability of a person using drugs" (Burrow-Sanchez, 2006, p. 284). For example, living in poverty, failing in school, or associating with drug users are all risk factors. In contrast, there is a so-called *protective factor*, which is "anything that protects or decreases the probability of a person using drugs" (p. 284). Examples of protective factors are a well-monitored and stable family, an association with friends who do not use drugs, and high achievement in school. *Triggers*, environmental events, are involved in both risk and protective behaviors.

To try to prevent drug abuse and avoid addiction, a number of programs have been developed, some of which are more successful than others. On the simpler side are programs such as **"Just Say No,"** which focus on trying to help preteens and teenagers say "no" when offered a potentially addictive or dangerous substance. The focus is to learn how to be assertive and how to refuse offers of harmful drugs in an appropriate way—for example, simply ignoring an offer, walking away from drug-related situations, saying "No thanks," or making an excuse for refusing an offer of drugs.

Individuals who are addicted to drugs other than alcohol or nicotine, such as cocaine, other illegal drugs, or even prescriptive drugs, often receive treatment based on the AA model. However, because of society's greater disapproval of "drug addicts," the context in which treatment is offered is often not the same. For example, one context in which treating drug abuse and addiction is jail because many drug substances are illegal and many laws are antiquated. Thus drug abusers are often tried as criminals and incarcerated.

There are some treatment programs within prisons. A prototype of a jail treatment program that works well is "Stay'n Out" in Staten Island, New York. "Its secret is a captive audience; participants don't have any choice about showing up for therapy. It's be there—or you're off to a meaner cellblock" (Alter, 1995, pp. 20–21). Although the ethical dimensions of this program are debatable, the results are a recidivism rate of only 25%, much lower than the average. A substance abuse program such as Stay'n Out saves money for communities to use in other ways because recovering addicts require lower health care and criminal justice costs. However, the sad fact is that many individuals who are addicted to drugs do not receive any treatment at all.

PROCESS ADDICTIONS

As opposed to alcohol, nicotine, and drug substances, the idea of addiction to non-behaviors, that is behaviors that are not interpersonally abusive, is relatively new. "These behaviors, often called "*process addictions*," include addictions to such things as sexuality, Internet use, gaming, and gambling" (Hagedorm & Young, 2011, p. 251). Behavior moves from normal to addictive when it both produces pleasure and reduces negative moods and includes two key features: (a) the individual is unable to control, cut back, or stop the behavior, and (b) the individual continues to use the behavior despite substantial negative consequences (Goodman, 2001). According to Hagedorm and Young (2011) the most common and problematic addictive nonviolent or abusive behaviors found among children and adolescents include "(a) food, (b) gambling, (c) exercise, (d) sex, (e) spending, (f) the Internet, and (g) video/computer games" (p. 251). The same types of behaviors are unfortunately common and problematic for many adults as well with work being an additional factor. Compulsive gambling and workaholism will be covered in this section of the chapter.

Compulsive Gambling

Moderate gambling, like moderate use of alcohol, is an accepted part of North American society and usually causes little concern. However, compulsive gambling is a serious problem (Maske, 2007). In such cases gambling is not glitzy, glamorous, or fun. It is pathological and may tragically take the form of illegal and dehumanizing activities as in the case of Michael Vick and betting on dog fights.

Compulsive gambling is found in about 2.5% of the population. Members of adolescent and young adult populations are at a higher risk for the development of gambling-relate problems than are older adults, largely due to the increases in accessibility of gambling activities via the Internet (Hardoon & Derevensky, 2002; Shaffer, 2003) and due to their being the first generation raised on video gaming (Messerlian, Byrne, & Derevensky, 2004). In addition to gambling, net (Internet) addiction or compulsion may result in the excessive use of computers when they interfere with daily life. Regardless, compulsive gambling and Internet compulsion leave in their wake broken homes, shattered dreams, empty lives, and financial ruin.

Compulsive gambling and Internet compulsion parallel alcohol, nicotine, and drug addiction in numerous ways. Those who become compulsive lose control over their behaviors. They commonly lie and cheat in order to continue their compulsion. In the process, their social interaction, mood, personality, work ethic, relationships, and thought process are negatively affected. Like other addicts, they frequently try, unsuccessfully, to cut down or quit only to usually be swept back up in their nonproductive behavior again.

The pattern of behavior in compulsive gambling revolves around the "action" that occurs when placing a bet. Compulsive gamblers experience an aroused, euphoric state comparable to the "high" sought by drug users. This state includes a change in brain chemistry and often a "rush," which is sometimes characterized by sweaty palms, rapid heartbeat, and nausea experienced during the period of anticipation. Just like in other addictions, compulsive gamblers develop "tolerance" for the "action." Thus they must increase the size of their bets or the odds against them to create the same amount of excitement.

TREATING COMPULSIVE GAMBLING. Compulsive gambling is treatable, just like other addictive behaviors. However, many problem gamblers are reluctant to seek treatment because they do not understand the nature of the addiction involved, and they do not want to lose self-esteem from admitting they cannot handle their problem.

One major source of help is **Gamblers Anonymous** (www.gamblersanonymous.org). It follows the same pattern as Alcoholics Anonymous, including the same 12-step treatment program. The success rate is comparable to that for other addictions. However, sometimes the nature of treatment is longer and more complicated because a number of compulsive gamblers also suffer from other addictions such as alcoholism, drug abuse, compulsive shopping, or bulimia.

Work Addiction (Workaholism)

Work is like any other activity in that it can become all consuming to the point where the person in the midst of it abandons other opportunities that could be beneficial. Robinson, Flowers, and Ng (2006) define *workaholism* as "a compulsive and progressive, potentially fatal disorder characterized by self-imposed demands, compulsive overworking, inability to regulate work habits, and overindulgence in work to the exclusion and detriment of intimate relationships and major life activities" (p. 213). Workaholism negatively affects families of those involved and can lead to mental health problems in marriages, including marital dissatisfaction associated with over-controlling tendencies in a spouse and impaired communication (Robinson, 2001; Robinson et al., 2006). Those who compulsively overwork, sometimes known as "workaholics," focus primarily on their careers for self-validation, while ignoring other important aspects of themselves or their environments. "Workaholics have been compared with alcoholics in that these two groups share some of the same symptoms, such as reality distortion, need to control, denial, anxiety, depression, withdrawal, irritability, and relationship problems with friends and family members" (Chamberlin & Naijian, 2009, p. 159). A few successful public figures, like Andrew Lloyd Webber, confess to being workaholics but most individuals who adopt this lifestyle do not flourish either personally or professionally.

TREATING WORK ADDICTION.   Robinson (1995, p. 33) recommends the following steps for working with clients who are addicted to work, especially those who are recovering.

- *"Help them slow down their pace."*   Give them examples of how they can make a conscious effort to slow down their daily lives through deliberate means.
- *"Teach them to learn to relax."*   Learning meditation or yoga, reading an inspirational book, or even soaking in a hot tub is healthy and helpful in moderation.
- *"Assist them in evaluating their family climate."*   Interactions with family members, especially of a positive nature, can be meaningful and relaxing. Therefore, it behooves recovering addicts to explore ways they "can strengthen family ties."
- *"Stress the importance of celebrations and rituals."*   Activities such as celebrations and rituals are the glue that holds families together and makes life personally rich and rewarding.
- *"Help them [clients] get back into the social swing."*   This strategy involves devising a plan for developing social lives and friendship. If successful, it "explores ways of building social networks outside of work."
- *"Address living in the now."*   By appreciating the present, recovering addicts can enjoy experiences more and not become anxious about or preoccupied with the future.
- *"Encourage clients to nurture themselves."*   Often individuals who have become addicts find it hard, if not impossible, to indulge themselves even in healthy ways. However, the practice of self-nurturing can be beneficial.

- *"Stress the importance of proper diet, rest, and exercise."*   It is hard to function if a person is running on a deficit either physically or emotionally. Therefore, getting clients to balance their lives in regard to diet, rest, and exercise can go a long way to helping them recover from their addiction.
- *"Help clients grieve the loss of their childhoods" and "address self-esteem."*   Many addicts feel ashamed, saddened, angry, or even determined by their past. Helping them realize they can recover from past times and experiences can go a long way in assisting clients to become functional.
- *"Inform clients [that] 12-step programs [are] available as a complement to the individual work you do with them."*   Almost all addicts in recovery can benefit from a 12-step program that emphasizes human relationships in concert with a higher power.

To this extensive list Chamberlin & Naijian (2009) add "**help clients identify their individual reinforcement history**" and assist workaholics in "**exploring consequences and rewards of workaholic behavior**" (p. 167).

PERSONAL REFLECTION

Robinson and Chamberlin & Naijian have laid out some excellent ideas for slowing down the pace of life and enjoying people. How might you use these ideas in other venues of counseling besides dealing with workaholics?

TREATING WOMEN AND MINORITY CULTURAL GROUPS IN ABUSE AND ADDICTION

Women who abuse alcohol or who are addicted to it, approximately 5 to 7 million in the United States alone, may have an especially difficult time seeking and finding appropriate treatment. The same is true for women who abuse or are addicted to other substances. This is because of societal rebuke and chastisement of them and because of barriers to treatment faced by women such as the need for child care, cost, family opposition, and inadequate diagnosis (Van der Wade, Urgenson, Weltz, & Hanna, 2002). Although female alcohol abusers constitute about one third of the membership in Alcoholics Anonymous, "there is little empirical evidence on the benefits of AA and NA to the female alcoholic or addict" (Manhal-Baugus, 1998, p. 82). Therefore, new theories and alternative treatment strategies are developing for women that reflect the broader context of women's lives, especially difficulties they face regarding alcohol addiction. These programs draw on community resources in a different way from traditional approaches. One of these programs is "Women for Sobriety," a mutual help group based on a cognitive-behavior modification approach that helps teach women to change their thinking so they may overcome feelings of helplessness, powerlessness, guilt, and dependence. It has 13 affirmations that promote positive thinking in a supportive relationship environment run by women for women (Manhal-Baugus, 1998; Shallcross, 2011c).

In addition to gender differences, cultural differences play a part, too, in the recovery process. In most cases, special considerations are required for treating members of minority cultures. For instance, Native Americans may find spiritual elements different from non–Native American traditions important in helping them. Therefore, counselors who work with this population may want to consult a medicine man or medicine woman before trying to work with persons or groups seeking recovery (Vick, Smith, & Herrera, 1998). In addition, there seems to be a growing body of evidence on the significant relationship "between discrimination and historical loss and substance abuse and physical and mental health in minority groups" (Hinson, 2010, p. 22).

Thus, this factor needs to become part of the equation in considering how to work with African Americans and Native Americans in particular during recovery.

Affiliation, Certification, and Education of Counselors Who Work in Abuse and Addiction

The **International Association of Addictions and Offender Counseling (IAAOC)** is one of the leading groups that focuses on the prevention, treatment, and description of abusive and addictive behaviors. This association publishes materials, such as the *Journal of Addictions & Offender Counseling*, that informs professional counselors about the latest developments in the field. Another major organization is the **National Association of Alcoholism and Drug Abuse Counselors (NAADAC)**, a national organization that certifies addiction counselors.

Interestingly, NAADAC membership is almost equally divided between members who have master's and doctoral degrees and those who do not (West, Mustaine, & Wyrick, 2002). The number of academic programs that educate counselors with an emphasis on substance abuse counseling continues to grow, and since 1994 the National Board for Certified Counselors (NBCC) has had a certification process for becoming a master addiction counselor. However, at present the field of substance abuse counseling is split between *recovering counselors*, those who have been abusers, now are dry, and have taken specialized courses to qualify for a NAADAC certification; and *nonrecovering counselors*, those who have earned at least a master's degree in counseling, usually with a concentration in substance abuse.

The effectiveness of the two groups varies and the ways they work are distinct. Recovering counselors are more likely to engage in activities that are consistent with the philosophy described in the 12 steps of Alcoholics Anonymous (Culbreth & Borders, 1999). Thus, they are "prone to be involved in community education programs, socialize with clients away from the work environment, and visit clients in the hospital," whereas nonrecovering counselors do not and, in addition, are more prone to see alcohol and drug problems on a continuum rather than as a yes or no diagnosis. With the trend being for more professional counselors than paraprofessionals to enter the field in the future, a number of procedures will change, including the way supervision is delivered (Culbreth & Borders, 1999). In addition, as this transition occurs, counselors from both traditions who are presently in the field will need intensive training to learn even more treatment interventions so they can work effectively with diverse clients presenting complex issues (Thombs & Osborn, 2001).

COUNSELING AND DISABILITY

Ability is a natural tendency to do something well such as carry out tasks in daily life (e.g., dress or feed oneself), work at a job/attend school, or be mobile. *Disability* is an inability or a limitation that prevents a person from performing some or all of the tasks of daily life, such as taking care of bodily functions, walking, talking, or being independent of a caretaker. Disabilities are prevalent in American life. About 20% of Americans "have physical, sensory, psychiatric, or cognitive disabilities that interfere with daily living" (Livneh & Antonah, 2005, p. 12). Overall, "disabilities affect 54 million people in the United States, of whom 4.4 million are children" (Roskam, Zech, Nils, & Nader-Grosbois, 2008, p. 132). Broken down even further,

- more than 9 million Americans with disabilities are unable to work or attend school;
- costs of annual income support . . . and medical care provided by the U.S. government to assist people with disabilities is about $60 billion;
- disabilities are higher among older people, minorities, and lower socioeconomic groups; and
- 8 of the 10 most common causes of death in the United States are associated with chronic illness.

As if these figures were not bad enough, ethnic minority populations suffer from disabilities more than the general population (Smith, Foley, & Chaney, 2008). The reasons are numerous and include low income and poverty, employment in physically dangerous jobs, lack of health insurance coverage, low educational attainment, and faculty and inaccurate testing and assessment (Wilson & Senices, 2005, p. 87).

The Nature of Disabilities

Clients who have disabilities include those whose manifestations are physical, emotional, mental, and behavioral. Disabilities vary widely and include a number of diagnoses such as alcoholism, arthritis, blindness, cardiovascular disease, deafness, cerebral palsy, epilepsy, intellectual disabilities, drug abuse, neurological disorders, orthopedic disabilities, psychiatric disabilities, renal failure, speech impairments, and spinal cord conditions. Not all disabilities are visible, however, and thereby go unnoticed.

Unfortunately, people who have disabilities often encounter others who have misconceptions and biases about their limitations (Smith et al., 2008). These individuals may even harass those who are disabled about their disabilities, especially if the persons have other characteristics, such as a minority sexual orientation (e.g., being lesbian or gay) (Hunt, Matthews, Milsom, & Lammel, 2006). This type of treatment is cruel and may well affect the person's "everyday social interactions" (Leierer, Strohmer, Leclere, Cornwell, & Whitten, 1996, p. 89).

As a result of the treatment they receive in public, a large percentage of persons with disabilities tend to withdraw from mainstream interactions with others and are unemployed or unable to achieve an independent-living status (Blackorby & Wagner, 1996). In fact, "individuals with disabilities as a group may have the highest rate of unemployment and underemployment in the United States" (Clarke & Crowe, 2000, p. 58). Thus, people with disabilities may suffer from low self-esteem, lack of confidence in decision making, social stigma, a restricted range of available occupations, and few successful role models (Enright, 1997). They may also have limited early life experiences.

Linked to, but distinct from, a disability is a **handicap** which is "an observable or discernible limitation that is made so by the presence of various barriers" (Schumacher, 1983, p. 320). An example of a person who is disabled and who has a handicap is someone who is a quadriplegic assigned to a third-floor apartment in a building without an elevator, or a partially deaf person receiving instructions orally.

Working with People Who Have Disabilities

Services for those with disabilities have been strongly influenced by government legislation. In turn, counselors who work with this specific population have been active in supporting federal and state legislation. Yet there have been other influences as well.

A distinguishing aspect of counseling with people who have disabilities is the historical link with the *medical model* of delivering services (Ehrle, 1979). The prominence of the medical model is easy to understand when one recalls how closely professionals who were first involved with persons with disabilities treated those who were physically challenged. However, a number of different models for helping people who are disabled have emerged (Smart & Smart, 2006). There are four that are most prominent.

The most popular of these models and the closest associated with the medical model is the *biomedical model*. This model is steeped in the language of medicine, but it is silent in the language of social justice. According to this model, "disabilities are objective conditions that exist in and of themselves" (p. 30). They are considered deficiencies and residing within an individual who is totally responsible for the problem. This model basically equates disability with pathology. Whereas the model may work best when dealing with physical disabilities, it is "less useful with mental and psychiatric disabilities" (p. 31).

The second conception of disability is the ***environmental and functional model***. Its focus is more appropriate for chronic disabilities (i.e., what most disabilities are). In this model, people carry a label with them (i.e., "disabled"). The label may lead to some degree of social prejudice and discrimination. Yet, it also places the blame for disabilities outside the individual.

The ***sociopolitical model*** is the third model and is sometimes referred to as the ***minority model***. It assumes that persons with disabilities are a minority group rather than people with pathologies. "The hallmarks of this model include self-definition, the elimination (or reduction) of the prejudice and discrimination (sometimes referred to as *'handicapism'*), rejection of medical diagnoses and categories, and the drive to achieve full equality and civil rights under U.S. law" (p. 34).

The fourth model is the ***peer counselor model***. It assumes that people with direct experience with disabilities are best able to help those who have recently acquired disabilities.

In working with clients with disabilities to develop or to restore adjustment, the role of counselor is to assess the clients' current level of functioning and environmental situation that either hinder or enhance functionality. After such an assessment is made, counselors use a wide variety of counseling theories and techniques. Virtually all the affective, behavioral, cognitive, and systemic theories of counseling are employed. Systems theories in such work have become especially popular in recent years (Cottone, Grelle, & Wilson, 1988; Hershenson, 1996).

The actual theories and techniques used are dictated by the skills of counselors as well as the needs of clients. For example, a client with disabilities who has sexual feelings may need a psychoeducational approach on how to handle these emotions, whereas another client with disabilities who is depressed may need a more cognitive or behavioral intervention (Boyle, 1994). An action-oriented approach such as Gestalt psychodrama can be especially powerful in helping clients become more involved in the counseling process and accept responsibility for their lives (Coven, 1977; Gatta et al., 2010). Techniques from this tradition, such as role-playing, may be especially helpful.

Clients with Specific Disabilities

There are a number of specific disabilities that counselors work with, too many to cover here. Thus, only four—physical disabilities, intellectual disabilities, ADD/ADHD, and posttraumatic stress disorder—will be briefly highlighted as examples of specific disabilities counselors encounter.

PHYSICAL DISABILITIES.   Physical injuries such as spinal cord damage, mild traumatic brain injury (MTBI), limb loss, or blindness produce a major loss for an individual and consequently have a tremendous physical and emotional impact (Jones, Young, & Leppma, 2010; Krause & Anson, 1997). Counseling in such cases may require some combination of occupational, physical, and cognitive therapies as well as concentration and cooperation on both the client's and the family's part to adjust to the situation.

Livneh and Evans (1984) point out that clients who have physical disabilities go through **12 phases of adjustment** that may distinguish them from others: **shock, anxiety, bargaining, denial, mourning, depression, withdrawal, internalized anger, externalized aggression, acknowledgment, acceptance, and adjustment/adaptation**. There are behavioral correlates that accompany each phase and intervention strategies appropriate for each as well. For example, the client who has lost a limb is often in a state of shock and disbelief and may be immobilized and cognitively disorganized initially. Intervention strategies most helpful during this time include comforting the person (both physically and verbally), listening and attending, offering support and reassurance, and allowing the person to ventilate feelings (Knittel, 2010). Later strategies focus on treating the person as a person and not an amputee and encouraging the individual to take appropriate risks in life.

In addition to serving as counselors, professionals working with persons who are physically disabled must be advocates, consultants, and educators. They must confront disabled persons in developing an internal locus of control for their lives. The task is comprehensive and involves a complex relationship among job functions. Caretakers and support personnel involved in helping persons with physical disabilities need help themselves in working through the recovery process and should be included as much as possible in making evaluations and developing plans.

INTELLECTUAL DISABILITIES. Clients with intellectual disabilities include those who have mild to severely limited cognitive abilities. In some cases, counselors' tasks and techniques may be similar to those employed with adults or adolescents who have physical disabilities (supportive counseling and life-planning activities), but young clients with intellectual deficiencies may require different activities and services. For instance, counselors can help parents of these children in working through their feelings about having children with intellectual disabilities. In the process they help the children as well through promoting positive parental interactions that encourage maximum development (Huber, 1979).

When working with adolescents or military personnel who have intellectual difficulties due to head injuries, counselors must address social issues as well as therapeutic activities (Bergland & Thomas, 1991). As a general rule, increased time and effort in attending to psychosocial issues are required for working with anyone who has been intellectual impaired, regardless of age or the cause of the impairment (Kaplan, 1993).

ADD OR ADHD. **Attention deficit disorder (ADD)** and **attention deficit/hyperactivity disorder (ADHD)** are disorders that interfere with learning and day-to-day functioning. These disabilities have a neurological base and begin in childhood, influencing the emotional, social, and behavioral adjustment of children, with more boys than girls impacted. ADD and ADHD are found in various forms (e.g., ADHD, which affects between 3% and 5% of school-age children, has three subtypes: **inattentive, hyperactivity-impulsivity,** or **a combination of the first two subtypes**) (Brown, 2000). Unfortunately, 50% to 80% of children with ADHD continue to have symptoms into adolescence and some even into adulthood (Wender, 1998).

Difficulties associated with ADHD such as "distractibility, impulsivity, disorganization, and interpersonal problems . . . persist and sometimes worsen with age" (Schwiebert, Sealander, & Dennison, 2002, p. 5). Thus, ADHD can have an impact throughout the life span. Heightened levels of frustration, anxiety, distress, depression, and diminished self-concepts are other symptoms that may happen as a result.

Since ADD and ADHD have become more widely known in recent years, a number of strategies for working with children and adults who are so impaired have been developed by clinicians in educational and community settings. For instance, counselors may help students with ADHD prepare for postsecondary education and vocational entry by giving them cues in mnemonic form on how to behave in certain situations. One such cue is the mnemonic ***SLANT***, which may be used to help those who have learning problems focus on classroom lectures (Mercer, Mercer, & Pullen, 2011). The letters stand for

S = "Sit up straight"

L = "Lean forward"

A = "Activate thinking and Ask questions"

N = "Name key information and Nod your head to validate the teacher/speaker"

T = "Track the teacher or speaker"

Overall, counselors who work with clients with ADD and ADHD need to be aware that many facets of personality may be shaped by the multiple effects of these disorders. Treatment may be a long-term process that is multidimensional in nature (Erk, 2000). Interventions for children or adolescents with ADHD include, but are not limited to, (a) parent counseling and training, (b) client education, (c) individual and group counseling, and (d) social skills training (Brown, 2000).

Medical treatment may also be necessary. Proper medication "often results in increased attentiveness and decreased impulsivity and overactivity" (Brown, 2000). Stimulant medications, such as methylphenidate (Ritalin), dextroamphetamine (Dexedrine), and pemoline (Cylert), are usually the first medications chosen for ADHD. However, not all children who have ADHD need medications. In addition, if medications are prescribed, they should always be given first in small dosages. Counselors need to be up-to-date on the latest medications and other treatments for this disability in order to enhance the lives of clients they serve and their families.

Posttraumatic Stress Disorder or ***PTSD*** is "characterized by the reexperiencing of an extremely traumatic event, usually by way of nightmares and intrusive thoughts of the incident. In addition, symptoms of increased arousal and avoidance of stimuli associated with the trauma must be present" (Jones, Young, & Leppma, 2010, p. 373). PTSD is often prevalent in soldiers returning from a war zone and in such situations is the result of the intense horrors and traumas such individuals have experienced. However, PTSD is found among all segments of the populations and is more common among women than men. There are approximately 7 million people in the United States with PTSD (Shallcross, 2009b).

PTSD is usually treated with counseling and antianxiety or antidepressant medications. Sometimes eye movement desensitization and reprocessing (EMDR) is used.

Clearly, counselors with clients who have disabilities must be versatile. They must not only provide services directly but also coordinate services with other professionals and monitor clients' progress in gaining independence and self-control. Thus, counselors need skills from an array of theories and techniques and adaptability in shifting professional roles.

AFFILIATION, CERTIFICATION, AND EDUCATION OF COUNSELORS WHO WORK WITH THE DISABLED

Rehabilitation Counseling

Rehabilitation counseling, a specialty in the counseling profession, is particularly focused on serving individuals with disabilities (Parker, 2012). Those who specialize as rehabilitation counselors must have knowledge of medical terminology to be effective (Emener & Cottone, 1989). *Rehabilitation* is defined as the reeducation of individuals with disabilities who have previously lived independent lives. A related area, ***habilitation***, focuses on educating clients who have been disabled from early life and have never been self-sufficient. Rehabilitation counseling is a multidimensional task whose success is dependent on many things. "The rehabilitation counselor is expected to be a competent case manager as well as a skilled therapeutic counselor" (Cook, Bolton, Bellini, & Neath, 1997, p. 193). The ultimate goals of rehabilitation services are successful employment, independent living, and community participation (Bolton, 2001).

Many rehabilitation counselors belong to the **American Rehabilitation Counselor Association (ARCA;** www.arcaweb.org/). Before the founding of ARCA, there was a void for a professional counseling organization within rehabilitation. Soon after World War II, ARCA was organized as an interest group of the National Vocational Guidance Association (NVGA). ARCA became a part of ACA (then APGA) as the Division of Rehabilitation Counseling (DRC) in 1958 and as ARCA in 1961.

The **Council of Rehabilitation Education (CORE)** has traditionally accredited institutions that offered rehabilitation counseling, whereas the **Commission of Rehabilitation Counselor Certification (CRCC)** has certified rehabilitation counselors who complete CORE-accredited programs. That certification requires applicants to complete specific courses and experience requirements.

Traditionally, most rehabilitation counselors have been hired by federal, state, and local agencies. Since the late 1960s, however, more have moved into for-profit agencies and private practice. The movement from the public sector into private employment is the result of several developments, such as economic changes, new emphases by businesses and insurance companies, national professional certification requirements, and state licensure laws that have affected all counselors.

Federal legislation has been an impetus through the years in establishing services for people who are disabled. For example, in 1920 Congress passed the **Vocational Rehabilitation Act**, which was mainly focused on working with physically disabled Americans. In more recent times, the **Americans with Disabilities Act** (ADA) of 1990 is another key piece of legislation. This act helped heighten awareness of the needs of millions of people in the United States with disabilities and increased national efforts in providing multiple services for people with mental, behavioral, and physical disabilities. The **Individuals with Disabilities Education Act** (IDEA) of 2004 was another important measure, especially in regard to education. IDEA requires educational institutions to provide a *free and appropriate public education* (*FAPE*) for all students with disabilities. According to the U.S. Department of Education, this act has opened up education to approximately 12% of students between the ages of 6 and 17 years (Lambie & Milsom, 2010). Likewise, the **Ticket to Work** and **Work Incentives Improvement Act** (WIIA) of 1999 enhanced the ability of consumers with disabilities to make a choice of service providers between private nonprofit, state rehabilitation agency, and private proprietary providers (Kosclulek, 2000).

Work as a Rehabilitation Counselor

A rehabilitation counselor must be a professional with a clear sense of purpose (Parker, 2012; Wright, 1980, 1987). There are several competing, but not necessarily mutually exclusive, ideas about what roles and functions rehabilitation counselors should assume. In the late 1960s, Muthard and Salomone conducted the first systematic investigation of rehabilitation counselors' work activities (Bolton & Jaques, 1978). They found eight major activities that characterize the counselor's role and noted a high degree of importance attached to affective counseling, vocational counseling, and placement duties (Muthard & Salomone, 1978). In this survey, rehabilitation counselors reported spending the majority of their time in counseling and counseling-related activities. The same appears to be true today, although there is more paperwork.

In 1970 the U.S. Labor Department listed 12 major functions of rehabilitation counselors, which are still relevant (Schumacher, 1983).

1. *Personal counseling.*   This function entails working with clients individually from one or more theoretical models. It plays a vital part in helping clients make complete social and emotional adjustments to their circumstances.
2. *Case finding.*   Rehabilitation counselors attempt to make their services known to agencies and potential clients through promotional and educational materials.
3. *Eligibility determination.*   Rehabilitation counselors determine, through a standard set of guidelines, whether a potential client meets the criteria for funding.
4. *Training.*   Primary aspects of training involve identifying client skills and purchasing educational or training resources to help clients enhance them. In some cases, it is necessary to provide training for clients to make them eligible for employment in a specific area.
5. *Provision of restoration.*   The counselor arranges for needed devices (e.g., artificial limbs or wheelchairs) and medical services that will make the client eligible for employment and increase his or her general independence.
6. *Support services.*   These services range from providing medication to offering individual and group counseling. They help the client develop in personal and interpersonal areas while receiving training or other services.
7. *Job placement.*   This function involves directly helping the client find employment. Activities range from supporting clients who initiate a search for work to helping less motivated clients prepare to exert more initiative.
8. *Planning.*   The planning process requires the counselor to include the client as an equal. The plan they work out together should change the client from a recipient of services to an initiator of services.
9. *Evaluation.*   This function is continuous and self-correcting. The counselor combines information from all aspects of the client's life to determine needs and priorities.
10. *Agency consultation.*   The counselor works with agencies and individuals to set up or coordinate client services, such as job placement or evaluation. Much of the counselor's work is done jointly with other professionals.
11. *Public relations.*   The counselor is an advocate for clients and executes this role by informing community leaders about the nature and scope of rehabilitation services.
12. *Follow-along.*   This function involves the counselor's constant interaction with agencies and individuals who are serving the client. It also includes maintaining contact with the clients themselves to ensure steady progress toward rehabilitation.

CASE EXAMPLE

George and the Game

George was an energetic rehabilitation counselor. He liked working with people who needed rehabilitation services. He was exemplary at placing these people in proper educational and job settings. The problem with George was that he had no follow-through. Although he was interested in those he helped, he thought that follow-up was a waste of time. As a result, many of his clients were not as successful as they might have been.

What do you see as the place of follow-up in counseling, especially rehabilitation counseling? Are there ethical considerations to keep in mind? Is a failure to follow-up with a client the same as abandonment? Why or why not?

MyCounselingLab™

Go to Topic 16: *Substance Abuse Counseling* in the MyCounselingLab™ site (www.MyCounselingLab.com) for *Counseling: A Comprehensive Profession,* Seventh Edition, where you can:

- Find learning outcomes for *Substance Abuse Counseling* along with the national standards that connect to these outcomes.
- Complete Assignments and Activities that can help you more deeply understand the chapter content.
- Apply and practice your understanding of the core skills identified in the chapter with the Building Counseling Skills unit.
- Prepare yourself for professional certification with a Practice for Certification quiz.
- Connect to videos through the Video and Resource Library.

Summary and Conclusion

The specialty areas of abuse counseling, addiction counseling, and counseling with those who have disabilities are unique and yet interrelated. They emphasize the dynamics and differences behind wellness and adjustments as opposed to dysfunctional behaviors and maladjustment. Prevention programs and treatment strategies are crucial in working in these three areas.

The treatment of abusers, whether it is for physical or substance abuse, is an important focus in counseling. The abuse of individuals (children, siblings, spouse/partners, or the elderly) is all too prevalent and carries with it physical and psychological scars that have deep and negative consequences for those involved. Abuse of substances, such as alcohol, tobacco, and drugs (whether legal or not), has a deleterious impact on individuals, families, and society in general. When abuse transitions into addiction, the result is even more devastating. Physiological as well as process addiction carries with it neglect of important human functions and interactions, and the cost in personal development and interpersonal fulfillment and enjoyment is tremendous.

To work with members of abuse and addiction populations, counselors must focus on prevention and treatment. Prevention can come through educational programs warning of dangers associated with these two ways of behaving. Treatment programs, on the other hand, focus on interrupting dysfunctional actions in a systematic way. They may include individual counseling; cognitive, behavioral, or spiritually oriented groups such as Alcoholics Anonymous; or family counseling and programs run by professionals who have been involved in the same maladies. Treatment facilities include those for both inpatient and outpatient clients.

Counseling with people who are disabled is similar to abuse and addiction counseling in that it focuses on both prevention and the provision of treatment services. Counselors who work in this area are distinct in their client population and in some of their terminology and treatment techniques but are universal in working with all those affected by the disabilities involved. Rehabilitation counseling is the specialty that has traditionally been tied in with working with people who have disabilities, just as addiction and offender counseling is most associated in working with abusers and those who are addicted.

Counselors should remember that people who are abusers, addicted, or have disabilities are more than the actions or symptoms that bring them to counseling. The people behind the focus of treatment have thoughts, feelings, and needs as well as potentials that counseling can constructively address. Empowering these individuals and the society in which they live to be more productive is crucial. Thus, the emphasis of counseling in these special areas is the same as counseling otherwise—to promote wellness and well-being on multiple levels.

Clinical Mental Health and Private Practice Counseling

20

It comes in slowly like a whisper
  aching into the marrow of the bone
    like the chill of dull gray winter mornings.
Quietly it rests
  heavy on the heart in motion
    creating a subtle pressure
      that throws the rhythmic beat
        ever so slightly
          off.
Depression rules in silence
  unseen but deeply felt,
A shadow of despair in the hourglass of life
  cleverly disguised at times
    with a smile.

Reprinted from "Depression," by S. T. Gladding, 1978, *The School Counselor, 26,* p. 45. © 1978 S. T. Gladding.

Chapter Overview

From this chapter you will learn about

- The uniqueness of clinical mental health counseling and how it developed

- The advantages and limitations of working as a clinical mental health counselor in various work settings and emphases

- Preventive and remedial aspects of clinical mental health counseling

- The challenges and benefits of private practice and ways of establishing such a practice

As you read consider

- Why clinical mental health developed and how it differs from other counseling specialties

- What rewards and drawbacks are inherent in working as a clinical mental health counselor

- The different strategies a clinical mental health counselor would use in prevention as opposed to remediation

- How you might feel, think, and behave if you were in private practice as opposed to working in a public clinic

MyCounselingLab™

Visit the MyCounselingLab™ site (www.MyCounselingLab.com) for *Counseling: A Comprehensive Profession,* Seventh Edition to enhance your understanding of chapter concepts. You'll have the opportunity to practice your skills through video- and case-based Assignments and Activities as well as Building Counseling Skills units and to prepare for your certification exam with Practice for Certification quizzes.

Working as a clinical mental health counselor and in a setting such as a private practice is a goal for many counselors. Those who choose this route usually do so for various reasons. Among the factors that clinical mental health counseling environments provide are opportunities to work with the public and governmental organizations in the promotion of wellness, the prevention and treatment of mental illnesses, and sometimes the opportunity to be an independent contractor or consultant. The chance to make a difference in any of these ways is exciting and stimulating for many clinicians. A number of practitioners in clinical mental health counseling, including those in private practice, belong to the **American Mental Health Counselor Association** (AMHCA; www.amhca.org). Most also end up joining an association that reflects their specialty in practice or their philosophical orientation to treatment.

Counselors who choose private practice, regardless of their background, also are attracted to such a practice for various reasons including autonomy and opportunity to specialize in certain areas. In examining private practice, particular attention will be focused on prevention and the promotion of positive health, as well as the treatment of disorders. However, first we will look at how clinical mental health counseling developed and is practiced today.

THE DEVELOPMENT OF CLINICAL MENTAL HEALTH COUNSELING

Mental health has been defined as follows by the Surgeon General of the United States as

> The successful performance of mental function, resulting in productive activities, fulfilling relationships with other people, and the ability to adapt to change and to cope with adversity; from early childhood until later life, mental health is the springboard of thinking and communication skills, learning, emotional growth, resilience, and self esteem. (U.S. Department of Health and Human Services, 1999, p. vii)

While mental health has never received as much attention and funding as physical health, it has been a major focus within the nation at various times.

The most significant early piece of federal legislation that brought mental health much more on par with other health services in the United States was the **Community Mental Health Centers Act of 1963**. This act was intended to promote local mental health initiatives. Through it the mental health counselor movement became full blown. It provided funding for the establishment of more than 2,000 community mental health centers nationwide. It also made it possible for local communities to employ mental health professionals from a variety of backgrounds and focus on mental health education in the form of outreach programs. As time went on, the focus of mental health centers began to change from one of prevention (the original intent) to one of treatment. The treatment emphasis was especially highlighted in the late 1970s and early 1980s as state and federal mental hospitals were deinstitutionalized, and individuals with a variety of mental problems, some quite severe, were picked up by these centers or left to cope on their own.

Mental health counseling has been defined in many ways during its relatively brief history. Initially, it was described as a specialized form of counseling performed in noneducational, community-based, or mental health settings (Seiler & Messina, 1979). Over the years, however, different views of mental health counseling have evolved, including those that are developmental (Ivey, 1989); relationship focused (Ginter, 1989); and slanted toward treatment, advocacy, or personal and environmental coping (Hershenson, Power, & Seligman, 1989). The Council for Accreditation of Counseling and Related Educational Programs (CACREP, 2009) has developed a detailed description of this specialty, along with requirements for coursework, basic knowledge, and skills.

Advocates for the profession have suggested that, despite some drawbacks, clinical mental health counseling is distinct due to its curriculum (which includes psychodiagnosis, psychopathology, psychopharmacology, and treatment planning); its collaborative affiliation with ACA; the intent of its founders, leaders, and followers; its publications; and its accreditation requirements (i.e., a 60-hour program) (Pistole & Roberts, 2002). Presently, clinical mental health counseling "is a master's level, primarily practice-oriented profession. It shares a border with professional counseling [and is a part of counseling] in its conceptual and philosophical perspective that is more educational-developmental-preventive than clinical remedial" (p. 15). Overall, clinical mental health counseling is a specialty within the field of professional counseling.

CLINICAL MENTAL HEALTH COUNSELING AS A SPECIALTY

Clinical mental health counseling is interdisciplinary in its history, practice settings, skills/knowledge, and roles performed (Gladding & Newsome, 2010). This interdisciplinary nature is an asset in generating new ideas and energy. At the same time, it is a drawback in helping those who identify themselves as clinical mental health counselors distinguish themselves from some closely related mental health practitioners (Wilcoxon & Puleo, 1992).

Regardless, many practitioners within the counseling profession use the term *mental health counselor* or *clinical mental health counselor* to describe themselves, and some states, such as Florida, designate licensed counselors under these titles. As a group, clinical mental health counselors work with a diverse group of clients, including rape victims, eating disorders, depressives, families, potential suicide victims, and those with diagnosable disorders. In addition, they consult, educate, and at times perform administrative duties. Thus, it is crucial that these counselors know psychopathology as defined by the *Diagnostic and Statistical Manual* (DSM) classifications so they can converse intelligently with other health professionals and skillfully treat dysfunctional clients (Hinkle, 1994a; Vacc, Loesch, & Guilbert, 1997).

Clinical mental health counselors have basic counseling skills as well as specialty skills related to the needs and interests of particular populations or problems. Major duties of counselors in mental health are assessing and analyzing background and current information on clients, diagnosing mental and emotional conditions, exploring possible solutions, and developing treatment plans. Preventive mental health activities and recognition of the relationship between physical and mental health are prominent in their work.

As a group, clinical mental health counselors are interested in professional development and counseling topics related to applied areas of counseling such as marriage and family counseling; substance abuse/chemical dependency; third-party reimbursement; small-group counseling; grief, loss, and bereavement; as well as mindfulness and posttraumatic growth just to name a few (Chopko & Schwartz, 2009; Prieto, 2011; Wilcoxon & Puleo, 1992). Such interests are understandable in light of the fact that most clinical mental health counselors are practitioners and earn a living by offering services for remuneration.

The **American Mental Health Counselor Association (AMHCA**, 801 N. Fairfax Street, Suite 304, Alexandria, VA 22314) has initiated a number of task forces and committees over the years to help its members broaden their horizons and develop practical skills and knowledge. These task forces cover such areas as business and industry, aging and adult development, treatment of various disorders, and prevention. Such concentrations are important because they allow clinical mental health counselors to obtain in-depth knowledge and skills in particular domains.

AMHCA also emphasizes total health and wellness including wellness counseling. This aspect of clinical mental health counseling is vital because changes made within a community can be upsetting or cause regressive behaviors if people are unprepared. By providing clients and communities with health information and support, counselors can prevent more serious problems (e.g., alcoholism or depression) from occurring. Such an emphasis is unique in many helping professions, which as a whole tend to be treatment based.

In addition, AMHCA has set up certification standards for counselors to become *Certified Clinical Mental Health Counselors* (CCMHC). This procedure initially involved the establishment of the National Academy of Certified Clinical Mental Health Counselors (NACCMHC) as an independently incorporated certification group in 1978. In 1993, NACCMHC merged with the National Board for Certified Counselors (NBCC), and now professionals who wish to obtain the CCMHC credential must first become national certified counselors (NCCs).

PERSONAL REFLECTION

At this point in time, clinical mental health counseling appears to be formulated on a philosophy and have legislative support. From what you have read so far, why do you think many students find this specialty so attractive? What are the drawbacks to becoming a clinical mental health counselor?

Interests, Theories, and Functions

As indicated previously, clinical mental health counselors are diverse in their interests and the ways they use theories and techniques in their practices. This diversity is due in part to the varied settings in which they work and the wide range of functions they have. Thus, some clinical mental health counselors focus on concepts such as forgiveness (Wade, 2010) and self-care, while others look at non-suicidal self-injury (Trepal, 2010). One theoretical position, existential theory, has been advocated as "congruent with the essential principles of mental health counseling" (Bauman & Waldo, 1998, p. 27), but a large number of theories have been used by practitioners in the field. The selection of theories by clinical mental health counselors depends on their clients' needs. Generally, the literature about clinical mental health counseling focuses on two major issues that have theoretical implications: (a) prevention and promotion of mental health and (b) treatment of disorders and dysfunctions. Both topics are likely to continue attracting attention because they are considered primary roles of clinical mental health counselors.

PRIMARY PREVENTION AND THE PROMOTION OF MENTAL HEALTH. A primary philosophical emphasis throughout the history of clinical mental health counseling has been on prevention and promotion of mental health services. Many clinical mental health counselors are actively involved in primary prevention types of programs through schools, colleges, churches, community health centers, and public and private agencies. **Primary prevention** is characterized by its "before the fact quality"; it is intentional and "group- or mass-, rather than individually, oriented" (Baker & Shaw, 1987, p. 2). It may be directly or indirectly implemented, but it is based on a sound theoretical foundation. For example, the establishment of over 1,200 suicide and emotional help lines worldwide and on the net (Internet) to deal with the warning signs of suicide is a primary prevention approach to dealing with this problem (Befrienders International, 2007). When successful, primary prevention ultimately results in healthier and better adjusted individuals and communities.

Hall and Torres (2002) recommend two primary prevention models appropriate for communitywide implementation with adolescents. They are Bloom's (1996) **configural model of prevention** and Albee's **incidence formula** (Albee & Gullotta, 1997).

Bloom's model focuses on three dimensions:

1. First, counselors need to work to increase individual strengths and decrease individual limitations.
2. Second, they must increase social support (e.g., through parents and peers) and decrease social stress.
3. Finally, environmental variables, such as poverty, natural disasters, and community programming for youth, must be addressed.

Albee's model is equally global in scope and emphasizes that counselors must decrease the negative effects of biology and stress while simultaneously increasing the positive effects of adolescents' coping skills, self-esteem, and supportive systems. Both models require a willingness by counselors to network with other agencies and individuals. They must invest considerable time and energy in program construction that may not have an immediate payoff.

CASE EXAMPLE

Ned and the Network

Ned was much more interested in doing preventive work than in doing treatment. However, it was not easy to support himself because there were few positions for prevention specialists. Therefore, he had to string together a series of grants that periodically either ran out or required renewal.

One day, exhausted from his work, Ned came to the office to find a grant agent there questioning his facts and figures. At first Ned was intimidated. Then he thought, "I have a network of professionals who know my work and can vouch for my statistics." They did exactly that, and Ned actually received a larger grant from the foundation that had questioned him.

What other strategies could Ned have used in this case? Why do you think prevention is so difficult to fund at times?

One place where primary prevention is emphasized is in the area of **suicide** (Granello & Juhnke, 2009). In the United States, suicide is "the ninth-ranking cause of death for adults and third for young people ages 17 and under" (Carney & Hazler, 1998, p. 28). Suicide is also the fifth-leading cause of death among Canadians (Paulson & Worth, 2002).

When assessing clients for suicide, clinical mental health counselors need to be mindful that there are various factors that influence the rates and lethality of suicide attempts

(Granello, 2010b). For instance, three times as many females as males attempt suicide, but about three times as many males as females are successful (McWhirter, McWhirter, McWhirter, & McWhirter, 2007). Tragically, the likelihood of suicide for gay and lesbian youth is two to three times higher than for heterosexual youth. In addition, different ethnic groups are more at risk for suicidal behavior than others. Native Americans have the highest adolescent suicide rate, and Latino adolescents have a higher rate of suicide than European American youth (McWhirter et al., 2007).

In addition to gender, sexual orientation, and multicultural variables, clinicians need to use assessment instruments to evaluate more accurately suicidal ideation. One global scale they may use is the **SAD PERSONS scale** (Patterson, Dohn, Bird, & Patterson, 1983) for adults or the **Adapted-SAD PERSONS scale** (A-SPS) for children (Juhnke, 1996) to determine which individuals are most likely to be at high risk. The letters in this scale stand for the following:

*S*ex (male)

*A*ge (older clients)

*D*epression

*P*revious attempt

*E*thanol (alcohol) abuse

*R*ational thinking loss

*S*ocial support system lacking (lonely, isolated)

*O*rganized plan

*N*o spouse

*S*ickness (particularly chronic or terminal illness)

It is the combination of these factors in an interactive process that is likely to yield information pertinent for clinical mental health counselors to use in prevention. In addition to these specifics, Granello (2010b) has constructed a list of 12 core process principles that clinicians should keep in mind when working with a client who is suicidal. These include such factors as recognizing the uniqueness of each person and realizing that suicide risk assessment is complex, relies on clinical judgment, should be collaborative with others, and is an ongoing process with all threats and warning signs being taken seriously. Granello also reminds clinicians that almost all counselors during their careers will work with a client who makes a suicide attempt. Therefore, tough questions are called for in assessment, sensitivity to the cultural context is critical, and documentation of assessment is essential.

PERSONAL REFLECTION

Do you know someone who has either attempted or committed suicide? Try to put yourself in that person's place. What might keep you from taking your own life? What would make such an act attractive?

Another form of primary prevention is emphasizing **healthy development**—that is, positive coping and growth so that individuals are able to deal effectively with crises they may face (Hershenson, 1982, 1992a). "Insofar as counseling derives from a model based on healthy development, it can reasonably hope to achieve its purpose of promoting healthy development in its clients" (Hershenson, 1982, p. 409). Erik Erikson (1963) and Abraham Maslow (1962) offer basic premises from which clinical mental health counselors can work. The writings of these theorists were based on observations about human development and emphasized the promotion of healthy growth and development. The integration of these two systems of thought yields **six personal development trends: survival, growth, communication, recognition, mastery, and understanding**. The first two trends focus on the self, the middle two on interpersonal functions, and the final two on the accomplishment of tasks. Clinical mental health counseling is geared toward the improvement of the self in interpersonal relationships and task performances.

In an important article on healthy personal development, Heath (1980) outlined a comprehensive model of healthy maturation. He pointed out that research demonstrates that an adolescent's psychological maturity is a major predictor of adult mental health and vocational adaptation and that the degree of adult maturity is related to marital sexual adjustment and vocational adaptation. Heath then proposed practical **general principles that counselors can apply in promoting client development**. Four are listed here (Heath, 1980, p. 395):

1. *"Encourage the anticipatory rehearsal of new adaptations,"* such as those that deal with jobs and intimate relationships.
2. *"Require constant externalization of what is learned and its correction by action."* In essence, Heath believes practice makes perfect in the accomplishment of all human tasks. Learning is accomplished through feedback.
3. *"Allow a person to experience the consequences of his or her decisions and acts."* Heath agrees with Alfred Adler on this idea. He notes that inappropriate or excessive rewards may have an unhealthy effect on a person's development.
4. *"Appreciate and affirm strengths."* Reinforcement, according to behaviorist principles, is crucial to new learning. Heath agrees and says that the acknowledgment and acceptance of people's strengths can bolster self-confidence and help them take the risks necessary for new learning.

Focusing on persons' environments is another preventive emphasis of clinical mental health counselors whether it is conducted globally or more individually. Environments have personalities just as people do. Some environments are controlling and rigid, whereas others are more flexible and supportive. To make effective use of this *social-ecological perspective*, clinical mental health counselors should do the following:

- Identify the problem as one essentially connected with a particular setting. Some environments elicit or encourage specific behaviors that may not be healthy.
- Gain the agreement of clients and significant others that the environment is the client. It is much easier for most people to see a difficulty as simply a matter related to the individual.
- Assess the dynamic variables within an environment. Moos (1973) developed a number of ways to evaluate environments. Counselors can work with clients to determine how environments function in favor of or counter to the clients' needs.
- Institute social change and social justice initiatives where needed. Counselors can help clients with specific methods for improving the present environment.
- Evaluate the outcome. There is no one way to do this, but the more clearly the client states his or her criteria for the ideal environment, the better the evaluation possibility.

Related to the social-ecological perspective is *ecosystemic thinking:* "thinking that recognizes the indivisible interconnectedness of individual, family, and sociocultural context" (Sherrard & Amatea, 1994, p. 5). In this view, clinical mental health counseling is enlarged to consider the cultural contexts in which people relate and communicate. The meaning that individuals give to their interpersonal and environmental interactions becomes a consideration in counseling (Conyne & Cook, 2004).

Marriage is a situation that illustrates the importance of both personal and environmental factors in individuals' well-being (Gladding, 2011). A study conducted by Wiggins, Moody, and Lederer (1983) on marital satisfaction found that the most significant predictor of such satisfaction was the compatibility of couples' tested personality typologies. They concluded that individuals express "satisfaction with and seek interaction in environments that meet their psychological needs" (p. 177). In interracial marriages, which are increasing in American society and worldwide for that matter, clinical mental health counselors can be therapeutic in helping couples identify and address predictable stressors in their lives. Such stressors may manifest themselves in the form of prejudice or identity issues regarding the marriage relationship and biracial children, among others. In these matters, clinical mental health counselors help couples find support within each other, within groups in the communities in which they live, or in special programs such as marriage enrichment (Solsberry, 1994).

CASE EXAMPLE

Eileen and the Environment

Eileen grew up in a small, midwestern town where people were friendly and the pace was slow. However, when she married George, she left the town and moved to a large city where no one spoke to strangers and the pace was very fast. Eileen hated it, but she loved George and wanted to adjust to her new environment if at all possible.

Because she had never finished college, Eileen enrolled in a nearby community college. Besides being stimulated by the environment, she found a support group of young women in the same situation she was in. The support group expanded to not only meeting on campus but holding socials with spouses and partners. At the end of the first year, Eileen realized she actually liked her new surroundings.

Although Eileen may not have intentionally worked to shape her environment, ecologically minded counselors do. What are some ways you can shape your environment to make it and you healthier?

An overall emphasis in clinical mental health prevention related to health is on **wellness** or *positive wellness* (health-related activities that are both preventive and remedial and have a therapeutic value to individuals who practice them consistently). Such activities include eating natural foods, taking vitamins, going to health spas, meditating, participating in regular exercise, and exploring a variety of humanistic and transpersonal approaches to helping (Granello, 2012; O'Donnell, 1988). "For the person to be a whole, healthy, functioning organism, one must evaluate the physical, psychological, intellectual, social, emotional, and environmental processes" (Carlson & Ardell, 1988, p. 383).

Signs of the holistic movement toward health, well-being, and wellness are apparent everywhere in counseling and becoming more prevalent. For instance, the Spring 2007 issue of the *Journal of Humanistic Counseling, Development and Education* was devoted completely to wellness and ways of promoting health. In general, Americans of all ages have become more aware of positive and negative habits with an increased emphasis on increasing the former and decreasing the latter.

Research backs up the basis for this movement toward health, well-being, and wellness and in some ways leads it (Myers & Sweeney, 2005). For instance, in an extensive review of the literature on the effectiveness of physical fitness on measures of personality, Doan and Scherman (1987) found strong support for the idea that regular exercise can have a beneficial effect on people's physical and psychological health. Their review supports counselors who prescribe health habits to accompany regular counseling practices. Their findings have had more recent support from the review of research in this field by Penedo and Dahn (2005).

In addition to the emphasis on physical wellness, research has confirmed that wellness counseling can increase wellness among law enforcement officers (Tanigoshi, Kontos, & Remley, 2008). Furthermore, wellness factors explain a significant portion of the variance in components of self-esteem in adolescents (Myers, Willise, & Villalba, 2011).

The most extensive evidence-based work in the area of wellness has been conducted by Myers and Sweeney (e.g., 2008). They have developed two instruments to measure wellness: the Wheel of Wellness and the Indivisible Self models. At the center of the **Wheel of Wellness** is spirituality, the most important characteristic of well-being. It includes a sense of meaning and purpose in life that is very much in line with Alfred Adler's theoretical emphasis, which is the basis for this model. Radiating from the center of the wheel are 12 spokes in the life task of self direction: sense of worth, sense of control, realistic beliefs, emotional awareness and coping, sense of humor, nutrition, exercise, self-care, problem-solving and creativity, stress management, gender identity, and cultural identity. The **Indivisible Self** model is empirical, as opposed to hypothetical, like the Wheel of Wellness. It is interactive and composed of the creative self, the coping self, the social self, the essential self, and the physical self. The Indivisible Self is ecological as well, "with four contexts presented as integral to individual wellness: *local*, *instructional*, *global*, and *chronometrical*" (p. 485).

Roscoe (2009) states that "when using wellness in counseling, counselors should first educate clients on its multidimensional, synergistic nature. Furthermore, counselors need to stress the idea that optimal functioning is not just the absence of illness. After introducing the general ideas of wellness, counselors can explore each of the dimensions with clients, who will benefit from considering how each wellness dimension relates to their experiences and goals" (p. 224). In the process, clients can visualize or brainstorm activities that will promote wellness in their lives. They can also rate themselves on wellness using a 1–10 scale and make a bar graph to represent how they are presently functioning. Such a graph can lead to the exploration and generation of goals as well as obstacles for achieving wellness. Homework can then be assigned. Such a process works well in individual as well as group settings.

Other strategies for working from a wellness perspective besides those already provided include:

- having counselors dwell on positive, life-enhancing actions clients have done and how such behaviors can be repeated in different settings or times in life;
- altering traditional screening to include more emphasis on overall health and wellness by developing intake forms and questions that underscore the wellness dimension of life; and
- highlighting the multiple features of clients' lives from the perspective of what Lazarus (1989) calls *multimodal therapy* in which he uses the acronym **BASIC I.D.** to explore the multiple dimensions of clients' lives as they relate to wellness: **behavior, affect, sensation, imagery, cognition, interpersonal relationships, and drugs/biology**.

SECONDARY AND TERTIARY PREVENTION. In addition to primary prevention, clinical mental health counselors concentrate on *secondary prevention* (controlling mental health problems that have already surfaced but are not severe) and **tertiary prevention** (controlling serious mental health problems to keep them from becoming chronic or life threatening). In such cases (in contrast to primary prevention), clinical mental health counselors assess client functioning and then, if appropriate, use theories and techniques developed by major theorists such as Rogers, Ellis, Skinner, and Glasser to treat symptoms and core conditions.

Clinical mental health counselors who work in treatment face a number of challenges. One is responding adequately to the number of people who need and seek mental health services. The nation's mental health providers such as counselors, psychiatrists, psychologists, and social workers cannot adequately deal with everyone who needs treatment services for minor or major disorders. Even if the treatment of clients were the only activity in which these professionals were engaged, they would still not be able to take care of those in need (Lichtenberg, 1986; Meehl, 1973). For example, an estimated 7.5 million children, or 12% of the residents of the United States, "under 18 years of age have a diagnosable mental disorder, and nearly half of these are severely handicapped by their disabilities. The population of children with serious emotional and behavioral problems has been growing dramatically, concomitant with the growth of such social problems as poverty, homelessness, and substance abuse" (Collins & Collins, 1994, p. 239).

Another challenge for clinicians in mental health counseling is the trend in inpatient psychiatric hospitals to shorten the length of stays for severely disturbed clients. This trend is known as **deinstitutionalization**. These shortened stays mean more disturbed individuals are either not receiving the treatment they need or being seen in outpatient facilities, where many clinical mental health counselors work and are often restricted by managed care regulations.

A survey of articles in the *Journal of Mental Health Counseling* in the early 1990s revealed that clinical mental health counselors have a stronger tendency to deal with treatment as a major emphasis of clinical mental health counseling (Kiselica & Look, 1993). The situation has changed little since, except for the increased amounts of paperwork and regulations brought on by managed care companies and government regulations such as HIPAA. In this respect, clinical mental health counseling is more like other helping disciplines, such as psychology, social work, and psychiatric nursing (Hansen, 1998; Hershenson & Berger, 2001; Waldo, Horswill, & Brotherton, 1993). Some of the areas clinical mental health counselors focus on in treatment are general and specific life-span disorders, such as grief and loss (Prieto, 2011), mild depression (Kolenc, Hartley, & Murdock, 1990), self-injury (Trepal, 2010), smoking cessation (Pinto & Morrell, 1988), forgiveness (Wade, 2010), obsessive-compulsive behavior (Dattilio, 1993), trauma and resilience (Goodman & West-Olatunji, 2008), and at-risk youth (Hill, 2007).

Clinical mental health counselors assess and treat disorders using the *Diagnostic and Statistical Manual* (DSM). Some deal with severe mental disorders (Perham & Accordino, 2007), whereas others specialize in working with either less severely disturbed persons or specific populations and the disorders that impact these groups most. Regardless, those who are diagnosed with mental disorders are among the most stigmatized, marginalized, and disadvantaged in society. In order to get a feel for what treatment is like to have such a disorder or to work with someone who does, novice counselors should view films such as *Three Faces of Eve,* and *A Beautiful Mind.*

Counselors can work to mitigate the **stigma of mental disorders** in three ways: protest, education, and contact (Overton & Medina, 2008). **Protest** is an attempt to suppress stereotypes and can actually backfire since there are those in society who have different views and may counterprotest. **Education** is a means of conveying factual information about specific populations. It often changes beliefs but not behaviors. Information distributed by mental health associations and other advocacy groups promoting positive mental health is educational in nature. **Contact**, on the other hand—personal interaction with someone from a stigmatized group—does seem effective in changing both beliefs and behaviors. Increasing education and challenging people in community settings to have contact with those less fortunate than themselves can often lead to an increase in understanding and actions. The same is true with counselors, especially those in the early stages of their clinical training. Contact with those who are living with mental disorders is essential. Such exposure helps to develop higher levels of cognitive complexity in individuals who have such interaction along with exposing them in interactive ways to clients who have mental disorders. Thus the behavioral and cognitive component of understanding come together to increase empathy as well as the reality that textbook descriptions of disorders are not generally what a person sees when working with another human being who has a diagnosis.

PERSONAL REFLECTION

You have most likely read a number of books or seen television shows, as well as movies, that portray individuals with various mental disorders. What is your opinion about how realistically these characters are presented? As you ponder this question reflect also about the life of Clifford Beers, as presented in Chapter 1, and his struggle in getting the general public to understand mental disorders.

Two General Clinical Disorders: Depression and Anxiety

The list of disorders that people have has grown almost exponentially since the *Diagnostic and Statistical Manual* was first published in the 1950s. Therefore, covering the bulk of these disorders is a specialty course. However, underlying or integrated into almost all disorders and standing on their own are two clinical components, depression and anxiety, which are "the most common clinical symptoms associated with presentation for counseling services" (Hinkle, 1999, p. 475).

Depression seems to be especially rampant, having increased to epidemic proportions with "roughly 10% to 25% of the population" experiencing "some form of depression" and with depression being "10 times as prevalent now as it was in 1960!" (Paradise & Kirby, 2005, p. 116). In addition, depression "may be the most common disorder of mental health workers themselves . . . with research suggesting that from one third to more than 60% of mental health professionals" report "a significant episode of depression within the previous year" (p. 116).

Mental health counselors need to continually educate themselves on the latest treatments of depression including those that have a proven psychological track record, such as cognitive–behavioral counseling methods (e.g., mindfulness), and those that may be more physiologically based, such as exercise. It has usually been found that a combination of "talk therapy" and medication work best in treating individuals who suffer from this malady. However, mental health counselors need to keep in mind that there are various forms of depression, and acute depression differs from chronic depression just as depression resulting from the loss of a loved one differs significantly from depression that is pervasive due to a chemical imbalance in the brain.

Anxiety affects 40 million adults or 18 percent of the adult population. The disorder has both a genetic and a behavioral component. Anxiety disorders take on a number of forms, and **generalized anxiety** (characterized by at least 6 months of persistent and excessive anxiety, worry), **social anxiety** (characterized by emotional discomfort or apprehension over social situations that require interaction with others), and **panic disorder** (intense fear, usually accompanied by physical symptoms, such as heart palpitations, sweating, or dizziness, that something bad will happen that is unexpected) are among the most common (Shallcross, 2009b).

Like depression, there are a number of proven treatments that help clients deal with anxiety, such as those that are cognitive–behavioral based like systematic desensitization and exposure therapies. Medications may also be prescribed, but like depression, anxiety disorders are best treated with a combination of "talk therapy" and prescriptive medicines. Since anxiety disorders differ from mild to severe, treatment methods must be tailored to clients.

Regardless of the exact figures on populations affected, depression and anxiety are common in society for a number of reasons, many of which are featured nightly on the evening news or talk radio. Mental health counselors, like other counselors, will find themselves working with individuals who manifest these symptoms regardless of their clinical setting. The good news, as mentioned earlier, is that there are a number of treatments for both depression and anxiety. All seem to work well in the treatment (i.e., recovery) and prevention of these maladies (Dixon, 2000; Gladding, 2005; Paradise & Kirby, 2005).

Trauma and Hopelessness

In addition to treating depression and anxiety disorders, clinical mental health counselors, like many counselors in other settings, are called on to work with individuals who have suffered trauma and may feel hopeless. There are several models for working with clients who have so been affected, but two that are most prominent are the **crisis intervention model** and the **continuing-therapy model** (Paulson & Worth, 2002). "Both models stress the significance of a positive therapeutic relationship and the understanding and validation of client's feelings" (p. 87), which may be intense. They emphasize the importance of helping those who have gone through trauma develop self-awareness, construct a new identity, and deal with loss. The focus is to restore equilibrium to clients' **biopsychosocial functioning** (i.e., the combination of biological, psychological, and social factors that make up and influence how a person operates within a society) with the realization that many people will need longer term therapeutic interventions and that healing from the afteraffects of a flood, tornado, hurricane, fire, or other natural or manmade disaster takes time as well as work. Whereas both approaches are effective, the continuing-therapy model is more advantageous because it provides a lengthier time frame for counselor–client interactions.

In addition to these two models, counselors can also help those who have a sense of hopelessness from a traumatic event create meaning through the use of an **existential-constructivist framework** (Rogers, 2001). This theoretical approach delves into an "increased understanding of . . . individuals from a phenomenological meaning perspective" (p. 16). It requires the counselor and client to commit to long-term therapeutic work and deal with the community and others as well as intrapersonal thoughts and feelings.

EMPLOYMENT OF CLINICAL MENTAL HEALTH COUNSELORS

As a group, clinical mental health counselors work in a variety of settings, including mental health centers, community agencies, psychiatric hospitals, health maintenance organizations (HMOs), health and wellness promotion programs (HWPs), geriatric centers, crisis control agencies, and child guidance clinics. They often work closely with other helping professionals, such as psychiatrists, psychologists, clinical social workers, psychiatric nurses, and other counseling specialists to become part of a team effort.

One place where clinical mental health counselors are being hired in increasing numbers is *employee assistance programs (EAPs)* (Gladding & Newsome, 2010). These programs are found in many businesses and institutions across the United States. Their purpose is to work with employees in preventive and remedial ways in order to help them avoid or work through problems that might detrimentally affect their on-the-job behavior. To be effective, EAP counselors set up programs that deal with a variety of subjects that employees have an interest in, such as wellness or retirement. They invite outside experts to make presentations at convenient times and arrange for follow-up material or input if needed. EAP counselors also offer short-term counseling services to employees who may be experiencing difficulties. These services are usually time limited (e.g., three sessions). However, as experts in community resources, EAP counselors are able to make referrals to mental health professionals who can offer employees more expertise. As an overall rule, large companies and institutions will offer EAP services on their premises (i.e., in-house), whereas smaller operations will usually rely on EAP counselors who serve a number of companies and institutions (i.e., outsource).

Another place where clinical mental health counselors may be employed is with **crises-oriented organizations**, such as the Red Cross or local emergency telephone and walk-in counseling centers. In crisis situations, respondents must take care of a multitude of needs ranging from physical to mental health. Thus, local communities, and even international groups, hire counselors and other mental health professionals who can offer needed counseling and supportive services to victims of disasters whether natural or human-made. Individuals who work in these situations may have jobs that differ from the norm in regard to hours and activities. They also have above-average excitement and challenges in the work they perform.

Clinical mental health counselors are also found in settings where many other helping specialists work. For example, counselors with this background may be employed in substance abuse, hospice, child guidance clinics, wellness centers, colleges, hospitals, and private practice. The reason they are hired and retained in so many settings is their solid training in CACREP-required counseling areas and their versatility in regard to helping people with a wide variety of difficulties or concerns. With experience, clinical mental health counselors may obtain specialized training in a theoretical or treatment modality. They may stay generalists in mental health, too. There are advantages as well as limitations for clinical mental health counselors depending on their degree of specialization.

PRIVATE PRACTICE AS A SPECIALTY

Private practice counselors have less of a formalized history than mental health counseling. There have been such professionals from various backgrounds since the beginning of counseling. Private practitioners aspire to work for themselves in an individual or group practice unaffiliated with an agency. Before insurance, third-party payments, managed care, and HIPAA, the professional lives of such individuals were less complicated. They were like physicians in working on a **fee-for-service** basis (i.e., paying for services separately as opposed to paying for services in an integrative way). That arrangement changed dramatically in the 1980s as fee-for-service arrangements began to disappear.

Despite changes in the ways clinicians are now reimbursed for service, private practice is still popular (Shallcross, 2011). When many students first enroll in a counseling program, they aspire to set up a private practice. Indeed, doctoral graduates of counseling programs indicate that private practice is their preferred venue of service delivery (Zimpfer, 1996; Zimpfer & DeTrude, 1990). Often counselors conceptualize that a private practice setting will give them more control over their lives and be more financially rewarding. Indeed, a private practice can be a wonderful experience. However, it usually takes a great deal of work to begin such a practice unless a professional buys, or is invited into, an already established practice.

Difficulties in Setting Up a Private Practice

To be successful as a private practitioner, a counselor needs a number of abilities beyond clinical expertise. Among the most salient of these abilities, he or she

- must be able to balance business skills, such as marketing, billing, and hiring a secretary, with those of counseling or else find a competent business manager;
- must be patient, persistent, and prepared for the time it takes to build up a clientele that is sufficient to make a living;
- must network and build up an outside clinical support system in a way not as necessary in agency work, where one is often surrounded by colleagues who can supply needed information on treatment, supervision, or referrals to appropriate specialists;
- must become technologically savvy in developing a website, using e-mail, iPhones, and other technology to both make oneself known and to keep up with clients and referrals;
- must overcome or avoid the use of restrictive covenants or noncompetitive agreements that some agencies put in their contracts with counselors that prohibit them from setting up a private practice within a certain geographical area or within a certain time period after leaving the agency (Wyatt, Daniels, & White, 2000);
- must invest time and hard work in **"pull marketing" relationships** (i.e., making oneself attractive by generating referrals through offering needed services to people in groups [such as singles, the divorced, or the widowed]) and meeting other community professionals regularly in order to learn about them and to introduce oneself (Crodzki, 2002);
- must find a way to make sure emergency situations and the unexpected crisis some clients have are covered when out of town or out of the office; and
- must be willing to donate services and participate in endeavors for the public good in order to build up a reputation and a practice, for as Allen Ivey remarked: "There is just a very small window for private practitioners to make big money" (Littrell, 2001, p. 117).

CASE EXAMPLE

Sicily Sends Out Notices of Her Private Practice

Sicily could hardly wait to finish her course of study in counseling. She had always dreamed of being independent, and as soon as she passed the National Counselor Exam she threw a party with the theme "Independence Day!" At the party she announced that within the next few months she would start her new life as a private practitioner.

After the announcement, Sicily realized she could not become a private practitioner until she was licensed, which was many months away. She also realized she had no specialty, and therefore she doubted that people would line up to see her. Finally, she confessed that she did not have a clue as to how to go about setting up a business, which a private practice is. Putting away her dreams of practicing independently, Sicily went to work for a mental health agency.

Have you ever had dreams like Sicily's? If so, what do you think you will have to do to make them come true? If not, what do you think of Sicily's decision to work for a mental health agency?

Advantages in Setting Up a Private Practice

There are opportunities for counselors to enter private practice and succeed. Indeed, mental health agency administrators view "private practitioners . . . as the greatest competitors for insured clients" (Wyatt et al., 2000, p. 19). Among the advantages private practitioners have are the following:

- A growing dissatisfaction among consumers with mental health managed care. In such an environment, consumers are most likely to begin paying directly for services when they can afford it and not go through a managed care arrangement. Such an arrangement may benefit counselors in private practice and portions of the public.
- A chance for counselors to develop a niche or a specialty and become known in their communities as professionals who provide quality service in a distinct area and in the process gain excellent reputations as clinicians (Paterson, 2008).
- An opportunity for counselors to set up their office hours for times most convenient for them.
- A chance for counselors to branch out in treatment services, such as coaching or consulting, especially if they live in large urban areas where there are abundant numbers of clients with business and other specific problems that are not necessarily traditionally counseling.
- An opportunity to be entrepreneurial, using the enterprising aspect of their personality to advertise their services, and artistic using the creative side of their personality to develop products, such as books and videos. Clinicians usually cannot use these aspects of themselves as fully in agency settings because of other demands (Shallcross, 2011a).

Overall, whereas private practice has some drawbacks, it will continue as a place where counselors elect to work. It simply requires a commitment and the development of different skills than counselors in more traditional settings have.

MyCounselingLab™

Go to Topic 4: *Counseling in Mental Health and Private Practice* in the MyCounselingLab™ site (www.MyCounselingLab.com) for *Counseling: A Comprehensive Profession,* Seventh Edition, where you can:

- Find learning outcomes for *Counseling in Mental Health and Private Practice* along with the national standards that connect to these outcomes.
- Complete Assignments and Activities that can help you more deeply understand the chapter content.
- Apply and practice your understanding of the core skills identified in the chapter with the Building Counseling Skills unit.
- Prepare yourself for professional certification with a Practice for Certification quiz.
- Connect to videos through the Video and Resource Library.

Summary and Conclusion

Clinical mental health counseling originated in the 1970s primarily due to legislative initiatives of the time, specifically the Community Mental Health Centers Act of 1963. This act established mental health centers nationwide. Master's level counselors who worked in these centers were basically disenfranchised because they lacked credentials and a group to represent them. Thus, the main initiators behind the founding of the American Mental Health Counselors Association (AMHCA) were those of recognition and empowerment.

Clinical mental health counselors today are well established and work with a number of clients needing general and specialized treatment. Their work includes primary, secondary, and tertiary prevention with a focus on wellness. The specialty of clinical mental health counseling is accredited by CACREP on the master's level.

Those who concentrate their studies in this area work in settings that are varied. As a group,

clinical mental health counselors identify themselves strongly as counselors who specialize in some of the same areas, such as depression, anxiety, and trauma, as other helping professionals such as psychiatrists and psychologists. They know the DSM well, but they are attuned to prevention, wellness, and development as well.

Finally, this chapter has covered counselors in private practice, where there are opportunities and pitfalls. Counselors who work as private practitioners must have business and counseling abilities to be successful and be entrepreneurial. There are a number of difficulties associated with private practice, such as finding support and supervision. There are numerous rewards as well, such as setting one's own hours and skirting the headaches of managed care regulations if one wishes. Overall, private practice continues to be a popular alternative for counselors.

Epilogue

It is over! You've read some or all of the 20 chapters in this book. You have most likely had a test or two (or maybe three or four) on this material, and you may have explored some of the topics in more depth through brief or extensive research or reaction papers. The most important part of what has occurred, however, involves the question: "What have you learned?"

It is relatively easy for the majority of us to briefly memorize facts and spit them back. It is quite another matter though to integrate knowledge into the essence of our being so that it makes a difference in our lives. I always tell my students I do not want them to get an understanding of counseling into their heads. I want them to get it into the marrow of their bones! If they do that, counseling can be transformative in their lives personally and professionally. My wish for you is that your appreciation of this profession you are entering, or at least considering, has grown exponentially, and you understand what counseling is and is not on the deepest level possible.

For review purposes let me highlight a few of the more salient parts of this text. First, counseling is a unique profession that traces its roots back for over a century but which has really become a strong entity with a distinct identity in the last few decades. Second, most associated with the profession agree that the definition of counseling is as follows: "Counseling is a professional relationship that empowers diverse individuals, families, and groups to accomplish mental health, wellness, education, and career goals." As such, counseling deals with both prevention and remediation. It is an active process, multicultural in nature, encompassing a variety of intrapersonal and interpersonal developmental and situational difficulties from persons, groups, families, and even society. Thus, counseling involves advocacy and social justice causes within community settings, as well as actions that lead to adjustment and growth on a smaller personal and interpersonal scale.

The American Counseling Association is the organization that counselors join and identify with as a professional home. Its divisions encompass areas that counselors have an interest in—from creativity to career development. Most of the main foci and settings of counselors have been covered in this text including those involving schools, colleges, cultures, human development, groups, families, rehabilitation, addiction, abuse, careers, assessment, research, ethics, spirituality, sexual orientation, and mental health. As of 2010 all states in the

United States, plus Puerto Rico and the District of Columbia, licensed counselors, and since 1985 counselors have had their own honor society that promotes excellence in the profession: Chi Sigma Iota.

However, counseling is more than just organizations, associations, settings, and topics. It is people and a way of life! Those who practice it benefit from it through developing a larger worldview and a greater depth of empathy and understanding of others than the vast majority of individuals on the planet. Unmentioned so far but significant is that counselors are some of the nicest people in the world, and the conventions and conferences of the American Counseling Association and its divisions are extremely informative and fun! Nevertheless, counseling has its drawbacks, and one is the continued focus counselors must bring to sessions in order to concentrate on clients. What seems so simple is not. It takes effort and commitment to really be with somebody. Second, counselors will at times build up toxicity from listening to the difficulties of clients. Therefore, maintaining your personal health as well as your professional credentials takes time, sweat, and a willingness to be vulnerable and open in ways most professions do not require.

In closing, let me return to the initial question I began with: "What have you learned?" Hopefully, your answer will be one that is currently before you and one that unfolds in time. You have some answers now, and those will guide you as you enter the profession or decide to pursue another field of interest. Some responses to this query will come later as you reflect on or reread portions of this book and your class experiences related to it. The important point is to remember that counseling and becoming a counselor are continuous endeavors. Counseling as a profession is evolving, and where it is now will not be where it is tomorrow, next week, or in years to come. That is positive because most individuals who want to work with people sincerely believe there is growth and development in humankind. Likewise, people attracted to the profession of counseling almost always want to become more than they are now. That happens if individuals work at it and do not assume a passive role in their own growth. Thus, learning occurs on multiple, interactional, and even international levels.

Regardless of what you do with what you have learned and what you will learn in the future, I wish you well. I am glad I have been able to share words with you that will hopefully make a difference in your life and the lives of those with whom you work. I am always open to your ideas, stories, and feedback. My e-mail is stg@wfu.edu.

Sincerely,

Samuel T. Gladding

APPENDIX A

Counseling-Related Organizations

American Association for Marriage and Family Therapy
www.AAMFT.org
112 South Alfred St.
Alexandria, VA 22314
(703) 838-9808

American Association of Pastoral Counselors
aapc.org/content/what-pastoral-counseling
9504A Lee Highway
Fairfax, VA 22031-2303
(703) 385-6967

American Counseling Association
www.counseling.org
5999 Stevenson Avenue
Alexandria, VA 22304
(703) 823-9800

American Psychiatric Association
www.psych.org
1000 Wilson Boulevard, Suite 1825,
Arlington, VA 22209-3901
(703) 907-7300

American Psychological Association
www.APA.org
750 First Street, N.E.
Washington, DC 20002-4242
(202) 336-5500

Chi Sigma Iota
www.csi-net.org
P.O. Box 35448
Greensboro, NC 27425-5448
(336) 841-8180

Council for Accreditation of Counseling
and Related Educational Programs (CACREP)
www.cacrep.org
1001 North Fairfax Street, Suite 510
Alexandria, VA 22314
(703) 535-5990

National Association of School Psychologists
www.nasponline.org/about_sp/whatis.aspx
4340 East West Highway, Suite 402,
Bethesda, MD 20814
(301) 657-0270

National Association of Social Workers
www.socialworkers.org
750 First Street, NE • Suite 700
Washington, DC 20002-4241
(202) 408-8600

National Board for Certified Counselors, Inc.
www.nbcc.org
3 Terrace Way
Greensboro, NC 27403-3660
(336) 547-0607

REFERENCES

AA World Services, Inc. (2002). *Alcoholics Anonymous: The story of how many thousands of men and women have recovered from alcoholism* (4th ed.). New York: Author.

Abudabeth, N., & Aseel, H. A. (1999). Transcultural counseling and Arab Americans. In J. McFadden (Ed.), *Transcultural counseling* (2nd ed., pp. 283–296). Alexandria, VA: American Counseling Association.

ACES-ASCA Joint Committee on the Elementary School Counselor. (1966). The elementary school counselor: Preliminary statement. *Personnel and Guidance Journal, 44,* 658–661.

Ackerman, N. W. (1958). *The psychodynamics of family life.* New York: Basic Books.

ACT, Inc. (1998). *DISCOVER.* Hunt Valley, MD: Author.

Adelman, H. S., & Taylor, L. (2002). School counselors and school reform: New directions. *Professional School Counseling, 5,* 235–248.

Adler, A. (1927). *Understanding human nature.* Greenwich, CT: Fawcett.

Adler, A. (1931). *What life should mean to you.* Boston: Little, Brown.

Adler, A. (1956). *The individual psychology of Alfred Adler: A systematic presentation in selections from his writings* (H. L. Ansbacher & R. R. Ansbacher, Eds.). New York: Norton.

Adler, A. (1964). *Social interest: A challenge to mankind.* New York: Capricorn.

Ahia, C. E. (2006). A cultural framework for counseling African Americans. In C. C. Lee (Ed.), *Multicultural issues in counseling* (3rd ed., pp. 57–62). Alexandria, VA: American Counseling Association.

Akos, P., Cockman, C. R., & Strickland, C. A. (2007). Differentiating classroom guidance. *Professional School Counseling, 10,* 455–463.

Akos, P., Hamm, J. V., Mack, S. G., & Dunaway, F. (2007). Utilizing the development influence of peers in middle school groups. *Journal for Specialists in Group Work, 32,* 51–60.

Albee, G. W., & Gullotta, T. P. (1997). *Primary prevention works.* Thousand Oaks, CA: Sage.

Albert, K. A., & Luzzo, D. A. (1999). The role of perceived barriers in career development: A social cognitive perspective. *Journal of Counseling & Development, 77,* 431–436.

Alberti, R. E., & Emmons, M. L. (2008). *Your perfect right: Assertive and equality in your life and relationships* (9th ed.). San Luis Obispo, CA: Impact.

Aldridge, D. (1994). Single-case research designs for the creative art therapist. *Arts in Psychotherapy, 21,* 333–342.

Ali, S. R., & Saunders, J. L. (2006). College expectations of rural Appalachian youth: An exploration of social cognitive career theory factors. *Career Development Quarterly, 55,* 38–51.

Allan, J., & Brown, K. (1993). Jungian play therapy in elementary schools. *Elementary School Guidance and Counseling, 28,* 30–41.

Allen, G. (1977). *Understanding psychotherapy: Comparative perspectives.* Champaign, IL: Research Press.

Allen, V. B. (1986). A historical perspective of the AACD ethics committee. *Journal of Counseling & Development, 64,* 293.

Alter, G. (1995, May 29). What works. *Newsweek,* 18–24.

Altmaier, E. M., Greiner, M., & Griffin-Pierson, S. (1988). The new scholarship on women. *Journal of Counseling & Development, 66,* 345–346.

Alyn, J. H. (1988). The politics of touch in therapy: A response to Willison and Masson. *Journal of Counseling & Development, 66,* 432–433.

Ambler, D. A. (1989). Designing and managing programs: The administrator role. In U. Delworth, G. R. Hanson, & Associates (Eds.), *Student services: A handbook for the profession* (2nd ed., pp. 247–264). San Francisco: Jossey-Bass.

American Academy of Pediatrics. (2007). Child Abuse. (Retrieved December 28, 2007 from http://www.aap.org/publiced/BK0_ChildAbuse.htm)

American Counseling Association. (2005). *ACA Code of Ethics.* Alexandria, VA: Author.

American Educational Research Association, American Psychological Association, and National Council on Measurement in Education. (1999, March). *Standards for educational and psychological tests* (Rev.). Washington, DC: American Educational Research Association.

American Psychiatric Association. (1994). *Diagnostic and statistical manual of mental disorders* (4th ed.). Washington, DC: Author.

American Psychiatric Association. (2000). *Diagnostic and statistical manual of mental disorders* (4th ed., text revision), *DSM-IV-TR.* Washington, DC: Author.

American Psychiatric Association. (2013). *Diagnostic and statistical manual of mental disorders* (5th ed.). Washington, DC: Author.

American School Counselor Association. (2005). *ASCA's national model: A foundation for school counseling programs* (2nd ed.). Alexandria, VA: Author.

Americans with Disabilities Act. (1990, July 26). Public Law 101-336. Washington, DC: Government Printing Office.

Amundson, N. E. (1996). Supporting clients through a change in perspective. *Journal of Employment Counseling, 33,* 155–162.

Anastasi, A. (1982). *Psychological testing* (5th ed.). New York: Macmillan.

Anastasi, A. (1992b). What counselors should know about the use and interpretation of psychological tests. *Journal of Counseling & Development, 70,* 610–615.

Anastasi, A., & Urbina, S. (1997). *Psychological testing* (7th ed.). Upper Saddle River, NJ: Prentice Hall.

Ancis, J. R., Sedlacek, W. E., & Mohr, J. J. (2000). Student perceptions of campus cultural climate by race. *Journal of Counseling & Development, 78,* 180–185.

Andersen, P., & Vandehey, M. (2012). *Career counseling and development in a global economy* (2nd ed.). Belmont, CA: Brooks/Cole.

Anderson, C. M., & Stewart, S. (1983). *Mastering resistance: A practical guide to family therapy.* New York: Guilford.

Anderson, D., & Swanson, C. (1994). *Legal issues in licensure.* Alexandria, VA: American Counseling Association.

Andronico, M. P. (Ed.). (1996). *Men in groups: Insights, interventions, and psychoeducational work.* Washington, DC: American Psychological Association.

Angus, J., & Reeve, P. (2006). Ageism: A treat to 'aging well' in the 21st century. *Journal of Applied Gerontology, 25,* 137–152.

Anton, J. L. (1978). Intensive experimental designs: A model for the counselor/researcher. *Personnel and Guidance Journal, 56,* 273–278.

Anton, W. D., & Reed, J. R. (1991). *College adjustment*

scales professional manual. Odessa, FL: Psychological Assessment Resources.

Aplin, J. C. (1985). Business realities and organizational consultation. *Counseling Psychologist, 13,* 396–402.

Aprahamian, M., Kaplan, D. M., Windham, A. M., Sutter, J. A., & Visser, J. (2011). The relationship between acculturation and mental health of Arab Americans. *Journal of Mental Health Counseling, 33,* 80–92.

Arias, E. (2011, September 28). United States Life Tables, 2007.: *National Vital Statistics Report, 59* (9), pp. 1–61.

Arnett, J. J. (2007). *Emerging adulthood: The winding road from the late teens through the twenties.* New York: Oxford.

Arredondo, P. (1998). Integrating multicultural counseling competencies and universal helping conditions in culture-specific contexts. *Counseling Psychologist, 26,* 592–601.

Arredondo, P., Rosen, D. C., Rice, T., Perez, P., & Tovar-Gamero, Z. G. (2005). Multicultural counseling: A 10-year content analysis of the *Journal of Counseling & Development. Journal of Counseling & Development, 83,* 155–161.

Arredondo, P., Toporek, R., Brown, S., Jones, J., Locke, D. C., Sanchez, J., et al. (1996). *Operationalization of the multicultural counseling competencies.* Alexandria, VA: Association for Multicultural Counseling and Development.

Arthur, G. L., & Swanson, C. D. (1993). *Confidentiality and privileged communication.* Alexandria, VA: American Counseling Association.

Ary, D., Jacobs, L. C., Sorensen, C., & Razavieh, A. (2010). *Introduction to research in education* (9th ed.). Belmont, CA: Wadsworth.

Ashby, J. S., & Rice, K. G. (2002). Perfectionism, dysfunctional attitudes, and self-esteem: A structural equations analysis. *Journal of Counseling & Development, 80,* 197–203.

Aslanian, C. B., & Brickell, H. M. (1980). *Americans in transition: Life changes as reasons for adult learning.* New York: College Entrance Examination Board.

Association for Specialists in Group Work. (1992). Professional standards for the training of group workers. *Journal for Specialists in Group Work, 17,* 12–19.

Association for Specialists in Group Work. (1998). Best practice guidelines. *Journal for Specialists in Group Work, 23,* 237–244.

Association for Specialists in Group Work. (2000). Professional standards for the training of group workers. *Journal for Specialists in Group Work, 25,* 327–342.

Astramovich, R. L., & Coker, K. (2007). Program evaluation: The accountability bridge model for counselors. *Journal of Counseling & Development, 85,* 162–172.

Astramovich, R. L., & Harris, K. R. (2007). Promoting self-advocacy among minority students in school counseling. *Journal of Counseling & Development, 85,* 269–276.

Atlas, G., & Morier, D. (1994). The sorority rush process: Self-selection, acceptance criteria, and the effect of rejection. *Journal of College Student Development, 35,* 346–353.

Atkinson, D. R. (2004). *Counseling American minorities: A cross-cultural perspective* (6th ed.). New York: McGraw-Hill.

Aubrey, R. F. (1977). Historical development of guidance and counseling and implications for the future. *Personnel and Guidance Journal, 55,* 288–295.

Aubrey, R. F. (1979). Relationship of guidance and counseling to the established and emerging school curriculum. *School Counselor, 26,* 150–162.

Aubrey, R. F. (1982). A house divided: Guidance and counseling in twentieth-century America. *Personnel and Guidance Journal, 60,* 198–204.

Aubrey, R. F. (1983). The odyssey of counseling and images of the future. *Personnel and Guidance Journal, 61,* 78–82.

Austin, J. T. (1994). Minnesota Multiphasic Personality Inventory (MMPI-2). *Measurement and Evaluation in Counseling and Development, 27,* 178–185.

Auvenshine, D., & Noffsinger, A. L. (1984). *Counseling: An introduction for the health and human services.* Baltimore: University Park Press.

Avasthi, S. (1990). Native American students targeted for math and sciences. *Guidepost, 33*(6), 1, 6, 8.

Axelson, J. A. (1999). *Counseling and development in a multicultural society* (3rd ed.). Pacific Grove, CA: Brooks/Cole.

Azar, B. (1994, June). Could "policing" test use improve assessment? *APA Monitor, 25,* 16.

Bachman, R. W. (1975). Elementary school children's perceptions of helpers and their characteristics. *Elementary School Guidance and Counseling, 10,* 103–109.

Baggerly, J., & Parker, M. (2005). Child-centered group play therapy with African American boys at the elementary school level. *Journal of Counseling & Development, 83,* 387–396.

Bailey, W. R., Deery, N. K., Gehrke, M., Perry, N., & Whitledge, J. (1989). Issues in elementary school counseling: Discussion with American School Counselor Association leaders. *Elementary School Guidance and Counseling, 24,* 4–13.

Baim, C., Burmeister, J., & Manuela, M. (2007). *Psychodrama: Advances in theory and practice.* New York: Routledge.

Baker, S. (1996). Recollections of the boom era in school counseling. *School Counselor, 43,* 163–164.

Baker, S. B., & Gerler, E. R., Jr. (2008). *School counseling for the twenty-first century* (4th ed.). Upper Saddle River, NJ: Merrill/Prentice Hall.

Baker, S. B., & Shaw, M. C. (1987). *Improving counseling through primary prevention.* Upper Saddle River, NJ: Prentice Hall.

Baker, S. B., Swisher, J. D., Nadenichek, P. E., & Popowicz, C. L. (1984). Measured effects of primary prevention strategies. *Personnel and Guidance Journal, 62,* 459–464.

Baldwin, C. (1989). Peaceful alternatives: Inner peace. *Journal of Humanistic Education and Development, 28,* 86–92.

Balkin, R. S., & Roland, C. B. (2007). Reconceptualizing stabilization for counseling adolescents in brief psychiatric hospitalization: A new model. *Journal of Counseling & Development, 85,* 64–72.

Bandura, A. (1976). Effecting change through participant modeling. In J. D. Krumboltz & C. E. Thoresen (Eds.), *Counseling methods* (pp. 248–265). New York: Holt, Rinehart & Winston.

Bandura, A. (1982). The psychology of chance encounters and life paths. *American Psychologist, 37,* 747–755.

Bankart, C. P. (1997). *Talking cures.* Pacific Grove, CA: Brooks/Cole.

Barkley, W. M. (1982). Introducing research to graduate students in the helping professions. *Counselor Education and Supervision, 21,* 327–331.

Barna, J. S. & Brott, P. E. (2011). How important is personal/social development to academic achievement? The elementary school counselor's perspective. *Professional School Counseling, 43,* 242–249.

Barnett, J. E, & Johnson, W. B. (2010). *Ethics desk reference for counselors.* Alexander, VA: American Counseling Association.

Barret, R. L., & Logan, C. (2002). *Counseling gay men and lesbians: A practice primer.* Pacific Grove, CA: Brooks/Cole.

Barrett-Kruse, C., Martinez, E., & Carll, N. (1998). Beyond reporting suspected abuse: Positively influencing the development of the student within the classroom. *Professional School Counseling, 1,* 57–60.

Barrow, J. C., & Prosen, S. S. (1981). A model of stress and counseling interventions. *Personnel and Guidance Journal, 60,* 5–10.

Barstow, S. (1998, June). Managed care debate heats up in Congress. *Counseling Today, 1,* 26.

Baruth, L. G., & Manning, M. L. (2012). *Multicultural counseling and psychotherapy: A lifespan perspective* (5th ed.). Upper Saddle River, NJ: Pearson/Prentice Hall.

Bateson, G. H., Jackson, D. D., Haley, J., & Weakland, J. (1956). Toward a theory of schizophrenia. *Behavioral Science, 1,* 251–264.

Bateson, G. H. (1971). The cybernetics of "self": A theory of alcoholism. *Psychiatry, 34,* 1–18.

Bauman, S. (2008). The role of the elementary school counselor in reducing school bullying. *Elementary School Journal, 108,* 362–375.

Bauman, S., & Waldo, M. (1998). Existential theory and mental health counseling: If it were a snake it would have bitten! *Journal of Mental Health Counseling, 20,* 13–27.

Beale, A. V., & Nugent, D. G. (1996). The pizza connection: Enhancing career awareness. *Elementary School Guidance and Counseling, 30,* 294–303.

Beale, A. V., & Scott, P. C. (2001). "Bullybusters": Using drama to empower students to take a stand against bullying behavior. *Professional School Counseling, 4,* 300–305.

Beane, J. A. (1986). The self-enhancing middle-grade school. *School Counselor, 33,* 189–195.

Beaver, M. L. (1991). Life review/reminiscent therapy. In P. K. H. Kim (Ed.), *Serving the elderly: Skills for practice* (pp. 67–89). New York: Aldine de Gruyter.

Beck, A. T., & Weishaar, M. (2008). Cognitive therapy. In R. J. Corsini & D. Wedding (Eds.), *Current psychotherapies* (8th ed., pp. 263–294). Belmont, CA: Thomson Brooks/Cole.

Becky, D., & Farren, P. M. (1997). Teaching students how to understand and avoid abusive relationships. *School Counselor, 44,* 303–308.

Becvar, D. S. (1982). The family is not a group: Or is it? *Journal for Specialists in Group Work, 7,* 88–95.

Becvar, D. S., & Becvar, R. J. (2009). *Family therapy: A systematic integration* (7th ed.). Boston: Allyn & Bacon.

Beers, C. (1908). *A mind that found itself.* New York: Longman Green.

Befrienders International. (2007). *Befrienders Worldwide.* Retrieved August 7, 2007, from http://www.befrienders.org/index.asp

Beiten, B. K., & Allen, K. R. (2005). Resilience in Arab American couples after September 11, 2001: A systems perspective. *Journal of Marital and Family Therapy, 31,* 251–267.

Bell, D. A. (1985, July 15 and 22). America's great success story: The triumph of Asian Americans. *The New Republic, 3678/3679,* 24–31.

Bell, J. E. (1975). *Family therapy.* New York: Aronson.

Bell, J. E. (1976). A theoretical framework for family group therapy. In P. J. Guerin (Ed.), *Family therapy: Theory and practice* (pp. 129–143). New York: Gardner.

Bemak, F. (1998, February 13). *Counseling at-risk students.* Presentation at Wake Forest University Institute for Ethics and Leadership in Counseling, Winston-Salem, NC.

Bemak, F., & Chung, R. C-Y. (2008). New professional roles and advocacy strategies for school counselors: A multicultural/social justice perspective to move beyond the nice counselor syndrome. *Journal of Counseling & Development, 86,* 372–382.

Bemak, F., & Keys, S. (2000). *Violence and aggressive youth: Intervention and prevention strategies for changing times.* Thousand Oaks, CA: Sage.

Benjamin, A. (1987). *The helping interview* (4th ed.). Boston: Houghton Mifflin.

Benshoff, J. M., & Paisley, P. O. (1996). The structured peer consultation model for school counselors. *Journal of Counseling & Development, 74,* 314–318.

Benson, L. T., & Deeter, T. E. (1992). Moderators of the relation between stress and depression in adolescence. *School Counselor, 39,* 189–194.

Berenson, B. G., & Mitchell, K. M. (1974). *Confrontation: For better or worse.* Amherst, MA: Human Resource Development Press.

Berenson, D. (1992). The therapist's relationship with couples with an alcoholic member. In E. Kaufman & P. Kaufman (Eds.), *Family therapy of drug and alcohol abuse* (pp. 224–235). Boston: Allyn & Bacon.

Berg, B. (1986). *The assertiveness game.* Dayton, OH: Cognitive Counseling Resources.

Berg, B. (1989). *The anger control game.* Dayton, OH: Cognitive Counseling Resources.

Berg, B. (1990a). *The anxiety management game.* Dayton, OH: Cognitive Counseling Resources.

Berg, B. (1990b). *The depression management game.* Dayton, OH: Cognitive Counseling Resources.

Berg, B. (1990c). *The self-control game.* Dayton, OH: Cognitive Counseling Resources.

Berg-Cross, L. (2002). *Couples therapy* (2nd ed.). Thousand Oaks, CA: Sage.

Bergin, A. E. (1985). Proposed values for guiding and evaluating counseling and psychotherapy. *Counseling and Values, 29,* 99–115.

Bergin, A. E. (1992). Three contributions of a spiritual perspective to counseling, psychotherapy, and behavior change. In M. T. Burke & J. G. Miranti (Eds.), *Ethical and spiritual values in counseling* (pp. 5–15). Alexandria, VA: American Counseling Association.

Bergland, M. M., & Thomas, K. R. (1991). Psychosocial issues following severe head injury of adolescence: Individual and family perceptions. *Rehabilitation Counseling Bulletin, 35,* 5–22.

Bergman, J. S. (1985). *Fishing for barracuda.* New York: Norton.

Berkel, L. A., & Constantine, M. G. (2005). Relational variables and life satisfaction in African American and Asian American college women. *Journal of College Counseling, 8,* 5–13.

Bernard, J. M. (1986). Laura Perls: From ground to figure. *Journal of Counseling & Development, 64,* 367–373.

Bernard, J. M., & Goodyear, R. K. (2009). *Fundamentals of clinical supervision* (4th ed.). Boston: Allyn & Bacon.

Berne, E. (1964). *Games people play.* New York: Grove.

Berrios, R., & Lucca, N. (2006). Qualitative methodology in counseling research: Recent contributions and challenges for a new century. *Journal of Counseling & Development, 84,* 174–186.

Bertalanffy, L. von (1968). *General systems theory: Foundations, development, application.* New York: Brazillier.

Berube, E., & Berube, L. (1997). Creating small groups using school and community resources to meet student needs. *The School Counselor, 44,* 300–302.

Betsworth, D. G., & Fouad, N. A. (1997). Vocational interests: A look at the past 70 years and a glance at the future. *Career Development Quarterly, 46,* 23–47.

Betz, N., & Fitzgerald, L. (1987). *The career psychology of women.* New York: Academic Press.

Beymer, L. (1971). Who killed George Washington? *Personnel and Guidance Journal, 50,* 249–253.

Bieschke, K. J., Perez, R. M., & DeBord, K. A. (Eds.). (2007). *Handbook of counseling and psychotherapy with lesbian, gay, bisexual, and transgender clients* (2nd ed.). Washington, DC: American Psychological Association.

Bishop, J. B. (1990). The university counseling center: An agenda for the 1990s. *Journal of Counseling & Development, 68,* 408–413.

Bishop, J. B. (1992). The changing student culture: Implications for counselors and administrators. *Journal of College Student Psychotherapy, 6,* 37–57.

Blackorby, J., & Wagner, M. (1996). Longitudinal postschool outcomes of youth with disabilities: Findings from the national longitudinal transition study. *Exceptional Children, 62,* 399–413.

Blair, R. G. (2004). Helping older adolescents search for meaning in depression. *Journal of Mental Health Counseling, 26*(4), 333–347.

Blake, R. (1975). Counseling in gerontology. *Personnel and Guidance Journal, 53,* 733–737.

Blake, R. (1982). Assessing the counseling needs of older persons. *Measurement and Evaluation in Guidance, 15,* 188–193.

Blanck, G., & Blanck, R. (1979). *Egopsychology II: Psychoanalytic developmental psychology.* New York: Columbia University Press.

Blando, J. (2011). *Counseling older adults.* New York: Routledge.

Blatner, A. (2004). *Foundations for psychodrama: History, theory, and practice* (4th ed.). New York: Springer.

Blimling, G. S. (2003). *The resident assistant: Applications and strategies for working with college students in residence halls* (6th ed.). Dubuque, IA: Kendall/Hunt.

Bloch, D. P. (1988). *Reducing the risk: Using career information with at-risk youth.* Eugene, OR: Career Information Systems.

Bloch, D. P. (1989). Using career information with dropouts and at-risk youth. *Career Development Quarterly, 38,* 160–171.

Bloland, P. A. (1986). Student development: The new orthodoxy? Part 1. *ACPA Developments, 13,* 1, 13.

Bloland, P. A. (1992, December). Qualitative research in student affairs. *CAPS Digest,* EDO-CG-92-26.

Bloom, M. (1996). *Primary prevention practices.* Thousand Oaks, CA: Sage.

Bobo, M., Hildreth, B. L., & Durodoye, B. (1998). Changing patterns in career choices among African-American, Hispanic, and Anglo children. *Professional School Counseling, 1*(4), 37–42.

Boesch, R., & Cimbolic, P. (1994). Black students' use of college and university counseling centers. *Journal of College Student Development, 35,* 212–216.

Bohart, A. C. & Watson, J. C. (2011). The person-centered psychotherapy and related experiential approaches. In S. B. Messer & A. S. Gurman (Eds.), *Essential psychotherapies* (pp. 223–260). New York: Guilford.

Bohlmeijer, E., Smit, F., & Cuijpers, P. (2003). Effects of reminiscence and life review on late-life depression: A meta-analysis. *International Journal of Geriatric Psychiatry, 18,* 1088–1094.

Bolles, R. N. (2012). *What color is your parachute? 2012: A practical manual for job hunters and career changers.* Berkeley, CA: Ten Speed Press.

Bolton, B. (2001). Measuring rehabilitation outcomes. *Rehabilitation Counseling Bulletin, 44,* 67–75.

Bolton, B., & Jaques, M. E. (1978). Rehabilitation counseling research: Editorial introduction. In B. Bolton & M. E. Jaques (Eds.), *Rehabilitation counseling: Theory and practice* (pp. 163–165). Baltimore: University Park Press.

Bolton, R. (1979). *People skills: How to assert yourself, listen to others, and resolve conflicts.* Upper Saddle River, NJ: Prentice Hall.

Bonebrake, C. R., & Borgers, S. B. (1984). Counselor role as perceived by counselors and principals. *Elementary School Guidance and Counseling, 18,* 194–199.

Borders, L. D. (2002). School counseling in the 21st century: Personal and professional reflections. *Professional School Counseling, 5,* 180–185.

Borders, L. D., & Brown, L. L. (2005). *The new handbook of counseling supervision.* Mahwah, NJ: Erlbaum.

Borders, L. D., & Drury, S. M. (1992). Comprehensive school counseling programs: A review for policymakers and practitioners. *Journal of Counseling & Development, 70,* 487–498.

Borders, L. D., & Leddick, G. R. (1988). A nationwide survey of supervision training. *Counselor Education and Supervision, 27,* 271–283.

Borders, L. D. (Ed.). (1994). *Supervision: Exploring the effective components.* Greensboro, NC: ERIC/CASS.

Borders, S., & Paisley, P. O. (1992). Children's literature as a resource for classroom guidance. *Elementary School Guidance and Counseling, 27,* 131–139.

Bostick, D., & Anderson, R. (2009). Evaluating a small-group counseling program—A model for program planning and improvement in the elementary setting. *Professional School Counseling, 12,* 428–433.

Bowen, M. (1960). A family concept of schizophrenia. In D. D. Jackson (Ed.), *The etiology of schizophrenia* (pp. 346–372). New York: Basic Books.

Bowen, M. (1976). Theory in the practice of psychotherapy. In P. J. Guerin, Jr. (Ed.), *Family therapy: Theory and practice* (pp. 42–90). New York: Gardner.

Bowen, M. (1978). *Family therapy in clinical practice.* New York: Aronson.

Bowman, J. T., & Reeves, T. G. (1987). Moral development and empathy in counseling. *Counselor Education and Supervision, 26,* 293–298.

Bowman, R. P. (1986). Peer facilitator programs for middle graders: Students helping each other grow up. *School Counselor, 33,* 221–229.

Boy, A. V., & Pine, G. J. (1968). *The counselor in the schools: A reconceptualization.* Boston: Houghton Mifflin.

Boy, A. V., & Pine, G. J. (1983). Counseling: Fundamentals of theoretical renewal. *Counseling and Values, 27,* 248–255.

Boyer, S. P., & Sedlacek, W. E. (1989). Noncognitive predictors of counseling center use by international students. *Journal of Counseling & Development, 67,* 404–407.

Boyle, P. S. (1994). Rehabilitation counselors as providers: The issue of sexuality. *Journal of Applied Rehabilitation Counseling, 25,* 6–10.

Braaten, L. J. (1986). Thirty years with Rogers's necessary and sufficient conditions of therapeutic personality change. *Person-Centered Review, 1,* 37–49.

Bradley, L. J. (1984). Lifespan career assessment for counselors and educators. *Counseling and Human Development, 16,* 1–16.

Bradley, R. W. (1994). Tests and counseling: How did we ever become partners? *Measurement and Evaluation in Counseling and Development, 26,* 224–226.

Bradley, R. W., & Cox, J. A. (2001). Counseling: Evolution of the profession. In D. C. Locke, J. E. Myers, & E. L. Herr (Eds.), *The handbook of counseling* (pp. 27–41). Thousand Oaks, CA: Sage.

Brammer, L. M., Abrego, P., & Shostrom, E. (1993). *Therapeutic counseling and psychotherapy* (6th ed.). Upper Saddle River, NJ: Merrill/Prentice Hall.

Brammer, L. M., & MacDonald, G. (2003). *The helping relationship* (8th ed.). Boston: Allyn & Bacon.

Brammer, R. (2012). *Diversity in counseling* (2nd ed.). Belmont, CA: Thomson Brooks/Cole.

Brandt, R. (1959). *Ethical theory.* Upper Saddle River, NJ: Prentice Hall.

Bratcher, W. E. (1982). The influence of the family on career selection: A family systems perspective. *Personnel and Guidance Journal, 61,* 87–91.

Braun, S. A., & Cox, J. A. (2005). Managed mental health care: Intentional misdiagnosis of mental disorders. *Journal of Counseling & Development, 83,* 425–433.

Brewer, J. M. (1932). *Education as guidance.* New York: Macmillan.

Brewer, J. M. (1942). *History of vocational guidance.* New York: Harper.

Briere, J., & Scott, C. (2006). *Principles of trauma counseling: A guide to symptoms, evaluation, and treatment.* Thousand Oaks, CA: Sage.

Briggs, M. K, & Rayle, A. D. (2005). Incorporating spirituality into core counseling courses: Ideas for classroom application. *Counseling and Values, 50,* 63–75.

Brinson, J. A. (1996). Cultural sensitivity for counselors: Our challenge for the twenty-first century. *Journal of Humanistic Education and Development, 34,* 195–206.

Brooks, F., & McHenry, B. (2009). *A contemporary approach to substance abuse and addiction counseling: A counselor's guide to application and understanding.* Alexandria, VA: American Counseling Association.

Broverman, I., Broverman, D., Clarkson, F., Rosenkrantz, P., & Vogel, S. (1970). Sex-role stereotypes and clinical judgments of mental health. *Journal of Consulting and Clinical Psychology, 34,* 1–7.

Brown, D. (1985). Career counseling: Before, after or instead of personal counseling. *Vocational Guidance Quarterly, 33,* 197–201.

Brown, D. (1989). The preservice training and supervision of consultants. *Counseling Psychologist, 13,* 410–425.

Brown, D. (1993). Training consultants: A call to action. *Journal of Counseling & Development, 72,* 139–143.

Brown, D. (1997). Implications of cultural values for cross-cultural consultation with families. *Journal of Counseling & Development, 76,* 29–35.

Brown, D. (2002). The role of work and cultural values in occupational choice, satisfaction, and success: A theoretical statement. *Journal of Counseling & Development, 80,* 48–56.

Brown, D. (2012). *Career information, care, and career development* (10th ed.). Upper Saddle River, NJ: Pearson.

Brown, D., Pryzwansky, W. B., & Schulte, A. C. (2011). *Psychological consultation* (7th ed.). Boston: Allyn & Bacon.

Brown, J. A. (1983). Consultation. In J. A. Brown & R. H. Pate, Jr. (Eds.), *Being a counselor: Directions and challenges* (pp. 124–146). Pacific Grove, CA: Brooks/Cole.

Brown, L. S. (2010). *Feminist therapy.* Washington, DC: American Psychological Association.

Brown, M. B. (2000). Diagnosis and treatment of children and adolescents with attention-deficit/hyperactivity disorder. *Journal of Counseling & Development, 78,* 195–203.

Brown, M. B. (2006). School-based health centers: Implications for counselors. *Journal of Counseling & Development, 84,* 187–191.

Brown, N. M. (1990). Men nurturing men. *Family Therapy Networker, 14,* 11.

Brown, N. W. (2011). *Psycho-educational groups* (3rd ed.). Philadelphia: Routledge.

Brown, R. D. (1986). Editorial. *Journal of College Student Personnel, 27,* 99.

Brown, T., & Helms, J. (1986). The relationship between psychological development issues and anticipated self-disclosure. *Journal of College Student Personnel, 27,* 136–141.

Bruce, A. M., Getch, Y. Q., Ziomek-Daigle, J. (2009). Closing the gap: A group counseling approach to improve test performance of African American students. *Professional School Counseling, 12,* 450–457.

Bryan, J. (2009). Engaging clients, families, and communities as partners in mental health. *Journal of Counseling & Development, 87,* 507–512.

Bubenzer, D., Zimpfer, D., & Mahrle, C. (1990). Standardized individual appraisal in agency and private practice: A survey. *Journal of Mental Health Counseling, 12,* 51–66.

Buelow, G. (1995). Comparing students from substance abusing and dysfunctional families: Implications for counseling. *Journal of Counseling & Development, 73,* 327–330.

Buhler, C., & Allen, M. (1972). *Introduction to humanistic psychology.* Pacific Grove, CA: Brooks/Cole.

Bulkeley, C. (2009). The enigma of endings. *Psychodynamic Practice: Individuals, Groups and Organisations, 15*(3), 303–310.

Bullis, R. K. (1993). *Law and the management of a counseling agency or private practice.* Alexandria, VA: American Counseling Association.

Bundy, M. L., & Poppen, W. A. (1986). School counselors' effectiveness as consultants: A research review. *Elementary School Guidance and Counseling, 20,* 215–222.

Burch, M. A., & Skovholt, T. M. (1982). Counseling services and men in need: A problem in person-environment matching. *AMHCA Journal, 4,* 89–96.

Burck, H. D., & Peterson, G. W. (1975). Needed: More evaluation, not research. *Personnel and Guidance Journal, 53,* 563–569.

Burgess, A. W., & Holstrom, L. L. (1974). Rape trauma syndrome. *American Journal of Psychiatry, 131,* 981–986.

Burke, J. F. (1989). *Contemporary approaches to psychotherapy and counseling.* Pacific Grove, CA: Brooks/Cole.

Burke, K. L. (1993). The negative stereotyping of student athletes. In W. D. Kirk & S. V. Kirk (Eds.), *Student athletes: Shattering the myths and sharing the realities* (pp. 93–98). Alexandria, VA: American Counseling Association.

Burke, M. T., Hackney, H., Hudson, P., Miranti, J., Watts, G. A., & Epp, L. (1999). Spirituality, religion, and CACREP curriculum standards. *Journal of Counseling & Development, 77,* 251–257.

Burke, M. T., & Miranti, J. G. (1995). *Counseling: The spiritual dimension.* Alexandria, VA: American Counseling Association.

Burrow-Sanchez, J. J. (2006). Understanding adolescent substance abuse: Prevalence, risk factors, and clinical implications. *Journal of Counseling & Development, 84,* 283–290.

Burrow-Sanchez, J. J., Jenson, W. R., & Clark, E. (2008). School-based interventions for students with substance abuse. *Psychology in the Schools, 46,* 238–245.

Burrow-Sanchez, J. J., & Lopez, A. L. (2009). Identifying substance abuse issues in high schools: A national survey of high school counselors. *Journal of Counseling & Development, 87,* 72–79.

Butin, D. W. (2010). *Service-learning in theory and practice: The future of community engagement in higher education.* New York: Palgrave Macmillan

Butler, K. (1990). Spirituality reconsidered. *Family Therapy Networker, 14,* 26–37.

Butler, K. (1994, July/August). Duty of care. *Family Therapy Networker, 18,* 10–11.

Butler, R. N. (2001). Ageism. In G. L. Maddox (Ed.), *Encyclopedia of aging* (Vol. A-L, 3rd ed., p. 38). New York: Springer.

Bynner, J. M. (1997). Basic skills in adolescents' occupational preparation. *Career Development Quarterly, 45,* 300–321.

Calhoun, L. G., & Tedeschi, R. G. (Eds.). (2006). *The handbook of posttraumatic growth: Research and practice.* Mahwah, NJ: Lawrence Earlbaum Associates.

Calley, N. G. (2007). Integrating theory and research: The development of a research-based treatment program for juvenile male sex offenders. *Journal of Counseling & Development, 85,* 131–142.

Calley, N. G. (2009). Promoting a contextual perspective in the application of the ACA Code of Ethics: The ethics into action map. *Journal of Counseling & Development, 87,* 476–482.

Callis, R. (1985). Minnesota School Attitude Survey, Lower and Upper Forms. *Journal of Counseling & Development, 63,* 382.

Campbell, A., & Katona, G. (1953). The sample survey: A technique for social science research. In L. Festinger & D. Katz (Eds.), *Research methods in the behavioral sciences* (pp. 15–55). New York: Dryden.

Campbell, C. (1993a). Strategies for reducing parent resistance to consultation in the schools. *Elementary School Guidance and Counseling, 28,* 83–90.

Campbell, C. A. (1993b). Play, the fabric of elementary school counseling programs. *Elementary School Guidance and Counseling, 28,* 10–16.

Campbell, C. A., & Dahir, C. A. (1997). *Sharing the vision: The national standard for school counseling programs.* Alexandria, VA: American School Counselors Association.

Campbell, D. (1974). *If you don't know where you're going you'll probably end up somewhere else.* Niles, IL: Argus.

Campbell, D. T., & Stanley, J. C. (1963). *Experimental and quasi-experimental designs for research.* Chicago: Rand McNally.

Canaff, A. L. (1997). Later life career planning: A new challenge for career counselors. *Journal of Employment Counseling, 34,* 85–93.

Canon, H. J. (1985). Ethical problems in daily practice. In H. J. Canon & R. D. Brown (Eds.), *Applied ethics in student services* (pp. 5–15). San Francisco: Jossey-Bass.

Canon, H. J. (1988). Nevitt Sanford: Gentle prophet, Jeffersonian rebel. *Journal of Counseling & Development, 66,* 451–457.

Canon, H. J. (1989). Guiding standards and principles. In U. Delworth, G. R. Hanson, & Associates (Eds.), *Student services: A handbook for the professional* (2nd ed., pp. 57–79). San Francisco: Jossey-Bass.

Caplan, G. (1964). *Principles of preventive psychiatry.* New York: Basic Books.

Caplan, G. (1970). *The theory and practice of mental health consultation.* New York: Basic Books.

Caplan, G., & Caplan, R. (1993). *Mental health consultation and collaboration.* San Francisco: Jossey-Bass.

Capuzzi, D. (2009). *Suicide prevention in the schools: Guidelines for middle and high school settings* (2nd ed.). Alexandria, VA: American Counseling Association.

Capuzzi, D. (Ed.). (2008). *Youth at risk: A preventive resource for counselors, teachers, and parents* (4th ed). Alexandria, VA: American Counseling Association.

Carey, J. C., & Dimmit, C. (2006). Resources for school counselors and counselor educators: The Center for School Counseling and Outcome Research. *Professional School Counseling, 9,* 416–420.

Carey, J., & Dimmitt, C. (2008). A model for evidence-based elementary school counseling: Using school data, research, and evaluation to enhance practice. *The Elementary School Journal, 108,* 422–430.

Carey, J. C., Williams, K. S., & Wells, M. (1988). Relationships between dimensions of supervisors' influence and counselor trainees' performance. *Counselor Education and Supervision, 28,* 130–139.

Carkhuff, R. R. (1969). *Helping and human relations* (Vols. 1 & 2). New York: Holt, Rinehart & Winston.

Carkhuff, R. R. (1972). *The art of helping.* Amherst, MA: Human Resource Development Press.

Carkhuff, R. R. (2000). *The art of helping* (8th ed.). Amherst, MA: Human Resource Development Press.

Carkhuff, R. R., & Anthony, W. A. (1979). *The skills of helping.* Amherst, MA: Human Resource Development Press.

Carkhuff, R. R., & Berenson, B. G. (1967). *Beyond counseling and psychotherapy.* New York: Holt, Rinehart & Winston.

Carlson, J., & Ardell, D. E. (1988). Physical fitness as a pathway to wellness and effective counseling. In R. Hayes & R. Aubrey (Eds.), *New directions for counseling and human development* (pp. 383–396). Denver: Love.

Carlson, J., & Dinkmeyer, D., Jr. (2006). *Consultation: Creating school-based interventions* (3rd ed.). New York: Routledge.

Carlson, J., Watts, R. E., & Maniacci, M. (Eds.). (2006). *Adlerian therapy: Theory and practice.* Washington, DC: American Psychological Association.

Carlson, J. G. (1989). Rebuttal. The MBTI: Not ready for routine use in counseling. A reply. *Journal of Counseling & Development, 67,* 489.

Carmichael, K. D. (1994). Sand play as an elementary school strategy. *Elementary School Guidance and Counseling, 28,* 302–307.

Carnegie Task Force on Meeting the Needs of Young Children. (1994). *Starting points: Meeting the needs of our youngest children.* New York: Author.

Carney, J. V., & Hazler, R. J. (1998). Suicide and cognitive-behavioral counseling: Implications for mental health counselors. *Journal of Mental Health Counseling, 20,* 28–41.

Carrese, M. A. (1998). Managing stress for college success through self-hypnosis. *Journal of Humanistic Education and Development, 36,* 134–142.

Carroll, L., Gilroy, P. J., & Ryan, J. (2002). Counseling transgendered, transsexual, and gender-variant clients. *Journal of Counseling & Development, 80,* 131–139.

Carroll, M. R., & Levo, L. (1985). The association for specialists in group work. *Journal of Counseling & Development, 63,* 453–454.

Carruthers, W. L., Sweeney, B., Kmitta, D., & Harris, G. (1996). Conflict resolution: An examination of the research literature and a model for program evaluation. *School Counselor, 44,* 5–18.

Carson, R. C., Butcher, J. N., & Mineka, S. (2000). Mood disorder and suicide. In *Abnormal psychology and modern life* (11th ed., pp. 209–267). Boston: Allyn & Bacon.

Carter, R. T. (1990). The relationship between racism and racial identity among white

Americans: An exploratory investigation. *Journal of Counseling & Development, 69,* 46–50.

Casey, J. M. (1996). Gail F. Farwell: A developmentalist who lives his ideas. *School Counselor, 43,* 174–180.

Cashwell, C. S., & Vacc, N. A. (1996). Family functioning and risk behaviors: Influences on adolescent delinquency. *School Counselor, 44,* 105–114.

Cashwell, C. S., & Watts, R. E. (2010). The new ASERVIC competencies for addressing spiritual and religious issues in counseling. *Counseling and Values, 55,* 2–5.

Cashwell, C. S., & Young, J. S. (Eds.). (2011). *Integrating spirituality and religion into counseling: A guide to competent practice* (2nd ed.). Alexandria, VA: American Counseling Association.

Cautilli, J., & Skinner, L. (1996, September). Combating youth violence through wrap-around service. *Counseling Today,* 12.

Cavanagh, M. E., & Levitov, J. E. (2002). *The counseling experience: A theoretical and practical approach* (2nd ed). Prospect Heights, IL: Waveland.

Cavanaugh, J. C., & Blanchard-Fields, F. (2011). *Adult development and aging* (6th ed.). Belmont, CA: Wadsworth.

Cavazos-Rehg, P. A., & DeLucia-Waack, J. L. (2009). Education, ethnic identity, and acculturation as predictors of self-esteem in Latino adolescents. *Journal of Counseling & Development, 87,* 47–54.

Center for Credentialing and Education (CCE). (2011). *Board certified coach.* http://www.cce-global.org/BCC

Chamberlin, C. M., & Najijian, Z. (2009). Workaholism, health, and self-acceptance. *Journal of Counseling & Development, 87,* 159–169.

Chandler, C. K., Holden, J. M., & Kolander, C. A. (1992). Counseling for spiritual wellness: Theory and practice. *Journal of Counseling & Development, 71,* 168–175.

Chang, D. F., Tong, H., Shi, Q., & Zeng, Q. (2005). Letting a hundred flowers bloom: Counseling and psychotherapy in the People's Republic of China. *Journal of Mental Health Counseling, 27,* 104–116.

Chao, R., & Good, G. E. (2004). Nontraditional students' perspectives on college education: A qualitative study. *Journal of College Counseling, 7,* 5–12.

Chauvin, J. C., & Remley, T. P., Jr. (1996). Responding to allegations of unethical conduct. *Journal of Counseling & Development, 74,* 563–568.

Chen, X. (2007). *Part-time undergraduates in post secondary education 2003–04.* Washington, DC: U.S. Department of Education.

Chen-Hayes, S. F. (1997). Counseling lesbian, bisexual, and gay persons in couple and family relationships: Overcoming the stereotypes. *The Family Journal, 5,* 236–240.

Chernin, J., Holden, J. M., & Chandler, C. (1997). Bias in psychological assessment: Heterosexism. *Measurement and Evaluation in Counseling and Development, 30,* 68–76.

Chesley, G. L., Gillett, D. A., & Wagner, W. G. (2008). Verbal and nonverbal metaphor with children in counseling. *Journal of Counseling & Development, 86,* 399–411.

Cheston, S. E. (2000). A new paradigm for teaching counseling theory and practice. *Counselor Education and Supervision, 39,* 254–269.

Chew, A. L. (1984). Training counselors to interpret psychoeducational evaluations: A course model. *Counselor Education and Supervision, 24,* 114–119.

Chickering, A. W., & Reisser, L. (1993). *Education and identity* (2nd ed.). San Francisco: Jossey-Bass.

Childers, J. H., Jr., & Couch, R. D. (1989). Myths about group counseling: Identifying and challenging misconceptions. *Journal for Specialists in Group Work, 14,* 105–111.

Chisolm, M. S. (1998, May 15). Colleges need to provide early treatment of students' mental illnesses. *Chronicle of Higher Education, 44,* B6–B7.

Chojnacki, J. T., & Gelberg, S. (1994). Toward a conceptualization of career counseling with gay/lesbian/bisexual persons. *Journal of Career Development, 21,* 3–9.

Chope, R. C. (2006). *Family matters: The influence of the family in career decision making.* Austin, TX: Pro-Ed.

Chopko, B. A., & Schwartz, R. C. (2009). The relation between mindfulness and posttraumatic growth: A study of first responders to trauma-inducing incidents. *Journal of Mental Health Counseling, 31,* 363–376.

Christenbury, L. (Ed.). (1995). *Books for you.* Chicago: National Council of Teachers of English.

Christenbury, L., Beale, A. V., & Patch, S. S. (1996). Interactive bibliocounseling: Recent fiction and nonfiction for adolescents and their counselors. *School Counselor, 44,* 133–145.

Christopher, J. C. (1996). Counseling's inescapable moral visions. *Journal of Counseling & Development, 75,* 17–25.

Chung, R., C-Y. (2005). Women, human rights, and counseling: Crossing international boundaries. *Journal of Counseling & Development, 83,* 262–268.

Chung, R., C-Y., & Bemak, F. (2002). The relationship of culture and empathy in cross-cultural counseling. *Journal of Counseling & Development, 80,* 154–159.

Chusmir, L. H. (1990). Men who make nontraditional career choices. *Journal of Counseling & Development, 69,* 11–16.

Claiborn, C. D. (1979). Counselor verbal intervention, non-verbal behavior and social power. *Journal of Counseling Psychology, 26,* 378–383.

Clark, A. J. (2004). Empathy: Implications of three ways of knowing in counseling. *Journal of Humanistic Counseling, Education and Development, 43,* 141–151.

Clark, A. J. (2007). *Empathy in counseling and psychotherapy: Perspectives and practices.* Mahwah, NJ: Erlbaum.

Clark, A. J. (2010a). Empathy: An integral model in the counseling process. *Journal of Counseling & Development, 88*(3), 348–356.

Clarke, N. E., & Crowe, N. M. (2000). Stakeholder attitudes toward ADA title I: Development of an indirect measurement method. *Rehabilitation Counseling Bulletin, 43,* 58–65.

Clawson, T. W., & Wildermuth, V. (1992, December). The counselor and NBCC. *CAPS Digest,* EDO-CG-92-14.

Clay, D. L., Anderson, W. P., & Dixon, W. A. (1993). Relationship between anger expression and stress in predicting depression. *Journal of Counseling & Development, 72,* 91–94.

Clemens, E. (2007). Developmental counseling and therapy as a model for school counselor consultation with teachers. *Professional School Counseling, 10,* 352–359.

Cleveland, P. H., & Lindsey, E. W. (1995). Solution-focused family interventions. In A. C. Kilpatrick & T. P. Holland (Eds.), *Working with families* (pp. 145–160). Boston: Allyn & Bacon.

Cobia, D. C., & Henderson, D. A. (2007). *Developing an effective and accountable school counseling program* (2nd ed). Upper Saddle River, NJ: Prentice Hall.

Cobia, D. C., & Pipes, R. B. (2002). Mandated supervision: An intervention for disciplined professionals. *Journal of Counseling & Development, 80,* 140–144.

Cobia, D. C., Sobansky, R. R., & Ingram, M. (2004). Female survivors of childhood sexual abuse: Implications for couples' therapists. *The Family Journal: Counseling and Therapy for Couples and Families, 12,* 312–318.

Cochran, J. L. (1996). Using play and art therapy to help culturally diverse students overcome barriers to school success. *School Counselor, 43,* 287–298.

Cohen, G. D. (2000). *The creative age.* New York: Avon.

Cohen, J. (1990). Things I have learned (so far). *American Psychologist, 45,* 1304–1312.

Cohen, M. N. (1998, April 17). Culture, not race, explains human diversity. *Chronicle of Higher Education,* B4–B5.

Cohen, R. J., & Swerdik, M. (2009). *Psychological testing and assessment* (7th ed.). New York: McGraw-Hill.

Colangelo, N. (1985). Overview. *Elementary School Guidance and Counseling, 19,* 244–245.

Colangelo, N., & Pulvino, C. J. (1980). Some basic concerns in counseling the elderly. *Counseling and Values, 24,* 68–73.

Colapinto, J. (2000). Structural family therapy. In A. M. Horne (Ed.), *Family counseling and therapy* (3rd ed., pp. 140–169). Itasca, IL: F. E. Peacock.

Colbert, R. D., Vernon-Jones, R., & Pransky, K. (2006). The school change feedback process: Creating a new role for counselors in education reform. *Journal of Counseling & Development, 84,* 72–82.

Cole, C. G. (1982). Career guidance for middle junior high school students. *Vocational Guidance Quarterly, 30,* 308–314.

Cole, C. G. (1988). *Guidance in middle level schools: Everyone's responsibility.* Columbus, OH: National Middle School Association.

Coll, K. M. (1993). Student attitudinal changes in a counseling ethics course. *Counseling and Values, 37,* 165–170.

Coll, K. M., Thobro, P., & Hass, R. (2004). Relational and purpose development in youth offenders. *Journal of Humanistic Counseling, Education and Development, 43,* 41–49.

Collins, B. G., & Collins, T. M. (1994). Child and adolescent mental health: Building a system of care. *Journal of Counseling & Development, 72,* 239–243.

Collison, B. B. (1981). Counseling adult males. *Personnel and Guidance Journal, 60,* 219–222.

Collison, B. B. (1982). Needs assessment for guidance program planning: A procedure. *School Counselor, 30,* 115–121.

Columbia University's Mailman School of Public Health (2011, January 7). Many survivors of World Trade Center suffered PTSD. *HealthDay News* (http://consumer. healthday.com/Article. asp?AID=648660).

Combs, A. (1982). *A personal approach to teaching: Beliefs that make a difference.* Boston: Allyn & Bacon.

Commission on Substance Abuse at Colleges and Universities. (1994). *Rethinking rites of passage: Substance abuse on America's campuses.* New York: Center on Addiction and Substance Abuse at Columbia University.

Compass, B. E., Connor-Smith, J. K., Saltzman, H., Thomsen, A. H., & Wadsworth, M. E. (2001). Coping with stress during childhood and adolescence: Problems, progress, and potential in theory and research. *Psychological Bulletin, 127,* 87–127.

Conoley, J. C. (1981). Emergent training issues in consultation. In J. C. Conoley (Ed.), *Consultation in schools: Theory, research procedures* (pp. 223–263). New York: Academic Press.

Conoley, J. C., & Conoley, C. W. (1992). *School consultation: Practice and training* (2nd ed.). Boston: Allyn & Bacon.

Constantine, M. G., Hage, S. M., Kindaichi, M. M., & Bryant, R. M. (2007). Social justice and multicultural issues: Implications for the practice and training of counselors and counseling psychologists. *Journal of Counseling & Development, 85,* 24–29.

Conyne, R. K. (1975). Environmental assessment: Mapping for counselor action. *Personnel and Guidance Journal, 54,* 150–154.

Conyne, R. K. (1998). What to look for in groups: Helping trainees become more sensitive to multicultural issues. *Journal for Specialists in Group Work, 23,* 22–32.

Conyne, R. K., & Cook, E. (2004). *Ecological counseling: An innovative approach to conceptualizing person-environment interaction.* Alexandria, VA: American Counseling Association.

Cook, D., Bolton, B., Bellini, J., & Neath, J. (1997). A statewide investigation of the rehabilitation counselor generalist hypothesis. *Rehabilitation Counseling Bulletin, 40,* 192–201.

Cook, D. W. (1989). Systematic need assessment: A primer. *Journal of Counseling & Development, 67,* 462–464.

Cook, E. P. (Ed.). (1993). *Women, relationships, and power: Implications for counseling.* Alexandria, VA: American Counseling Association.

Cook, E. P., Heppner, M. J., & O'Brien, K. M. (2002). Career development of women of color and White women: Assumptions, conceptualizations, and interventions from an ecological perspective. *Career Development Quarterly, 50,* 291–305.

Cooley, L. (2009). *The power of groups: Solution-focused group counseling in the schools.* Thousand Oaks, CA: Corwin.

Cooper, D. L., Healy, M., & Simpson, J. (1994). Student development through involvement: Specific changes over time. *Journal of College Student Development, 35,* 98–101.

Coppock, M. W. (1993). Small group plan for improving friendships and self-esteem. *Elementary School Guidance and Counseling, 28,* 152–154.

Corcoran, K. O., & Mallinckrodt, B. (2000). Adult attachment, self-efficacy, perspective taking, and conflict resolution. *Journal of Counseling & Development, 78,* 473–483.

Corey, G. (2009). *Theory and practice of counseling and psychotherapy* (8th ed.). Belmont, CA: Thomson Brooks/ Cole.

Corey, G. (2012). *Theory and practice of group counseling* (8th ed). Belmont, CA: Thomson Brooks/Cole.

Corey, G., Corey, M. S., & Callanan, P. (2011). *Issues and ethics in the helping professions* (8th ed.). Belmont, CA: Thomson Brooks/ Cole.

Cormier, L. S., Nurius, P. S., & Osborn, C. J. (2009). *Interviewing and change strategies for helpers* (6th ed.). Belmont, CA: Brooks/Cole.

Cormier, L. S., & Hackney, H. (2012). *Counseling strategies and interventions* (8th ed.). Boston: Pearson.

Cornelius-White, J. H. D. (2005). Teaching person-centered multicultural counseling: Collaborative endeavors to transcend resistance and increase awareness. *Journal of Humanistic Counseling, Education and Development, 44,* 225–236.

Corsini, R. J. (2008). Introduction. In R. J. Corsini & D. Wedding (Eds.), *Current psychotherapies* (8th ed., pp. 1–13). Belmont, CA: Thomson Brooks/Cole.

Corsini, R. J., & Wedding, D. (Eds.). (2010). *Current psychotherapies* (9th ed.). Belmont, CA: Cengage.

Costa, L., & Altekruse, M. (1994). Duty-to-warn guidelines for mental health counselors. *Journal of Counseling & Development, 72,* 346–350.

Cottone, R. R., & Claus, R. E. (2000). Ethical decision-making counseling: A review of the literature. *Journal of Counseling & Development, 78,* 279.

Cottone, R. R., Grelle, M., & Wilson, W. C. (1988). The accuracy of systemic versus psychological evidence in judging vocational evaluator recommendations: A preliminary test of a systemic theory of vocational rehabilitation. *Journal of Rehabilitation, 54,* 45–52.

Cottone, R. R., & Tarvydas, V. M. (2007). *Ethical and professional issues in counseling* (3rd ed.). Upper Saddle River, NJ: Merrill/Prentice Hall.

Couch, R. D. (1995). Four steps for conducting a pregroup screening interview. *Journal for Specialists in Group Work, 20,* 18–25.

Council for Accreditation of Counseling and Related Educational Programs. (2009). *CACREP accreditation manual.* Alexandria, VA: Author.

Council for the Advancement of Standards in Higher Education. (2009). *CAS professional standards for higher education* (7th ed.). Washington, DC: Author.

Coven, A. B. (1977). Using Gestalt psychodrama experiments in rehabilitation counseling. *Personnel and Guidance Journal, 56,* 143–147.

Cowan, E. W., & Presbury, J. H. (2000). Meeting client resistance and reactance with reverence. *Journal of Counseling & Development, 78,* 411–419.

Cox, B. J., & Waller, L. L. (1991). *Bridging the communication gap with the elderly.* Chicago: American Hospital Association.

Cox, H. G. (2009). *Later life: The realities of aging* (6th ed.). Upper Saddle River, NJ: Prentice Hall.

Cozby, P. C. (2009). *Methods in behavioral research* (10th ed.). New York: McGraw-Hill.

Craig, M. P., Contreras, M., & Peterson, N. (2000). Multicultural career exploration with adolescent females. In N. Peterson & R. C. Gonzalez (Eds.), *Career counseling models for diverse populations* (pp. 20–35). Pacific Grove, CA: Brooks/Cole.

Crawford, R. L. (1994). *Avoiding counselor malpractice.* Alexandria, VA: American Counseling Association.

Crawford, R. L., & Phyfer, A. Q. (1988). Adult children of alcoholics: A counseling model. *Journal of College Student Development, 29,* 105–111.

Creamer, D. G., & Associates (1990). *College student development: Theory and practices for the 1990s.* Alexandria, VA: American College Personnel Association.

Crespi, T. D., & Howe, E. A. (2000, March). Families in crisis: Considerations and implications for school counselors. *Counseling Today, 42*(9), 6.

Creswell, J. W. (2012). *Educational research: Planning, conducting, and evaluating quantitative and qualitative research* (4th ed.). Boston: Addison Wesley/Pearson.

Crites, J. O. (1969). *Vocational psychology.* New York: McGraw-Hill.

Crites, J. O. (1981). *Career counseling: Models, methods, and materials.* New York: McGraw-Hill.

Crodzki, L. (2002, May/June). Practice strategies. *Family Therapy Magazine, 1,* 43–44.

Cronbach, L. J. (1979). The Armed Services Vocational Aptitude Battery: A test battery in transition. *Personnel and Guidance Journal, 57,* 232–237.

Crosbie-Burnett, M., & Newcomer, L. L. (1989). A multimodal intervention for group counseling with children of divorce. *Elementary School Guidance and Counseling, 23,* 155–166.

Croteau, J. M., & Thiel, M. J. (1993). Integrating sexual orientation in career counseling: Acting to end a form of the personal-career dichotomy. *Career Development Quarterly, 42,* 174–179.

Culbreth, J. R., & Borders, L. D. (1999). Perceptions of the supervisory relationship: Recovering and nonrecovering substance abuse counselors. *Journal of Counseling & Development, 77,* 330–338.

Cunradi, C., Caetano, R., & Schafer, J. (2002). Socioeconomic predictors of intimate partner violence among White, Black, and Hispanic couples in the United States. *Journal of Family Violence, 17,* 377–389.

Curtis, J. M. (1981). Indications and contraindications in the use of therapist's self-disclosure. *Psychological Reports, 49,* 449–507.

Curtis, R., & Sherlock, J. J. (2006). Wearing two hats: Counselors working as managerial leaders in agencies and schools. *Journal of Counseling & Development, 84,* 120–126.

Curtis, R., Van Horne, J. W., Robertson, P., & Karvonen, M. (2010). Outcomes of a school-wide positive behavioral support program. *Professional School Counseling, 13,* 159–164.

Dahir, C. A. (2009). School Counseling in the 21st Century: Where lies the future? *Journal of Counseling & Development, 87*(1), 3–5.

Dahir, C. A., & Stone, C. B. (2009). School counselor accountability: The path to social justice and systemic change. *Journal of Counseling & Development, 87,* 12–20.

Daire, A. P., LaMothe, S., & Fuller, D. P. (2007). Differences between Black/African American and White college students regarding influences on high school completion, college attendance, and career choice. *Career Development Quarterly, 55,* 275–279.

D'Andrea, M., & Daniels, J. (2001). RESPECTFUL counseling: An integrative multidimensional model for counselors. In D. B. Pope-Davis and H. L. K. Coleman (Eds.), *The intersection of race, class, and gender in multicultural counseling* (pp. 417–466). Thousand Oaks, CA: Sage.

D'Andrea, M., & Heckman, E. (2008). A 40-year review of multicultural counseling outcome research: Outlining a future research agenda for the multicultural counseling movement. *Journal of Counseling & Development, 86,* 356–363.

Daniel, T., & Ivey, A. E. (2007). *Microcounseling: Making skills work in a multicultural world.* Springfield, IL: Thomas.

Daniels, J. A. (2001). Managed care, ethics, and counseling. *Journal of Counseling & Development, 79,* 119–122.

Daniels, J. A. (2002). Assessing threats of school violence: Implications for counselors. *Journal of Counseling & Development, 80,* 215–218.

Daniels, M. H., Mines, R., & Gressard, C. (1981). A meta-model for evaluating counseling programs. *Personnel and Guidance Journal, 5*(9), 578–582.

Daniluk, J. C., & Haverkamp, B. E. (1993). Ethical issues in counseling adult survivors of incest. *Journal of Counseling & Development, 72,* 16–22.

Das, A. K. (1987). Indigenous models of therapy in traditional Asian societies. *Journal of Multicultural Counseling and Development, 15,* 25–37.

Das, A. K. (1998). Frankl and the realm of meaning. *Journal of Humanistic Education and Development, 36,* 199–211.

Dattilio, F. M. (1993). A practical update on the treatment of obsessive-compulsive disorders. *Journal of Mental Health Counseling, 15,* 244–259.

Daugherty, D. A., Murphy, M. J., & Paugh, J. (2001). An examination of the Adlerian construct of social interest with criminal offenders. *Journal of Counseling & Development, 79,* 465–471.

Davenport, D. S., & Yurich, J. M. (1991). Multicultural gender issues. *Journal of Counseling & Development, 70,* 64–71.

Davidson, J. P., III. (1986, March). *Developing an effective evaluation plan.* Paper presented at the Jefferson County (Alabama) Model School Program, Birmingham, AL.

Davis, D. C. (1998). The American College Counseling Association: A historical view. *Journal of College Counseling, 1,* 7–9.

Davis, H. V. (1988). *Frank Parsons: Prophet, innovator, counselor.* Carbondale: University of Southern Illinois Press.

Davis, J. (1914). *Vocational and moral guidance.* Boston: Ginn.

Davis, M. S., Wester, K. L., & King, B. (2008). Narcissism, entitlement, and questionable research practices in counseling: A pilot study. *Journal of Counseling & Development, 86,* 200–210.

Davis, T., & Ritchie, M. (1993). Confidentiality and the school counselor: A challenge for the 1990s. *School Counselor, 41,* 23–30.

Day, R. W., & Sparacio, R. T. (1980). Structuring the counseling process. *Personnel and Guidance Journal, 59,* 246–249.

Day, S. X. (2008). *Theory and design in counseling and psychotherapy* (2nd ed.). Boston: Houghton Miffline.

Dean, L. A. (1994, June). Chimney building. *Visions, 2,* 3–4.

DeAngelis, T. (1992, November). Best psychological treatment for many men: Group therapy. *APA Monitor, 23,* 31.

Degges-White, S., & Shoffner, M. F. (2002). Career counseling with lesbian clients: Using the theory of work adjustment as a framework. *Career Development Quarterly, 51,* 87–96.

Del Prete, T. (1998). Getting back in touch with students: Should we risk it? *Professional School Counseling, 1*(4), 62–65.

DeLaszlo, V. S. (1994). *The basic writings of C. G. Jung.* New York: Modern Library.

DeLucia-Waack, J. L. (1996). Multiculturalism is inherent in all group work. *Journal for Specialists in Group Work, 21,* 218–223.

DeLucia-Waack, J. L. (1999). Supervision for counselors working with eating disorders groups: Countertransference issues related to body image, food, and weight. *Journal of Counseling & Development, 77,* 379–388.

Delve, C. I., Mintz, S. D., & Stewart, G. M. (1990). *Community service as values education.* San Francisco: Jossey-Bass.

Denzin, N. K., & Lincoln, Y. S. E. (Eds.). (2011). *The SAGE handbook of qualitative research* (4th ed.). Thousand Oaks, CA: Sage.

DeRidder, L. M. (1993). Teenage pregnancy: Etiology and educational interventions. *Educational Psychology Review, 5,* 87–103.

Dermer, S. B., Smith, S. D., & Barto, K. K. (2010). Identifying and correctly labeling sexual prejudice, discrimination, and oppression. *Journal of Counseling & Development, 88*(3), 325–331.

deShazer, S. (1984). The death of resistance. *Family Process, 23,* 11–17.

deShazer, S. (1991). *Putting differences to work.* New York: Norton.

DeVoe, M. W., & McClam, T. (1982). Service coordination: The school counselor. *School Counselor, 30,* 95–100.

Dickson, G. L., & Parmerlee, J. R. (1980). The occupation family tree: A career counseling technique. *School Counselor, 28,* 99–104.

Dingman, R. L. (1990, November). *Counselor credentialing laws.* Paper presented at the Southern Association for Counselor Education and Supervision Conference, Norfolk, VA.

Dinkmeyer, D. (1973a). Elementary school counseling: Prospects and potentials. *School Counselor, 52,* 171–174.

Dinkmeyer, D. (1989). Beginnings of "Elementary School Guidance and Counseling." *Elementary School Guidance and Counseling, 24,* 99–101.

Dinkmeyer, D., & Losoncy, L. E. (1980). *The encouragement book: Becoming a positive person.* Upper Saddle River, NJ: Prentice Hall.

Dinkmeyer, D. C. (1971). The "C" group: Integrating knowledge and experience to change behavior. *Counseling Psychologist, 3,* 63–72.

Dinkmeyer, D. C. (1973b). The parent C group. *Personnel and Guidance Journal, 52,* 4.

Dinkmeyer, D. C., & Caldwell, C. E. (1970). *Developmental counseling and guidance: A comprehensive school approach.* New York: McGraw-Hill.

Dinkmeyer, D. C., & Carlson, J. (1973). *Consulting: Facilitating human potential and processes.* Upper Saddle River, NJ: Prentice Hall.

Dinkmeyer, D. C., & Muro, J. J. (1979). *Group counseling: Theory and practice* (2nd ed.). Itasca, IL: F. E. Peacock.

Dinkmeyer, D. C., Jr., & Carlson, J. (2006). Consultation: Creating school-based interventions (3rd ed.). New York: Routledge.

Dixon, A. L., Scheidegger, C., & McWhirter, J. (2009). The adolescent mattering experience: Gender variations in perceived mattering, anxiety, and depression. *Journal of Counseling & Development, 87,* 302–310.

Dixon, D. N., & Glover, J. A. (1984). *Counseling: A problem-solving approach.* New York: Wiley.

Dixon, W. A. (2000). Problem-solving appraisal and depression: Evidence for a recovery model. *Journal of Counseling & Development, 78,* 87–91.

Dixon, W. A., & Reid, J. K. (2000). Positive life events as a moderator of stress-related depressive symptoms. *Journal of Counseling & Development, 78,* 343–347.

Doan, R. E., & Scherman, A. (1987). The therapeutic effect of physical fitness on measures of personality: A literature review. *Journal of Counseling & Development, 66,* 28–36.

Dobson, J. E., & Campbell, N. J. (1986). Laboratory outcomes of personal growth groups. *Journal for Specialists in Group Work, 11,* 9–15.

Doherty, W. J., & Simmons, D. S. (1996). Clinical practice patterns of marriage and family therapists: A national survey of therapists and their clients. *Journal of Marital and Family Therapy, 22,* 9–25.

Dollarhide, C. T. (1997). Counseling for meaning in work and life: An integrated approach. *Journal of Humanistic Education and Development, 35,* 178–187.

Dollarhide, C. T., & Saginak, K. A. (2012). *Comprehensive school counseling programs* (2nd ed.). Upper Saddle River, NJ: Pearson.

Donigian, J., & Malnati, R. (1997). *Systemic group therapy: A triadic model.* Pacific Grove, CA: Brooks/Cole.

Donnay, D. A. C. (1997). E. K. Strong's legacy and beyond: 70 years of the Strong Interest Inventory. *Career Development Quarterly, 46,* 2–22.

Dorn, F. J. (1984). The social influence model: A social psychological approach to counseling. *Personnel and Guidance Journal, 62,* 342–345.

Doster, J. A., & Nesbitt, J. G. (1979). Psychotherapy and self-disclosure. In G. J. Chelune (Ed.), *Self-disclosure: Origins, patterns, and implications and openness in interpersonal relationships* (pp. 177–224). San Francisco: Jossey-Bass.

Dougherty, A. M. (1986). The blossoming of youth: Middle

graders "on the grow." *School Counselor, 33,* 167–169.

Dougherty, A. M. (2009). *Psychological consultation and collaboration in school and community settings* (5th ed.). Belmont, CA: Brooks/Cole.

Doyle, K. (1997). Substance abuse counselors in recovery: Implications for the ethical issue of dual relationships. *Journal of Counseling & Development, 75,* 428–432.

Drapela, V. J. (1983). Counseling, consultation, and supervision: A visual clarification of their relationship. *Personnel and Guidance Journal, 62,* 158–162.

Dreikurs, R. R. (1950). *Fundamentals of Adlerian psychology.* Chicago: Alfred Adler Institute.

Dreikurs, R. R. (1967). *Psychodynamics, psychotherapy, and counseling.* Chicago: Alfred Adler Institute.

Dreikurs, R. R., & Mosak, H. H. (1966). The tasks of life: I. Adler's three tests. *Individual Psychologist, 4,* 18–22.

Dreikurs, R. R., & Soltz, V. (1964). *Children: The challenge.* New York: Hawthorne.

Dreisbach, V. M. (2003). Post-traumatic stress disorder in fire and rescue personnel. *Journal of the American Academy of Psychiatry and the Law, 31,* 120–123.

Drummond, R. J., & Jones, K. D. (2010). *Appraisal procedures for counselors and helping professionals* (7th ed.). Upper Saddle River, NJ: Prentice Hall.

Drummond, R. J., & Ryan, C. W. (1995). *Career counseling: A developmental approach.* Upper Saddle River, NJ: Merrill/Prentice Hall.

Dryden, W. (1994). Reason and emotion in psychotherapy: Thirty years on. *Journal of Rational Emotive and Cognitive Behavior Therapy, 12,* 83–89.

Dunn, C. W., & Veltman, G. C. (1989). Addressing the restrictive career maturity patterns of minority youth:

A program evaluation. *Journal of Multicultural Counseling and Development, 17,* 156–164.

Dustin, D., & Ehly, S. (1984). Skills for effective consultation. *School Counselor, 31,* 23–29.

Duys, D. K., & Hobson, S. M. (2004). Reconceptualizing self-esteem: Implications of Kegan's constructive-developmental model for school counselors. *Journal of Humanistic Counseling, Education, and Development, 43,* 152–162.

Dyer, W. W., & Vriend, J. (1977). A goal-setting checklist for counselors. *Personnel and Guidance Journal, 55,* 469–471.

Dykeman, C., Daehlin, W., Doyle, S., & Flamer, H. S. (1996). Psychological predictors of school-based violence: Implications for school counselors. *School Counselor, 44,* 35–47.

Edgemon, A. W., Remley, T. P., Jr., & Snoddy, H. N. (1985). Integrating the counselor's point of view. *School Counselor, 32,* 296–301.

Education Trust. (1997). *The national guidance and counseling reform program.* Washington, DC: Author.

Edwards, J. (2012). *Working with families: Guidelines and techniques.* Hoboken, NJ: Wiley.

Egan, G. (2010). *The skilled helper* (9th ed.). Belmont, CA: Thomson Brooks/Cole.

Ehrle, R. A. (1979). Rehabilitation counselors on the threshold of the 1980s. *Counselor Education and Supervision, 18,* 174–180.

Elam, G. A., & Kleist, D. M. (1999). Research on the long-term effects of child abuse. *The Family Journal: Counseling and Therapy for Couples and Families, 7,* 154–160.

El Nasser, H., & Overberg, P. (2002, June 5). More people identify themselves as simply 'American.' *USA Today,* p. A1.

Elkind, D. (1986). Stress and the middle grader. *School Counselor, 33,* 196–206.

Ellis, A. (1962). *Reason and emotion in psychotherapy.* New York: Stuart.

Ellis, A. (1971). *Growth through reason.* Palo Alto, CA: Science and Behavior Books.

Ellis, A. (1980). Foreword. In S. R. Walen, R. DiGiuseppe, & R. L. Wesslon (Eds.), *A practitioner's guide to rational-emotive therapy* (pp. vii–xii). New York: Oxford University Press.

Ellis, A. (1984). Must most psychotherapists remain as incompetent as they are now? In J. Hariman (Ed.), *Does psychotherapy really help people?* Springfield, IL: Thomas.

Ellis, A. (2008). Rational-emotive behavior therapy. In R. J. Corsini & D. Wedding (Eds.), *Current psychotherapies* (8th ed., pp. 187–222). Belmont, CA: Thomson Brooks/Cole.

Elmore, P. B., Ekstrom, R. B., Diamond, E. E., & Whittaker, S. (1993). School counselors' test use patterns and practices. *School Counselor, 41,* 73–80.

Elmore, T. M. (1984). Counselor education and counseling psychology: A house divided? *ACES Newsletter, 44,* 4, 6.

Elmore, T. M., & Roberge, L. P. (1982). Assessment and experiencing: On measuring the marigolds. *Measurement and Evaluation in Guidance, 15,* 95–102.

Elstein, A. S., Shulman, A. S., & Sprafka, S. A. (1978). *Medical problem solving: An analysis of clinical reasoning.* Cambridge, MA: Harvard University Press.

Emener, W. G., & Cottone, R. R. (1989). Professionalization, deprofessionalization, and reprofessionalization of rehabilitation counseling according to criteria of professions. *Journal of Counseling & Development, 67,* 576–581.

Emerson, S., & Markos, P. A. (1996). Signs and symptoms of the impaired counselor. *Journal of Humanistic Education and Development, 34,* 108–117.

Engels, D. W., Jacobs, B. C., & Kern, C. W. (2000). Life-career developmental

counseling. In D. C. Davis & K. M. Hemphrey (Eds.), *College counseling: Issues and strategies for a new millennium* (pp. 187–203). Alexandria, VA: American Counseling Association.

Engen, H. B., Lamb, R. R., & Prediger, D. J. (1982). Are secondary schools still using standardized tests? *Personnel and Guidance Journal, 60,* 287–290.

English, H. B., & English, A. C. (1956). *A comprehensive dictionary of psychological and psychoanalytical terms.* New York: Longman Green.

Engstrom, C. M., & Sedlacek, W. E. (1991). A study of prejudice toward university student-athletes. *Journal of Counseling & Development, 70,* 189–193.

Enns, C. Z. (1993). Twenty years of feminist counseling and therapy. *Counseling Psychologist, 21,* 3–87.

Enns, C. Z. (1996). Counselors and the backlash: "Rape hype" and "false-memory syndrome." *Journal of Counseling & Development, 74,* 358–367.

Enns, C. Z., & Hackett, G. (1993). A comparison of feminist and nonfeminist women's and men's reactions to nonsexist and feminist counseling: A replication and extension. *Journal of Counseling & Development, 71,* 499–509.

Enright, M. S. (1997). The impact of short-term career development programs on people with disabilities. *Rehabilitation Counseling Bulletin, 40,* 285–300.

Epp, L. R. (1998). The courage to be an existential counselor: An interview with Clemmont E. Vontress. *Journal of Mental Health Counseling, 20,* 1–12.

Eppler, C., Olsen, J. A., & Hidano, L. (2009). Using stories in elementary school counseling: Brief narrative techniques. *Professional School Counseling, 12,* 387–391.

Erber, J. T. (2010). *Aging and older adulthood* (2nd ed).

Belmont, CA: Thomson Wadsworth.

Erchul, W. P., & Martens, B. K. (2010). *School consultation: Conceptual and empirical bases of practice* (3rd ed). New York: Springer.

Erdman, P., & Lampe, R. (1996). Adapting basic skills to counsel children. *Journal of Counseling & Development, 74,* 374–377.

Erford, B. T. (2008). *Therapeutic dinosaur games.* Alexandria, VA: American Counseling Association.

Erford, B. T., Miller, E. M., Schein, H., McDonald, A., Ludwig, L., & Leishear, K. (2011). Journal of Counseling & Development publication patterns: Author and article characteristics from 1994 to 2009. *Journal of Counseling & Development, 89,* 73–80.

Erickson, M. (1954). Special techniques of brief hypnotherapy. *Journal of Clinical and Experimental Hypnosis, 2,* 109–129.

Eriksen, K., & Kress, V. E. (2008). Gender and diagnosis: Struggles and suggestions for counselors. *Journal of Counseling & Development, 86,* 152–162.

Erikson, E. H. (1958). *Young man Luther.* New York: Norton.

Erikson, E. H. (1963). *Childhood and society* (2nd ed.). New York: Norton.

Erikson, E. H. (1968). *Identity, youth and crisis.* New York: Norton.

Erk, R. R. (2000). Five frameworks for increasing understanding and effective treatment of attention-deficit/hyperactivity disorder: Predominately inattentive type. *Journal of Counseling & Development, 78,* 389–399.

Erkel, R. T. (1990, May/June). The birth of a movement. *Family Therapy Networker, 14,* 26–35.

Erwin, T. M. (2006). A qualitative analysis of the Lesbian Connection's discussion forum. *Journal of Counseling & Development, 84,* 95–107.

Espelage, D. L., Bosworth, K., & Simon, T. R. (2000). Examining the social context of bullying behaviors in early adolescence. *Journal of Counseling & Development, 78,* 326–333.

Evanoski, P. O., & Tse, F. W. (1989). Career awareness programs for Chinese and Korean American parents. *Journal of Counseling & Development, 67,* 472–474.

Evans, C.C. & Gladding, S.T. (2010). A comparison of counselor education and counseling psychology master's degree programs: Are they really different? Retrieved from http://counselingoutfitters.com/vistas/vistas10/article_24.pdf

Evans, D. R., Hearn, M. T., Uhlemann, M. R., & Ivey, A. E. (2011). *Essential interviewing* (8th ed.). Belmont, CA: Thomson Brooks/Cole.

Evans, J. E., & Hines, P. L. (1997). Lunch with school counselors: Reaching parents through their workplace. *Professional School Counseling, 1,* 45–47.

Evans, K. M., Kincade, E. A., Marbley, A. F., & Seem, S. R. (2005). Feminism and feminist therapy: Lessons from the past and hopes for the future. *Journal of Counseling & Development, 83,* 269–277.

Evans, N. J., Carr, J., & Stone, J. E. (1982). Developmental programming: A collaborative effort of residence life and counseling center staff. *Journal of College Student Personnel, 23,* 48–53.

Evelyn, J. (2002, June 14). Nontraditional students dominate undergraduate enrollments, study finds. *Chronicle of Higher Education 48*(40), A34.

Everall, R. D., Altrows, K. J., & Paulson, B. L. (2006). Creating a future: A study of resilience in suicidal female adolescents. *Journal of Counseling & Development, 84,* 461–470.

Everly, G. S., Lating, J. M., & Mitchell, J. T. (2000). Innovations in group intervention: Critical Incident Stress Debriefing (CISD) and Critical Incident Stress Management (CISM). In A. R. Roberts (Eds.), *Crisis intervention handbook: Assessment, treatment, and research.* New York: Oxford Press.

Ewing, D. B. (1990). Direct from Minnesota: E. G. Williamson. In P. P. Heppner (Ed.), *Pioneers in counseling and development: Personal and professional perspectives* (pp. 104–111). Alexandria, VA: American Counseling Association.

Exner, J. E. (2003). *The Rorschach: A comprehensive system* (4th ed.). New York: Wiley.

Fagan, J. (1970). The task of the therapist. In J. Fagan & I. L. Shepherd (Eds.), *Gestalt therapy now* (pp. 88–106). Palo Alto, CA: Science and Behavior Books.

Fagan, J., & Shepherd, I. L. (1970). Theory of Gestalt therapy. In J. Fagan & I. L. Shepherd (Eds.), *Gestalt therapy now* (pp. 1–7). Palo Alto, CA: Science and Behavior Books.

Fagan, R. (2006). Counseling and treating adolescents with alcohol and other substance use problems and their families. *The Family Journal: Counseling and Therapy for Couples and Families, 14,* 326–333.

Faiver, C., Eisengart, S., & Colonna, R. (2004). *The counselor intern's handbook* (3rd ed.). Pacific Grove, CA: Brooks/Cole.

Falco, L. D., Bauman, S., Sumnicht, Z., & Engelstad, A. (2011). Content analysis of the *Professional School Counseling* journal: The first 10 years. *Professional School Counseling, 14,* 271–277.

Fall, M., & VanZandt, C. E. Z. (1997). Partners in research: School counselors and counselor educators working together. *Professional School Counseling, 1,* 2–3.

Fallon, M. V. (1997). The school counselor's role in first generation students' college plans. *School Counselor, 44,* 384–393.

Fals-Stewart, W. (2003). The occurrence of partner physical aggression on days of alcohol consumption: A longitudinal diary study. *Journal of Consulting and Clinical Psychology, 71,* 41–51.

Faust, V. (1968). *History of elementary school counseling: Overview and critique.* Boston: Houghton Mifflin.

Fauth, J., & Hayes, J. A. (2006). Counselors' stress appraisal as predictors of countertransference behavior with male clients. *Journal of Counseling & Development, 84,* 430–439.

Fenske, R. H. (1989). Evolution of the student services professional. In U. Delworth, G. R. Hanson, & Associates (Eds.), *Student services: A handbook for the profession* (2nd ed., pp. 25–56). San Francisco: Jossey-Bass.

Fernando, D. M. (2007). Existential theory and solution-focused strategies: Integration and application. *Journal of Mental Health Counseling, 29,* 226–241.

Fiedler, F. (1950). The concept of the ideal therapeutic relationship. *Journal of Consulting Psychology, 45,* 659–666.

Fischer, A. R., Jome, L. M., & Atkinson, R. A. (1998). Back to the future of multicultural psychotherapy with a common factors approach. *Counseling Psychologist, 26,* 602–606.

Fishman, C. H. (1988). *Treating troubled adolescents: A family therapy approach.* New York: Basic Books.

Fitzpatrick, M. R., & Irannejad, S. (2008). Adolescent Readiness for Change and the Working Alliance in Counseling. *Journal of Counseling & Development, 86,* 438–445.

Fleming, J. S., & Rickord, B. (1997). Solution-focused brief therapy: One answer to managed mental health care. *Family Journal, 5,* 286–294.

Fogle, D. O. (1979). Preparing students for the worst: The

power of negative thinking. *Personnel and Guidance Journal, 57,* 364–367.

Fong, M. L. (1992). When a survey isn't research. *Counselor Education and Supervision, 31,* 194–195.

Fong, M. L., & Cox, B. G. (1983). Trust as an underlying dynamic in the counseling process: How clients test trust. *Personnel and Guidance Journal, 62,* 163–166.

Fontes, L. A. (2002). Child discipline and physical abuse in immigrant Latino families: Reducing violence and misunderstandings. *Journal of Counseling & Development, 80,* 31–40.

Ford, D., & Urban, H. (1998). *Systems of psychotherapy: A comparative study* (2nd ed.). New York: Wiley.

Ford, D. Y., Harris, J. J., III, & Schuerger, J. M. (1993). Racial identity development among gifted Black students. *Journal of Counseling & Development, 71,* 409–417.

Forester-Miller, H., & Davis, T. E. (1996). *A practitioner's guide to ethical decision making.* Alexandria, VA: American Counseling Association.

Forrest, D. V. (1983). Depression: Information and interventions for school counselors. *School Counselor, 30,* 269–279.

Forrest, L. (1989). Guiding, supporting, and advising students: The counselor role. In U. Delworth, G. R. Hanson, & Associates (Eds.), *Student services: A handbook for the profession* (2nd ed., pp. 265–283). San Francisco: Jossey-Bass.

Forsyth, D. R., & Strong, S. R. (1986). The scientific study of counseling and psychotherapy. *American Psychologist, 41,* 113–119.

Foster, S. (1996, December). Characteristics of an effective counselor. *Counseling Today,* 21.

Fouad, N. A., & Byars-Winston, A. M. (2005). Cultural context of career choice: Meta-analysis of race/ethnicity differences.

Career Development Quarterly, 53, 223–233.

Foubert, J. D. (2007). *Lessons learned: How to avoid the biggest mistakes made by college resident assistants.* New York; Routledege.

Fowler, F. J. (2009). *Survey research methods* (4th ed.). Thousand Oaks, CA: Sage.

Fowler, J. (1995). Stages of faith (Rev. ed.). San Francisco, CA: Harper & Row.

Fox, M. (1994). *The reinvention of work: A new vision of livelihood for our time.* San Francisco: Harper.

Framo, J. L. (1996). A personal retrospective of the family therapy field: Then and now. *Journal of Marital and Family Therapy, 22,* 289–316.

Frankl, V. (1962). *Man's search for meaning: An introduction to logotherapy.* New York: Washington Square Press.

Frankl, V. (1967). *Psychotherapy and existentialism: Selected papers on logotherapy.* New York: Washington Square Press.

Frankl, V. (1969). *Psychotherapy and existentialism: Selected papers on logotherapy.* New York: Simon & Schuster.

Freeman, F. H., Knott, K. B., & Schwartz, M. K. (1996). *Leadership education: A source book.* Greensboro, NC: Center for Creative Leadership.

Freeman, S. C. (1990). C. H. Patterson on client-centered career counseling: An interview. *Career Development Quarterly, 38,* 291–301.

Fretz, B. R., & Mills, D. H. (1980). *Licensing and certification of psychologists and counselors.* San Francisco: Jossey-Bass.

Freud, A. (1936). *The ego and the mechanisms of defense* (J. Strachey, Trans.). New York: International Universities Press.

Freud, A. (1958). Adolescence. *Psychoanalytic Study of the Child, 13,* 255–278.

Frey, D. H. (1972). Conceptualizing counseling theories.

Counselor Education and Supervision, 11, 243–250.

Frey, D. H. (1978). Science and the single case in counseling research. *Personnel and Guidance Journal, 56,* 263–268.

Friedan, B. (1994). *The fountain of age.* New York: Touchstone.

Friedberg, R. D. (1996). Cognitive-behavioral games and workbooks: Tips for school counselors. *Elementary School Guidance and Counseling, 31,* 11–19.

Friedlander, M. L., Wildman, J., Heatherington, L., & Skowron, E. A. (1994). What we do and don't know about the process of family therapy. *Journal of Family Psychology, 8,* 390–416.

Friedman, E. H. (1991). Bowen theory and therapy. In A. S. Gurman & D. P. Kniskern (Eds.), *Handbook of family therapy* (Vol. 2, pp.134–170). New York: Brunner/Mazel.

Frieman, B. B. (1994). Children of divorced parents: Action steps for the counselor to involve fathers. *The School Counselor, 28,* 197–205.

Friesen, J. D. (1985). *Structural-strategic marriage and family therapy.* New York: Gardner.

Friskopp, A., & Silverstein, S. (1995). *Straight jobs gay lives.* New York: Scribner.

Frone, M. R. (2003). Work-family balance. In J. C. Quick & L. E. Terrick (Eds.), *Handbook of occupational health psychology* (pp. 143–162). Washington, DC: American Psychological Association.

Fuqua, D. R., & Newman, J. L. (1985). Individual consultation. *Counseling Psychologist, 13,* 390–395.

Furlong, M. J., Atkinson, D. R., & Janoff, D. S. (1979). Elementary school counselors' perceptions of their actual and ideal roles. *Elementary School Guidance and Counseling, 14,* 4–11.

Gade, E., Fuqua, D., & Hurlburt, G. (1988). The relationship of Holland's personality types to educational satisfaction

with a Native-American high school population. *Journal of Counseling Psychology, 35,* 183–186.

Galassi, J. P., Griffin, D., & Akos, P. (2008). Strengths-Based School Counseling and the ASCA National Model®. *Professional School Counseling, 12,* 176–181.

Galassi, J. P., & Gulledge, S. A. (1997). The middle school counselor and teacher-advisor programs. *Professional School Counseling, 1,* 55–60.

Gale, A. U. (1998). Carl McDaniels: A life of transitions. *Journal of Counseling & Development, 76,* 202–207.

Galfo, A. J., & Miller, E. (1976). *Interpreting educational research* (3rd ed.). Dubuque, IA: Wm. C. Brown.

Gallessich, J. (1974). Training the school psychologist for consultation. *Journal of School Psychology, 12,* 138–149.

Gallessich, J. (1982). *The profession and practice of consultation.* San Francisco: Jossey-Bass.

Gallessich, J. (1985). Toward a meta-theory of consultation. *Counseling Psychologist, 13,* 336–354.

Galvin, M., & Ivey, A. E. (1981). Researching one's own interviewing style: Does your theory of choice match your actual practice? *Personnel and Guidance Journal, 59,* 536–542.

Ganje-Fling, M. A., & McCarthy, P. (1996). Impact of childhood sexual abuse on client spiritual development: Counseling implications. *Journal of Counseling & Development, 74,* 253–258.

Gardner, H. (2011). *Frames of mind: The theory of multiple intelligences* (3rd ed.). New York: Basic Books.

Garner, R., Martin, D., & Martin, M. (1989). The PALS program: A peer counseling training program for junior high school. *Elementary School Guidance and Counseling, 24,* 68–76.

Garretson, D. J. (1993). Psychological misdiagnosis of

African Americans. *Journal of Multicultural Counseling and Development, 21,* 119–126.

Garrett, M. T. (2006). When eagle speaks: Counseling Native Americans. In C. C. Lee (Ed.), *Multicultural issues in counseling* (3rd ed., pp. 25–54). Alexandria, VA: American Counseling Association.

Garrett, M. T., & Carroll, J. J. (2000). Mending the broken circle: Treatment of substance dependence among Native Americans. *Journal of Counseling & Development, 78,* 379–388.

Garrett, M. T., & Pichette, E. F. (2000). Red as an apple: Native American acculturation and counseling with or without reservation. *Journal of Counseling & Development, 78,* 3–13.

Garza, Y., & Watts, R. E. (2010). Filial Therapy and Hispanic values: Common ground for culturally sensitive helping. *Journal of Counseling & Development, 88*(1), 108–113.

Gatta, M., Lara, D., Lara, D., Andrea, S., Paolo, T., Giovanni, C., & PierAntonio, B. (2010). Analytical psychodrama with adolescents suffering from psycho behavioral disorder: Short-term effects on psychiatric symptoms. *The Arts in Psychotherapy, 37,* 240–247.

Gaushell, H., & Lawson, D. (1994, November). *Counselor trainee family-of-origin structure and current intergenerational family relationships: Implications for counselor training.* Paper presented at the Southern Association of Counselor Education and Supervision Convention, Charlotte, NC.

Gay, L. R., Mills, G. E., & Airasian, P. (2009). *Educational research* (9th ed.). Upper Saddle River, NJ: Merrill/Prentice Hall.

Gazda, G. M. (1989). *Group counseling: A developmental approach* (4th ed.). Boston: Allyn & Bacon.

Gazda, G. M., Ginter, E. J., & Horne, A. M. (2001). *Group counseling and group psychotherapy: Theory and application.* Boston: Allyn & Bacon.

Geertz, C. (1973). *The interpretation of cultures.* New York: Basic Books.

Geis, G. L., & Chapman, R. (1971). Knowledge of results and other possible reinforcers in self-instructional systems. *Educational Technology, 2,* 38–50.

Gelso, C. J. (1979). Research in counseling: Methodological and professional issues. *Counseling Psychologist, 8,* 7–36.

Gelso, C. J. (1985). Rigor, relevance, and counseling research: On the need to maintain our course between Scylla and Charybdis. *Journal of Counseling & Development, 63,* 551–553.

Gelso, C. J. (2011). *The real relationship in psychotherapy: The hidden foundation of change.* Washington, DC: American Psychological Association.

Gelso, C. J., & Carter, J. A. (1985). The relationship in counseling and psychotherapy: Components, consequences, and theoretical antecedents. *Counseling Psychologist, 13,* 155–243.

Gemignani, M., & Gliiberto, M. (2005). Counseling and psychotherapy in Italy: A profession in constant change. *Journal of Mental Health Counseling, 27,* 168–184.

Gerdes, H., & Mallinckrodt, B. (1994). Emotional, social, and academic adjustment of college students: A longitudinal study of retention. *Journal of Counseling & Development, 72,* 281–288.

Gerler, E. R. (1987). Classroom guidance for success in overseas schools. *International Quarterly, 5,* 18–22.

Gerler, E. R., & Anderson, R. F. (1986). The effects of classroom guidance on children's success in school. *Journal of Counseling & Development, 65,* 78–81.

Gerler, E. R., Drew, N. S., & Mohr, P. (1990). Succeeding in middle school: A multimodal approach. *Elementary School Guidance and Counseling, 24,* 263–271.

Gerler, E. R., Jr. (1985). Elementary school counseling research and the classroom learning environment. *Elementary School Guidance and Counseling, 20,* 39–48.

Geroski, A. M., Rodgers, K. A., & Breen, D. T. (1997). Using the DSM-IV to enhance collaboration among school counselors, clinical counselors, and primary care physicians. *Journal of Counseling & Development, 75,* 231–239.

Gertner, D. M. (1994). Understanding and serving the needs of men. *Counseling and Human Development, 27,* 1–16.

Gibbons, M. M., & Shoffner, M. F. (2004). Perspective first-generation college students: Meeting their needs through social cognitive career theory. *Professional School Counseling, 8,* 91–97.

Gibson, D. M., & Myers, J. E. (2000). Gender and infertility: A relational approach to counseling women. *Journal of Counseling & Development, 78,* 400–410.

Giles, T. A. (1983). Counseling services and men in need: A response to Burch and Skovholt. *AMHCA Journal, 5,* 39–43.

Gill, C. S., Barrio Minton, C. A., & Myers, J. E. (2010). Spirituality and religiosity: Factors affecting wellness among low-income, rural women. *Journal of Counseling & Development, 88,* 293–302.

Gillies, R. M. (1993). Action research in school counseling. *School Counselor, 41,* 69–72.

Gilligan, C. (1982). *In a different voice: Psychological theory and women's development.* Cambridge, MA: Harvard University Press.

Gill-Wigal, J., Heaton, J., Burke, J., & Gleason, J. (1988). When too much is too much.

Journal of College Student Development, 29, 274–275.

Ginter, E. J. (1989). Slayers of monster watermelons found in the mental health patch. *Journal of Mental Health Counseling, 11,* 77–85.

Ginter, E. J. (2002). *Journal of Counseling & Development* (JCD) and counseling's interwoven nature: Achieving a more complete understanding of the present through "historization" (Musings of an exiting editor—an editorial postscript). *Journal of Counseling & Development, 80,* 219–222.

Ginzberg, E. (1972). Toward a theory of occupational choice: A restatement. *Vocational Guidance Quarterly, 20,* 169–176.

Ginzberg, E., Ginsburg, S. W., Axelrad, S., & Herma, J. L. (1951). *Occupational choice.* New York: Columbia University Press.

Giordano, F. G., Schwiebert, V. L., & Brotherton, W. D. (1997). School counselors' perceptions of the usefulness of standardized test, frequency of their use, and assessment training needs. *School Counselor, 44,* 198–205.

Gladding, S. T. (1990a). Coming full cycle: Reentry after the group. *Journal for Specialists in Group Work, 15,* 130–131.

Gladding, S. T. (1990b). Let us not grow weary of theory. *Journal for Specialists in Group Work, 15,* 194.

Gladding, S. T. (1995). Humor in counseling: Using a natural resource. *Journal of Humanistic Education and Development, 34,* 3–12.

Gladding, S. T. (2005). *Counseling theories: Essential concepts and applications.* Upper Saddle River, NJ: Pearson Merrill Prentice Hall.

Gladding, S. T. (2009). *Becoming a counselor: The light, the bright, and the serious* (2nd ed.) Alexandria, VA: American Counseling Association.

Gladding, S. T. (2011). *The creative arts in counseling* (4th ed.). Alexandria, VA: American Counseling Association.

Gladding, S. T. (2012). *Groups: A counseling specialty* (6th ed.). Upper Saddle River, NJ: Merrill/Prentice Hall.

Gladding, S. T., & Gladding, C. (1991). The ABCs of bibliotherapy for school counselors. *School Counselor, 39,* 7–13.

Gladding, S. T., & Hood, W. D. (1974). Five cents, please. *School Counselor, 21,* 40–43.

Gladding, S. T., Lewis, E. L., & Adkins, L. (1981). Religious beliefs and positive mental health: The GLA scale and counseling. *Counseling and Values, 25,* 206–215.

Gladding, S. T., & Newsome, D. (2010). *Clinical mental health counseling in community and agency settings.* (3rd ed.). Upper Saddle River, NJ: Merrill/Prentice Hall.

Gladstein, G. A. (1983). Understanding empathy: Integrating counseling, developmental, and social psychology perspectives. *Journal of Counseling Psychology, 30,* 467–482.

Gladstein, G. A., & Apfel, F. S. (1987). A theoretically based adult career counseling center. *Career Development Quarterly, 36,* 178–185.

Glass, G. V. (1976). Primary, secondary, and meta-analyses of research. *Educational Researcher, 5,* 3–8.

Glasser, W. (1965). *Reality therapy: A new approach to psychiatry.* New York: Harper & Row.

Glasser, W. (1980). Reality therapy: An explanation of the steps of reality therapy. In W. Glasser (Ed.), *What are you doing? How people are helped through reality therapy.* New York: Harper & Row.

Glasser, W. (1981). *Stations of the mind.* New York: Harper & Row.

Glasser, W. (1984). *Control theory: A new explanation of how we control our lives.* New York: Harper & Row.

Glasser, W. (1988, November). *Reality therapy.* Workshop presented at the Alabama Association for Counseling and Development, Fall Conference, Birmingham.

Glasser, W. (1998). *Choice theory.* New York: HarperCollins.

Glasser, W. (2000). School violence from the perspective of William Glasser. *Professional School Counseling, 4,* 77–80.

Glasser, W. (2005, February). *Reality therapy today.* Presentation at the Wake Forest University Counseling Winter Forum. Winston-Salem, NC.

Glasser, W., & Wubbolding, R. (1995). Reality therapy. In R. Corsini & D. Wedding (Eds.), *Current psychotherapies* (5th ed., pp. 293–321). Itasca, IL: F. E. Peacock.

Glauser, A. S., & Bozarth, J. D. (2001). Person-centered counseling: The culture within. *Journal of Counseling & Development, 79,* 142–147.

Gloria, A. M., & Kurpius Robinson, S. E. (2000). I can't live without it: Adolescent substance abuse from a cultural and contextual framework. In D. Capuzzi & D. R. Gross (Eds.), *Youth at risk* (3rd ed., pp. 409–439). Alexandria, VA: American Counseling Association.

Gloria, A. M., & Rodriguez, E. R. (2000). Counseling Latino university students: Psychosociocultural issues for consideration. *Journal of Counseling & Development, 78,* 145–154.

Gloria, A. M., Castellanos, J., Park, Y. S., & Kim, D. (2008). Adherence to Asian cultural values and cultural fit in Korean American undergraduates' help-seeking attitudes. *Journal of Counseling & Development, 86*(4), 419–428.

Glosoff, H. L., Herlihy, B., & Spence, E. B. (2000). Privileged communication in the counselor-client relationship.

Glosoff, H. L., & Koprowicz, C. L. (1990). *Children achieving potential.* Alexandria, VA: American Counseling Association.

Goetz, B. (1998, May 27). *An inside/outsider's view of the counseling profession today.* Paper presented at the Chi Sigma Iota Invitational Counselor Advocacy Conference, Greensboro, NC.

Gold, J. (2009). Assessment terminology in counseling. In B. Erford (Ed.), *ACA Encyclopedia of Counseling* (pp. 39–40). Alexandria, VA: American Counseling Association.

Gold, J., & Pitariu, G. V. (2004). Opening the eyes of counselors to the emotional abuse of men: An overlooked dynamic in dysfunctional families. *Journal of Humanistic Counseling, Education and Development, 43,* 178–187.

Gold, L. (1979). Adler's theory of dreams: An holistic approach to interpretation. In B. B. Wolman (Ed.), *Handbook of dreams: Research, theories, and applications.* New York: Van Nostrand Reinhold.

Goldberg, C. (1975). Termination: A meaningful pseudo-dilemma in psychotherapy. *Psychotherapy, 12,* 341–343.

Golden, L. (2009). *Case studies in counseling older adults.* Upper Saddle River, NJ: Prentice Hall.

Goldenberg, H., & Goldenberg, I. (2002). *Counseling today's family* (4th ed.). Pacific Grove, CA: Brooks/Cole.

Goldiamond, I. (1976). Self-reinforcement. *Journal of Applied Behavior Analysis, 9,* 509–514.

Goldin, E., & Bordan, T. (1999). The use of humor in counseling: The laughing cure. *Journal of Counseling & Development, 77,* 405–410.

Goldin, E., Bordan, T., Araoz, D. L., Gladding, S. T., Kaplan, D., Krumboltz, J., et al. (2006). Humor in counseling: Leader

Journal of Counseling & Development, 78, 454–462.

perpectives. *Journal of Counseling & Development, 84,* 397–404.

Goldman, L. (1971). *Using tests in counseling* (2nd ed.). New York: Appleton-Century-Crofts.

Goldman, L. (1972a). Introduction. *Personnel and Guidance Journal, 51,* 85.

Goldman, L. (1972b). Tests and counseling: The marriage that failed. *Measurement and Evaluation in Guidance, 4,* 213–220.

Goldman, L. G. (1976). A revolution in counseling research. *Journal of Counseling Psychology, 23,* 543–552.

Goldman, L. G. (1977). Toward more meaningful research. *Personnel and Guidance Journal, 55,* 363–368.

Goldman, L. G. (1978). Science, research, and practice: Confusing the issues. *Personnel and Guidance Journal, 56,* 641–642.

Goldman, L. G. (1979). Research is more than technology. *Counseling Psychologist, 8,* 41–44.

Goldman, L. G. (1986). Research and evaluation. In M. D. Lewis, R. L. Hayes, & J. A. Lewis (Eds.), *The counseling profession* (pp. 278–300). Itasca, IL: F. E. Peacock.

Goldman, L. G. (1992). Qualitative assessment: An approach for counselors. *Journal of Counseling & Development, 70,* 616–621.

Goldman, L. (1994a). The marriage between tests and counseling redux: Summary of the 1972 article. *Measurement and Evaluation in Counseling and Development, 26,* 214–216.

Goldman, L. (1994b). The marriage is over . . . for most of us. *Measurement and Evaluation in Counseling and Development, 26,* 217–218.

Goldstein, A. (1971). *Psychotherapeutic attraction.* New York: Pergamon.

Goldstein, A. P. (1973). *Structural learning therapy: Toward a psychotherapy for the poor*. New York: Academic Press.

Gonzalez, G. M. (1997). The emergence of Chicanos in the twenty-first century: Implications for counseling, research, and policy. *Journal of Multicultural Counseling and Development, 25,* 94–106.

Goodman, A. (2001). What's in a name? Terminology for designating a syndrome of driven sexual behavior. *Sexual Addiction & Compulsivity, 8,* 191–213.

Goodman, J. (2009). Starfish, salmon, and whales: An introduction to the special section. *Journal of Counseling & Development, 87,* 259.

Goodman, J., Schlossberg, N. K., & Anderson, M. L. (2006). *Counseling adults in transition: Linking practice with theory* (3rd ed.). New York: Springer.

Goodman, R. D., & West-Olatunji, C. (2008). Transgenerational trauma and resilience: Improving mental health counseling for survivors of Hurricane Katrina. *Journal of Mental Health Counseling, 30,* 121–136.

Goodnough, G. E., & Ripley, V. (1997). Structured groups for high school seniors making the transition to college and to military service. *School Counselor, 44,* 230–234.

Goodyear, R. K. (1976). Counselors as community psychologists. *Personnel and Guidance Journal, 54,* 512–516.

Goodyear, R. K. (1981). Termination as a loss experience for the counselor. *Personnel and Guidance Journal, 59,* 349–350.

Goodyear, R. K. (1984). On our journal's evolution: Historical developments, transitions, and future directions. *Journal of Counseling & Development, 63,* 3–9.

Goodyear, R. K. (1987). In memory of Carl Ransom Rogers. *Journal of Counseling & Development, 65,* 523–524.

Goodyear, R. K., & Bradley, F. O. (1980). The helping process as contractual. *Personnel and Guidance Journal, 58,* 512–515.

Goodyear, R. K., & Watkins, C. E., Jr. (1983). C. H. Patterson: The counselor's counselor. *Personnel and Guidance Journal, 61,* 592–597.

Gottfredson, L., & Saklofske, D. H. (2009). Intelligence: Foundations and issues in assessment. *Canadian Psychology/Psychologie Canadienne, 50*(3), 183–195.

Gottfredson, L. S. (1981). Circumscription and compromise: A developmental theory of occupational aspirations. *Journal of Counseling Psychology, 28,* 545–579.

Gottfredson, L. S. (2005). Applying Gottfredson's theory of circumscription and compromise in career guidance and counseling. In S. D. Brown & R. W. Lent (Eds.), *Career development and counseling: Putting theory and research to work* (pp. 71–100). Hoboken, NJ: Wiley.

Granello, D. H. (2004). Assisting beginning counselors in becoming gay affirmative: A workshop approach. *Journal of Humanistic Counseling, Education and Development, 43,* 50–64.

Granello, D. (2010a). Cognitive complexity among practicing counselors: How thinking changes with experience. *Journal of Counseling & Development, 88,* 92–100.

Granello, D. (2010b). The process of suicide risk assessment: Twelve core principles. *Journal of Counseling & Development, 88,* 363–371.

Granello, P. (2012). *Wellness counseling*. Upper Saddle River, NJ: Pearson.

Granello, P., & Juhnke, G. A. (2009). *Case studies in suicide: Experiences of mental health professionals*. Upper Saddle River, NJ: Prentice Hall.

Grant, B. (1992). The moral nature of psychotherapy. In M. T. Burke & J. G. Miranti (Eds.), *Ethical and spiritual values in counseling* (pp. 27–35). Alexandria, VA: American Counseling Association.

Green, A., & Keys, S. G. (2001). Expanding the developmental school counseling paradigm: Meeting the needs of the 21st century student. *Professional School Counseling, 5,* 84–95.

Greene, G. J., Hamilton, N., & Rolling, M. (1986). Differentiation of self and psychiatric dialogue: An empirical study. *Family Therapy, 8,* 187–194.

Greene, M. (2006). Helping build lives: Career and life development of gifted and talented students. *Professional School Counseling, 10*(1), 34–42.

Greenstone, M., & Looney, A. (2011, June 19). Women in the workforce: Is wage stagnation catching up with them too? Brookings Institute, Up Front Block, http://www.brookings .edu/opinions/2011/0401_ jobs_greenstone_looney .aspx

Griswold, K. S., Aronoff, H., Kernan, J. B., & Kahn, L. S. (2008). Adolescent substance use and abuse: Recognition and management. *American Family Physician, 77*(3), 331–336.

Grites, T. J. (1979). Between high school counselor and college advisor: A void. *Personnel and Guidance Journal, 58,* 200–204.

Grosch, W. N., & Olsen, D. C. (1994). *When helping starts to hurt*. New York: Norton.

Grosse, S. J. (2002). Children and post traumatic stress disorder: What classroom teachers should know. In G. R. Walz & C. J. Kirkman (Eds.), *Helping people cope with tragedy and grief* (pp. 23–27). Greensboro, NC: ERIC & NBCC.

Groth-Marnat, G. (2010). *Handbook of psychological assessment* (5th ed.). New York: Wiley.

Guerney, L. (1983). Client-centered (nondirective) play therapy. In C. E. Schaeffer & K. J. O'Connor (Eds.), *Handbook of play therapy* (pp. 21–64). New York: Wiley.

Guerra, P. (1998, January). Advocating for school counseling. *Counseling Today, 20.*

Guiffrida, D. A., & Douthit, K. Z. (2010). The Black student experience at predominantly White colleges: Implications for school and college counselors. *Journal of Counseling & Development, 88,* 311–318.

Guindon, M. H., & Hanna, F. J. (2002). Coincidence, happenstance, serendipity, fate, or the hand of God: Case studies in synchronicity. *Career Development Quarterly, 50,* 195–208.

Gumaer, J., & Scott, L. (1985). Training group leaders in ethical decision making. *Journal for Specialists in Group Work, 10,* 198–204.

Gummere, R. M., Jr. (1988). The counselor as prophet: Frank Parsons, 1854–1908. *Journal of Counseling & Development, 66,* 402–405.

Gurman, A., & Kniskern, D. (1981). Family therapy outcome research: Knowns and unknowns. In A. Gurman & D. Kniskern (Eds.), *Handbook of family therapy* (pp. 742–775). New York: Brunner/Mazel.

Gurman, A. S. (Ed.). (2008). *Clinical handbook of couple therapy* (4th ed.). New York: Guilford.

Guy, J. D. (1987). *The personal life of the psychotherapist*. New York: Wiley.

Gysbers, N. C. (2001). School guidance and counseling in the 21st century: Remember the past into the future. *Professional School Counseling, 5,* 96–105.

Gysbers, N. C. (2011). *School Counseling Principles: Remembering the Past, Shaping the Future, A History of School Counseling*. Alexandria, VA: American School Counseling Association.

Gysbers, N. C., & Guidance Program Field Writers. (1990).

Comprehensive guidance programs that work. Ann Arbor, MI: ERIC/CAPS.

Gysbers, N. C., & Henderson, P. (2006b). *Developing and managing your school guidance and counseling program* (4th ed). Alexandria, VA: American Counseling Association.

Gysbers, N. C., Heppner, J. A., & Johnstone, J. A. (2003). *Career counseling: Process, issues, & techniques* (2nd ed.). Boston: Allyn & Bacon.

Haase, R. F. (1970). The relationship of sex and instructional set to the regulation of interpersonal interaction distance in a counseling analogue. *Journal of Counseling Psychology, 17,* 233–236.

Haase, R. F., & DiMattia, D. J. (1976). Spatial environments and verbal conditioning in a quasi-counseling interview. *Journal of Counseling Psychology, 23,* 414–421.

Haber, R. A. (1983). The family dance around drug abuse. *Personnel and Guidance Journal, 61,* 428–430.

Haberstroh, S., Duffey, T., Evans, M., Gee, R., & Trepal, H. (2007). The experience of online counseling. *Journal of Mental Health Counseling, 29,* 269–282.

Haberstroh, S., Parr, G., Bradley, L., Morgan-Fleming, B., & Gee, R. (2008). Facilitating online counseling: Perspectives from counselors in training. *Journal of Counseling & Development, 86,* 460–470.

Hackler, A., Vogel, D. L., & Wade, N. G. (2010). Attitudes toward seeking professional help for an eating disorder: The role of stigma and anticipated outcomes. *Journal of Counseling & Development, 88,* 424–431.

Hackney, H. (1978). The evolution of empathy. *Personnel and Guidance Journal, 57,* 35–38.

Hadley, R. G., & Mitchell, L. K. (1995). *Counseling research and program evaluation*. Pacific Grove, CA: Brooks/Cole.

Hage, S. M. (2006). Profiles of women survivors: The development of agency in abusive relationships. *Journal of Counseling & Development, 84,* 83–94.

Hagedorm, W. B. & Young, T. (2011). Identifying and intervening with students exhibiting signs of gaming addiction and other addictive behaviors: Implications for professional school counselors. *Professional School Counseling, 14,* 250–260.

Haggard-Grann, U. (2007). Assessing violence risk: A review and clinical recommendation. *Journal of Counseling & Development, 85,* 294–301.

Hall, A. S., & Torres, I. (2002). Partnerships in preventing adolescent stress: Increasing self-esteem, coping, and support through effective counseling. *Journal of Mental Health Counseling, 24,* 97–109.

Hall, C. S. (1954). *A primer of Freudian psychology*. New York: New American Library.

Hamachek, D. E. (1988). Evaluating self-concept and ego development within Erikson's psychosocial framework: A formulation. *Journal of Counseling & Development, 66,* 354–360.

Hamann, E. E. (1994). Clinicians and diagnosis: Ethical concerns and clinical competence. *Journal of Counseling & Development, 72,* 259–260.

Hammel, J. (Ed.) (2008). *Intimate partner and family abuse: A casebook of gender-inclusive therapy*. New York: Springer.

Hammerschlag, C. A. (1988). *The dancing healers*. San Francisco: Harper & Row.

Hanna, C. A., Hanna, F. J., Giordano, F. G., & Tollerud, T. (1998). Meeting the needs of women in counseling: Implications of a review of the literature. *Journal of Humanistic Education and Development, 36,* 160–170.

Hanna, G. S. (1988). Using percentile bands for meaningful

descriptive test score interpretations. *Journal of Counseling & Development, 66,* 477–483.

Hansen, J. C., & Prather, F. (1980). The impact of values and attitudes in counseling the aged. *Counseling and Values, 24,* 74–85.

Hansen, J. C., Rossberg, R. H., & Cramer, S. H. (1994). *Counseling: Theory and process* (5th ed.). Boston: Allyn & Bacon.

Hansen, J. C., Stevic, R. R., & Warner, R. W. (1986). *Counseling: Theory and process* (4th ed.). Boston: Allyn & Bacon.

Hansen, J. C., Warner, R. W., & Smith, E. J. (1980). *Group counseling* (2nd ed.). Chicago: Rand McNally.

Hansen, J-I. C. (1994). Multiculturalism in assessment. *Measurement and Evaluation in Counseling and Development, 27,* 67.

Hansen, J. T. (1998). Do mental health counselors require training in the treatment of mentally disordered clients? A challenge to the conclusions of Vacc, Loesch, and Guilbert. *Journal of Mental Health Counseling, 20,* 183–188.

Hansen, J. T. (2006). Counseling theories within a postmodernist epistemology: New roles for theories in counseling practice. *Journal of Counseling & Development, 84,* 291–297.

Hansen, J. T. (2009). Self-awareness revisited: Reconsidering a core value of the counseling profession. *Journal of Counseling & Development, 87*(2), 186–193.

Hansen, J. T. (2010). Consequences of the postmodernist vision: Diversity as the guiding value for the counseling profession. *Journal of Counseling & Development, 88,* 101–107.

Hanson, P. (1972). What to look for in groups: An observation guide. In J. Pfeiffer & J. Jones (Eds.), *The 1972 annual handbook for group*

facilitators (pp. 21–24). San Diego: Pfeiffer.

Hanson, W. E., & Claiborn, C. D. (2006). Effects of test interpretation style and favorability in the counseling process. *Journal of Counseling & Development, 84,* 349–357.

Harding, A. K., Gray, L. A., & Neal, M. (1993). Confidentiality limits with clients who have HIV: A review of ethical and legal guidelines and professional policies. *Journal of Counseling & Development, 71,* 297–304.

Hardoon, K. K., & Derevensky, J. L. (2002). Child and adolescent gambling behavior: Current knowledge. *Clinical Child Psychology and Psychiatry, 7,* 263–281.

Hare-Mustin, R. T. (1983). An appraisal of the relationship between women and psychotherapy. *American Psychologist, 38,* 593–599.

Harman, R. L. (1977). Beyond techniques. *Counselor Education and Supervision, 17,* 157–158.

Harman, R. L. (1997). *Gestalt therapy techniques: Working with groups, couples, and sexually dysfunctional men*. Northvale, NJ: Aronson.

Harold, M. (1985). Council's history examined after 50 years. *Guidepost, 27*(10), 4.

Harper, F. D. (1994). Afrinesians of the Americas: A new concept of ethnic identity. *Journal of Multicultural Counseling and Development, 22,* 3–6.

Harris, A. H. S., Thoresen, C. E., & Lopez, S. J. (2007). Integrating positive psychology into counseling: Why and (when appropriate) how. *Journal of Counseling & Development, 85,* 3–13.

Harris, F. (1994, April). Everyday ethics. *ACCA Visions, 2,* 7–8, 10.

Harris, S. M., & Busby, D. M. (1998). Therapist physical attractiveness: An unexplored influence on client disclosure. *Journal of Marital and Family Therapy, 24,* 251–257.

Harris-Bowlsbey, J. (1992, December). Building blocks of computer-based career planning systems. *CAPS Digest,* EDO-CG-92-7.

Harris-Bowlsbey, J., Dikel, M. R., & Sampson, J. P. (Eds.). (2002). *The Internet: A tool for career planning* (2nd ed.). Alexandria, VA: American Counseling Association.

Hartung, P. J., & Blustein, D. L. (2002). Reason, intuition, and social justice: Elaborating on Parsons' career decision-making model. *Journal of Counseling & Development, 80,* 41–47.

Hashimi, J. (1991). Counseling older adults. In P. K. H. Kim (Ed.), *Serving the elderly: Skills for practice* (pp. 33–51). New York: Aldine de Gruyter.

Hatcher, C., & Himelsteint, P. (Eds.). (1997). *The handbook of Gestalt therapy.* Northvale, NJ: Aronson.

Havighurst, R. J. (1959). Social and psychological needs of the aging. In L. Gorlow & W. Katkovsky (Eds.), *Reading in the psychology of adjustment* (pp. 443–447). New York: McGraw-Hill.

Hawes, D. J. (1989). Communication between teachers and children: A counselor consultant/trainer model. *Elementary School Guidance and Counseling, 24,* 58–67.

Hay, C. E., & Kinnier, R. T. (1998). Homework in counseling. *Journal of Mental Health Counseling, 20,* 122–132.

Hayes, J. A., Gelso, C. J., & Hummel, A. M. (2011). Managing countertransference. *Psychotherapy, 48*(1), 88–97.

Hayes, P. A. (1996). Addressing the complexities of culture and gender in counseling. *Journal of Counseling & Development, 74,* 332–338.

Hayes, R. L. (1981). High school graduation: The case for identity loss. *Personnel and Guidance Journal, 59,* 369–371.

Hayes, R. L. (1993). Life, death, and reconstructive self. *Journal of Humanistic Education and Development, 32,* 85–88.

Hayman, P. M., & Covert, J. A. (1986). Ethical dilemmas in college counseling centers. *Journal of Counseling & Development, 64,* 318–320.

Hays, D. G. (2008). Assessing multicultural competence in counselor trainees: A review of instrumentation and future directions. *Journal of Counseling & Development, 86,* 95–101.

Hays, D. G., Prosek, E. A., & McLeod, A. L. (2010). A mixed methodological analysis of the role of culture in the clinical decision-making process. *Journal of Counseling & Development, 88*(1), 114–121.

Health Providers Service Organization (HPSO). (February 24, 2011). Documentation: An important step in avoiding malpractice. *HPSO Newsletter.* Hatboro, PA: Author.

Healy, C. C., & Woodward, G. A. (1998). The Myers-Briggs Type Indicator and career obstacles. *Measurement and Evaluation in Counseling and Development, 31,* 74–85.

Heath, D. H. (1980). Wanted: A comprehensive model of healthy development. *Personnel and Guidance Journal, 58,* 391–399.

Heinrich, R. K., Corbin, J. L., & Thomas, K. R. (1990). Counseling Native Americans. *Journal of Counseling & Development, 69,* 128–133.

Helwig, A. (2002, Summer). New Orleans workshop highlights. *NECA Newsletter, 2.*

Henderson, D. A. (2007). School counseling. In R. R. Cottone & V. M. Tarvydas, *Ethical and professional issues in counseling* (3rd ed., pp. 241–267). Upper Saddle River, NJ: Prentice Hall.

Henderson, D. A., & Thompson, C. D. (2011). *Counseling children* (8th ed.). Belmont, CA: Thomson Brooks/Cole.

Henderson, S. J. (2000). "Follow your bliss": A process for career happiness. *Journal of Counseling & Development, 78,* 305–315.

Hendrick, S. S. (1988). Counselor self-disclosure. *Journal of Counseling & Development, 66,* 419–424.

Henkin, W. A. (1985). Toward counseling the Japanese in America: A cross-cultural primer. *Journal of Counseling & Development, 63,* 500–503.

Heppner, P. P. (1990a). Life lines: Institutional perspectives [Feature editor's introduction]. *Journal of Counseling & Development, 68,* 246.

Heppner, P. P. (1990b). *Pioneers in counseling and development: Personal and professional perspectives.* Alexandria, VA: American Counseling Association.

Heppner, P. P., & Anderson, W. P. (1985). On the perceived nonutility of research in counseling. *Journal of Counseling & Development, 63,* 545–547.

Heppner, P. P., Wampold, B. E., & Kivlighan, D. M., Jr. (2008). *Research design in counseling* (3rd ed). Belmont, CA: Thomson Brooks/Cole.

Herlihy, B. (1996). When a colleague is impaired: The individual counselor's response. *Journal of Humanistic Education and Development, 34,* 118–127.

Herlihy, B., & Corey, C. (2006). *ACA ethical standards casebook* (6th ed.). Alexandria, VA: American Counseling Association.

Herlihy, B., & Sheeley, V. L. (1987). Privileged communication in selected helping professions: A comparison among statutes. *Journal of Counseling & Development, 64,* 479–483.

Herman, K. C. (1993). Reassessing predictors of therapist competence. *Journal of Counseling & Development, 72,* 29–32.

Herman, W. E. (1997). Values acquisition: Some critical distinctions and implications. *Journal of Humanistic Education and Development, 35,* 146–155.

Hermann, M. A., & Herlihy, B. R. (2006). Legal and ethical implications of refusing to counsel homosexual clients. *Journal of Counseling & Development, 84,* 414–418.

Hermann, M. A. (2011a, April 29). *Legal and ethical issues in counseling, Session 1.* Winston-Salem, North Carolina.

Hermann, M. A. (2011b, April 29). *Legal and ethical issues in counseling, Session 2.* Winston-Salem, North Carolina.

Hermann, M. A. (2011c, Winter). Protect yourself, protect your students. *VSCA Voice,* 9–10.

Herr, E. L. (1985). AACD: An association committed to unity through diversity. *Journal of Counseling & Development, 63,* 395–404.

Herr, E. L. (1997). Super's life-span, life-space and its outlook for refinement. *Career Development Quarterly, 45,* 238–246.

Herr, E. L. (2002). School reform and perspectives on the role of school counselors: A century of proposals for change. *Professional School Counseling, 5,* 220–234.

Herr, E. L., Cramer, S. H., & Niles, S. G. (2004). *Career guidance and counseling through the lifespan: Systematic approaches* (6th ed.). Boston: Allyn & Bacon.

Herr, E. L., & Fabian, E. S. (1993). The *Journal of Counseling & Development:* Its legacy and its aspirations. *Journal of Counseling & Development, 72,* 3–4.

Herring, R. D. (1996). Synergetic counseling and Native American Indian students. *Journal of Counseling & Development, 74,* 542–547.

Herring, R. D. (1997). The creative arts: An avenue to wellness among Native American Indians. *Journal of Humanistic Education and Development, 36,* 106–113.

Herring, R. D., & White, L. M. (1995). School counselors,

teachers, and the culturally compatible classroom: Partnerships in multicultural education. *Journal of Humanistic Education and Development, 34,* 52–64.

Hershenson, D. B. (1982). A formulation of counseling based on the healthy personality. *Personnel and Guidance Journal, 60,* 406–409.

Hershenson, D. B. (1992a). A genuine copy of a fake Dior: Mental health counseling's pursuit of pathology. *Journal of Mental Health Counseling, 14,* 419–421.

Hershenson, D. B. (1996). A systems reformulation of a developmental model of work adjustment. *Rehabilitation Counseling Bulletin, 40,* 2–10.

Hershenson, D. B., & Berger, G. P. (2001). The state of community counseling: A survey of directors of CACREP-accredited programs. *Journal of Counseling & Development, 79,* 188–193.

Hershenson, D. B., Power, P. W., & Seligman, L. (1989). Mental health counseling theory: Present status and future prospects. *Journal of Mental Health Counseling, 11,* 44–69.

Hetherington, C., Hillerbrand, E., & Etringer, B. D. (1989). Career counseling with gay men: Issues and recommendations for research. *Journal of Counseling & Development, 67,* 452–453.

Hetzel, R. D., Barton, D. A., & Davenport, D. S. (1994). Helping men change: A group counseling model for male clients. *Journal for Specialists in Group Work, 19,* 52–64.

Hill, C. (2009). *Helping skills: Facilitating exploration, insight, and action* (3rd ed.). Washington, DC: American Psychological Association.

Hill, C. E. (1982). Counseling process research: Philosophical and methodological dilemmas. *Counseling Psychologist, 10,* 7–19.

Hill, C. E. (1991). Almost everything you ever wanted to know about how to do process research on counseling and psychotherapy but didn't know who to ask. In C. E. Watkins, Jr., & L. J. Schneider (Eds.), *Research in counseling* (pp. 85–118). Hillsdale, NJ: Erlbaum.

Hill, C. E., Carter, J. A., & O'Farrell, M. K. (1983). A case study of the process and outcomes of time-limited counseling. *Journal of Counseling Psychology, 30,* 3–18.

Hill, C. L., & Ridley, C. R. (2001). Diagnostic decision making: Do counselors delay final judgment? *Journal of Counseling & Development, 79,* 98–104.

Hill, N. R. (2007). Wilderness therapy as a treatment modality for at-risk youth: A primer for mental health counselors. *Journal of Mental Health Counseling, 29,* 338–349.

Hilts, P. J. (1996). *Smokescreen: The truth behind the tobacco industry cover-up.* Reading, MA: Addison-Wesley.

Hines, M. (1988). Similarities and differences in group and family therapy. *Journal for Specialists in Group Work, 13,* 173–179.

Hinkelman, J. M., & Luzzo, D. A. (2007). Mental health and career development of college students. *Journal of Counseling & Development, 85,* 143–147.

Hinkle, J. S. (1994b, September). *Psychodiagnosis and treatment planning under the DSM-IV.* Workshop presentation of the North Carolina Counseling Association, Greensboro, NC.

Hinkle, J. S. (1999). A voice from the trenches: A reaction to Ivey and Ivey (1998). *Journal of Counseling & Development, 77,* 474–483.

Hinson, J. A., & Swanson, J. L. (1993). Willingness to seek help as a function of self-disclosure and problem severity. *Journal of Counseling & Development, 71,* 465–470.

Hinson, W. R. (2010, November/December). A look at addiction and ethnicity. *Family Therapy, 9*(6), 20–23.

Hinterkopf, E. (1998). *Integrating spirituality in counseling: A manual for using the experiential focusing method.* Alexandria, VA: American Counseling Association.

Hipple, T., Comer, M., & Boren, D. (1997). Twenty recent novels (and more) about adolescents for bibliotherapy. *Professional School Counseling, 1,* 65–67.

Hitchcock, A. A. (1984). Work, aging, and counseling. *Journal of Counseling & Development, 63,* 258–259.

Hobson, S. M., & Kanitz, H. M. (1996). Multicultural counseling: An ethical issue for school counselors. *School Counselor, 43,* 245–255.

Hoffman, R. M. (2006). Gender self-definition and gender self-acceptance in women: Intersections with feminist, womanist, and ethnic identities. *Journal of Counseling & Development, 84,* 358–372.

Hogan, T. P. (2007). *Psychological testing: A practical introduction* (2nd ed). New York: Wiley.

Hohenshil, T. H. (1993). Assessment and diagnosis in the *Journal of Counseling & Development. Journal of Counseling & Development, 72,* 7.

Hohenshil, T. H. (1996). Role of assessment and diagnosis in counseling. *Journal of Counseling & Development, 75,* 64–67.

Hohenshil, T. H. (2000). High tech counseling. *Journal of Counseling & Development, 78,* 365–368.

Hohenshil, T. H., & Hohenshil, S. B. (1989). Preschool counseling. *Journal of Counseling & Development, 67,* 430–431.

Holcomb-McCoy, C., & Bryan, J. (2010). Advocacy and Empowerment in Parent Consultation: Implications for Theory and Practice. *Journal of Counseling & Development, 88,* 259–268.

Holden, J. (1993). *Behavioral consequences on behavior.* Unpublished manuscript, University of North Texas, Denton.

Holden, J. (2001). Cognitive-behavioral counseling. In D. C. Locke, J. E. Myers, & E. L. Herr (Eds.), *The handbook of counseling* (pp. 131–150). Thousand Oaks, CA: Sage.

Holiday, M., Leach, M. M., & Davidson, M. (1994). Multicultural counseling and intrapersonal value conflict: A case study. *Counseling and Values, 38,* 136–142.

Holland, J. L. (1994). *Self-directed search.* Odessa, FL: Psychological Assessment Resources.

Holland, J. L. (1997). *Making vocational choices: A theory of vocational preferences and work environments* (3rd ed.). Odessa, FL: Psychological Assessment Resources.

Holland, J. L., & Gottfredson, G. D. (1976). Using a typology of persons and environments to explain careers: Some extensions and clarifications. *Counseling Psychologist, 6,* 20–29.

Hollander, S. K. (1989). Coping with child sexual abuse through children's books. *Elementary School Guidance and Counseling, 23,* 183–193.

Hollis, J. W. (1997). *Counselor preparation 1996–1998* (9th ed.). Muncie, IN: Accelerated Development.

Hollis, J. W. (2000). *Counselor preparation 1999–2001: Programs, faculty, trends* (10th ed.). Philadelphia: Taylor & Francis.

Holmes, T. H., & Rahe, R. H. (1967). The social readjustment rating scale. *Journal of Psychosomatic Research, 11,* 213–218.

Hood, A. B., & Johnson, R. W. (2007). *Assessment in counseling* (4th ed.). Alexandria, VA: American Counseling Association.

Horne, A. M. (2000). *Family counseling and therapy* (3rd ed.). Itasca, IL: F. E. Peacock.

Horne, A. M., & Mason, J. (1991, August). *Counseling men.* Paper presented at the Annual Convention of the American Psychological Association, San Francisco.

Hosie, T. W. (1994). Program evaluation: A potential area of expertise for counselors. *Counselor Education and Supervision, 33,* 349–355.

House, R. M., & Hayes, R. L. (2002). School counselors: Becoming key players in school reform. *Professional School Counseling, 5,* 249–256.

House, R. M., & Miller, J. L. (1997). Counseling gay, lesbian, and bisexual clients. In D. Capuzzi & D. R. Gross (Eds.), *Introduction to the counseling profession* (2nd ed., pp. 397–432). Boston: Allyn & Bacon.

Howard, G. S. (1985). Can research in the human sciences become more relevant to practice? *Journal of Counseling & Development, 63,* 539–544.

Hoyt, K. B. (1989). Policy implications of selected data from adult employed workers in the 1987 Gallup Career Development Survey. In D. Brown & C. W. Minor (Eds.), *Working in America: A status report on planning and problems* (pp. 6–24). Alexandria, VA: National Career Development Association.

Hoyt, K. B. (1994). Youth apprenticeship "American style" and career development. *Career Development Quarterly, 42,* 216–223.

Hoyt, K. B. (2005). *Career education: History and future.* Broken Arrow, OK: National Career Development Association.

Hubble, M. A., & Gelso, C. J. (1978). Effects of counselor attire in an initial interview. *Journal of Counseling Psychology, 25,* 581–584.

Huber, C. H. (1979). Parents of the handicapped child: Facilitating acceptance through group counseling. *Personnel and Guidance Journal, 57,* 267–269.

Huber, C. H. (1980). Research and the school counselor. *School Counselor, 27,* 210–216.

Huber, C. H. (1989). Paradox-orthodox: Brief pastoral psychotherapy. *Individual Psychology, 45,* 230–237.

Hudson, P. (1998, April/May). Spirituality: A growing resource. *Family Therapy News, 29*(2), 10–11.

Huey, W. C. (1986). Ethical concerns in school counseling. *Journal of Counseling & Development, 64,* 321–322.

Huffman, S. B., & Myers, J. E. (1999). Counseling women in midlife: An integrative approach to menopause. *Journal of Counseling & Development, 77,* 258–266.

Hughey, K. F., & Akos, P. (2005). Foreword: Developmentally responsive middle school counseling. *Professional School Counseling, 9,* 93–103.

Hulse-Killacky, D. (1993). Personal and professional endings. *Journal of Humanistic Education and Development, 32,* 92–94.

Hulse-Killacky, D., Killacky, J., & Donigian, J. (2001). *Making task groups work in your world.* Upper Saddle River, NJ: Prentice Hall.

Humes, C. W., II. (1972). Accountability: A boon to guidance. *Personnel and Guidance Journal, 51,* 21–26.

Humes, C. W., II. (1978). School counselors and P.L. 94–142. *School Counselor, 25,* 192–195.

Hummell, D. L., Talbutt, L. C., & Alexander, M. D. (1985). *Law and ethics in counseling.* New York: Van Nostrand Reinhold.

Hunt, B., Matthews, C., Milsom, A., & Lammel, J. A. (2006). Lesbians with physical disabilities: A qualitative study of their experiences with counseling. *Journal of Counseling & Development, 84,* 163–173.

Hunter, S. V. (2006). Understanding the complexity of child sexual abuse: A review of the literature with implications for family counseling. *The Family Journal: Counseling and Therapy for Couples and Families, 14,* 349–358.

Husband, R., & Foster, W. (1987). Understanding qualitative research: A strategic approach to qualitative methodology. *Journal of Humanistic Education and Development, 26,* 50–63.

Huskey, H. H. (1994, April). Counseling the senior student. *Visions, 2,* 10–11.

Hutchins, D. E., & Vaught, C. G. (1997). *Helping relationships and strategies* (3rd ed.). Pacific Grove, CA: Brooks/Cole.

Hutchins, J. (1995, December). Barrett calls for MFT mediation for false memory families. *Family Therapy News, 26,* 21.

Hutchins, R. M. (1936). *The higher learning in America.* New Haven, CT: Yale University Press.

Hyde, C., Bentovim, A., & Monck, E. (1995). Some clinical and methodological implications of a treatment outcome study of sexually abused children. *Child Abuse and Neglect, 19,* 1387–1399.

Imbimbo, P. V. (1994). Integrating personal and career counseling: A challenge for counselors. *Journal of Employment Counseling, 31,* 50–59.

Ingersoll, R. E. (1994). Spirituality, religion, and counseling: Dimensions and relationships. *Counseling and Values, 38,* 98–111.

Israelashvili, M. (1998). Preventive school counseling: A stress inoculation perspective. *Professional School Counseling, 1,* 21–25.

Ivey, A. E. (1971). *Microcounseling.* Springfield, IL: Thomas.

Ivey, A. E. (1980). *Counseling and psychotherapy: Skills, theories, and practice.* Upper Saddle River, NJ: Prentice Hall.

Ivey, A. E. (1989). Mental health counseling: A developmental process and profession. *Journal of Mental Health Counseling, 11,* 26–35.

Ivey, A. E. (1990). Prejudice in the profession. *Guidepost, 33*(6), 2.

Ivey, A. E., & Goncalves, O. F. (1988). Developmental therapy: Integrating developmental processes into the clinical practice. *Journal of Counseling & Development, 66,* 406–413.

Ivey, A. E., & Ivey, M. B. (1990). Assessing and facilitating children's cognitive development: Developmental counseling and therapy in a case of child abuse. *Journal of Counseling & Development, 68,* 299–305.

Ivey, A. E., Ivey, M. B., & Zalaquett, C. P. (2010). *Intentional interviewing and counseling* (7th ed.). Belmont, CA: Brooks/Cole.

Ivey, A. E., Ivey, M. B., Myers, J. E., & Sweeney, T. J. (2005). *Developmental counseling and therapy: Promoting wellness over the lifespan.* Boston: Houghton Mifflin.

Iwasaki, M. (2005). Mental health and counseling in Japan: A path toward societal transformation. *Journal of Mental Health Counseling, 27,* 129–141.

Jackson, A. P., & Scharman, J. S. (2002). Constructing family-friendly careers: Mothers' experiences. *Journal of Counseling & Development, 80,* 180–187.

Jackson, D. N., & Hayes, D. H. (1993). Multicultural issues in consultation. *Journal of Counseling & Development, 72,* 144–147.

Jackson, M. L. (1987). Cross-cultural counseling at the crossroads: A dialogue with Clemmont E. Vontress. *Journal of Counseling & Development, 66,* 20–23.

Jacobs, E. E., Masson, R. L., Harvill, R. L., & Schimmel, C. J. (2012). *Group counseling*

(7th ed.). Belmont, CA: Thomson Brooks/Cole.

James, I. A. (2008). Psychotherapy with older people. In S. Curran, & J. P. Wattis (Eds). *Practical Management of Affective Disorders in Older People: A Multi-Professional Approach* (pp. 108–125). London: Radcliffe.

James, M. D., & Hazler, R. J. (1998). Using metaphors to soften resistance in chemically dependent clients. *Journal of Humanistic Education and Development, 36,* 122–133.

James, R. K. (2008). *Crisis intervention strategies* (6th ed.). Belmont, CA: Thomson Brooks/Cole.

James, R. K. & Gilliland, B. E., (2003). *Theories and strategies in counseling and psychotherapy* (5th ed.). Boston: Allyn & Bacon.

James, S. H., & Greenwalt, B. C. (2001). Documenting success and achievement: Presentation and working portfolios for counselors. *Journal of Counseling & Development, 79,* 161–165.

Janson, G. R., Carney, J. V., Hazier, R. J., & Insoo, O. (2009). Bystanders' reactions to witnessing repetitive abuse experiences. *Journal of Counseling & Development, 87,* 319–326.

Jencius, M., & Rotter, J. C. (1998, March). *Applying naturalistic studies in counseling.* Paper presented at the American Counseling Association Conference, Indianapolis, IN.

Jepsen, D. A. (1982). Test usage in the 1970s: A summary and interpretation. *Measurement and Evaluation in Guidance, 15,* 164–168.

Jesser, D. L. (1983). Career education: Challenges and issues. *Journal of Career Education, 10,* 70–79.

Johnson, C. S. (1985). The American College Personnel Association. *Journal of Counseling & Development, 63,* 405–410.

Johnson, D. W., & Johnson, F. P. (2009). *Joining together*

(10th ed.). Boston: Allyn & Bacon.

Johnson, M., & Scarato, A. M. (1979). A knowledge base for counselors of women. *Counseling Psychologist, 8,* 14–16.

Johnson, W. B., & Hayes, D. N. (1997). An identity-focused counseling group for men. *Journal of Mental Health Counseling, 19,* 295–303.

Johnson, D. H., Nelson, S. E., & Wooden, D. J. (1985). Faculty and student knowledge of university counseling center services. *Journal of College Student Personnel, 26,* 27–32.

Johnson, W., & Kottman, T. (1992). Developmental needs of middle school students: Implications for counselors. *Elementary School Guidance and Counseling, 27,* 3–14.

Jolliff, D. (1994). Group work with men. *Journal for Specialists in Group Work, 19,* 50–51.

Jome, L. M., Surething, N. A., & Taylor, K. K. (2005). Relationally oriented masculinity, gender nontraditional interests, and occupational traditionality of employed men. *Journal of Career Development, 32,* 183–197.

Jones, K. D., & Robinson, E. H. (2000). Psychoeducational groups: A model for choosing topics and exercises appropriate to group stages. *Journal for Specialists in Group Work, 25,* 356–365.

Jones, K., Young, T., & Leppma, M. (2010). Mild Traumatic Brain Injury and Posttraumatic Stress Disorder in returning Iraq and Afghanistan war veterans: Implications for assessment and diagnosis. *Journal of Counseling & Development, 88*(3), 372–376.

Jones, R. M. (1979). Freudian and post-Freudian theories of dreams. In B. B. Wolman (Ed.), *Handbook of dreams: Research, theories, and applications.* New York: Litton.

Jongsma, A. E., Jr., & Peterson, L. M. (1995). *The complete*

psychotherapy treatment planner. New York: Wiley.

Jordan, J. V. (1995). A relational approach to psychotherapy. *Women and Therapy, 16,* 51–61.

Jordan, K. (2002). Providing crisis counseling to New Yorkers after the terrorist attack on the World Trade Center. *The Family Journal: Counseling and Therapy for Couples and Families, 10,* 139–144.

Jourard, S. (1971). *The transparent self.* Princeton, NJ: Van Nostrand.

Jourard, S. M. (1958). *Personal adjustment: An approach through the study of healthy personality.* New York: Macmillan.

Jourard, S. M. (1964). *The transparent self: Self-disclosure and well-being.* Princeton, NJ: Van Nostrand.

Jourard, S. M. (1968). *Disclosing man to himself.* Princeton, NJ: Van Nostrand.

Jourdan, A. (2006). The impact of the family environment on the ethnic identity development of multiethnic college students. *Journal of Counseling & Development, 84,* 328–340.

Joynt, D. F. (1993). *A peer counseling primer.* Danbury, CT: Author.

Juhnke, G. A. (1996). The adapted-SAD PERSONS: A suicide assessment scale designed for use with children. *Elementary School Guidance and Counseling, 30,* 252–258.

Juhnke, G. A. (2002). *Substance abuse assessment and diagnosis: A comprehensive guide for counselors and helping professionals.* New York: Brunner-Routledge.

Juhnke, G. A., & Hagedorn, B. (2006). *Counseling addicted families: An integrated approach.* New York: Routledge.

Juhnke, G. A., & Kelly, V. A. (Eds.) (2005). *Critical incidents in addictions counseling.* Alexandria, VA: American Counseling Association.

Kadison, R., & DiGeronimo, T. F. (2004). *College of the overwhelmed: The campus mental health crisis and what to do about it.* San Francisco: Jossey-Bass.

Kahn, W. J. (1976). Self-management: Learning to be our own counselor. *Personnel and Guidance Journal, 55,* 176–180.

Kahnweiler, W. M. (1979). The school counselor as consultant: A historical review. *Personnel and Guidance Journal, 57,* 374–380.

Kampfe, C. M. (2002). Older adults' perceptions of residential relocation. *Journal of Humanistic Counseling, Education and Development, 41,* 103–113.

Kamphaus, R. W., Beres, K. A., Kaufman, A. S., & Kaufman, N. L. (1996). The Kaufman Assessment Battery for Children (K-ABC). In C. S. Newmark (Ed.), *Major psychological assessment instruments* (2nd ed.). Boston: Allyn & Bacon.

Kampwirth, T. J., & Powers, K. M. (2012). *Collaborative consultation in the schools* (4th ed.). Upper Saddle River, NJ: Merrill/Prentice Hall.

Kaplan, A. (1964). *The conduct of inquiry.* San Francisco: Chandler.

Kaplan, D. M., & Gladding, S. T. (2011). A vision for the future of counseling: The 20/20 principles for unifying and strengthening the profession. *Journal of Counseling & Development, 89,* 367–372.

Kaplan, R. M., & Saccuzzo, D. P. (2009). *Psychological testing: Principles, applications, and issues* (7th ed.). Belmont, CA: Thomson Brooks/Cole.

Kaplan, S. P. (1993). Five year tracking of psychosocial changes in people with severe traumatic brain injury. *Rehabilitation Counseling Bulletin, 36,* 151–159.

Karcher, M. J. (2008). The cross-age mentoring program: A developmental intervention for promoting intervention for promoting students' connectedness across grade levels. *Professional School Counseling, 12*(2), 137–143.

Kasper, L. B., Hill, C. E., & Kivlighan, D. R. (2008). Therapist immediacy in brief psychotherapy: Case study I. *Psychotherapy: Theory, Research, Practice, Training, 45*(3), 281–297.

Katz, M. R. (1975). *SIGI: A computer-based system of interactive guidance and information.* Princeton, NJ: Educational Testing Service.

Katz, M. R. (1993). *Computer-assisted career decision-making: The guide in the machine.* Hillsdale, NJ: Erlbaum.

Kay, A. (2006). *Life's a bitch and then you change careers. 9 steps to get out of your funk and on to the future.* New York: STC Paperbacks.

Keat, D. B., II (1990). Change in child multimodal counseling. *Elementary School Guidance and Counseling, 24,* 248–262.

Keeling, R. P. (1993). HIV disease: Current concepts. *Journal of Counseling & Development, 71,* 261–274.

Kees, N. L. (2005). Women's voices, women's lives: An introduction to the special issue on women and counseling. *Journal of Counseling & Development, 83,* 259–261.

Keirsey, D., & Bates, M. (1984). *Please understand me: Character and temperament types.* Del Mar, CA: Prometheus Nemesis Book Company.

Kelly, E. W., Jr. (1995). *Spirituality and religion in counseling and psychotherapy.* Alexandria, VA: American Counseling Association.

Kelly, K. R. (1988). Defending eclecticism: The utility of informed choice. *Journal of Mental Health Counseling, 10,* 210–213.

Kelly, K. R., & Hall, A. S. (1994). Affirming the developmental model for counseling men. *Journal of Mental Health Counseling, 16,* 475–482.

Kemp, A. (1998). *Abuse in the family: An introduction.* Pacific Grove, CA: Brooks/Cole.

Kemp, J. T. (1984). Learning from clients: Counseling the frail and dying elderly. *Personnel and Guidance Journal, 62,* 270–272.

Kempler, W. (1973). Gestalt therapy. In R. Corsini (Ed.), *Current psychotherapies* (pp. 251–286). Itasca, IL: F. E. Peacock.

Kendall, P. C. (1990). *Coping cat workbook.* Philadelphia: Temple University.

Kennedy, A. (2008, July). Next stop, adulthood. *Counseling Today, 51*(1), 42–43, 45.

Kennedy, A. (2008b, August). Plugged in, turned on and wired up. *Counseling Today, 51*(2), 34–38.

Kerka, S. (1991). Adults in career transition. *ERIC Digest,* ED338896.

Kerlinger, F. N., & Lee, H. B. (2000). *Foundations of behavioral research* (4th ed.). New York: Harcourt.

Kern, C. W., & Watts, R. E. (1993). Adlerian counseling. *Texas Counseling Association Journal, 21,* 85–95.

Kernberg, O. (1975). *Borderline conditions and pathological narcissism.* New York: Aronson.

Kernes, J. L., & McWhirter, J. J. (2001). Counselors' attribution of responsibility, etiology, and counseling strategy. *Journal of Counseling & Development, 79,* 304–313.

Kerr, B. A., Claiborn, C. D., & Dixon, D. N. (1982). Training counselors in persuasion. *Counselor Education and Supervision, 22,* 138–147.

Kerr, M. E. (1988). Chronic anxiety and defining a self. *The Atlantic Monthly, 262,* 35–37, 40–44, 46–58.

Kerr, M. E., & Bowen, M. (1988). *Family evaluation: An approach based on Bowen theory.* New York: Norton.

Keyes, C. L. M., & Lopez, S. J. (2002). Toward a science of mental health: Positive directions in psychodiagnosis and treatment. In C. R. Snyder & S. J. Lopez (Eds.), *The handbook of positive psychology* (pp. 45–62). New York: Oxford University Press.

Keys, S. G., & Bemak, F. (1997). School-family-community linked services: A school counseling role for changing times. *School Counselor, 44,* 255–263.

Keys, S. G., Bemak, F., Carpenter, S. L., & King-Sears, M. E. (1998). Collaborative consultant: A new role for counselors serving at-risk youths. *Journal of Counseling & Development, 76,* 123–133.

Kim, B. K., Ng, G. F., & Ahn, A. J. (2009). Client adherence to Asian cultural values, common factors in counseling, and session outcome with Asian American clients at a university counseling center. *Journal of Counseling & Development, 87*(2), 131–142.

Kim-Appel, D., Appel, J., Newman, I., & Parr, P. (2007). Testing the effectiveness of Bowen's concept of differentiation in predicting psychological distress in individuals age 62 years or older. *The Family Journal: Counseling and Therapy for Couples and Families, 15,* 224–233.

King, E. B., & Knight, J. L. (2011). *How women can make it work: The science of success.* Santa Barbara, CA: Praeger.

Kinnier, R. T., Brigman, S. L., & Noble, F. C. (1990). Career indecision and family enmeshment. *Journal of Counseling & Development, 68,* 309–312.

Kiracofe, N. M., & Wells, L. (2007). Mandated disciplinary counseling on campus: Problems and possibilities. *Journal of Counseling & Development, 85,* 259–268.

Kirk, W. D., & Kirk, S. V. (1993). The African American student athlete. In W. D. Kirk & S. V. Kirk (Eds.), *Student athletes: Shattering the myths and sharing the realities* (pp. 99–112). Alexandria, VA: American Counseling Association.

Kisch, R. M. (1977). Client as "consultant-observer" in the role-play model. *Personnel and Guidance Journal, 55,* 494–495.

Kiselica, M. S., & Look, C. T. (1993). Mental health counseling and prevention: Disparity between philosophy and practice? *Journal of Mental Health Counseling, 15,* 3–14.

Kiselica, M. S., & Morrill-Richards, M. (2007). Sibling maltreatment: The forgotten abuse. *Journal of Counseling & Development, 85,* 148–161.

Kiselica, M. S., & Pfaller, J. (1993). Helping teenage parents: The independent and collaborative roles of counselor educators and school counselors. *Journal of Counseling & Development, 72,* 42–48.

Kiselica, M. S., & Robinson, M. (2001). Bringing advocacy counseling to life: The history, issues, and human dramas of social justice working in counseling. *Journal of Counseling & Development, 79,* 387–397.

Kitchener, K. S. (1985). Ethical principles and ethical decisions in student affairs. In H. J. Canon & R. D. Brown (Eds.), *Applied ethics in student services* (pp. 17–29). San Francisco: Jossey-Bass.

Kitchener, K. S. (1986). Teaching applied ethics in counselor education: An integration of psychological processes and philosophical analysis. *Journal of Counseling & Development, 64,* 306–310.

Kitchener, K. S. (1994, May). Doing good well: The wisdom behind ethical supervision. *Counseling and Human Development,* 1–8.

Klaw, E., & Humphreys, K. (2004). The role of peer-led mutual help groups promoting health and well-being. In J. L. DeLucia-Waack, D. A. Gerrity, C. R. Kalodner, & M. T. Riva (Eds.),

Handbook of group counseling and psychotherapy (pp. 630–640). Thousand Oaks, CA: Sage.

Kleist, D. M., & White, L. J. (1997). The values of counseling: A disparity between a philosophy of prevention in counseling and counselor practice and training. *Counseling and Values, 41,* 128–140.

Kline, W. B. (1986). The risks of client self-disclosure. *AMHCA Journal, 8,* 94–99.

Knapp, S., & Vandecreek, L. (1982). *Tarasoff:* Five years later. *Professional Psychology, 13,* 511–516.

Knittel, M. (2010, December). Helping clients with limb loss. *Counseling Today, 53*(6), 44–45.

Knowles, D. (1979). On the tendency of volunteer helpers to give advice. *Journal of Counseling Psychology, 26,* 352–354.

Kocet, M. M. (2006). Ethical challenges in a complex world: Highlights of the 2005 ACA Code of Ethics. *Journal of Counseling & Development, 84,* 228–234.

Kohatsu, E. L., Victoria, R., Lau, A., Flores, M., & Salazar, A. (2011). Analyzing anti-Asian prejudice from a racial identity and color-blind perspective. *Journal of Counseling & Development, 89*(1), 63–72.

Kohlberg, L. (1969). *Stages in the development of moral thought and action.* New York: Holt, Rinehart & Winston.

Kohlberg, L. (1984). *Essays on moral development: Vol. 2. The psychology of moral development: The nature and validity of moral stages.* New York: Harper & Row.

Kolenc, K. M., Hartley, D. L., & Murdock, N. L. (1990). The relationship of mild depression to stress and coping. *Journal of Mental Health Counseling, 12,* 76–92.

Komives, S. R., Dugan, J. P., Owen, J. E., Slack, C., Wagner, W., & Associates (Eds.). (2011). *The handbook for student leadership development* (2nd ed.). San Francisco: Jossey-Bass.

Kopla, M., & Keitel, M. A. (Eds.). (2003). *Handbook of counseling women.* Thousand Oaks, CA: Sage.

Kosclulek, J. F. (2000). The Ticket to Work and Work Incentives Improvement Act (WIIA) of 1999. *Rehabilitation Counselors Bulletin, 43,* 1–2.

Kottler, J. A. (1991). *The complete therapist.* San Francisco: Jossey-Bass.

Kottler, J. A. (1994a). *Advanced group leadership.* Pacific Grove, CA: Brooks/Cole.

Kottler, J. A. (1994b). Working with difficult group members. *Journal for Specialists in Group Work, 19,* 3–10.

Kottler, J. A. (2010). *On being a therapist* (4th ed.). San Francisco: Jossey-Bass.

Kottler, J. A., Sexton, T. L., & Whiston, S. C. (1994). *The heart of healing.* San Francisco: Jossey-Bass.

Kovacs, A. L. (1965). The intimate relationship: A therapeutic paradox. *Psychotherapy, 2,* 97–103.

Kovacs, A. L. (1976). The emotional hazards of teaching psychotherapy. *Psychotherapy, 13,* 321–334.

Kraus, K., & Hulse-Killacky, D. (1996). Balancing process and content in groups: A metaphor. *Journal for Specialists in Group Work, 21,* 90–93.

Krause, J. S., & Anson, C. A. (1997). Adjustment after spinal cord injury: Relationship to participation in employment or educational activities. *Rehabilitation Counseling Bulletin, 40,* 202–214.

Krauskopf, C. J. (1982). Science and evaluation research. *Counseling Psychologist, 10,* 71–72.

Kreider, R. M., & Ellis, R. (2011, May). Number, timing, and duration of marriages and divorces: 2009. *Current Population Reports, United State Census Bureau.* Washington, DC: U.S. Government Printing Office.

Kress, V. E., & Shoffner, M. F. (2007). Focus groups: A practical and applied research approach for counselors. *Journal of Counseling & Development, 85,* 189–195.

Kress, V. E. W., Eriksen, K. P., Rayle, A. D., & Ford, S. J. W. (2005). The DSM-IV-TR and culture: Considerations for counselors. *Journal of Counseling & Development, 83,* 97–104.

Krieshok, T. S. (1987). Review of the self-directed search. *Journal of Counseling & Development, 65,* 512–514.

Krieshok, T. S. (1998). An antiintrospectivist view of career decision making. *Career Development Quarterly, 46,* 210–229.

Kroll, J. (2003). Posttraumatic symptoms and the complexity of responses to trauma. *Journal of the American Medical Association, 290,* 667–670.

Krumboltz, J. D. (1966a). Behavioral goals of counseling. *Journal of Counseling Psychology, 13,* 153–159.

Krumboltz, J. D. (1979). *Social learning and career decision making.* New York: Carroll.

Krumboltz, J. D. (1991). *Manual for the Career Beliefs Inventory.* Palo Alto, CA: Consulting Psychologists Press.

Krumboltz, J. D. (1992, December). Challenging troublesome career beliefs. *CAPS Digest,* EDO-CG-92-4.

Krumboltz, J. D. (1994). Integrating career and personal counseling. *Career Development Quarterly, 42,* 143–148.

Krumboltz, J. D. (1996). A learning theory of career counseling. In M. Savickas & B. Walsh (Eds.), *Integrating career theory and practice* (pp. 233–280). Palo Alto, CA: CPP Books.

Krumboltz, J. D. (Ed.). (1966b). *Revolution in counseling.* Boston: Houghton Mifflin.

Krumboltz, J. D., & Levin, A. S. (2004). *Luck is no accident.* Atascadero, CA: Impact Publishers.

Krumboltz, J. D., & Mitchell, L. K. (1979). Relevant rigorous research. *Counseling Psychologist, 8,* 50–52.

Krumboltz, J. D., & Thoresen, C. E. (Eds.). (1969). *Behavioral counseling: Cases and techniques.* New York: Holt, Rinehart and Winston.

Krumboltz, J. D., & Thoresen, C. E. (1976). *Counseling methods.* New York: Holt, Rinehart & Winston.

Kubler-Ross, E. (1969). *On death and dying.* New York: Macmillan.

Kuder, F. (1939). *Manual for the Preference Record.* Chicago: Science Research Associates.

Kuder, F. (1977). *Activity interest and occupational choice.* Chicago: Science Research Associates.

Kuh, G. D. (1996). *Student learning outside the classroom: Transcending artificial boundaries.* Washington, DC: George Washington University.

Kuh, G. D., Bean, J. R., Bradley, R. K., & Coomes, M. D. (1986). Contributions of student affairs journals to the literature on college students. *Journal of College Student Personnel, 27,* 292–304.

Kurpius, D. J. (1978). Consultation theory and process: An integrated model. *Personnel and Guidance Journal, 56,* 335–338.

Kurpius, D. J. (1986a). Consultation: An important human and organizational intervention. *Journal of Counseling and Human Service Professions, 1,* 58–66.

Kurpius, D. J. (1986b). The helping relationship. In M. D. Lewis, R. L. Hayes, & J. A. Lewis (Eds.), *The counseling profession* (pp. 96–129). Itasca, IL: F. E. Peacock.

Kurpius, D. J. (1988). *Handbook of consultation: An intervention for advocacy and outreach.* Alexandria, VA: American Counseling Association.

Kurpius, D. J., & Brubaker, J. C. (1976). *Psycho-educational consultation: Definitions-functions-preparation*. Bloomington: Indiana University Press.

Kurpius, D. J., & Fuqua, D. R. (1993). Fundamental issues in defining consultation. *Journal of Counseling & Development, 71,* 598–600.

Kurpius, D. J., Fuqua, D. R., & Rozecki, T. (1993). The consulting process: A multidimensional approach. *Journal of Counseling & Development, 71,* 601–606.

Kurpius, D. J., & Robinson, S. E. (1978). An overview of consultation. *Personnel and Guidance Journal, 56,* 321–323.

Kurtz, P. D., & Tandy, C. C. (1995). Narrative family interventions. In A. C. Kilpatrick & T. P. Holland (Eds.), *Working with families* (pp. 177–197). Boston: Allyn & Bacon.

Kushman, J. W., Sieber, C., & Heariold-Kinney, P. (2000). This isn't the place for me: School dropout. In D. Capuzzi & D. R. Gross (Eds.), *Youth at risk* (3rd ed., pp. 471–507). Alexandria, VA: American Counseling Association.

L'Abate, L. (1992). Introduction. In L. L'Abate, G. E. Farrar, & D. A. Serritella (Eds.), *Handbook of differential treatments for addiction* (pp. 1–4). Boston: Allyn & Bacon.

L'Abate, L., & Thaxton, M. L. (1981). Differentiation of resources in mental health delivery: Implications of training. *Professional Psychology, 12,* 761–767.

LaBarge, E. (1981). Counseling patients with senile dementia of the Alzheimer type and their families. *Personnel and Guidance Journal, 60,* 139–142.

LaCross, M. B. (1975). Non-verbal behavior and perceived counselor attractiveness and persuasiveness. *Journal of Counseling Psychology, 22,* 563–566.

Ladany, N., & Bradley, L. J. (2010). *Counselor Supervision*. Philadelphia: Routledge.

Ladd, E. T. (1971). Counselors, confidences, and the civil liberties of clients. *Personnel and Guidance Journal, 50,* 261–268.

LaFountain, R. M., & Bartos, R. B. (2002). *Research and statistics made meaningful in counseling and student affairs*. Pacific Grove, CA: Brooks/Cole.

LaFountain, R. M., Garner, N. E., & Eliason, G. T. (1996). Solution-focused counseling groups: A key for school counselors. *School Counselor, 43,* 256–267.

Laker, D. R. (2002). The career wheel: An exercise for exploring and validating one's career choices. *Journal of Employment Counseling, 39,* 61–71.

Lambert, M. J., Masters, K. S., & Ogles, B. M. (1991). Outcome research in counseling. In C. E. Watkins, Jr., & L. J. Schneider (Eds.), *Research in counseling* (pp. 51–83). Hillsdale, NJ: Erlbaum.

Lambie, G. W. (2007). The contribution of ego development level to burnout in school counselors: Implications for professional school counseling. *Journal of Counseling & Development, 85,* 82–88.

Lambie, G. W., & Milsom, A. (2010). A narrative approach to supporting students diagnosed with learning disabilities. *Journal of Counseling & Development, 88,* 196–203.

Lampropoulos, G. K., Schneider, M. K., & Spengler, P. M. (2009). Predictors of early termination in a university counseling training clinic. *Journal of Counseling & Development, 87*(1), 36–46.

Landis, L. L., & Young, M. E. (1994). The reflective team in counselor education. *Counselor Education and Supervision, 33,* 210–218.

Landreth, G. L. (2002). *Play therapy: The art of the relationship* (2nd ed.). New York: Brunner-Routledge.

Lanning, W. (1992, December). Ethical codes and responsible decision-making. *ACA Guidepost, 35,* 21.

Lapan, R. T., Gysbers, N. C., & Petroski, G. F. (2001). Helping seventh graders be safe and successful: A statewide study of the impact of comprehensive guidance and counseling programs. *Journal of Counseling & Development, 79,* 320–330.

Lapsley, D. K., & Quintana, S. M. (1985). Recent approaches to the moral and social education of children. *Elementary School Guidance and Counseling, 19,* 246–259.

Laux, J. M., Salyers, K. M., & Kotova, E. (2005). A psychometric evaluation of the SASSI-3 in a college sample. *Journal of College Counseling, 8,* 41–51.

Lawler, A. C. (1990). The healthy self: Variations on a theme. *Journal of Counseling & Development, 68,* 652–654.

Lawless, L. L., Ginter, E. J., & Kelly, K. R. (1999). Managed care: What mental health counselors need to know. *Journal of Mental Health Counseling, 21,* 50–65.

Lawrence, G., & Kurpius, S. E. R. (2000). Legal and ethical issues involved when counseling minors in nonschool settings. *Journal of Counseling & Development, 78,* 130–136.

Lawson, A. W. (1994). Family therapy and addictions. In J. A. Lewis (Ed.), *Addiction: Concepts and strategies for treatment* (pp. 211–232). Gathersburg, MD: Aspen.

Lawson, D. (1994). Identifying pretreatment change. *Journal of Counseling & Development, 72,* 244–248.

Lawson, D. M. (2009). Understanding and treating children who experience interpersonal maltreatment: Empirical findings. *Journal of Counseling & Development, 87,* 204–215.

Lawson, G., Hein, S. F., & Stuart, C. L. (2009). A qualitative investigation of supervisees' experiences of triadic supervision. *Journal of Counseling & Development, 87,* 449–457.

Lawson, G., Venart, E., Hazler, R. J., & Kottler, J. A. (2007). Toward a culture of counselor wellness. *Journal of Humanistic Counseling, Education and Development, 46,* 5–19.

Layne, C. M., & Hohenshil, T. H. (2005). High tech counseling: Revisited. *Journal of Counseling & Development, 83,* 222–226.

Lazarus, A. A. (1985). Behavior rehearsal. In A. S. Bellack & M. Hersen (Eds.), *Dictionary of behavior therapy techniques* (p. 22). New York: Pergamon.

Lazarus, A. A. (2008). *Multimodal therapy*. In R. J. Corsini & D. Wedding (Eds.), *Current psychotherapies* (8th ed., pp. 368–401). Belmont, CA: Thomson Brooks/Cole.

Lazarus, A. A., & Beutler, L. E. (1993). On technical eclecticism. *Journal of Counseling & Development, 71,* 381–385.

Lazarus, A. P. (1989). *The practice of multimodal therapy: Systematic, comprehensive, and effective psychotherapy*. Baltimore: Johns Hopkins University Press.

Leaman, D. R. (1978). Confrontation in counseling. *Personnel and Guidance Journal, 56,* 630–633.

Learner, B. (1981). Representative democracy, "men of zeal," and testing legislation. *American Psychologist, 36,* 270–275.

Leder, S., Grinstead, L. N., & Torres, E. (2007). Grandparents raising grandchildren: Stressors, social support, and health outcomes. *Journal of Family Nursing, 13,* 333–352.

Lee, C. C. (1989). AMCD: The next generation. *Journal of Multicultural Counseling and Development, 17,* 165–170.

Lee, C. C. (1998). Professional counseling in a global

context: Collaboration for international social action. In C. C. Lee & G. R. Walz (Eds.), *Social action: A mandate for counselors* (pp. 293–306). Alexandria, VA: American Counseling Association.

Lee, C. C. (2001). Culturally responsive school counselors and programs: Addressing the needs of all students. *Professional School Counseling, 4,* 257–261.

Lee, C. C. (Ed.). (2006a). *Counseling for social justice* (2nd ed.). Alexandria, VA: American Counseling Association.

Lee, C. C. (Ed.). (2006b). *Multicultural issues in counseling: New approaches to diversity* (3rd ed.). Alexandria, VA: American Counseling Association.

Lee, C. C., & Rodgers, R. A. (2009). Counselor advocacy: Affecting systemic change in the public arena. *Journal of Counseling & Development, 87,* 284–287.

Lee, C. C., & Walz, G. R. (Eds.). (1998). *Social action: A mandate for counselors.* Alexandria, VA: American Counseling Association.

Lee, J. M. (1966). Issues and emphases in guidance: A historical perspective. In J. M. Lee & N. J. Pallone (Eds.), *Readings in guidance and counseling.* New York: Sheed & Ward.

Lee, R. M., & Robbins, S. B. (2000). Understanding social connectedness in college women and men. *Journal of Counseling & Development, 78,* 484–491.

Leech, N. L., & Kees, N. L. (2005). Researching women's groups: Findings, limitations, and recommendations. *Journal of Counseling & Development, 83,* 367–373.

Leech, N. L., & Onwuegbuzie, A. J. (2010). Guidelines for conducting and reporting mixed research in the field of counseling and beyond. *Journal of Counseling & Development, 88*(1), 61–69.

Leedy, P. D., & Ormrod, J. E. (2010). *Practical research* (9th ed.). Upper Saddle River, NJ: Merrill/Prentice Hall.

Lefrancois, G. R. (1999). *The lifespan* (6th ed.). Belmont, CA: Wadsworth.

Leibert, T. W. (2006). Making change visible: The possibilities in assessing mental health counseling outcomes. *Journal of Counseling & Development, 84,* 108–113.

Leierer, S. J., Strohmer, D. C., Leclere, W. A., Cornwell, B. J., & Whitten, S. L. (1996). The effect of counselor disability, attending behavior, and client problem on counseling. *Rehabilitation Counseling Bulletin, 40,* 92–96.

Lemoire, S. J., & Chen, C. P. (2005). Applying person-centered counseling to sexual minority adolescents. *Journal of Counseling & Development, 83,* 146–154.

Leonard, M. M., & Collins, A. M. (1979). Woman as footnote. *Counseling Psychologist, 8,* 6–7.

Leong, F. T. L. (Ed.). (1995). *Career development and vocational behavior of racial and ethnic minorities.* Hillsdale, NJ: Erlbaum.

Lerner, S., & Lerner, H. (1983). A systematic approach to resistance: Theoretical and technical considerations. *American Journal of Psychotherapy, 37,* 387–399.

Leslie, R. S. (2004, July/August). Minimizing liability. *Family Therapy Magazine, 3*(4), 46–48.

Levine, E. (1983). A training model that stresses the dynamic dimensions of counseling. *Personnel and Guidance Journal, 61,* 431–433.

Lewin, K. (1936). *Principles of topological psychology.* New York: McGraw-Hill.

Lewing, R. J., Jr., & Cowger, E. L., Jr. (1982). Time spent on college counselor functions. *Journal of College Student Personnel, 23,* 41–48.

Lewis, J. A., Hayes, B. A., & Bradley, L. J. (Eds.). (1992). *Counseling women over the life span.* Denver: Love.

Lewis, J. A., & Lewis, M. D. (1977). *Community counseling: A human service approach.* New York: Wiley.

Lewis, R. A., & Gilhousen, M. R. (1981). Myths of career development: A cognitive approach to vocational counseling. *Personnel and Guidance Journal, 59,* 296–299.

Lewis, R. E., & Borunda, R. (2006). Lived stories: Participatory leadership in school counseling. *Journal of Counseling & Development, 84,* 406–413.

Lewis, W. (1996). A proposal for initiating family counseling interventions by school counselors. *School Counselor, 44,* 93–99.

Lichtenberg, J. W. (1986). Counseling research: Irrelevant or ignored? *Journal of Counseling & Development, 64,* 365–366.

Lieberman, M. A. (1991). Group methods. In F. H. Kanfer & A. P. Goldstein (Eds.), *Helping people change: A textbook of methods* (4th ed.). Boston: Allyn & Bacon.

Lieberman, M. A. (1994). Self-help groups. In H. I. Kaplan & B. J. Sadock (Eds.), *Comprehensive group psychotherapy* (3rd ed.). Baltimore: Williams & Wilkins.

Lindemann, E. (1944). Symptomatology and management of acute grief. *American Journal of Psychiatry, 101,* 141–148.

Lindemann, E. (1956). The meaning of crisis in individual and family. *Teachers College Record, 57,* 310.

Lippert, L. (1997). Women at midlife: Implications for theories of women's adult development. *Journal of Counseling & Development, 76,* 16–22.

Littrell, J. M. (2001). Allen E. Ivey: Transforming counseling theory and practice. *Journal of Counseling & Development, 79,* 105–118.

Littrell, J. M., & Peterson, J. S. (2001). Transforming the school culture: A model based on an exemplary counselor. *Professional School Counseling, 4,* 310–313.

Lively, K. (1998, May 15). At Michigan State, a protest escalated into a night of fires, tear gas, and arrests.

Chronicle of Higher Education, 44, A46.

Livneh, H., & Antonak, R. F. (2005). Psychosocial adaptation to chronic illness and disability: A primer for counselors. *Journal of Counseling & Development, 83,* 12–20.

Livneh, H., & Evans, J. (1984). Adjusting to disability: Behavioral correlates and intervention strategies. *Personnel and Guidance Journal, 62,* 363–368.

Livneh, H., & Sherwood-Hawes, A. (1993). Group counseling approaches with persons who have sustained myocardial infarction. *Journal of Counseling & Development, 72,* 57–61.

Locke, D. C. (1990). A not so provincial view of multicultural counseling. *Counselor Education and Supervision, 30,* 18–25.

Locke, D. C. (1998, Spring). Beyond U.S. borders. *American Counselor, 1,* 13–16.

Locke, D. C., & Faubert, M. (1993). Getting on the right track: A program for African American high school students. *School Counselor, 41,* 129–133.

Lockhart, E. J., & Keys, S. G. (1998). The mental health counseling role of school counselors. *Professional School Counseling, 1*(4), 3–6.

Loesch, L. (1977). Guest editorial. *Elementary School Guidance and Counseling, 12,* 74–75.

Loesch, L. (1984). Professional credentialing in counseling: 1984. *Counseling and Human Development, 17,* 1–11.

Loewenstein, S. F. (1979). Helping family members cope with divorce. In S. Eisenberg & L. E. Patterson (Eds.), *Helping clients with special concerns* (pp. 193–217). Boston: Houghton Mifflin.

Logan, W. L. (1997). Peer consultation group: Doing what works for counselors. *Professional School Counseling, 1,* 4–6.

London, M. (1982). How do you say good-bye after you've said hello? *Personnel and Guidance Journal, 60,* 412–414.

Long, L. L., & Young, M. E. (2007). *Counseling and therapy for couples* (2nd ed.). Belmont, CA: Thomson Brooks/Cole.

Lopez, S. J., Edwards, L. M., Pedrotti, J. T., Prosser, E. C., LaRue, S., Spalitto, S. V., et al. (2006). Beyond the DSM-IV: Assumptions, alternatives, and alterations. *Journal of Counseling & Development, 84,* 259–267.

Lopez-Baez, S. I. (2006). Counseling Latinas: Culturally responsive interventions. In C. C. Lee (Ed.), *Multicultural issues in counseling* (3rd ed., pp. 187–194). Alexandria, VA: American Counseling Association.

Loughary, J. W., Stripling, R. O., & Fitzgerald, P. W. (Eds.). (1965). *Counseling: A growing profession.* Washington, DC: American Personnel and Guidance Association.

Lowman, R. L. (1993). The interdomain model of career assessment and counseling. *Journal of Counseling & Development, 71,* 549–554.

Loxley, J. C., & Whiteley, J. M. (1986). *Character development in college students.* Alexandria, VA: American Counseling Association.

Luborsky, E. B., O'Reilly-Landry, M., & Arlow, J. A. (2008). Psychoanalysis. In R. J. Corsini & D. Wedding (Eds.), *Current psychotherapies* (8th ed., pp. 15–62). Belmont, CA: Thomson Brooks/Cole.

Lucas, M. S., Skokowski, C. T., & Ancis, J. R. (2000). Contextual themes in career decision making of female clients who indicate depression. *Journal of Counseling & Development, 78,* 316–325.

Luft, J. (1970). *Group process: An introduction to group dynamics.* Palo Alto, CA: National Press Books.

Lum, D. (2007). *Culturally competent practice: A framework for understanding diverse groups and justice issues* (3rd ed.). Belmont, CA: Thomson Brooks/Cole.

Lundervold, D. A., & Belwood, M. F. (2000). The best kept secret in counseling: Single-case (N = 1) experimental design. *Journal of Counseling & Development, 78,* 92–102.

Lusky, M. B., & Hayes, R. L. (2001). Collaborative consultation and program evaluation. *Journal of Counseling & Development, 79,* 26–38.

Luzzo, D. A., & McWhirter, E. H. (2001). Sex and ethnic differences in the perception of educational and career-related barriers and levels of coping efficacy. *Journal of Counseling & Development, 79,* 61–67.

Lyddon, W. J., Clay, A. L., & Sparks, C. L. (2001). Metaphor and change in counseling. *Journal of Counseling & Development, 79,* 269–274.

Lynch, A. Q. (1985). The Myers-Briggs Type Indicator: A tool for appreciating employee and client diversity. *Journal of Employment Counseling, 22,* 104–109.

Lynch, R. T., & Gussel, L. (1996). Disclosure and self-advocacy regarding disability-related needs: Strategies to maximize integration in postsecondary education. *Journal of Counseling & Development, 74,* 352–357.

Lynch, R. K., & Maki, D. (1981). Searching for structure: A trait-factor approach to vocational rehabilitation. *Vocational Guidance Quarterly, 30,* 61–68.

Lynn, S. J., & Frauman, D. (1985). Group psychotherapy. In S. J. Lynn & J. P. Garske (Eds.), *Contemporary psychotherapies: Models and methods* (pp. 419–458). Upper Saddle River, NJ: Merrill/Prentice Hall.

MacCluskie, K. C., & Ingersoll, R. E. (2001). *Becoming a 21st century agency counselor.* Pacific Grove, CA: Brooks/Cole.

Mackenzie, S., Wiegel, J. R., Mundt, M., Brown, D., Saewyc, E., Heiligenstein, E., Harahan, B., Fleming, B. (2011).

Depression and suicide ideation among students accessing campus health care. *American Journal of Orthopsychiatry, 81,* 101–107.

Madanes, C. (1984). *Behind the one-way mirror: Advances in the practice of strategic therapy.* San Francisco: Jossey-Bass.

Magnuson, S. (1996). Charlotte's web: Expanding a classroom activity for a guidance lesson. *Elementary School Guidance and Counseling, 31,* 75–76.

Maholick, L. T., & Turner, D. W. (1979). Termination: The difficult farewell. *American Journal of Psychotherapy, 33,* 583–591.

Manderscheid, R. W., & Sonnenschein, M. A. (1992). *Mental health in the United States, 1992* (DHHS Publication No. [SMA] 92–1942). Washington, DC: U.S. Government Printing Office.

Manhal-Baugus, M. (1998). The self-in-relation theory and Women for Sobriety: Female-specific theory and mutual help group for chemically dependent women. *Journal of Addiction and Offender Counseling, 18,* 78–87.

Mann, D. (1986). Dropout prevention: Getting serious about programs that work. *NASSP Bulletin, 70,* 66–73.

Manthei, R. J. (1983). Client choice of therapist or therapy. *Personnel and Guidance Journal, 61,* 334–340.

Maples, M. F., & Abney, P. C. (2006). Baby boomers mature and gerontological counseling comes of age. *Journal of Counseling & Development, 84,* 3–9.

Maples, M., & Han, J. (2008). Cybercounseling in the United States and South Korea: Implications for counseling college students of the Millennial Generation and the Networked Generation. *Journal of Counseling & Development, 86,* 178–183.

Maples, M. F., Dupey, P., Torres-Rivera, E., Phan, L. T., Vereen, L., & Garrett, M. T. (2001).

Ethnic diversity and the use of humor in counseling: Appropriate or inappropriate? *Journal of Counseling & Development, 79,* 53–60.

Maples, M. F., Packman, J., Abney, P., Daugherty, R. F., Casey, J. A., & Pirtle, L. (2005). Suicide by teenagers in middle school: A postvention team approach. *Journal of Counseling & Development, 83,* 397–405.

Maples, M. R., & Luzzo, D. A. (2005). Evaluating DISCOVER's effectiveness in enhancing college students' social cognitive career development. *Career Development Quarterly, 53,* 274–285.

Marczinski, C. A., Grant, E. C.,& Grant, V. J. (2009). *Binge drinking in adolescents and college students.* Hauppauge NY: Nova Science Publications.

Margolin, G. (1982). Ethical and legal considerations in marital and family therapy. *American Psychologist, 37,* 788–801.

Margolis, R. D., Zweben, J. E. (2011). *Treating patients with alcohol and other drug problems: An integrated approach* (2nd ed.). Washington, DC: American Psychological Association.

Marino, T. M. (1979). Resensitizing men: A male perspective. *Personnel and Guidance Journal, 58,* 102–105.

Marino, T. M. (1994, December). Starving for acceptance. *Counseling Today, 37,* 1, 4.

Marino, T. W. (1996, July). Looking for greener pastures. *Counseling Today, 16.*

Marinoble, R. M. (1998). Homosexuality: A blind spot in the school mirror. *Professional School Counseling, 1,* 4–7.

Markowitz, L. M. (1994, July/August). The cross-culture of multiculturalism. *Family Therapy Networker, 18,* 18–27, 69.

Marks, L. I., & McLaughlin, R. H. (2005). Outreach by college counselors: Increasing student attendance at presentations. *Journal of College Counseling, 8,* 86–96.

Marotta, S. A. (2000). Best practices for counselors who treat posttraumatic stress disorder. *Journal of Counseling & Development, 78,* 492–495.

Marotta, S. A., & Asner, K. K. (1999). Group psychotherapy for women with a history of incest: The research base. *Journal of Counseling & Development, 77,* 315–323.

Martell, C. R., Safren, S. A., & Prince, S. E. (2004). *Cognitive behavioral therapies with lesbian, gay, and bisexual clients.* New York: Guilford.

Maske, M. (2007, July 18). Falcons' Vick indicted in dog fighting case. *Washington Post,* p. E1.

Maslow, A. H. (1962). *Toward a psychology of being.* Princeton, NJ: Van Nostrand.

Mason, M. J. (2009). Rogers redux: Relevance and outcomes of motivational interviewing across behavioral problems. *Journal of Counseling & Development, 87*(3), 357–362.

Mason, C., & Duba, J. D. (2009). Using reality therapy in schools: Its potential impact on the effectiveness of the ASCA national model. *International Journal of Reality Therapy, 29*(1), 5–12.

Mathewson, R. H. (1949). *Guidance policy and practice.* New York: Harper.

Mathiasen, R. E. (1984). Attitudes and needs of the college student-client. *Journal of College Student Personnel, 25,* 274–275.

Matthews, C. R. (2005). Infusing lesbian, gay, and bisexual issues into counselor education. *Journal of Humanistic Counseling, Education and Development, 44,* 168–184.

Matthews, C. R., Lorah, P., & Fenton, J. (2006). Treatment experiences of gays and lesbians in recovery from addiction: A qualitative inquiry. *Journal of Mental Health Counseling, 28,* 110–132.

Matthews, D. B., & Burnett, D. D. (1989). Anxiety: An achievement component. *Journal of Humanistic Education and Development, 27,* 122–131.

Maultsby, M. C., Jr. (1984). *Rational behavior therapy.* Upper Saddle River, NJ: Prentice Hall.

Maultsby, M. C., Jr. (1986). Teaching rational self-counseling to middle graders. *School Counselor, 33,* 207–219.

Maxwell, M. (2007). Career counseling is personal counseling: A constructivist approach to nurturing the development of gifted female adolescents. *Career Development Quarterly, 55,* 206–224.

May, J. C. (2005). Family attachment narrative therapy: Healing the experience of early childhood maltreatment. *Journal of Marital and Family Therapy, 31,* 221–237.

May, K. M. (1996). Naturalistic inquiry and counseling: Contemplating commonalities. *Counseling and Values, 40,* 219–229.

May, R. (1939). *The art of counseling.* New York: Abingdon-Cokesbury.

May, R. (1975). *The courage to create.* New York: Norton.

May, R. (1977). *The meaning of anxiety* (Rev. ed.). New York: Norton.

May, R., Angel, E., & Ellenberger, H. (Eds.). (1958). *Existence.* New York: Simon & Schuster.

May, R., Remen, N., Young, D., & Berland, W. (1985). The wounded healer. *Saybrook Review, 5,* 84–93.

Maynard, P. E., & Olson, D. H. (1987). Circumplex model of family systems: A treatment tool in family counseling. *Journal of Counseling & Development, 65,* 502–504.

Mays, D. T., & Franks, C. M. (1980). Getting worse: Psychotherapy or no treatment: The jury should still be out. *Professional Psychology, 2,* 78–92.

McAdams III, C. R., & Keener, H. J. (2008). Preparation, Action, Recovery: A Conceptual Framework for Counselor Preparation and Response in Client Crises. *Journal of Counseling & Development, 86,* 388–398.

McAuliffe, G., & Lovell, C. (2006). The influence of counselor epistemology on the helping interview: A qualitative study. *Journal of Counseling & Development, 84,* 308–317.

McBride, M. C., & Martin, G. E. (1990). A framework for eclecticism: The importance of theory to mental health counseling. *Journal of Mental Health Counseling, 12,* 495–505.

McCarthy, C. J., Brack, C. J., Lambert, R. G., Brack, G., & Orr, D. P. (1996). Predicting emotional and behavioral risk factors in adolescents. *School Counselor, 43,* 277–286.

McCarthy, M., & Sorenson, G. (1993). School counselors and consultants: Legal duties and liabilities. *Journal of Counseling & Development, 72,* 159–167.

McCarthy, P., DeBell, C., Kanuha, V., & McLeod, J. (1988). Myths of supervision: Identifying the gaps between theory and practice. *Counselor Education and Supervision, 28,* 22–28.

McClellan, G. S., & Stringer, J. (Eds.). (2009). *The handbook of student affairs administration.* San Francisco, CA: Jossey-Bass.

McClure, B. A. (1990). The group mind: Generative and regressive groups. *Journal for Specialists in Group Work, 15,* 159–170.

McClure, B. A. (1994). The shadow side of regressive groups. *Counseling and Values, 38,* 77–89.

McClure, B. A., & Russo, T. R. (1996). The politics of counseling: Looking back and forward. *Counseling and Values, 40,* 162–174.

McCormick, J. F. (1998). Ten summer rejuvenators for school counselors. *Professional School Counseling, 1,* 61–63.

McCoy, G. A. (1994, April). A plan for the first group session. *ASCA Counselor, 31,* 18.

McCracken, J. E., Hayes, J. A., & Dell, D. (1997). Attributions of responsibility for memory problems in older and younger adults. *Journal of Counseling & Development, 75,* 385–391.

McDaniels, C. (1984). The work/leisure connection. *Vocational Guidance Quarterly, 33,* 35–44.

McEachern, A. G., Aluede, O., & Kenny, M. C. (2008). Emotional abuse in the classroom: Implications and interventions for counselors. *Journal of Counseling & Development, 86,* 3–10.

McFadden, J. (Ed.). (1999). *Transcultural counseling* (2nd ed.). Alexandria, VA: American Counseling Association.

McFadden, J., & Lipscomb, W. D. (1985). History of the Association for Non-white Concerns in Personnel and Guidance. *Journal of Counseling & Development, 63,* 444–447.

McGannon, W., Carey, J., & Dimmitt, C. (2005). *The current status of school counseling outcome research* (Research Monograph No. 2). Amherst: Center for School Counseling Outcome Research, University of Massachusetts, School of Education.

McGee, T. F., Schuman, B. N., & Racusen, F. (1972). Termination in group psychotherapy. *American Journal of Psychotherapy, 26,* 521–532.

McGlynn, A. P. (2007). *Teaching today's college student widening the circle of success.* Madison, WI: Atwood.

McGoldrick, M., Carter, B., & Garcia-Preto (Eds.) (2011). *The expanded family life cycle: Individual, family, and social perspectives* (4th ed.). Upper Saddle River, NJ: Pearson.

McGoldrick, M., Gerson, R., & Petry, S. (2008). *Genograms: Assessment and intervention* (3rd ed.). New York: Norton.

McGoldrick, M., Giordano, J., & Garcia-Preto, N. (Eds.). (2005). *Ethnicity and family therapy* (3rd ed.). New York: Guilford.

McGowan, A. S. (1995). "Suffer the little children": A developmental perspective.

Journal of Humanistic Education and Development, 34, 50–51.

McHugh, M. C., Koeske, R. D., & Frieze, I. H. (1986). Issues to consider in conducting non-sexist psychological research. *American Psychologist, 41,* 879–890.

McIllroy, J. H. (1979). Career as life-style: An existential view. *Personnel and Guidance Journal, 57,* 351–354.

McLeod, J. (2003). *Doing counselling research* (2nd ed.). Thousand Oaks, CA: Sage.

McMahon, M., & Patton, W. (1997). Gender differences in children and adolescents' perceptions of influences on their career development. *School Counselor, 44,* 368–376.

McRae, M. B., Thompson, D. A., & Cooper, S. (1999). Black churches as therapeutic groups. *Journal of Multicultural Counseling and Development, 27,* 207–220.

McWey, L. M. (2004). Predictors of attachment styles of children in foster care: An attachment theory model for working with families. *Journal of Marital and Family Therapy, 30,* 439–452.

McWhirter, J. J., McWhirter, B. T., McWhirter, A. M., & McWhirter, E. H. (1994). High- and low-risk characteristics of youth: The five Cs of competency. *School Counselor, 28,* 188–196.

McWhirter, J. J., McWhirter, B. T., McWhirter, E. H., & McWhirter, R. J. (2007). *At-risk youth: A comprehensive response for counselors, psychologists, and human services professionals* (4th ed.). Belmont, CA: Thomson Brooks/Cole.

Means, B. L. (1973). Levels of empathic response. *Personnel and Guidance Journal, 52,* 23–28.

Meehl, P. (1973). *Psychodiagnosis: Selected papers.* New York: Norton.

Mehrabian, A. (1970). Some determinants of affiliation and conformity. *Psychological Reports, 27,* 19–29.

Mehrabian, A. (1971). *Silent messages.* Belmont, CA: Wadsworth.

Meichenbaum, D. (1993). Changing conceptions of cognitive behavior modification: Retrospect and prospect. *Journal of Consulting and Clinical Psychology, 61,* 202–204.

Meier, S. T., & Davis, S. R. (2011). *The elements of counseling* (7th ed.). Belmont, CA: Thomson Brooks/Cole.

Mejia, X. E. (2005). Gender matters: Working with adult male survivors of trauma. *Journal of Counseling & Development, 83,* 29–40.

Mellin, E. A. (2009). Responding to the crisis in children's mental health: Potential roles for the counseling profession. *Journal of Counseling & Development, 87,* 501–506.

Mencken, F. C., & Winfield, I. (2000). Job search and sex segregation: Does sex of social contact matter? *Sex Roles, 42,* 847–865.

Mendelowitz, E., & Schneider, K. (2008). Existential psychotherapy. In R. J. Corsini & D. Wedding (Eds.), *Current psychotherapies* (8th ed., pp. 295–327). Belmont, CA: Thomson Brooks/Cole.

Mercer, C. D., Mercer, A. R., & Pullen, P. C. (2011). *Teaching students with learning problems* (8th ed.). Upper Saddle River, NJ: Prentice Hall.

Merchant, N., & Dupuy, P. (1996). Multicultural counseling and qualitative research: Shared worldview and skills. *Journal of Counseling & Development, 74,* 537–541.

Merriam, S. B. (2002). Assessing and evaluating qualitative research. In S. B. Merriam (Ed.), *Qualitative research in practice* (pp. 18–33). San Francisco: Jossey-Bass.

Merrill Education. (2007). *A guide to ethical conduct for the helping professions* (2nd ed.). Upper Saddle River, NJ: Author.

Merta, R. J. (1995). Group work: Multicultural perspectives. In J. G. Ponterotto, J. M. Casas, L. A. Suzuki, & C. M. Alexander (Eds.), *Handbook of multicultural counseling* (pp. 567–585). Thousand Oaks, CA: Sage.

Mertens, D. M. (2005). *Research methods in education and psychology* (2nd ed.). Thousand Oaks, CA: Sage.

Messerlian, C., Byrne, A., & Derevensky, J. (2004). Gambling, youth and the Internet: Should we be concerned? *The Canadian Child and Adolescent Psychiatry Review, 13,* 12–15.

Meyer, D., Helwig, A., Gjernes, O., & Chickering, J. (1985). The National Employment Counselors Association. *Journal of Counseling & Development, 63,* 440–443.

Meyer, D. F. (2005). Psychological correlates of help seeking for eating-disorder symptoms in female college students. *Journal of College Counseling, 8,* 20–30.

Meyer, D. F., & Russell, R. K. (1998). Caretaking, separation from parents, and the development of eating disorders. *Journal of Counseling & Development, 76,* 166–173.

Meyer, G. J., Finn, S. E., Eyde, L. D., Kay, G. G., Moreland, K. L., Dies, R. R., et al. (2001). Psychological testing and psychological assessment: A review of evidence and issues. *American Psychologist, 56,* 128–165.

Middleton, R. A., Flowers, C., & Zawaiza, T. (1996). Multiculturalism, affirmative action, and section 21 of the 1992 Rehabilitation Act amendments: Fact or fiction? *Rehabilitation Counseling Bulletin, 40,* 11–30.

Miller, G. A. (2003). *Incorporating spirituality in counseling and psychotherapy: Theory and technique.* Hoboken, NJ: Wiley.

Miller, G. A., Wagner, A., Britton, T. P., & Gridley, B. E. (1998). A framework for understanding the wounding of healers. *Counseling and Values, 42,* 124–132.

Miller, G. M. (1982). Deriving meaning from standardized tests: Interpreting test results to clients. *Measurement and Evaluation in Guidance, 15,* 87–94.

Miller, J. B., & Stiver, I. R. (1997). *The healing connection: How women form relationships in therapy and in life.* Northvale, NJ: Aronson.

Miller, K. L., Miller, S. M., & Stull, J. C. (2007). Predictors of counselor educators' cultural discriminatory behavior. *Journal of Counseling & Development, 85,* 325–336.

Miller, M. J. (1985). Analyzing client change graphically. *Journal of Counseling & Development, 63,* 491–494.

Miller, M. J. (1996). Client-centered reflections on career decision making. *Journal of Employment Counseling, 33,* 43–46.

Miller, M. J. (1998). Broadening the use of Holland's hexagon with specific implications for career counselors. *Journal of Employment Counseling, 35,* 2–6.

Miller, M. J. (2002). Longitudinal examination of a three-letter Holland code. *Journal of Employment Counseling, 39,* 43–48.

Miller, W. R., & Brown, S. A. (1997). Why psychologists should treat alcohol and drug problems. *American Psychologist, 52,* 1269–1279.

Miller, W. R., & Rollnick, S. (2002). *Motivational interviewing: Preparing people for change* (2nd ed). New York: Guilford.

Minuchin, P., Colapinto, J., & Minuchin, S. (1999). *Working with families of the poor.* New York: Guilford.

Minuchin, S. (1974). *Families and family therapy.* Cambridge, MA: Harvard University Press.

Minuchin, S., & Fishman, H. C. (1981). *Family therapy techniques.* Cambridge, MA: Harvard University Press.

Minuchin, S., Montalvo, B., Guerney, B., Rosman, B., & Schumer, F. (1967). *Families of the slums.* New York: Basic Books.

Miranda, A. O., Bilot, J. M., Peluso, P. R., Berman, K., & Van Meek, L. G (2006). Latino families: The relevance of the connection among acculturation, family dynamics, and health for family counseling research and practice. *The Family Journal: Counseling and Therapy for Couples and Families, 14,* 268–273.

Mitchell, R. (2007). *Documentation in counseling records: An overview of ethical, legal, and clinical issues* (3rd ed.). Alexandria, VA: American Counseling Association.

Miwa, Y., & Hanyu, K. (2006). The effects of interior design on communication and impressions of a counselor in a counseling room. *Environment and Behavior, 38,* 484–502.

Modak, R., & Sheperis, C. J. (2009). White racial identity models. In B. Erford (Ed.). *ACA Encyclopedia of Counseling* (pp. 565–566). Alexandria, VA: American Counseling Association.

Mohai, C. E. (1991). *Are school-based drug prevention programs working?* Ann Arbor, MI: CAPS Digest (EDO-CG-91-1).

Moleski, S. M., & Kiselica, M. S. (2005). Dual relationships: A continuum ranging from the destructive to the therapeutic. *Journal of Counseling & Development, 83,* 3–11.

Mollen, D. (2006). Voluntarily childfree women: Experiences and counseling consideration. *Journal of Mental Health Counseling, 28,* 269–284.

Monk, G. (1998). Narrative therapy: An exemplar of the postmodern breed of therapies. *Counseling and Human Development, 30*(5), 1–14.

Moon, K. A. (2007). A client-centered review of Rogers with Gloria. *Journal of Counseling & Development, 85,* 277–285.

Moore, D., & Haverkamp, B. E. (1989). Measured increases in male emotional expressiveness following a structured group intervention. *Journal of Counseling & Development, 67,* 513–517.

Moore, D., & Leafgren, F. (Eds.). (1990). *Problem solving strategies and interventions for men in conflict.* Alexandria, VA: American Counseling Association.

Moore, D. D., & Forster, J. R. (1993). Student assistance programs: New approaches for reducing adolescent substance abuse. *Journal of Counseling & Development, 71,* 326–329.

Moos, R. (1973). Conceptualization of human environments. *American Psychologist, 28,* 652–665.

Morgan, J. I., & Skovholt, T. M. (1977). Using inner experience: Fantasy and daydreams in career counseling. *Journal of Counseling Psychology, 24,* 391–397.

Morgan, J. P., Jr. (1994). Bereavement in older adults. *Journal of Mental Health Counseling, 16,* 318–326.

Mori, S. (2000). Addressing the mental health concerns of international students. *Journal of Counseling & Development, 78,* 137–144.

Morkides, C. (2009, May). From burning bright to simply burned out. *Counseling Today, 51*(11), 42–46.

Morran, D. K. (1982). Leader and member self-disclosing behavior in counseling groups. *Journal for Specialists in Group Work, 7,* 218–223.

Morrill, W. H., Oetting, E. R., & Hurst, J. C. (1974). Dimensions of counselor functioning. *Personnel and Guidance Journal, 53,* 354–359.

Morrissey, M. (1997, October). The invisible minority: Counseling Asian Americans. *Counseling Today, 1,* 21.

Morrissey, M. (1998, January). The growing problem of elder abuse. *Counseling Today,* 14.

Morse, C. L., & Russell, T. (1988). How elementary counselors see their role: An empirical study. *Elementary School Guidance and Counseling, 23,* 54–62.

Mosak, H., & Maniacci, M. P. (2008). Adlerian psychotherapy. In R. J. Corsini & D. Wedding (Eds.), *Current psychotherapies* (8th ed., pp. 63–106). Belmont, CA: Thomson Brooks/Cole.

Mostert, D. L., Johnson, E., & Mostert, M. P. (1997). The utility of solution-focused, brief counseling in schools: Potential from an initial study. *Professional School Counseling, 1,* 21–24.

Moundas, S., Singh, A., Hosea, J., Pickering, D., Roan, A. & Burnes, T. (2009, January). Counseling transgender adults. *Counseling Today, 51*(7), 61–63.

Moursund, J., & Kenny, M. C. (2002). *The process of counseling and therapy* (4th ed.). Upper Saddle River, NJ: Prentice Hall.

Mudore, C. F. (1997). Assisting young people in quitting tobacco. *Professional School Counseling, 1,* 61–62.

Mullen, P. E., Martin, J. L., Anderson, J. C., Romans, S. E., & Herbison, G. P. (1995). The long-term impact of physical, emotional, and sexual abuse of children: A community study. *Child Abuse and Neglect, 20,* 7–21.

Muro, J. J. (1981). On target: On top. *Elementary School Guidance and Counseling, 15,* 307–314.

Murphy, J. J. (2008). *Solution-focused counseling in the schools* (2nd ed.). Alexandria, VA: American Counseling Association.

Murphy, K. A., Blustein, D. L., Bohlig, A. J., & Platt, M. G. (2010). The college-to-career transition: An exploration of emerging adulthood. *Journal of Counseling & Development, 88,* 174–181.

Murphy, K. E. (1998). Is managed care unethical? *IAMFC Family Digest, 11*(1), 3.

Murphy, S. N. (2011, February). Your witness. *Counseling Today, 53*(8), 36–40.

Murray, C. E. (2009). Diffusion of innovation theory: A bridge for the research-practice gap in counseling. *Journal of Counseling & Development, 87,* 108–116.

Murray, H. A. (1938). *Explorations in personality.* New York: Oxford University Press.

Muthard, J. E., & Salomone, P. R. (1978). The role and function of the rehabilitation counselor. In B. Bolton & M. E. Jaques (Eds.), *Rehabilitation counseling: Theory and practice* (pp. 166–175). Baltimore: University Park Press.

Myers, I. B. (1962). *Manual for the Myers-Briggs Type Indicator.* Palo Alto, CA: Consulting Psychologists Press.

Myers, I. B. (1980). *Gifts differing.* Palo Alto, CA: Consulting Psychologists Press.

Myers, J., & Sweeney, T. J. (2005). *Counseling for wellness: Theory, research, and practice.* Alexandria, VA: American Counseling Association.

Myers, J. E. (1983). A national survey of geriatric mental health services. *AMHCA Journal, 5,* 69–74.

Myers, J. E. (1990). Aging: An overview for mental health counselors. *Journal of Mental Health Counseling, 12,* 245–259.

Myers, J. E. (1995). From "forgotten and ignored" to standards and certification: Gerontological counseling comes of age. *Journal of Counseling & Development, 74,* 143.

Myers, J. E. (1998). Combatting ageism: The rights of older persons. In C. C. Lee & G. Walz (Eds.), *Social action for counselors.* Alexandria, VA: American Counseling Association.

Myers, J. E., Poidevant, J. M., & Dean, L. A. (1991). Groups for older persons and their caregivers: A review of the literature. *Journal for Specialists in Group Work, 16,* 197–205.

Myers, J. E., & Sweeney, T. J. (2001). Specialties in counseling. In D. C. Locke, J. E. Myers, & E. L. Herr (Eds.), *The handbook of counseling* (pp. 43–54). Thousand Oaks, CA: Sage.

Myers, J. E., & Sweeney, T. J. (2008). Wellness counseling: The evidence base for practice. *Journal of Counseling & Development, 86*, 482–493.

Myers, J. E., Sweeney, T. J., & Witmer, J. M. (2000). The wheel of wellness: Counseling for wellness: A holistic model for treatment planning. *Journal of Counseling & Development, 78*, 251–266.

Myers, J. E., Shoffner, M. F., & Briggs, M. K. (2002). Developmental counseling and therapy: An effective approach to understanding and counseling children. *Professional School Counseling, 5*, 194–202.

Myers, J. E., Willise, J. T., & Villalba, J. A. (2011). Promoting self-esteem in adolescents: The influence of wellness factors. *Journal of Counseling & Development, 89*, 28–36.

Myers, S. (2000). Empathetic listening: Reports on the experience of being heard. *Journal of Humanistic Psychology, 40*, 148–173.

Myrick, R. D. (1997). Traveling together on the road ahead. *Professional School Counseling, 1*, 4–8.

Myrick, R. D. (2003). *Developmental guidance and counseling: A practical approach* (4th ed.). Minneapolis: Educational Media Corporation.

Napier, A., & Whitaker, C. (1978). *The family crucible.* New York: Harper & Row.

Napier, A. Y. (1988). *The fragile bond.* New York: Harper & Row.

Nasser-McMillan, S. C., & Hakim-Larson, J. (2003). Counseling considerations among Arab Americans. *Journal of Counseling & Development, 81*, 150–159.

National Career Development Association. (1990). *National survey of working America, 1990: Selected findings.* Alexandria, VA: Author.

National Center on Addiction and Substance Abuse at Columbia University. (2003). *CASA 2003 teen survey: High stress, frequent boredom, too much spending money: Triple threat that hikes risk of teen substance abuse.* New York: Author.

National Center on Addiction and Substance Abuse at Columbia University. (2007). *Wasting the best and brightest.* New York: Author.

National Occupational Information Coordinating Committee. (1994). *Program guide: Planning to meet career development needs in school-to-work transition programs.* Washington, DC: U.S. Government Printing Office.

Negy, C. (2008). *Cross-cultural psychotherapy: Toward a critical understanding of diverse clients* (2nd ed.). Reno, NV: Bent Tree Press.

Nelligan, A. (1994, Fall). Balancing process and content: A collaborative experience. *Together, 23*, 8–9.

Nelson, J. (2008). Laugh and the world laughs with you: An attachment perspective on the meaning of laughter in psychotherapy. *Clinical Social Work Journal, 36*(1), 41–49.

Nelson, J. A. (2006). For parents only: A strategic family therapy approach in school counseling. *The Family Journal: Counseling and Therapy for Couples and Families, 14*, 180–183.

Nelson, M. L. (1996). Separation versus connection: The gender controversy: Implications for counseling women. *Journal of Counseling & Development, 74*, 339–344.

Nelson, R. C., & Shifron, R. (1985). Choice awareness in consultation. *Counselor Education and Supervision, 24*, 298–306.

Nerenberg, L. (2008). *Elder abuse prevention: Emerging trends and promising strategies.* New York: Springer.

Ness, M. E. (1989). The use of humorous journal articles in counselor training. *Counselor Education and Supervision, 29*, 35–43.

Neugarten, B. L. (1971, December). Grow old along with me! The best is yet to be. *Psychology Today*, 48–56.

Neugarten, B. L. (1978). The rise of the young-old. In R. Gross, B. Gross, & S. Seidman (Eds.), *The new old: Struggling for decent aging* (pp. 47–49). New York: Doubleday.

Newman, J. L. (1993). Ethical issues in consultation. *Journal of Counseling & Development, 72*, 148–156.

Newman, J. L., Fuqua, D. R., Gray, E. A., & Simpson, D. B. (2006). Gender differences in the relationship of anger and depression in a clinical sample. *Journal of Counseling & Development, 84*, 157–162.

Nicholas, D. R., Gobble, D. C., Crose, R. G., & Frank, B. (1992). A systems view of health, wellness, and gender: Implications for mental health counseling. *Journal of Mental Health Counseling, 14*, 8–19.

Nichols, D. S., & Kaufman, A. (2011). *Essentials of MMPI-2 assessment* (2nd ed). Hoboken, NJ: Wiley.

Nichols, M. (1988). *The self in the system: Expanding the limits of family therapy.* New York: Brunner/Mazel.

Nichols, M. (2010). *Family therapy: Concepts and methods* (9th ed.). Boston: Allyn & Bacon.

Nichols, M. P. (1998). The lost art of listening. *IAMFC Family Digest, 11*(1), 1–2, 4, 11.

Nichols, W. C. (1993). *The AAMFGC: 50 years of marital and family therapy.* Washington, DC: American Association of Marriage and Family Therapists.

Nielsen, S., Okiishi, J., Nielsen, D. L., Hawkins, E. J., Harmon, S., Pedersen, T., & . . . Jackson, A. P. (2009). Termination, appointment use, and outcome patterns associated with intake therapist discontinuity. *Professional Psychology: Research and Practice, 40*(3), 272–278.

Niles, S. G., & Harris-Bowlsbey, J. H. (2009). *Career development interventions in the 21st century* (3rd ed.). Upper Saddle River, NJ: Merrill/Prentice Hall.

Nims, D. R. (1998). Searching for self: A theoretical model for applying family systems to adolescent group work. *Journal for Specialists in Group Work, 23*, 133–144.

Nisson, J. E., Love, K. M., Taylor, K. J., & Slusher, A. L. (2007). A content and sample analysis of quantitative articles published in the *Journal of Counseling & Development* between 1991 and 2000. *Journal of Counseling & Development, 85*, 357–363.

Noll, V. (1997). Cross-age mentoring program for social skills development. *School Counselor, 44*, 239–242.

Norcross, J. C., & Beutler, L. E. (2008). Integrative psychotherapies. In R. J. Corsini & D. Wedding (Eds.), *Current psychotherapies* (8th ed., pp. 481–511). Belmont, CA: Thomson Brooks/Cole.

Nordal, K. C. (2010). Where has all the psychotherapy gone? *APA Monitor, 41*(10), 17.

North, C. S., & Pferrerbaum, B. (2002). Research on the mental health effects of terrorism. *Journal of the American Medical Association, 288*, 633–636.

Nugent, F. A. (1981). *Professional counseling.* Pacific Grove, CA: Brooks/Cole.

Nugent, F. A., & Jones, K. D. (2009). *An introduction to the profession of counseling* (5th ed.). Upper Saddle River, NJ: Merrill/Prentice Hall.

Nwachuku, U., & Ivey, A. (1991). Culture-specific counseling: An alternative model. *Journal of Counseling & Development, 70*, 106–111.

Nye, R. D. (2000). *Three psychologies: Perspectives from*

Freud, Skinner, and Rogers (6th ed.). Pacific Grove, CA: Brooks/Cole.

Nystul, M. S. (2011). *The art and science of counseling and psychotherapy* (4th ed.). Upper Saddle River, NJ: Pearson.

Oates, R. K., & Bross, D. C. (1995). What have we learned about treating child physical abuse? A literature review of the last decade. *Child Abuse and Neglect, 19,* 463–473.

Oakland, T. (1982). Nonbiased assessment in counseling: Issues and guidelines. *Measurement and Evaluation in Guidance, 15,* 107–116.

O'Brien, B. A., & Lewis, M. (1975). A community adolescent self-help center. *Personnel and Guidance Journal, 54,* 212–216.

Odell, M., & Quinn, W. H. (1998). Therapist and client behaviors in the first interview: Effect on session impact and treatment duration. *Journal of Marital and Family Therapy, 24,* 369–388.

O'Donnell, J. M. (1988). The holistic health movement: Implications for counseling theory and practice. In R. Hayes & R. Aubrey (Eds.), *New directions for counseling and human development* (pp. 365–382). Denver: Love.

Ohlsen, M. M. (1977). *Group counseling* (2nd ed.). New York: Holt, Rinehart & Winston.

Ohlsen, M. M. (1979). *Marriage counseling in groups.* Champaign, IL: Research Press.

Ohlsen, M. M. (1982). Family therapy with the triad model. In A. M. Horne & M. M. Ohlsen (Eds.), *Family counseling and therapy* (pp. 412–434). Itasca, IL: F. E. Peacock.

Ohlsen, M. M. (1983). *Introduction to counseling.* Itasca, IL: F. E. Peacock.

Okun, B. F. (1984). *Working with adults: Individual, family, and career development.* Pacific Grove, CA: Brooks/Cole.

Okun, B. F. (1990). *Seeking connections in psychotherapy.* San Francisco: Jossey-Bass.

Okun, B. R. (1997). *Effective helping: Interviewing and counseling techniques* (5th ed.). Belmont, CA: Thomson.

Okun, B. F., Fried, J., & Okun, M. L. (1999). *Understanding diversity: A learning-as-practice primer.* Pacific Grove, CA: Brooks/Cole.

Okun, B. F., & Kantrowitz, R. E. (2008). *Effective helping: Interviewing and counseling techniques* (7th ed.). Belmont, CA: Thomson Brooks/Cole.

Oldham, J. M., & Morris, L. B. (1995). *New personality self-portrait: Why you think, work, love, and act the way you do.* New York: Bantam.

O'Leary, K. D., & Murphy, C. (1999). Clinical issues in the assessment of partner violence. In R. Ammerman & M. Hersen (Eds.), *Assessment of family violence: A clinical and legal sourcebook* (pp. 46–94). New York: Wiley.

Oliver, K. (2010). *Secrets of happy couples: Loving yourself, your partner, and your life.* Country Club Hills, IL: InsideOut Press.

Olsen, L. D. (1971). Ethical standards for group leaders. *Personnel and Guidance Journal, 50,* 288.

Olson, D. H. (1986). Circumplex model VII: Validation studies and FACES III. *Family Process, 25,* 337–351.

Onedera, J. D., & Greenwalt, B. (2007). Choice theory: An interview with Dr. William Glasser. *The Family Journal: Counseling and Therapy for Couples and Families, 15,* 79–86.

O'Neil, J. M., & Carroll, M. R. (1988). A gender role workshop focused on sexism, gender role conflict, and the gender role journey. *Journal of Counseling & Development, 67,* 193–197.

Openlander, P., & Searight, R. (1983). Family counseling perspectives in the college counseling center. *Journal of College Student Personnel, 24,* 423–427.

Orfield, G. (Ed.). (2004). *Dropouts in America: Confronting the graduation rate crisis.* Cambridge, MA: Harvard Education Press.

O'Ryan, L. W., & McFarland, W. P. (2010). A phenomenological exploration of the experiences of dual-career lesbian and gay couples. *Journal of Counseling & Development, 88,* 71–79.

Osborn, D. S., Howard, D. K., & Leierer, S. J. (2007). The effect of a career development course on the dysfunctional career thoughts of racially and ethnically diverse college freshment. *Career Development Quarterly, 55,* 365–377.

Osborne, J. L., Collison, B. B., House, R. M., Gray, L. A., Firth, J., & Lou, M. (1998). Developing a social advocacy model for counselor education. *Counselor Education and Supervision, 37,* 190–202.

Osborne, W. L. (1982). Group counseling: Direction and intention. *Journal for Specialists in Group Work, 7,* 275–280.

Osborne, W. L., Brown, S., Niles, S., & Miner, C. U. (1997). *Career development assessment and counseling.* Alexandria, VA: ACA.

Osipow, S. H., & Fitzgerald, L. F. (1996). *Theories of career development* (4th ed.). Boston: Allyn & Bacon.

Ostlund, D. R., & Kinnier, R. T. (1997). Values of youth: Messages from the most popular songs of four decades. *Journal of Humanistic Education and Development, 36,* 83–91.

Otani, A. (1989). Client resistance in counseling: Its theoretical rationale and taxonomic classification. *Journal of Counseling & Development, 67,* 458–461.

Ottens, A. J., & Klein, J. F. (2005). Common factors: Where the soul of counseling and psychotherapy resides. *Journal of Humanistic Counseling, Education and Development, 44,* 32–45.

Otwell, P. S., & Mullis, F. (1997). Counselor-led staff development: An efficient approach to teacher consultation. *Professional School Counseling, 1,* 25–30.

Overholser, J. C. (2010). Psychotherapy that strives to encourage social interest: A simulated interview with Alfred Adler. *Journal of Psychotherapy Integration, 20,* 347–363.

Overton, S. L., & Medina, S. L. (2008). The stigma of mental illness. *Journal of Counseling & Development, 86,* 143–151.

Pace, D., Stamler, V. L., Yarris, E., & June, L. (1996). Rounding out the cube: Evolution to a global model for counseling centers. *Journal of Counseling & Development, 74,* 321–325.

Pachis, B., Rettman, S., & Gotthoffer, D. (2001). *Counseling on the net 2001.* Boston: Allyn & Bacon.

Pack-Brown, S. P., Whittington-Clark, L. E., & Parker, W. M. (1998). *Images of me: A guide to group work with African-American women.* Boston: Allyn & Bacon.

Paisley, P. O., & Hubbard, G. T. (1994). *Developmental school counseling programs: From theory to practice.* Alexandria, VA: American Counseling Association.

Paisley, P. O., & McMahon, H. G. (2001). School counseling for the 21st century: Challenges and opportunities. *Professional School Counseling, 5,* 106–115.

Paisley, P. O., & Milsom, A. (2007). Group work as an essential contribution to transforming school counseling. *Journal for Specialists in Group Work, 32,* 9–17.

Palladino Schultheiss, D. E., Palma, T. V., & Manzi, A. J. (2005). Career development in middle childhood: A qualitative inquiry. *Career Development Quarterly, 53,* 246–262.

Papero, D. V. (1996). Bowen family systems and marriage. In N. S. Jacobson & A. S. Gurman (Eds.), *Clinical* handbook of marital therapy. New York: Guilford.

Paradise, L. V., & Kirby, P. C. (2005). The treatment and prevention of depression: Implications for counseling and counselor training. *Journal of Counseling & Development, 83,* 116–119.

Paramore, B., Hopke, W. E., & Drier, H. N. (2004). *Children's dictionary of occupations* (4th ed.). Bloomington, IL: Meridian Education Corp.

Parham, T. A. (2002). Counseling models for African Americans: The what and how of counseling. In T. A. Parham (Ed.), *Counseling persons of African descent: Raising the bar of practitioner competence* (pp. 100–118). Thousand Oaks, CA: Sage.

Parham, T. A., White, J. L., & Ajamu, A. (2000). *The psychology of Blacks: An African centered perspective* (3rd ed.). Upper Saddle River, NJ: Prentice Hall.

Parker, K. (2011, January 18). A portrait of stepfamilies. pew social & demographic trends project. Washington, DC: Pew Research Center.

Parker, M. (1994, March). SIG updates. *Career Developments, 9,* 14–15.

Parker, R. M. (2012). *Rehabilitation counseling: Basics and beyond* (5th ed.). Austin, TX: Pro-Ed.

Parker, R. M., & Szymanski, E. M. (1996). Ethics and publications. *Rehabilitation Counseling Bulletin, 39,* 162–163.

Parker, S. (2011). Spirituality in counseling: A faith development perspective. *Journal of Counseling & Development, 89,* 112–119.

Parker, W. M., Archer, J., & Scott, J. (1992). *Multicultural relations on campus.* Muncie, IN: Accelerated Development.

Parsons, F. (1909). *Choosing a vocation.* Boston: Houghton Mifflin.

Parsons, R. D. (1996). *The skilled consultant: A systematic approach to the theory and practice of consultation.* Boston: Allyn & Bacon.

Paterson, D. J., & Darley, J. (1936). *Men, women, and jobs.* Minneapolis: University of Minnesota Press.

Paterson, J. (2008, September). Pitch your niche. *Counseling Today, 51*(3), 52–54.

Paterson, J. (2009, June). Beyond an elementary approach. *Counseling Today, 51*(12), 34–37.

Patterson, C. H. (1971). Are ethics different in different settings? *Personnel and Guidance Journal, 50,* 254–259.

Patterson, C. H. (1985). *The therapeutic relationship.* Pacific Grove, CA: Brooks/Cole.

Patterson, G. R. (1971). *Families: Applications of social learning to family life.* Champaign, IL: Research Press.

Patterson, W., Dohn, H., Bird, J., & Patterson, G. (1983). Evaluation of suicide patients: The SAD PERSONS scale. *Psychosomatics, 24,* 343–349.

Paul, E. L., & Brier, S. (2001). Friendsickness in the transition to college: Precollege predictors and college adjustment correlates. *Journal of Counseling & Development, 79,* 77–89.

Paul, G. L. (1967). Strategy of outcome research in psychotherapy. *Journal of Consulting Psychology, 31,* 109–118.

Paulson, B. L., & Worth, M. (2002). Counseling for suicide: Client perspectives. *Journal of Counseling & Development, 80,* 86–93.

Peach, L., & Reddick, T. L. (1991). Counselors can make a difference in preventing adolescent suicide. *School Counselor, 39,* 107–110.

Pearson, J. E. (1988). A support group for women with relationship dependency. *Journal of Counseling & Development, 66,* 394–396.

Pearson, Q. M. (1998). Terminating before counseling has ended: Counseling implications and strategies for counselor relocation. *Journal of Mental Health Counseling, 20,* 55–63.

Pearson, Q. M. (2000). Opportunities and challenges in the supervisory relationship: Implications for counselor supervision. *Journal of Mental Health Counseling, 22,* 283.

Pearson, Q. M. (2008). Role overload, job satisfaction, leisure satisfaction, and psychological health among employed women. *Journal of Counseling & Development, 86,* 57–63.

Peck, L. D., & Lightsey Jr, O. (2008). The eating disorders continuum, self-esteem, and perfectionism. *Journal of Counseling & Development, 86,* 184–192.

Peck, M. S. (1978). *The road less traveled.* New York: Simon & Schuster.

Pedersen, P. (1987). Ten frequent assumptions of cultural bias in counseling. *Journal of Multicultural Counseling and Development, 15,* 16–22.

Pedersen, P. (1990). The constructs of complexity and balance in multicultural counseling theory and practice. *Journal of Counseling & Development, 68,* 550–554.

Pedersen, P. B. (1977). The triad model of cross-cultural counselor training. *Personnel and Guidance Journal, 56,* 94–100.

Pedersen, P. B. (1978). Four dimensions of cross-cultural skill in counselor training. *Personnel and Guidance Journal, 56,* 480–484.

Pedersen, P. B. (1982). Cross-cultural training for counselors and therapists. In E. Marshall & D. Kurtz (Eds.), *Interpersonal helping skills: A guide to training methods, programs, and resources.* San Francisco: Jossey-Bass.

Pedersen, P., Lonner, W. J., Draguns, J. G., & Trimble, J. E. (Eds.). (2007). *Counseling across cultures* (6th ed.). Thousand Oaks, CA: Sage.

Pedrotti, J., Edwards, L. M., & Lopez, S. J. (2008). Promoting hope: Suggestions for school counselors. *Professional*

School Counseling, 12(2), 100–107.

Peer, G. G. (1985). The status of secondary school guidance: A national survey. *School Counselor, 32,* 181–189.

Pelsma, D. M., & Borgers, S. B. (1986). Experience-based ethics: A developmental model of learning ethical reasoning. *Journal of Counseling & Development, 64,* 311–314.

Pence, E., Paymar, M., Ritmeester, T., & Shepard, M. (1998). *Education groups for men who batter: The Duluth model.* New York: Springer.

Penedo, F. J., & Dahn, J. R. (2005). Exercise and well-being: A review of mental and physical health benefits associated with physical activity. *Current Opinions in Psychiatry, 18,* 189–193.

Perls, F. S. (1969). *Gestalt therapy verbation.* Lafayette, CA: Real People Press.

Perham, A. S., & Accordino, M. P. (2007). Exercise and functional level of individuals with severe mental illness: A comparison of two groups. *Journal of Mental Health Counseling, 29,* 350–362.

Perry, W. G., Jr. (1970). *Forms of intellectual and ethical development in the college years.* New York: Holt, Rinehart & Winston.

Pérusse, R., Goodnough, G. E., & Lee, V. V. (2009). Group counseling in the schools. *Psychology in the Schools, 46*(3), 225–231.

Peterman, L. M., & Dixon, C. G. (2003). Domestic violence between same-sex partners: Implications for counseling. *Journal of Counseling & Development, 81,* 40–47.

Peters, H. J. (1980). *Guidance in the elementary schools.* New York: Macmillan.

Petersen, S. (2000). Multicultural perspective on middle-class women's identity development. *Journal of Counseling & Development, 78,* 63–71.

Peterson, C., & Seligman, M. E. P. (2004). *Character strength and virtues: A handbook and classification.* Washington,

DC: American Psychological Association.

Peterson, K. S. (2002, July 15). For better sex: Less conflict, more friendship. *USA Today,* p. 6D.

Peterson, K. S., & O'Neal, G. (1998, March 25). Society more violent; so are its children. *USA Today,* p. 3A.

Peterson, N., & Gonzalez, R. C. (Eds.). (2000). *Career counseling models for diverse populations.* Pacific Grove, CA: Brooks/Cole.

Peterson, N., & Priour, G. (2000). Battered women: A group vocational counseling model. In N. Peterson & R. C. Gonzalez (Eds.), *Career counseling models for diverse populations* (pp. 205–218). Pacific Grove, CA: Brooks/Cole.

Petrocelli, J. V. (2002). Processes and stages of change: Counseling with the transtheoretical model of change. *Journal of Counseling & Development, 80,* 22–30.

Phelps, R. E., Tranakos-Howe, S., Dagley, J. C., & Lyn, M. K. (2001). Encouragement and ethnicity in African American college students. *Journal of Counseling & Development, 79,* 90–97.

Piazza, N. J., & Baruth, N. E. (1990). Client record guidelines. *Journal of Counseling & Development, 68,* 313–316.

Piercy, F. P. (2010). *Working with aging families: Therapeutic solutions for caregivers, spouses, and adult children.* New York: W. W. Norton.

Piercy, F. P., & Lobsenz, N. M. (1994). *Stop marital fights before they start.* New York: Berkeley.

Pietrofesa, J. J., Hoffman, A., & Splete, H. H. (1984). *Counseling: An introduction* (2nd ed.). Boston: Houghton Mifflin.

Pinjala, A., & Pierce, J. (2010, November/December). Bullying. *Family Therapy, 9*(6), 32–37.

Pinsof, W. M., & Wynne, L. C. (1995). The efficacy of marital and family therapy: An empirical overview, conclusions and recommendations. *Journal of Marital and Family Therapy, 21,* 585–614.

Pinson-Milburn, N. M., Fabian, E. S., Schlossberg, N. K., & Pyle, M. (1996). Grandparents raising grandchildren. *Journal of Counseling & Development, 74,* 548–554.

Pinterits, E. J., & Atkinson, D. R. (1998). The diversity video forum: An adjunct to diversity sensitive training in the classroom. *Counselor Education and Supervision, 37,* 203–216.

Pinto, R. P. & Morrell, E. M. (1988). Current approaches and future trends in smoking cessation programs. *Journal of Mental Health Counseling, 10,* 95–110.

Piotrowski, C., & Keller, J. (1989). Psychological testing in outpatient mental health facilities: A national study. *Professional Psychology: Research and Practice, 20,* 423–425.

Pistole, M. C. (1997a). Attachment theory: Contributions to group work. *Journal for Specialists in Group Work, 22,* 7–21.

Pistole, M. C. (1997b). Using the genogram to teach systems thinking. *Family Journal, 5,* 337–341.

Pistole, M. C., & Roberts, A. (2002). Mental health counseling: Toward resolving identity confusion. *Journal of Mental Health Counseling, 24,* 1–19.

Pistorello, J., & Follette, V. M. (1998). Childhood sexual abuse and couples' relationships: Female survivors' reports in therapy group. *Journal of Marital and Family Therapy, 24,* 473–485.

Polanski, P. J., & Hinkle, J. S. (2000). The mental status examination: Its use by professional counselors. *Journal of Counseling & Development, 78,* 357–364.

Polansky, J., Horan, J. J., & Hanish, C. (1993). Experimental construct validity of the outcomes of study skills training and career counseling as treatments for the retention of at-risk students. *Journal of Counseling & Development, 71,* 488–492.

Pollack, W. S., & Levant, R. F. (Eds.). (1998). *New psychotherapies for men.* New York: Wiley.

Pollock, S. L. (2006). Internet counseling and its feasibility for marriage and family counseling. *The Family Journal: Counseling and Therapy for Couples and Families, 14,* 65–70.

Polster, E., & Polster, M. (1973). *Gestalt therapy integrated: Contours of theory and practice.* New York: Brunner/Mazel.

Ponterotto, J. G., & Casas, J. M. (1987). In search of multicultural competence within counselor education programs. *Journal of Counseling & Development, 65,* 430–434.

Ponterotto, J. G., & Sabnani, H. B. (1989). "Classics" in multicultural counseling: A systematic five-year content analysis. *Journal of Multicultural Counseling and Development, 17,* 23–37.

Ponton, R. F., & Duba, J. D. (2009). The ACA Code of Ethics: Articulating counseling's professional covenant. *Journal of Counseling & Development, 87,* 117–121.

Ponzetti, J. J., Jr., & Cate, R. M. (1988). The relationship of personal attributes and friendship variables in predicting loneliness. *Journal of College Student Development, 29,* 292–298.

Ponzo, Z. (1978). Age prejudice of "act your age." *Personnel and Guidance Journal, 57,* 140–144.

Ponzo, Z. (1985). The counselor and physical attractiveness. *Journal of Counseling & Development, 63,* 482–485.

Pope, M., & Sweinsdottir, M. (2005). *Frank,* We Hardly Knew Ye: The Very Personal Side of *Frank Parsons. Journal of Counseling & Development, 83,* 105–115.

Popenhagen, M. P., & Qualley, R. M. (1998). Adolescent suicide: Detection, intervention, and prevention. *Professional School Counseling, 1,* 30–35.

Portman, T. (2009). Faces of the future: School counselors as cultural mediators. *Journal of Counseling & Development, 87,* 21–27.

Posthuma, B. W. (2002). *Small groups in counseling and therapy: Process and leadership* (4th ed.). Boston: Allyn & Bacon.

Prediger, D. J. (1994). Tests and counseling: The marriage that prevailed. *Measurement and Evaluation in Counseling and Development, 26,* 227–234.

Prediger, D. J. (Ed.). (1993). *Multicultural assessment standards: A compilation for counselors.* Alexandria, VA: Association for Assessment in Counseling.

Presbury, J. H., Echterling, L. G., & McKee, J. E. (2008). *Beyond brief counseling and therapy: An integrative approach* (2nd ed.). Upper Saddle River, NJ: Prentice Hall.

Pressly, P. K., & Heesacker, M. (2001). The physical environment and counseling: A review of theory and research. *Journal of Counseling & Development, 79,* 148–160.

Priest, R. (1991). Racism and prejudice as negative impacts on African American clients in therapy. *Journal of Counseling & Development, 70,* 213–215.

Prieto, L. R. (2011). Introduction to the special section on grief, loss, and bereavement. *Journal of Mental Health Counseling, 33,* 1–3.

Prieto, L. R., & Scheel, K. R. (2002). Using case documentation to strengthen counselor trainees' case conceptualization skills. *Journal of Counseling & Development, 80,* 11–21.

Prochaska, J. O. (1999). How do people change, and how can we change to help many more people? In M. A. Hubble, B. L. Duncan, & S. D. Miller (Eds.), *The heart and soul of change: What works in therapy* (pp. 227–255). Washington,

DC: American Psychological Association.

Prochaska, J. O., & DiClemente, C. C. (1992). The transtheoretical approach. In J. C. Norcross & M. R. Goldfried (Eds.), *Handbook of psychotherapy integration* (pp. 300–334). New York: Basic Books.

Prochaska, J. O., & Norcross, J. C. (2010). *Systems of psychotherapy: A transtheoretical analysis* (7th ed.). Belmont, CA: Brooks/Cole.

Purkey, W. W., & Schmidt, J. J. (1987). *The inviting relationship.* Upper Saddle River, NJ: Prentice Hall.

Puterbaugh, D. T. (2006). Communication counseling as a part of a treatment plan for depression. *Journal of Counseling & Development, 84,* 373–380.

Putman, S. E. (2009). The monsters in my head: Posttraumatic stress disorder and the child survivor of sexual abuse. *Journal of Counseling & Development, 87,* 80–89.

Pyle, K. R. (2000). A group approach to career decision making. In N. Peterson & R. C. Gonzalez (Eds.), *Career counseling models for diverse populations* (pp. 121–136). Pacific Grove, CA: Brooks/Cole.

Quintana, S. M., & Kerr, J. (1993). Relational needs in late adolescent separation-individuation. *Journal of Counseling & Development, 71,* 349–354.

Ragle, J., & Krone, K. (1985). Extending orientation: Telephone contacts by peer advisors. *Journal of College Student Personnel, 26,* 80–81.

Rainey, L. M., Hensley, F. A., & Crutchfield, L. B. (1997). Implementation of support groups in elementary and middle school student assistant programs. *Professional School Counseling, 1,* 36–40.

Rak, C. F., & Patterson, L. E. (1996). Promoting resilience in at-risk children. *Journal of Counseling & Development, 74,* 368–373.

Ramos-Sánchez, L., & Atkinson, D. R. (2009). The relationships between Mexican American acculturation, cultural values, gender, and help-seeking intentions. *Journal of Counseling & Development, 87,* 62–71.

Rampell, C. (March 2, 2010). More college students take public sector jobs, *The New York Times,* B1.

Randolph, D. L., & Graun, K. (1988). Resistance to consultation: A synthesis for counselor-consultants. *Journal of Counseling & Development, 67,* 182–184.

Raney, S., & Cinarbas, D. C. (2005). Counseling in developing countries: Turkey and India as examples. *Journal of Mental Health Counseling, 27,* 149–160.

Range, L. M. (2006). Women and suicide. In J. Worrell & C. D. Goodheart (Eds.). *Handbook of girls' and women's psychological health* (pp. 129–137). New York: Oxford.

Ratts, M. J., Toporek, R. L., & Lewis, J. A. (2010). *ACA advocacy competencies: A social justice framework for counselors.* Alexandria, VA: American Counseling Association.

Rayle, A. D. (2006). Mattering to others: Implications for the counseling relationship. *Journal of Counseling & Development, 84,* 483–487.

Reardon, R. C., Bullock, E. E., & Meyer, K. E. (2007). A Holland perspective on the U.S. workforce from 1960 to 2000. *Career Development Quarterly, 55,* 262–274.

Reese, R. J., Conoley, C. W., & Brossart, D. F. (2006). The attractiveness of telephone counseling: An empirical investigation of current perceptions. *Journal of Counseling & Development, 84,* 54–60.

Remer, R. (1981). The counselor and research: An introduction. *Personnel and Guidance Journal, 59,* 567–571.

Remley, T. P., Jr. (1985). The law and ethical practices

in elementary and middle schools. *Elementary School Guidance and Counseling, 19,* 181–189.

Remley, T. P., Jr. (1991). *Preparing for court appearances.* Alexandria, VA: American Counseling Association.

Remley, T. P., Jr. (1992, Spring). You and the law. *American Counselor, 1,* 33.

Remley, T. P., Jr., & Herlihy, B. (2010). *Ethical, legal, and professional issues in counseling* (3rd ed.). Upper Saddle River, NJ: Prentice Hall.

Remley, T. P., Jr., Herlihy, B., & Herlihy, S. B. (1997). The U.S. Supreme Court decision in *Jaffee* v. *Redmond*: Implications for counselors. *Journal of Counseling & Development, 75,* 213–218.

Remley, T. P., Jr., Hermann, M. A., & Huey, W. C. (Eds.). (2011). *Ethical and legal issues in school counseling* (3rd ed.). Alexandria, VA: American School Counselor Association.

Remley, T. P., Jr., & Sparkman, L. B. (1993). Student suicides: The counselor's limited legal liability. *School Counselor, 40,* 164–169.

Resnikoff, R. D. (1981). Teaching family therapy: Ten key questions for understanding the family as patient. *Journal of Marital and Family Therapy, 7,* 135–142.

Ribak-Rosenthal, N. (1994). Reasons individuals become school administrators, school counselors, and teachers. *School Counselor, 41,* 158–164.

Rice, K. G., & Dellwo, J. P. (2002). Perfectionism and self-development: Implications for college adjustment. *Journal of Counseling & Development, 80,* 188–196.

Rice, K. G., & Whaley, T. J. (1994). A short term longitudinal study of within-semester stability and change in attachment and college student adjustment. *Journal of College Student Development, 35,* 324–330.

Richardson, E. H. (1981). Cultural and historical

perspectives in counseling American Indians. In D. W. Sue (Ed.), *Counseling the culturally different* (pp. 216–249). New York: Wiley.

Richardson, R. C., & Norman, K. I. (1997). "Rita dearest, it's OK to be different": Teaching children acceptance and tolerance. *Journal of Humanistic Education and Development, 35,* 188–197.

Richmond, L. J., & Guindon, M. H. (2010). Self-esteem and the third phase of life. In M. H. Guindon (Ed.). *Self-esteem across the lifespan* (pp. 281–294). New York: Routledge.

Richter-Antion, D. (1986). Qualitative differences between adult and younger students. *NASPA Journal, 23,* 58–62.

Ridley, C. R. (2005). *Overcoming unintentional racism in counseling and therapy: A practitioner's guide to intentional intervention* (2nd ed.). Thousand Oaks, CA: Sage.

Rimm, D. C., & Cunningham, H. M. (1985). Behavior therapies. In S. J. Lynn & J. P. Garske (Eds.), *Contemporary psychotherapies: Models and methods* (pp. 221–259). Upper Saddle River, NJ: Prentice Hall.

Riordan, R. J., & Beggs, M. S. (1987). Counselors and self-help groups. *Journal of Counseling & Development, 65,* 427–429.

Ritchie, M. H. (1986). Counseling the involuntary client. *Journal of Counseling & Development, 64,* 516–518.

Ritchie, M. H. (1989). Enhancing the public image of school counseling: A marketing approach. *School Counselor, 37,* 54–61.

Ritchie, M. H., & Partin, R. L. (1994). Parent education and consultation activities of school counselors. *School Counselor, 41,* 165–170.

Riva, M. T., Lippert, L., & Tackett, M. J. (2000). Selection practices of group leaders: A national survey. *Journal for Specialists in Group Work, 25,* 157–169.

Rivera, E., Nash, S., Chun Wah, B., & Ibrahim, S. (2008). Training school counselors in Singapore: First impressions of a multicultural challenge. *Journal of Counseling & Development, 86*(2), 219–223.

Roark, M. L. (1987). Preventing violence on college campuses. *Journal of Counseling & Development, 65,* 367–371.

Robert, T., & Kelly, V. A. (2010). Metaphor as an instrument for orchestrating change in counselor training and the counseling process. *Journal of Counseling & Development, 88,* 182–188.

Roberti, J. W., & Storch, E. A. (2005). Psychosocial adjustment of college students with tattoos and piercings. *Journal of College Counseling, 8,* 14–19.

Roberts, A. R. (2005). *Crisis intervention handbook: Assessment, treatment, and research* (3rd ed). New York: Oxford Press.

Roberts, A. R. (Ed.). (2007). *Battered women and their families: Intervention strategies and treatment programs* (3rd ed.). New York: Springer.

Roberts, D., & Ullom, C. (1989). Student leadership program model. *NASPA Journal, 27,* 67–74.

Roberts, S. (2007, August 9). Minorities now form majority in one-third of most-populous countries. *The New York Times* [online]. Retrieved August 9, 2007, from http://www.nytimes.com/2007/08/09us/09census.html?th&emc=th

Robinson, B. E. (1995, July). Helping clients with work addiction: Don't overdo it. *Counseling Today, 38,* 31–32.

Robinson, B. E. (2001). Workaholism and family functioning: A profile of familial relationships, psychological outcomes, and research considerations. *Contemporary Family Research, 23,* 123–135.

Robinson, B. E., Flowers, C., & Ng, K-M (2006). The relationship between workaholism and marital disaffection: Husbands' perspective. *The Family Journal: Counseling and Therapy for Couples and Families, 14,* 213–220.

Robinson, E. H., III. (1994). Critical issues in counselor education: Mentors, models, and money. *Counselor Education and Supervision, 33,* 339–343.

Robinson, F. P. (1950). *Principles and procedures of student counseling.* New York: Harper.

Robinson, S. E., & Gross, D. R. (1986). Counseling research: Ethics and issues. *Journal of Counseling & Development, 64,* 331–333.

Robinson, S. E., & Kinnier, R. T. (1988). Self-instructional versus traditional training for teaching basic counseling skills. *Counselor Education and Supervision, 28,* 140–145.

Robinson-Wood, T. L. (2009). *The convergence of race, ethnicity, and gender: Multiple identities in counseling* (3rd ed.). Upper Saddle River, NJ: Merrill/Prentice Hall.

Rodgers, R. F. (1980). Theories underlying student development. In D. G. Creamer (Ed.), *Student development in higher education* (pp. 10–96). Cincinnati, OH: American College Personnel Association.

Rodgers, R. F. (1989). Student development. In U. Delworth, G. R. Hanson, & Associates (Eds.), *Student services: A handbook for the profession* (2nd ed., pp. 117–164). San Francisco: Jossey-Bass.

Roehlke, H. J. (1988). Critical incidents in counselor development: Examples of Jung's concept of synchronicity. *Journal of Counseling & Development, 67,* 133–134.

Rogers, C. R. (1942). *Counseling and psychotherapy.* Boston: Houghton Mifflin.

Rogers, C. R. (1951). *Client-centered therapy.* Boston: Houghton Mifflin.

Rogers, C. R. (1955). Persons or science? A philosophical question. *American Psychologist, 10,* 267–278.

Rogers, C. R. (1957). The necessary and sufficient conditions of therapeutic personality change. *Journal of Consulting Psychology, 21,* 95–103.

Rogers, C. R. (1961). *On becoming a person.* Boston: Houghton Mifflin.

Rogers, C. R. (1964). Toward a science of the person. In T. W. Wann (Ed.), *Behaviorism and phenomenology: Contrasting bases for modern psychology* (pp. 109–140). Chicago: University of Chicago Press.

Rogers, C. R. (1967). The conditions of change from a client-centered view. In B. Berenson & R. Cankhuff (Eds.), *Sources of gain in counseling and psychotherapy* (pp. 71–86). New York: Holt, Rinehart & Winston.

Rogers, C. R. (1970). *Carl Rogers on encounter groups.* New York: Harper & Row.

Rogers, C. R. (1975). Empathic: An unappreciated way of being. *Counseling Psychologist, 5,* 2–10.

Rogers, C. R. (1977). *Carl Rogers on personal power: Inner strength and its revolutionary impact.* New York: Delacorte.

Rogers, C. R. (1980). *A way of being.* Boston: Houghton Mifflin.

Rogers, C. R. (1987). The underlying theory: Drawn from experience with individuals and groups. *Counseling and Values, 32,* 38–46.

Rogers, J. R. (2001). Theoretical grounding: The "missing link" in suicide research. *Journal of Counseling & Development, 79,* 16–25.

Rollins, J. (2009a, July). Crossing the great divide. *Counseling Today, 52*(1), 28–33.

Rollins, J. (2009b, August). Connecting with clients of faith.

Counseling Today, 52(2), 34–37.

Roloff, M. E., & Miller, G. R. (Eds.). (1980). *Persuasion: New directions in theory and research.* Beverly Hills, CA: Sage.

Romero, D., Silva, S. M., & Romero, P. S. (1989). In memory: Rene A. Ruiz. *Journal of Counseling & Development, 67,* 498–505.

Ronnestad, M. H., & Skovholt, T. M. (1993). Supervision of beginning and advanced graduate students of counseling and psychotherapy. *Journal of Counseling & Development, 71,* 396–405.

Roscoe, L. J. (2009). Wellness: A review of theory and measurement for counselors. *Journal of Counseling & Development, 87,* 216–226.

Rosen, S., & Tesser, A. (1970). On the reluctance to communicate undesirable information: The MUM effect. *Sociometry, 33,* 253–263.

Rosenthal, H. (2005). *Before you see your first client.* Philadelphia: Brunner-Routledge.

Rosenthal, J. A. (2001). *Statistics and data interpretation for the helping professions.* Pacific Grove, CA: Brooks/Cole.

Roskam, I., Zech, E., Nils, F., & Nader-Grosbois, N. (2008). School reorientation of children with disabilities: A stressful life event challenging parental cognitive and behavioral adjustment. *Journal of Counseling & Development, 86,* 132–142.

Rossi, P. H., Lipsey, M. W., & Freeman, H. E. (2004). *Evaluation: A systematic approach* (7th ed.). Thousand Oaks, CA: Sage.

Roudebush, S. (2011, June 1). Where do I begin? *Career Convergence Magazine Web Magazine,* http://associationdatabase.com/aws/NCDA/pt/sp/career_convergence

Rowley, W. J., & MacDonald, D. (2001). Counseling and the law: A cross-cultural perspective. *Journal of Counseling & Development, 79,* 422–429.

Roysircar, G. (2009). The big picture of advocacy: counselor, heal society and thyself. *Journal of Counseling & Development, 87,* 288–294.

Rubin, S. G. (1990). Transforming the university through service learning. In C. I. Delve, S. D. Mintz, & G. M. Stewart (Eds.), *Community services as values education* (pp. 111–124). San Francisco: Jossey-Bass.

Rudolph, J. (1989). The impact of contemporary ideology and AIDS on the counseling of gay clients. *Counseling and Values, 33,* 96–108.

Rueth, T., Demmitt, A., & Burger, S. (1998, March). *Counselors and the DSM-IV: Intentional and unintentional consequences of diagnosis.* Paper presented at the American Counseling Association Convention, Indianapolis, IN.

Ruiz, R. A. (1981). Cultural and historical perspectives in counseling Hispanics. In D. W. Sue (Ed.), *Counseling the culturally different* (pp. 186–215). New York: Wiley.

Ruiz, R. A., & Padilla, A. M. (1977). Counseling Latinos. *Personnel and Guidance Journal, 55,* 401–408.

Rule, W. R. (1982). Pursuing the horizon: Striving for elusive goals. *Personnel and Guidance Journal, 61,* 195–197.

Rumberger, R. W. (1987). High school dropouts. *Review of Educational Research, 57,* 101–122.

Rybak, C. J., & Brown, B. M. (1997). Group conflict: Communication patterns and group development. *Journal for Specialists in Group Work, 22,* 31–42.

Rybak, C. J., Eastin, C. L., & Robbins, I. (2004). Native American healing practices and counseling. *Journal of Humanistic Counseling, Education and Development, 43,* 25–32.

Sack, R. T. (1985). On giving advice. *AMHCA Journal, 7,* 127–132.

Sack, R. T. (1988). Counseling responses when clients say "I don't know." *Journal of Mental Health Counseling, 10,* 179–187.

Saidla, D. D. (1990). Cognitive development and group stages. *Journal for Specialists in Group Work, 15,* 15–20.

Salisbury, A. (1975). Counseling older persons: A neglected area in counselor education and supervision. *Counselor Education and Supervision, 4,* 237–238.

Salomone, P. R., & McKenna, P. (1982). Difficult career counseling cases. I: Unrealistic vocational aspirations. *Personnel and Guidance Journal, 60,* 283–286.

Salomone, P. R., & Sheehan, M. C. (1985). Vocational stability and congruence: An examination of Holland's proposition. *Vocational Guidance Quarterly, 34,* 91–98.

Sampson, J. P., Kolodinsky, R. W., & Greeno, B. P. (1997). Counseling on the information highway: Future possibilities and potential problems. *Journal of Counseling & Development, 75,* 203–212.

Sampson, J. P., Jr., & Bloom, J. W. (2001). The potential for success and failure of computer applications in counseling and guidance. In D. C. Locke, J. E. Myers, & E. L. Herr (Eds.), *The handbook of counseling* (pp. 613–627). Thousand Oaks, CA: Sage.

Sandeen, A. (1988). *Student affairs: Issues, problems and trends.* Ann Arbor, MI: ERIC/CAPS.

Sandell, D. S., & Hudson, L. (2010). *Ending elder abuse: A family guide.* Fort Bragg, CA: Cypress House.

Sanders, D. (1987). Cultural conflicts: An important factor in the academic failures of American Indian students. *Journal of Multicultural Counseling and Development, 15,* 81–90.

Sandhu, D. S. (1997). Psychocultural profiles of Asian and Pacific Islander Americans: Implications for counseling and psychotherapy. *Journal of Multicultural Counseling and Development, 25,* 7–22.

Sanford, N. (1962). *The American college.* New York: Wiley.

Sanford, N. (1979). Freshman personality: A stage in human development. In N. Sanford & J. Axelrod (Eds.), *College and character.* Berkeley, CA: Montaigne.

Sang Min, L., Seong Ho, C., Kissinger, D., & Ogle, N. T. (2010). A typology of burnout in professional counselors. *Journal of Counseling & Development, 88,* 131–138.

Savage, T. A., Harley, D. A., & Nowak, T. M. (2005). Applying social empowerment strategies as tools for self-advocacy in counseling lesbian and gay male clients. *Journal of Counseling & Development, 83,* 131–137.

Savickas, M. L. (1989). Annual review: Practice and research in career counseling and development, 1988. *Career Development Quarterly, 38,* 100–134.

Savickas, M. L. (1998). Interpreting interest inventories: A case example. *Career Development Quarterly, 46,* 307–319.

Savickas, M. L. (2005). The theory and practice of career construction. In S. D. Brown & R. W. Lent (Eds.), *Career development and counseling: Putting theory and research to work* (pp. 42–70). New York: Wiley.

Savickas, M. L. (2012). *Career counseling.* Washington, DC: American Psychological Association.

Saxton, J. W. (2008). *The satisfied patient: A guide to preventing malpractice claims by providing excellent customer service* (2nd ed.). Danvers, MA: HealthLeaders Media.

Scarborough, J. L. (1997). The SOS Club: A practical peer helper program. *Professional School Counseling, 1,* 25–28.

Scarborough, J. L., & Culbreth, J. R. (2008). Examining discrepancies between actual and preferred practice of school counselors. *Journal of Counseling & Development, 86*(4), 446–459.

Schaie, K. W., & Willis, S. L. (Eds.). (2011). *Handbook of the psychology of aging* (7th ed.). San Diego: Academic Press.

Schecter, S., & Ganley, A. (1995). *Domestic violence: A national curriculum for family preservation practitioners.* San Francisco: Family Violence Prevention Fund.

Schein, E. H. (1978). The role of the consultant: Content expert or process facilitator? *Personnel and Guidance Journal, 56,* 339–343.

Schellenberg, R. C., Parks-Savage, A., & Rehfuss, M. (2007). Reducing levels of elementary school violence with peer mediation. *Professional School Counseling, 10,* 475–481.

Scher, M. (1979). On counseling men. *Personnel and Guidance Journal, 57,* 252–254.

Scher, M. (1981). Men in hiding: A challenge for the counselor. *Personnel and Guidance Journal, 60,* 199–202.

Scher, M., & Stevens, M. (1987). Men and violence. *Journal of Counseling & Development, 65,* 351–355.

Schlossberg, N. K. (1990). Training counselors to work with older adults. *Generations, 15,* 7–10.

Schmidt, J. A. (1974). Research techniques for counselors: The multiple baseline. *Personnel and Guidance Journal, 53,* 200–206.

Schmidt, C. K., & Welsh, A. C. (2010). College adjustment and subjective well-being when coping with a family member's illness. *Journal of Counseling & Development, 88,* 397–406.

Schmidt, J. J. (2007). *Counseling in schools: Comprehensive programs of responsive services for all students* (5th ed.). Boston: Allyn & Bacon.

Schmidt, J. J. (2010). *The elementary/middle school*

counselor's survival guide (3rd ed). San Francisco: Jossey-Bass.

Schmidt, J. J., & Osborne, W. L. (1981). Counseling and consultation: Separate processes or the same? *Personnel and Guidance Journal, 60,* 168–170.

Schmidt, J. J., & Osborne, W. L. (1982). The way we were (and are): A profile of elementary counselors in North Carolina. *Elementary School Guidance and Counseling, 16,* 163–171.

Schneller, G., & Chalungsooth, P. (2002, June). Development of a multilingual tool to assess client presenting problems. *American College Counseling Association Visions,* 5–7.

Schofield, W. (1964). *Psychotherapy: The purchase of friendship.* Upper Saddle River, NJ: Prentice Hall.

Schrank, F. A. (1982). Bibliotherapy as an elementary school counseling tool. *Elementary School Guidance and Counseling, 16,* 218–227.

Schuh, J. J., Shipton, W. C., & Edman, N. (1986). Counseling problems encountered by resident assistants: An update. *Journal of College Student Personnel, 27,* 26–33.

Schuh, J. J., Jones, S. R., Harper, S. R., & Associates (Eds.). (2011). *Student services: A handbook* (5th ed.). San Francisco: Jossey-Bass.

Schultheiss, D. E. P. (2003). A relational approach to career counseling: Theoretical integration and practical application. *Journal of Counseling & Development, 81,* 301–310.

Schumacher, B. (1983). Rehabilitation counseling. In M. M. Ohlsen (Ed.), *Introduction to counseling* (pp. 313–324). Itasca, IL: F. E. Peacock.

Schutz, W. (1971). *Here comes everybody: Bodymind and encounter culture.* New York: Harper & Row.

Schwartz, R. C., & Feisthamel, K. P. (2009). Disproportionate diagnosis of mental disorders among African American versus European American clients: Implications for counseling theory, research, and practice. *Journal of Counseling & Development, 87,* 295–301.

Schwartz, S. J., & Finley, G. E. (2010). Troubled ruminations about parents: Conceptualization and validation with emerging adults. *Journal of Counseling and Development, 88,* 80–91.

Schwiebert, V. L., Myers, J. E., & Dice, C. (2000). Ethical guidelines for counselors working with older adults. *Journal of Counseling & Development, 78,* 123–129.

Schwiebert, V. L., Sealander, K. A., & Dennison, J. L. (2002). Strategies for counselors working with high school students with attention-deficit/hyperactivity disorder. *Journal of Counseling & Development, 80,* 3–10.

Scrignar, C. B. (1997). *Posttraumatic stress disorder, diagnosis, treatment and legal issues* (3rd ed.). New York: Bruno.

Sears, R., Rudisill, J., & Mason-Sear, C. (2006). *Consultation skills for mental health professionals.* New York: Wiley.

Sears, S. (1982). A definition of career guidance terms: A National Vocational Guidance Association perspective. *Vocational Guidance Quarterly, 31,* 137–143.

Sears, S. J., & Granello, D. H. (2002). School counseling now and in the future: A reaction. *Professional School Counseling, 5,* 164–171.

Seiler, G., Brooks, D. K., Jr., & Beck, E. S. (1987). Training standards of the American Mental Health Counselors Association: History, rationale, and implications. *Journal of Mental Health Counseling, 9,* 199–209.

Seiler, G., & Messina, J. J. (1979). Toward professional identity: The dimensions of mental health counseling in perspective. *AMHCA Journal, 1,* 3–8.

Seligman, L. (1984). Temporary termination. *Journal of Counseling & Development, 63,* 43–44.

Seligman, L. (1999). Twenty years of diagnosis and the DSM. *Journal of Mental Health Counseling, 21,* 229–239.

Seligman, L. (2004). *Diagnosis and treatment planning in counseling* (3rd ed.). New York: Springer.

Seligman, L. W. & Reichenberg, L. W. (2010). *Theories of counseling and psychotherapy: Systems, strategies, and skills* (3rd ed.). Upper Saddle River, NJ: Prentice Hall.

Senour, M. N. (1982). How counselors influence clients. *Personnel and Guidance Journal, 60,* 345–349.

Seto, A., Becker, K. W., & Akutsu, M. (2006). Counseling Japanese men on fathering. *Journal of Counseling & Development, 84,* 488–492.

Sexton, T. L. (1993). A review of the counseling outcome research. In G. R. Walz & J. C. Bleuer (Eds.), *Counselor efficacy* (pp. 79–119). Ann Arbor, MI: ERIC/CAPS.

Sexton, T. L. (1994). Systemic thinking in a linear world: Issues in the application of interactional counseling. *Journal of Counseling & Development, 72,* 249–258.

Sexton, T. L. (1996). The relevance of counseling outcome research: Current trends and practical implications. *Journal of Counseling & Development, 74,* 590–600.

Sexton, T. L., & Whiston, S. C. (1994). The status of the counseling relationship: An empirical review, theoretical implications, and research directions. *Counseling Psychology, 22,* 6–78.

Sexton, T. L., & Whiston, S. C. (1996). Integrating counseling research and practice. *Journal of Counseling & Development, 74,* 588–589.

Shadley, M. L. (2010, November/December). The way it was: Challenging the myths of addiction and how treatment and research have changed. *Family Therapy, 9*(6), 16–19.

Shaffer, H. J. (2003). The emergence of gambling among youth: The prevalence of underage lottery use and the impact of gambling. In H. J. Shaffer, M. N. Hall, J. Vander Bilt, and E. George (Eds.), *Future at stake: Youth, gambling, and severity,* (pp. 25–38). Reno, NV: University of Nevada Press.

Shallcross, L. (2009b, August). Living an uneasy existence. *Counseling Today, 52*(2), 38–43.

Shallcross, L. (2009c, August). Confronting addiction. *Counseling Today, 52*(2), 28–33.

Shallcross, L. (2010, April). Treating trauma. *Counseling Today, 52*(10), 26–35.

Shallcross, L. (2011a, March). Breaking away from the pack. *Counseling Today, 53*(9), 28–36.

Shallcross, L. (2011b, January). Taking care of yourself as a counselor. *Counseling Today, 53*(7), 30–37.

Shallcross, L. (2011c, June). Don't turn away. *Counseling Today, 53*(12), 30–38.

Shapiro, J. L., Peltz, L. S., & Bernadett-Shapiro, S. (1998). *Brief group treatment: Practical training for therapists and counselors.* Pacific Grove, CA: Brooks/Cole.

Sharf, J., Primavera, L. H., & Diener, M. J. (2010). Dropout and therapeutic alliance: A meta-analysis of adult individual psychotherapy. *Psychotherapy: Theory, Research, Practice, Training, 47*(4), 637–645.

Sharkin, B. S. (1997). Increasing severity of presenting problems in college counseling centers: A closer look. *Journal of Counseling & Development, 75,* 275–281.

Sharpley, C. F. (2007). So why aren't counselors reporting n = 1 research designs? *Journal of Counseling & Development, 85,* 349–356.

Shaw, H. E., & Shaw, S. F. (2006). Critical ethical issues in online counseling: Assessing current practices with an ethical intent checklist. *Journal of Counseling & Development, 84*, 41–53.

Sheehy, G. (1976). *Passages: Predictable crises of adult life.* New York: Bantam.

Sheeley, V. L. (1978). *Career guidance leadership in America: Pioneering professionals.* Falls Church, VA: National Vocational Guidance Association.

Sheeley, V. L. (1983). NADW and NAAS: 60 years of organizational relationships. In B. A. Belson & L. E. Fitzgerald (Eds.), *Thus, we spoke: ACPA-NAWDAC, 1958–1975.* Alexandria, VA: American College Personnel Association.

Sheeley, V. L. (1988). Historical perspectives on NVGA/NCDA: What our leaders think. *Career Development Quarterly, 36*, 307–320.

Sheeley, V. L. (2002). American Counseling Association: The 50th year celebration of excellence. *Journal of Counseling & Development, 80*, 387–393.

Sheeley, V. L., & Eberly, C. G. (1985). Two decades of leadership in measurement and evaluation. *Journal of Counseling & Development, 63*, 436–439.

Sheeley, V. L., & Herlihy, B. (1989). Counseling suicidal teens: A duty to warn and protect. *School Counselor, 37*, 89–97.

Sheeley, V., & Stickle, F. E. (2008). Gone but not forgotten: Council leaders, 1934–1952. *Journal of Counseling & Development, 86*, 211–218.

Sherman, R. (1993). The intimacy genogram. *The Family Journal: Counseling and Therapy for Couples and Families, 1*, 91–93.

Sherrard, P. A. D., & Amatea, E. S. (1994). Through the looking glass: A preview. *Journal of Mental Health Counseling, 16*, 3–5.

Sherrod, M., Getch, Y. Q., & Ziomek-Daigle, J. (2009).

The impact of positive behavior support to decrease discipline referrals with elementary students. *Professional School Counseling, 12*(6), 421–427.

Sherry, A., Lyddon, W. J., & Henson, R. K. (2007). Adult attachment and developmental personalities styles: An empirical study. *Journal of Counseling & Development, 85*, 337–348.

Shertzer, B., & Linden, J. D. (1979). *Fundamentals of individual appraisal, assessment techniques for counselors.* Boston: Houghton Mifflin.

Shertzer, B., & Stone, S. C. (1974). *Fundamentals of counseling* (2nd ed.). Boston: Houghton Mifflin.

Shertzer, B., & Stone, S. C. (1980). *Fundamentals of counseling* (3rd ed.). Boston: Houghton Mifflin.

Shertzer, B., & Stone, S. C. (1981). *Fundamentals of guidance* (4th ed.). Boston: Houghton Mifflin.

Shorman, J. (2011, July 21). 1 in 4 Americans binge-drink. *USAToday*, 3D.

Shulman, L. (2009). *The skills of helping individuals, families, groups, and communities* (6th ed.). Belmont, CA: Brooks Cole.

Siegal, J. C., & Sell, J. M. (1978). Effects of objective evidence of expertness and nonverbal behavior on client perceived expertness. *Journal of Counseling Psychology, 25*, 188–192.

Sielski, L. M. (1979). Understanding body language. *Personnel and Guidance Journal, 57*, 238–242.

Simkin, J. S. (1975). An introduction to Gestalt therapy. In F. D. Stephenson (Ed.), *Gestalt therapy primer* (pp. 3–12). Springfield, IL: Thomas.

Simon, G. M. (1989). An alternative defense of eclecticism: Responding to Kelly and Ginter. *Journal of Mental Health Counseling, 2*, 280–288.

Simon, L., Gaul, R., Friedlander, M. L., & Heatherington, L. (1992). Client gender and sex role: Predictors of counselors' impressions and expectations. *Journal of Counseling & Development, 71*, 48–52.

Simone, D. H., McCarthy, P., & Skay, C. L. (1998). An investigation of client and counselor variables that influence the likelihood of counselor self-disclosure. *Journal of Counseling & Development, 76*, 174–182.

Singh, A. A., Hays, D. G., & Watson, L. S. (2011). Strength in the face of adversity: Resilience strategies of transgender individuals. *Journal of Counseling & Development, 89*, 20–27.

Singleton, M. G., & Pope, M. (2000). A comparison of successful smoking cessation interventions for adults and adolescents. *Journal of Counseling & Development, 78*, 448–453.

Singley, D. B., & Sedlacek, W. E. (2009). Differences in universal-diverse orientation by race-ethnicity and gender. *Journal of Counseling & Development, 87*, 404–411.

Sinick, D. (1980). Attitudes and values in aging. *Counseling and Values, 24*, 148–154.

Skinner, B. F. (1953). *Science and human behavior.* New York: Macmillan.

Sklare, G., Keener, R., & Mas, C. (1990). Preparing members for "here-and-now" group counseling. *Journal for Specialists in Group Work, 15*, 141–148.

Sklare, G., Petrosko, J., & Howell, S. (1993). The effect of pre-group training on members' level of anxiety. *Journal for Specialists in Group Work, 18*, 109–114.

Skovholt, T. M., & McCarthy, P. R. (1988). Critical incidents: Catalysts for counselor development. *Journal of Counseling & Development, 67*, 69–72.

Skowron, E. A., & Platt, L. F. (2005). Differentiation of self

and child abuse potential in young adulthood. *The Family Journal: Counseling and Therapy for Couples and Families, 13*, 281–290.

Slavik, S. (1991). Early memories as a guide to client movement through life. *Canadian Journal of Counseling, 25*, 331–337.

Slan-Jerusalim, R., & Chen, C. P. (2009). Work–family conflict and career development theories: A search for helping strategies. *Journal of Counseling & Development, 87*, 492–500.

Smart, J. F., & Smart, D. W. (2006). Models of disability: Implications for the counseling profession. *Journal of Counseling & Development, 84*, 29–40.

Smead, R. (1995). *Skills and techniques for group work with children and adolescents.* Champaign, IL: Research Press.

Smith, E. J. (1977). Counseling black individuals: Some stereotypes. *Personnel and Guidance Journal, 55*, 390–396.

Smith, E. M. J., & Vasquez, M. J. T. (1985). Introduction. *Counseling Psychologist, 13*, 531–536.

Smith, H. (2001). Professional identity for counselors. In D. C. Locke, J. E. Myers, & E. L. Herr (Eds.), *The handbook of counseling* (pp. 569–579). Thousand Oaks, CA: Sage.

Smith, H. B., Sexton, T. H., & Bradley, L. J. (2005). The practice research network: Research into practice, practice into research. *Counseling and Psychotherapy Research, 5*, 285–290.

Smith, L., Foley, P. F., & Chaney, M. P. (2008). Addressing classism, ableism, and heterosexism in Counselor Education. *Journal of Counseling & Development, 86*, 303–309.

Smith, M. L. (1981). Naturalistic research. *Personnel and Guidance Journal, 59*, 585–589.

Smith, R. L., Engels, D. W., & Bonk, E. C. (1985). The

past and future: The National Vocational Guidance Association. *Journal of Counseling & Development, 63,* 420–423.

Snider, M. (1992). *Process family therapy.* Boston: Allyn & Bacon.

Snider, P. D. (1987). Client records: Inexpensive liability protection for mental health counselors. *Journal of Mental Health Counseling, 9,* 134–141.

Snyder, B. A. (2005). Aging and spirituality: Reclaiming connection through storytelling. *Adultspan Journal, 4,* 49–55.

Snyder, B. A., & Daly, T. P. (1993). Restructuring guidance and counseling programs. *School Counselor, 41,* 36–42.

Solomon, C. (1982). Special issue on political action: Introduction. *Personnel and Guidance Journal, 60,* 580.

Solsberry, P. W. (1994). Interracial couples in the United States of America: Implications for mental health counseling. *Journal of Mental Health Counseling, 16,* 304–316.

Sommer, C. A., Ward, J. E., & Scofield, T. (2010). Metaphoric stories in supervision of internship: A qualitative study. *Journal of Counseling & Development, 88*(4), 500–507.

Sommers-Flanagan, J. (2007). The development and evolution of person-centered expressive art therapy: A conversation with Natalie Rogers. *Journal of Counseling & Development, 85,* 120–125.

Sommers-Flanagan, J., & Sommers-Flanagan, R. (1998). Assessment and diagnosis of conduct disorder. *Journal of Counseling & Development, 76,* 189–197.

Southwick, S. M., Gilmartin, R., Mcdonough, P., & Morrissey, P. (2006). Logotherapy as an adjunctive treatment for chronic combat-related PTSD: A meaning-based

intervention. *American Journal of Psychotherapy, 60,* 161–174.

Splete, H. H. (1982a). Consultation by the counselor. *Counseling and Human Development, 15,* 1–7.

Splete, H. H. (1982b). Planning for a comprehensive career guidance program in the elementary schools. *Vocational Guidance Quarterly, 30,* 300–307.

Spokane, A. R., & Catalano, M. (2000). The self-directed search: A theory-driven array of self-guided career interventions. In C. E. Watkins, Jr., & V. I. Campbell (Eds.), *Testing and assessment in counseling practice* (2nd ed., pp. 339–370). Mahwah, NJ: Erlbaum.

Springer, C. A., Britt, T. W., & Schlenker, B. R. (1998). Codependency: Clarifying the construct. *Journal of Mental Health Counseling, 20,* 141–158.

Springer, C. A., & Lease, S. H. (2000). The impact of multiple AIDS related bereavement in the gay male population. *Journal of Counseling & Development, 78,* 297–304.

Sprinthall, N. A. (1981). A new model for research in service of guidance and counseling. *Personnel and Guidance Journal, 59,* 487–496.

Sprinthall, N. A. (1984). Primary prevention: A road paved with a plethora of promises and procrastinations. *Personnel and Guidance Journal, 62,* 491–495.

Sprinthall, N. A., Hall, J. S., & Gerler, E. R., Jr. (1992). Peer counseling for middle school students experiencing family divorce: A deliberate psychological education model. *Elementary School Guidance and Counseling, 26,* 279–294.

St. Clair, K. L. (1989). Middle school counseling research: A resource for school counselors. *Elementary School Guidance and Counseling, 23,* 219–226.

St. Germaine, J. (1993). Dual relationships: What's wrong with them? *American Counselor, 2,* 25–30.

Stadler, H. (1986). Preface to the special issue. *Journal of Counseling & Development, 64,* 291.

Staley, W. L., & Carey, A. L. (1997). The role of school counselors in facilitating a quality twenty-first century workforce. *School Counselor, 44,* 377–383.

Stamm, M. L., & Nissman, B. S. (1979). *Improving middle school guidance.* Boston: Allyn & Bacon.

Stanard, R. P., Sandhu, D. S., & Painter, L. C. (2000). Assessment of spirituality in counseling. *Journal of Counseling & Development, 78,* 204–210.

Stanton, M., & Todd, T. (1982). *The family therapy of drug abuse and addiction.* New York: Guilford.

Statton, J. E., & Wilborn, B. (1991). Adlerian counseling and the early recollections of children. *Individual Psychology, 47,* 338–347.

Steen, S., & Kaffenberger, C. J. (2007). Integrating academic interventions into small group counseling in elementary school. *Professional School Counseling, 10,* 516–519.

Steenbarger, B. N. (1998). Alcohol abuse and college counseling: An overview of research and practice. *Journal of College Counseling, 1,* 81–92.

Steinglass, P. (1979). Family therapy with alcoholics: A review. In E. Kaufman & P. N. Kaufman (Eds.), *Family therapy of drug and alcohol abuse* (pp. 147–186). New York: Gardner.

Steinhauser, L., & Bradley, R. (1983). Accreditation of counselor education programs. *Counselor Education and Supervision, 25,* 98–108.

Stephens, W. R. (1988). Birth of the National Vocational Guidance Association. *Career Development Quarterly, 36,* 293–306.

Stevens, P., & Smith, R. L. (2009). *Substance abuse counseling: Theory and practice* (4th ed.). Upper Saddle River, NJ: Merrill/Prentice Hall.

Stevens-Smith, P., & Hughes, M. M. (1993). *Legal issues in marriage and family counseling.* Alexandria, VA: American Counseling Association.

Stevens-Smith, P., & Remley, T. P., Jr. (1994). Drugs, AIDS, and teens: Intervention and the school counselor. *School Counselor, 41,* 180–184.

Stevenson, O. (2007). *Neglected children and their families* (2nd ed.). Malden, MA: Blackwell.

Stinnett, N. (1998). *Good families.* New York: Doubleday.

Stinnett, N., & DeFrain, J. (1985). *Secrets of strong families.* Boston: Little, Brown.

Stockton, R., Barr, J. E., & Klein, R. (1981). Identifying the group dropout: A review of the literature. *Journal for Specialists in Group Work, 6,* 75–82.

Stone, C. B. (2010). *School counseling principles: Ethics and law* (2nd ed.) Alexandria, VA: American School Counselors Association.

Strahan, R. F., & Kelly, A. E. (1994). Showing clients what their profiles mean. *Journal of Counseling & Development, 72,* 329–331.

Street, S., & Isaacs, M. (1998). Self-esteem: Justifying its existence. *Professional School Counseling, 1,* 46–50.

Stripling, R. O. (1978). ACES guidelines for doctoral preparation in counselor education. *Counselor Education and Supervision, 17,* 163–166.

Strong, E. K., Jr. (1943). *Vocational interests of men and women.* Stanford, CA: Stanford University Press.

Strong, S. R. (1968). Counseling: An interpersonal influence process. *Journal of Counseling Psychology, 15,* 215–224.

Strong, S. R. (1982). Emerging integrations of clinical and social psychology: A clinician's perspective. In

G. Weary & H. Mirels (Eds.), *Integrations of clinical and social psychology* (pp. 181–213). New York: Oxford University Press.

Strong, T., & Zeman, D. (2010). Dialogic considerations of confrontation as a counseling activity: An examination of Allen Ivey's use of confronting as a microskill. *Journal of Counseling & Development, 88,* 332–339.

Stude, E. W., & McKelvey, J. (1979). Ethics and the law: Friend or foe? *Personnel and Guidance Journal, 57,* 453–456.

Stufflebeam, D. L., Foley, W. J., Gephart, W. J., Guba, E. G., Hammond, R. L., Merriman, H. D., et al. (1971). *Educational evaluation and decision-making.* Bloomington, IN: Phi Delta Kappa.

Stum, D. (1982). DIRECT: A consultation skills training model. *Personnel and Guidance Journal, 60,* 296–302.

Sue, D. W. (1978a). Counseling across cultures. *Personnel and Guidance Journal, 56,* 451.

Sue, D. W. (1978b). Editorial. *Personnel and Guidance Journal, 56,* 260.

Sue, D. W. (1992, Winter). The challenge of multiculturalism. *American Counselor, 1,* 6–14.

Sue, D. W., Arredondo, P., & McDavis, R. J. (1992). Multicultural counseling competencies and standards: A call to the profession. *Journal of Counseling & Development, 70,* 477–486.

Sue, D. W., Ivey, A. E., & Pedersen, P. (2009). *A theory of multicultural counseling and therapy.* Pacific Grove, CA: Brooks/Cole.

Sue, D. W., & Sue, D. (1973). Understanding Asian-Americans: The neglected minority: An overview. *Personnel and Guidance Journal, 51,* 387–389.

Sue, D. W., & Sue, D. (2008). *Counseling the culturally different: Theory and practice* (5th ed.). New York: Wiley.

Sue, D. W., & Sue, S. (1972). Counseling Chinese-Americans. *Personnel and Guidance Journal, 50,* 637–644.

Sue, D. W., Nadal, K. L., Capodilupo, C. M., Lin, A. I., Torino, G. C., & Rivera, D. P. (2008). Racial microaggressions against black Americans: Implications for counseling. *Journal of Counseling & Development, 86,* 330–338.

Sullivan, C., & Cottone, R. R. (2010). Emergent characteristics of effective cross-cultural research: A review of the literature. *Journal of Counseling & Development, 88,* 357–362.

Sullivan, K. R., & Mahalik, J. R. (2000). Increasing career self-efficacy for women: Evaluating a group intervention. *Journal of Counseling & Development, 78,* 54–62.

Sunich, M. F., & Doster, J. (1995, June). Cocaine—Part II. *Amethyst Journal, 1,* 1–2.

Super, D. E. (1954a). Career patterns as a basis for vocational counseling. *Journal of Counseling Psychology, 1,* 12–19.

Super, D. E. (1954b). Guidance: Manpower utilization or human development? *Personnel and Guidance Journal, 33,* 8–14.

Super, D. E. (1955). Transition: From vocational guidance to counseling psychology. *Journal of Counseling Psychology, 2,* 3–9.

Super, D. E. (1957). *The psychology of careers.* New York: Harper.

Super, D. E. (1983). Synthesis: Or is it distillation? *Personnel and Guidance Journal, 61,* 511–514.

Super, D. E. (1990). A life-span, life-space approach to career development. In D. Brown, L. Brooks, & Associates (Eds.), *Career choice and development: Applying contemporary theories to practice* (2nd ed., pp. 197–261). San Francisco: Jossey-Bass.

Super, D. E., Thompson, A. S., & Lindeman, R. H. (1988).

Adult career concerns inventory. Palo Alto, CA: Consulting Psychologists Press.

Suzuki, L. A., & Kugler, J. F. (1995). Intelligence and personality assessment. In J. G. Ponterotto, J. M. Casas, L. A. Suzuki, & C. M. Alexander (Eds.), *Handbook of multicultural counseling* (pp. 493–515). Thousand Oaks, CA: Sage.

Suzuki, L. A., Meller, P. J., & Ponterotto, J. G. (Eds.). (2001). *Handbook of multicultural assessment: Clinical, psychological, and educational applications* (2nd ed.). San Francisco: Jossey-Bass.

Swanson, C. D. (1983a). Ethics and the counselor. In J. A. Brown & R. H. Pate, Jr. (Eds.), *Being a counselor* (pp. 47–65). Pacific Grove, CA: Brooks/Cole.

Swanson, C. D. (1983b). The law and the counselor. In J. A. Brown & R. H. Pate, Jr. (Eds.), *Being a counselor* (pp. 26–46). Pacific Grove, CA: Brooks/Cole.

Swanson, J. L., & Hansen, J. C. (1988). Stability of vocational interests over 4-year, 8-year, and 12-year intervals. *Journal of Vocational Behavior, 33,* 185–202.

Swartz-Kulstad, J. L., & Martin, W. E., Jr. (1999). Impact on culture and context on psychosocial adaptation: The cultural and contextual guide process. *Journal of Counseling & Development, 77,* 281–293.

Sweeney, T. J. (1989). Excellence vs. elitism. *Newsletter of Chi Sigma Iota, 5,* 1, 11.

Sweeney, T. J. (1991). Counseling credentialing: Purpose and origin. In F. O. Bradley (Ed.), *Credentialing in counseling* (pp. 1–12). Alexandria, VA: Association for Counselor Education and Supervision.

Sweeney, T. J. (2001). Counseling: Historical origins and philosophical roots. In D. C. Locke, J. E. Myers, & E. L. Herr (Eds.), *The handbook of*

counseling (pp. 3–26). Thousand Oaks, CA: Sage.

Sweeney, T. J. (2009). *Adlerian counseling and psychotherapy: A practitioner's approach* (5th ed.). New York: Routledge.

Sylvania, K. C. (1956). Test usage in counseling centers. *Personnel and Guidance Journal, 34,* 559–564.

Talbutt, L. C. (1981). Ethical standards: Assets and limitations. *Personnel and Guidance Journal, 60,* 110–112.

Talbutt, L. C. (1983). The counselor and testing: Some legal concerns. *School Counselor, 30,* 245–250.

Talleyrand, R. M. (2010). Eating disorders in African American Girls: Implications for counselors. *Journal of Counseling & Development, 88,* 319–324.

Tamminen, A. W., & Smaby, M. H. (1981). Helping counselors learn to confront. *Personnel and Guidance Journal, 60,* 41–45.

Tanigoshi, H., Kontos, A. P., & Remley Jr., T. P. (2008). The effectiveness of individual wellness counseling on the wellness of law enforcement officers. *Journal of Counseling & Development, 86*(1), 64–74.

Tate, D. S., & Schwartz, C. L. (1993). Increasing the retention of American Indian students in professional programs in higher education. *Journal of American Indian Education, 32,* 21–31.

Taub, D. J. (1998). Promoting student development through psychoeducational groups: A perspective on the goals and process matrix. *Journal for Specialists in Group Work, 23,* 196–201.

Taylor, J. G., & Baker, S. B. (2007). Psychosocial and moral development of PTSD-diagnosed combat veterans. *Journal of Counseling & Development, 85,* 364–369.

Tedeschi, G. J., Zhu, S-H, Anderson, C. M., Cummins, S., & Ribner, N. G. (2005).

Putting it on the line: Telephone counseling for adolescent smokers. *Journal of Counseling & Development, 83,* 416–424.

Tennyson, W. W., & Strom, S. M. (1986). Beyond professional standards: Developing responsibleness. *Journal of Counseling & Development, 64,* 298–302.

Terres, C. K., & Larrabee, M. J. (1985). Ethical issues and group work with children. *Elementary School Guidance and Counseling, 19,* 190–197.

Terry, L. L. (1989). Assessing and constructing a meaningful system: Systemic perspective in a college counseling center. *Journal of Counseling & Development, 67,* 352–355.

Teyber, E. (2000). *Interpersonal process in psychotherapy: A relational approach.* Belmont, CA: Wadsworth/ Thomson.

Thames, T. B., & Hill, C. E. (1979). Are special skills necessary for counseling women? *Counseling Psychologist, 8,* 17–18.

Thomas, A. J. (1998). Understanding culture and worldview in family systems: Use of the multicultural genogram. *The Family Journal, 6,* 24–32.

Thomas, G. P., & Ezell, B. (1972). The contract as counseling technique. *Personnel and Guidance Journal, 51,* 27–31.

Thomas, S. C. (1996). A sociological perspective on contextualism. *Journal of Counseling & Development, 74,* 529–536.

Thomas, V. (1994). Value analysis: A model of personal and professional ethics in marriage and family counseling. *Counseling and Values, 38,* 193–203.

Thombs, D. L., & Osborn, C. J. (2001). A cluster analysis study of clinical orientations among chemical dependency counselors. *Journal of Counseling & Development, 79,* 450–458.

Thompson, A. (1990). *Guide to ethical practice in psychotherapy.* New York: Wiley.

Thompson, B. (1996). *Personal Preferences Self-Description Questionnaire.* College Station, TX: Psychometrics Group.

Thompson, B. (2002). 'Statistical,' 'practical,' and 'clinical': How many kinds of significance do counselors need to consider? *Journal of Counseling & Development, 80,* 64–71.

Thoresen, C. E. (1978). Making better science, intensively. *Personnel and Guidance Journal, 56,* 279–282.

Thornburg, H. D. (1978). *The bubblegum years: Sticking with kids from 9 to 13.* Tucson: HELP Books.

Thornburg, H. D. (1986). The counselor's impact on middle-grade students. *School Counselor, 33,* 170–177.

Thorndike, R. M., & Thorndike-Christ, T. M. (2010). *Measurement and evaluation in psychology and education* (8th ed.). Upper Saddle River, NJ: Merrill/Prentice Hall.

Thurman, C. (1983). Effects of a rational-emotive treatment program on Type A behavior among college students. *Journal of College Student Personnel, 24,* 417–423.

Tinsley, H. E. A., & Bradley, R. W. (1986). Test interpretation. *Journal of Counseling & Development, 65,* 462–466.

Todd, T. C. (1986). Structural-strategic marital therapy. In N. S. Jacobson & A. S. Gurman (Eds.), *Clinical handbook of marital therapy* (pp. 71–105). New York: Guilford.

Tomes, H. (1996, August). Are we in denial about child abuse? *APA Monitor, 27,* 55.

Tomine, S. (1986). Private practice in gerontological counseling. *Journal of Counseling & Development, 64,* 406–409.

Tomlinson, S. M., & Evans-Hughes, G. (1991). Gender, ethnicity, and college

students' responses to the Strong-Campbell Interest Inventory. *Journal of Counseling & Development, 70,* 151–155.

Tracey, T. J. (1983). Single case research: An added tool for counselors and supervisors. *Counselor Education and Supervision, 22,* 185–196.

Tracey, T. J. (1991). Counseling research as an applied science. In C. E. Watkins, Jr., & L. J. Schneider (Eds.), *Research in counseling* (pp. 3–32). Hillsdale, NJ: Erlbaum.

Trepal, H. (2010). Introduction to the special section on nonsuicidal self-injury. *Journal of Mental Health Counseling, 32,* 288–289.

Trotzer, J. P. (1988). Family theory as a group resource. *Journal for Specialists in Group Work, 13,* 180–185.

Truax, C., & Mitchell, K. (1971). Research on certain therapist interpersonal skills in relation to process and outcome. In A. E. Bergin & S. L. Garfield (Eds.), *Handbook of psychotherapy and behavior change: An empirical analysis.* New York: Wiley.

Truax, C. B., & Carkhuff, R. R. (1967). *Toward effective counseling and psychotherapy: Training and practice.* Chicago: Aldine.

Trusty, J., Robinson, C. R., Plata, M., & Ng, K-M. (2000). Effects of gender, socioeconomic status, and early academic performance on postsecondary educational choice. *Journal of Counseling & Development, 78,* 463–472.

Tuckman, B. (1965). Developmental sequence in small groups. *Psychological Bulletin, 63,* 384–399.

Tuckman, B. W., & Jensen, M. A. (1977). Stages of small group development revisited. *Group and Organizational Studies, 2,* 419–427.

Turner, S. L., & Conkel, J. L. (2010). Evaluation of a career development skills intervention with adolescents living in an inner city. *Journal of*

Counseling & Development, 88, 457–465.

Turock, A. (1978). Effective challenging through additive empathy. *Personnel and Guidance Journal, 57,* 144–149.

Turock, A. (1980). Immediacy in counseling: Recognizing clients' unspoken messages. *Personnel and Guidance Journal, 59,* 168–172.

Tursi, M. M., & Cochran, J. L. (2006). Cognitive-behavioral tasks accomplished in a person-centered relational framework. *Journal of Counseling & Development, 84,* 387–396.

Tyler, L. E. (1984). What tests don't measure. *Journal of Counseling & Development, 63,* 48–50.

Tyler, L. E. (1986). Farewell to guidance. *Journal of Counseling and Human Service Professions, 1,* 152–155.

Tylka, T. L., & Subich, L. M. (2002). Exploring young women's perceptions of the effectiveness and safety of maladaptive weight control techniques. *Journal of Counseling & Development, 80,* 101–110.

Tymchuk, A. J. (1986). Guidelines for ethical decision making. *Canadian Psychology, 27,* 36–43.

Tymofievich, M., & Leroux, J. A. (2000). Counselors' competencies in using assessments. *Measurement and Evaluation in Counseling and Development, 33,* 50–59.

Tysl, L. (1997, January). Counselors have a responsibility to promote the counseling profession. *Counseling Today,* 16.

Umansky, D. L., & Holloway, E. L. (1984). The counselor as consultant: From model to practice. *School Counselor, 31,* 329–338.

Ungersma, A. J. (1961). *The search for meaning.* Philadelphia: Westminster.

Urbina, S. (2005). *Essentials of psychological testing.* New York: Wiley.

U.S. Census Department (2009). *Number, timing, and*

duration of marriages and divorces: 2009. Washington, DC: Author.

U.S. Census Bureau. (2010). 2010 U. S. Census Data. http://2010.census.gov/2010census/data/

U.S. Department of Health and Human Services, National Institute of Mental Health. (1999). *Mental health: A report of the Surgeon General–Executive Summary*. Rockville, MD: Author.

U.S. Employment Service. (1939). *Dictionary of occupational titles*. Washington, DC: Author.

Utsey, S. O., Ponterotto, J. G., Reynolds, A. L., & Cancelli, A. A. (2000). Racial discrimination, coping, life satisfaction, and self-esteem among African Americans. *Journal of Counseling & Development, 78,* 72–80.

Utsey, S. O., Ponterotto, J. G., & Porter, J. S. (2008). Prejudice and racism, year 2008—Still going strong: Research on reducing prejudice with recommended methodological advances. *Journal of Counseling & Development, 86,* 339–347.

Vacc, N., Loesch, L., & Guilbert, D. (1997). The clientele of certified clinical mental health counselors. *Journal of Mental Health Counseling, 19,* 165–170.

Vacc, N. A., & Juhnke, G. A. (1997). The use of structured clinical interviews for assessment in counseling. *Journal of Counseling & Development, 75,* 470–480.

Vacc, N. A., Juhnke, G. A., & Nilsen, K. A. (2001). Community mental health service providers' code of ethics and the *Standards for Educational and Psychological Testing. Journal of Counseling & Development, 79,* 217–224.

Vacc, N. A., & Loesch, L. C. (2001). *A professional orientation to counseling* (3rd ed.). Philadelphia: Brunner-Routledge.

Vacha-Haase, T., & Thompson, B. (2002). Alternative ways of measuring counselees' Jungian psychological-type preferences. *Journal of Counseling & Development, 80,* 173–179.

Vaihinger, H. (1911). *The philosophy of "as if."* New York: Harcourt, Brace, & World.

Valle, R. (1986). Cross-cultural competence in minority communities: A curriculum implementation strategy. In M. R. Miranda & H. H. L. Kitano (Eds.), *Mental health research and practice in minority communities: Development of culturally sensitive training programs* (pp. 29–49). Rockville, MD: National Institute of Mental Health. (ERIC Document Reproduction Service No. ED278754)

van Asselt, K. W., & Baldo Senstock, T. D. (2009). Influence of counselor spirituality and training on treatment focus and self-perceived competence. *Journal of Counseling & Development, 87*(4), 412–419.

VanBoven, A. M., & Espelage, D. L. (2006). Depressive symptoms, coping strategies, and disordered eating among college women. *Journal of Counseling & Development, 84,* 341–348.

Van Brunt, B., & Manley, E. D. (2009). Research and evaluation, key people in. In B. Erford (Ed.), *ACA Encyclopedia of Counseling* (pp. 455–456). Alexandria, VA: American Counseling Association.

Van Buren, J. B., Kelly, K. R., & Hall, A. S. (1993). Modeling nontraditional career choices: Effects of gender and school location on response to a brief videotape. *Journal of Counseling & Development, 72,* 101–104.

Van der Wade, H., Urgenson, F. T., Weltz, S. H., & Hanna, F. J. (2002). Women and alcoholism: A biopsychosocial perspective and treatment approaches. *Journal of Counseling & Development, 80,* 145–153.

Van Hoose, W. H., & Kottler, J. (1985). *Ethical and legal issues in counseling and psychotherapy* (2nd ed.). San Francisco: Jossey-Bass.

Van Hoose, W. H., & Paradise, L. V. (1979). *Ethics in counseling and psychotherapy*. Cranston, RI: Carroll.

Van Veisor, P. (2009). School counselors as social-emotional learning consultants: Where do we begin? *Professional School Counseling, 13*(1), 50–58.

Vandenbos, G. R., Cummings, N., & Deleon, P. H. (1992). A century of psychotherapy: Economic and environmental influences. In D. K. Freedheim (Ed.), *History of psychotherapy: A century of change* (pp. 65–102). Washington, DC: American Psychological Association.

Vereen, L. G., Butler, S. K., Williams, F. C., Darg, J. A., & Downing, T. K. E. (2006). The use of humor when counseling African American college students. *Journal of Counseling & Development, 84,* 10–15.

Vernon, A. (2006). *Thinking, feeling, and behaving: An emotional education curriculum for children (grades 1–6)—revised edition.* Champaign, IL: Research Press.

Vick, R. D., Smith, L. M., & Herrera, C. I. R. (1998). The healing circle: An alternative path to alcoholism recovery. *Counseling and Values, 42,* 133–141.

Vickio, C. J. (1990). The goodbye brochure: Helping students to cope with transition and loss. *Journal of Counseling & Development, 68,* 575–577.

Viney, L. L., Henry, R. M., & Campbell, J. (2001). The impact of group work on offender adolescents. *Journal of Counseling & Development, 79,* 373–381.

Voight, N. L., Lawler, A., & Fulkerson, K. F. (1980). Community-based guidance: A "Tupperware party" approach to mid-life decision making. *Personnel and Guidance Journal, 59,* 106–107.

Vontress, C. E. (1966). Counseling the culturally different adolescent: A school-community approach. In J. C. Gowan & G. Demos (Eds.), *The disadvantaged and potential dropout* (pp. 357–366). Springfield, IL: Thomas.

Vontress, C. E. (1967). The culturally different. *Employment Service Review, 4,* 35–36.

Vontress, C. E. (1996). A personal retrospective on cross-cultural counseling. *Journal of Multicultural Counseling and Development, 16,* 73–83.

Vontress, C. E., & Epp, L. R. (1997). Historical hostility in the African client: Implications for counseling. *Journal of Multicultural Counseling and Development, 25,* 170–184.

Vriend, J., & Dyer, W. W. (1973). Counseling the reluctant client. *Journal of Counseling Psychology, 20,* 240–246.

Wade, J. C. (1998). Male reference group identity dependence: A theory of male identity. *Counseling Psychologist, 26,* 349–383.

Wade, N. G. (2010). Introduction to the special issue on forgiveness in therapy. *Journal of Mental Health Counseling, 32,* 1–4.

Wahl, K. H., & Blackhurst, A. (2000). Factors affecting the occupational and educational aspirations of children and adolescents. *Profesional School Counseling, 3,* 367–374.

Wakefield, J. C. (1992). The concept of mental disorder: On the boundary between biological facts and social values. *American Psychologist, 47,* 373–388.

Waldo, M. (1985). Curative factor framework for conceptualizing group counseling. *Journal for Counseling and Development, 64,* 52–58.

Waldo, M. (1989). Primary prevention in university residence halls: Paraprofessional-led relationship enhancement groups for college roommates. *Journal of Counseling & Development, 67,* 465–471.

Waldo, M., & Bauman, S. (1998). Regrouping the categorization of group work: A goal and process (GAP) matrix for groups. *Journal for Specialists in Group Work, 23,* 164–176.

Waldo, M., Horswill, R. K., & Brotherton, W. D. (1993). Collaborating with state departments to achieve recognition of mental health counselors. *Journal of Mental Health Counseling, 15,* 342–346.

Walen, S. R., DiGuiseppe, R., & Dryden, W. (1992). *A practitioner's guide to rational-emotive therapy.* New York: Oxford University Press.

Walker-Staggs, J. (2000). DISCOVER. In N. Peterson & R. C. Gonzalez (Eds.), *Career counseling models for diverse populations* (pp. 112–120). Pacific Grove, CA: Brooks/Cole.

Wall, J. E., & Walz, G. R. (Eds.). (2004). *Measuring up: Assessment issues for teachers, counselors, and administators.* Greensboro, NC: CAPS Press.

Wallace, W. A., & Hall, D. L. (1996). *Psychological consultation: Perspectives and applications.* Pacific Grove, CA: Brooks/Cole.

Walls, R. T., & Fullmer, S. L. (1996). Comparing rehabilitated workers with the United States workforce. *Rehabilitation Counseling Bulletin, 40*(2), 153–164.

Walsh, F. (1993). Conceptualizations of normal family functioning. In F. Walsh (Ed.), *Normal family process* (2nd ed., pp. 3–42). New York: Guilford.

Walsh, R. (2000). Asian psychotherapies. In R. J. Corsini & D. Wedding (Eds.), *Current psychotherapies* (6th ed., pp. 407–444). Itasca, IL: F. E. Peacock.

Walsh, W. B., & Heppner, M. (2006). *Handbook of career counseling for women* (2nd ed). Hillsdale, NJ: Erlbaum.

Walsh, W. B., & Savickas, M. (Eds.). (2005). *Handbook of vocational psychology* (3rd ed.). Hillsdale, NJ: Erlbaum.

Walsh, W. M., & Keenan, R. (1997). Narrative family therapy. *Family Journal, 5,* 332–336.

Walter, J., & Peller, J. (1992). *Becoming solution-focused in brief therapy.* New York: Brunner/Mazel.

Walz, G. R., & Kirkman, C. J. (Eds.). (2002). *Helping people cope with tragedy and grief.* Greensboro, NC: ERIC & NBCC.

Ward, C. (2010, October). *Counseling supervision.* Paper presented at the Southern Association of Counselor Education and Supervision Counselor Education, Williamsburg, VA.

Ward, D. E. (1982). A model for the more effective use of theory in group work. *Journal for Specialists in Group Work, 7,* 224–230.

Ward, D. E. (1984). Termination of individual counseling: Concepts and strategies. *Journal of Counseling & Development, 63,* 21–25.

Ward, D. E. (2002). Like old friends, old familiar terms and concepts need attention. *Journal for Specialists in Group Work, 27,* 119–121.

Warfield, R. D., & Goldstein, M. B. (1996). Spirituality: The key to recovery from alcoholism. *Counseling and Values, 40,* 196–205.

Warnath, C. F. (1977). Relationship and growth theories and agency counseling. *Counselor Education and Supervision, 17,* 84–91.

Warner, C. B. (2009). Racial identity development models, minority. In B. Erford (Ed.), *ACA Encyclopedia of Counseling* (pp. 437–439). Alexandria, VA: American Counseling Association.

Wastell, C. A. (1996). Feminist development theory: Implications for counseling. *Journal of Counseling & Development, 74,* 575–581.

Watanabe, C. (1973). Self-expression and the Asian

American experience. *Personnel and Guidance Journal, 51,* 390–396.

Watkins, C. (2001). Comprehensive guidance programs in an international context. *Professional School Counseling, 4,* 262–270.

Watkins, C. E., Jr. (1983b). Counselor acting out in the counseling situation: An exploratory analysis. *Personnel and Guidance Journal, 61,* 417–423.

Watkins, C. E., Jr. (1985). Early recollections as a projective technique in counseling: An Adlerian view. *AMHCA Journal, 7,* 32–40.

Watkins, C. E., Jr. (1990a). The effects of counselor self-disclosure: A research review. *Counseling Psychologist, 18,* 477–500.

Watkins, C. E., Jr. (1990b). The testing of the test section of the *Journal of Counseling & Development:* Historical, contemporary, and future perspectives. *Journal of Counseling & Development, 69,* 70–74.

Watkins, C. E., Jr., & Schneider, L. J. (1989). Self-involving versus self-disclosing counselor statements during an initial interview. *Journal of Counseling & Development, 67,* 345–349.

Watkins, C. E., Jr., & Schneider, L. J. (1991). Research in counseling: Some concluding thoughts and ideas. In C. E. Watkins, Jr., & L. J. Schneider (Eds.), *Research in counseling* (pp. 287–299). Hillsdale, NJ: Erlbaum.

Watkins, E. (1983). Project retain: A client centered approach to student retention. *Journal of College Student Personnel, 24,* 81.

Watson, J. C. (2005). College student-athletes' attitudes toward help-seeking behavior and expectations of counseling services. *Journal of College Student Development, 46,* 442–429.

Watt, H. M. G., & Eccles, J. S. (Eds.). (2008). *Gender and occupational outcome: Longitudinal assessment*

of individual, social and cultural influences. Washington, DC: American Psychological Association.

Watzlawick, P. (1983). *The situation is hopeless, but not serious.* New York: Norton.

Watzlawick, P., Weakland, J. H., & Fisch, R. (1974). *Change: Principles of problem formation and problem resolution.* New York: W.W. Norton.

Webb, W. (1992). Empowering at-risk children. *Elementary School Guidance and Counseling, 27,* 96–103.

Webber, J., & Mascari, B. (Eds.). (2010). *Terrorism, trauma, and tragedies: A counselor's guide to preparing and responding* (3rd ed.). Alexandria, VA: American Counseling Association.

Wechsler, D. (2008). *Wechsler Adult Intelligence Scale— Fourth Edition.* San Antonio, TX: Pearson Education.

Wedding, D., & Pope, K. S. (2008). Contemporary challenges and controversies. In R. J. Corsini & D. Wedding (Eds.), *Current psychotherapies* (8th ed., pp. 512–540). Belmont, CA: Thomson Brooks/Cole.

Weigel, D. J., Donovan, K. A., Krug, K. S., & Dixon, W. A. (2007). Prescription opioid abuse and dependence: Assessment strategies for counselors. *Journal of Counseling & Development, 85,* 211–215.

Weinrach, S. G. (1980). Unconventional therapist: Albert Ellis. *Personnel and Guidance Journal, 59,* 152–160.

Weinrach, S. G. (1987). Microcounseling and beyond: A dialogue with Allen Ivey. *Journal of Counseling & Development, 65,* 532–537.

Weinrach, S. G. (1996). The psychological and vocational interest patterns of Donald Super and John Holland. *Journal of Counseling & Development, 75,* 5–16.

Weinrach, S. G., Ellis, A., MacLaren, C., DiGiuseppe, R., Vernon, A., Wolfe, J., et al. (2001). Rational emotive behavior therapy successes and failures: Eight personal perspectives. *Journal of Counseling & Development, 79,* 259–268.

Weinrach, S. G., & Thomas, K. R. (1998). Diversity-sensitive counseling today: A postmodern clash of values. *Journal of Counseling & Development, 76,* 115–122.

Weiss, R. S. (Ed.). (1973). *Loneliness.* Cambridge, MA: MIT Press.

Welfel, E. R. (2010). *Ethics in counseling and psychotherapy* (4th ed.). Belmont, CA: Brooks/Cole.

Welfel, E. R., Danziger, P. R., & Santoro, S. (2000). Mandated reporting of abuse/maltreatment of older adults: A primer for counselors. *Journal of Counseling & Development, 78,* 284–292.

Welfel, E. R., & Lipsitz, N. E. (1983a). Ethical orientation of counselors: Its relationship to moral reasoning and level of training. *Counselor Education and Supervision, 23,* 35–45.

Welfel, E. R., & Lipsitz, N. E. (1983b). Wanted: A comprehensive approach to ethics research and education. *Counselor Education and Supervision, 22,* 320–332.

Welfel, E. R., & Patterson, L. E. (2005). *The counseling process: A multitheoretical integrative approach* (6th ed.). Belmont, CA: Thomson Brooks/Cole.

Wendel, P. (1997, October). Cultural bias among minority counselors. *Counseling Today, 1,* 20.

Wender, P. (1998). Attention-deficit hyperactivity disorder in adults. *Psychiatric Clinics of North America, 21,* 761–774.

Werner, J. L. (1978). Community mental health consultation with agencies. *Personnel and Guidance Journal, 56,* 364–368.

Werth, J. L., Jr., & Gordon, J. R. (2002). Amicus Curiae Brief for the United States Supreme Court on mental health issues associated with 'physician-assisted suicides.'

Journal of Counseling & Development, 80, 160–172.

West, J. D., Bubenzer, D. L., Smith, J. M., & Hamm, T. L. (1997). Insoo Kim Berg and solution-focused therapy. *Family Journal, 5,* 286–294.

West, P. L., Mustaine, B. L., & Wyrick, B. (2002). Apples and oranges make a nice start for a fruit salad: A response to Culbreth and Borders (1999). *Journal of Counseling & Development, 80,* 72–76.

Westbrook, B. W. (1988). Suggestions for selecting appropriate career assessment instruments. *Measurement and Evaluation in Counseling and Development, 20,* 181–186.

Westbrook, F. D., Kandell, J. J., Kirkland, S. E., Phillips, P. E., Regan, A. M., Medvene, A., et al. (1993). University campus consultation: Opportunities and limitations. *Journal of Counseling & Development, 71,* 684–688.

Wester, S. R., McDonough, T. A., White, M., Vogel, D. L., & Taylor, L. (2010). Using gender role conflict theory in counseling male-to-female transgender individuals. *Journal of Counseling & Development, 88,* 214–219.

Wester, S. R., Vogel, D. L., Wei, M., & McLain, R. (2006). African American men, gender role conflict, and psychological distress: The role of racial identity. *Journal of Counseling & Development, 84,* 419–429.

Westgate, C. E. (1996). Spiritual wellness and depression. *Journal of Counseling & Development, 75,* 26–35.

Westmacott, R., & Hunsley, J. (2010). Reasons for terminating psychotherapy: A general population study. *Journal of Clinical Psychology, 66*(9), 965–977.

Wexler, D. P. (2009). *Men in therapy: New approaches to effective treatment.* New York: W. W. Norton.

Wheeler, A. M., & Bertram, B. (2012). *The counselor and*

the law: A guide to legal and ethical practice (6th ed.). Alexandria, VA: American Counseling Association.

Wheeler, C. D., & D'Andrea, L. M. (2004). Teaching counseling students to understand and use immediacy. *Journal of Humanistic Counseling, Education and Development, 43,* 117–128.

Wheeler, P. T., & Loesch, L. (1981). Program evaluation and counseling: Yesterday, today, and tomorrow. *Personnel and Guidance Journal, 59,* 573–578.

Whiston, S. C. (1996). Accountability through action research: Research methods for practitioners. *Journal of Counseling & Development, 74,* 616–623.

Whiston, S. C. (2002). Response to the past, present, and future of school counseling: Raising some issues. *Professional School Counseling, 5,* 148–155.

Whiston, S. C., & Sexton, T. L. (1998). A review of school counseling outcome research: Implications for practice. *Journal of Counseling & Development, 76,* 412–426.

Whiston, S. C., Wendi Lee, T., Rahardja, D., & Eder, K. (2011). School counseling outcome: A meta-analytic examination of interventions. *Journal of Counseling & Development, 89*(1), 37–55.

Whitaker, C. (1977). Process techniques of family therapy. *Interaction, 1,* 4–19.

White, E. B. (1952). *Charlotte's web.* New York: Trophy.

White, M. (1995). *Re-authoring lives.* Adelaide, Australia: Dulwich Centre Publications.

White, M., & Epston, D. (1990). *Narrative means to therapeutic ends.* New York: Norton.

Whitehead, B. D. (1997). *The divorce culture.* New York: Knopf.

Whiteley, J. M. (1982). *Character development in college students.* Alexandria, VA: American Counseling Association.

Whiteley, J. M. (1984). Counseling psychology: A historical

perspective. *Counseling Psychologist, 12,* 2–109.

Whitfield, E. A., Feller, R. W., & Wood, C. (2009). *A counselor's guide to career assessment instruments* (5th ed.). Broken Arrow, OK: National Career Development Association.

Whitmarsh, L., Brown, D., Cooper, J., Hawkins-Rodgers, Y., & Wentworth, D. K. (2007). Choices and challenges: A qualitative exploration of professional women's career patterns. *Career Development Quarterly, 55,* 225–236.

Wiehe, V. R. (2000). Sibling abuse. In H. Henderson (Ed.), *Domestic violence and child abuse resource sourcebook* (pp. 409–492). Detroit, MI: Omnigraphics.

Wiggins, J., & Weslander, D. (1979). Personality characteristics of counselors rated as effective or ineffective. *Journal of Vocational Behavior, 15,* 175–185.

Wiggins, J. D., Moody, A. D., & Lederer, D. A. (1983). Personality typologies related to marital satisfaction. *AMHCA Journal, 5,* 169–178.

Wilcox-Matthew, L., Ottens, A., & Minor, C. W. (1997). An analysis of significant events in counseling. *Journal of Counseling & Development, 75,* 282–291.

Wilcoxon, S. A. (1985). Healthy family functioning: The other side of family pathology. *Journal of Counseling & Development, 63,* 495–499.

Wilcoxon, S. A. (1986). Engaging nonattending family members in marital and family counseling: Ethical issues. *Journal of Counseling & Development, 64,* 323–324.

Wilcoxon, S. A. (1987). Ethical standards: A study of application and utility. *Journal of Counseling & Development, 65,* 510–511.

Wilcoxon, S. A., & Fenell, D. (1983). Engaging the non-attending spouse in marital therapy through the use of therapist-initiated written communication. *Journal of*

Marital and Family Therapy, 9, 199–203.

Wilcoxon, S. A., & Puleo, S. G. (1992). Professional-development needs of mental health counselors: Results of a national survey. *Journal of Mental Health Counseling, 14,* 187–195.

Wilcoxon, S. A., Remley, T. P., Jr., &, Gladding, S. T. (2012). *Ethical, legal and professional issues in the practice of marriage and family therapy* (5th ed.). Upper Saddle River, NJ: Merrill/Prentice Hall.

Wilkerson, K., & Bellini, J.(2006). Interpersonal and organizational factors associated with burnout among school counselors. *Journal of Counseling & Development, 84,* 440–450.

Williams, C. B., & Freeman, L. T. (2002). Report of the ACA Ethics Committee: 2000–2001. *Journal of Counseling & Development, 80,* 251–254.

Williams, J. M., Ballard, M. B., & Alessi, H. (2005). Aging and alcohol abuse: Increasing counselor awareness. *Adultspan Journal, 4,* 7–18.

Williamson, E. G. (1939). *How to counsel students: A manual of techniques for clinical counselors.* New York: McGraw-Hill.

Williamson, E. G. (1961). *Student personnel services in colleges and universities.* New York: McGraw-Hill.

Williamson, E. G. (1972). Trait-and-factor theory and individual differences. In B. Stefflre & W. H. Grant (Eds.), *Theories of counseling* (2nd ed., pp. 136–176). New York: McGraw-Hill.

Williamson, E. G., & Biggs, D. A. (1979). Trait-factor theory and individual differences. In H. M. Burks, Jr. & B. Stefflre (Eds.), *Theories of counseling* (3rd ed., pp. 91–131). New York: McGraw-Hill.

Willison, B., & Masson, R. (1986). The role of touch in therapy: An adjunct to communications. *Journal of Counseling & Development, 65,* 497–500.

Wilmarth, R. R. (1985, Summer). Historical perspective, part two. *AMHCA News, 8,* 21.

Wilson, F. R., & Yager, G. G. (1981). A process model for prevention program research. *Personnel and Guidance Journal, 59,* 590–595.

Wilson, G. T. (2008). Behavior therapy. In R. J. Corsini & D. Wedding (Eds.), *Current psychotherapies* (8th ed., pp. 223–262). Belmont, CA: Thomson Brooks/Cole.

Wilson, K. B., & Senices, J. (2005). Exploring the vocational rehabilitation acceptance rates for Hispanics versus Non-Hispanics in the United States. *Journal of Counseling & Development, 83,* 86–96.

Winston, R. B., Jr., & Creamer, D. G. (1997). *Improving staffing practices in student affairs.* San Francisco: Jossey-Bass.

Winston, R. B., Jr., & Ender, S. C. (1988). Use of student paraprofessionals in divisions of college student affairs. *Journal of Counseling & Development, 66,* 466–473.

Witmer, J. M., & Young, M. E. (1996). Preventing counselor impairment: A wellness model. *Journal of Humanistic Education and Development, 34,* 141–155.

Wittmer, J., & Adorno, G. (2000). *Managing your school counseling program: Developmental strategies* (2nd ed.). Minneapolis: Educational Media Corporation.

Wohlman, B., & Stricker, G. (1983). *Handbook of family and marital therapy.* New York: Plenum.

Woody, R. H. (1988). *Fifty ways to avoid malpractice.* Sarasota, FL: Professional Resource Exchange.

Woody, R. H., Hansen, J. C., & Rossberg, R. H. (1989). *Counseling psychology.* Pacific Grove, CA: Brooks/Cole.

Wooten, H. R. (1994). Cutting losses for student-athletes in transition: An integrative transition model. *Journal of Employment Counseling, 31,* 2–9.

Worden, M. (2003). *Family therapy basics* (3rd ed.). Pacific Grove, CA: Brooks/Cole.

Worrell, J., & Goodheart, C. D. (Eds.). (2006). *Handbook of girls' and women's psychological health.* New York: Oxford.

Worth, M. R. (1983). Adults. In J. A. Brown & R. H. Pate, Jr., (Eds.), *Being a counselor* (pp. 230–252). Pacific Grove, CA: Brooks/Cole.

Wrenn, C. G. (1962a). *The counselor in a changing world.* Washington, DC: American Personnel and Guidance Association.

Wrenn, C. G. (1962b). The culturally encapsulated counselor. *Harvard Educational Review, 32,* 444–449.

Wright, G. N. (1980). *Total rehabilitation.* Boston: Little, Brown.

Wright, G. N. (1987). Rehabilitation counselors' qualifications and client responsibilities structure their professional relationships. *Journal of Applied Rehabilitation Counseling, 18,* 18–20.

Wubbolding, R. E. (1988). *Using reality therapy.* New York: Harper/Collins.

Wubbolding, R. E. (1991). *Understanding reality therapy: A metaphorical approach.* New York: Harper.

Wubbolding, R. E. (1998). *Cycle of managing, supervising, counseling, and coaching using reality therapy.* Cincinnati: Center for Reality Therapy.

Wubbolding, R. E. (2000). *Reality therapy for the 21st century.* New York: Brunner-Routledge.

Wyatt, T., Daniels, M. H., & White, L. J. (2000). Noncompetition agreements and the counseling profession: An unrecognized reality for private practitioners. *Journal of Counseling & Development, 78,* 14–20.

Wylie, M. S. (1991, March/April). Family therapy's neglected prophet. *Family Therapy Networker, 15,* 24–37, 77.

Wynne, L. C., Ryckoff, I., Day, J., & Hirsch, S. I. (1958).

Pseudomutuality in the family relationships of schizophrenics. *Psychiatry, 21,* 205–220.

Xu, J. (2010). Logotherapy: A balm of Gilead for aging? *Journal of Religion, Spirituality & Aging, 22,* 180–195.

Yalom, I. D. (2005). *The theory and practice of group psychotherapy* (5th ed.). New York: Basic Books.

Yalom, I. & Josselson, R. (2011). Existential psychotherapy. In R. J. Corsini & D. Wedding (Eds.), *Current psychotherapies* (9th ed., pp. 310–341). Belmont, CA: Brooks Cole.

Yalom, I. D., & Lieberman, M. (1971). A study of encounter group casualties. *Archives of General Psychiatry, 25,* 16–30.

Yamawaki, N. (2010). The effects of self-construal and masculinity vs. femininity: A comparison of American and Japanese attitudes toward mental health services. *Journal of Mental Health Counseling, 32,* 154–167.

Yeh, C. J., & Hwang, M. Y. (2000). Interdependence in ethnic identity and self: Implications for theory and practice. *Journal of Counseling & Development, 78,* 420–429.

Young, J. S., Wiggins-Frame, M., & Cashwell, C. S. (2007). Spirituality and counselor competence: A national survey of American Counseling Association members. *Journal of Counseling & Development, 85,* 47–52.

Young, M. E. (2009). *Learning the art of helping: Building blocks and techniques* (4th ed.). Upper Saddle River, NJ: Merrill/Pearson.

Young, R. A. (1988). Ordinary explanations and career theories. *Journal of Counseling & Development, 66,* 336–339.

Zalaquett, C. P., & Stens, A. N. (2006). Psychosocial treatment for major depression and dysthymia in older adults: A review of the research literature. *Journal of Counseling & Development, 84,* 192–201.

Zautra, A. J., Hall, J. S., & Murray, K. E. (2010). Resilience: A new definition of health for people and communities. In J. W. Reich, A. J. Zautra, & J. S. Hall (Eds.), *Handbook of Adult Resilience* (pp. 3–34). New York: Guilford.

Zimpfer, D. (1996). Five-year follow-up of doctoral graduates in counseling. *Counselor Education and Supervision, 35,* 218–229.

Zimpfer, D., & DeTrude, J. (1990). Follow-up of doctoral graduates in counseling. *Journal of Counseling & Development, 69,* 51–55.

Zinck, K., & Littrell, J. M. (2000). Action research shows group counseling effective with at-risk adolescent girls. *Professional School Counseling, 4,* 50–59.

Zinker, J. (1978). *Creative process in Gestalt therapy.* New York: Random House.

Zinnbauer, B. J., & Pargament, K. I. (2000). Working with the sacred: Four approaches to religious and spiritual issues in counseling. *Journal of Counseling & Development, 78,* 162–171.

Zins, J. E. (1993). Enhancing consultee problem-solving skills in consultative interactions. *Journal of Counseling & Development, 72,* 185–188.

Zunker, V. G. (2012). *Career counseling* (8th ed.). Pacific Grove, CA: Brooks/Cole.

Zytowski, D. (1985). Frank! Frank! Where are you now that we need you? *Counseling Psychologist, 13,* 129–135.

Zytowski, D. G. (1992). Three generations: The continuing evolution of Frederic Kuder's interest inventories. *Journal of Counseling & Development, 71,* 245–248.

Zytowski, D. G., & Holmberg, K. S. (1988). Preferences: Frederic Kuder's contributions to the counseling profession. *Journal of Counseling & Development, 67,* 150–156.

NAME INDEX

SUBJECT INDEX